ENCYCLOPEDIA OF
CATHOLIC LITERATURE

Advisory Board

ENCYCLOPEDIA OF CATHOLIC LITERATURE

VOLUME I

Edited by Mary R. Reichardt

GREENWOOD PRESS
Westport, Connecticut • London

Library of Congress Cataloging-in-Publication Data

Encyclopedia of Catholic literature/edited by Mary R. Reichardt.
   p. cm.
  Includes bibliographical references.
  ISBN 0-313-32802-1 (v. 1 : alk. paper)—ISBN 0-313-32803-X (v. 2 : alk. paper)—
ISBN 0-313-32289-9 (set : alk. paper)
  1. Catholic literature—History and criticism. 2. Catholic literature—
Bio-bibliography—Dictionaries. I. Reichardt, Mary R.
PN485.E53 2004
809'.933822—dc22   2004047511

British Library Cataloguing in Publication Data is available.

Library of Congress Catalog Card Number: 2004047511
ISBN: 0-313-32289-9 (Set)
     0-313-32802-1 (Vol. I)
     0-313-32803-X (Vol. II)

First published in 2004

Greenwood Press, 88 Post Road West, Westport, CT 06881
An imprint of Greenwood Publishing Group, Inc.
www.greenwood.com

Printed in the United States of America

The paper used in this book complies with the
Permanent Paper Standard issued by the National
Information Standards Organization (Z39.48-1984).

10 9 8 7 6 5 4 3 2 1

Contents

CONTENTS

Works Listed by Chronology

Note: Most works are listed by publication date. For some works, an approximate writing date, or both a writing date and a publication date, may be listed if the work was published long after it was written. An approximate range of writing dates is listed for an essay that covers a variety of works (for example, Flannery O'Connor's short stories).

1916 James Joyce, *A Portrait of the Artist as a Young Man*
1920–1922 Sigrid Undset, *Kristin Lavransdatter*
1925 G. K. Chesterton, *The Everlasting Man*
1927 Willa Cather, *Death Comes for the Archbishop*
1928–1932 (published 1987) Edith Stein, *Essays on Woman*
c. 1930–1988 Jessica Powers, Poems
1931 Gertrud von le Fort, *The Song at the Scaffold*
1932 François Mauriac, *Viper's Tangle*
1933 Antonia White, *Frost in May*
1936 Georges Bernanos, *The Diary of a Country Priest*
1936–1942 T. S. Eliot, *Four Quartets*
1940 Graham Greene, *The Power and the Glory*
1941 François Mauriac, *A Woman of the Pharisees*
1941 Dorothy L. Sayers, *The Man Born to Be King*
1945 Evelyn Waugh, *Brideshead Revisited*
c. 1947–1964 Flannery O'Connor, Short Stories
1948 Thomas Merton, *The Seven Storey Mountain*
1949–1966 (published 1978) William Everson (Brother Antoninus), *The Veritable Years: Poems 1949–1966*
1950 Isak Dinesen (Karen Blixen), *Babette's Feast*
1951 Simone Weil, *Waiting for God*
1952 Dorothy Day, *The Long Loneliness*
1952 Flannery O'Connor, *Wise Blood*
1954 J. R. R. Tolkien, *The Lord of the Rings*
1956 Caroline Gordon, *The Malefactors*
1959 Robert Lax, *The Circus of the Sun*
1959 Mary Lavin, *Selected Stories*
1959 Muriel Spark, *Memento Mori*
1962 Katherine Anne Porter, *Ship of Fools*
1962 J. F. Powers, *Morte d'Urban*
1965 Evelyn Waugh, *Sword of Honor*
1966 Shusaku Endo, *Silence*
1966 Jean Sulivan, *Eternity, My Beloved*
1969 Rumer Godden, *In This House of Brede*
1970 Elizabeth Cullinan, *House of Gold*
1971 Heinrich Böll, *Group Portrait with Lady*
1972 Brian Moore, *Catholics*
1975 Larry Woiwode, *Beyond the Bedroom Wall*
1977 Annie Dillard, *Holy the Firm*
1977 Walker Percy, *Lancelot*
1978 Mary Gordon, *Final Payments*
1978 Christopher J. Koch, *The Year of Living Dangerously*
1984 Sandra Cisneros, *The House on Mango Street*
1984 Andre Dubus, *Voices from the Moon*
1988 Piers Paul Read, *A Season in the West*
1990 Jon Hassler, *North of Hope*
1991 Ron Hansen, *Mariette in Ecstasy*
1996 Kathleen Norris, *The Cloister Walk*
1997 Denise Levertov, *The Stream and the Sapphire*

Works Listed by Author's Gender

WORKS BY MEN

Peter Abelard, *The Letters of Abelard and Heloise*

Augustine of Hippo, *Confessions of St. Augustine*

Hilaire Belloc, *The Path to Rome*

Georges Bernanos, *The Diary of a Country Priest*

Heinrich Böll, *Group Portrait with Lady*

Orestes Brownson, *The Spirit-Rapper; An Autobiography*

Geoffrey Chaucer, *The Canterbury Tales*

G. K. Chesterton, *The Everlasting Man*

Paul Claudel, *Break of Noon*

Dante Alighieri, *The Divine Comedy*

John Dryden, *The Hind and the Panther*

Andre Dubus, *Voices from the Moon*

William Dunbar, Poems

T. S. Eliot, *Four Quartets*

Shusaku Endo, *Silence*

Desiderius Erasmus, *The Praise of Folly*

William Everson (Brother Antoninus), *The Veritable Years: Poems 1949–1966*

Graham Greene, *The Power and the Glory*

Ron Hansen, *Mariette in Ecstasy*

Jon Hassler, *North of Hope*

Gerard Manley Hopkins, Poems

John of the Cross, *The Dark Night of the Soul*

James Joyce, *A Portrait of the Artist as a Young Man*

Christopher J. Koch, *The Year of Living Dangerously*

Robert Lax, *The Circus of the Sun*

François Mauriac, *A Woman of the Pharisees*

François Mauriac, *Viper's Tangle*

Thomas Merton, *The Seven Storey Mountain*

Brian Moore, *Catholics*

Thomas More, *Utopia*

John Henry Newman, *Apologia Pro Vita Sua*

John Henry Newman, *Callista, A Sketch of the Third Century*

John Henry Newman, *Loss and Gain, The Story of a Convert*

Walker Percy, *Lancelot*

Alexander Pope, *Essay on Man*

J. F. Powers, *Morte d'Urban*

Piers Paul Read, *A Season in the West*

Henryk Sienkiewicz, *Quo Vadis?*

Jean Sulivan, *Eternity, My Beloved*

Henry Suso, *Exemplar*

J. R. R. Tolkien, *The Lord of the Rings*

Evelyn Waugh, *Brideshead Revisited*

Evelyn Waugh, *Sword of Honor*

Larry Woiwode, *Beyond the Bedroom Wall*

WORKS BY WOMEN

Angela of Foligno, *The Book of the Blessed Angela of Foligno*
Willa Cather, *Death Comes for the Archbishop*
Catherine of Siena, *Dialogue*
Sandra Cisneros, *The House on Mango Street*
Elizabeth Cullinan, *House of Gold*
Dorothy Day, *The Long Loneliness*
Annie Dillard, *Holy the Firm*
Isak Dinesen (Karen Blixen), *Babette's Feast*
Rumer Godden, *In This House of Brede*
Caroline Gordon, *The Malefactors*
Mary Gordon, *Final Payments*
Hildegard of Bingen, *Scivias*
Sor Juana Inés de la Cruz, *Response to Sor Filotea*
Julian of Norwich, *Revelations of Divine Love*
Mary Lavin, *Selected Stories*

Gertrud von le Fort, *The Song at the Scaffold*
Denise Levertov, *The Stream and the Sapphire*
Alice Meynell, Poems
Kathleen Norris, *The Cloister Walk*
Flannery O'Connor, Short Stories
Flannery O'Connor, *Wise Blood*
Katherine Anne Porter, *Ship of Fools*
Jessica Powers, Poems
Christina Rossetti, Poems
Dorothy L. Sayers, *The Man Born to Be King*
Elizabeth Ann Seton, *Letters of Mother Seton to Mrs. Julianna Scott*
Muriel Spark, *Memento Mori*
Edith Stein, *Essays on Woman*
Teresa of Avila, *The Interior Castle*
Thérèse of Lisieux, *Story of a Soul*
Sigrid Undset, *Kristin Lavransdatter*
Simone Weil, *Waiting for God*
Antonia White, *Frost in May*

Works Listed by Genre

Note: Some works cross genres and are therefore not easy to categorize. For the sake of simplicity, however, they are placed here in the category they best represent.

Autobiography

Augustine of Hippo, *Confessions of St. Augustine*

Dorothy Day, *The Long Loneliness*

Thomas Merton, *The Seven Storey Mountain*

John Henry Newman, *Apologia Pro Vita Sua*

Kathleen Norris, *The Cloister Walk*

Thérèse of Lisieux, *Story of a Soul*

Collected Letters

Peter Abelard, *The Letters of Abelard and Heloise*

Elizabeth Ann Seton, *Letters of Mother Seton to Mrs. Julianna Scott*

Drama

Paul Claudel, *Break of Noon*

Dorothy L. Sayers, *The Man Born to Be King*

Literary Nonfiction

Hilaire Belloc, *The Path to Rome*

Annie Dillard, *Holy the Firm*

Mystical Works/Spiritual Instruction

Angela of Foligno, *The Book of the Blessed Angela of Foligno*

Catherine of Siena, *Dialogue*

Hildegard of Bingen, *Scivias*

John of the Cross, *The Dark Night of the Soul*

Julian of Norwich, *Revelations of Divine Love*

Henry Suso, *Exemplar*

Teresa of Avila, *The Interior Castle*

Simone Weil, *Waiting for God*

Novels

Georges Bernanos, *The Diary of a Country Priest*

Heinrich Böll, *Group Portrait with Lady*

Orestes Brownson, *The Spirit-Rapper; An Autobiography*

Willa Cather, *Death Comes for the Archbishop*

Sandra Cisneros, *The House on Mango Street*

Elizabeth Cullinan, *House of Gold*

Shusaku Endo, *Silence*

Rumer Godden, *In This House of Brede*

Caroline Gordon, *The Malefactors*

Mary Gordon, *Final Payments*

Graham Greene, *The Power and the Glory*

Ron Hansen, *Mariette in Ecstasy*

Jon Hassler, *North of Hope*

James Joyce, *A Portrait of the Artist as a Young Man*

Christopher J. Koch, *The Year of Living Dangerously*

François Mauriac, *Viper's Tangle*

François Mauriac, *A Woman of the Pharisees*

Brian Moore, *Catholics*
John Henry Newman, *Loss and Gain,*
The Story of a Convert
John Henry Newman, *Callista, A Sketch*
of the Third Century
Flannery O'Connor, *Wise Blood*
Walker Percy, *Lancelot*
Katherine Anne Porter, *Ship of Fools*
J. F. Powers, *Morte d'Urban*
Piers Paul Read, *A Season in the West*
Henryk Sienkiewicz, *Quo Vadis?*
Muriel Spark, *Memento Mori*
Jean Sulivan, *Eternity, My Beloved*
J. R. R. Tolkien, *The Lord of the Rings*
Sigrid Undset, *Kristin Lavransdatter*
Evelyn Waugh, *Brideshead Revisited*
Evelyn Waugh, *Sword of Honor*
Antonia White, *Frost in May*
Larry Woiwode, *Beyond the Bedroom Wall*

Novellas

Isak Dinesen (Karen Blixen), *Babette's*
Feast
Andre Dubus, *Voices from the Moon*
Gertrud von le Fort, *The Song at the*
Scaffold

Poems

Geoffrey Chaucer, *The Canterbury*
Tales
Dante Alighieri, *The Divine Comedy*

John Dryden, *The Hind and the*
Panther
William Dunbar, Poems
T. S. Eliot, *Four Quartets*
William Everson (Brother Antoninus),
The Veritable Years: Poems
1949–1966
Gerard Manley Hopkins, Poems
Robert Lax, *The Circus of the Sun*
Denise Levertov, *The Stream and the*
Sapphire
Alice Meynell, Poems
Alexander Pope, *Essay on Man*
Jessica Powers, Poems
Christina Rossetti, Poems

Short Stories

Mary Lavin, *Selected Stories*
Flannery O'Connor, Short Stories

Social/Political Satires

Desiderius Erasmus, *The Praise of Folly*
Thomas More, *Utopia*

Theological/Philosophical Writings

G. K. Chesterton, *The Everlasting Man*
Sor Juana Inés de la Cruz, *Response to*
Sor Filotea
Edith Stein, *Essays on Woman*

Preface

The Catholic literary tradition is the longest and most diverse written literary tradition in history. Consisting of works as unique and influential as Augustine's *Confessions*, Dante's *Divine Comedy*, Erasmus's *The Praise of Folly*, James Joyce's *A Portrait of the Artist as a Young Man*, Christina Rossetti's poetry, and Flannery O'Connor's short stories, this tradition has strongly shaped the development of western letters and culture and, to a lesser degree, also that of the East.

This double-volume set consists of essays on seventy-seven major works that form part of this tradition. Arranged alphabetically by last name of author, these works span seventeen centuries, from the fourth to the twentieth, and were composed by writers from numerous cultures and countries, including France, England, Ireland, Africa, Spain, Mexico, Norway, the United States, Germany, Japan, Australia, and Poland. In addition, they represent a wide variety of literary genres, including fiction, nonfiction, autobiography, poetry, drama, satire, mysticism, and fantasy.

Each of the volumes' essays is written by a noted scholar in the field and is divided into several sections: a biography of the author; a summary of the plot (if the work is a narrative); an extended critical discussion examining, in particular, the work's Catholic themes and content; a survey of the work's critical reception over time; a note on the edition of the work that is profiled in the essay; works cited; and, usually, a bibliography. As a further help to readers, the works described are listed by date of composition, by the author's gender, and by genre. A selected, general bibliography is also provided to direct further reading and study in the areas of Catholic literature and Catholic thought.

BACKGROUND ON THIS ENCYCLOPEDIA

Following the publication of *Catholic Women Writers: A Bio-Bibliographical Sourcebook* (Greenwood, 2001), I was asked by editor George Butler to compile a more comprehensive survey of Catholic writing, this time focused on texts written by both male and female authors and providing much-expanded essays. True to its name, readers will find that this volume is indeed "encyclopedic" in scope and size. Although the prospect of editing a book of this magnitude was a daunting one, I was delighted to accept the challenge, for the need for such a reference volume is clear. As a professor of literature in my university's Catholic Studies program responsible for teaching both undergraduate and graduate students, I have participated over the last several years in the current wave of new scholarship on Catholicism taking place both in the United States and abroad. Importantly, this research has focused—and is focusing—not only on traditional areas of theology and philosophy but also on the rich and heretofore often unmined veins of Catholic history, culture, and the arts. As new programs and advanced courses on the Catholic intellectual tradition continue to flourish, and as the Catholic population worldwide continues to increase, the need for contemporary critical materials in a variety of disciplines related to that tradition is acute. The situation in the field of Catholic literary studies mirrors, to a great extent, that in academia as a whole. Although Catholic literature has been produced for nearly two millennia and is alive and well today, the relative paucity of modern critical scholarship on it can be traced to the dominant direction of academia toward poststructuralist theories over the last three decades. While at best contributing a laudable ethical dimension, these theories have often been antithetical, if not downright hostile, to religious values and hence also to the literature that lends itself unequivocally to a religiously based criticism. Since Catholic literature is literature that, by definition, is open to the existence of the supernatural, deterministic theories cannot suffice for full and accurate interpretations. The last heyday for Catholic literary criticism was, in fact, in the 1950s and early 1960s, an era ripe to assess the then-recent rise of mature Catholic fiction produced by such authors as Graham Greene, Hilaire Belloc, Evelyn Waugh, T. S. Eliot, and Sigrid Undset. This lag in scholarship is now being remedied, however, with a number of important critical texts on Catholic literature appearing since the early 1990s.

SCOPE OF THE WORK

Bringing together biographical, critical, and bibliographical information on a substantial body of writing, *Encyclopedia of Catholic Literature* is the most comprehensive and detailed reference book on Catholic literature ever produced. Readers will find it a convenient "first stop" guide, a useful tool to gain information on a text or an author that they are interested in but may know little about. Scholars who wish to attain an overview of the Catholic literary tradition and of the huge sweep and variety of its writings will likewise find the essays here helpful in directing their teaching and research. It should be noted, however, that this book does not claim to be complete, nor does it attempt to define a specific canon of Catholic literature. Rather, its more modest goal is to assemble in one place critical essays on a body of literature widely acknowledged as among the most significant works in the Catholic tradition—the literary "A" list, if you will. Without question, other works also deserve a place here, including multiple texts by the same author. Assembling any such collection necessitates a difficult selection process. To arrive at a manageable number of essays, I relied on several selection criteria. First, as in *Catholic Women Writers*, I evolved a working definition of "Catholic literature." No precise meaning of this term exists, and it may be configured in different ways for different situations. For my purposes, I deemed a literary work suitable for inclusion if it was informed in a substantial and meaningful way by the structures, traditions, history, spirituality, and/or culture of Catholicism. As will be noted, this definition is not based on the author's biography—that is, on whether he or she was a professing Catholic or not—but rather on the nature of the literary text itself, a far more reliable measure. In fact, Catholic literature has been written by baptized, practicing Catholics, by lapsed or dissenting Catholics, and by non-Catholics. In addition, my definition of Catholic literature is purposely broad. Because it is such a long and diverse tradition, Catholic literature conforms to no single pattern. Some works are didactic, some apologetic. Some are confessional or autobiographical. Some are visionary or mystical. Some uphold an orthodox view of the faith whereas others are critical of Catholicism's doctrines or practices, or they view the Church as merely a historical or cultural artifact. Some, including the majority of works here, are "literary" in the best sense of the word; that is, excellently rendered, complexly drawn, and profound works steeped in a deep yet realistic understanding of the Catholic faith and the Catholic Church.

Once this definition was in place, I queried a number of scholars around the nation and abroad who research Catholic literature regarding those works they would recommend for inclusion. A long list was generated—about twice as long as the offerings here—and then winnowed according to the most frequently mentioned choices and to those works either written in or translated into English and available in accessible editions. The list was further pared with an eye to broad representation of historical eras and as wide a scope of countries and ethnicities as possible. Finally, from a practical standpoint, the list was also narrowed to those works for which I could locate willing and able contributors.

TYPES OF WORK INCLUDED

Although the literary works included here are too numerous to mention, sketching some broad historical or generic categories may help readers place them in context. Written in the year 397, Augustine's *Confessions* is not only the first work in terms of historical date that will be found here but also one of the most influential. This autobiographical account of the African saint's conversion to the Catholic faith set the tone and shape of the human pilgrimage to God for all Christian writers to come; echoes of it resound through other spiritual narratives, such as Dante's *Divine Comedy* (c. 1321), John Henry Newman's *Apologia Pro Vita Sua* (1864), Thomas Merton's *The Seven Story Mountain* (1948), and Dorothy Day's *The Long Loneliness* (1952). Although represented by a number of significant works, including the *Letters of Abelard and Heloise* (c. 1130) and Chaucer's *The Canterbury Tales* (c. 1389), Catholic literature in the Middle Ages is best characterized by the flourishing of mystical or visionary works, such as Hildegard of Bingen's *Scivias* (c. 1152), Angela of Foligno's *Book* (c. 1309), Julian of Norwich's *Revelations of Divine Love* (c. 1393), and Catherine of Siena's *Dialogue* (c. 1398). A unique literary genre and a major contribution to the spiritual tradition of the Church, mystical writing emphasizes a direct, emotional approach to the divine that paralleled the simultaneous development of the rational, abstract scholasticism of such scholars as Thomas Aquinas (died 1274). Later mystical or visionary works represented here include Teresa of Avila's

The Interior Castle (1577), John of the Cross's *The Dark Night of the Soul* (c. 1586), and Simone Weil's *Waiting for God* (1951).

New strains of Renaissance humanism influenced the satires of Desiderius Erasmus (*The Praise of Folly*, 1511) and Thomas More (*Utopia*, 1516), while the seventeenth and eighteenth centuries saw long narrative poems defending the Roman Catholic faith in a reformed England such as John Dryden's *The Hind and the Panther* (1687) and Alexander Pope's *Essay on Man* (1734). The product of secular, pluralistic society, the novel arose in the nineteenth century and makes its first appearance here, in terms of date, with John Henry Newman's *Loss and Gain, The Story of a Convert* (1848) followed by Newman's American counterpart, Orestes Brownson's, *The Spirit-Rapper; An Autobiography* (1854). More significant as milestones in the development of Catholic fiction than as accomplished literary pieces, these early novels tended toward didacticism, a result of their authors' uneasy status in non-Catholic societies. Newman's support of the Oxford Movement, culminating in his embrace of Roman Catholicism in 1845, influenced numerous other conversions as well as the writing of such artists as Christina Rossetti, Gerard Manley Hopkins, and Alice Meynell, all poets of the late nineteenth and early twentieth centuries.

Imaginative writing in the Catholic tradition came of its own during the first half of the twentieth century with a remarkable outpouring of mature fiction, drama, and poetry by such well-known figures as Paul Claudel (*Break of Noon*, 1905, 1948), James Joyce (*A Portrait of the Artist as a Young Man*, 1916), Sigrid Undset (*Kristin Lavransdatter*, 1922), Willa Cather (*Death Comes for the Archbishop*, 1927), François Mauriac (*Viper's Tangle*, 1932, and *A Woman of the Pharisees*, 1941), Georges Bernanos (*The Diary of a Country Priest*, 1936), Graham Greene (*The Power and the Glory*, 1940), Dorothy L. Sayers (*The Man Born to Be King*, 1941), T. S. Eliot (*Four Quartets*, 1942), Evelyn Waugh (*Brideshead Revisited*, 1945, and *Sword of Honor*, 1965), Flannery O'Connor (*Wise Blood*, 1952), J. R. R. Tolkien (*The Lord of the Rings*, 1954), and Muriel Spark (*Memento Mori*, 1959). As some critics have suggested, the stable, unchanging rituals and doctrines of the Catholic Church of the period, a seeming bulwark against encroaching modernism, provided writers with the security to leave off the defensiveness that characterized the previous generation's fiction and venture into new artistic territory, portraying Catholicism in a complex, sophisticated manner. This secure image changed, however, with the advent of Vatican II (1962–1965). Some of the fiction produced soon after the historic Church Council shows an eagerness to shake off the stultifying past and "open the windows" to the modern world, the very goal of the Council's *aggiornamento*. But it also registers a tremendous sense of disorientation in the face of change. Novels such as Elizabeth Cullinan's *House of Gold* (1970), Brian Moore's *Catholics* (1972), and Mary Gordon's *Final Payments* (1978) well reflect these anxious times. "The Catholics in these [post-Vatican II] novels stand like a bankrupt urban renewal project, unable to revert to their former state and without the resources to build the new," critic Michael Quillan has aptly observed (1975, 34).

Since the 1970s, literature in the Catholic tradition has continued to thrive in a wide variety of modes and genres. Authors such as Heinrich Böll (*Group Portrait with Lady*, 1971), Walker Percy (*Lancelot*, 1977), Annie Dillard (*Holy the Firm*,

1977), Andre Dubus (*Voices from the Moon*, 1984), Sandra Cisneros (*The House on Mango Street*, 1984), Piers Paul Read (*A Season in the West*, 1988), Jon Hassler (*North of Hope*, 1990), and Denise Levertov (*The Stream and the Sapphire*, 1997) are read and enjoyed today by a wide audience, both Catholic and non-Catholic. Recent fiction such as Ron Hansen's *Mariette in Ecstasy* (1991) succeeds in uniting the Catholic literary past with the present, incorporating the long tradition of Catholic autobiography and mystical works into a postmodern form.

WORK CITED

Quillan, Michael. 1975. "Since Blue Died: American Catholic Novels Since 1961." *The Critic* (Fall): 25–35.

Acknowledgments

A reference volume of this magnitude is the collaborative effort of many people. I especially thank the sixty-six scholars who have contributed essays, many of whom also recommended authors and works for inclusion. A delightful benefit of such collaborative scholarship is the number of friendships formed and stimulating conversations held—many over e-mail—on teaching and researching Catholic literature and on the impact of such literature on readers' lives. I also thank Greenwood editor George Butler, who commissioned the project, and developmental editor Anne Thompson, who answered questions and expedited its production. Finally, I am grateful to the University of St. Thomas for a generous University Scholars Grant that provided me with release time over a three-year period to complete (among other projects) the compilation and editing of this book.

Introduction

CATHOLIC LITERATURE

Readers who pick up an *Encyclopedia of Catholic Literature* expecting to discover uniformly sentimental, moralistic, or smugly sectarian tales of priests and nuns, saintly children, or pious churchgoers will be surprised at what they actually encounter here. With good reason, a certain stigma hovers over any piece of writing labeled "religious," but a narrow use of this word does not apply to the literary works profiled in this volume. Adhering to no single pattern, each of these works, nevertheless, is informed to one degree or another by a Catholic Christian view of the world. Yet this Catholic perspective, or vision, varies tremendously according to the creativity, sensibility, and purposes of the individual author. "Certainly the imagination of a Catholic will be profoundly affected by his religion, but the manner in which it will be affected is not easy to predict," states Donat O'Donnell (1952, vii). Likewise, author and critic Flannery O'Connor maintained that a Catholic literary work "is not necessarily about a Christianized or Catholicized world, but simply . . . one in which the truth as Christians know it has been used as a light to see the world by. This may or may not be a Catholic world, and it may or may not have been seen by a Catholic" (1969, 173). In short, although Catholic literature does not lend itself to an external unity based on ideology, it does manifest a particular way of seeing the world.

While the ancient faith of Catholicism rests on a bedrock of doctrinal truths that have remained little altered over two thousand years, its practice of those doctrines and its outward expressions have proven to be highly adaptable to all historical eras and to numerous cultures throughout the world. Still, in its core teachings—and despite the fact that individual practitioners of the faith and the institutional Church have failed and will continue to fail many times in this regard—Catholicism's tenets consistently run counter to the general direction of secular society, which tends, in every age, toward increasing materialism, selfishness, greed, and violence. As such, the Christianity practiced by Christ and held up by the Catholic Church as the ideal is always countercultural, even as its more malleable teachings and expressions may adapt to particular times and places. Such tensions—being *in* the world yet simultaneously not *of* the world—have provided writers in the Catholic tradition with the kind of double sightedness that so often fuels artistic creativity. It is fair to say, I think, that all of the literary works represented in this volume arise in some way from this tension.

Let us now explore, in broad outlines, what is meant by a "Catholic perspective." Catholicism traces its roots to the Incarnation of Jesus Christ, the God-Man who came to earth to fulfill the ancient Jewish law, not abolish it, by establishing a new, higher law of Love. Christ's crucifixion and resurrection opened the gates of heaven to all who believe and who keep the commandments. Catholicism teaches the immortality of the soul, the redemptive nature of suffering, and the fellowship of all believers, living and dead, in the Body of Christ. It also asserts the unity of doctrine passed down in an unbroken line of authority through the institution of the papacy and the Church hierarchy.

In its teachings, Catholicism emphasizes God's immanence in the world rather than absence from it. This fact is seen most clearly in the Church's seven sacraments (Baptism, Confirmation, Penance, Eucharist, Marriage, Holy Orders, and Anointing of the Sick), in which the supernatural meets the natural and grace is conferred. The Church's central sacrament, the Eucharist—the natural elements of bread and wine transformed into the actual body and blood of Christ—which believers may receive each day, especially signifies God's intimate presence among his people. By contrast, Protestantism, to various degrees depending on the denomination, downplays or eliminates altogether such stress on sacramentality, thus placing more emphasis on God's distance from the world rather than presence in it. The result is a tendency to see more of a radical dualism between the human and the divine, the flesh and the spirit, sin and grace. Catholics may be characterized as possessing a more integrative, anagogical habit of mind than non-Catholics, one that, because of the faith's strongly sacramental basis, tends to see a unity between the secular and spiritual, a continuum of sorts rather than a sharp division. In the Catholic perspective, all created things emanate from Christ and reveal Christ "for whom and through whom all things were made." Thus, all of creation is essentially good, although wounded by the Fall. The extreme Protestant Calvinist sense of innate depravity is, therefore, as foreign to Catholic thought as is its opposite, the Romantic idealist view of an unfallen and endlessly perfectible world. To Catholics, in a famous formula, grace builds upon nature; it does not obliterate it or destroy it but transforms it. To a secular world now largely demystified and rationalistic, this habit of seeing the spiritual in the material—of constantly looking through surface reality to the supernatural— appears radical indeed.

At its most fundamental level, then, one can say that Catholic literature is that which will at least be open to the possibility of the supernatural, of more than meets the eye. And this vision naturally leads to a reconsideration of the purpose and meaning of human life. Catholicism takes as its premise the fact that humans are created beings, purposely and carefully designed by a Creator for a noble end. Human life, therefore, is precious, and existence on earth an important yet transient one, a journey or a pilgrimage rather than a final destination. Human life gets somewhere—it is positively oriented toward growth to an end and not merely meaningless or chaotic. And the human will is free to accept the challenge of the arduous journey to a high and dignified calling or not—that is, to accept redemption through Christ or to turn toward self and sin. As such, human life on earth becomes intensely dramatic, with the forces of evil a reality, not an illusion, and the struggles of each individual toward God or away from God immensely significant. "The . . . advantage religion gives us [writers] is Drama," author Paul Claudel once stated. "In a world where you do not know the yes or the no of anything, where there is no law, moral or intellectual, where everything is lawful, where there is nothing to hope and nothing to lose, where evil brings no punishment, and good no recompense—in such a world there is no drama, because there is no struggle, and there is no struggle because there is nothing worth the trouble" (1933, 12). It is precisely this dramatic sense that many writers in the Catholic tradition have found to be a powerful impetus to the creation of literature.

Because life on earth is but a journey toward a goal and not the goal itself, the Catholic imagination tends to express itself in terms of exile, perhaps especially in the alien environment of modern materialistic society. "The cry of many of our writers," says Frank O'Malley (quoting Nicholas Berdyaev), "is 'Save us from the deadly melancholy of our triumphant civilization'" (1951, 33). But this sense of exile and the interior drama of the soul are actually nothing new: Saint Augustine spoke eloquently of the restless heart resting, finally, in God alone. A sense of exile is especially pronounced in the large group of Catholic authors who were, at heart, satirists and who tended to regard modern life with a jaundiced eye, as a world gone mad. These include Muriel Spark, Walker Percy, Evelyn Waugh, J. F. Powers, and Flannery O'Connor.

One major tenet of the Catholic faith that has strongly affected its literature is its incarnationalism. Because Christ chose to save humankind by becoming a person and going through all human things, from birth to death, he sanctified human life on earth in all its aspects. As a result, the Christian faith is relentlessly historical, grounded in a real time and place even while emphasizing its eternal and spiritual dimensions. Salvation is not to be found by closing one's eyes, Buddha-like, to all that is human or by attempting to bypass it but rather by going through it. The body, too, with all its limitations, is not to be scorned but to be treated with reverence and care. Moreover, the inevitable suffering of life is considered an intimate part of God's plan, mysteriously tied to salvation in imitation of Christ, who chose to suffer in order to redeem. Thus, the idea of the Cross—of crucifixion—is at the core of the Catholic imagination. Due to the Incarnation, the basic pattern of Catholic thought, then, is that of descending in order to ascend—to go up one must first go down. One sees this pattern at work, for example, in Dante's *Divine Comedy*, a sophisticated allegory in which, in the opening scene, Dante's pilgrim is thwarted when he tries to climb directly up to the light. To reach the summit he must, rather, follow his heaven-sent guide on the longer, more difficult road, which first descends into the "hell" of self-knowledge and repentance.

Because of its strongly incarnational basis, the Catholic imagination does not shy away from all that is truly human. Catholic literature feels at liberty to describe the depths of evil and sin as well as the heights of the good and beautiful, for both form the truth about humankind. All of life may be embraced as it is, here and now, without any artificial need, as Flannery O'Connor once put it, to "tidy up" reality for the sake of a pious or uplifting story. "If the writer uses his eyes in the real security of his Faith, he will be obliged to use them honestly, and his sense of mystery, and acceptance of it, will be increased," O'Connor wrote. "To look at the worst will be for him no more than an act of trust in God" (1969, 148). Another critic summed up the incarnational perspective this way: "A writer for whom the universe is an undelivered unredeemed bewilderment can hardly look upon time or history or nature or man with a profoundly dynamic response. . . . The Catholic [writer], however, knows that Christ, the Son of God, has entered into the world, into time, and redeemed history and mankind. This incarnational awareness, this grasp of liturgical, factual reality, of Christ-in-time, Christ-in-the-universe, can enliven the poet's vision and illumine, inform, his words" (O'Malley 1951, 64–65). We can expect, therefore, that writers in the Catholic tradition will pay particularly close attention to reality—to existing things, to events, to others, to their own shifting moods—scrutinizing *what is* with the double sight that leads to a higher vision. The Psalms, in fact, are a marvelous literary model for the inherent tension of human life on earth—the rhythm of lofty, noble sentiments of praise, joy, and thanksgiving followed closely by sorrow, guilt, and humble petition. Conversion, in a Catholic sense, is not a one-time matter but an ongoing daily struggle, the "long road" of ups and downs, fits and starts. The remarkable poetry of Gerard Manley Hopkins, in its close concentration on the natural world, intense probing of the inner self, and abiding supernatural perspective, provides a fine example of literature written from a deeply incarnational perspective.

Because Christianity is an optimistic faith, the natural tendency of literary works written in the Catholic tradition is toward comedy (in the classic sense of the word) rather than tragedy. Hope is, after all, one of the cardinal virtues, and where there is life, there is hope. While much modern literature views the world as deterministic, random, or chaotic, the Catholic vision, as a result of its incarnational and sacramental bases, rejects despair no matter how inexorably tragic life may appear at any given time. This imagination "is, indeed, affirmative—radically affirmative—in its attitude toward nature and time and history," writes Nathan Scott. "[T]he religion which finds its main fulcrum in the Incarnational event is one which does not take us out of this world: it takes us, rather, deeper and deeper into it. . . . [T]he Christian mind has no desire to be an angel, but, rather, to the scandalization of idealists and angelists, it persists in wallowing about in all the temporal, creatural stuff of human life, for it was in this stuff that God Himself became Incarnate" (1966, 115–16).

The Catholic vision, then, is a richly imaginative one, both delighting in creation and steeped in mystery. At once lofty and sensual, heaven directed and earth bound, it has inspired countless artists with ready material to engage their hearts and minds throughout the centuries. Yet, of course, the Catholic beliefs and tendencies outlined above rarely, if ever, translate in undiluted form into literary art. Rather, a work of literature is always a unique amalgamation not only of the author's experiences and skills but also of his or her degree of understanding, acceptance, or rejection of such beliefs and tendencies. Contemporary writers in the Catholic tradition who have thought about the matter have insisted, in fact, that literature must never degenerate into a mouthpiece for dogma. This guideline is especially true of imaginative literature. Any work of art that bows to societal or institutional pressure for "correctness," however defined, quickly becomes mere propaganda. As noted, truly absorbing a Catholic sense of incarnationalism and sacramentality—the essential goodness of physical reality and the need to first penetrate it before transforming it—allows writers in the Catholic tradition to explore all possible topics, even those that challenge or push the limits of orthodoxy. Literature is, after all, not theology, but something quite different from it. Famously, Graham Greene claimed that an artist has the duty to embrace the "virtue of disloyalty"—that is, the obligation to say "no" to any institution, church or state, that tries to impose restrictions on the creative imagination. Such disloyalty, he maintained, gave him the freedom to roam through the minds of even the least sympathetic of characters, to play the devil's advocate in defending even despised humanity. For a like reason, writers have often refused the label "Catholic author," finding that the phrase pigeonholes their endeavors in uncomfortably narrow ways. "I am not a Catholic writer," Heinrich Böll emphatically exclaimed. "I am a Catholic who writes." Still, a number of authors, such as Flannery O'Connor, have insisted that their orthodox beliefs actually liberate them in their quest to explore unconventional territory. "If the writer believes that our life is and will remain essentially mysterious, if he looks upon us as beings existing in a created order to whose laws we freely respond, then what he sees on the surface will be of interest to him only as he can go through it into an experience of mystery itself. His kind of fiction will always be pushing its own limits outward toward the limits of mystery," she wrote (1969, 41).

As I have argued, Catholic literature is defined less by a specifically Catholic content than by a particular Catholic perspective applied to its subject matter. Moreover, a tendency to view things in a Catholic way may diminish but probably does not depart fully from a lapsed Catholic or one who has renounced the faith altogether. Several works in this volume, in fact, were written long after their authors had left off religious practice. "There is a distinctly, recognizably Catholic way of looking at and responding to experience mentally and imaginatively that operates prior to and deeper than doctrinal adherence and so remains operative even if doctrinal adherence moves into indifference or rejection," Albert Gelpi has correctly noted (1999, 205). In addition, various writers who were, or are, not Catholic have contributed in major ways to the development of the Catholic literary tradition. Writers in the High Church Anglican tradition, such as Christina Rossetti, Dorothy L. Sayers, and T. S. Eliot, strongly share the Roman Catholic perspective on such fundamental matters as incarnationalism, sacramentality, and the importance of liturgy. An author such as the contemporary Midwest poet and memoirist Kathleen Norris (*The Cloister Walk*, 1996) finds herself drawn to Catholic communal life and spiritual practice even while committed to her Protestant faith; her writing lends a valuable ecumenical perspective. Although not a Catholic, American writer Willa Cather wrote sensitively about the Catholic pioneer experience in such works as *Death Comes for the Archbishop*, a fictionalized historical account of the founding of the southwest missions. While Cather's novel is "Catholic" in content, on a much more integral level it also evinces a Catholic perspective. "Willa Cather makes the good—its nature, what it points to, and what protects it—the subject of her work," writes Michael Platt. While Cather loves the land, "she loves human beings more than regions, and she understands them as souls, not selfs, because she loves eternity more than all" (1991, 132, 146). Yet other non-Catholic authors, such as Norwegian writer Isak Dinesen (the pen name for Karen Blixen), have composed works that resonate strongly with a Catholic sensibility, whether intended or not. In her sparse, gemlike tale *Babette's Feast* (1950), Dinesen manages to capture the power of sacrament to unite the sensual and spiritual and to demonstrate the meaning of sacrifice for a higher good. Told with great good humor, this work never preaches but endlessly suggests, a hallmark of its excellence.

Given such broad parameters, one may indeed wonder just how useful the term "Catholic literature" is. In a larger sense, perhaps all literature expresses something deeply Catholic, especially western literature, the foundations of which are strongly marked by Roman Catholic influence. Certainly, the faith's viability two millennia after its founding indicates its continuing ability to address the human condition in its most profound aspects—as great literature also does. "Indeed, I have come to think that a case can be made for maintaining that all literature is Catholic," Ralph McInerny (1991) has stated. "The case is a bit forced, needless to say, but it would begin with Flannery O'Connor's contention that all literature—*all* literature—must have an anagogic sense. By this she meant that the actions depicted in the story have a meaning beyond the temporal realm in which they occur" (9–10). To press the case one step further, perhaps all the liberal arts are, on some level, at once "catholic" and "Catholic." Art, in a Catholic sense, is a wholly appropriate endeavor, a valid way of tapping the highest aspirations of humankind. "Even beyond its typically religious expressions, true art has a close affinity with the world of faith," Pope John Paul II has written, "so that, even in situations where culture and the Church are far apart, art remains a kind of bridge to religious experience. In so far as it seeks the beautiful, fruit of an imagination which rises above the everyday, art is by its nature a kind of appeal to the mystery. Even when they explore the darkest depths of the soul or the most unsettling aspects of evil, artists give voice in a way to the universal desire for redemption" (1999, 8). In a recent study, sociologist Andrew Greeley (2000) found a strong positive correlation between regular Catholic church attendance and appreciation of and participation in the fine arts. There is little to surprise here, for at Mass week in and week out Catholics are immersed in ritual and sacrament, in metaphor and symbol, in the sensory "smells and bells" of the liturgy as well as its lofty supernatural purpose. To Catholics, the habit of seamlessly merging the world of sense with the world of spirit is as natural as breathing.

Moreover, as are all Christians, Catholics are people of the Word, convinced of the intrinsic power of language and story. The Bible presents a God who delights in correspondences, associations, allusions, symbol, and metaphor. Events, images, and prophecies from the Old Testament are repeatedly echoed and given new meaning in the New Testament. Jesus' parables, too, are models of good literature, grounded in reality, open-ended, and multilayered. Several writers in the Catholic tradition have credited church attendance with the necessary inspiration for their art. "Looking back on my childhood now, I find that church-going and religion were in good part the origin of my vocation as a writer," says Ron Hansen, "for along with Catholicism's feast for the senses, its ethical concerns, its insistence on seeing God in all things and the high status it gave to Scripture, drama and art, there was a connotation in Catholicism's liturgies that storytelling mattered. Each Mass was a narrative steeped in meaning and metaphor" (2001, 7). A large number of Catholic authors have also credited Saint Ignatius's classic text, *Spiritual Exercises*, with helping nurture not only their spiritual life but also their art. Ignatius's exercises are disciplined approaches to prayer that first engage and center the imagination on certain Gospel scenes, asking the participant to "enter into" the scene, reenacting it in the mind's eye. It is precisely this kind of focused concentration on every detail of an imagined or recollected scene that underscores the artist's technique. A healthy and active imagination is central to both the practice of faith and the creation of literature. Faith is nourished by story, and a mind steeped in narrative finds its imaginative faculty constantly expanding. The literature described in this volume serves as a testament to the integral relationship between literature and religious faith.

WORKS CITED

Claudel, Paul. 1933. *Ways and Crossways*, trans. Rev. John O'Connor. London: Sheed and Ward.

Gelpi, Albert. 1999. "The Catholic Presence in American Culture." *American Literary History* 11, no. 1 (Spring): 196–212.

Greeley, Andrew. 2000. *The Catholic Imagination*. Berkeley: University of California Press.

Hansen, Ron. 2001. "Hotly in Pursuit of the Real." *America* 185, no. 15 (November 12): 6–10.

John Paul II. 1999. "Letter of His Holiness Pope John Paul II to Artists." April 4. Available at http://adoremus.org/7-899ArtistLetter.html.

McInerny, Ralph. 1991. "Preface." In *The Catholic Writer*, ed. Ralph McInerny, vol. 2, 9–11. San Francisco: Ignatius Press.

O'Connor, Flannery. 1969. *Mystery and Manners*, ed. Sally and Robert Fitzgerald. New York: Farrar, Straus, and Giroux.

O'Donnell, Donat. 1952. *Maria Cross: Imaginative Patterns in a Group of Modern Catholic Writers*. New York: Oxford University Press.

O'Malley, Frank. 1951. "The Renascence of the Novelist and the Poet." In *The Catholic Renascence in a Disintegrating World*, ed. Norman Weyand, 25–88. Chicago: Loyola University Press.

Platt, Michael. 1991. "The Happiness of Willa Cather." In *The Catholic Writer*, ed. Ralph McInerny, vol. 2. 129–50. San Francisco: Ignatius Press.

Scott, Nathan A. 1966. "The Bias of Comedy and the Narrow Escape into Faith." In *The Broken Center: Studies in the Theological Horizon of Modern Literature*, ed. Nathan A. Scott, 77–118. New Haven, CT: Yale University Press.

Peter Abelard [1079–1142]

The Letters of Abelard and Heloise

BIOGRAPHY

Peter Abelard was born in 1079, the son of a Breton knight. He gave up the life of a knight for learning, becoming a teacher of rhetoric and dialectic. By 1113, Abelard was a master in the cathedral school of Notre Dame renowned for his argumentative skills and his spotless reputation. But then around 1115, he entered into a passionate love affair with Heloise, the intellectually precocious niece and ward of Fulbert, a canon of Notre Dame. The affair lasted less than two years, but its consequences dramatically changed both their lives. When it was over, Abelard decided to enter a monastery and instructed Heloise to do the same.

As a monk, Abelard found himself in troubled circumstances many times. His history, his uncompromising precision, and his challenging intellectual methods infuriated many of the monks and clerics he met, including some very powerful people. While in the monastery, Abelard faced heresy prosecutions, physical assaults, and threats to his life. Nevertheless, he continued to study, teach, and write on theology for more than twenty years. Among his many learned writings, three were particularly important: the autobiographical *Historia calamitatum* (The History of My Calamities), which tells about his life up to around 1132; *Scito te ipsum* (Know Thyself), a work of moral philosophy asserting that intention should be the essential standard for evaluating sin; and *Sic et non* (Yes and No), a collection of patristic and Scriptural excerpts arranged under 158 theological and ecclesiological questions. The latter work made plain the necessity of developing a method to deal with the problem of conflicting sources; by example, it also offered such a method based on careful definition and dialectical argument. Scholars after Abelard developed this into the so-called "scholastic method" used by philosophers, theologians, and jurists, including Albertus Magnus, Thomas Aquinas, Gratian, and many others. Abelard was a brilliant albeit frequently arrogant thinker who made enemies and suffered for it.

Abelard died in 1142, about a decade after completing the *Historia calamitatum*. Late in life, he had become a target of Bernard of Clairvaux, a monk, preacher, and probably the most influential man in Christendom at the time. Bernard instigated a heresy proceeding against Abelard at Sens in 1140. Abelard was not permitted to defend himself properly and was convicted of heresy and sentenced to confinement, a sentence he immediately appealed to the papal curia. But while Abelard was resting at the monastery of Cluny on his way to Rome, word reached him that Pope Innocent II had confirmed the sentence at Bernard's request. He spent the last eighteen months of his life effectively in the custody of the abbot, Peter the Venerable. Peter endeavored to ameliorate Abelard's circumstances; he began a correspondence with Heloise and managed to reconcile Abelard and Bernard before the former's death. Upon his death, Abelard was buried at the oratory he had founded near Troyes, the Paraclete, as he had wished.

Almost nothing is known about Heloise before she met Abelard. She seems to have been in her early twenties when their affair began. In 1118, Heloise gave birth to a son by Abelard whom the couple named Astrolabe. When Fulbert began to humiliate her publicly even after the couple had married, Heloise retreated to a convent at Argenteuil for protection at her husband's urging. Heloise followed Abelard's command: she took vows and became a nun. At Argenteuil, she gained a reputation for piety and learning, eventually becoming prioress. To judge from her letters, Heloise was also an excellent Latin stylist, well versed in classical and Christian literature. After a long, distinguished career as abbess at the Paraclete, Heloise was buried alongside Abelard in 1164.

SUMMARY

The Letters of Abelard and Heloise is a collection of eight letters written in Latin in the 1130s and surviving in nine manuscripts, most of which date from the fourteenth century or later, but at least one of which dates from the late thirteenth century. Jeun de Meun, the thirteenth-century author who continued the *Romance of the Rose*, popularized the "tragic" love story of Abelard and Heloise in a section of his work that criticized marriage. The fourteenth-century Italian poet Petrarch also possessed a manuscript of the *Letters* in which he placed numerous glosses. Through Jean de Meun and others, Abelard and Heloise, and especially Heloise, became iconic figures in the courtly love tradition.

The first of the eight letters (letter I) is, in form, a work of consolation written by Abelard not to Heloise but ostensibly to a friend of his also in a religious order. A sort of autobiography, it has long been referred to by scholars as the *Historia calamitatum*. It is an important work not only because it reveals so much about the life and personality of this major twelfth-century thinker but also because it is an autobiography, one of the very first works in this genre written in the West since Saint Augustine's *Confessions*, composed about 400 A.D.

In the *Historia*, Abelard describes his rise to the top of his intellectual world, the affair with Heloise, and its aftermath. In 1117, when she became pregnant, Abelard decided to confess the affair to Fulbert. He promised to marry Heloise to placate her uncle, but on condition that the marriage be kept secret. When Abelard told this to Heloise, she argued against the marriage, doubting that it would satisfy Fulbert or fail to harm Abelard's career. And she was correct. Fulbert and his kinsmen spread word about the marriage and humiliated Heloise publicly. When Heloise, at Abelard's urging, took refuge at a convent at Argenteuil, where she had been educated, Fulbert and some of his kinsmen captured Abelard in his home and castrated him. In shock and shame, Abelard decided to become a monk. He entered the great monastery of St. Denis north of Paris after Heloise took the veil at Argenteuil.

Trouble continued to follow Abelard at St. Denis. He turned to theological studies and regained his writing and teaching prowess. But enemies he had made on his way up and some of the monks now vexed him. When Abelard wrote a treatise on the Trinity, one of the knottiest problems in the theology of the time, his enemies brought heresy charges against him, and not for the last time. At a council at Soissons in 1121, Abelard was forced to burn his treatise and was sentenced to confinement even though no specific claim of heresy had been proven. The sentence was soon lifted, but for his opponents, the stain would never be erased. Abelard reported that he quickly got into more trouble with Adam, the abbot of St. Denis. Abelard wanted to leave the abbey because it contained many enemies and was rich and worldly in a way he thought unseemly; however, the abbot placed him under censures that bound him there. Abelard then circulated information calling into question the rank and reputation of the monastery's patron, Saint Denis. The monks and the abbot attacked him and he fled to the Count of Champagne, who mediated the conflict. Abelard was eventually permitted to move to a quiet spot near Troyes, where he was followed by students anxious to hear him teach. There, Abelard was able to build an oratory for his students. He dedicated it to the Paraclete, the Holy Spirit, protesting in this way his mistreatment over his writing on the Trinity.

In 1122, Adam of St. Denis died and Suger, the new abbot, made peace with the scholar, allowing him to enter another monastic house. When the monks of St. Gildas in Brittany offered Abelard the abbacy in 1125, he accepted it. But St. Gildas proved to be ungovernable, corrupt, beset with poverty, and preyed upon by the community. Abelard's attempts to enforce discipline made him many enemies at St. Gildas. After several years, it was clear he was facing yet another failure.

But around 1130, Abelard heard that the nuns of Argenteuil had been expelled by Suger, who had seized their convent and its lands. He offered the women refuge at the Paraclete, eventually donating the site to them for a new convent (confirmed by Pope Innocent II in 1131). As far as we know, this was the first time he had contact with his wife in more than ten years. Abelard notes that the nuns experienced difficulties at first but that soon the local people became more generous and their situation gradually became more secure. At the same time, he notes that Heloise spent more and more time alone in her cell, even while her reputation for piety and wisdom grew.

Abelard involved himself with the nuns little at first, but in the penultimate section of the *Historia* he rehearses his thoughts leading to a decision to work with the women and to guide them, even though by doing so he courted further attacks upon his reputation and his person. The attacks came from the monks of St. Gildas. He endured their physical assaults and anticipated their attempts to poison him. The calumnies regarding Heloise and his assistance to the sisters at the Paraclete intensified his sense of shame. Abelard ends the *Historia calamitatum* with a meditation on the necessity of accepting what Shakespeare later called "the slings and arrows of outrageous fortune" in a spirit of gratitude:

> And so fortified by this evidence and these examples, let us endure our crosses with greater resignation as they are the more unjust. . . . Wherefore in all things we are right saying to Him: *Thy will be done.* . . . they clearly depart from righteousness who are wroth at some hardship which they have to bear, knowing full well that it comes upon them by divine dispensation. These follow their own will, not that of God, and through their secret desires they range themselves against the import of the words: *Thy will be done*, putting their own before the will of God. (Muckle 1964, 79–80)

The seven other letters in the collection constitute the correspondence initiated by Heloise, who, having seen the *Historia calamitatum*, wrote to request the same sort of consolation in view of their marriage. This correspondence is in two parts: four so-called "personal letters" (letters II–V), two each from Heloise and Abelard; and three so-called "letters of direction" (letters VI–VIII), one from Heloise and two responses from Abelard.

The personal letters, especially Heloise's, are full of pathos and pain. She was still desperately in love with Abelard and tried vainly to evoke from him some remnant of the tenderness and companionship they had once shared. But Abelard had come to loathe the whole love affair and to blame his feelings, particularly his lust, for his fall. The only relationship Abelard would agree to carry on with Heloise was one based on their lives and responsibilities as members of monastic orders.

Heloise's first letter (II) is a compelling, honest plea for Abelard to communicate with her. She notes that she had discovered the *Historia* and had been moved to tears by it. She asks for the same consideration as Abelard has given the friend for whom he wrote the *Historia*. Heloise holds out to her husband the emotional benefit of sharing the burden of their tragedy. She recalls their affair, correcting details from the *Historia* and showing the depth and honesty of her love: "I invoke God as witness that if Augustus, ruler of the whole world, would think me worthy of the honor of marriage and would confer upon me the whole world to possess forever, it would seem more dear and honorable to me to be called your harlot rather than his empress" (my translation). She reproaches Abelard for seeing to it that she took the veil before he became a monk, as if he had not trusted her then. Now, by contrast, he seems to trust her so much that he gives her no care at all: "the more I have made you feel secure in me, the more I have to bear with your neglect," she complains (Radice 1974, 117).

Abelard's first response to Heloise (III) is tentative and full of self-contempt. He excuses his silence by praising Heloise loftily for her accomplishments and reputation. As Abelard saw it, Heloise needed no help that he could give. He expresses a willingness to correspond with her, but only to the extent of answering questions on religious matters. The rest of Abelard's letter is a meditation on prayer: his need for it and its efficaciousness (especially when offered by pious women). Finally, he contemplates his own death and burial among women dedicated to Christ, asking only for prayers from Heloise and her sisters: "Finally, I ask this of you above all else: at present you are over-anxious about the danger to my body, but then your chief concern must be for the salvation of my soul" (126).

Heloise's second letter (IV) is the most wrenching of the collection; Abelard's response appears to have unhinged her. Heloise rejects Abelard's lofty praise of her and remonstrates with him against his preoccupation with death: "And so, I beg you, spare us—spare her at least who is yours alone, by refraining from words like these. They pierce our hearts with swords of death so that what comes before is more painful than death itself" (128). Heloise then slips into a reverie of pain and self-pity concerning Abelard's mutilation, their entry into religious life, and his pointed failure to return any of the tenderness they had shared years before:

> But if I lose you, what is left for me to hope for? What reason for continuing on life's pilgrimage for which I have no support but you, and none in you save the knowledge that you are alive, now that I am forbidden all other pleasures in you and denied even the joy of your presence which from time to time could restore me to myself?... Of all wretched women I am the most wretched, and amongst the unhappy, I am the unhappiest. (129)

Hurt and love and need are all swirled together in this letter. Heloise objects to Abelard's placement of her name before his in his salutation. She pleads with him not to praise her because, blasphemously, she proclaims herself devoted to him before God. And Heloise declares her persisting physical passion for Abelard and the falsity of her outwardly chaste life: "These pleasures of loving that we practiced together were so sweet to me that neither could they ever displease me nor could I ever forget them... They acclaim me as chaste; they have not found out I am a hypocrite" (my translation). The reader cannot help but be haunted by these words. Heloise's two letters seem to challenge the moral monopoly of ascetic religious values thought to be in place in the early twelfth century. Heloise here anticipated the ideas of courtly love that are critical of those values, which would not arise for decades. Indeed, it seems difficult to believe that a woman of Heloise's time could have written these words.

In Abelard's second letter to Heloise (V), he calmly yet determinedly refuses to return the emotional solace for which she was hoping. He responds to her complaints point by point. If he placed her name before his and praised her, this was because she was more elevated than he and worthy of praise. If he spoke of his death, this was because she asked about whatever perils might trouble him. And then Abelard turns Heloise's reasoning back upon her. She had argued that avoiding communication with her would validate the calumny that their affair had been only about sex. Abelard recalls the moment he had described in the *Historia* when Heloise took her vows and became a nun. Through her tears, he had recited the words of Pompey's wife, Cornelia (from Lucan's *Pharsalia*), who had requested that Pompey slay her so as to appease the gods and grant him victory over Caesar. Now Abelard answers that Heloise risked falling under Pompey's reproach and that perhaps it was only what her husband had once had and lost—in Heloise's case, the means to satisfy their lust rather than power and glory—that she truly loved. Abelard urges her to accept her lot as nun and abbess as a far better destiny than the life they might have had together, and he calls upon Heloise to redirect her misplaced love toward Christ.

In Heloise's third letter (VI), the first of the so-called letters of direction, her tone appears to be completely changed. The letter's opening is somewhat ambiguous: "*God's own in species, his own as an individual....* I would not want to give cause for finding me disobedient in anything, so I have set the bridle of your injunction on the words which issue from my unbounded grief; thus in writing at least I may moderate what it is difficult or rather impossible to forestall in speech. For nothing is less under our control than our heart" (Radice 1974, 159). Heloise tells Abelard that he has the capacity to remedy her grief. And then in this her longest letter, she conforms her words to his wishes. In a probing analysis, Heloise raises only questions about monastic regulations as they might be applied to women, asking Abelard for information, advice, and assistance in creating a better rule for her nuns at the Paraclete. The last two letters are Abelard's responses to Heloise's request. In the first (VII), Abelard discourses upon the history of nuns; in the second (VIII), he discusses various aspects of monastic life pursuant to the creation of an improved rule for nuns. None of the three letters of direction makes for compelling reading, except perhaps to someone with a special interest in monastic regulations.

MAJOR THEMES

The twenty-first-century reader can hardly avoid understanding the *Letters* as a romantic tragedy, alternately being infuriated by and pitying Abelard while being dazzled by and weeping for Heloise. But the reader must be cautious about anachronism; Heloise's enduring passion for Abelard was completely at odds with the prevailing moral precepts of her time. It anticipated by several decades the medieval courtly love tradition that elevated love against conventional values, but there is none of that here. Heloise considered her passion sinful; her letters never question the moral teachings her emotions resisted.

The indispensable context of *The Letters of Abelard and Heloise* is that of early twelfth-century monasticism. It was monasticism that had powered the great ecclesiastical reform movement of the eleventh century, through which ascetic monastic values and reformist monks captured the papacy and reshaped the institutions of the Roman Catholic Church. The election of bishops and of the pope, a stricter formal separation of spiritual and secular institutions, the insistence on a celibate priesthood, and even the Crusades were all signs of an intensified "ascetification" of the Church and of society comparable to the rise of fundamentalist movements in various religious traditions in the later twentieth century.

The triumph of monastic values in western European society was so complete by the early twelfth century that there was simply no secular lifestyle that could compare in moral and spiritual eminence to that of the monk. The Church also held, at that moment, a de facto monopoly on learning and scholarship. Consequently, there was no career path for a learned person outside the Church that Abelard might have followed. Even within the Church, the affair with and subsequent marriage to Heloise placed his career prospects in grave doubt.

The triumph of monastic values by the early twelfth century was not without a dark side. As the leading cultural institutions in society, some monasteries grew rich and some monks became influential and powerful. Contrary to their ideals of humility and of alienation from the secular world, some leaders of the monastic movement pursued policies that were patently worldly and aggrandizing. Like a fruit that has reached its full ripeness, early twelfth-century monasticism was showing signs of corruption. One consequence of this was another wave of reform within monasticism, led by Bernard of Clairvaux and others. But the tensions within the monastic movement at this time manifested themselves in personal animosities as well as in more constructive initiatives. That an arrogant personality and notorious fornicator such as Abelard could be a brilliant teacher and theologian must have been intolerably annoying to some.

When Fulbert discovered the affair, Abelard's career and the life he had known were, therefore, put in grave peril. His marriage to Heloise would likely not have preserved the life they knew, which is why Abelard had insisted it be kept secret. As a secular cleric, Abelard's career might well have culminated with a bishopric. But in an age in which celibacy was beginning to be required for priests as well as bishops, secrecy would not have been enough. As Heloise argued, Abelard's career prospects would have been far better without the marriage. Fulbert merely accelerated Abelard's fall by publicizing it, humiliating Heloise, and emasculating the man. After this, the choices Abelard made—taking monastic vows and compelling Heloise to do likewise, avoiding contact with her for years, taking up theology seriously, writing the *Historia* to make his contrition public, and then refusing to reciprocate in any open way the love his wife poured out to him—amounted to a consistent strategy for separating himself from his scandalous past. He attempted to surrender completely to the preeminent cultural institution of his day. Abelard's actions may have been driven by a sincere moral conversion, but they were also the only reasonable course he could have followed that might allow him to hold onto his career.

Not only does monasticism provide the necessary context for understanding the *Letters*, it is also treated in them in various aspects. This is not surprising given that the *Letters* are largely a correspondence between two members of religious orders. The letters of direction, discussed here only briefly, trace the history of women in monastic life (VI and VII) and describe how a monastic rule written for men might be better tailored to women (VI and VIII). In the *Historia*, there are examples of monastic excess, corruption, and petty politics, as in Abelard's discussion of his experience at St. Gildas (Radice 1974, 94–96) and his difficulties in the "depraved" monastery of St. Denis (77–88).

Between the *Historia* and the beginning of letter VI, in which Heloise restricts herself to matters of religion and monastic life, the *Letters* also constitute a drama of monastic values and lifestyle triumphing over sin. Abelard describes himself as a man destined for a fall, too clever by half and filled with irrepressible pride. When he dared to indulge his lust, Abelard's obsession with this sin, he tells us, corrupted Heloise and nearly ruined his career. He fell. The marriage was by no means a solution because marriage was regarded as a state far inferior to celibacy in moral terms. And so Abelard took monastic vows and began the slow process of turning from a secular to a fully religious lifestyle. Abelard presents the ongoing "calamities" that afflicted him both as the deferred wages of his sin and as the means by which he learned humility and put his priorities in proper order. At the end of the *Historia*, he seems to believe that he had turned a corner and repaired his soul. Whether this was sincere belief or artifice is not known; but either way, Heloise's letters must have hit him hard, either as yet one more catastrophic consequence of his sin or as an unwelcome intrusion from the past that would threaten his chance to regain respectability.

Abelard's answer to Heloise was to refuse her *sentimental* consolation and to insist that she instead seek *spiritual* consolation—and she must seek it from Christ rather than from himself. His first letter to Heloise is tentative and a bit morose, both on account of the St. Gildas monks and because her revelation no doubt troubled Abelard deeply. In his second letter, Abelard is less troubled and more firm, perhaps because the shock had worn off. And his approach worked. The personal letters (II–V) and the first of the letters of direction (VI), Heloise's detailed request for guidance on monastic matters, are sometimes said to map her conversion from a worldly to a truly spiritual outlook. According to this theory, Heloise changed inwardly and willed herself to become the nun of immaculate reputation that she was thought to be but professed to be only outwardly in her second letter (IV). Ironically, this sort of "conversion" on the part of Heloise follows a conception about love first enunciated in Bernard of Clairvaux's mystical treatise *De diligendo Deo* (On Loving God). There, Bernard defined four stages of love; the fourth and highest degree is reached when one recognizes those qualities in oneself that God (or, shall we say, the Beloved) prizes and consciously reforms one's life to emphasize those qualities. Abelard insisted that Heloise accept her destiny as an abbess, and so she became a renowned abbess, splendid in every respect.

Another theme raised in the *Historia* is the conflict between religious authority and intellectual inquiry. Rhetorically, Abelard depicts himself as a scholar pursuing the truth and believing his ideas to be fully orthodox; by contrast, he portrays many other churchmen as caring much less about honest inquiry in pursuit of understanding than about conformity to established authority. Constant Mews has speculated persuasively that the *Historia* may have been written as a means by which Abelard could acknowledge responsibility for his sins and put his past behind him so that he could resume his teaching in Paris (1999, 156–57). But Abelard often fails in containing his contempt for his opponents: the work fairly sparkles with the author's winks and nods to humility. This attitude resonates in the *Historia*: Abelard takes responsibility in a general way for his calamities, but he defends himself on many points when petty, misguided colleagues act out of ignorance or malice. Clearly, Abelard struggled, often without success, to embrace humility.

The *Letters of Abelard and Heloise* explore aspects of human emotion and the human condition from a fundamentally Catholic perspective, but it is a rarified one—that of monasticism and monastic values. Although Heloise became a part of the courtly love tradition in the thirteenth century, a tradition that helped broaden Catholic approaches to human passion, the feelings and attitudes reflected in the *Letters* betray the narrow, hostile attitude of her time. They were a harbinger, a precocious example of how classical literature would provide the raw materials with which western Europeans could create a mental world that was more positive about human feelings and earthly life. But not for Heloise and not for Abelard.

CRITICAL RECEPTION

The Letters of Abelard and Heloise did not receive much critical attention at all until the publication of Abelard's works in the early seventeenth century.

The "story" of Abelard and Heloise retold in the *Romance of the Rose* was known, but the letters themselves were not. A collection that survives in only nine manuscripts must not have been widely read. Peter Dronke has demonstrated that medieval testimonies about Abelard and Heloise were generally sympathetic and that Heloise especially became an iconic figure in the courtly love tradition.

From the early nineteenth century until the late twentieth century, the primary scholarly issue regarding the *Letters* concerned their authenticity. Although there is no hard evidence that anyone other than Abelard and Heloise wrote these letters (or at least some parts of them), a number of scholars have expressed doubts about their authorship for two reasons. First, they have noted that Heloise's claims of being devoted to Abelard even over her devotion to God and of cherishing the memory of their sexual experience is unprecedented in their time. Such concepts seem much closer to the ideas of courtly love that would have been current in the mid-thirteenth century. Moreover, given the fact that the earliest surviving manuscript dates from that period, some have speculated that the *Letters* were actually written or perhaps substantially revised at that time. Second, some scholars have found Heloise's dramatic shift from letters II and IV to letter VI difficult to accept. Her astonishing admissions, together with the suddenness of her conversion, make some suspect that perhaps Abelard or someone else fabricated the whole correspondence as a drama of conversion.

Although the authenticity debate is not closed, the common opinion among scholars today is that the *Letters* are indeed authentic, partly because of two more recent developments. Since the 1980s, the *Letters* have been investigated by scholars interested in gender and gender relationships in the twelfth century. Feminist scholars have embraced Heloise as a highly accomplished, eloquent, and heroic figure, one whose sensibility seems positively modern in comparison with her contemporaries. But the most intriguing development in the scholarly study of these letters has been Ewald Könsgen's publication (1974) of more than one hundred *Epistolae duorum amantium* (Letters of Two Lovers) discovered in Troyes. Könsgen suggested that these letters were written by Abelard and Heloise, and Constant Mews (1999) demonstrated that his hypothesis is almost certainly true. These letters were written by Abelard and Heloise in the years of their love affair, and they are filled with the tender sensuality that Abelard so utterly rejected in the *Historia* and his two personal letters (III and V) in the standard collection. Their discovery and Mews's interpretation may render the authenticity question regarding the standard collection moot. But they will only increase the interest in both Abelard and Heloise, two people of astonishing ability and individuality in an age in which we can see very few such people in any depth.

Closely related to the authenticity debate has been a line of criticism, which might be called "Catholic" from a certain perspective, supporting the principle that the values and culture of the early twelfth century were thoroughly monastic. Bernhard Schmeidler (1935) pointed out a number of internal contradictions in the *Letters* and argued that they are a fiction created by Abelard. In his Latin edition of the "Personal Letters," Joseph T. Muckle (1953) asserted that they are authentic in large part but must have been altered later on the theory that Heloise could not have carried on the "double life" revealed in the *Letters*. In his collection of essays, *Medieval Humanism*, the eminent medievalist Richard Southern accepted the *Letters*' authenticity and Heloise's double life, but he came to a similar conclusion: "Outside the monastic ethic there were only fragments of a classical ethic, difficult to combine in a coherent system and still more difficult to combine with the needs of secular activity . . . in the end [Abelard] had only one central code of conduct to fall back on—the code of monastic Christianity" (1970, 95).

NOTE

Peter Abelard, *The Letters of Abelard and Heloise*, trans. Betty Radice (New York: Penguin Books, 1974). Unless otherwise noted, all references are to this edition.

WORKS CITED

Dronke, Peter. 1976. *Abelard and Heloise in Medieval Testimonies*. Glasgow: University of Glasgow Press.

Könsgen, Ewald. 1974. *Epistolae Duorum Amantium: Briefe Abaelards und Heloises?* Mittellateinische Studien und Texte viii. Leiden, The Netherlands: E. J. Brill.

Mews, Constant J. 1999. *The Lost Love Letters of Heloise and Abelard*. New York: St. Martin's Press.

Muckle, Joseph T. 1953. "The Personal Letters between Abelard and Heloise." *Mediaeval Studies* 15: 47–94.

———. 1964. *The Story of Abelard's Adversities: A Translation with Notes of the "Historia Calamitatum."* Toronto: Pontifical Institute of Medieval Studies.

Schmeidler, Bernhard. 1935. "Der Briefwechsel zwischen Abälard und Heloise als eine literarische Fiktion Abälards." *Zeitschrift für Kirchengeschichte* Band 54 (III, Folge V), Hefte II–III: 323–38.

Southern, Richard W. 1970. "The Letters of Abelard and Heloise." In *Medieval Humanism*, 86–104. New York: Harper Torchbooks.

BIBLIOGRAPHY

Clanchy, Michael T. *Abelard: A Medieval Life*. New York and London: Blackwell, 1997.

McLaughlin, T. P. "Abelard's Rule for Religious Women" *Mediaeval Studies* 18 (1956): 241–92.

Monfrin, Jacque, ed. *Abélard. Historia calamitatum: Texte critique avec une introduction*. Bibliothèque des textes Philosophìques. Paris: Vrin, 1959.

Muckle, Joseph T. "Abelard's Letter of Consolation to a Friend (*Historia Calamitatum*)." *Mediaeval Studies* 12 (1950): 163–213.

———. "The Letter of Heloise on Religious Life and Abelard's First Reply." *Mediaeval Studies* 17 (1955): 240–81.

Wheeler, Bonnie, ed. *Listening to Heloise: The Voice of a Twelfth-Century Woman*. New York: St. Martin's Press, 2000.

— **Brendan McManus**

Angela of Foligno [c. 1248–1309]

The Book of the Blessed Angela of Foligno

BIOGRAPHY

Angela, an Italian mystic of the Franciscan tradition, was born in Foligno, a town near Assisi in the region of Umbria. While scholars have speculated on various details about her life, almost everything we actually know about her is narrated in *The Book of the Blessed Angela of Foligno*.

Unfortunately, we know almost nothing regarding her life before 1285. According to local tradition, she was most likely born in 1248 into a wealthy and noble family. Her father probably died while she was still very young. Angela married and had several sons. Her husband remains anonymous. Sometime in the 1280s, Angela underwent a dramatic conversion, and soon thereafter her children, husband, and mother all died. According to her own account in her *Book*, she had prayed for their deaths. Although this seems extraordinary, her writings indicate that her family had seemed an obstacle to her. She had encountered a good deal of hostility from them, and it is likely that she felt this prevented her from making spiritual progress.

Angela's *Book* implies that before her conversion she enjoyed the extravagant pleasures of the wealthy—fancy food, beautiful and expensive clothing, and fine perfumes. Her writings also indicate that she had a tendency toward anger, pride, and gossiping. According to local tradition, she was unfaithful to her husband, but no document exists to confirm this claim. Nevertheless, a close examination of her writings suggests that the sin she felt obligated to confess at the onset of her conversion may have been of a sexual nature.

The only explicit motives for her conversion that are mentioned in the *Book* indicate that in 1285 she wept sorrowfully, fearing damnation. Although inspired to go to confession, she was unable to confess some of her sins due to her shame. Utterly desperate, she prayed to Saint Francis and asked him to help her find a confessor. The next morning, she encountered a Franciscan friar who was chaplain to the local bishop. Angela then decided that this was the man for whom she had prayed and made a full confession to him. Biographical tradition refers to him simply as Brother A. This confessor may have been her relative, Brother Arnaldo, who would later become her scribe and literary collaborator.

It is likely that Angela did not receive a formal education, but it is clear from her *Book* that she was an exceptionally cultivated woman. Not unlike other women of her time, she was probably able to read but not write. It is possible that she may have learned to write (either in Latin or in her Umbrian dialect) only later in life. She dictated part of her *Book* to Brother Arnaldo. From probably 1292 to 1296, Arnaldo, as her confessor, met regularly with Angela in a local church in Foligno, writing down what she told him of her spiritual journey.

After her conversion, Angela began a new life of penance. Initially, it was a slow and difficult process, and from 1285 until 1291, Angela struggled to fully liberate herself from her sinful past. Against the counsel of her religious advisors, she decided to follow the example of Saint Francis in his poverty, giving up her extravagant way of life and distributing most of her belongings to the needy. She made a pilgrimage to Rome in 1291, where she asked the apostle Peter to help her become truly poor. Upon her return to Foligno, she gave up almost all of her remaining possessions and sold her home to give to the destitute. At some time during that same year, Angela became a Franciscan Tertiary. She also went on a pilgrimage to Assisi to pray to Saint Francis that he might help her faithfully observe the Franciscan Third Order rule.

Angela had a companion whom later manuscripts of the *Book* refer to as Masazuola. Although very little is known about her, it is thought that initially she may have been Angela's servant. From the numerous references to her in the *Book*, it is clear that she became Angela's constant companion and spiritual confidante. Passages of the *Book* highlight Masazuola's exceptional purity and piety. We know that she was in direct rapport with Arnaldo and also related to him some of the mystical phenomena she had observed in Angela. Both Angela and her companion cared for the sick and the poor.

Angela experienced intense, startling visions and mystical ecstasies that she narrated to Brother Arnaldo. She also underwent intermittent periods of agony and joy. Very little is known of her life from 1296 until her death in 1309. In 1300, she made another pilgrimage to Assisi. Later, a group of disciples and devotees began to gather around her to listen to her teachings. Angela was never canonized by the Church but was given the title of "Blessed" in 1701.

SUMMARY

Angela's *Book* consists of two parts. She dictated the first part, the *Memorial*, to Brother Arnaldo. Drawing from her own experience, Angela's *Memorial* narrates the steps or transformations the soul makes as it advances in its spiritual journey. The first twenty steps trace the early phases of her spiritual development. It is a difficult process of purification that is characterized by great struggle, effort, and suffering. The remaining stages are divided into seven "supplementary" steps. They describe her greater mystical ascent in her spiritual journey.

The second part of her *Book*, the *Instructions*, were dictated to anonymous disciples. The thirty-six *Instructions* contain Angela's teachings, admonitions, and letters that were offered to her devotees, to whom she had become a spiritual mother. They also include other mystical experiences that presumably occurred after the first part of her *Book* was written. The last of the *Instructions* narrates what she told her disciples during her final illness before her death. It is followed by an obituary notice and an epilogue.

MAJOR THEMES

The *Memorial* actually contains three narrators: God, Angela, and Arnaldo. The result is a complex, interpretation-laden account of what Angela actually experiences. God reveals himself to Angela, and she attempts to communicate her experiences to Arnaldo, who writes down what he hears. It was usually men (spiritual directors, confessors) who recorded the experiences of women mystics of the period. Deciphering exactly how much these men influenced the thinking (and the texts) of the women they wrote about is difficult. As Angela's spiritual director, Arnaldo would have exerted some influence over her life and thinking. However, as she advanced along the way of spiritual perfection, it is likely that their roles may have shifted. It appears that he became more of a disciple and she a spiritual mother.

What is clear is that Angela's own voice, personality, and experiences dominate the *Memorial*. Steps one through twenty describe Angela's progressive spiritual catharsis through suffering and her subsequent intimacy with God. At the onset of her conversion, Angela is painfully aware of her sinful past and greatly fears condemnation. The first seven steps along the way of perfection represent the initial phases of her development. They entail painful struggle and, above all, extraordinary anguish and distress. A complete surrender of her heart to God is achieved through a gradual process, and Angela emphasizes more than once that the soul's progress takes time.

In the early stages of Angela's development (steps eight through seventeen), we see that it is this suffering that effects her purification and enables her to reorient her affections and rid herself of possessions. In a dramatic gesture, Angela physically strips herself before a crucifix, offering herself to Christ. Determined to align her life with the Savior's, she pledges perpetual chastity and ardently desires poverty. Her actions clearly recall the example of Saint Francis, who unrobed himself publicly at the onset of his conversion. Angela's spirituality is much indebted to the Poverello. It was to Saint Francis that Angela prayed at the very start of her transformation, and he remained a central figure of inspiration to her during her spiritual development. In addition, Umbria was fresh with the religious fervor of the Franciscans, and it is not unlikely that they were the ones who initially influenced her to change her life. Angela's understanding of poverty involves both a lack of material things and a stripping of attachments to friends and relatives.

Saint Francis appears to her at various points throughout the *Book*, and it is largely due to his influence over her as spiritual father that Christ's humanity, passion, and crucifixion are of primary importance throughout her journey. During steps ten through fifteen, she experiences visions of Christ's passion. Angela's emphasis on the Crucified echoes those of other women mystics of the time. Many of them were influenced by the medieval diffusion of devotion to Christ's humanity, particularly in all its most pathetic elements (bleeding wounds, suffering, and torment). It is at this point that, like Catherine of Siena, Angela has a vision of herself drinking blood freshly flowing from Christ's side. Women mystics often ardently desired the Eucharist, and occasionally this manifested itself in visions of blood drinking. In step sixteen, Angela emphasizes her awareness of divine mercy and her understanding of the meaning of the Cross. Here, she more fully understands God's goodness and is acutely aware of her own unworthiness. This theme of knowledge of God and self continues to develop throughout Angela's *Book*. It is by meditating on Christ crucified and leading a life in conformity with his that Angela grows in her knowledge of God's goodness. In essence, all of the steps demonstrate her ongoing progress toward self-knowledge. In this manner, Angela's *Memorial* is a kind of spiritual biography, like Augustine's *Confessions*, in which self-knowledge is presented as an important aspect of one's pursuit of God.

It is in the seventeenth step that Angela's faith acquires a new dimension. She says that the Virgin Mary gives her a faith that is different from the one she had before. Here, Angela gains a greater certainty in her love of God and passes into a mystical state that alters her level of contemplation. Now more mature, her numerous mystical consolations occur both in visions while she is awake and in dreams when she is asleep. In step eighteen, she begins to exhibit intense physical manifestations as a result of her impassioned absorption into the Divine. If she hears someone speak about God, she screams. Upon viewing paintings of Christ's passion, she becomes feverish and falls sick. Finally, in step nineteen, she receives such a great mystical consolation that she loses her power of speech. At the end of the nineteenth step, Angela desires to find God so completely that she wants nothing else, and he promises her that the Trinity will come into her when she has finished divulging herself of her possessions. At the beginning of the twentieth step the promise is fulfilled, and Angela manages to dispossess herself of almost everything. By his own admission, Arnaldo abandons the process of describing the twentieth step, saying simply that it is filled with great divine revelations.

At this point, there is a notable break in the narrative structure of Angela's *Memorial*, which highlights the key role Arnaldo played in the organization of the text itself. Here, Arnaldo feels compelled to explain his rationale for having condensed the rest of Angela's transformations. Arnaldo's special role as Angela's scribe and confessor merits particular attention. The process of creating her text generally followed a pattern: Angela dictated her visions in the Umbrian dialect to Arnaldo, who recorded and translated her words into Latin. Sometimes Arnaldo had trouble understanding the meaning of some of Angela's revelations and mystical experiences. Although he states that he was very conscientious while copying Angela's *Memorial*, he often had to reread to her what she had dictated in order to be sure he had copied it correctly. Arnaldo compares himself to a sifter that retains only the coarsest flour. Angela acknowledged that, while what he wrote was somehow "weakened," it was basically faithful to what she had told him. However, she states that on occasion what he writes and then rereads to her is "obscure" and "bland."

Although Angela had originally designated thirty steps in her spiritual journey, Arnaldo had such difficulty describing the remaining material that he decided to assemble the following revelations into seven supplementary steps. The first five supplementary steps demonstrate Angela's heightened perception of Christ's passion and a further penetration into the mystery of the Cross. Angela's ascension is characterized by increasingly intense visions and experiences of Christ crucified, the Eucharist, the universe filled with the presence of God, and various other formless visions of the Godhead. Through these powerful and even shocking divine revelations, Angela grows even more intimate with Christ, who she calls the suffering "God-Man." Despite the nature of her intense visions, she endures periods of emptiness, doubts and uncertainties, and temptations from the devil. These periods are interspersed with feelings of immense joy and certitude of God's love. With these steps, Angela begins to enter into the mystical life proper.

The first supplementary step initially takes place on the road during a pilgrimage to Assisi. While traveling, she becomes aware of the Holy Spirit, who promises her a great consolation. The Holy Spirit then enters into her deepest self, along with an intense feeling of the crucified Christ and God the Father. This experience of the Trinity stays with her until, while contemplating a church window depicting Saint Francis, she feels it gently withdraw. This represents an important landmark for Angela. Once back in her home in Foligno, she remains in a state of rapture for eight days, which concludes with her mystical betrothal to Christ. During this first supplementary step, Angela also describes visions of Christ's flesh on the cross, including his throat and arms. Occasionally the Host appears to her as containing the Christ child or even the Savior's eyes themselves. Several other extraordinary visions involving the Eucharist occur throughout the *Memorial*. Angela's experiences recall those of many medieval mystics, and in particular women, who also saw Christ (in various forms) appear in the Host while it was elevated.

In the second supplementary step, Angela has a vision of God in Paradise. The theme of the ineffability of her religious experiences is introduced and continues with numerous references that appear throughout her *Book*. Here, since her vision of God is indescribable, she says simply that he appeared as a full brightness surrounded by praising saints and angels. God manifests himself to Angela through revelations and defines himself as the love of the soul. It is revealed to Angela that all can and must love God. Reassuring her of his love for both her and her companion, God gives her a permanent sign of his love. He removes Angela's doubt and deposits in her an ardent desire for him that will burn continuously. In this step, Angela speaks of Christ as a physician of the soul. This theme of Christ as physician is grounded in patristic writings, in particular those of Saint Bernard and Saint Bonaventure. Angela maintains that, if one is ill, one must do whatever the doctor says and must refuse to rely on medicines other than those that he prescribes. Christ's blood is the medicine that he himself administers to the sick.

In the third supplementary step, God reveals knowledge to Angela through various teachings. This stage is dominated by the theme of the "sons" of God. In response to Angela's request that he show her his true sons, God tells her a parable about a banquet. The Lord loves all his guests, but some he loves more. Some eat at the table near him, and still others are allowed to eat from his plate and drink from his cup. Those special sons who eat from his table are those who wish to please him. God explains the "descent" of Christ, who suffered indignity and vileness but who then "ascended" to dignity. Likewise, God grants special tribulations to his sons for their own benefit so that they too might ascend to dignity. These tribulations become sweet, and works of charity represent an ascent into joy. Here, Angela provides Arnaldo with a shocking example from her own life. After drinking the water she and her companion had used to wash a leper's decaying wounds, she declared that it tasted as sweet as communion. It should be noted that this radical gesture of ingesting the filth of lepers' sores is anchored in the life of Saint Francis, and it is repeated in the lives of various other saints, including Catherine of Genoa and Catherine of Siena.

In the fourth supplementary step, Angela experiences intermittent periods of intense and continuous contemplation of God followed by feelings of dejection and despair. During her high points, she claims to have comprehended the entire creation and God's power that is everywhere and fills everything. At her low points, she is assailed by doubts, physical illness, and tribulation. Angela describes these intervals as God "playing" with and in the soul. This metaphor of the "game" that God plays with the soul is one often used in mystical literature of the period. Angela states that when the soul tries to "seize" God, he will immediately withdraw. Finally liberated, she is then elevated to a mystical state after having received the Eucharist. This is followed by a total immersion within Christ. Her extreme delight in the Passion expresses itself in various visions, including one in which her soul enters into the wound in Christ's side. During this step, God also responds to various questions and through a vision reveals his power, will, goodness, and justice, which provides Angela with a complete and certain understanding never felt before. Angela describes the soul as being in a state of "darkness" that is then illumined to understanding. Her use of darkness to describe her lofty mystical states recalls the theology of the Pseudo-Dionysius, a fifth-century neoplatonic author whose writings are fundamental to Christian mystical tradition. In the Middle Ages, they enjoyed an authority almost equivalent to that of Scripture. Terminology from Pseudo-Dionysius's writings was widespread among mystics of the time. Formless visions of the Godhead peppered with descriptions of some of his divine attributes (such as the "All Good") also bear the Dionysian imprint and suggest Angela's freshly attained heights of mysticism.

Profound ecstasies and visions of the Passion of Christ characterize the fifth supplementary step. The transformation of Angela's soul through her participation in Christ's sufferings prepares her for union with God. During this step, Angela is given a deep understanding of Christ's poverty, humility, and physical and emotional suffering. Her visions include one in which she is united with Christ in his tomb. She kisses his breast and his mouth while he embraces her tightly. It is worth noting that the use of such erotic imagery drawn from the Song of Songs was not uncommon among some medieval holy women. Their use of such metaphors affirmed the importance of love as a means of access to deep union with the Divine. Often extremely poetic, these types of descriptions occasionally caused ecclesiastical suspicion, particularly because they seemed to deny the need of any intermediary between God and the self. Angela's visions of God's love become so intense that she undergoes a three-day state of rapture and loses the power of speech. During this step, Angela also enumerates seven ways in which God enters the soul to reveal his presence. These are described with increasing intensity, the greatest being when the soul grants hospitality to Christ the Pilgrim. In this last way, one's soul reaches such a profound understanding of God that one is incapable of speaking about it because it is so far beyond words or thoughts.

The sixth supplementary step at first appears to be an unexpected reversal of her progress, as Angela practically collapses under countless bodily assailments and demonic torments of her soul. Sunk to the depths of despair, Angela's emotions range from hopelessness to rage. She battles against pride and experiences persistent feelings of damnation. She describes this period as a "horrible darkness" in which she is assailed with sexual temptations and ghastly suffering for which she finds no consolation. Her intense feelings of abandonment are comparable to those that Christ suffered on the cross. During this step, Angela is enduring the "dark night of the soul," a stage of spiritual development common among great mystics and later described by Saint John of the Cross. The result of this step is that Angela's soul undergoes extreme purgation and purification. She comes to the understanding that without humility, salvation is virtually impossible. This step prepares her for her final transforming union with the Divine.

It is from the depths of despair that Angela is finally catapulted into the highest point of her mystical ascent, the seventh and final supplementary step. It begins with a lofty vision of God in darkness, where she sees both "nothing" and "everything" simultaneously. Although it is almost inexpressible, Angela explains that her soul sees the creation that overflows with God's presence. She understands his power and wisdom, and in the darkness, she is made totally sure of God. Angela says that her soul becomes elevated to such exalted heights that she sees God in a darkness that is altogether ineffable. God's transcendence is beyond conceptualization, and any attempt to describe it seems to be blasphemy. The language that Angela uses throughout the seventh supplementary step recalls the "negative theology" of the Pseudo-Dionysius, which defines God in terms of our ignorance rather than of our knowledge. While in this state, God draws Angela to himself and her soul "lies" in the Trinity, where she becomes one with the Divine. She affirms that there is no intermediary between God and herself. During this period, Angela describes mystical elevations and visions in which she is immersed in the love of God and of the Crucified, lies on the "bed" of the Cross, where she finds rest, and "swims" in a deep abyss. Angela comprehends God's justice and the meaning of difficult Scriptures. In a series of Eucharistic revelations, she understands how Christ's body is present in the sacrament of the altar yet is also simultaneously everywhere, filling everything. During this final step, Angela also describes a state that surpasses all others in which she is given a greater awareness of God. It appears to be beyond even the divine darkness. Angela claims to understand the complete truth in the entire universe, including heaven and hell. Finally, she experiences her own soul's presentation before God, which is accomplished with no fear or hesitation. Angela rests in the profound knowledge that nothing can ever separate her from God.

As the heart of Angela's *Book*, the *Memorial* is the most widely read and studied and provides us with more information on her own inner world. The *Memorial* ultimately derives its unity from Angela's personal account of a spiritual journey toward oneness with God. The wisdom that she gains from the journey is then offered to her followers in the *Instructions* for their spiritual benefit. We know very little about Angela's immediate disciples, but it appears that many of them were most likely among the Franciscan First and Third Orders. It is not clear to whom the *Instructions* (particularly the letters) were addressed. Nevertheless, we do know that Angela intended her teachings for those disciples near her as well as those far and wide who extended beyond the boundaries of Umbria. It is the concern for the spiritual formation of her sons and daughters that is the unifying principle behind the *Instructions*.

Angela's various letters are addressed to both groups and individuals, although the recipients are not named. They indicate that she had a close relationship with her spiritual entourage. The scribes of the *Instructions* also remain anonymous, but differing styles indicate that there were many of them. It is likely that Arnaldo may have written several of the first *Instructions*. The manuscript history of the *Instructions* is a complicated one. Many of them circulated independently of one another and the *Memorial*. Their numerical arrangement varies considerably among the manuscripts.

Most of the *Instructions* are undated, and some may be additions and glosses composed by various disciple scribes. The themes developed in the various steps of Angela's *Memorial* are repeated and expanded in the *Instructions*. Although they are frequently amplified, the teachings are firmly grounded in the *Memorial*. The themes of the *Instructions* include the following: Christ, the suffering God-Man and his cross; Christ's poverty; prayer; the Eucharist; and knowledge of God and self.

CRITICAL RECEPTION

Angela has been called a "teacher of theologians," and her *Book* is regarded as a work of great importance in the literature of Christian mysticism. Her influence extended beyond the group of followers to whom her teachings were addressed. It is likely that many penitents came to Foligno seeking to keep company with her and to benefit from her experience as a spiritual mother. The most notable of these was Ubertino of Casale, leader of the Franciscan Spirituals. To Angela he credits his conversion to a more radical ascetic life. Her writings also inspired several saints, including Teresa of Avila, Ignatius of Loyola, Francis de Sales, Alphonsus Liguori, and the French philosopher Ernest Hello.

Angela's writings, either as selections or in their entirety, have been translated several times into English. Paul Lachance's recent translation and critical edition, *Angela of Foligno: Complete Works* (1993), contains an extensive introduction that offers a panorama of Angela's life and times. Various chapters discuss the importance of the historical, cultural, and spiritual currents surrounding Angela and her *Book*. Other chapters develop further the major motifs of her spirituality and inner journey. Lachance examines Angela's direct influence on her contemporary disciples and concludes that her *Book* was perhaps used for polemical purposes in the struggle between the various factions of the early fourteenth-century Franciscan movement. Additionally, he discusses the early manuscripts of her writings and the influence of her teachings through the centuries. Cristina Mazzoni's edition, *Angela of Foligno: Memorial* (1999), contains John Cirignano's creative translation as well as a critical introduction and interpretative essay by Mazzoni. Her thought-provoking essay compares Angela's experience with current feminist theology. An annotated bibliography of selected studies on Angela is provided.

Angela's *Book*, particularly the *Memorial*, has lately enjoyed a good deal of critical interest. Caroline Walker Bynum (1991) examines Angela in the framework of other medieval holy women, emphasizing the role of food, the Eucharist, female imagery, and the body in their writings and religious devotional practices. Elizabeth Petroff's works also discuss Angela alongside other medieval female religious (1986, 1994). Mary Ann Sagnella (1995) investigates Angela's writings in light of the negative medieval perception of the female body as vile, while Tiziana Arcangeli (1995) attempts to disentangle Angela's voice from that of Arnaldo in the *Memorial*. Arcangeli argues that Angela's voice is filtered; thus, we as readers remain somewhat removed from it. Catherine Mooney (1994) also examines the role of Arnaldo in the transcribing of the *Memorial*. Rosamaria Lavalva (1992) considers the role of language in Angela's attempt to narrate her mystical visions to Arnaldo. Finally, in my article "A Mystic's Drama: The Paschal Mystery in the Visions of Angela da Foligno" (2001), I explore how many of Angela's visions were inspired by ceremonies and dramatizations common in the Middle Ages during Holy Week.

NOTE

Angela of Foligno, *Angela of Foligno: Complete Works*, ed. and trans. Paul Lachance (New York: Paulist Press, 1993). This edition of Angela of Foligno's works is recommended.

WORKS CITED

Arcangeli, Tiziana. 1995. "Re-reading a Mis-known and Mis-read Mystic: Angela da Foligno." *Annali d'Italianisica* 13: 41–78.

Bynum, Caroline Walker. 1991. *Fragmentation and Redemption: Essays on Gender and the Human Body in Medieval Religion*. New York: Zone.

Lavalva, Rosamaria. 1992. "The Language of Vision in Angela da Foligno's *Liber de vera fidelium experientia*." *Stanford Italian Review* 11, nos. 1–2: 103–22.

Mazzoni, Cristina, ed. 1999. *Angela of Foligno: Memorial*, trans. John Cirignano. Cambridge: D. S. Brewer.

Mooney, Catherine M. 1994. "The Authorial Role of Brother A. in the Composition of Angela of Foligno's Revelations." In *Creative Women in Medieval and Early Modern Italy*, ed. Ann E. Matter and John Coakley, 34–63. Philadelphia: University of Pennsylvania Press.

Morrison, Molly. 2001. "A Mystic's Drama: The Paschal Mystery in the Visions of Angela da Foligno." *Italica* 78, no. 1: 36–52.

Petroff, Elizabeth Alvilda. 1986. *Medieval Women's Visionary Literature*. New York: Oxford University Press.

———. 1994. *Body and Soul: Essays on Medieval Women and Mysticism*. New York: Oxford University Press.

Sagnella, Mary Ann. 1995. "Carnal Metaphors and Mystical Discourse in Angela da Foligno's *Liber*." *Annali d'Italianistica* 13: 79–90.

— **Molly Morrison**

Augustine of Hippo [354–430]

Confessions of St. Augustine

BIOGRAPHY

Saint Augustine, bishop, confessor, and Doctor of the Church, was born Aurelius Augustinus on November 13, 354, in Thagaste in northern Africa, a prosperous town developed by the Romans in a lush agricultural district. His father, Patricius, a pagan, was a property owner and a town official. His mother, Monica, was a faithful Catholic who later converted her husband to Catholicism. Augustine had at least two older siblings: a brother, Navigius, who appears briefly in the *Confessions*, and a sister, Perpetua, who entered the religious life. In Augustine's home there existed the dichotomy between pagan and Christian cultures, sensuality and piety, tensions that affected a large part of Augustine's life.

Augustine was fascinated by human development and language acquisition, and thus he devotes the beginning of the *Confessions* to his infancy and to childhood in general. He takes the reader through his boyhood and school days, his enjoyment of the Latin language, his respect for Greek culture and language, his adolescence and the famous episode of stealing from a pear tree, and his young adulthood, when he took a concubine, a nameless girl who shared his life for fifteen years. (It is important to remember that Augustine was living in a milieu that encouraged an epicurean lifestyle.) As a young adult, Augustine also became associated with a gang known as the Wreckers: as he states, he "sometimes delighted in their friendship" (*Confessions*, 38). But in the midst of his studies, he encountered Cicero's *Hortensius*, which changed his outlook on life and aroused in him a quest for wisdom and learning that prompted him to study both the Christian Scriptures and the heresies rampant at that time. When he was eighteen years old, he became a father and named his son Adeodatus, which means "gift of God." While Roman law permitted infanticide and would grant Augustine permission to turn away mother and child and refuse any provision for the baby, Augustine declined to do so and, instead, loved his son. Augustine and Adeodatus later even coauthored *On the Teacher*, a Christocentric theological treatise written in the form of a dialogue between father and son. Augustine once said of Adeodatus, "his intelligence left me awestruck" (164).

In the year 383, Augustine traveled to Rome against his mother's wishes, tricking her in order to depart (she followed him there two years later). He then traveled farther north to Milan, where he befriended Ambrose, who had served as bishop of Milan for eleven years prior to Augustine's arrival. Ambrose's oratorical style and Scriptural erudition greatly edified Augustine and caused him to experience and accept a new spirituality, that of Christianity. Book six of the *Confessions*, titled "Years of Struggle," describes the turning point in Augustine's life and provides an exemplary description of "the dark night of the soul": that is, of the buffetings of his heart and soul as he wrestled with the Catholicism of Ambrose and Monica. In book eight, he recounts how he heard a childlike voice that told him to "take up and read" (*"tolle, lege"*) while he was in a garden in Milan in September 386, an epiphanic experience that prompted him to read Romans 13:13: "not on carousing and drunkenness, not in sexual excess and lust, not in quarrelling and jealousy. Rather, put on the Lord Jesus Christ and make no provision for the desires of the flesh" (202). This text silenced all his questions. Soon thereafter, he decided to abandon marriage and secular ambition; under Ambrose's instruction, he was baptized on Holy Thursday, April 22, 387. He returned to Carthage in 388 and became a priest a year later. He was granted a leave of several months for intensive Bible study and published several Scriptural treatises. In 396, Augustine was consecrated bishop of Hippo, an office he held for the next thirty-four years. The sack of Rome in 410 inspired him to write *The City of God* (413–426 A.D.). His other major works include *On the Trinity* (416), the *Enchiridion* (421), *On Christian Doctrine* (425), and *Retractions* (427). He also penned treatises against heresies, biblical commentaries, theological and philosophical tracts, works on ethics and moral theology, and letters. In 428, the Vandals invaded Hippo. Augustine died on August 28, 430, during that siege.

Augustine was a prolific and accessible writer. Indeed, the *Confessions* speaks to the modern reader as it describes the anxieties, conflicts, shortcomings, temptations, and spiritual journey of a man who, of all the early Church fathers, seems most like us. His psychological self-analysis and autobiographical writing style, which were uncommon prior to the nineteenth century, are more in keeping with a modern sensibility. Yet he was not just a converted sinner whose writings resound meaningfully in the personal lives of Christians. He wrote substantially and substantively on a wide range of topics that greatly influenced western Christianity, including the doctrine of original sin, the place of the Church in the world, and the believer's dependence on divine grace.

Augustine's desire to bear witness to the God he wrestled with, experienced, and ultimately accepted is the structuring principle of the *Confessions* and is what distinguishes spiritual autobiography from other literary genres. The *Confessions* significantly influenced later authors and cultures and served as a model for an articulation of the conversion process. Many subsequent works of literary autobiography, including William Wordsworth's *Prelude*, secularized the religious ideas and themes of Augustine's text. The *Confessions* stands as a masterpiece of devotional literature in its beauty of language, honesty of personal expression, and praise of God.

Augustine is recognized in the lexicon of Roman Catholic saints on August 28, the day of his death. He is often referred to as *the* great Doctor of the Latin Church for his philosophical, Scriptural, and dogmatic influence on the ancient world as well as on other periods, such as the Middle Ages, the Renaissance, and the Enlightenment. A writer of tremendous depth and perspective and a leading theologian, he holds one of the highest positions not only in the Roman Catholic tradition but in the entire Christian tradition. His place in western history is secure.

PLOT SUMMARY

Saint Augustine's *Confessions* is the first and, unequivocally, the most influential religious autobiography in the Christian tradition. Considered one of the great masterpieces of world literature and western Christianity, this work was written in 397 A.D., when Augustine was forty-three years of age. Like many individuals who arrive at middle age, he began writing reflectively, having been a baptized Catholic for ten years, a priest for six, and the bishop of Hippo for only two. This classic spiritual autobiography of a great saint is a theocentric testimonial of his conversion experience and his growing understanding of God. It is a moving depiction of the life and experiences of an early Catholic believer, conveyed to us across the sixteen centuries that separate us from his writing and its context. The *Confessions* has been translated into more languages than any Latin writings except Virgil's.

In this intensely personal narrative, Augustine relates the story of his soul: his infancy and childhood on a humble Algerian farm; his youthful indiscretions, struggles with sexuality, and hedonism; his thoughts on friendship, especially with Ambrose, eloquent preacher and bishop of Milan; his conversion experience; his tributes to his mother Monica; his renunciation of secular ambition and marriage; his encounters with ecclesiastical power in Milan; and, ultimately, the recovery of the faith his mother had taught him as a child. The *Confessions* also contains Augustine's philosophical musings on Platonism and the nature of God; his fascination with astrology and Manichaeism; and his skepticism and disillusion with pagan myths until he finally arrives at belief in the Christian faith.

In the 400 years between the time of Jesus and Augustine, the Hebraic sex-positive view was gradually rejected in favor of the sex-negative Greek philosophies of Stoicism and Gnosticism, which renounced sexual passion and erotic pleasure. Except for procreation, sex was deemed a sin; joy and pleasure in sex even within marriage were considered antithetical to God's will. When the Roman emperor Constantine adopted Christianity, it abruptly shifted from counterculture to mainstream religious dogma and was integrated into the social hierarchy. By the fourth century, Ambrose, Jerome, and Augustine established the ideal of virginity and sexual purity as the highest of Christian virtues. Augustine, however, was the central architect of the sexual credo most identified with western Christendom. In the *Confessions*, he discusses his perception that one's moral stature and value as a human being is a function of the mind's ability to control the body. Thus, to be fully human and spiritual was to be at war with oneself, to fight against one's sexual impulses.

The *Confessions* is composed of thirteen books, or chapters, and is written as a colloquy or direct address to God. The work can be read on a number of levels, all of which guarantee its wide appeal. On one level, it provides a compendium of many of the religious trends and philosophies competing for acclaim in the fifth century. Augustine's religious ambivalence is apparent in the chapters that explicate his thoughts on the Manichees, a missionary-minded Gnostic movement of Persian origin; the Neoplatonists; and, finally, Catholic thinkers. On another level, the *Confessions* may also be read as a psychological description of a mother-son relationship as well as a narrative of friendship between Augustine and Ambrose, Augustine's mentor in his return to the faith. The book contains many passages detailing theological concepts that perplexed Augustine and many sections of such tenderness and beauty that they are reminiscent of the Psalms in their poetic lyricism. The *Confessions* also succeeds in conveying the pull or draw toward divine love that the author encountered, and it invites the reader to consider his or her own religious experiences from a similar perspective.

The narrative style of the *Confessions* may be viewed as a tripartite structure: the first nine books are autobiographical, relating the story of how Augustine rejected the Catholicism of his childhood and how he returned to it in his early thirties. In book ten, Augustine returns to the present time of his writing, twelve years after the last scenes of book nine, and begins a series of theological reflections. Books eleven through thirteen continue in this meditative style but are more focused on how to understand God's Word in creation. These three sections may be viewed as parallel to the three stages of mystical ascent to God described by Saint John of the Cross—purgation, or overcoming obstacles to the will of God; illumination, or growing in passionate love for God; and union, or gaining alliance with God—thus providing the *Confessions* with a unifying principle and accounting for the shift in compositional style. Like all authentic works of spiritual autobiography, the *Confessions* is, principally, not about the author but about the ultimate Author—God—with whom the writer finds union and intimate encounter: "You have made us for yourself, and our heart is restless until it rests in you" (3).

In the *Confessions*, Augustine defines his place in God's creation and describes his awareness of sin, repentance, and submission to the divine will. Augustine wrote from memory, a dozen years or more after his conversion and baptism. The narrative thread, therefore, follows no neat chronological sequence. He wrote as a sinner who has been saved and redeemed, selectively tracing his spiritual journey to God. He was not burdened by any self-conscious regard for literary style or the publication market. This spiritual autobiography, therefore, offers no finished patterns. What it does offer is a chronicle that has the capacity to radically alter the reader's perspective on the truth of life as it is experienced by the soul. In this respect, regarding the *Confessions* as spiritual autobiography reaffirms its claim to authentic literary and spiritual interpretation and argues for the critical importance, extreme versatility, change, and continuity of this genre in the hallmark of literary and spiritual achievement. A consideration of the *Confessions* as spiritual autobiography helps to define the tension, conflict, and resolution of the two poles of sin and love and allows the reader to recover the experiential side of two vital traditions: the spiritual and the literary.

Thomas Merton paid fitting tribute to the *Confessions* when he stated,

In plain words—if you can accept them as plain—Christianity is the life and death and resurrection of Christ going on day after day in the souls of individual men and in the heart of society. It is this Christ-life, this incorporation into the Body of Christ, this union with His death and resurrection as a matter of conscious experience, that St. Augustine wrote of in his *Confessions*.[1]

MAJOR THEMES

Saint Augustine was, perhaps, more responsible than anyone else for the doctrinal advancement of Christianity. In his youth, he rejected Christianity because of certain inconsistencies he found in the Bible and because of what he considered the too simplistic teachings of the apostles. As he grew older, he pondered the intellectual and spiritual controversies of his age, the concept of time, and his place in the universe. The *Confessions* addresses these topics. An articulation of these issues is important in providing the reader with a framework and a foundation for reading the *Confessions*.

One controversy that Augustine took on in his text was Manichaeism, a dualistic world view founded by the Persian prophet Mani around 216 A.D. that maintained that evil vied with God for power in the world and that the body was but an evil necessity that housed the soul. After his conversion and in opposition to the Manichees, Augustine believed that, with the Fall, humanity freely turned away from God and towards the self and so fell into original sin; this explained the appearance of evil in creation. Augustine was the first theologian to incorporate a theory of the Fall as an essential doctrine of Christian faith. The Manichees also did not believe in the Incarnation, death, and Resurrection of Christ, a point to which Augustine takes exception in book nine when he states that "by a true physical death 'he who intercedes for us died for us'" (161), authenticating his stance by alluding to Romans 8:34. This evokes for Augustine a conception of Christ's identity and explains why he had previously "loved vanity and sought after a lie" (161). Before his conversion and while involved with the Manichees, he had not known that God had done three important and interrelated things: God had raised Christ from the dead; God had put Christ at God's right hand; and Christ had sent the Holy Spirit. As the bishop now states, "And you Lord had already 'magnified your holy one' (Ps. 4:4), raising him from the dead and setting him at your right hand (Eph. 1:20), whence he sent from on high his promise, the Paraclete, the Spirit of truth (John 14:16f.). He had already sent him but I did not know it" (161).

The second controversy that Augustine confronted was the heresy of the Donatists, a fourth-century North African Christian sect founded by the bishop of Casae Nigrae that held extremely rigorous views concerning purity and sanctity. Donatism maintained that the true Church was set apart from the surrounding society because it had the sacraments and that these sacraments were to be dispensed only by clergy who were "perfect" or completely sinless, otherwise they would not only be invalid but even harmful to the recipients. Augustine, on the other hand, formulated a sacramental theology that regarded the sacraments as given by Christ rather than distributed solely by the priest (*ex opere operandi*). Thus, he formulated a theological basis for the Church as an institution of well-meaning but imperfect people who would achieve perfection only in the city of God but who are helped while on this journey by Christ's sacraments. Indeed, as some critics suggest, the *Confessions* may have been written as a type of response to the Donatists, who insisted that bishops such as Augustine must be perfect in order to be "true" bishops.

The third controversy that Augustine took on was Pelagianism, founded by Pelagius, a British monk and theologian, in the fifth century. Pelagius denied the primitive state in Paradise and original sin, insisted on the naturalness of concupiscence and the death of the body, and ascribed the actual existence and universality of sin to the bad example that Adam set by his first sin. Since his ideas were chiefly rooted in Stoicism rather than in Christianity, he regarded the moral strength of the will, when rooted in asceticism, as sufficient in attaining virtue. By justification, we are cleansed of our sins through faith alone (the doctrine of *sola fides*), but this pardon, according to Pelagius, implies no interior renovation or sanctification of the soul. This controversy enabled Augustine to articulate a doctrine of grace that replaced the Pelagian view that individuals can achieve perfection through their own effort with a doctrine that underscored the necessity of both human effort and divine grace in a world weakened by sin. The *Confessions* also provides a more careful development of the dogmas of original sin and grace.

Augustine also struggled with the concept of time. As he makes quite clear, the fact that the world is created "out of nothing" is one of the topics he wants to address with God. The intrinsically temporal nature of creation is problematic to him, since "temporal" implies the capability of being destroyed—created out of nothing and returning to nothing. Augustine understands that, through the power of memory, all time—past, present, and future—is available to us simultaneously and that all time is actually measured against eternal time. This paradox resulting from his definition of time grounds the *Confessions* not in a chronologically autobiographical framework but in a narrative and plot structure that attempts to capture and approximate a *kairos*, or God-centered view of time. Such structural bifurcation—temporal and eternal—underscores the unique documentation of the journey of a soul.

For Augustine, time *is* and time *is not*: the pressure of eternity on the present is pervasive. Since storytelling and narrative are the ultimate safeguards against the threat of death and temporality, in the *Confessions* Augustine focuses on the nature of sin and its various manifestations to demonstrate the temporality and the restlessness of creation. Augustine frames most of the *Confessions* in narrated time. As a matter of fact, in book eleven, he poses the question, "What is time?" not as a philosophical injunction but as an overview of the project of this work: to relate his "lived" experience in and about time to God and to eternity. He thus uses the literary trope of direct address to God to generate a narrative wherein the vertical and horizontal meet. This concept of time is considered a theological and philosophical masterpiece in that it attempts to describe not only the question of time but more so the ascent of the soul to God through the "circular" process of time: "But no time is wholly present. It will see that all past time is driven backwards by the future, and all future time is the consequent of the past, and all past and future are created and set on their course by that which is always present" (228–29). Rather than being organized according to the principle of succession usually seen in narrative, then, Augustine's confessional story is organized around a much wider parameter: "the extensionless present of the moment" (Pranger 2001, 8). Commenting on the relationship between

Augustine's account of his conversion and his concept of time, critic M. B. Pranger states:

> [W]hat [Augustine] now is and what he once was are far from being an orderly succession of events. [The *Confessions*] is neither a story of a successful conversion, nor a story of ups and downs, nor even a tragic account of utter failure. In a sense, there are neither plans nor bounds. Addressing himself to God, the source of being and the embodiment of eternity, Augustine cannot but blur distinctions between sooner and later, before and after. Tied to timeless eternity, the present as lacking extension is all there is left. As such, it reveals itself as the black hole in the heart of human existence, as the ever-present and ever-evasive moment that cannot be grasped. (8)

Moreover, such an understanding of Augustine's complex notion of time is crucial to an embedding of the *Confessions* in the genre of spiritual autobiography. The *Confessions* abounds with Augustine's descriptions of his procrastination, delays, hesitation, lapses—all characteristics of spiritual autobiography implicit in the stages of purgation, illumination, and union with God, which, because they are not necessarily distinct steps, suggest the interplay and simultaneity of the past, present, and future. The classic tripartite way articulated in the *Confessions* is the basic model of the conversion archetype. In fact, Augustine observes that what is lacking in the Platonist's writings is precisely the emotional and spiritual ups and downs of the soul progressing along this way to God: a "face of this devotion, the tears of confession . . . a troubled spirit, a contrite and humble spirit. . . . In the Platonic books no one sings. . . . In surprising ways these thoughts had a visceral effect on me as I read 'the least' of your apostles [Paul]. I meditated upon your works and trembled" (131–32).

Besides noting Augustine's view of religious controversies and his concept of time, there are numerous other ways of reading the *Confessions*. In her article, "The Symbolic Structure of Augustine's *Confessions*," critic Marjorie Suchocki (1982) argues that the *Confessions* is focused around two trees—the pear tree in book two and the fig tree in book eight—which correspond symbolically to the two trees in the Garden of Eden, the tree of the knowledge of good and evil and the tree of life. She confirms the universal appeal of the *Confessions* by showing how Augustine and all persons repeat the story of Adam, and she suggests thereby that Augustine is an Everyman figure. Other critics claim that Augustine's journey to God is organized into two parts, with the first part (books one through eight) describing the search for God and the second part (books nine through thirteen) demonstrating the mind of the person who has found God. Still other critics consider Augustine's use of imagery in describing God (warming winds, father, doctor, nurse, mother); his various alimentary images that convey the search of a starved soul for God, the source of true nourishment; his conflating of biblical and Neoplatonic notions of the divine; and his extensive Scriptural allusions and citations, especially from the Psalms.

The *Confessions* may also be considered from an archetypal perspective with such motifs as the pilgrimage, the psychomachic struggle, the masculine archetype (father, God, wise counselor, tutor), the feminine archetype (mother, spouse, Church, divine wisdom, temptress), the child archetype (inner child)—all of which Augustine suggests in his spiritual quest. The work may likewise be interpreted as conveying the conversion process by using images of chaos and creation to depict the soul's progression toward salvation, postconversion unity, and recovery from chaos; or it may be seen in terms of the four themes intrinsic to spiritual autobiography: rebellion, revelation, redemption, and regeneration. Still other critics claim that the *Confessions* is a revisiting of Virgil's *Aeneid*, which Augustine frequently cites. Indeed, "the hero of the *Confessions* is a spiritual Aeneas, and his journey from Africa to Italy represents the movement from the profane to the spiritual, from the city of the world to the city of God" (Hawkins 1978, vi). In the *Confessions*, Augustine's trials and initiation render him a citizen of both cities.

But no matter how it is considered, the *Confessions* has broad genre appeal; it may be read as a work of theology, spirituality, autobiography, psychology, history, or literature. In it, we see how religious discourse actually becomes part of lived experience and how personal narrative serves as a significant and authentic resource for theology. Augustine openly describes the good things and the bad things in his life and confesses much sin and wrongdoing, but he does so to magnify the grace of God and not merely to record a solipsistic struggle.

Rather than just a continuous and chronological unfolding of the public life of the author, spiritual autobiography interprets an individual's life from a larger perspective, thereby imbuing ordinary experiences and events with spiritual meaning and magnitude. The *Confessions*, in particular, invites the reader to be attentive to the ways by which Augustine imparts order and meaning to his daily experiences. Moreover, it demands a disciplined and reflective attention to the reader's own spiritual journey. Augustine looked at his youthful past through the lens of his adult experience, wrote about it from a spiritual perspective, and consequently came to understand that past in a new way. The *Confessions* is a retrospective record of the creative and dynamic tension implicit in one's evolving relationship with a God who is tireless in pursuit of a wandering spirit. Augustine's engagement in the search for God brings him some release of tension but ultimately no true rest. As Peter Brown puts it, Augustine's quest is therefore the endless quest of the romantic:

> If to be a Romantic means to be acutely aware of being caught in an existence that denies [a person] the fullness for which he craves, to feel that he is defined by his tension toward something else, by his capacity for faith, for hope, for longing, to think of himself as a wanderer seeking a country that is always distant, but made ever present to him by the quality of love that groans for it, then Augustine has imperceptibly become a Romantic. (1967, 156)

A consideration of the *Confessions* as a verbal portrait written in the *schola cordis* tradition—an expression of the inward groaning and groping for the God of creation and for a refashioning of the writer—posits it as not merely a biographical record of Augustine's life but as a spiritual record of the Christian disciple. The book is an acknowledgment that creation is a continuous outpouring of God's being and that God himself is both dynamic and changeable yet never changing. In the *Confessions*, Augustine attempts to articulate "the groaning that cannot be expressed in speech" (Rom. 8:26).

It is ironic that devotional works such as the *Confessions* that record struggles and conflicts can establish a sense of the sacred that is more apparent than works that merely attempt to reinforce and redefine religious tradition and doctrine. Writing in the genre of spiritual autobiography provides both a refashioning of the self and a record of God's transforming grace.

CRITICAL RECEPTION

The American philosopher William James published the first psychological evaluation of the *Confessions*. In his 1902 *Varieties of Religious Experience: A Study in Human Nature* (1958), James views Augustine as a perfect example of the "divided self," a psychomachic character. While it is not always appropriate to use psychoanalytic language to explain religious experience, the use of the psychomachic struggle to capture the essence of the religious quest is defensible when applied to Augustine, the prototypical spiritual autobiographer.

Peter Brown's *Augustine of Hippo: A Biography* (1967) may be considered the best historical biography of Augustine. Brown considers not only the Mediterranean world of Augustine's time but also significant cultural influences on his character and personality. This book is a psychobiography of Augustine. Henry Chadwick, an eminent scholar of early Christianity and general editor of the *Oxford History of the Christian Church* and *Oxford Early Christian Texts*, provides in the Oxford World's Classics edition (1998) the first translation of Augustine's *Confessions* in forty years. His notes are informative, and his translation renders this classic accessible to the contemporary reader.

In *Recherches sur les confessions de saint Augustin*, Pierre Courcelle (1950), considered one of the greatest Augustine scholars of the twentieth century, interprets the *Confessions* as a literary construct rather than as providing a historically accurate account of the conversion experience.

James J. O'Donnell's *Augustine: Confessions* (1992) is a valuable and comprehensive three-volume study that contains the text of the *Confessions*; an introduction to and commentary on each of its books; a discussion of Augustine's use and interpretation of Scripture; and passages from Augustine's other works, thereby allowing Augustine to be his own commentator. He reports the findings of modern scholarship and enables the reader to read from the Latin Bible and other patristic and classical sources in Greek, French, German, Spanish, Italian, and Latin. Also included are indices to Augustine's works, other ancient authors, Scriptural passages, and a four-page general index. The book provides a working bibliography of 594 scholarly sources of Augustinian studies from around the world. O'Donnell gives noteworthy credit to the Paris Institute, Etudes Augustiniennes, for its holdings of bibliographical resources. This study makes a significant contribution to criticism on Augustine's *Confessions* and enables the reader to better appreciate a great saint and a fascinating intellect.

Richard Severson (1996), who holds a doctorate in theology and a professional degree in library science, evaluates the literature and anglophone works on the *Confessions* in *The Confessions of Saint Augustine: An Annotated Bibliography of Modern Criticism, 1888–1999*. Eight subject categories, all key elements of the *Confessions*—autobiography, literary criticism, conversion experience, philosophy, psychology, spirituality, textual unity, and theological issues—are annotated in this treatment of 468 items. The study focuses on scholarly articles or books on the *Confessions* written in English between the years 1888 and 1995 and a few written in French.

NOTES

Augustine of Hippo, *The Confessions of St. Augustine*, Oxford World's Classics, trans. Henry Chadwick (New York: Oxford University Press, 1998). All references are to this edition.

1. Thomas Merton, quotation taken from the cover of John Kenneth Ryan's translation of *The Confessions of St. Augustine* (New York: Doubleday, 1960).

WORKS CITED

Brown, Peter. 1967. *Augustine of Hippo: A Biography*. Berkeley: University of California Press.

Courcelle, Pierre. 1950. *Recherches sur les confessions de saint Augustin*. Paris: E. de Boccard.

Hawkins, Anne Olivia. 1978. Archetypes in the Spiritual Autobiographies of St. Augustine, John Bunyan, and Thomas Merton. Ph.D. diss., University of Rochester.

James, William. 1958. *The Varieties of Religious Experience: A Study in Human Nature*. New York: New American Library Books.

O'Donnell, James J., ed. 1992. *Augustine: Confessions*. New York: Oxford/ Clarendon.

Pranger, M. B. 2001. "Time and Narrative in Augustine's *Confessions*." *Journal of Religion* 81, no. 3 (July): 8.

Severson, Richard. 1996. *The Confessions of Saint Augustine: An Annotated Bibliography of Modern Criticism, 1888–1995*. Westport, CT: Greenwood.

Suchocki, Marjorie. 1982. "The Symbolic Structure of Augustine's *Confessions*." *Journal of the American Academy of Religion* 50, no. 3 (September): 367–70.

BIBLIOGRAPHY

Elledge, W. Paul. "Embracing Augustine: Reach, Restraint, and Romantic Resolution in *The Confessions*." *Journal for the Scientific Study of Religion* 27, no. 1 (March 1988): 75–76.

Manville, Brook. "Donatism and St. Augustine: *The Confessions* of a Fourth-Century Bishop." *Augustinian Studies* 7 (1977): 125–37.

— Mary Theresa Hall

Hilaire Belloc [1870–1953]

The Path to Rome

BIOGRAPHY

Hilaire Belloc was born at La Celle Saint Cloud, twelve miles outside Paris, on July 27, 1870. His birth coincided with the outbreak of the Franco-Prussian war, forcing his parents to evacuate the family home a few weeks later. They fled to Paris to escape the advancing Prussian army, and as the Prussians prepared to lay siege to the French capital, the Bellocs managed to catch the last train to Dieppe, on the Normandy coast, from whence they sailed to the safety of England.

Belloc was educated in the benevolent shadow of the aging Cardinal Newman at the Oratory School in Birmingham and at Balliol College, Oxford. As an undergraduate, his considerable presence and oratory prowess gained him a degree of preeminence among his peers that culminated in his election to the presidency of the Oxford Union. In June 1895, he crowned his exceptionally brilliant career at Oxford with a First Class Honors degree in history.

Even before going to Oxford, the young Belloc had commenced his wanderlust-like perambulations, tramping through his beloved France and traveling across the United States. The latter journey was undertaken in an endeavor to persuade Elodie Hogan, a young Irish American girl whom he had met in London, to marry him. Having traveled the breadth of the United States, Belloc arrived in California to be informed that his beloved was intent on trying her vocation with the Sisters of Charity. Returning brokenhearted and empty-handed to Europe, he enlisted for national service in the French army.

Belloc never lost touch with his apparently lost love in America, and in the summer of 1896, he returned to California and married Elodie at St. John the Baptist Church in Napa on June 15. The newlyweds returned to England, where they would be blessed with five children before Elodie's tragic death in 1914.

The commencement of Belloc's married life coincided with the commencement of his literary career. In 1896, his first two books were published, *Verses and Sonnets* and *The Bad Child's Book of Beasts*. The latter became an instant popular success, prompting more of the same, including *More Beasts (for Worse Children)* in 1897 and *Cautionary Tales for Children* ten years later. Although these books for children (of all ages) are indubitably charming and enduringly funny, it is perhaps unfortunate that, for many, Belloc is remembered primarily for these relatively trivial sorties into children's literature rather than for the vast body of work, transcending several genres, that represents his true and lasting legacy.

His first biography, *Danton*, was published in 1899, and thereafter Belloc would continue to write biographies of historical figures, specializing particularly, although by no means exclusively, on figures of the English Reformation. These included studies of Oliver Cromwell, James the Second, Cardinal Wolsey, Thomas Cranmer, Charles the First, and John Milton. He also published panoramic studies of the whole period, such as *How the Reformation Happened* and *Characters of the Reformation*, as well as a four-volume *History of England*. His motivation for this prodigious output of what might be termed historical revisionism was a personal crusade to fight the "enormous mountain of ignorant wickedness" that constituted "tom-fool Protestant history" (Pearce 2002, 230).

Belloc was also interested in questions of politics and economics and was a resolute and vociferous champion of the social teaching of the Catholic Church as espoused by Pope Leo XIII in the encyclical *Rerum Novarum* (1891). His principal works in this area are *The Servile State* (1912) and *An Essay on the Restoration of Property* (1936). Belloc should also be remembered for his works of apologetics, particularly perhaps for his late masterpiece *Survivals and New Arrivals* (1929), a much underrated book that rivals in lucidity and potency the better known apologetic works of G. K. Chesterton, such as *Orthodoxy* (1908) and *The Everlasting Man* (1925).

As a novelist, Belloc was prolific although not always particularly adept. Most of his excursions into fiction were bogged down by stolid prose and stagnant story lines. The one notable exception, *Belinda* (1928), fulfilled his potential as a novelist, which had hitherto been frustrated. He was far more successful as an essayist and as the writer of what might be termed (inadequately) "farragoes," or literary miscellanies. These farragoes, such as *The Path to Rome* (1902), *The Four Men* (1912), and *The Cruise of the "Nona"* (1925), are among the most loved and most popular of all his works. It was, however, as a poet that Belloc achieved true greatness in the literary sphere. "Tarantella," "Ha'nacker Mill," "Lines to a Don," "The End of the Road," and several of his sonnets guarantee his place among the *eminenti* of twentieth-century English poets.

Apart from his prolific and prodigious career as a writer, Belloc was also a great controversialist and was, for a time, a member of Parliament. He continued to travel widely, both nationally and internationally, but always returned to King's Land, his rural haven in Sussex. Having suffered a stroke in the early years of World War II, possibly as a result of learning of the death of his youngest son, killed on active service with the Royal Marines, Belloc's powers began to fail. Thereafter, he ceased to write and spent the last years of his life in increasingly solitary senility. He died in 1953.

Lastly, Belloc must be remembered for the gargantuan nature of his personality. In his case, to an extraordinary degree, it is the man himself who breathes life and exhilaration into the work. When he is writing at his best, every page exudes the charisma of the author, spilling over with the excess of exuberance for which he was famous among his contemporaries. From his legendary and fruitful friendship with G. K. Chesterton to his vituperative enmity toward H. G. Wells, Belloc always emerges as the sort of man who is often described as larger than life. Strictly speaking, of course, no man is larger than life. In Belloc's case, however, perhaps more than almost any other literary figure of his generation, the man can be considered truly greater than his oeuvre. As such, his greatest works are those that reflect his personality to the greatest degree. Whether he is loved or loathed, and he is loved or loathed more than most, he cannot be easily ignored.

PLOT SUMMARY

Belloc considered *The Path to Rome* to be perhaps his finest work. Six years after its publication, he wrote in his own personal copy of the book the final wistful lines of a ballade, the first part of which was presumably never written:

> *Alas! I never shall so write again!*
>   Envoi
> *Prince, bow yourself to God and bow to Time,*
> *Which is God's servant for the use of men,*
> *To bend them to his purpose sublime.*
> *Alas! I never shall so write again.* (quoted in Pearce 2002, 84)

It could be considered a trifle presumptuous to assume that these lines of verse prove that Belloc thought that he "never wrote so well thereafter." After all, he wrote a great deal thereafter. The lines were written in 1908, before he wrote *The Four Men* and many years before he wrote *Belinda*. Writing of *Belinda* to his friend Maurice Baring, Belloc stated that it was "the only thing I ever finished in my life and the only piece of my writing that I have liked for more than 40 years" (Pearce 2002, 234). Belloc informed another friend, however, that *Belinda* was "certainly the book of mine which I like best since I wrote *The Path to Rome*" (234). These words, written in 1930, would appear to confirm the lines inscribed in his own copy of *The Path to Rome* twenty-two years earlier. It is clear, therefore, that in the opinion of the author himself, and regardless of the dissenting views of some of his admirers, the "best of Belloc" is to be found on the path to Rome.

At its most basic, *The Path to Rome* is a firsthand account of the author's pilgrimage to Rome in 1901. He sets off from Toul, in France, and journeys through the valley of the Moselle, heading for Switzerland and from there traversing the Alps to Italy. The book itself, although ostensibly an account of the author's pilgrimage, is much more. In its pages we see Europe at the turn of a new century through the eyes of a poet besotted with its beauty. We see it through the lens of a historian who understands the living majesty of its past. We see it through the faithful heart of a Catholic who beholds a vision of the Europe of the present in vibrant communion with the Europe of the past. We see it in the transcendence of all these visions united in one mystical flesh: the poet and the historian and the Catholic forming a united trinity beholding something greater than itself. As such, it is a work of humility and awe, of gratitude and hope, of faith and love. Yet it is more, and less, than this. It is incarnational. Its flesh, mystically communing with, and exiled from, heaven, is also rooted in the earth. It is pithy and earthy, anecdotal and tangential; it is both prayerfully reverent and playfully irreverent, at one and the same time. It is a faith loved and lived within the constraints of the fallible and fallen nature of the author.

From the pregnant poignancy of Belloc's superb preface, with its delightful combination of the wistful and the whimsical, to the dash and dare of the wonderful poem that serves as the book's, and the pilgrim's, conclusion, *The Path to Rome* takes the reader on a journey into himself and out of himself, a voyage of discovery in which home and exile are interwoven in a mystical dance of contemplation. In its pages we discover the Europe of the Faith, which was, and is, the heart of Christendom, and the Faith of Europe, which was, and is, the heart of all.

As for Belloc's motivation for writing *The Path to Rome*, the inscription in his own personal copy of the book, dated March 29, 1904, says it all: "I wrote this book for the glory of God" (Pearce 2002, 84).

MAJOR THEMES

The Path to Rome is both a travelogue and a farrago, which is to say that it is, at one and the same time, a linear narrative connected to a journey and a seemingly random dispersal of anecdotal thoughts and musings. Its overriding structure is, therefore, animated by the tension between the forward momentum maintained by the author's account of his pilgrimage and the inertial force of the tangential interruptions. This singular literary combination constitutes a distinct literary genre and one in which Belloc excelled. Having experimented with what may be dubbed the travel-farrago in the writing of *The Path to Rome*, Belloc would return to it with great success in *The Four Men* and *The Cruise of the "Nona."*

Perhaps the best way of discussing the major themes in a work of this sort is to follow the line of the narrative, while pausing as needed to study the ponderable, and sometimes ponderous, interruptions with which Belloc punctuates his narrative. In other words, it is not my intention to analyze the work thematically but, rather, to study the themes as they emerge from the narrative in the order in which they are presented to the reader. To put the matter succinctly, we shall follow the author along the route of his pilgrimage and shall not attempt to remain aloof by dissecting it thematically from a disengaged distance.

Belloc begins his narrative by recounting an unexpected encounter with the valley of his birth. He is surprised to see "the old tumble-down and gaping church" that he had loved in his youth renovated so that it appeared "noble and new" (*Path to Rome*, xvii). This pleases him "as much as though a fortune had been left to us all; for one's native place is the shell of one's soul, and one's church is the kernel of that nut" (xviii). At the very outset, therefore, Belloc has laid the foundations of what might be termed a "theology of place." This concept, which can be said to be truly at the heart of Belloc's work, is quintessentially incarnational. A sense of "place" is linked to the love of home, and the love of home is itself salted by the home's temporary absence or unattainability. Paradoxically, it is the sense of exile that gives the love of home its intensity and its power. The theology of place is therefore rooted in the earth and yet reaching to heaven. It is expressed most sublimely in the *Salve Regina*, in which the "poor banished children of Eve" lost in "this vale of tears" hope that, "after this our exile," we might behold the Blessed Fruit of our Mother's womb. Heaven is our haven; Jesus is our home. And where Jesus is at home, in his Mother's arms and in her womb, we shall be at home also. One's earthly home, or "native place," is "the shell of one's soul" because it is an incarnated inkling of the home for which we are made and toward which we are mystically directed. It is for that reason that "one's church is the kernel of that nut."

Nowhere has Belloc encapsulated the theology of place better than in a letter he wrote to Katherine Asquith:

> The Faith, the Catholic Church, is discovered, is recognized, triumphantly enters reality like a landfall at sea which first was thought a cloud. The nearer it is seen, the more it is real, the less imaginary: the more direct and external its voice, the more indubitable its representative character, its "persona," its voice. The metaphor is not that men fall in love with it: the metaphor is that they discover home. "This was what I sought. This was my need." It is the very mold of the mind, the matrix to which corresponds in every outline the outcast and unprotected contour of the soul. It is Verlaine's "Oh! Rome—oh! Mere!" And that not only to those who had it in childhood and have returned, but much more—and what a proof!—to those who come upon it from the hills of life and say to themselves, "Here is the town." (quoted in Pearce 1999, 319)

This theology of place is such a recurrent theme in Belloc's work that it could be said to be almost omnipresent. Few writers have felt so intensely the sense of exile, and hence the love of home, to the degree to which it is invoked by Belloc. From the love of Sussex evoked in *The Four Men* and in poems such as "Ha'nacker Mill" or "The South Country," to the love of Europe in general, and France in particular, evoked in *The Path to Rome* and in poems such as "Tarantella," his work resonates with the love of earth as a foreshadowing of the love of heaven.

Seen in this light, the renovation of the church in his native valley, which Belloc proclaims as the very "kernel of that nut" which is his soul, takes on metaphorical, and therefore metaphysical, significance. Is the church itself a metaphor for Belloc's soul? Is its renovation a symbol of the renewal of the author's spirit inherent in his pilgrimage to Rome? Is the church of home (the soul of the author) retracing its source, its meaning and its purpose, to the Church of Rome (the Mystical Body of Christ)? Is home paying homage to Home?

Those intent on a strictly two-dimensional reading of the text might insist that this metaphorical interpretation goes too far. Isn't the book simply a straightforward factual account of the author's pilgrimage to Rome in the late spring and early summer of 1901? Certainly there is ample documentation, particularly in the contemporaneous correspondence with his wife, to verify that Belloc actually followed the route recounted in the book, yet the factual foundation does not exclude the metaphorical ascent into higher levels of meaning. On the contrary, if we accept that facts are physical whereas truth is metaphysical, it follows that facts serve the truth and that metaphor or allegory is the means by which the applicability of physical facts to metaphysical truth is conveyed. Indeed, these were the very principles upon which Saint Augustine and Saint Thomas Aquinas built their understanding of Scriptural exegesis. Belloc, as a lifelong practicing Catholic educated by the Oratorians, would have been well versed in such concepts. It is, therefore, hardly controversial to suggest that Belloc perceived that the facts of his pilgrimage served the truth toward which the pilgrimage was directed. As Belloc insisted, the book itself was written "for the glory of God."

Perhaps the best way to illustrate Belloc's employment of metaphor in *The Path to Rome* is to compare it with *The Four Men*. These two books are remarkably similar in style and structure. Both are travel-farragoes recounting a journey by the author, on foot, through land that he loves. In *The Four Men*, the men in question are Grizzlebeard, the Sailor, the Poet, and Myself. It seems likely that each character was not an individual whom Belloc had actually met en route but that they were in fact, or in truth, allegorical representations of various facets of Belloc's own character. It can be seen, therefore, that Belloc was not averse to the use of allegory and metaphor but that he employed them liberally throughout his work.

Having ascertained the meaning of the initial metaphor that, in turn, is the key to understanding the deeper meaning of the work, the reader can proceed with the author along the path to Rome.

Inspired by the vision of the renovated church in his native valley, Belloc makes a prayerful vow "to go to Rome on Pilgrimage and see all Europe which the Christian Faith has saved" (xviii). Furthermore, he pledges that he will set off from Toul, the garrison town in which he had served in the army; that he will walk all the way and take advantage of no wheeled thing; that he will sleep rough, will cover thirty miles a day, and will hear Mass every morning; and that he will arrive in Rome in time to attend High Mass at St. Peter's on the Feast of Saints Peter and Paul. As the narrative unfolds, we see that he breaks many of these vows, one by one. He sets off as he intended from the French garrison town of Toul but he does not sleep rough every night, he does not attend Mass daily, and he eventually succumbs to the temptation of "wheeled things." Again, the parallels with the life of the proverbial Everyman are obvious. We set out with good intentions and with a set goal in mind but fail to live up to the standards we set for ourselves. The author's pilgrimage to Rome is a microcosmic metaphor for Everyman's pilgrimage through life.

The metaphor recurs at various times and in various guises, as, for instance, in Belloc's description of the Moselle near its source. The young river was "full of the positive innocence that attaches to virgins": "There was about that scene something of creation and of a beginning, and as I drew it, it gave me like a gift the freshness of the first experiences of living and filled me with remembered springs. I mused upon the birth of rivers, and how they were persons and had a name—were kings, and grew strong and ruled great countries, and how at last they reached the sea" (84–85).

Belloc's portrayal of the people he encounters is always engaging and displays a genuine love for humankind. In the Ballon d'Alsace, he finds his prejudiced presuppositions against those of Germanic culture challenged by the experience of meeting a German-speaking family. Having described "the Germanies" as "a great sea of confused and dreaming people, lost in philosophies" (93), he is humbled by the civilized customs of his Germanic hosts: "In good-nights they had a ceremony; for they all rose together and curtsied. Upon my soul I believe such people to be the salt of the earth. I bowed with real contrition, for at several moments I had believed myself better than they" (98). He is also graphically effective in his depiction of pain, describing how his feet "were so martyrized that I doubted if I could walk at all on the morrow." In the morning, as he "fearlessly forced" (99) his boots onto his feet, the reader almost winces in sympathy, especially if he or she has also experienced the pain of a protracted perambulation.

Possibly the most subtle metaphoric suggestiveness in the whole work emerges following the author's musing upon the nature of the human soul, which was "a puzzling thought, very proper to a pilgrimage." What exactly is it? he wonders. Describing himself as knowing nothing of "pleasures . . . in which my senses have had no part," he is baffled by the saints and the mystics who speak of the pleasures of the spirit as being distinct from, and superior to, the pleasures of the flesh:

> As I was pondering on these things in this land of pastures and lonely ponds . . . (my pain seemed gone for a moment, yet I was hobbling slowly)—I say as I was considering this complex doctrine, I felt my sack suddenly much lighter, and I had hardly time to rejoice at the miracle when I heard immediately a very loud crash, and turning half round I saw on the blurred white of the twilit road my quart of Open Wine all broken to atoms. My disappointment was so great that I sat down on a milestone to consider the accident and to see if a little thought would not lighten my acute annoyance. Consider that I had carefully cherished this bottle and had not drunk throughout a painful march all that afternoon, thinking that there would be no wine worth drinking after I had passed the frontier

> . . . I rose to go on into the night. As it turned out I was to find beyond the frontier a wine in whose presence this wasted wine would have seemed a wretched jest, and whose wonderful taste was to colour all my memories of the Mount Terrible. It is always thus with sorrows if one will only wait.

> So, lighter in the sack but heavier in the heart, I went forward to cross the frontier in the dark. (117–20)

In this short passage, Belloc's use of metaphor becomes a parable. Having described himself as a sensualist, Belloc discovers that the immediate objects of his senses, both the painful and the pleasurable, are taken away. First his pain "seemed gone," and then his pleasure, the quart of wine, is "broken to atoms." If the wine is taken as a symbol of worldly pleasures, for those that pay no heed to the pleasures of the soul its destruction or removal becomes a symbol for pain or suffering and, ultimately, death. He had cherished it on the assumption that it would be unavailable once he had "passed the frontier." The frontier is itself a symbol for the moment of suffering, or the point of death, and, although he could not know it at the time, he was destined to discover that the unknown wine over the frontier would make his cherished possession on this side of the frontier seem "a wretched jest": "It is always thus with sorrows if one will only wait." The allegorical intent is also demonstrated by other uses of religious imagery. His burden becomes miraculously light; he crosses the frontier "in the dark"; and his destination over the frontier is Mount Terrible, surely an allusion to purgatory, particularly in relation to the sentence that follows in which Belloc speaks of the healing of sorrows "if one will only wait."

The fact that these events, presumably, happened in actuality in the manner in which Belloc describes them does not in the least negate the allegorical interpretation of the parable. It merely indicates a providential connection between the experience of life and its deeper meaning, the apprehension of which is something "very proper to a pilgrimage." As J. R. R. Tolkien once remarked, life is a study for eternity for those so gifted. Clearly, Belloc is one so gifted.

Throughout *The Path to Rome*, Belloc continually bestows upon the reader the fruits of his considerable wisdom. Thus, he informs us that "economics are but an expression of the mind and do not (as the poor blind slaves of the great cities think) mold the mind": "What is more, nothing makes property run into a few hands but the worst of the capital sins, and you who say it is 'the modern facility of distribution'. . . are like men who should say that their drunkenness was due to their drink, or that arson was caused by matches" (131). The insistence that economics is merely a derivative of philosophical presumptions, coupled with an exposé of the folly of deterministic analyses of economic "laws," foreshadows the work of the Catholic economist E. F. Schumacher, whose best-seller *Small is Beautiful* reiterated these very same conclusions seventy years later.

An intermittent recurrence throughout the narrative of *The Path to Rome* is the dialogue between the author ("Auctor") and the reader ("Lector"). Apart from Belloc's use of the Lector as a foil, he is also employed as a symbol of modernity. Whenever the discussion strays into the area of philosophy or religion, the Lector invariably acts as the voice of shallow skepticism or agnostic indifference. He is a child of his age, a slave to intellectual fashion. "I see that all the religion I have stuck into the book has no more effect on you than had Rousseau upon Sir Henry Maine. You are as full of Pride as a minor Devil" (162): thus does the Auctor upbraid the Lector, berating his superficiality.

Whereas the Lector plods, clod-laden, unable to lift his mind and heart above the sea level of ground zero, the lowest common denominator world of presumed materialism, the Auctor rises to the heights of mysticism, never more so than in his first vision of the Alps:

> Their sharp steadfastness and their clean uplifted lines compelled my adoration. Up there, the sky above and below them, part of the sky, but part of us, the great peaks made communion between that homing creeping part of me which loves vineyards and dances and a slow movement among pastures, and that other part which is only properly at home in Heaven. (180)

Once again, the theology of place places the mysticism of the alpine vision into the vision of home. And once again, the very vision of nature resplendent inspires the author's prose to metamorphose into metaphor:

> Since I could now see such a wonder and it could work such things in my mind, therefore, some day I should be part of it.

> That is what I felt. This it is also which leads some men to climb mountaintops, but not me, for I am afraid of slipping down. (181)

The mountain summits having become a celestial vision, the saints have become mystical mountaineers whose abilities to attain the spiritual heights outstrip the author's backsliding and earthbound spirituality: "For it is the saddest thing about us that this bright spirit with which we are lit from within like lanterns, can suffer dimness. Such frailty makes one fear that extinction is our final destiny, and it saps us with numbness, and we are less than ourselves" (190). The days in which the author suffers such "dimness" are described as days "without salt," days in which the pilgrimage becomes a "trudge," days in which "[t]he air was ordinary, the colors common; men, animals, and trees indifferent." On such days "[s]omething had stopped working." The "salt" to which Belloc is referring is the joy of surprise, an energy from God: "I say our energy also is from God, and we should never be proud of it as though it were from ourselves, but we should accept it as a kind of present, and we should be thankful for it; just as a man should thank God for his reason" (193–94). On such days it is only "Duty" (capitalized) that keeps the pilgrim resolutely on his path to Rome (191). Again, it is difficult not to see autobiographical parallels between the author's present journey and his life's journey, parallels that are, of course, equally applicable to the lives of his readers.

Once the sense of gratitude for the salt of life is lost, the salt itself is soon lost. Thereafter, the unsalted lapse into intellectual pride, "than which no sin is more offensive to the angels":

> What! here are we with the jolly world of God all round us, able to sing, to draw, to paint, to hammer and build, to sail, to ride horses, to run, to leap; having for our splendid inheritance love in youth and memory in old age, and we are to take one miserable little faculty, our one-legged, knock-kneed, gimcrack, purblind, rough-skinned, underfed, and perpetually irritated and grumpy intellect, or analytical curiosity rather (a diseased appetite), and let it swell till it eats up every other function? Away with such foolery. (234–35)

By contrast, the words of the creed contain "a power of synthesis that can jam all their analytical dust-heap into such a fine, tight, and compact body as would make them stare to see" (235). Here Belloc might indeed have descended to the level of bombast, but it is not the bombast of relativism, the bombast of mere opinion, sanitized by self-righteousness, but the bombast of absolutes, the bombast of certitude, sanctified by servitude to the objective righteousness beyond the self.

The high point, literally and literarily, of *The Path to Rome* is Belloc's description of his foolhardy attempt to cross the Alps in a snowstorm, an attempt that ended in heroic failure. In these pages, the prose soars as loftily as the peaks it describes and as powerfully as the elements that beat him back in sullen defeat. Again, the whole episode resonates with moral applicability. His proud and self-willed determination to conquer the peaks ends in the sort of humiliation that points to humility: "Indeed it is a bitter thing to have to give up one's sword" (249).

The other high point, literarily, is not prose but poetry: it is the verse with which Belloc chooses to conclude his book and his pilgrimage. "The End of the Road" is effectively a summary of the whole book distilled into thirty-four energy-charged lines. Although deceptively simple in structure, it exhibits masterful metrical acrobatics. At the outset it surges and soars, filled with the freshness of the first days of the pilgrimage; it marches, pants, swings, and dashes. Slowly it slows; plodding, hobbling, trudging, and sauntering to a standstill. There is a pregnant pause, followed by a parenthetical penitential prayer orated bilingually in Latin and English, leading into a confession of broken vows. Finally, it glides unhurriedly to its destination. Throughout the poem, the metrics are controlled by an ingenious combination of iambic dexterity, variations in scansion, and, equally important, the dynamics of the verbs employed in the text itself. Rarely has Belloc achieved such heights in verse; indeed, rarely are such heights reached by any poet. And, of course, the ascent from prose to poetry, especially when executed so expertly, represents the perfect finishing touch to the work of literature, a finish with finesse. A climax.

With characteristic humor hinting at a more serious intention, Belloc describes the poem as a "dithyrambic epithalamium or threnody." It is certainly dithyrambic, reeling wildly and ecstatically, almost drunkenly, toward its destination; but can anything be both an epithalamium *and* a threnody? Can one sing of marriage and death in the same breath? Aren't nuptial bliss and the *Nunc dimittis* unacceptable bedfellows? Clearly, Belloc is concluding his path to Rome with a provocative paradox, but the apparent contradictions point profoundly to a greater truth. His arrival in Rome resonates with the joy of the marriage bed. The Church is both the Mystical Body of Christ and, at the same time, the bride of Christ. The pilgrim, at his most Christlike, is mystically married to the bride; he is wedded to the Church; he is at one with her. At the same time, as a loyal and suppliant member of the Church, he is mystically married to Christ. More soberly and somberly, the arrival in Rome, the end of the pilgrimage, also signifies death, the end of our earthly pilgrimage. Ultimately, the marriage bed and the grave represent a consummation. The joys and sorrows of life and death find their true consummation in the glory of eternity, represented symbolically in *The Path to Rome* by the Eternal City itself.

> *Drinking when I had a mind to,*
> *Singing when I felt inclined to;*
> *Nor ever turned my face to home*
> *Till I had slaked my heart at Rome.*

CRITICAL RECEPTION

The Path to Rome was published in April 1902. It would eventually sell more than 100,000 copies and is still reprinted regularly today. Something of its spirit, and perhaps part of the secret of its success, was captured by G. K. Chesterton in a review for *The World* in which Chesterton contrasted Belloc's rambunctious *joie de vivre* with the ennui of the Decadents:

> *The Path to Rome* is the product of the actual and genuine buoyancy and thoughtlessness of a rich intellect. . . . The dandies in *The Green Carnation* stand on their heads for the same reason that the dandies in Bond Street stand on their feet—because it is the thing that is done; but they do it with the same expression of fixed despair on their faces, the expression of fixed despair which you will find everywhere and always on the faces of frivolous people and men of pleasure. He will be a lucky man who can escape out of that world of freezing folly into the flaming and reverberating folly of *The Path to Rome*. (quoted in Pearce 2002, 83–84)

Other critics were also as fulsome in their praise. Reviewers in periodicals as diverse as the *Athenaeum*, the *Literary World*, the *Daily Chronicle*, the *Manchester*

Guardian, and the *New York Times* queued up to salute the arrival of an exciting new author, comparing his creative credentials to those of writers as rare and distinguished as Robert Burton, Samuel Butler, William Cobbett, Heinrich Heine, Rabelais, Lawrence Sterne, Robert Lewis Stevenson, and Isaac Walton. More recently, Dom Philip Jebb, former abbot of Downside and Belloc's grandson, opined that the descriptive passages of the Alps in *The Path to Rome* confirm Belloc's status as a genuine mystic (Pearce 2002, 83).

Nobody has summed up the importance of this classic work better than Belloc's friend, admirer, and biographer, Robert Speaight:

> More than any other book he ever wrote, *The Path to Rome* made Belloc's name; more than any other, it has been lovingly thumbed and pondered. It was a new kind of book, just as Belloc was a new kind of man. It gave a vital personality, rich and complex, bracing and abundant, to the tired Edwardian world. Above all, it brought back the sense of Europe, physical and spiritual, into English letters. Vividly and personally experienced, the centuries returned. (Pearce 2002, 84)

NOTE

Hilaire Belloc, *The Path to Rome* (San Francisco: Ignatius Press, 2003). All references are to this edition.

WORKS CITED

Pearce, Joseph. 1999. *Literary Converts: Spiritual Inspiration in an Age of Unbelief.* San Francisco: Ignatius Press.

———. 2002. *Old Thunder: A Life of Hilaire Belloc.* San Francisco: Ignatius Press.

— Joseph Pearce

Georges Bernanos [1888–1948]

The Diary of a Country Priest

BIOGRAPHY

Georges Bernanos was born on February 20, 1888, in Paris, where his father was a successful interior decorator. From an early age, he showed intense religious fervor. When in 1899 he received his First communion, an event that was to remain an ever-luminous memory, he expressed an earnest desire to be a witness for Jesus Christ. School, on the other hand, cast a pall over his early years. Georges had a difficult time adjusting to various boarding schools, although his teachers recognized his literary gift. In 1906 he began his university studies in Paris, preparing for a degree in law and letters. It was during this time that he became involved with the royalist movement *Action française*, which involved rough street demonstrations and brief sojourns in jail. With the outbreak of World War I, Bernanos joined the army for the duration and was wounded and decorated. In 1917, he married Jeanne Talbert d'Arc, a direct descendant of a brother of Joan of Arc, and the following year the first of six children was born.

After the war, Bernanos became an insurance inspector, employment that involved much train travel throughout northwestern France, during which he snatched the time to write his first novel, *Under Satan's Sun*. Its publication in 1926 brought immediate critical and popular success, and Bernanos decided to quit his job and live by his pen, a decision that guaranteed years of peripatetic penury for him and his family. His second novel, *The Impostor*, appeared in 1927, and the 1929 *Joy* received the prestigious literary award, the *Prix Femina*. In 1933, a motorcycle accident left him crippled for life, able to walk only with the assistance of two canes. (Bernanos's passion for motorcycles was a celebration of freedom and adventure, an exhilaration that no doubt faintly echoed the spiritual liberty he sought in Christ. This is reflected in a beautiful passage in *The Diary of a Country Priest* in which the Curé, only days from death, experiences the joy of friendship and a fleeting emancipation as a passenger on the motorcycle of the Countess's nephew, Olivier.) At the same time, persistent money problems began to worsen and, seeking cheaper living, he and his large family moved in 1934 to the Spanish island of Majorca, leaving behind unpaid rent and all their furnishings. It was there that he began to write *The Diary of a Country Priest*. By 1936, the Spanish Civil War had reached the island, and the Bernanos family found itself embroiled in the dress rehearsal for the coming struggle between two totalitarian giants.

Still plagued by money troubles, Bernanos and his family left Majorca in 1938 to settle in Brazil, where he abandoned fiction to devote himself to polemical writing, much of it directed against Nazi Germany. He rallied behind the Resistance movement after the fall of his homeland in 1940, and his radio messages were broadcast by the BBC into occupied France. In 1945, General de Gaulle cabled him, "Bernanos, your place is with us." Within two months he and his family returned to France, where he politely but persistently refused to accept de Gaulle's offer of the Legion of Honor, anxious to avoid anything that would compromise his ability to, as he put it, "tell the truth" to his country (he had already discouraged the offering of the honor in 1926, 1937, and 1940). Similarly, he rebuffed François Mauriac's efforts to secure him a seat in the French Academy, no doubt perceiving that his inveterate nonconformism precluded membership in that most tradition-bound body. Finally, disgusted by France's postwar political climate, he and his family soon left for Tunisia, where he wrote *The Carmelites*, a work originally intended as the screenplay for a projected film and that later became the libretto for Francis Poulenc's celebrated opera. In 1948, Bernanos returned to France for unsuccessful cancer surgery. He died in the American Hospital in Paris on July 5th of that year. His other novels are *A Crime* (1935), *Mouchette* (1937), *Monsieur Ouine* (1943), and the posthumously published *Night is Darkest* (1950).

PLOT SUMMARY

In a letter to a friend in 1935, Bernanos himself provided a succinct summation of the novel he was then writing. He indicated his intention of composing the diary of a young priest fresh from seminary whose first parish assignment is marked by ineptitude in administration, naiveté in his interactions with those who seek to exploit and dupe him, and failure in the implementation of unrealistic projects. In the end, though, Bernanos assures his correspondent, the priest's failures will prove God's victory, and he will die peacefully of cancer.

The young Curé (parish priest) of the village of Ambricourt is certainly unworldly, and his guileless enthusiasm is dampened at every turn, whether in a futile attempt to begin a sports club for boys or in his ingenuous belief, quickly disabused, in the natural goodness of the children who attend his catechism class. He is seriously ill with excruciating stomach pains that allow him to take only bread and wine, a diet of obvious sacramental imagery, although one that prompts rumors of drunkenness. He bares his soul to his diary, which, save for a letter at the end, constitutes the novel's entire first-person narrative. He also seeks support and advice from his only friend, the older and experienced Curé of Torcy, an important and imposing character.

The two poles of the novel's action are the village, a rural parish of peasants and petit-bourgeois merchants, and the château where the Count and Countess, their daughter Chantal, and her governess Mlle Louise reside. We learn that the Count, an inveterate adulterer, is conducting an affair with Mlle Louise. Chantal, long believing herself the sole apple of her father's eye, is enraged by jealousy upon discovering the truth, while her embittered mother affects indifference. The novel's central scene transpires during a visit the priest pays to the château to confront the Countess about her treatment of Chantal, whose imminent banishment to England has provoked threats of suicide. He discovers that, since the death of her infant son, the *châtelaine* has hardened her heart, not only against her family but against God. The dramatic encounter between her and the priest is a literary tour de force. In the end, the Countess finds peace in abandonment to God's will, dying that very night of a heart attack. Her vindictive daughter, who had secretly witnessed the conversation, spreads the calumny that the priest had precipitated her mother's death by relentless provocation.

Eventually, the Curé goes to the city of Lille to consult a physician, who diagnoses terminal stomach cancer, and to call upon a defrocked priest and one-time fellow seminarian who has been writing him frequent letters imploring a visit. It is in the company of this former priest and his mistress that he dies.

MAJOR THEMES

In 1954, the eminent Swiss-German theologian, Hans Urs von Balthasar, made a rather sweeping statement: "St. Thérèse is everywhere is Bernanos's work." He was, of course, referring to Saint Thérèse of Lisieux (1873–1897), the "Little Flower," one of the most popular and revered saints of modern times. This statement provoked a surge of critical assessment. Anyone who has read the many thousands of pages of Bernanos's essays and polemical works would have already appreciated the depth of his devotion to this young Carmelite nun from Lisieux, although the important question was to what extent, if any, it had influenced his fiction. The consensus among scholars was that the saint's imprint on the novels was pervasive, but nowhere more so than on *The Diary of a Country Priest*.

At age fifteen, Saint Thérèse of the Child Jesus and of the Holy Face (born Thérèse Martin) entered the Carmelite monastery in Lisieux in northwestern France, where she rejected the harsh Jansenist spirituality of the time and set about finding her own way, a "little way," to holiness. Under obedience, she wrote what would become a classic of its kind, her spiritual autobiography, *The Story of a Soul*. She contracted tuberculosis and, after months of terrible suffering, died at the age of twenty-four. She was canonized in 1925.

Certainly, there are a number of striking biographical similarities between the life of Bernanos's fictional saint and Saint Thérèse. Both suffer from painful terminal illnesses and die while still very young; in fact, neither can even imagine themselves in old age. As well, both pass from this life with what Bernanos once described as Thérèse's "incomprehensible" smile. However, his intention in writing *The Diary of a Country Priest* was not to duplicate biographical data from the Carmelite nun's life but rather to delve deeply into her inner self. The Curé of Ambricourt represents, in large measure, an attempt to incarnate in a fictional character the spirituality of the woman Pope Pius X called "the greatest saint of modern times."

Thérèsian spirituality rests, paradoxically, upon a notion of irreducible simplicity: weakness. As a young nun, Thérèse Martin longed for holiness, yet the insurmountable obstacle was her powerlessness. Comparing herself with the saints was like comparing "a mountain whose summit is lost in the clouds and an obscure grain of sand trodden underneath by all who pass by" (*Story of a Soul*, 135). It was while meditating on sacred Scripture that the answer was revealed to her. She would not attempt to climb the ladder of perfection; rather, she would let go of its daunting flow of rungs and allow herself to fall into the arms of the living God. She would accept her weakness and imperfections so that God himself could be her strength and holiness. This was her famous little way, a path to heaven that required only that one remain always childlike and small, hidden within the life of the Father.

The hero of *Diary of a Country Priest* is also discomfited by a sense of personal weakness that stokes his fears and threatens to undermine his courage. His incompetence in the practical duties of parish administration constitutes a frustrating element of this awareness. He alienates the village merchants with his naiveté in money matters and, as mentioned above, his efforts to establish a boys' club come to naught, while his catechism class is sabotaged by juvenile cruelty. He, like Thérèse, is also instinctively aware of his childlikeness, so much so that when he attends meetings with his fellow priests he feels like a little boy who has strayed into a room of gabbling grown-ups (33). If the full significance of this sensation and its relationship to his weakness initially escape him, it is not lost on his mentor, the Curé of Torcy, who understands that powerlessness is the true wellspring of human joy, as with a child who gladly and confidently relies upon its mother (19).

These two central Thérèsian themes of weakness and childhood fuse most dramatically in the novel's central scene, in which the priest confronts the disaffected Countess. He seeks to bring her to resignation to the divine will, but his efforts, so it seems, are undermined by his inner poverty. His words are spoken so "clumsily" and "haltingly" that they seem "ridiculous," and his exhaustion makes intelligent formulations next to impossible (164). Yet, it is precisely at this crucial juncture that the hand of God intervenes with a gesture that is both powerful and poignantly subtle. Gripped by a sadness that renders him "powerless," a single tear flows across the Curé's cheek and the Countess watches it fall (164). It is this tear, born of weakness yet pregnant with divine charity, that opens the smallest of breaches in her despair.

As their dialogue continues, the Curé becomes ever more aware of a heightened eloquence of speech, which, he well knows, is not his own. In this respect, the scene represents not so much an encounter between the priest and the Countess as one between herself and God. And so, as the Curé, nearly paralyzed by the fearful consequences of the spiritual battle in which he is engaged, surrenders to his weakness, the divine presence assumes the ascendancy. While exhausted by a struggle against doubt and growing terror, he senses a return in his heart to a spirit of prayer, not prayer as the "shallow" Christian understands it, but an infusion of divine energy like the wind that swells the sails of a creaking ship. It is soon after he is imbued this imbuement that the Countess is able to pray "Thy will be done," an unthinkable utterance since the death of her son. Her emergence into the light allows her to perceive in the Curé that essential element of his character that he himself only intuits. In a note that she sends him after his departure from the château, she writes that his childlikeness had delivered her from years of terrible solitude spent with the desperate memory of her dead child. The loss of one child had brought her a kind of living death, and another child had brought her back to life. She assures the Curé that he is indeed a child and prays God to keep him so always. Childhood and holiness are as inextricably linked for Bernanos as they were for Saint Thérèse.

One other particularly painful aspect of spiritual poverty that both the Curé and Thérèse share is an experience of the dark night of the soul. Saint Thérèse, for example, writes frequently about her "great dryness" in prayer; the Curé admits that he prays badly and too little (102). She refers to the "thick darkness" that surrounds her, while he both "inhales" the night and is himself the night (105). The Carmelite confesses in her autobiography that her faith had become no longer a sail that swept her along but a "wall"; the young priest confides to his diary that behind him is a void and before him stands a "wall" of darkness (103).

Finally, one further Thérèsian imprint upon Bernanos's hero, and a very pointed one at that, needs to be mentioned. Throughout her monastic life, the saint wished to remain unnoticed by the other nuns, and her prayer was well answered. She was misunderstood by her religious sisters, who, blind to her heroic charity, believed that she had entered Carmel to enjoy herself; even as she lay dying, many in the monastery, as she knew, did not believe she was sick at all. Cast in the same mold, the Curé of Ambricourt's remarkable inner life remains hidden from all but a few, and as he succumbs to cancer, he wishes that even his death might be unheroic and "as small as possible" (280). His strength lies in knowing he has none.

And so it is that he dies in the dark slumlike flat of a defrocked priest and his mistress. When it appears that the priest who had been summoned to administer the Last Rites will not arrive on time, the Curé speaks his last words, "Does it matter? All is grace" (298). "All is grace" is a direct quotation of Saint Thérèse of Lisieux recorded in a collection of her final words, the *Last Conversations*. She uttered the words "*tout est grâce*" in response to concerns that no priest might be available at the moment of her death. This is the only occasion on which Bernanos directly quoted the saint in any of his novels. However, it must be pointed out to readers of the sole English version of the novel that translator Pamela Morris woefully mistranslates Saint Thérèse's words as "Grace is everywhere," thus subverting the theology that underpins it, one that echoes Saint Paul's pronouncement in Romans 8:28 that "all things work to the good for those who love God."

The novel's most prominent secondary character is the diarist's worldly-wise, robust mentor, the Curé of Torcy. His importance lies in the length of his discourses, the undoubted authority of his voice, and his role as foil for his naive protégé. On the other hand, he serves as a spokesman for some of Bernanos's most cherished themes: the historical, cultural, and theological critiques that appear regularly in his nonfiction. Torcy delivers two long monologues in the novel, the first of which expands upon Bernanos's great love for the Middle Ages and, by contrast, his relentlessly negative evaluation of modern western society. Bernanos's admiration for the Middle Ages was not naive nostalgia for a golden age of faith; as Torcy puts it, the people of the thirteenth century were not "plaster saints" or "goodie-goodies" (18). They were, however, a "Christian people" (18). The opposite of a Christian people, he asserts, is a people "grown old and sad" (18). What Bernanos saw as essential to the glory of the medieval period, and the vision that Torcy articulates, was the building of the empire that was Christendom. This is no "fairytale" (18), Torcy tells his young friend, but rather a moment in history when the social consciousness was infused with the divine reality. During this period, Torcy states, man knew that he was a son of God, and this idea was the solid foundation of all else: "habits and customs, relaxation and pleasure, down to the very simplest needs" (19). The Middle Ages, Torcy declares in the unmistakable voice of Bernanos himself, "understood everything" (210).

This perception stands in opposition to the judgments pronounced against contemporary society that run like a thread through the novel. Modern man is an orphan, crippled by a "sense of his own loneliness" (19). His essential characteristic is "ennui," a term that appears in the English translation as "boredom." In this context, however, it signifies much more: a profound spiritual and moral torpor, the *acedia* of which the Desert Fathers wrote. This is the motif with which the novel begins: "My parish is bored stiff . . . eaten up by boredom" (1). It is, the Curé of Ambricourt confides to his diary, "a cancerous growth within us" (1). Torcy observes that modern man, in his desperate pursuit of distraction, has transformed even sin into something trite and stale. It is this boredom, he believes, that explains the obsession with evasion, the artificial paradise offered by a "tiny pinch of morphia" (19). This theme is again taken up when we meet Dr. Laville, who, holding up a syringe of opiate, assures the Curé of Ambricourt that with the drug he can "do without God" (266). Ennui also sheds light upon the contemporary fixation on technology, the "mechanical toys" (19) of a culture in dire need of distraction. We suffer from a "softening of the soul" (75), a spiritual slumber, the consequences of which extend to eternity. In the din of the whirring wheels of industry, the clamor of the machines that fabricate our prosperity and the toys of our pleasure, we may continue to deceive ourselves. But, warns Torcy, in the first few minutes of silence we will finally hear the voice of the demon who has for so long been whispering in our ear: "'I am the door forever locked, the road which leads nowhere, the lie, the everlasting dark'" (20–21). Modern ennui is symptomatic of "essential evil" (145) because it signifies a "vast yearning for the void, for emptiness" (145). "This contagion, this leprosy of boredom: an aborted despair, a shameful form of despair," writes the Curé of Ambricourt, is the "fermentation of a Christianity in decay" (3).

Torcy's second monologue, which also appears early in the novel, introduces the important theme of poverty and articulates its primacy in Bernanos's spiritual vision, although it should be noted that the author always distinguished between poverty, an honored Christian state, and "misery," a plight of utter destitution. Christ, Torcy tells his protégé, took poverty as his bride and bestowed upon her a dignity of which she can never be deprived (50). He shocks Ambricourt when he speaks of the necessity of preaching poverty to the poor: "Here is your Queen, recognize her, swear to honor her and be faithful" (56). This imperative recognizes the peril of those in whose ear the demon whispers his primordial promise of riches if only "you prostrate yourself in homage before me" (Matt. 4:9). The monologue also expresses Bernanos's deep distaste for the socialist experiment and its chimera of eliminating poverty, "the filthy thing," a fanciful project that only results in the poor experiencing their state as "a shameful illness" (56). He also castigates bourgeois solicitude, personified by, of all people, Judas Iscariot, who "like any millionaire" is interested in the "pauper problem" (61). It is Judas, embezzler of the common purse, who objects to the cost of the expensive nard with which the sinful woman anoints Jesus' feet. Torcy imagines Christ's rebuke to Judas, who demonstrates the kind of bourgeois righteousness that allows a beggar a few pennies but cries foul when he heads for the nearest pub instead of the bakery for a piece of stale bread (62).

The theme of poverty is again taken up during a conversation between Ambricourt and Dr. Delbende, an honorable atheist who suffers from his inability to believe. Delbende upbraids a Church that proclaims the nobility of the poor while pandering in fact to the rich and powerful. After twenty centuries of Christianity, he scolds the priest, being poor should not be shameful, and to the degree the Church has allowed such a stigma to endure it has betrayed its Christ (81). If indeed it is true that the poor man is the living image of Christ himself, why is he seated at the back of the church instead of being led to the gates of the sanctuary like the prince he is? (82). Still later, Ambricourt himself reflects upon the "Poor," capitalized to underscore Bernanos's belief that the "Poor Man" is indeed a privileged incarnation of God (93). At the novel's end, on the evening of the Curé's death, a soliloquy of exquisite tenderness and beauty is delivered by the defrocked priest's mistress, who speaks of poverty in the ageless voice, both brave and long-suffering, of the poor working woman (287). The simplicity of her acceptance and its lyrical expression of the universal cry of the poor recalls the One who assumed the condition of a slave and who loves them as equals.

This brings us to the work's theological core, the Incarnation itself. Just as it constitutes for Christians the watershed event of history, so its centrality in *Diary of a Country Priest* affords the novel its thematic unity. As Torcy puts it, the Incarnation is "the one and only drama, the drama of dramas" (210). Ambricourt too alludes recurrently to this mystery in his diary, insisting upon the actual fact of God's entrance into the human experience. Our God, he asserts, is not a reticent Godhead, the supreme but distant being proclaimed by Enlightenment Deism, but an intimate friend who shares our joys and sorrows and, in our last hour, will take us into his arms and press us to his heart. The Curé protests that he is not a philosopher, the "mouthpiece" of some geometrical God, but the servant of a master who shares our very life.

On the deepest level, the significance of the Incarnation leitmotif is intimately bound up with the protagonist's own story, and here we touch upon a crucial point of Bernanos's theology, namely, the process of "divinization." To understand its significance, it would be helpful to cite an English translation of Bernanos's favorite prayer from the Roman liturgy, one to which he averred frequently and with great urgency in his nonfiction, although always, of course, in the Latin of the Tridentine liturgy:

> O God, who didst wonderfully create, and yet more wondrously renew the dignity of man's nature; grant that by the mystery of this water and wine we may be made partakers of his divinity, who vouchsafed to share our humanity, Jesus Christ thy Son, our Lord: who liveth and reigneth with thee in the unity of the Holy Ghost, God throughout all ages, world without end. Amen.

Spoken by the priest during the Offertory of the Mass while pouring a small amount of water into the chalice of wine, this invocation articulated for Bernanos the essence of the Christian vocation: not to imitate Christ but to *become* him.

We are to participate in his very divinity and thus share in the Incarnation itself, or, as Saint Paul puts it, "I live now, not I, but Christ" (Gal. 2:20).

It is in this light that we are to understand the Curé of Ambricourt. His acute suffering, physical, emotional, and spiritual, demonstrates two critical aspects that make it distinctive. Like the Savior who "suffers our pain," he takes upon himself the suffering of others. Yet, more significantly still, this personal Calvary proves invariably redemptive for those whose pain he thus assumes. So it is, for example, with Chantal, the rebellious daughter of the Count and Countess, who has been consumed by a demonic spite since learning of her father's affair with the governess. During a tense encounter with the priest, she declares her hatred of her parents and her intention to disgrace herself to punish her unfaithful father. In an instance of sacerdotal clairvoyance, the Curé discerns her soul and beholds its misery. It afflicts him with a sadness that is scarcely bearable, although he is keen not only to share it but also to embrace it wholly so that it might fill his very being, his "heart" and his "bones" (134). It is no coincidence that, almost immediately after this experience of supernatural compassion, the Curé notes in his diary that the pain in his stomach, which had subsided, now returned with unprecedented ferocity (136). His suffering intensifies until at the summit of this spiritual combat the priest divines with prophetic certitude that Chantal's last great struggle against God had ended and that the evil that possessed her was departing (139). Later, after bringing peace and reconciliation to the girl's mother, he observes, "surely that must be paid for," and indeed it is (200). The payment is the Cross, and the Curé is Christ crucified. The priest himself is vaguely, intuitively, aware of this fact. Like Christ lamenting over Jerusalem, he had earlier looked down from a hilltop upon his parish and confessed that he sometimes imagines that the village had nailed him to a cross and was watching him die (40). He subsequently comes to understand that he is, eternally, a "prisoner" of the Lord's agony in the garden (203).

In Bernanos's theology, the grace of divinization—this intimate participation in the Incarnation—is the substance of the Church. To describe its inverse, Bernanos coined the term "disincarnation," which first appeared in his most famous polemical work, *A Diary of My Times*, ostensibly a memoir of the Spanish Civil War but in fact a penetrating meditation on the state of the Christian West. In a memorable scene from that essay, Bernanos imagines an agnostic preaching a sermon to a congregation of complacent Catholics (on the feast day of Saint Thérèse of Lisieux, no less!). This improbable homilist tells his bourgeois flock, "because you have not lived your faith, your faith is no longer alive; it has become abstract; it is as it were, disincarnate. Perhaps we will discover in this disincarnation of the Word the true cause of our misfortunes" (my translation). *Diary of My Times* is worth mentioning here because both it and *Diary of a Country Priest* were written during the same fecund few years of the mid-1930s and share many of the same preoccupations. This is especially true of the idea of disincarnation. Although the term as such is never used in the novel, it is clear that the fatal contagion it connotes was much on Bernanos's mind as he wrote it, as when the Curé condemns intellectualized faith as an "abstraction" (122).

Whereas the Curé of Ambricourt represents the Church's true vocation, others in the novel epitomize an ersatz church, a disincarnate Christianity. Bernanos was a perceptive and prophetic critic of "Christianity in decay," and there are characters throughout the novel, some of them minor, who personify it. There is, for example, the Count, who regards the Church as a policing organ whose first duty is to preserve social order, to discourage public excess, and to restrain dissolute behavior (195). His wife, whose heart seethes with enmity, insists that she is a Catholic in good standing and declares to a scandalized Curé that hers is a Christian household (159). He reminds her that while she may invite Christ into her home, so did Caiaphas.

While the Countess views Christianity as a habit of ritual and duty, Arsène, the aged parish sacristan, deems it a social and ancestral convention (197). As for the clergy, there are various exemplars of degeneration within their ranks. This should come as no surprise, since Bernanos was known as an essayist whose rebuke of clerical malfeasance was scathing. (His indictment of the Spanish hierarchy and clergy in *Diary of My Times* spurred the Spanish Church to do everything in its power to have the book placed on the *Index* of forbidden books. According to Bernanos, it was Pope Pius XI himself who intervened to prevent such a measure.) Says Ambricourt of his fellow priests, "Their serene security appalls me" (32). Isn't it true, he asks, that the real reason that so many of the poor have such a deep dislike of priests is the fact that they are so often mediocre, and a mediocre priest is "ugly"? (74). Several such clerics appear in the novel. There is, of course, the Curé's rather pathetic defrocked friend of seminary days. There is also a vignette about the retired bishop of Bailloeil, who represents one for whom Bernanos had a particular disdain, the so-called "intellectual" priest, who is embarrassed before the secular intelligentsia by the apparent lack of rational sophistication of religious faith. Such a one feels compelled to apologize "for Almighty God, Whose style leaves so much to be desired" (4). The Curé confesses that the "lettered" priest has always been repugnant to him (4). It is worth noting that Father Cénabre, the evil protagonist of Bernanos's second novel, *The Impostor*, is a celebrated scholar. His sinister presence also permeates *Joy*.

There is, however, a third cleric in *Diary of a Country Priest* who, beyond personal mediocrity, espouses a vision of the Church that is at odds with Ambricourt's. For the Dean of Blangermont, the Church is above all a political entity that, to survive, must make compromises with the rapacious merchant middle class. This class may do its best to exploit the Church, he tells the Curé, but at least it respects her. This makes for a certain solidarity between the ecclesial institution and its cynical backers (68). The solid families of the bourgeoisie provide the Church with priests, while the Church is for them an instrument of social cohesion, a buffer against the forces of disorder that threaten their privilege. However, the Dean's most revealing comment does not appear in the English text; in fact, Pamela Morris failed to translate an entire page of his conversation with Ambricourt. One suspects that she feared to offend English Catholic sensibilities. At any rate, in that missing page, to the younger priest's amazement, the Dean exclaims, "May God preserve us from saints too." He claims that among the secular clergy in particular, God discourages saints. They are "supernatural adventurers" who cause problems for the hierarchy. Worse, by their words, their attitude, even their silence, they cause scandal to those who are half-hearted and mediocre, by which he means the lukewarm Catholic middle class who are an indispensable source of ecclesial revenue. The Dean asserts that what the Church needs, finally employing the operative word, is money. The saint, therefore, disturbs the "solidarity" between the Church and her backers. However distasteful this machiavellianism may be, it is principally Blangermont's inherent advocacy of the disincarnation of the Word that Bernanos decries in this character. After all, sanctity is essentially a participation in the Incarnation.

The Diary of a Country Priest ends on a note of reconciliation, not with God, as might be expected, but with the self, although the two are inextricably linked. The need for such reconciliation reflects the primacy of the theme of self-hatred that figures in all of Bernanos's novels, none perhaps more than this one. It emerges very early on, when the Curé reflects upon the difficulty of relating to the peasant class that believes itself to be incorrigible and makes no effort to improve but rather endures vice "stolidly," despising gestures of love because "a peasant seldom loves himself" (22). In Bernanos's catalog of sins, this self-hatred is primal, one for which there is no forgiveness (23).

The novel relates Christian faith itself, or its lack, to the same question. The Curé defines faith as "that supernatural knowledge of ourselves in the Divine" (126), while its rejection or conceptualization betrays a lack of interest in one's own profound truth, the loss of any real desire to know oneself. He views the death of faith as the manifestation of some fundamental alienation with eternal consequences. In his imagination, the Curé addresses himself to just such a creature set against himself, one who no longer wishes to "possess" himself, who no longer aspires to his own joy. Not loving God, in whom alone the love of self is possible, he cannot love himself and never will, not in this world or the one to come (126). Self-hatred is a way that leads to perdition, one that Chantal, for example, has chosen to follow. The priest quickly recognizes that her revolt is primarily directed against herself, and during their principal confrontation he reveals to her the unwelcome truth: "Well—it's your own self you hate, just you" (191).

Given the uncompromising nature of his censure of self-hatred, it is perhaps surprising to discover that the Curé is himself similarly tempted. He acknowledges the essence of his "dark night": "My solitude is complete and hateful. I can feel no pity for myself. Suppose I were never to love again!" (105–06). When, near the novel's end, he is diagnosed with cancer of the stomach, he stands weeping before the doctor and avows to his diary that he could have "died of self-loathing" (275). Why self-loathing? Because of tears of weakness shed before a stranger? That is hardly in the Curé's character. When he candidly confesses that he had never been so close to hating himself, it is more precisely true to say that it is his body, exposed in all its vulnerability and weakness, that he is tempted to hate. This is later made explicit when he admits, "Already I was too inclined to be disgusted with my own body" (278). He realizes that, as he faces death, his first task is to become reconciled with himself, and the penultimate paragraph of his diary, entered on the day of his death, records just such a restoration of harmony. Here, once again, Pamela Morris's translation, "I am reconciled to myself, to the poor, poor shell of me," is not particularly helpful (296). The French text would be better translated literally: "I am reconciled with myself, with this poor carcass." The pointed inclusion of "carcass" (*dépouille*) emphasizes the final acceptance of his incarnate being. How is this made possible? The last entry provides the answer: "How easy it is to hate oneself! True grace is to forget. Yet if pride could die in us, the supreme grace would be to love oneself in all simplicity—as one would love any one of those who themselves have suffered and loved in

Christ" (296). In this theology, a vital reconciliation with the self, and perhaps especially with one's own body, is realized only within the Body of Christ.

CRITICAL RECEPTION

When *The Diary of a Country Priest* appeared in March 1936, the French literary establishment welcomed it with enormous enthusiasm, although it took time to catch on with the public. Its success was crowned when the French Academy awarded it its *Grand Prix du Roman*. When the English translation was published the following year, it was greeted with similar enthusiasm by British and American critics. "In daring to describe the awareness of the supernatural, M. Bernanos has successfully brought to birth a kind of fiction which had seemed inconceivable," wrote a reviewer in the *Times Literary Supplement* (1937). And the *New York Times Book Review* called the novel "a work of deep, subtle and singularly encompassing art" (Woods 1937, 1).

Also to be noted is that, in 1950, France's brilliant and idiosyncratic *cinéaste* Robert Bresson made a film version of *The Diary of a Country Priest* that is considered by critics of the cinema to be one of his masterpieces.

NOTE

Georges Bernanos, *The Diary of a Country Priest*, trans. Pamela Morris (New York: Carroll and Graf, 1983). All references are to this edition.

WORKS CITED

Review of *Diary of a Country Priest*, by Georges Bernanos. 1937. *Times Literary Supplement* (September 18): 674.
Thérèse of Lisieux. 1951. *Story of a Soul*. London: Burns and Oates.
Woods, Katherine. 1937. Review of *Diary of a Country Priest*, by Georges Bernanos. *New York Times Book Review* (October 24): 1.

BIBLIOGRAPHY

Bush, William. *Georges Bernanos*. New York: Twayne, 1969.
Dorschell, Mary Frances. *Georges Bernanos's Debt to Thérèse of Lisieux*. Lewiston, PA: Mellen University Press, 1996.
O'Sharkey, Eithne M. *The Role of the Priest in the Novels of Georges Bernanos*. New York: Vantage, 1983.
Speaight, Robert. *Georges Bernanos: A Study of the Man and the Writer*. London: Collens and Harvill, 1973.

— Michael R. Tobin

Heinrich Böll [1917–1985]

Group Portrait with Lady

BIOGRAPHY

By 1971, when Heinrich Böll's award-winning novel, *Group Portrait with Lady* (*Gruppenbild mit Dame*) was published, he was already an established writer, well known on the literary scene and respected nationally and internationally. By many, he was considered the "chronicler of German history" and the "conscience of the nation," labels he personally rejected in his modesty and simplicity. He was a man of highest integrity, profound kindness, outspoken honesty, deeply rooted religiosity, and great love for his family. Three important factors influenced his literary development: his biography, the Catholic Rhineland, and his social and political involvement as a citizen of the Federal Republic of Germany.

Böll was born on December 21, 1917, in Cologne into a devout Catholic family. His father, Viktor Böll, who was a skilled, self-employed master cabinetmaker, and his mother Maria, née Hermanns, to whom he referred throughout his life as a "wonderful, great woman," raised their children with respect for the teaching of the Church but also with a critical attitude to it as an institution. In the few autobiographical sketches that he wrote, Böll confirms his love for his parents, those two admired persons who had provided him with a happy childhood.

Born during World War I, Böll experienced poverty and hunger at an early age. The inflation of the 1920s and his father's unemployment during those years forced the family to move frequently within the different quarters of his native city or its vicinity. It also taught the young boy respect for the poor, and it allowed him to mix with youngsters of all classes and to play with the "red" children of the Socialist families in their new neighborhood. Böll's belief in a humane socialism can be traced back to those early years. He was also made aware of his parents' struggle to regain financial security and to remain strong in their political convictions.

The city of Cologne, with its old and beautiful buildings, streets, and churches; the nearby river Rhine, with its white ships and barges; the Rhenish dialect; and the almost proletarian lust for life of its inhabitants were other sources for Böll's colorful portrayal of people, landscape, and events in his fiction. His early formal education started in a Catholic elementary school (1924–1927). Of the 515 children taught by an exclusively Catholic team of twelve teachers, only one child was Jewish. From 1928 to 1937, Böll was a student at the Kaiser Wilhelm Gymnasium in Cologne, which was also an "extremely Catholic" institution, as he pointed out later in life. From 1929 on, initiated by the Wall Street stock market crash, a time of extreme hardship began in Germany that was accompanied by a growing radicalization of its population. The unemployment rate in Cologne reached 30.8 percent. Böll's father had to sell their house, and the large family moved into an apartment in the city.

As a sixteen year old, Böll witnessed the growing support for Hitler's National Socialist Party and, on May 1, 1933, observed the first Nazi march through the streets of Cologne followed by the boycott of Jewish shops. On May 17, 1933, seven days after the first public burning of books in Berlin, a similar event took place in his native city (Viktor Böll et al. 2002, 17).

In 1938, one year after the completion of his high school education, Böll's love for books sent him for a short while to the nearby city of Bonn, where he became an apprentice to a book dealer, employment that was later documented in his autobiographical sketch, *What's to Become of the Boy? Or, Something to Do with Books* (1984). He had received his early moral education not only in his parents' home but also through the discovery of the great thinkers and writers Heinrich von Kleist, Friedrich Hölderlin, Rainer Maria Rilke, Charles Dickens, Honoré de Balzac, and Homer. Also important for his intellectual formation at the time were the writings of the French Catholic authors of the *Renouveau Catholique*, or Catholic Renaissance: Georges Bernanos, François Mauriac, Charles Péguy, and Léon Bloy. As an adolescent, he had also been attracted by the German writers Gertrud von Le Fort and Werner Bergengruen.

In the winter of 1938–39, Böll was called to compulsory labor service. When war broke out, he was twenty-two. His early short stories reflect in the portrayal of the lives of the young protagonists the devastating experiences of their "call for duty" and their hated participation in war, which Böll denounced in all his fiction as the major evil of mankind. In July 1939, he was called into military service. He served for the full six years of World War II and was stationed in Germany, Poland, France, Russia, and Hungary. In 1940, he became severely sick with dysentery and returned to Germany. His experience of this period in his life was described in 1958 in a collection of essays, among them his *Brief an einen jungen Katholiken* (*Letter to a Young Catholic*), which is also a bitter polemic against the Catholic Church in the Third Reich and its failure to provide moral leadership under Hitler and after 1945. This letter is considered by many critics as one of the most effective moral and political essays of the 1950s (see Conard 1992, 162).

While on leave in Germany in March 1942, Böll married Annemarie Cech, who became his lifelong companion and partner. Like Böll a teacher and accomplished translator, she bore him four sons: Christoph Paul, who died soon after his birth in 1945, Raimund (1947–1982), René (1948–), and Vincent (1950–). Both his wife and two sons are still actively involved in the publishing of Böll's works and the preservation of his memory.

Böll was often severely injured and hospitalized during his years of military service, and the experience affected his physical health throughout his life. In the last weeks of war, on April 9, 1945, he was taken prisoner. Freed from a prisoner of war camp in France, he returned home on December 15, 1945. His mother had been killed during one of the many air raids on Cologne, and for his wife, who was expecting their first child, he had to find shelter in a totally destroyed city.

In 1947, Böll published his first short stories. During his career, he often mentioned the hardship he encountered when—after years of National Socialist propaganda and the abuse of the German language—the naming of things and events in his native language proved to be a difficult task. But once this barrier was broken, his stories and novels recounted without mercy the absurdity and daily suffering in times of war. His protagonists were not war heroes but only the simple people who had survived and had to reshape their lives in the rubble of their cities and homes. The times of restoration and the economic miracle were targeted in those first stories and novels with a merciless criticism of the old and new generation of profiteers and former Nazis regaining power in the Germany of the 1950s. He also criticized his countrymen for their "inability to mourn." He felt that, because of the enormous task of rebuilding their cities, they had neglected to rebuild their souls.

In 1951, Böll received the prize of the "Group 47." This group of writers of postwar Germany was founded in 1947, and its members were dedicated to democracy and a politically committed literature. The group held annual informal gatherings. The prize gave Böll not only the much-needed financial support of one thousand marks but also instant recognition. The event became the turning point in his career, followed by the successful publication of his first novel, *Adam, Where Art Thou?* The tragic fate of a returning soldier, the misery of the daily fight for bread and survival, and the loss of empathy and compassion were the themes of the numerous short stories and novels that followed. Among these are *The Bread of Those Early Years* (1955), *Billiards at Half-past Nine* (1959), *The Clown* (1963), *Absent without Leave* (1964), and *End of a Mission* (1966). When *Group Portrait with Lady* appeared in 1971, Böll had lived through the hectic decade of the 1960s. After this period, troubled by the turmoil of the student revolution, the feminist movement, the rise of neo-Nazi voices, and the open criticism of the Roman Catholic Church for its role during the Nazi regime, Böll became more radicalized. He had hoped that the Second Vatican Council, opened in 1963, would prepare the Catholic Church to play a more modern role in the world. But he saw his hope for a progressive Catholicism fading. In 1969, in an act of public protest, he and his wife refused to pay the obligatory Church tax and both left the Church. It was their way of objecting to the Church's support of the capitalist system. However, many awards had accompanied the publication of his books and had resulted in a growing national and international recognition. The demands for public engagement grew, which led to Böll's active participation in the election campaign for the Social Democrats and support for chancellor candidate Willy Brandt. His attacks had long been directed toward the state and its Christian Democratic representatives and toward the institutionalized powers of the Catholic Church, represented in the conservative and wealthy Catholic milieu of the Rhineland. He also repeatedly warned against the indoctrination and abuse of the increasingly powerful media and the influential right-wing press of Axel Springer, which found its literary documentation in his novel *The Lost Honour of Katharina Blum* (1974). In the 1970s, Germany was deeply troubled by a wave of terrorism, and Böll engaged in open and emotional criticism of the state's and the police's handling of the events. This was misinterpreted as sympathizing with the terrorist acts of the Red Army Faction, or RAF (also known as the Baader-Meinhof Group after two of its early leaders). The original group was a relatively small leftist organization, but due to the violent actions of the RAF, the state and mass media criticized the entire left in Germany as ruthless and destructive. The political climate became hysterical, and Böll called for a solution to the national crisis in an article that suggested justice and fairness for a small group of young bourgeois radicals who felt that the new German democracy was endangered by a repressive conservative state. As a result of his engagement in this affair, he became the open target of police and state powers.

Böll joined the peace movement, and he and his family reached out to the agencies that were dedicated to helping the peoples of the Third World and the poor and deprived of middle America. As a frequent traveler to Russia, he also helped many of the dissidents of the failing regime in that country. He served for a time as the president of the International P. E. N., and he was a leading defender of the intellectual freedom of writers when, in 1980 and 1984, he assisted Lew Kopelev and Aleksandr Solzhenitsyn to find not only shelter but also financial support in his home. As a recipient of national awards and honorary doctorates from many universities, Böll's greatest international recognition came on December 10, 1972, with the award of the Nobel Prize for Literature. He was the first German to win this prestigious prize since Thomas Mann in 1929.

In his private life, Böll was a very religious and modest man. A heavy smoker and suffering throughout his life from ill health, including diabetes, he nevertheless wrote and spoke out until the very end. When he died on July 16, 1985, as a result of complications after surgery, artists, politicians, fellow citizens, and other admirers came to accompany him on his last journey. The music of a gypsy band resounded through the rural setting where he was laid to rest under a great old oak tree in the cemetery of Bornheim-Merten, the small village between Bonn and Cologne to which he and his family had moved in 1982.

PLOT SUMMARY

As the title of *Group Portrait with Lady* indicates, the novel's central character—the "Lady"—is a woman, Leni Pfeiffer, née Gruyten. She is surrounded by a multitude of characters who are introduced by the narrator as "The Group." This group of persons is composed of various families, the Gruytens, Pfeiffers, Hoysers, Schweigerts, and Pelzers. They all have shaped Leni's past and some of them are still part of her present biography.

At the beginning, the narrator introduces himself as "the Author" (or "Au."). In fourteen chapters, he attempts to reveal the true story and character of his heroine. He incorporates in his story the testimonies of fifty-one informants, among them nuns, Jesuits, her fellow workers, camp guards, Soviet prisoners of war, and her lovers. His purpose is to present Leni Gruyten Pfeiffer—contrary to her negative public image—in the correct light. In the first chapter of the novel, the biographer describes her surroundings, her modest and threatened living conditions, in the year 1970. Leni finds herself attacked and ostracized by her neighbors due to, among other things, her past and present associations with "foreigners." Her daily life is endangered by verbal and physical attacks to the extent that she is afraid to leave her living quarters. After introducing Leni's physical appearance with considerable accuracy according to age (forty-eight), height (five foot six inches), weight (133 pounds), color of eyes (dark blue and black), and hair (very thick and blond), the author makes his task as researcher very clear and encourages the reader to become the judge of Leni's life against the background of Germany's troubled history between the years 1922 and 1970. This sets the framework for the story, in which flashbacks into public and private events involving the main character present a chronicle of German history. The major events take place in a West German city.

In the first paragraph of the novel, we find out important facts about Leni. She is a war widow. In 1941, she had been married for a period of three days to Alois Pfeiffer, a sergeant in the German army, who was killed soon after in battle. We are also informed that she had been a working woman for thirty-two years, of which she had spent five years as an unskilled employee in the engineering firm of her father and twenty-seven years as an unskilled worker in a nursery garden. Further facts reveal that she is impoverished due to the loss of her inherited property, an apartment house, which she had sold for a pittance during the war. She has given up her job, although she is still quite young and without sufficient monetary resources. The introductory portrait ends with the author's remark that Leni is finding life especially difficult because her beloved son Lev is in jail.

The chronology of Leni's life is short and rather uneventful, and she is repeatedly described in the novel as a "taciturn and reticent, proud woman" (*Group Portrait*, 238), a beautiful woman, with the "incomparable directness of Rhenish girls" (215). The Au. also remarks that her "religious gifts have remained as unrecognized as her sensuality" (32). Leni was born on August 17, 1922. Educated in the early years of war, followed by a short period in a Catholic boarding school, her formal and spiritual education have obviously not succeeded in making her an acceptable member of the upper-middle-class society into which she was born. Even though her family accepts her for what she is, her teachers declare her a "misfit" at an early and formative age. Leni rejects the way that institutionalized and organized religion is lived and taught at the Catholic boarding school. However, she is strongly influenced and touched by the life and fate of one of the nuns, the mystical Jewish nun Rahel Ginzburg. At the end of Leni's story, the reader finds out that she considered Sister Rahel her true friend and teacher. Sister Rahel encouraged the young adolescent girl to accept and acknowledge not only the spiritual side but also the sensual side of her existence.

Dismissed from further schooling in 1938, Leni starts to work in her father's firm, where she remains until 1943. The background of the Gruyten family is revealed in the following chapter with the first experience of loss for Leni due to the tragic deaths of her brother Heinrich and her cousin Erhard, her first love. Both young soldiers had been tried as saboteurs and shot in Denmark as a result of trying to sell an antitank gun to the Danes, an act of protest against the business of war.

The narrator continues to describe the slow material decline of the Gruyten family. Hubert Gruyten, the patriarch of this prosperous Rhenish family, cannot accept his son's senseless death. He loses interest in his position and his construction firm, which had prospered due to its contribution to the Nazi economy. As a result of his disillusionment, he rids himself of his wealth and possessions and creates a fictitious "Dead Souls" company which enables him to drain the Nazi system. However, the fraud is soon discovered: Hubert is tried and convicted, imprisoned, and sent to a labor camp. The scandal and collapse of the Gruyten family at the end of 1942 and the beginning of 1943 leads to the death of Leni's mother and leaves the twenty-one-year-old protagonist alone in an unfriendly world marked by a violent war. Left without family and husband and far removed from an independent and protected lifestyle, she is forced to earn a living. She is assigned as a laborer to Pelzer's cemetery nursery, where she soon becomes an expert in wreath binding. It is there, and after she has been working for the opportunist Pelzer for a year, that she meets Boris Lvovic Koltowski. He joins the crew in Pelzer's shop as a Soviet prisoner of war. Leni offers him a cup of her precious, rationed coffee on his first day of work, which is forbidden in the eyes of most of her Fascist fellow workers. The frightened young Russian is considered an enemy by most of the workers, but Leni's act of kindness and generosity turns out to become the central event in her life. It is also the beginning of a great love story. During the heavy bombardment of the city in 1944, followed by numerous air raids, the couple secretly keeps on meeting in the cemetery's crypt, unnoticed by their fellow workers.

In the chaos of the ending war, Leni, who has become pregnant, and Boris take refuge among the tombs and await the birth of their child. On a crucial date, the day of the nine-hour Allied air raid on the city of Cologne on March 2, 1945, Leni and Boris's son Lev is born. His birth and baptism in the crypt by the nursery owner Pelzer is the highlight of their union. While the burning city is being evacuated, they decide to stay underground.

Boris's tragic fate results from his arrest by the Americans, who have occupied the city. He carries a German military passport and is believed to be a German soldier. Subsequently, he is handed over to the French, who put him to work in a mine in Lorraine, where he dies tragically in an accident. From that point on and after Leni has found Boris's grave in a foreign land, she devotes her life to raising and educating her beloved son. His early and adolescent years show young Lev in defiance of the norms and expectations of the established rules of postwar German society. In his refusal to become part of a world in which instant gratification is the norm, he starts to work for the state garbage collection. At age twenty-five, through his forging of a few checks, he comes in conflict with the state and ends up in prison. This criminal act was prompted by the insight he had acquired into the financial cheating of the Hoyser family and by the vulnerability of his mother.

Leni, who in the postwar game of profiteering is unable to repay an earlier loan that she had received from her father's former employee, Otto Hoyser, is under pressure to leave her parental home, now owned by the same Hoyser. As a result of her debt, he repossesses her property and threatens to evict her. She had been subletting her few rooms cheaply to foreign workers and had started a small classless community with them, trying to help them establish a new life in a foreign country. With one of them, the Turkish worker Mehmet, she starts a love affair. At the close of the novel and the time of her imminent eviction, she is, at the age of forty-eight, pregnant with his child. In this precarious situation, her friends create a "help Leni" committee. They collect money to cover her debts and even organize a traffic jam to gain time to prevent her eviction.

Before the story's ending, the reader is informed of the death of Leni's former classmate and most compassionate friend, who, as the other major female character in the novel, is most strongly contrasted with Leni. She has died of venereal disease.

The biographer, researcher, and author of Leni's life story has, in the meantime, traveled to a convent in Rome, where he meets Sister Klementina, who reveals more details about the mysterious Sister Rahel Ginzburg. The author falls in love with the attractive nun, and from then on they join forces and try to follow the traces of Rahel and Leni and unravel Leni's story. They actually meet Leni personally. The several happy endings to the novel include the union of Leni and Mehmet, of their friends Lotte and Bogakov, and of Sister Klementina, who leaves the convent in order to be with the author. Lev will soon be released from prison to join his mother and to contribute to this microcosm of a new community, which both of them hope will become a reality.

MAJOR THEMES

When *Group Portrait with Lady* appeared in 1971, Böll's belief in the constructive strength of the individual opposing the tyrannical forces of institutionalized powers had grown. In essays and lectures between 1963 and 1971, he had expressed his viewpoints on the viability of a new Christian ethic before they appeared in a crystallized and fictionalized form in his longest and richest text. In one of several interviews, he stated that his writings deal with religion and love and that he had tried in this latest novel "to describe or write about the fate of a German woman in her late forties who had taken on herself the burden of history between 1922 and 1970" (quoted in Matthaei 1975, 141).

All of the novel's events center on Leni and a narrator and the narrator's attempt to grasp her essence of being. Leni is an instinctively good woman: innocent, humane, sensuous, proud, and a true Christian. Her character, however, contains elements of contradictions. Her image is, according to Böll's poetic wishes, "anti-iconographic," but she shows similarities with biblical figures and displays their mythical qualities. Böll had acknowledged that her image may well be rooted in a specific regional tradition: the celebration of the Madonnas of the Rhineland. His familiarity with the many artistic representations and forms of adoration of the Madonna in his native city of Cologne may have been a creative influence in the shaping of the positive, almost saintly qualities of his protagonist. In the same interview, he also mentioned that he had wanted to portray in the figure of Leni "neither a positive nor a negative heroine" (quoted in Matthaei 1975, 154).

Leni Pfeiffer's full name is Helene Maria. She was born on August 17, 1922, two days after the Marian feast of the Assumption. She is repeatedly compared to "our Lady" in her virginal beauty, in her innocence and compassion for the people on the fringe of society, and in her belief in Christianity represented in the union of the Holy Family. The text is also filled with numerous comparisons of Leni's life with that of the Virgin Mary. Böll had addressed his conflict with society's and the Church's portrayal and interpretation of the role of women in his lectures at the University of Frankfurt in 1964. He had criticized the Church for its lack of explication of texts concerning women in the Scriptures. He saw the embodiment of femininity in the trinity of Eve, the Virgin Mary, and Mary Magdalene (Böll 1966, 101), and Leni does indeed represent all three of them in her spiritual, intellectual, and sensual desires.

The female counterpart to Leni can be found in her closest friend, Margret Schlömer, the obvious Mary Magdalene in the story, who, like Leni, gives of her love freely and selflessly, not sanctioned by the state's or the Church's legalized contracts. Both of these female figures give Böll the opportunity to criticize a society that views acts of sensuality as prostitution and marriage as a sacrament. There are a number of events that show Leni in her spiritual, almost saintly, dimension. The reader is especially reminded of her first encounter with the Russian prisoner Boris at the beginning of the love story. Considered an "enemy of the people," he is at first despised and rejected by the workers in Pelzer's wreath shop. Boris is referred to by the many witnesses as Leni's "Saint Joseph" (275), and he shares many of the human and spiritual features of the biblical figure of Joseph. When Leni offers him a cup of coffee on his first day of work, the reader is reminded of the ritual during communion when the priest offers the chalice to the community of believers. When one of the fellow workers, a Nazi, throws his artificial leg at the cup to object to Leni's acceptance of a foreigner in their midst, and the cup falls to the ground, Leni picks it up, carefully rinses it, dries it in a long period of "deathly silence," fills it again, and offers Boris a second cup "as if it was a sacred chalice" (184). The incident is considered by the Au. as Leni's second "birth" and as a decisive act of solidarity with the stranger, an open display of human kindness that eventually affected every one of the workers positively. From this day on, Boris also takes on a new role, that of educator for Leni as well as mentor to her fellow workers.

One of the most striking comparisons with the community of early Christians is also Leni and Boris's search for shelter among the tombs and crypts of the nearby cemetery during the heavy bombardments of the city. Fraternizing with the enemy could have endangered both of their lives and that of their fellow workers, who often refer to their hiding places as the "Soviet paradise in the vaults" (256). It is also underground, in hiding from the hostile world, that Leni gives birth to her child on a bed of peat moss, old blankets, and straw matting on March 2, 1945 (275). The reader is immediately reminded of the birth of the Christ child in a manger.

But Leni also embodies Eve-like tempting characteristics. All men in the novel—among them the narrator—are attracted to her. Her physical beauty at age forty-eight has likewise attracted the Mohammedan Turkish guest worker Mehmet, with whom she will have a child. Gifted with an intuitive and sensual appreciation of the world around her, Leni finds freedom of expression in art, poetry, and music.

The end of the story is revealing. Leni's life was filled with numerous casualties: the loss of her family and first husband; the loss of her friend Margret and her spiritual mentor, Sister Rahel; and the loss of her inherited property and material security. But she has handed down her qualities and belief in a humane, peace-loving, profitless and classless society to her son Lev. She has taught him and raised him according to her principles and, as a result, he also refuses to contribute to and take part in the ideals of a world of supermasculinity, which only rewards the overachiever. He rejects an educational system that leaves little room for the world of dreams and spirituality. He is also compared to the Man of Nazareth.

Robert C. Conard (1992, 101) suggests that "with Leni as Mary and Boris as Joseph, Lev must be Jesus and emerge as a savior." As his choice of profession clearly indicates, he intends to clean up the mess of the world as garbage collector with a team of sanitation workers.

This is Böll's way of suggesting that a new world order cannot be born without the destruction of the old. When questioned by Heinz Ludwig Arnold about the kind of society he had in mind, his answer was "a profitless and classless society." Provoked again by Arnold, who asked him whether he meant "a socialist society," Böll's answer was, "Yes, certainly!" (Conard 1992, 100).

CRITICAL RECEPTION

Group Portrait with Lady appeared in the summer of 1971. The newspaper *Frankfurter Allgemeine Zeitung* printed a serialized version in the same year. Within six months, 150,000 hardback copies were sold and the book became an instant best seller. The novel, with its unusual treatment of montage, collage, revolutionary messages, and utopian ideas, received mixed reviews. Reinhard K. Zachau (1994) has collected them in his study *Heinrich Böll: Forty Years of Criticism*. Most of the positive voices saw in the form and content of the novel "a mature masterpiece" (Karl Korn in Reid 1988, 172) and a kind of summary of all that Böll had achieved to that point. Helmut Heißenbüttel, one of the leading and most respected avant-garde writers, spoke for many others when he wrote that the label "masterpiece" could no longer do justice to the great qualities of the text (Reid 1988, 172). Some labeled the novel a "weak book," directing their criticism against the composition of the novel and arguing that a convincing explanation of the recorded events was missing. The legitimization, credibility, and research method of the narrator and "Author" were questioned by many (see chapter 2.3 in Sowinski 1993, 76–81). Böll had experimented with new narrative techniques, which were considered postmodern. The autonomous storyteller, the second protagonist in the story, also becomes an active player in the last of the fourteen chapters of the text. His involvement changes from researcher of Leni's life to reporter and finally to witness and participant in a utopian but Christian experiment. The utopian content of the novel and Böll's portrayal of a new society were found by many to be unrealistic.

A collection of the most significant critical essays on the text appeared in *Die subversive Madonna* (The Subversive Madonna), edited by Renate Matthaei in 1975. Most criticism was directed toward the portrayal of the leading "Lady" and her son Lev. Some critics saw in Leni "an ideal of timeless femininity" or a celebration of "the eternal German Kitsch" (Marcel Reich-Ranicki, quoted by Perraudin, in Butler 1994, 182). Others agreed that Böll's fictional figures of Leni and Lev displayed a wealth of *Menschlichkeit* (humaneness), which was anchored in their Christian existence. Robert C. Conard argued in his excellent study on Böll that the "radical message" of the novel could be reduced to the single explanation that "it is impossible to be a Christian (humanist) and support a society based on exploitation" (1981, 182). Among East German critics, Hans-Joachim Bernhard praised Böll's commitment to the "potential for proletarian solidarity" as depicted in the scene in which Turks, Germans, and Portuguese garbage collectors unite behind Leni at the end of the story (Reid 1988, 172).

Others found his attacks on an achievement-oriented society unacceptable. Most critics agreed, however, with Conard's assessment that Böll had succeeded in reshaping the "image of women" in his text and for his time. Conard (1992, 97) sees in the work "a manifesto of Böll's humanism, individualism, and socialism embodied in the novel's heroine Leni Pfeiffer, a new twentieth-century Madonna, a contemporary secular saint."

NOTE

Heinrich Böll, *Group Portrait with Lady*, trans. Leila Vennewitz (New York: McGraw-Hill, 1973). All references are to this edition.

WORKS CITED

Böll, Heinrich. 1961. *Brief an einen jungen Katholiken* (Letter to a Young Catholic). Cologne: Kiepenheuer and Witsch.
———. 1966. *Frankfurter Vorlesungen*. Cologne: Kiepenheuer and Witsch.
———. 1984. *What's to Become of the Boy? Or, Something to Do with Books*, trans. Leila Vennewitz. New York: Knopf.
Böll, Viktor, Markus Schäfer, and Jochen Schubert, eds. 2002. *Heinrich Böll*. Munich: Deutscher Taschenbuch Verlag.
Butler, Michael, ed. 1994. *The Narrative Fiction of Heinrich Böll: Social Conscience and Literary Achievement*. Cambridge: Cambridge University Press.
Conard, Robert C. 1981. *Heinrich Böll*. Twayne World Author Series. Boston: G. K. Hall.
———. 1992. *Understanding Heinrich Böll*. Columbia, SC: University of South Carolina Press.
Matthaei, Renate, ed. 1975. *Die subversive Madonna: Ein Schlüssel zum Werk Heinrich Bölls*. Cologne: Kiepenheuer and Witsch.
Reid, James Henderson. 1988. *Heinrich Böll: A German for His Time*. Oxford: Berg.
Sowinski, Bernhard. 1993. *Heinrich Böll*. Stuttgart: Metzler.
Zachau, Reinhard K. 1994. *Heinrich Böll: Forty Years of Criticism*. Columbia, SC: Camden House.

BIBLIOGRAPHY

Böll, Viktor, and Markus Schäfer, eds. *Fortschreibung: Bibliographie zum Werk Heinrich Bölls*. Cologne: Kiepenheuer and Witsch, 1997.

— Trudis E. Goldsmith-Reber

Orestes Brownson [1803–1876]

The Spirit-Rapper; An Autobiography

BIOGRAPHY

Orestes Brownson was one of the most important American Catholic figures of the nineteenth century. As the critic Russell Kirk has written, over his long life Brownson knew practically everyone and wrote about practically everything (Brownson 1990, 3). A prolific author, his collected works run to twenty volumes and include philosophy, political theory, fiction, reviews, and autobiography, among other subjects. Most of this output was published in journals for which Brownson served as editor and almost sole contributor—first the *Boston Quarterly Review*, which he published from 1838 to 1842, then *Brownson's Quarterly Review*, which appeared from 1844 to 1864. His most famous book-length work is probably the political treatise *The American Republic*, published in 1865 at the close of the Civil War. After Alexis de Tocqueville's *Democracy in America*, it has been called the best book on American democracy. Arthur Schlesinger Jr. and Woodrow Wilson are among those who considered Brownson one of the few true political thinkers America has produced. After a period of neglect, Brownson and his work are being republished and he is regaining his former reputation.

Brownson personified the religious and social upheavals that regularly convulsed nineteenth-century America. He lived during the religious revivals of the 1820s, the economic depression of the 1830s, the Civil War and its aftermath, and the growing role of Catholicism in America, all of which became subjects for his fertile pen. His decision to become a Catholic in 1844 was the end of a lifelong search for a truth that would satisfy his strong analytic mind as well as his social principles. At the time, Brownson's former friends and intellectual allies believed his conversion was only a temporary phase; he had changed beliefs so often in his path from Unitarian to Transcendentalist to philosophical Christian to Catholic that no decision he made was thought to be permanent. But he proved them wrong; Brownson was to remain a loyal, if occasionally controversial, Catholic for the rest of his life. Indeed, his standing was so great in the United States and abroad that John Henry Cardinal Newman offered him a post in his proposed Catholic University of Ireland. At his own death, Brownson himself would be called "America's Newman."

The fifth of six children, Orestes was born in Stockbridge, Vermont, where his family had settled upon moving from their native Connecticut. His father, Sylvester Brownson, died while Orestes was still a child. After some years of struggle, his mother, Relief Brownson, placed Orestes in the home of an older couple in the nearby town of Royalton. In his autobiography, *The Convert; or, Leaves from My Experience*, Brownson describes these foster parents as "plain country people" who "had been brought up in New England Congregationalism, were honest, upright, strictly moral and far more ready to suffer wrong than to do wrong, but had no particular religion, and seldom went to meeting" (1). While he was given very basic Christian religious instruction by his foster parents, religion does not seem to have been a focus of his home life. Brownson had his first "conversion experience" at a Methodist revival in Royalton that he attended on his own. It would be the first of many intense religious encounters.

When Brownson was about sixteen, Relief collected her children and went to live in Balston Spa, New York, in an area known for its religious enthusiasm. Young Orestes was enrolled in a school run by the Universalists. The Universalists emphasized the use of reason to unlock the meaning of Scripture; but rather than become more religious, the experience left Brownson without belief. Reason seemed to him to explain away rather than justify religion. After a brief flirtation with the Presbyterian Church in 1822 (following another conversion experience), Brownson returned to Universalism and entered a productive period of writing, publishing, and serving as a minister in New Hampshire and New York. However, he left the Universalists for good in 1829 because of his growing unorthodox beliefs. The reasons for his dissatisfaction were set out in two essays, "My Creed" and "Gospel Creed," in which Brownson separated religious faith from the supernatural or ideas about the afterlife. It was during this period, in 1827, that he married Sally Healy, with whom he had eight children.

For the next three years, Brownson charted his own course, first as a free thinker and proponent of a "religion of humanity" detached from any particular denomination, and then as an independent preacher coming to more orthodox Christian belief. The problem that occupied him during this period was the same as that in his Universalist years: how to reconcile religious belief with reason. Brownson found an initial solution in the works of William Ellery Channing (1780–1842), a prominent New England clergyman and writer. Channing attempted to develop, in the words of Patrick Carey, "a new understanding of the coherence or synthesis of the divine and the human in human nature" (Brownson 1991, 17). Humanity need not rely on reason alone, which Brownson had come to believe would never be fully open to religious truth. On the contrary, Channing taught that religious experience should be understood as "a gradual process of unfolding the divine within the human person" (17). Channing also held that God could intervene in the natural process, confirming divine power over the natural order. Reading Channing led Brownson to return to an established Christian Church, but this time it was the Unitarians of New Hampshire.

Brownson obtained a post as a Unitarian minister in Walpole, New Hampshire, in 1832. The free time this position provided allowed him to learn German and French and to focus his studying. (A few years later, he spent the summer reading

German with a young applicant for town schoolmaster, Henry David Thoreau, who was impressed with Brownson's intellect.) Brownson's wide reading exposed him to the leading philosophers and theologians of Europe, especially Saint-Simon, Benjamin Constant, and Victor Cousin. In particular, Cousin's philosophy allowed Brownson further basis to reconcile religious belief with reason and the empirical sciences. Cousin gave reason a status independent of the individual: it existed objectively and was able to unite the subject (the thinker), the object (the thing thought), and the relationship between them. Certain ideas, such as God, were independent of observation and represented an intuitive reaction to what Cousin termed "spontaneous reason." This explanation temporarily satisfied Brownson's worry that subjective belief would taint objective reason and render it unable to assess the claims of religion fairly.

Boston was a short carriage ride away, and its pull proved irresistible to Brownson and his need for constant intellectual stimulation. In the late 1830s, Brownson befriended some of the most eminent Bostonians of the day, including Bronson Alcott and Ralph Waldo Emerson. He often preached by invitation at the most prestigious Boston churches. Along with Emerson and George Ripley, Brownson was a founding member of the Transcendentalist Club, and he even published a strong defense of Emerson's work. Brownson became as well known as Emerson himself in some circles, and his writing had an avid and influential readership. When Ripley, Margaret Fuller, and others became involved with the utopian community of Brook Farm, Brownson became a frequent guest and wrote a favorable portrait of the community in 1842. During his visits to the farm, Brownson became friendly with Isaac Hecker, a young man living there at the time. Hecker, deeply impressed by Brownson, himself later converted to Catholicism and founded the Paulist order.

Brownson's interests extended beyond theology and included social and political reform. That interest had been sparked by his association with the Scottish reformer Frances "Fanny" Wright (1795–1852), whom Brownson had met sometime in 1828 or 1829. Wright was a radical who traveled to America with her associate, Robert Owen, to spread their platform. They advocated, among other radical measures, the redistribution of property and equal rights for women; for a time, Brownson became a correspondent for Wright's periodical the *Free Enquirer* and supported their efforts to create a workingman's party. But he soon lost interest in the political infighting and went his own way.

The influence of Wright and Owen never left Brownson, however, and he combined his philosophical reflections with practical politics throughout the 1830s. After leaving Walpole, for example, he helped found a society for workingmen in Massachusetts, and his sermons were marked by applications of the Christian Gospel to the problems of the age. Both before and after his conversion to Catholicism, Brownson had no love for quasi-feudal arrangements or inherited privilege. He did not believe that the Middle Ages represented a more authentic expression of Catholic political principles than democracy. Indeed, despite recasting his radical beliefs in the light of Catholic social teaching, he remained a believer in democratic government, which he argued was power granted to the people from God. Because of the divine source of its power, all of the individual members who constitute the people are equal. As scholar Peter Augustine Lawler phrased the question, "It is that affirmation, the very opposite of the Lockean principle of self-ownership, that is the foundation of the doctrine of human equal-ity" (Brownson, *American Republic*, xxv). Brownson's position also opposed him to reactionary Catholic thinkers who believed that a rigid social structure was in accordance with the natural law.

Throughout the 1830s, Brownson worked out his application of European philosophy to economics, culminating in the extraordinary essay, "The Laboring Classes," which he published in July 1840. The essay grew out of his dissatisfaction with the American capitalist system. Brownson had been a partisan of the Demo-cratic Party and believed that the will of the people would result in the election of the wisest leaders. He was to be sorely disappointed in the presidential election of 1840. In that election, the Whig candidate William Henry Harrison defeated Martin van Buren without any campaign platform other than demagoguery and appeal to the lowest popular sentiments. Some thought that "The Laboring Classes" had made the Democrats appear too radical and had cost van Buren the election. Thoroughly disillusioned, the experience inspired Brownson to engage in a decades-long search for the true bases of democracy, which eventually resulted in *The American Republic*.

By the 1840s, however, Brownson was once again growing restless in his faith. This time the question was ecclesiastical. Was there a true Church and, if so, which one was it? In 1844, he stated that such a true Church was not yet in existence. Soon afterward, however, Brownson began taking instruction as a Catholic. Once again, as with Channing and his return to liberal Christianity, Brownson found a writer who changed his understanding of religious belief. This time the author was Pierre Leroux (1797–1871). Leroux advocated a doctrine called "life by communion." Briefly, Leroux taught that each individual was a manifestation of a larger being and that all individuals were interconnected with each other, with nature, and with God. The progress of humanity was mediated through the work of exceptional individuals, such as Jesus or Confucius. Other individuals learned from them and absorbed something of their exceptional na-tures, thus improving humanity as a whole by their communion with one another.

Although Leroux was not Christian, his doctrine allowed Brownson to explain such complex theological ideas as the communion of saints. Brownson tried to adapt Leroux's theory to Christianity in an 1842 open letter to Channing entitled "The Mediatorial Life of Jesus." Although he condemned Leroux for being a pantheist, the doctrine of life by communion was able to surmount Brownson's final hesitations about becoming a Catholic. His conversion did not silence his controversial nature, however. Brownson became involved with controversies with other Catholics, including a fight with Newman over the development of Catholic doctrine. He also fought with other American Catholics in defense of American political institutions and with the growing anti-Catholic Know-Nothing party in defense of foreign-born Catholics. All the while, he was articulat-ing a Catholic understanding of American constitutionalism and trying to carve a place for the faith in the New World. These disputes, despite his fame, made him some enemies in the Catholic press and the hierarchy.

Through most of his early years as a Catholic, Brownson lived in Boston. But the restrictions placed upon him by the city's Bishop Fitzpatrick, including advance approval of his theological articles, proved too much. Brownson moved first to New York City, where he ran afoul of the powerful Archbishop Hughes, and then to Elizabeth, New Jersey. He died at the home of his son Henry in Detroit in 1876. Later, his remains were placed in a memorial at Notre Dame, Indiana.

PLOT SUMMARY

The Spirit-Rapper; An Autobiography (1854) is one of two fictionalized auto-biographical accounts, along with the earlier *Charles Elwood; or, the Infidel Converted* (1840), published before Brownson's conversion. His actual auto-biography, entitled *The Convert; or, Leaves from My Experience*, first appeared in 1857. Taken together, the three books provide an account of Brownson's disillusionment with the various competing religious options he considered, then rejected, before coming to Catholicism. *Charles Elwood* is the story of an unbeliever converted to a liberal form of Christianity. *The Convert* traces Brownson's dissatisfaction with the other theological alternatives available and his conviction that Catholicism solved the theological and social problems he saw in Protestantism. And *The Spirit-Rapper* shows us in a dramatic form what Brownson considered to be at stake in the choice.

The Spirit-Rapper is best described as a novel of the occult, or a fantasy novel. It centers on the discovery and exploitation of supernatural powers and the belief that mastery of these powers should be used for political purposes. The story is, as Brownson stated in his author's preface, based on factual information Brownson himself had confirmed; only the "mechanism" of the storytelling is fictional. Spirit rapping was believed to be a form of supernatural communication by which a medium allegedly communicates with the spirit world. Questions are posed to the spirit, who responds by a series of raps, or knocks, on a hard surface. This practice, a form of hypnotism, is related to mesmerism, a term derived from the name of Dr. Franz Anton Mesmer, a Viennese physician. Mesmer posited the existence of an invisible liquid that could be manipulated to permit the transmission of commands from one person to another and allowed the "mesmerizer" to control the "mesmerized." In other forms of mesmerism, the hypnotized state of the person mesmerized permitted communication with the dead.

The Spirit-Rapper is composed of twenty-six chapters and can be divided into three main sections. It is written as a deathbed recollection of the narrator, who is never named. The first section traces the involvement of the narrator's introduction to mesmerism and the supernatural. The narrator describes himself as a scientific man for whom "the moral and intellectual sciences were not much to my taste." In particular, the narrator devotes himself to chemistry, "which, by its subtle analyses, seemed to promise me an approach to the vital principle and to the essence of things" (*Spirit-Rapper*, 2). The introductory chapter, therefore, establishes the narrator as a man with no real interest in religious or spiritual questions. Indeed, before his exposure to mesmerism, he has little interest in much of anything. He says of himself, "I had had few strong or violent passions to trouble me, and few things had wounded me very deeply" (43). He is, in short, a typical nineteenth-century rationalist.

The narrator's interest in science, however, reflects a desire to measure and control the world around him; it is this desire that responds to his exposure to mesmerism and the supernatural. As a scientific man, he initially rejected its claims. But a chance meeting with an exiled Frenchman giving a course on mesmerism changes his mind, and the narrator soon discovers that he has a great aptitude for controlling spirits. Brownson devotes several chapters to illustrating this power. The narrator initially continues his studies "as a lover of science" to determine if these new powers could have any practical utility or be explained through normal scientific means. In a series of conversations, he discusses whether the powers could be used for evil as well as for good. This first part of the novel also introduces us to a number of characters who will become important to the narrator. Most significant among these are Priscilla, a "world-reformer" who exerts a strong influence on the narrator; Jack Wheatley, an old friend who has been overpowered by occult forces; and Mr. Merton, with whom the narrator engages in long discussions about philosophy and religion.

In the course of his studies, the narrator meets those who advocate philanthropic principles. For Brownson, the word "philanthropic" means any scheme to improve the world through philosophy or abstract principles, and it is usually joined with a rejection of traditional religion. Brownson uses the word somewhat interchangeably with "world-reformer." The narrator describes such advocates in this way:

> My friends and associates were nearly all philanthropists and world-reformers. There were among them seers and seeresses, enthusiasts and fanatics, socialists and communists, abolitionists and anti-hangmen, radicals and women's-rights men of both sexes; all professing the most deep and disinterested love for mankind, and claiming to be moved by the single desire to do good to the race. All agreed that hitherto every thing had gone wrong.... But beyond this I could scarcely find a point on which any two of them were not at loggerheads. (46–47)

The chapter describing the reformers is sharp and satiric, pointing out their hypocrisies and petty interests while portraying them as misguided dupes for those with more malicious purposes. And indeed, the narrator does use them as instruments for his own purposes.

Priscilla is described as the most persuasive and influential of these world reformers. She hosts a salon to which the narrator is invited. The two engage in an intense conversation, the thrust of which is that a world reformer must love and act for the world but not for individuals. Indeed, Priscilla denies value to the individual: "Individuals are nothing in themselves; they are real, substantial, only in humanity" (83). And humanity's progress cannot be restrained by antiquated ideas about morality or right and wrong; Priscilla tells the narrator that "[a]ll free activity is good, virtuous, right" whatever the result (86). With these arguments, Priscilla convinces the narrator to find a purpose for his growing power. The narrator confides that, by this point, his power had grown so great that he had come into contact with the source of mesmeric influence. This source (which we learn at the novel's end) is demonic, and it promises him even greater power. Priscilla suggests a political purpose: to help reform the world. With his power, and the alliance of the demonic forces, the narrator believes he can become the "Messiah of the nineteenth century" (68). He therefore decides to use his powers to become a philanthropist and overthrow the existing world order in favor of a new one.

The second part of *The Spirit-Rapper* traces the narrator's growing magical power and his efforts to control the world. The main action takes place in the middle and late 1840s, when revolutionary movements were coursing through Europe. At the instigation of a member of "Young Italy," a revolutionary movement, the narrator, Priscilla, and her husband travel overseas. By this point, Priscilla has become subservient to the narrator's power; her husband, James, in turn, is in thrall to Priscilla and does not protest his wife's strong spiritual and emotional bond with the narrator. They travel through much of Europe, establishing mesmeric "batteries" to unleash upon the continent at the appropriate time. During these years, Europe experienced much social and political unrest, culminating in the "revolutions" of 1848, during which liberalizing or revolutionary movements arose in several countries. The narrator explicitly connects his occultism with these movements by saying "without me and my accomplices you can just as little explain those [uprisings] of 1848" (162). To the narrator, revolution itself has a supernatural source.

Rome and the papacy are made a special target by the narrator; if they fall, he believes "the whole fabric of superstition and priestcraft would fall to the ground," opening a way for the new age (119). In a long chapter entitled "Worth Considering," the narrator describes how the destruction of Catholicism and Christianity was necessary for the success of his venture. Christianity believes in the existence of evil spirits and the power of the devil to tempt and persuade individuals. It also holds that some actions are morally wrong in themselves. If the world reformers could instead convince Christians that what they believed to be evil could be explained as merely natural through scientific or mesmeric means, that would go a long way to separate Christians from their faith. The narrator travels to Rome upon the death of Pope Gregory XVI, believing that his successor, Pius IX, would be susceptible to his mesmeric influences and eventually agree to the narrator's revolutionary program. He is mistaken, and in the end it is the new pope, through "passive courage," who becomes the fulcrum of resistance to the revolutionary movements of 1848. The narrator, acknowledging defeat, returns to America.

Upon arrival back in America, the narrator, now disillusioned, releases Priscilla from his power and returns to his home in New York. However, desire for Priscilla consumes him and he returns to Philadelphia, where she and her husband are living. Priscilla, he subsequently learns, had converted to Christianity secretly while in Europe, as has her husband. They have a child and have rejected mesmerism and repaired their marriage. She tries to convince the narrator of his error in maintaining his occult interests, but he believes there is no longer any hope of salvation for himself. When the narrator arrives at Priscilla's home, Priscilla's husband—now free of his earlier meekness and submission and under the impression that the narrator intends to assert control over Priscilla—mortally stabs him.

The final part of the book is recounted in the present as the narrator waits to die. It treats his final disillusion with the supernatural, his rejection of the powers he acquired, and his conversion to belief in something like the Christian God. Through a series of discussions with others, the narrator debates the source of the powers that have been granted him, which he had suspected were not fully natural in origin. But his scientific training was difficult, at first, to resist: "I felt that it would only be a proof of my ignorance and superstition to ascribe the mysterious phenomenon to any spiritual or supernatural agency" (318). Nor is the cause insanity, as sane people believe in these powers all too readily. The conclusion he arrives at is that the powers are indeed supernatural and, in fact, evil.

The narrator refutes his former beliefs, even going so far as to say that "[p]eople, speaking generally, are far better individually than they are collectively," a statement directly contrary to his former opinions (258). He summarizes his previous reflections on the existence of supernatural powers and whether these powers could be classified as good or evil. The final paragraphs leave us in some doubt regarding his redemption, but he receives Baptism and hopes for salvation.

MAJOR THEMES

The Spirit-Rapper is simple in its construction and techniques. Most of the action is internal and revolves around learned argument and illustration. Allowing the narrator to look back on events and replay them permits Brownson to draw attention to the moral of the story more easily. Because he is in effect omniscient, the narrator intersperses his opinions on the events of his past rather than providing a strict chronological narrative. The anonymity of the narrator also opens to the reader the possibility of believing either that this story is that of Brownson himself or that any one of us could be in the narrator's position if presented with such powers. The ubiquity of temptation, even among otherwise good-hearted people, is a strong Catholic theme that is present in *The Spirit-Rapper*.

The other major technique is the dialogue or conversation. There is not much formal action to speak of in the novel other than the development of the narrator's realization of the dangers of his powers. Each character in the dialogue fleshes out particular philosophical, theological, or social positions. Most of the characters bear names intending to give away their positions—Thomas Jefferson Hobbes, for example, or Increase Cotton Mather. Others represent the major figures of the day, such as the Fox sisters, who were famous for their mesmeric powers. The function of these characters is to lay out views commonly held at the time so that readers might recognize them and understand Brownson's critique.

At its most obvious level, *The Spirit-Rapper* is a story of grace and redemption. Brownson believes that the world is engaged in a struggle against evil. This evil is manifested not only in political evil but also within each individual. Moreover, individuals seek power, knowledge, and influence from pride or a belief in their own good intentions. *The Spirit-Rapper* explodes that belief and substitutes humility and charity as the foremost virtues. In the character of the narrator, Brownson illustrates the results of this Faustian bargain.

In particular, the book is a warning against those interested in pursuing occult practices and those who do not believe that those practices can be the work of evil forces. Brownson was writing at a time when interest in mesmeric phenomena was widespread and joined with a growing awareness that science could explain the otherwise inexplicable. Brownson needed to point out that an easy recourse to scientific answers would only disguise the reality of sin. Mastery over the physical world—either through chemistry or mesmerism—does not eliminate the need for moral choices. Furthermore, disbelief in demonic forces will only allow them to operate freely; Brownson's preface and the detailed asides in the novel about unrelated (but apparently factual) supernatural events are clearly intended to convince the reader of this fact.

The characters of Priscilla, Jack, and the narrator portray different reactions to the moral question these powers represent. None of these characters believe that such supernatural powers can master them or cause them harm. Jack treats them like a harmless prank but then is tortured by the memory of his wife, killed through their obsession with being mesmerized. Priscilla enters the novel as an independent woman seeking to reform the world according to more rational and purer principles. She and the narrator engage in a long disquisition on "spiritual marriage" and her inability to consign herself to just one man in light of her principles and devotion to the world. Yet she is eventually enslaved by the narrator's superior power. Even the narrator himself, although able to command great powers at least for a while, sinks into despair. He originally pursued his powers in the name of science, but eventually he becomes trapped by them.

Much of the third part of the book is taken up with answering specific objections to the narrator's conclusion that he had been mastered by the devil. The most important such objection concerns the nature of freedom. Brownson's reformers are always devoted to individual and collective freedom from every restraint. Indeed, Priscilla states as much when she says that the basis of her philanthropy is the ancient wisdom, which "the priests have branded as Satanic. Satan is my hero. He was a bold and daring rebel, and the first to set the example of resistance to despotism, and to assert unbounded freedom" (115–16). Brownson answers this objection in two ways. First, the fates of some of the main characters are meant as object lessons to where this kind of freedom can lead. But he also has his character Merton explain why what is believed to be freedom under the occult eventually leads to slavery and despair: "The indulgence of any of our morbid passions degrades us" (357). So pride, dominance, and "world reform," if continued, master us and render us more rather than less susceptible to evil. Brownson is relying on the orthodox Catholic teaching that the natural virtues can be formed by habit. Moreover, he confirms the force of free will; these demons, Brownson argues, cannot control us without our willing participation. We must want their assistance; but once we are allied with them, the narrator concludes, only a conscious act of will can free us. There must be full rejection and Christ's redemption before their power is dispelled. Where the narrator and Priscilla believe they have found freedom in the occult and liberation from religious belief, they are, in fact, trapped by their own weaknesses. The conversion of Priscilla occurs through the intercession of an old monk, who is later executed for his faith. Interestingly, Brownson leaves the fate of the narrator's soul unclear, which reinforces the Catholic vision of free will and the mystery of salvation.

On a larger scale, Brownson's work is also a warning against political Utopianism. When the novel was written, Brownson was working through his interpretation of Catholicism and political society; for him, the Church represented the ideal spiritual society and the necessary basis for political order. The political revolutions in Europe during the 1840s, which usually included attacks on Church property or religious faith itself, could not but seem destructive to Brownson. In his introduction to *The Spirit-Rapper*, Brownson makes the issue plain: "The connection of spirit-rapping, or the spirit-manifestations, with modern philanthropy, visionary reforms, socialism, and revolutionism, is not an imagination of my own. It is historical, and asserted by the Spiritists, or Spiritualists, themselves" (vi). Political radicalism, Brownson argues, inevitably accompanies religious radicalism. If the latter is based on an incorrect premise, the former will be as well. And as philanthropists seek to overthrow political arrangements, they also seek to overthrow all previous religious foundations.

The Catholic Church has a central role in this story. As we have seen, Brownson uses the Church as both a political and a moral force. The Church was able to resist the narrator's attempts to overthrow "superstition and priestcraft" because of its internal resources. Catholicism is the counterpoint to the world reformers' efforts to reverse the traditional understanding of good and evil. Indeed, all Christianity must be replaced with a false religion for any world reform to work. As the narrator explains in the chapter titled "The Ulterior Project," in the reformers' plan traditional Christian doctrines were to be subverted, slowly, by gradual deformation. Thus, the world reformers deliberately confuse the Christian resurrection with the pagan belief in the immortality of the soul. Charity is to be replaced by "a philanthropic, sentimental, and purely human morality" (234). But the Church can resist these encroachments on its teaching, as seen in the revolutions of 1848. It can also liberate individuals from entrapment by their own sinfulness, as in the person of the monk who converts Priscilla.

CRITICAL RECEPTION

When first published, *The Spirit-Rapper* merited some reviews in the Catholic press as well as in the Protestant journal *The Christian Examiner*, which often reviewed and published Brownson's work. Brownson's novel was perhaps the most prominent of a number of books appearing in the 1840s and 1850s that were concerned with the spiritualist and mesmerist phenomenon. *The Spirit-Rapper* was one of the earliest of the mesmerist novels, a popular genre that largely ended with Henry James's *The Bostonians* (1882), which contains mesmerist and spiritualist themes. Indeed, one scholar has noted that *The Spirit-Rapper* was perhaps the most influential novel of this kind in the nineteenth century, but its influence is seen more by imitation than commentary. The book spawned a number of imitators, the most famous of which is perhaps Herman Melville's *The Confidence-Man* (1857). Melville's book also features a "spirit-rapper" as the narrator, and some of the chapter titles and events in the novel indicate that Melville used Brownson's story as a model. Melville, however, was more sympathetic to the world reformers than was Brownson.

Among modern critics, the book has received muted or hostile reviews. While praising Brownson, Arthur Schlesinger called the novel "an overlong and oddly tedious tale, good-natured, but having throughout the air of a bad joke" (1966, 226). But others have found instead a sharp portrayal of the fads of the time and an incisive psychological portrait of the motivations of "reformers." Carolyn Karcher has noted that Brownson represents a tradition of American criticism that objects to any belief in human perfection (1979, 31–32). Brownson denied that the reformers' project could have any lasting value because it ignored the spiritual nature of existence. Unlike Melville, Brownson condemned the entire reform project as founded on false principles.

Despite its somewhat unfamiliar subject matter and historical references, *The Spirit-Rapper* has contemporary interest. The world-reformers Brownson describes hold opinions that would not seem unfamiliar to us in the twenty-first century. Their statements about the unrestrained nature of freedom have, in some cases, become even more prevalent today than in Brownson's time. Furthermore, New Age and occult movements continue to flourish, and some have descended from those Brownson attacked. Science continues to push boundaries with little thought for the moral dimensions of its growing power. And in our time's preference for rationality and a vague "compassion" over humility and charity, Brownson would recognize the likes of his narrator.

NOTE

Orestes Brownson, *The Spirit-Rapper; An Autobiography* (New York: Little, Brown and Co., 1854). All references are to this edition.

WORKS CITED

Brownson, Orestes A. 1877. *The Convert; or, Leaves from my Experience*. New York: D & J Sadlier.

———. 1990. *Orestes Brownson: Selected Political Writings*, ed. Russell Kirk. Rutgers, NJ: Transaction Books.

———. 1991. *Selected Writings*, ed. Patrick Carey. New York: Paulist Press.

———. 2002. *The American Republic*, introduction by Peter Augustine Lawler. Wilmington, DE: ISI Books.

Karcher, Carolyn L. 1979. "Spiritualism and Philanthropy in Brownson's *The Spirit-Rapper* and Melville's *The Confidence-Man*." *Emerson Studies Quarterly* 25, no. 1. 26–36.

Schlesinger, Arthur M., Jr. 1966. *A Pilgrim's Progress: Orestes A. Brownson*. Boston: Little, Brown.

BIBLIOGRAPHY

Herrera, Robert A. 1999. *A Sign of Contradiction*. Wilmington, DE: ISI Books.

— Gerald J. Russello

Willa Cather [1873–1947]

Death Comes for the Archbishop

BIOGRAPHY

Willa Cather, a preeminent twentieth-century American novelist, is best known for her works of fiction set on the Nebraska prairies and in the deserts of the American Southwest. In her Nebraska novels, such as *My Ántonia* and *O Pioneers!*, she portrayed the beauty of the frontier landscape, the joys and pains of pioneer life, and the struggles and victories of the new settlers. Although Cather was not a Catholic, two of her later works, *Death Comes for the Archbishop* and *Shadows on the Rock*, celebrate the triumph of Roman Catholicism in North America.

Cather was born in Back Creek Valley, Virginia, on December 7, 1873, and moved with her family to Webster County, Nebraska, in 1883. The region was being settled by people from the East Coast and immigrants from northern and eastern Europe. She spent most of her childhood and some of her young womanhood among these new settlers. After graduating from Red Cloud High School in Webster County, Cather entered the University of Nebraska in Lincoln. While attending the university, she wrote drama criticism for the *Nebraska State Journal*.

Upon graduation in 1895, Cather worked on the editorial staff of the *Home Monthly*, a Pittsburgh, Pennsylvania, magazine, and then as a copy editor and music and drama editor for the *Pittsburgh Leader*. From 1901 to 1906, she taught Latin and English at high schools in Pittsburgh. *April Twilights*, a collection of poems, was published in 1903 (enlarged in 1923), and *The Troll Garden*, a collection of short stories, in 1905. From 1906 to 1912, Cather served as a staffer, and then managing editor, of *McClure's Magazine*, a popular monthly in New York. She became a full-time creative writer with the publication of her first novel, *Alexander's Bridge* (1912); this was a tragic story of Bartley Alexander, a bridge builder who is torn between two women, his Bostonian wife and a beautiful Irish actress from his student years.

Acting upon local-color writer Sarah Orne Jewett's personal advice, Cather gave up her journalism career and began to write fiction full time, using materials familiar to her. She turned to her memories of Nebraska to tell life stories set on the western frontier. In *O Pioneers!* (1913), she chronicles the hardship and triumph of Alexandra Bergson, a young Swedish immigrant girl on the Nebraska prairie. After the death of her parents, she becomes the head of the family, tilling the land and holding the remaining family together. In *The Song of the Lark* (1915), Cather wrote about a woman in a small desert town in Colorado, Thea Kronberg. With a single-minded determination and iron will, she pursues and achieves her lifelong dream of a musical career and becomes an opera singer. She also learns that the life of an artist involves self-sacrifice. *My Ántonia* (1918), probably Cather's best-known work, is also set in Nebraska and tells the story of a Bohemian immigrant girl, Ántonia Shimerda. She becomes a hired girl and leaves the land but, after many trials and adversities, returns to the vast, lonely prairie as a wife and mother. *One of Ours* (1922), a winner of the Pulitzer Prize in 1923, records the story of Claude Wheeler, who escapes from his dreary life on a Nebraska farm and dies as a soldier in France during World War I. The protagonist of *A Lost Lady* (1923), Marian Forrester, differs from Cather's previous female characters in her grace and charm. The widow of a great railroad pioneer, she slowly degenerates in the face of difficult circumstances. *The Professor's House* (1925) concerns an earnest, middle-aged scholar's spiritual crisis as well as his brilliant student's discovery of the remains of the cliff dwellers in New Mexico. *My Mortal Enemy* (1926) is a novella about a woman who gives up everything for love, thus causing her own downfall.

Cather celebrated the pioneering days of Catholicism in the New World in *Death Comes for the Archbishop* (1927) and *Shadows on the Rock* (1931). *Death Comes for the Archbishop* is an episodic historical narrative based on the actual lives of Bishop Jean Baptiste Lamy and his vicar general, Father Joseph Machebeut. The novel chronicles the friendship, adventures, and missionary works of the two French priests, Bishop Latour and Vicar Father Vaillant, as they plant pioneer missions and the new Apostolic Vicariate in New Mexico Territory. In *Shadows on the Rock*, Cather records how French Catholicism took root in fifteenth-century Quebec. *Lucy Gayheart* (1935) focuses on a midwestern girl who leaves her beloved to pursue a musical career but dies an untimely death. Unlike Cather's pioneer novels, *Sapphira and the Slave Girl* (1940) is set in pre-Civil War Virginia and deals with a woman's excessive jealousy. *Obscure Destinies* (1932) contains three stories set in small communities of Nebraska, and *Youth and the Bright Medusa* (1920) is a collection of stories on artistic careers. *Not Under Forty* (1936) is a collection of Cather's literary essays. Cather, who never married, lived for many years with Edith Lewis in an apartment located in New York City. She died in New York City on April 24, 1947.

PLOT SUMMARY

In *Death Comes for the Archbishop*, Cather chronicles the spiritual pioneering of the Roman Catholic Church in New Mexico. In 1848, a missionary bishop from America convinces three cardinals in Rome to appoint a new vicar of New Mexico, a vast part of North America recently annexed to the United States. Since the time that the Spanish friars planted Catholicism and watered it with their blood in 1500, the Church in the territory has been neglected. Furthermore, the local priests there are ignorant and morally lax, the Indians are apathetic to the white man's religion, and the landscape is harsh. Father Jean Marie Latour, a Frenchman and current parish priest on the shores of Lake Ontario, is consecrated as Vicar Apostolic of New Mexico.

In 1851, after almost a year's perilous journey, Bishop Latour arrives at Santa Fe, New Mexico, alongside Father Joseph Vaillant, his boyhood friend from France. Because Latour has lost his appointment documents in a shipwreck in Galveston harbor, the Mexican priests refuse to acknowledge his authority. To obtain new papers from the bishop of Durango, Latour travels on horseback to Old Mexico, which is 1,500 miles away. Meanwhile, Father Vaillant endears himself to the local population, sets up an episcopal residence for Father Latour, and recovers a church bell dating from 1356.

The two priests take on many missionary journeys. Father Vaillant visits Albuquerque and the Indian pueblo of Santo Domingo to hold services. He successfully persuades a Mexican, Manuel Lujon, to donate two mules for mission trips. On the road to Mora, the two priests narrowly escape from Buck Scales, the murderous American who has already killed four travelers and their three babies. With the help of Scales's abused Mexican wife, Magdalena, Bishop Latour and Father Vaillant reach their destination safely. The following morning, Magdalena also escapes from her home, and Scales is captured and executed.

Five nuns arrive at Santa Fe to found the school of Our Lady of Light. Guided by Jacinto, a Native American, Bishop Latour visits Ácoma, a Pueblo Indian village near Albuquerque built on a sandstone mesa. Father Vaillant takes charge of the Albuquerque parish, replacing Father Gallegos, the popular but self-indulgent clergyman who enjoys dancing, poker games, and hunting. On the way from a business trip to Las Vegas, Father Vaillant visits the Pecos Mountains to dispense the sacraments; there, he catches black measles but is safely transported back to Santa Fe. Bishop Latour takes action against Father Martínez at Taos, who is not celibate, by excommunicating him; another corrupt priest, Father Lucero, is also expelled from the Church. Bishop Latour's excellent administrative skills are reported to Rome, and the vicariate of Santa Fe is formally elevated to a diocese. Under the bishop's leadership, a Romanesque cathedral is built in Santa Fe with large donations from the rich Mexican *rancheros*, especially Don Antonio Olivares.

With the 1853 Gadsden Purchase, the southern part of Arizona and New Mexico becomes part of the United States, hence part of Bishop Latour's diocese. Father Vaillant serves Tucson for several years and then is sent to Pike's Peak, Colorado, to minister to the miners there; later, he becomes the first bishop of Colorado. He briefly visits Santa Fe when Bishop Latour is promoted to an archbishop.

Upon retirement from his duties as archbishop, Father Latour lives in a little country estate, approximately four miles north of Santa Fe, domesticating and developing the native wild flowers. His main work, however, is to train the young missionaries from France, teaching them Spanish, the topography of the diocese, and acquainting them with the disposition and cultures of the different pueblos. In 1885, a young seminarian, Bernard Ducrot, arrives from France to look after the aging priest. After serving in Colorado for over twenty years, Father Vaillant dies, and the archbishop attends his funeral. Having lived a full life as a missionary priest, Archbishop Latour also meets his death in 1889. His last days are peaceful, graceful, and painless. The morning after his death, he is laid out before the high altar of the beautiful cathedral that he has built.

MAJOR THEMES

Death Comes for the Archbishop concerns the struggle and triumph of the two Catholic missionary priests, Latour and Vaillant, in the barren land of the American Southwest. As spiritual pioneers in the New World, Father Latour and Father Vaillant take up the Cross and minister to God's people in remote places; they give the sacraments, reform the clergy, and look after the needy. They live close not only to the believers but also to those who are hostile or indifferent to them. Early in the novel, Vaillant states that a missionary's life is "to plant where another shall reap" (*Death Comes for the Archbishop*, 39); the two clerics plant the seed of faith and harvest abundantly, winning the Southwest for Catholicism. The great cathedral Latour builds is a symbol of their combined success. Although the two clerics sometimes feel lonely, they finally adopt America as their home. In America, Latour misses France, but "in the Old World he [finds] himself homesick for the New" (274).

In their missionary life, Father Latour and Father Vaillant are confronted with and successfully overcome the rugged topography and the rebellious clergy. The landscape of the Southwest is harsh. The missionary bishop from America tells the three cardinals that the country will "dry up [Latour's] youth and strength as it does the rain" (10). Indeed, the territory is covered with mountain ranges, treacherous trails, trackless deserts, deep canyons, and mighty rivers. The two clerics are also challenged by the strong wind, sandstorms, snow, and cold.

Three corrupt native priests—Padre Gallegos of Albuquerque, Padre Martínez of Taos, and Padre Lucero of Arroyo Hondo—set bad examples for the Church and hinder the spread of the Word of God. Father Latour does not remove the powerful and popular Gallegos from his post immediately; a month after his initial confrontation with Gallegos, however, Latour suspends him and installs Vaillant as head of the parish. The womanizing Martínez and the miserly Lucero rebel against the authority of Latour by setting up a splinter church. Accordingly, these renegade clerics are excommunicated. Soon after, Martínez dies unrepentant, while Lucero confesses his sin and renounces heresy before his death.

In *Death Comes for the Archbishop*, Cather praises the European value of order. Before the priests' arrival at Santa Fe, the Catholic Church in the Southwest is in disarray. Father Latour has been chosen as New Mexico's Vicar Apostolic because he is "a man to whom order is necessary—as dear as life" (8). He does replace chaos with order—the order of the Catholic faith brought from Europe. He considers Father Martínez a man of the old order. Indeed, the word *order* is repeatedly used throughout the novel. When Latour wonders about the extent of his diocese, Vaillant reminds him, "Don't begin to worry about the diocese, Jean. For the present, Santa Fe is the diocese. Establish order at home" (40). When Manuel Lujon requests Vaillant to perform the sacrament of Baptism before the sacrament of Marriage, Vaillant replies, "No, I tell you, Lujon, the marriages first, the baptisms afterward; that order is but Christian" (55–56).

The wonder and beauty of the Catholic faith is another prominent theme of *Death Comes for the Archbishop*. During a hazardous trip to Old Mexico, Father Latour loses his way and almost dies of thirst. He is miraculously saved in the Mexican settlement called Agua Secreta (Hidden Water) by a young girl,

Josepha. When Latour sees Josepha for the first time, he thinks he has never seen a kindlier face. The girl states that their encounter was an answer to her father's prayers, and he acknowledges that it was a "miracle" to be found by her (29). Josepha's family is somewhat naïve about the outside world. They believe in only one Church, and anyone outside the Church is considered an infidel. They hold a particular grudge against Americans. The young boy, Jose, exclaims, "[Americans] destroyed our churches when they were fighting us, and stabled their horses in them. And now they will take our religion away from us. We want our own ways and our own religion" (27). Despite their simplicity, Latour finds them gentle and likable people who keep their simple faith. Latour feels thankful when "he [lies] in comfort and safety, with love for his fellow creatures flowing like peace about his heart" (29).

Cather often develops her novels by having her characters recount tales or stories. The story of the shrine of Our Lady of Guadalupe, narrated by a native priest, exemplifies the wonder and beauty of Catholicism. On December 9, 1531, Juan Diego, a neophyte of the monastery of St. James, was hurrying down Tapeyac hill to attend Mass in Mexico City when the Virgin Mary appeared as a young woman of great beauty. She told him to build a church where she stood. The incredulous bishop, however, demanded a sign of the Lady. The Virgin reappeared to Juan Diego and directed him to gather roses nearby. He found the unseasonable flowers, returned to the bishop, and showed the sign. The bishop and his vicar instantly knelt among the flowers. On the inside of Juan Diego's mantle was a painting of the Blessed Virgin, exactly as she had appeared to him upon the hillside. A shrine was built to contain this miraculous portrait, which since that day has drawn countless pilgrimages and has performed many miracles. A similar story, about the wonder-working portrait of Saint Joseph, is told by Father Jesus. The portrait was sent to the Ácoma Indians long ago by one of the Spanish kings. It has performed many miracles, including the production of rain. If the season is dry, the Ácoma people simply need to take the picture down to their farms. They have rain when no other rain appears in all the country, and they have crops when the Laguna Indians have none.

Clerical friendship is another important theme in Cather's novel. Father Latour and Father Vaillant have been companions since their seminary days. Their friendship recalls that of Paul and Barnabas in the New Testament; they minister together, encourage each other, and bless each other. The two characters are contrasted in their dispositions: Latour is intellectual and introverted, while Father Vaillant is practical and outgoing; Latour is a man of reflection, while Vaillant is a man of action; Latour is complex, while Vaillant is simple. Despite these differences, the two clergymen are equally dedicated to their mission. They use their own gifts—Latour's gift for leadership and Vaillant's gift for assistance—in furthering the kingdom of God. When Latour returns from his trip to Durango, for instance, he finds Santa Fe friendly because Vaillant has won everybody's trust. The two friends look after each other in difficult times. In his initial journey to Sante Fe, Latour is accompanied by Vaillant, who has shared his dangers. When Vaillant becomes gravely sick in the Pecos Mountains and later in a cactus desert in Arizona, Latour goes to him and brings him back home safely.

Another important idea Cather depicts is the need to respect native cultures and religions. Although Father Latour has come to the American Southwest to win the lost souls for Christ, he is sensitive to the native traditions and beliefs. He even finds similarities between his culture and the Indian culture: both are highly orderly societies and both respect mystery untouched by the crass materialism of the day. In his conversation with a trader named Orchard, Latour remarks that the Indians' veneration for old customs is a quality he likes in them and that it plays a great part in his own religion. It is no wonder that Latour recalls "vast cathedrals" when he observes "great rock mesas, generally Gothic in outline" in Ácoma (94) and that he finds "a lofty cavern" shaped "somewhat like a Gothic chapel" when he visits Jacinto's ceremonial cave (127, 135). Latour even sounds like a religious pluralist when he reflects on the Indians' right to live in the Canyon de Chelly: "[It] was their mother. Moreover, their gods dwelt there—in those inaccessible white houses set in caverns up in the face of the cliffs, which were older than the white man's world, and which no living man had ever entered. Their gods were there, just as the Padre's God was in his church" (294–95).

Although Father Vaillant initially considers the Indians "savages" and "heathens," he also learns to respect their cultures. After transferring from New Mexico to Colorado, he recalls the Indians' capacity for using the land, forest, and rivers without desecrating them. Unlike the Europeans, who desire to control and recreate nature, the Indians seem to live without spoiling it. The Indians hunt, but they do not slaughter. In a sense, life in the primitive environment has enabled the two European priests to humble themselves before nature and to live in communion with their environment.

As a Catholic novel, *Death Comes for the Archbishop* is valuable in understanding the history of nineteenth-century Catholicism in the American Southwest. The pioneering European missionaries were instrumental in bringing the Catholic faith to the vast land that seemed to have little room for evangelization. The Catholic Church had become the largest Christian denomination in Cather's time, and like many of her contemporaries, she embraced it as an American institution. Catholicism was no longer a "foreign" religion posing a threat to the mainstream Protestant culture. As a religious pluralist, however, Cather is not devotional or pious in her tone. She considers the two French priests in *Death Comes for the Archbishop* as distinctly American characters, pioneers who happen to be Catholic. It is noteworthy that Cather, as a non-Catholic, portrays Catholicism in a positive way, while some well-known twentieth-century novelists with Catholic backgrounds—James Joyce and Graham Greene in particular—at times approach the institution of Catholicism with suspicion and doubt.

CRITICAL RECEPTION

Once regarded as a regional writer, Willa Cather is now considered a major twentieth-century American novelist. Her fame reaches beyond the American borders; her fiction is studied extensively in such countries as France, Japan, and South Korea. Numerous books, dissertations, and scholarly articles on Cather testify to the popularity of her work.

Critical comments on Cather's novels are generally positive. According to Harold Bloom, Cather "has few rivals among the American novelists of [the twentieth] century" (1985, 1). He considers *My Ántonia*, *A Lost Lady*, and *The Professor's House* as "fictions worthy of a disciple of Flaubert and Henry James";

Death Comes for the Archbishop and *Shadows on the Rock* are rather less central than the previous three novels but are "equally beautiful and achieved" works (1). Philip Gerber observes that Cather, as stylist, "has had few peers among American authors"; her style—characterized by the use of plain English speech—is comparable to Ernest Hemingway's (1975, 161).

Although many critics consider *Death Comes for the Archbishop* Cather's finest work, others have attacked it for being an escapist novel. Granville Hicks, for example, accuses Cather of projecting her desires into the supposedly glorious past. To him, the novel lacks unity, thematic relevance, and artistic integrity. By retreating to the "security of an unquestioned faith" and to the "sheltered life" in the Southwest, Cather failed to examine "life as it is"—life in our industrial civilization (1933, 709, 710). David Daiches also questions Cather's resolve to tackle real-life issues in *Death Comes for the Archbishop*:

> [O]ne wonders whether this lively creation of a golden world in which all ideals are realized is not fundamentally a "softer" piece of writing than, say, *My Ántonia* with its frustrations counterbalancing successes, or than *The Professor's House*, whose main note is of heroic failure. There is, it is true, a splendid sympathy in the treatment of the characters and a most genuine feeling for the period and the natural setting in which the action is laid. However, there is no indication here of an artist wrestling successfully with intractable material. The material is all too tractable, and the success, though it is real enough, seems too easy. (1951, 105)

According to another critic, Alfred Kazin, Cather's Catholic fiction evinces the renunciation of her ideal in the face of the modern world. Completely turning her back on the world, she frankly and romantically submits to "the past, to the Catholic order and doctrine, and the deserts of California and New Mexico." Withdrawn into such an imagined world, the characters do not submit to failure; they live in "a charming and almost antediluvian world of their own" (1942, 256).

Much has been written about the Catholic elements in *Death Comes for the Archbishop*. Upon publication in 1927, the book was warmly received, especially by Catholic reviewers. The novel was viewed as a beautifully written Catholic novel significant in understanding United States Church history. One of these critics, Michael Williams, praised the novel for its stylistic beauty and its accurate portrayal of Catholic ideals. Cather is not a Catholic, Williams observed, "yet certainly no Catholic American writer that I know of has ever written so many pages so steeped in spiritual knowledge and understanding of Catholic motives and so sympathetically illustrative of the wonder and beauty of Catholic mysteries, as she has done in this book" (1927, 491). Catholics, Williams stressed, are obliged to purchase, read, and recommend Cather's masterpiece. Meanwhile, in his book *American Literature and Christian Doctrine*, Randall Stewart called *Death Comes for the Archbishop* "the outstanding explicitly Christian novel" (1958, 133).

Other critics focus on certain aspects of the novel in terms of its Catholicism. John H. Randall sees sharp contrasts between Cather's earlier novels and her Catholic fiction. In *Death Comes for the Archbishop* and *Shadows on the Rock*, the setting shifts from the present day to the more distant past, from the Calvinist, capitalist society to a Catholic society, from the democratic and individualistic American values to hierarchical and feudal ones. According to Randall, while

Cather's earlier pioneer novels focus on the life of heroic adventures, her Catholic fiction shows "an orderly, methodical, even ritualistic generation of men working within a rigidly hierarchical social framework" (1960, 256–57). To Catherine M. McLay, *Death Comes for the Archbishop* and *Shadows on the Rock* are aligned with "some form of religious experience." However, the affirmative tone in Cather's Catholic novels does not parallel her own spiritual life. Despite her deep admiration for Catholicism, Cather's Christian faith was clouded by constant religious skepticism. Her Catholic fiction, McLay concludes, is marked by her "underlying doubts, the shadows which obscure the rock of religion" as well as by "her desperate attempt to cling to a faith which will not founder, which outlives nature and art, and is not subject to time and decay" (1975, 144). In his analysis of the final phrase of *Death Comes for the Archbishop*, "in the church he had built," Donald Sutherland notes that Cather deliberately used "church" instead of "cathedral," for the former is more universal than the latter: "It was not a cathedral that Christ founded, but a church, and indeed it was a church, a religious congregation, that the Archbishop had founded in New Mexico" (1974, 179). John J. Murphy praises Cather's ability to distinguish between the priest as a living Christ on earth and the priest as a man. Cather was able to see the beauty of the Catholic faith—the "shared aspirations, ideals, visions"—which lies beyond the human weaknesses of the priests. "Many Catholics fail to make the distinctions she made, and few admire their tradition the way she could," adds Murphy. "Hers was the gift of sight as well as sympathy" (1982, 60).

Yet other critics view *Death Comes for the Archbishop* as a work of art having little to do with the Catholic faith per se. For example, Lionel Trilling sees Catholicism in Cather's fiction as "a Catholicism of culture, not of doctrine" (1964, 52). While the ideal of unrelenting individual quest (as exemplified in Herman Melville's *Moby Dick*) is fundamentally a Protestant one, the Catholic tradition turns to symbols for the ordered life, to the tangible tools that add meaning to life. To Trilling, the Catholic Church occupied a special but not central place in Cather's mind in her earlier novels; with the publication of *Death Comes for the Archbishop*, she now sees in Catholicism "permanence and certainty" (53)—a universal human desire for stability, durability, and order—that is symbolized by the image of the rock throughout the novel. Harold Bloom's view of Cather's novel is similar to that of Trilling. Bloom notes that too many critics have erroneously considered *Death Comes for the Archbishop* a Catholic novel, adding, "Herself a belated Aesthete, Cather emulated a familiar pattern of being attracted by the aura and not the substance of Roman Catholicism. New Mexico, and not Rome, is her place of the spirit, a spirit of the archaic and not of the supernatural" (1985, 2).

Finally, Morton Dauwen Zabel and Susan J. Rosowski see *Death Comes for the Archbishop* as a symbolist rather than a Catholic novel. According to Zabel, the Church appealed to Cather as "a human and historical constant"; the Church is "a cultural symbol, not a human or historical actuality, and the least real of any of the standards she invoked in her judgments and criticism of the modern world" (1957, 270). In Rosowski's view, the author of *Death Comes for the Archbishop* is not a Catholic or allegorical writer retreating from modern tensions but a symbolist. Cather's symbolic language, Rosowski maintains, goes beyond logic and empirical reality. The highly developed power of symbolism "provides meaning to the most ordinary acts and the most disparate objects: a wooden parrot, a desert rock, a tamarisk tree" (1986, 172). In Cather's fiction, such symbolism provides commonalities with sacramental qualities.

Perhaps an area that deserves further critical attention is Cather's depiction of Latour as a religious pluralist. Latour is represented as a quiet, intellectual Catholic with excellent organizational skills rather than as a zealous missionary (like Father Vaillant) whose passion is to convert "heathens" from "eternal damnation." One can reasonably label Cather a postmodern novelist in her affinity with such pluralists as Wilfred Cantwell Smith and John Hick, who claim that all ethical religions are equally valid.

NOTE

Willa Cather, *Death Comes for the Archbishop* (New York: Vintage Books, 1971). All references are to this edition.

WORKS CITED

Bloom, Harold, ed. and intro. 1985. *Willa Cather*. New York: Chelsea.

Daiches, David. 1951. *Willa Cather: A Critical Introduction*. Ithaca, NY: Cornell University Press.

Gerber, Philip. 1975. *Willa Cather*. Boston: Twayne.

Hicks, Granville. 1933. "The Case against Willa Cather." *English Journal* 22: 703–10.

Kazin, Alfred. 1942. *On Native Grounds: An Interpretation of Modern American Prose Literature*. New York: Harcourt, Brace and World.

McLay, Catherine M. 1975. "Religion in the Novels of Willa Cather." *Renascence* 27: 125–44.

Murphy, John J. 1982. "Willa Cather and Catholic Themes." *Western American Literature* 17: 53–60.

Randall, John H. 1960. *The Landscape and the Looking Glass: Willa Cather's Search for Value*. Boston: Houghton Mifflin.

Rosowski, Susan J. 1986. *The Voyage Perilous: Willa Cather's Romanticism*. Lincoln: University of Nebraska Press.

Stewart, Randall. 1958. *American Literature and Christian Doctrine*. Baton Rouge: Louisiana State University Press.

Sutherland, Donald. 1974. "Willa Cather: The Classic Voice." In *The Art of Willa Cather*, ed. Bernice Slote and Virginia Faulkner, 156–79. Lincoln: University of Nebraska Press.

Trilling, Lionel. 1964. "Willa Cather." In *After the Genteel Tradition: American Writers 1910–1930*, ed. Malcolm Cowley, 48–56. Carbondale: Southern Illinois University Press.

Williams, Michael. 1927. "Willa Cather's Masterpiece." *Commonweal* 6 (September 28): 490–92.

Zabel, Morton Dauwen. 1957. *Craft and Character: Texts, Method, and Vocation in Modern Fiction*. New York: Viking.

— John J. Han

Catherine of Siena [1347–1380]

Dialogue

BIOGRAPHY

Biographies of Saint Catherine of Siena, born Caterina di Giacomo di Benincasa, typically emphasize one of three aspects of her life: (1) her penitential practices, charitable works, and mystical experience; (2) her unusual, female apostleship, which included preaching, authorship of the *Dialogue*, and prodigious letter writing; or (3) her fearless efforts for peace and reform in an Italy of divided city-states and a Church torn by schism. What remains constant across these three domains and what helps to explain their interconnectedness is Catherine's original understanding of Dominican spirituality as a dialogic way of holiness open to women and characterized by a priestly mediation between God and humanity through prayer, preaching, and peacemaking. Catherine's personality structure as a conduit of grace, teaching, and prophecy equipped her to become the charismatic "second founder" of the Dominicans, a "mother" (*mama*) at the side of the "father" and founder of the Order of Preachers, Saint Dominic Guzman (who died in 1221).

In Catherine's case, grace not only built on nature (in accord with the well-known Thomistic principle) but also consumed it. Born in 1347 as the twenty-fourth of twenty-five children, Catherine was the youngest surviving offspring of a Sienese wool dyer. When her twin sister Giovanna died at birth, Catherine was literally formed from the womb to know the potential cost of mimetic strife among siblings, a tragic competition epitomized in ancient myth as a warfare between twin brothers and realized in her own time in the form of Florentine feuds and ecclesial schism. Surviving when her sister died, Catherine was also formed by that experience to mediate between heaven and earth, to occupy a certain psychological and spiritual threshold between the realms of time and eternity. A completely selfless love became her ideal. She was meant to be the one who brought people together, overcoming their enmities and uniting them with God.

The life of Saint Catherine, as related in the *Legenda maior* written by her Dominican disciple and confessor, Raymond of Capua, emphasizes her spiritual closeness to Saint Dominic, founder of the Order of Preachers, and to the Dominican family.[1] From her infancy, she attended the liturgies at the Church of Saint

Domenico in Siena. Her first confessor, the Dominican priest Tommaso della Fonte, was the brother of one of her brothers-in-law; orphaned during the Black Plague, he lived as a boy in the populous Benincasa household. At age five, Catherine was (miraculously) reading the lives of the saints, especially that of Saint Dominic, and she resolved to follow their example. At age six, she had her first vision of Christ, to whom she vowed her virginity. At thirteen, Catherine mourned the death of Bonaventura, the sister to whom she was closest. That same year she cut off her hair in stubborn defiance of her parents' plans for her to marry—a gesture that symbolically links her grieving for the dead with her own death to the world. In 1363, when her younger sister Nanna (named after her twin sister Giovanna) died, the fifteen-year-old Catherine began to abstain from food and openly declared that she would never marry.

What, then, would she do with her life? In her great desire to follow Saint Dominic as a preacher working for the salvation of souls, she considered disguising herself as a man in order to enter the Order. Later, in a vision, Saint Dominic addressed her as his dear daughter (*filia dulcissima*) and promised to clothe her in the garb of the Order. Eventually she did receive the mantle of a Dominican tertiary, joining the Order of Penitents founded by Saint Dominic. Admitted at age eighteen in 1364 to the *Mantellate* (the Dominican Third Order of the Sisters of Penance, called the *Mantellate* because of the distinctive black cape they wore), Catherine lived in seclusion in her parents' house for more than three years, devoting herself to prayer.

At the end of that time, she entered into a visionary, spiritual marriage with Christ, which was witnessed by Saint Dominic, in company with the Virgin Mary, Mary Magdalene, and other saints. Reminding her of her childhood zeal for souls and of her desire to be a Dominican preacher, even at the risk of disguising her sex, Christ called her at that time to leave her contemplative seclusion and embrace the active life as his apostle of charity in Siena. Catherine then emerged from her solitude to undertake corporal works of mercy, tending to Sienese victims of famine and plague. Fasting herself and feeding on the Eucharist, she fed the hungry poor and began to gather together a like-minded band of disciples, the *bella brigata* (beautiful brigade) or *famiglia* (family), with whom she had spiritual conversations.

These conversations fostered her desire to preach as a Dominican woman not only in the embodied form of charitable action but also in verbal instruction and exhortation. She continued to see Saint Dominic in visions, perhaps the most famous of which establishes a parallel between Christ as the *Verbum divinum*, sent from the Father's mouth, on the one hand, and Dominic, as the preacher of God's Word, on the other. In 1370, after an experience of "mystical death" during a prolonged trance of four hours, Catherine began to extend her public ministry. She traveled to Florence in 1374 and to Pisa in 1375. In Pisa, praying before a crucifix, she received an invisible stigmata. The execution in Siena in 1375 of Niccolò di Toldo, a political victim whom she consoled and with whom she identified, spurred her involvement in public mediation. She began her prolific writing of letters, 382 of which survive.

In a letter to her confessor, Raymond of Capua, Catherine relates a vision that she had on the night of April 1, 1376, in which she walked, in company with her "father Saint Dominic," into the open side of Jesus, from whom she received a commission to go forth to proclaim the Gospel joyfully to Christians and unbelievers alike, carrying "the cross on [her] shoulder" and an "olive branch in [her] hand" as iconic representations of her calling and message (*Letters*, 207). In realization of this vision, she made a historic trip to Avignon, appeared before Pope Gregory XI, and convinced him to return to Rome. With papal authorization, she preached the cause of peace in the Sienese countryside in 1377. During this time, she dictated her book, *Dialogue*. In 1378, she worked for months to smooth relations between Florence and the papacy, suffering an attempted assassination for her efforts. That same year saw the outbreak of the great schism that divided the Church between the forces of pope and antipope—a division Catherine died trying to heal. Pope Urban VI summoned her to Rome in November 1378, commissioning her to work for the unity of the Church. Exhausted by her many efforts and extreme fasting (she was no longer able to eat or even to swallow water), she died in Rome on April 29, 1380, at the age of thirty-three. On October 4, 1970, Pope Paul VI named her, along with Saint Teresa of Avila, a Doctor of the Church.

SUMMARY

According to her own account and that of contemporary witnesses, Saint Catherine of Siena, speaking in her native dialect, dictated her book to attendant scribes while in a trancelike ecstasy on several different occasions during the years 1377 and 1378. Having learned miraculously as a child to read and later also to write, Catherine subsequently edited the vernacular masterpiece known to future generations as her *Dialogue*. She herself did not so entitle it, calling it simply her "book" (*mi libro*).

The posthumous division of Catherine's *Dialogue* into chapters (by her close disciples) and later into four treatises (by Renaissance and modern editors) has served historically to obscure the actual genre of the work, which, as Giuliana Cavallini has demonstrated, is in fact a kind of continuous, overheard conversation between the mystic, who addresses a series of petitions and questions to God, and God the Father, who answers and instructs her at length, receiving her praises and thanksgiving in return (1980, xiii–xvi). The conversation begins with four petitions, to which Catherine's God refers again in the conclusion, but these four petitions—for the mystic's own growth in holiness and understanding; for the reform of the Church; for the salvation of the world and peace and protection for persecuted Christians; and for a providential direction of all things, general and particular—do not correspond to clearly marked, structural divisions within the *Dialogue*, nor do they match the editorial division of the work by Onorio Farri in 1579 into four separate treatises on discretion, prayer, providence, and obedience.

Finding the actual flow of conversational topics in the *Dialogue* best supported by the rubrics and chapter divisions in an early manuscript traceable to Barduccio Canigiana, one of Catherine's scribes, Cavallini in 1968 produced a revolutionary, new edition of the saint's book, which has since been translated into English. Cavallini distinguishes ten topical units in the *Dialogue*: the Prologue (chapters 1 and 2), the Way of Perfection (chapters 3 to 12), the Dialogue (chapters 13 to 25), the Bridge (chapters 26 to 87), the Tears (chapters 88 to 97), the Truth (chapters 98 to 109), the Mystic Body of the Church (chapters 110 to 134), Divine Providence (chapters 135 to 153), Obedience (chapters 154 to 165), and a Conclusion (chapters 166 and 167). The conversational shifts from one topic to another, as highlighted by the subtitles in Suzanne Noffke's translation of Cavallini's edition, are marked by the soul's thanksgivings to answered questions and her posing of new requests to God, whose truth she seeks to understand and to proclaim to others as a vital, spiritual food by which to live.

Dictated two years before her death, the *Dialogue* reflects Catherine's literal translation of prayer (for what is prayer but a conversation with God?) into teaching and preaching. This translation is remarkable in both its medium and message. The mystic herself is the medium, speaking God's own words to her (and through her to others) in her native, Sienese dialect, not in the Latin customarily used by theologians. In God's voice, she speaks and teaches Catholic doctrine as a woman in a world where such instruction belongs by office to clergymen. She does so, moreover, in a vivid, imagistic way that brings orthodox doctrine passionately to bear upon the contemporary conditions of the individual soul, the world, and the Church. A medium and spokesperson for God, Catherine also mediates for others. Not only Catherine's questions but also God's replies, which refer occasionally to specific happenings in her life, make her a vehicle for her audience, drawing them and their own experiences into her dialogue with God.

Catherine's *Dialogue* relates intertextually both to episodes in the *Legenda*, which records her life story, and to passages in her collected *Letters*, in which she similarly exhorts others and narrates her experience. Indeed, in the Prologue, Catherine mentions a letter from her beloved spiritual director and later biographer, Raymond of Capua (died 1399), whose expressed, timely concerns for the Church and world had served to inspire the petitions with which she enters into her prayerful dialogue with God. Raymond's voice thus merges into hers, even as God's merges with Catherine's. The dialogue is thus always triadic, as Catherine speaks for others and mediates God's Word to them. Her tireless conversations with others, epistolary and oral, are an animated outflow and continuation of her prayer with God, and vice versa. Indeed, her doctrine of charity makes them radically inseparable. As Catherine, speaking in God's voice, insists repeatedly throughout the book, "Every good and every evil is done by means of your neighbors," even the goods of prayer and prophecy (*Dialogue*, 56).

In the *Dialogue*, Catherine speaks literally and metaphorically the language of her life. To a large degree, her medium in the *Dialogue*—a medium of prayer and preaching inseparable from Catherine as mediator and peacemaker—is her message.

MAJOR THEMES

The themes and images of Saint Catherine's *Dialogue* are those of her life and letters. Whereas the monastic saint, Hildegard of Bingen (1098–1179), depicts the stages of ascent to heaven in the combined forms of the Tree of Life, the Tree of Virtues, and Jacob's Ladder, Catherine of Siena depicts the steps on the way of perfection in her *Dialogue* in the visionary images of (1) a flowering Christ-Tree of Life and Virtues, laden with juicy fruits; (2) a walled city bridge, similar to that spanning the River Arno in her native Florence, a bridge lined with shops, teeming with travelers, and built with variegated stones that represent virtues; and (3) the tiered zones of Christ's body—his feet, his pierced side, his mouth—extended on the cross as a priestly bridge or staircase of mediation between heaven and earth. The Cistercians similarly use the three bodily zones to represent stages in the spiritual life, but they see Christ's mouth primarily as the site of the mystic kiss sealing an intimate union between the soul and God, whereas Catherine emphasizes the mouth of Christ the preacher, speaking from the table of the cross. The mature disciple shares in Christ's evangelical mission by feeding on what Catherine likes to call "the food of souls."

The soul who "has arrived at [Christ's] Mouth . . . shows this by fulfilling the mouth's functions," declares Catherine (140). Since "the mouth speaks with its tongue and tastes flavors" (140), it has a double function. Speaking involves both prayer to God and preaching to others: "The tongue has an external and an internal language. Interiorly, the soul offers [Christ] tender loving desires for the salvation of souls. Externally, she proclaims the teaching of [Christ's] Truth, admonishing, advising, testifying, without any fear for the pain the world may please to inflict on her" (140). Tasting means eating "the food of souls, for [Christ's] honor, at the table of the most holy Cross" (140), that high pulpit of suffering whereon Jesus hung, declaring his longing for souls in the words "I thirst" (John 19:28).

As a sign of its arrival at the third stage of perfection, the soul takes "delight with [Christ] on the cross by feeding on souls for the glory and praise of [God's] name" (201). God explains to Catherine, "The soul begins to hunger for the honoring of me, God eternal, and for that food which is the salvation of souls. And because she is hungry, she feasts on that charity for her neighbors which she so hungers and hopes for, for her neighbors are indeed a food that, when she feeds on it, never satisfies her. She remains insatiably and continually hungry" (192).

In the multivalent expression "the food of souls," which is ubiquitous in Catherine's writings, the originality of her spiritual doctrine shows itself. Other saints had used the expression, to be sure, and it is in keeping with the traditional, biblical, and Dominican imagery of the preacher as the Lord's mouthpiece, who feeds and nourishes others with the Word he sows, the bread he consecrates. Following an Augustinian tradition, the Dominicans had always also emphasized the need for the preacher to eat spiritual food, to savor the Scriptures through meditation and study, feasting on them and on the Eucharist before feeding others. Catherine, however, places an extraordinary emphasis on the sacramental food of souls, which literally sustained the fasting saint, and on the mysterious circulation of the blood of Christ through the members of the Church. Nourished spiritually by her insatiable hunger and desire for the Eucharist, especially when she could not actually receive the Host (daily reception of the sacrament being discouraged by many priests at that time), Catherine in her *Dialogue* stresses that desire itself is also a food, a source of energy, a means of communion and atonement. This desire for Christ means for Catherine also a desire for Christ's desire, his thirst for souls, in which the disciple shares. Thus, the preacher feeds directly on the souls of those whom he longs to nourish, with whom he or she communicates.

Catherine stresses the reciprocal relationship, the communion between those who eat and those who are eaten, their mutual neediness, and the permeability of the "I" who lives for and by others. One can only feed souls if one also eats the food of souls, eagerly desiring the salvation of others. "Our souls must always be eating and savoring the souls of our brothers and sisters," Catherine wrote to Sano di Marco di Mazzacorno. "In no other food ought we ever to find pleasure. . . . This, after all, was our gentle Savior's food. I assure you, our Savior gives us plenty of them to eat!" (*Letters*, 95).

Indeed, according to Catherine, the proof that one has arrived at the third step, that is, the mouth, is that nothing limits the freedom of the apostolic soul, which is "clothed in [God's] loving charity and enjoying the food of the salvation of souls," to do and to suffer God's will in the fulfillment of his or her mission. Nothing can disturb her peace and quiet because "her selfish will [has] died" (141). The soul's virtues are so refined and perfected in charity that such people are prepared for martyrdom. Mature in Christ, they "go into battle, filled and inebriated with the blood of Christ crucified," which is placed in the tavern [*la bottiga*] of the Church "to give courage to those who would be true knights" (143).

Her linkage of inebriation with apostolic fearlessness in this passage harkens back to the Pentecostal scene described in Acts 2:13–15, but Catherine also sees in the wine of the Eucharist, which is Christ's blood, a literal, sacramental means to renew that same fervor in the present. On the bridge that represents for Catherine the mediation of Christ and the whole way of salvation, she imagines there to be a "Hostelry [*la bottiga*] . . . to serve the bread of life and the blood, lest the journeying pilgrims, [God's] creatures, grow weary and faint on the way" (66). In this same tavern, Catherine insists, one can also get drunk, if Christ's "blood inebriates the soul" and "clothes her in the fire of divine charity" (123).

Catherine describes the healing power of Christ's blood, which can melt a hardened heart, even as blood can soften (so she believed) a diamond (31). Comparing a hardened heart to a locked door, Catherine describes a door marked with the blood of Christ, the Passover Lamb, imploring God for the salvation of souls with these words: "In this blood you have washed away iniquity and drained the pus of Adam's sin. His blood is ours because you have made of it a bath for us, and you neither can nor will refuse it to those who ask it of you in truth" (275–76).

At one time the nurse of a dying, leprous woman, from whom she contracted a disfiguring skin disease (of which she was later miraculously healed), Catherine links the salvation of the Church and of the individual soul, leprous with sins, to an anointing with Christ's blood: "But look how my bride has disfigured her face! She is leprous with impurity and selfishness" (50). "Through the blessing of Christ's blood," God the Father continues, "I cleansed her face of the leprosy of sin" (180). Caring for plague victims and sickened by the stench of disease, Catherine and her companions had feared infection. "You could see," God reminds her, "nowhere that you . . . could go to escape being touched by this leprosy" until God showed her a "place of refuge" in "the cavern of [Christ's] open side" (238–39). Countering the suffocating stench of disease was "that fragrance of the blood" of the Eucharist, which remained "present to [Catherine's] mouth and . . . bodily taste for several days," allowing her to serve the sick (239).

Linking the flowing of Christ's blood to that of the penitent's sweat and tears, Catherine's God attributes to these holy liquids a related healing power: "Bring, then, your tears and your sweat . . . and use them to wash the face of my bride.

I promise you that thus her beauty will be restored" (54). Using six different kinds of tears to measure spiritual progress, Catherine compares "sweet tears" to "a milk that nourishes the soul in true patience" (163). Varying this metaphor, she declares, "[An] infant when quieted rests on its mother's breast, takes her nipple, and drinks her milk through her flesh. . . . This is how the soul . . . rests on the breast of my divine charity and takes into the mouth of her holy desire the flesh of Christ crucified" (179).

In sharp contrast to these life-giving foods and effluvia are the poisons that cause spiritual and physical disease. Since it is human nature to live and to feed upon what one desires, the object of one's desire determines one's very identity and well-being. In a scathing diagnosis of the ills of the clergy, Catherine's God denounces avaricious priests: "Your gullet is so ready to devour money that you have no appetite to eat souls for my honor" (247). Such clergymen administer the sacraments, but they do not feed their flock with their piety; instead, "they devour the souls who were bought with Christ's blood, eating them up in so many wretched ways, and feeding their own [illegitimate] children with what belongs to the poor" (233). Some Christians even persecute the Church and "persecute the blood," with the result that "both body and soul are eaten up by it. Their souls are eaten up because they are deprived of grace and chewed up by the worm of conscience. Their material possessions are consumed in the service of the devil. And their bodies die of it like animals" (217–18).

Such poisons must be expelled as pus or through vomiting if the sick sinner is to live. Catherine's God observes that the repentant sinner "opens the window and vomits out the rottenness in holy confession" (119): "It is just like a man who, once he has purged his stomach and vomited out the bile, has an appetite for food. So these souls wait for the hand of free choice to offer them lovingly the food of virtue, for as soon as it is offered, they are eager to eat it" (177).

CRITICAL RECEPTION

The striking orality of Catherine's imagery—which emphasizes the mouth of Christ, orifices (city gates, organ pipes, wounds), the food of souls, nursing, (in)digestion, and vomiting—has led scholars to interpret the *Dialogue* from the related perspectives of the saint's own fasting and Eucharistic devotion, on the one hand, and her remarkably influential preaching as a Dominican lay-woman, on the other. Some feminist scholars, arguing for gender differences in writing, find it significant that Catherine's habitual, extreme fasting is emphasized in Raymond of Capua's *Legenda*, whereas the *Dialogue* and *Letters* make little or no mention of it. In her own words, they say, the Catherine of agency and courageous leadership gains expression, whereas the saint of Raymond's *Legenda*, composed in support of her canonization and sensitive to criticism of Catherine's supposed presumption, is less a politically potent, peacemaking apostle than an ascetic, a penitent, and a mystic. These two Catherines are, however, inseparable.

Read with a knowledge of Catherine's inedia, that is, her inability to eat, the saint's words in her *Dialogue* and letters about eating the food of souls and drinking Eucharistic blood acquire a metonymic force, a palpable reality and a literalness that no mere metaphor or simple analogy could convey. At age fifteen, Catherine was eating only bread, water, and raw vegetables. By 1370 she could no longer tolerate bread. For the last eight years of her life, during which she was most active in ecclesiastical and civic politics and prolific in her writings, she subsisted on liquids and the Eucharist. When Catherine died at age thirty-three, she could not swallow even a drink of water. Truly she had arrived at what she called the stage of the mouth, making Christ's words on the cross her own: "I thirst!"

In recent years, the *Dialogue's* oral images and themes have been interpreted primarily against this biographical background. Many different theories have been advanced concerning Catherine's excessive fasting and that of other holy medieval women. Such theories have derived for the most part from a comparative understanding of medieval inedia and the modern eating disorder anorexia nervosa, even though, as William M. Davis observes, "the hallmark of anorexia nervosa, its single most telling diagnostic sign," is completely absent from the medieval accounts—namely, "a dread of fatness, and a self-conscious, unremitting pursuit of thinness" (1985, 181). Nor is there any evidence of the classic symptom of anorexia nervosa, described by Noelle Caskey as a "highly elaborated visual distortion . . . the anorexic's inability to 'see' her body as it truly is" (1986, 181–82). To equate the saint's striving for holiness with the anorectic's pursuit of thinness (as Rudolf Bell does in *Holy Anorexia* [1985]) reduces holiness, moreover, to nothing more than a culturally valued good—a materialist object of symbolic exchange—and denies to the present-day anorectic any unconscious quest for God as the real, underlying object of her desire (when, in fact, former anorectics not infrequently point to a personal experience of God's love as curative). Davis, responding to Bell, remarks, "Perhaps there is more here than disease. . . . Moreover, for a holy anorectic to be truly in control of herself might mean more, or other, than conquering her bodily needs and desires" (1985, 183–84). Richard Woods concurs with this objection: "If Catherine suffered from anorexia nervosa, it was in a form vastly different from that which afflicts young women in the twentieth century" (1998, 107).

In her influential study, *Holy Feast, Holy Fast,* Caroline Walker Bynum rejects Bell's notion of "holy anorexia" as a projection of the present upon the past. Her survey of late medieval female saints and mystics places particular emphasis on Saints Catherine of Siena and Catherine of Genoa (1447–1510) as examples of women who identified their bodies with the bleeding body of Christ on the cross and with the Host as food, and who were empowered through that symbolic identification to perform extraordinary works of corporal and spiritual charity. Bynum's major thesis concerns all medieval women, regardless of their spiritualities, because it takes the female body as a common denominator: "Religious women derived their basic symbols from such ordinary biological and social experiences as giving birth, lactating, suffering, and preparing and distributing food" (1987, 6). Rather than hating their bodies, they used them as symbols in order to draw closer to God: "Thus they gloried in the pain, the exudings, the somatic distortions that made their bodies parallel to the consecrated wafer on the altar and the man on the cross" (296).

Bynum admits that social setting affected this basic symbolism, causing some differences between "women who lived *in* the world (either as tertiaries or beguines or as laywomen) and . . . nuns raised in convents" (26), but she emphasizes what is common to medieval women as women, giving minimal attention to how the various spiritual "ways" of holiness nuanced feminine identification with the Eucharist and practices of fasting. Indeed, Bynum explicitly resists any attempt to distinguish among the women of the various orders, arguing, "the extent to which women of all life styles and affiliations revered the Eucharist . . . has been obscured" by the correlation of "eucharistic concern with factors other than gender. . . . Theologians and historians have failed to notice that food miracles, eucharistic piety, and abstinence are all food practices" (75). She thus cites Catherine of Siena as a prime example of womanly, rather than Dominican, spirituality.

Rudolf M. Bell notes that Dominican women of the Middle Ages were more prone than their Franciscan counterparts to what he calls "holy anorexia," but he explains this difference without reference to the major themes of Dominican spirituality and its internal logic, pointing rather to a complex of societal and psychological circumstances. Since Dominicans "were likely to come from Tuscany or the northeast, that is, from Florence and Venice, centers of opposition to the Papacy," Dominican women typically experienced greater opposition from their immediate environment, according to Bell: "The composite Dominican was more likely . . . to have struggled against parents opposed to her religious vocation who tried to force her to marry" (1985, 132–35). The "struggle for autonomy from the male world around them" translated into "detachment from their own bodies" in the form of "substantially higher levels of austerity, mystical contemplation, fasting, reclusion, and fortitude in bearing painful illnesses" (132–33). Blending the anthropologies of René Girard and Mary Douglas,[2] Martha Reinecke follows Bell but emphasizes instead "the different social positions of the Dominicans and Franciscans within the social body," wherein the Dominicans stood more exposed, as border guards on the frontiers of orthodoxy, and therefore were more inclined to exercise control over female bodily passages (1990, 256, n. 3).

Karen Scott criticizes Bell and Bynum alike for their heavy reliance on Raymond of Capua's *Legenda*, which, she contends, disassociates Catherine's asceticism and mysticism from her apostolic vocation and work. Whereas they stress Catherine's fasting and Eucharistic reception, Scott highlights the saint's preaching, writing, and prayer. According to Scott, Catherine "portrayed herself as an itinerant preacher and peace-maker, as a female apostle or *apostola*, and . . . this role enabled her to integrate the political and contemplative dimensions of her life" (1992, 37). Scott calls attention to Catherine's conscious self-identification with Mary Magdalene and the apostles. Citing Humbert of Romans, Scott also observes in passing that Catherine's letters of 1377 portray her "as a sower of grain and a guildsmember or artisan," using "imagery usually reserved for male preachers" (39).

Can a woman preach? Scott rightly emphasizes that Catherine was semiliterate and that her letters are best understood as reflecting an oral culture. Catherine dictated her letters to others, speaking in a personal, passionate way in her native Sienese dialect. Thus, "for Catherine the writing of letters was really a form of speech, in continuity with other kinds of words which she believed God called her to utter, and that is, informal preaching and prayer" (1993, 106). What Scott writes concerning Catherine's letters applies equally well to the *Dialogue* she dictated and edited, the "book" wherein God speaks with Catherine's prophetic voice and Sienese accent to direct souls and correct ecclesial abuses.

Despite this salutary emphasis on the preaching Catherine, Scott avoids seeing Catherine of Siena as a Dominican. The Dominicans proudly claim Catherine as a faithful follower of Saint Dominic and as a second founder of the Dominican family, attributing thousands of spiritual children, men and women, to her. Scott, by contrast, discounts Dominic's spiritual fathering of the Sienese saint (however much she herself points to him) as well as the formative influence of her Dominican pastors and directors, who certainly presented preaching as an ideal calling, however anxious they may have been to see a woman following it. Emphasizing the unusualness of a female preacher, she views Catherine's spirituality as unprecedented, *sui generis*, and dead-ended: "There were no religious institutions for lay people, especially women, who wanted to be apostles. . . . Her originality is underscored by the fact that she left no legacy as an apostle. . . . [S]he founded no new religious order for apostolic women; and after she died, her *famiglia* disintegrated" (1992, 44). In the sixteenth century, Scott acknowledges, Saint Catherine did become "a significant model for the lives of women in enclosed monasteries," but the Catherine they knew and followed was "the mystical Catherine" of Raymond of Capua's *Legenda* rather than the apostle she proclaimed herself to be in her own writings (36).

Certainly Catherine of Siena was unique, as all persons and especially all saints are, but Scott errs in misunderstanding the nature of saintly mimesis and in the related question of how medieval saints' lives were read. When Catherine of Siena named herself a daughter of Saint Dominic and determined to follow him, imitating him as he had imitated Christ (see 1 Cor. 11:1), she knew full well that she could never be exactly like him, nor did she desire to be. Instead, she viewed Dominic as an expressed form of Christ, an epiphany of Christ, which she impressed upon her soul in order that she might give it an entirely new and fresh expression, which differed in gender and historical context from his. The food images used by Catherine are those of the early Dominicans, but she renders them newly vibrant in her writings and literally embodies them to an unprecedented degree through metonymic gestures of preaching, fasting, feeding, and feasting that transform her life into a Dominican icon. What Saint Clare was for Saint Francis of Assisi during his lifetime, Saint Catherine became for Saint Dominic in the second century after his death, thereby taking her place at his side as his equal and giving the Order of Preachers a second, distinctly feminine, and mystical foundation.

NOTES

Catherine of Siena, *The Dialogue*, trans. and intro. Suzanne Noffke, The Classics of Western Spirituality (New York: Paulist Press, 1980). Used with permission of Paulist Press, www.paulistpress.com. All references are to this edition.

1. For a modern English translation of Raymond of Capua's *Legenda maior*, see Raymond of Capua, *The Life of Catherine of Siena*, trans. Conleth Kearns (Wilmington DE: Michael Glazier, 1980).

2. See Mary Douglas, *Purity and Danger: An Analysis of the Concepts of Pollution and Taboo* (Boston: Ark Paperbacks, 1985); and René Girard, *Things Hidden Since the Foundation of the World*, trans. Stephen Bann and Michael Metteer (Stanford, CA: Stanford University Press, 1987; reprint, 1997).

WORKS CITED

Bell, Rudolf M. 1985. *Holy Anorexia*. Chicago: University of Chicago Press.

Bynum, Caroline Walker. 1987. *Holy Feast and Holy Fast: The Religious Significance of Food to Medieval Women*. Berkeley: University of California Press.

Caskey, Noelle. 1986. "Interpreting Anorexia Nervosa." In *The Female Body in Western Culture: Contemporary Perspectives*, ed. Susan Rubin Suleiman, 175–89. Cambridge, MA: Harvard University Press.

Catherine of Siena. 1988. *The Letters of Catherine of Siena*, trans. and intro. Suzanne Noffke, vol. 1. Birmingham, NY: State University of New York at Birmingham.

Cavallini, Guiliana. 1980. Preface. In Catherine of Siena, *The Dialogue*, trans. Suzanne Noffke, xiii–xvi. Classics of Western Spirituality. New York: Paulist Press.

Davis, William M. 1985. Epilogue. In Rudolf M. Bell, *Holy Anorexia*, 180–90. Chicago: The University of Chicago Press.

Reinecke, Martha J. 1990. "'This Is My Body': Reflections on Abjection, Anorexia, and Medieval Women Mystics." *Journal of the American Academy of Religion* 58, no. 2: 245–65.

Scott, Karen. 1992. "St. Catherine of Siena, 'Apostola.'" *Church History* 61 (April): 34–46.

———. 1993. "'Io Catarina': Ecclesiastical Politics and Oral Culture in the Letters of Catherine of Siena." In *Dear Sister: Medieval Women and the Epistolary Genre*, ed. Karen Cherewatuk and Ulrike Wiethaus, 87–121. Philadelphia: University of Pennsylvania Press.

Woods, Richard. 1998. *Mysticism and Prophecy: The Dominican Tradition*. Maryknoll, MD: Orbis Press.

BIBLIOGRAPHY

Ashley, Benedict. *The Dominicans*. Collegeville, MN: Liturgical Press, 1990.

Catherine of Siena. *The Prayers of Catherine of Siena*, trans. Suzanne Noffke. New York: Paulist Press, 1983.

McAvoy, Jane. "Catherine of Siena: Contemplating the Fruitfulness of Christian Suffering." In *Women Christian Mystics Speak to Our Times*, ed. David B. Perrin, 55–70. Franklin, WI: Sheed and Ward, 2001.

Scott, Karen. "Mystical Death, Bodily Death: Catherine of Siena and Raymond of Capua on the Mystic's Encounter with God." In *Gendered Voices: Medieval Saints and Their Interpreters*, ed. Catherine M. Moony, 136–67. Philadelphia: University of Pennsylvania Press, 1999.

———. "Catherine of Siena and Lay Sanctity in Fourteenth-Century Italy." In *Lay Sanctity, Medieval and Modern: A Search for Models*, ed. Ann W. Astell, 77–90, 211–13. Notre Dame, IN: University of Notre Dame Press, 2000.

Tugwell, Simon, ed. and trans. *Early Dominicans: Selected Writings*. Classics of Western Spirituality. Mahwah, NJ: Paulist Press, 1982.

— Ann W. Astell

Geoffrey Chaucer [c. 1340–1400]

The Canterbury Tales

BIOGRAPHY

Geoffrey Chaucer is the first great English poet whose name is known to us. Earlier masterpieces such as the powerful epic *Beowulf* and the beautiful poetry of Chaucer's contemporary, known as the Pearl Poet, are anonymous.

Chaucer was born into a wealthy merchant family in London some time between 1340 and 1345. His is what was considered in the Middle Ages a long life; he died on October 25, 1400, and his burial in Westminster Abbey began what is known as Poets' Corner. Chaucer's life spans the reigns of three English kings. Born during the reign of Edward III, he already held the important position of controller of customs for the port of London when, in 1377, Richard II became king; the new king maintained Chaucer in this position and favored him in several other ways. From an early age, when he served as page to the Countess of Ulster, Chaucer was a favorite in the aristocratic milieu of the English court and was protected and rewarded by every monarch who ruled during his life.

Chaucer's ability to survive the various political rivalries of the era probably has much to do with his relationship to John of Gaunt, one of the richest and most powerful men in England and father of Henry Bolingbroke, who became King Henry IV. Chaucer's sister-in-law, Katherine Swynford, was John of Gaunt's third wife, and Chaucer himself was one of Gaunt's most famous protégés. Another was John Wyclif, an important figure in the religious controversies of Chaucer's time.

Chaucer's life spanned some of the most dramatic and disastrous events of early European history. In the eighteen months between summer 1348 and winter 1349, the Black Plague killed nearly half the population of England. Added to the moral and spiritual trauma of this event, the economic effects of the catastrophe included a severe shortage of manpower that contributed to the collapse of the feudal system. A further result was the violent Peasants' Revolt in 1381. It is also the time of the so-called Babylonian Captivity of the papacy at Avignon (1309–1377), an event that destabilized European Christianity. Greatest of all turmoils, and that which was to have the longest effect, was the dissolution of Christian unity brought about by the Great Schism (1378–1415).

England's Hundred Years' War with France lasted the whole of Chaucer's life and beyond and marked the final and complete independence of the island nation from its former conqueror, not only in political terms but, very importantly, in terms of national identity, culture, and language. It is of particular significance that when, at his coronation in 1399, Henry IV laid claim to the throne of England, he did so not in French, as had his predecessors since 1066, but "in English, the language that his friend Geoffrey Chaucer had done so much to establish as a medium capable of the highest artistic expression and, hence, worthy to be used on the most significant and solemn of public occasions" (Williams 1987, 4).

Chaucer's great literary achievement did not come about through a life dedicated exclusively to writing. Generally speaking, in the Middle Ages writing was not a profession but rather an avocation, and those who wrote poetry, like those who listened to it, did so as one of life's leisure activities. Chaucer was occupied in military service at the time he wrote his earliest works; later he was the king's ambassador on the Continent, and later still he took on the heavy responsibility of controller of customs for the port of London. He served as justice of the peace and was elected to Parliament in 1368; during all of this time, he was busy writing poetry. In 1389, Chaucer was appointed to the prestigious and profitable position of clerk of the king's works, and it is during this, the busiest time in his professional life, that he devoted himself to creating his last and greatest masterpiece, *The Canterbury Tales*.

PLOT SUMMARY

On a rainy day in April 1387, a motley group of Englishmen meet up in a tavern south of London and set out on a pilgrimage to the most sacred religious site in Britain, the tomb of Saint Thomas à Beckett in Canterbury Cathedral. The tavern owner, Herry Bailly, proposes to accompany the pilgrims and to manage a contest, so as to pass the time on the road pleasantly, in which the teller of the best story will win a free meal on the journey home, back at Bailly's tavern. This is the frame in which the tales of *The Canterbury Tales* are told.

MAJOR THEMES

A man of Chaucer's genius cannot be held up as typical of his time because he is unique, but we can, nevertheless, perceive something of the intellectual and spiritual climate of the Middle Ages through him. His literary works demonstrate familiarity with the great classics of Virgil, Cicero, Ovid, Boethius, Dante, and Boccaccio, to cite only the most important. As such a list suggests, Chaucer's interests are philosophical, and his translations into English of such philosophical works as Boethius's *Consolation of Philosophy* and the *Romance of the Rose* illustrate the point. Chaucer's England, the England of the fourteenth century, was a time of tremendous intellectual activity, of monumental spiritual creativity, of intense political and religious controversy, and all of this is mirrored to us in the works of Geoffrey Chaucer, nowhere more vividly or excitingly than in *The Canterbury Tales*.

The theme of freedom and predestination, an important theological and philosophical debate in his time and after, appears repeatedly in Chaucer's works: an omniscient God knows whether or not I will be saved; consequently, I am not free to determine my own salvation. Chaucer and Catholic theology found at least one orthodox answer to this conundrum in the works of Boethius. Another hot philosophical issue of the time, the theme of universals and particulars (whether universals such as justice or human nature exist ontologically or only as words for human abstractions), also known as the realist/nominalist debate, intrigued Chaucer and furnished material for his writing. The reason we can know a dog and name it despite all the differences between individual dogs is because there is something called "dogness" (the universal) in which all particular dogs "participate," says the realist. No, says the nominalist, what we call universals are merely abstractions that we make from the experience of seeing many dogs, and to that abstraction we give the name "dog."

Despite his strong philosophical leanings, Chaucer is primarily a comic poet working in a Christian tradition of redemptive comedy that conceives of the world as created by a good and loving God, a world in which, despite all its shortcomings, "all will be well." Chaucer's expression of this comic world view is squarely based on satire and irony, but his critique is never sarcastic or mocking; indeed, with perhaps one exception, Chaucer seems to smile rather than jeer at the flaws of his characters and takes them to task with affection rather than anathema. The fallen world of *The Canterbury Tales* is one in which the author makes us feel that the Redeemer is never far away.

The framing device of *The Canterbury Tales*, found in such ancient poems as *A Thousand and One Nights*, Chaucer borrows directly from Boccaccio, who used it in the *Decameron*. Boccaccio has a homogenous group of nobles travel into the countryside to flee the plague, telling stories to pass the time, but the tales seem to have little rapport with the tellers. Not only does Chaucer enliven the framing device by making the tale "fit" the character of the teller, he also variegates the company of pilgrims in terms of social class, intellectual level, and spiritual condition.

Although Chaucer, like other medievals, generally shunned novelty in art, a brilliant innovation in *The Canterbury Tales* is found in his use of the technique of the "naïve narrator." In a delicious irony, the first-person narrator of the pilgrimage is identified as Geoffrey Chaucer and then undermined throughout the work regarding the correctness of his perceptions and judgments and even his ability to tell a good story. This suggests another, hidden author and throws the audience back on its own wherewithal in finding him and the meaning of the text; indeed, as the text progresses, the device seems to call into question the reliability of human understanding and sends the audience on a quest for meaning that ends with Chaucer's beautiful description of Jesus Christ as the real, if hidden, author upon whom we may depend for all true meaning (*Riverside Chaucer* x [1], 1085f).

Since the Fall, the world has been an imperfect place, and although in his fictional self-portrait he may seem myopic and something of a Pollyanna, in real life Chaucer had a keen eye for human folly. The three estates represented on the pilgrimage to Canterbury, the aristocracy, the clergy, and the commons, are each portrayed as flawed as, indeed, they were in real life. The fourteenth century witnessed extensive corruption among the clergy, and several of Chaucer's clerics reflect that state. The Monk is dishonest and gluttonous; the Prioress, vain, disobedient, and self-indulgent. On the other hand, the Nun's Priest is an intellectually brilliant yet modest man; the Parson, a plain-living and morally upright figure. Chaucer does not exaggerate his criticism of any class. He does not engage in polemic.

The commons class is represented by a wide variety of characters, most of whom, like most of us, fall short morally, intellectually, and spiritually; yet only one is depicted as fundamentally evil. "The one lost soul" on the Canterbury pilgrimage, as the great Chaucerian scholar G. L. Kittredge called him, is the Pardoner (1960, 180). He bridges the clerical estate and the commons since, although most pardoners were clergy, some were laymen. Most were frauds, sellers of phony relics, mockers of simple piety, and exploiters of the poor.

The aristocratic class is sparsely represented on Chaucer's pilgrimage, and its main spokesman is described in terms that make him the single most virtuous character in the company. We cannot help but recall that Chaucer's audience was an aristocratic one and that he depended on the good will of the aristocracy for his livelihood. Nevertheless, the first estate does not escape criticism entirely, for the Knight's son, the Squire, is clearly depicted as a fop, more concerned with impressing the ladies than winning battles.

The "General Prologue" begins with an image of cosmic harmony in which all the elements of the physical universe—animal, vegetable, and mineral—are joined together in a union of parts and the whole is knitted together by the Creator of all. As the earth awakens to the life-renewing power of the April rains and spring winds bring the flowers and other vegetation to life, as the animals rouse themselves from a winter lethargy and birds begin to sing and to mate, so mankind awakens on the level appropriate to its nature—the spiritual level—and begins "to long for pilgrimage." Men and women setting out on a religious pilgrimage are the sign of human regeneration.

It is in this setting of cosmic unity, in which the spiritual longings of mankind are in harmony with and are a natural part of the longings of all Creation, that the Canterbury pilgrimage takes place. Still in keeping with this image of order and harmony, the representative of the highest social estate goes first in the order of tale tellers. A brief look at the Knight and his tale and three other pilgrims from different social classes and their tales may give something of the flavor of *The Canterbury Tales*.

The Knight

Part of the genius of Chaucer's art is found in his ability to match the tale to the spiritual and moral condition of the teller and to let it reflect this condition. The Knight is portrayed as the perfect Christian warrior who values "truth, reputation, generosity, and refinement" (I [A], 46). Although always victorious in battle, he is "meek as a maiden" (69); this is Chaucer's allusion to the Christian welding of the classical, pagan virtue of *audacia*, manly bravery, and the feminine virtue of *sapientia*, wisdom, in order to depict the perfect Christian knight. Despite his wealth, power, and superior social status, the Canterbury Knight "said never a haughty word to any man, whatever his condition" (70–71). This perfectly balanced man tells a tale of cosmic equilibrium and shows us a Neoplatonic, Christian world structured by the harmonious combination of opposites symbolized at both the beginning and the end of the tale by marriage, the classic Christian symbol of harmony.

Borrowing from the classical tradition of Theseus as found in Boccaccio, Chaucer's Knight constructs a philosophical and moral tale that begins with the pagan virtue of friendship, or *amicitias*, which is destroyed by the lower form of love, desire, or *cupiditas*, but which is ultimately redeemed and perfected by the higher virtue of *caritas*, Christian charity. Palamon and Arcite, two young knights sworn to sacred friendship, are captured and imprisoned by Theseus with the fall of Thebes. After years of incarceration, the psychically weakened friends perceive, one after the other, the beautiful Emilia, and conceive for her a passion that shatters their brotherly love. As passion grows, each degenerates morally and physically until death itself remains the only thing of value to them.

The tension between noble, disinterested love and erotic, self-indulgent love that the tale dramatizes seems almost to be a playing out of Saint Augustine's famous saying in his *Psalms*, "All love either ennobles or it degrades" ("*Omnia amor aut ascendit, aut descendit*"). Palamon and Arcite descend from the higher love of *amicitias* to the lower love of *cupiditas*. Whereas in Christian, Augustinian thought cupidity, or desire, is wholly good (indeed, it is the basis of life), its goodness is operative only in proper relation to other, higher forms of love. In the Christian philosophy of love, we refine cupidity into the more altruistic love of friendship, and we further refine friendship into the highest form of love, charity—a form of love given to us as a gift from God. It is from this point of view that the Christian philosophy of love conceived of the relation of husband and wife as one in which erotic love, friendship, and charity coexist as parts of a whole.

In the "Knight's Tale," the loss of harmony between the forms of love and the degradation of the lovers are resolved through the overarching symbol of marriage when Palamon, the surviving friend, weds Emilia, and Theseus explains the events through a thoroughly Christian philosophy under the guise of classical tropes:

> The First Mover of the cause above,
> When he first made the fair chain of love,
> Great was th'effect, and high was his intent. (I [A], 2986–88)

The Wyf of Bath

One of the most memorable of all of Chaucer's characters is the oft-married widow from Bath who is on the pilgrimage in hopes of finding a sixth husband. Through this extravagant character, Chaucer is able to dramatize, once again, much of the Augustinian theology of love, albeit from a negative perspective. The Wyf is a forthright sensualist and a materialist who, as a young woman, married exclusively for money and power and, in her later years, has married exclusively for sex. Her portrait, the most wistful of Chaucer's depictions, is of a divided self who cannot, even as she ages, unify her experience and fulfill her deepest longings. With her old rich husbands she got wealth and power but little or no sensual satisfaction; with her two younger husbands she gained plenty of sensual satisfaction but less and less power.

The governing metaphor of Chaucer's portrait of the Wyf is division and fragmentation; in her exuberant biblical exegesis, she divorces the letter of the text from its spirit; thus, the truth of the texts she cites always eludes her. She cleaves off the present from the past and future and thus loses the sense of the wholeness of reality; tragically, she also severs sex from love and thus bears the burden of a life of loneliness and frustration. The Wyf of Bath is a dramatic example of the Boethian perception that what all mankind yearns for is happiness but that we usually seek it in the wrong things.

Alys or Alisoun, as the Wyf is variously called, is full of nostalgia for a past that the audience suspects was not nearly so glorious as her memory of it:

> But—Lord God!—when I think back
> Upon my youth and all the joy,
> It does my heart good that I
> Have had my world in my own time.
> But old age, alas, that poisons all
> Has robbed me of my beauty and my pith. (III [D], 469)

Because of her self-obsession, this misguided character has identified sex and domination of others as the source of happiness. Because the real world will not bend itself to her desires, she constructs a fantasy of the "good old days" as a form of nostalgic consolation. While insisting on the superiority of "experience" over "authority," Alisoun destroys her own existential present, in which real experience takes place, by fabricating an ideal past and projecting from it a fantastic future. Her outburst at the end of still another nostalgic recollection of her life is one of Chaucer's most pathos-filled lines: "Alas, alas! That love was ever sin!" (III [D], 614). In the Christian world view that Chaucer projects, real love is never sin but rather its very opposite.

The same tragic misunderstanding of the nature of love, of the proper relation of men and women, and of the redemptive function of time is found in the Wyf's short tale, a rueful construction of a fantasy land where everything you want comes true, where rape is condoned if you can answer a riddle, where the elderly become young and beautiful, and where, finally, sex and power come together magically in the hands of the author's heroine, an old hag transformed through the subjugation of the male into the beautiful young woman the Wyf would like to be.

The Pardoner

The fascinating figure of the Pardoner reveals the drama of the abuses of religion in the late Middle Ages and, at the same time, the destructiveness of the heresies created by the misguided critics of those abuses. The Pardoner proffers pigs' bones and other junk as relics of Christ and the saints, a practice he defends by the relativist theory that, since there is no objective truth, whatever one wishes to believe is as good as truth. If the uneducated peasant to whom the Pardoner proffers an old rag believes that the rag is a piece of the Virgin's veil, where's the harm? Similarly, although he has no power to absolve, he offers absolution to the ignorant anyway, since, in the absence of any stable reality, their belief that they are forgiven is sufficient.

Chaucer's blatant description of the Pardoner as effeminate and apparently homosexual has encouraged many critics to interpret his viciousness of character in psychological terms. Whether viewed in psychological, moral, or philosophical terms, the Pardoner looms as a figure of hate, and the object of that hatred is life itself. His descriptions of the human body, of human desires and aspirations, are bitter and loathsome, expressing in shocking fashion his venomous spirit.

By his cynical abuse of the truthfulness of words, the efficacy of relics, and the spiritual power of pilgrimage itself, the Pardoner attacks the fundamentals of medieval Catholicism. However, it is in his ferocious attack on the sacrament of the Eucharist that he most clearly reveals himself as an archenemy of the Church. As a hater of everything life-giving, it is appropriate that the fullest expression of the Pardoner's malignity comes with his attack on the Eucharist, the very heart of Catholic spiritual life. In a wild denunciation of the human body as a putrid excrement machine, the Pardoner caps his description with an analogy between the transubstantiation of the bread and wine into the body and blood of Jesus and the digestive process of food into feces:

> Oh womb, oh belly, oh stinking bag,
> Full of dung and rotting flesh!
> At both ends of you the sound is foul.
> What great toil it is to feed you!
> These cooks, how they pound, and strain, and grind,
> And thus turn substance into accident! (VI [C], 534–39)

The most virulent opposition to the Catholic Church in Chaucer's time was expressed in the attack on the sacraments, particularly the Eucharist. It is surely significant that the Lollards, proto-Protestant dissenters and fourteenth-century England's most vociferous heretics, denounced the theory of transubstantiation in precisely the terms used by the Pardoner. It is also significant that it was over the issue of his heretical writings concerning the Eucharist that John Wyclif was denounced and disowned by his powerful patron, John of Gaunt. Chaucer, also a protégé of Gaunt, was probably writing the "Pardoner's Tale" at about the time of the conflict between his patron and fellow protégé. It has long been recognized that when writing the "Pardoner's Prologue" and "Tale," Chaucer had in mind the attack on the Catholic sacrament of the Eucharist by the Lollards. This becomes clear in the tale by the way in which three thugs, representative of the vices that the Pardoner himself cherishes, find the death that they have been seeking throughout their lives of sin. Having discovered money where death was said to reside ("the wages of sin is death"), the eldest of the trio sends the youngest to town "to bring us bread and wine" to celebrate their good luck. He conspires with the second to kill the youth when he returns so as to be able to divide the treasure in two rather than three. No less greedy or sly, the youngest heads for the apothecary, where he buys "some poison to kill the rats, and to avenge himself on the vermin that ate his goods by night" (VI [C], 854–58).

To the symbolism of bread and wine Chaucer now adds that of poison and vermin, and by doing so he alerts his original audience to contemporary anti-Catholic polemic, specifically to the widespread Lollard taunt against the orthodox: what if a rat or mouse, they sarcastically asked, were to get to the consecrated Host in the ciborium during the night and eat it? Would the vermin have received the body and blood of Jesus Christ? Would the sacrament work its power on the rat, giving it everlasting life? These were some of the degrading scenarios used to ridicule the Catholic belief in transubstantiation, and in this sense the Pardoner seems almost to have borrowed directly from John Wyclif's own necrotic imagery: "The sacrament of the altar is bread, but naturally considered it is worse than rat food; the sacrament of the chalice is wine, but naturally considered, it is worse than poison" (*De apostasia*, 172).

Adopting Wyclif's imagery of rat food and poison for the Eucharist, Chaucer seems to identify his Pardoner as a Wyclif figure and as spokesman for the heretical Lollards. Thus, the conclusion reached by Martin Stevens and Kathleen Falvey seems irresistible: "It is clear that the "Pardoner's Tale" is an attack on the Wyclifite position [on transubstantiation]: the Pardoner's materialism is the ultimate extension of the Wyclifite dogma. In this sense the "Pardoner's Tale" is a subtle refutation of the Lollard dialectic" (1982–83, 158, n. 17).

The Nun's Priest

Following the interruption of the "Monk's Tale," which Herry Bailly and the Knight have found to be an unbearably boring and depressing litany of lives foredoomed to tragic endings, the host calls upon "Sir John," the "sweete preest," to remedy the Monk's performance by telling a tale that will "make our hearts glad" (VIII, 2811). The Nun's Priest then tells a tale that in one way continues the theme of freedom and predestination that was inherent in the "Monk's Tale," but in a much more lighthearted manner. The simple style, we soon realize, turns out to be a veil for a highly complex and brilliant exercise in reflexive poetics revealing a world in which human freedom goes hand in hand with responsibility for our choices made in a world in which God's love and forgiveness are always within reach.

The setting is the prelapsarian world, where, according to legend, animals possessed the gift of speech, and where, in the Nun's Priest's version of the legend, matters of great philosophical importance are debated by chickens. We immediately recognize the tale as an allegory, but we are soon wondering what it is an allegory of. The setting of a farm supervised by a virtuous widow and her daughters who nurture and protect the animals suggests the standard allegory of the Church, temporarily widowed by the death of her spouse, Jesus, left to care for and protect the souls of his "estate."

But this theme is quickly abandoned as the author focuses in on the principal inhabitants of the microcosm, the regal cock Chauntecleer and his favorite paramour, Pertelote, a rather supercilious and domineering hen. Their relationship, which becomes the center of the narrative, is one in which the "woman" gives advice to her "husband" that might have led to his fatal error. Pertelote's advice to her anguished mate is that he eat herbs of her choosing that grow in their "garden." At this point we realize that the narrative is an allegory not of the Church as widow but of the Garden of Eden and the Fall, in which Pertelote is the Eve figure and Chauntecleer is the Adam figure. To make sure we do not miss the analogy, the Nun's Priest has Chauntecleer cite the popular maxim based on Genesis 3, "*in principio mulier est hominis confusion*" (in the beginning, woman caused the Fall of man). But then, as if to make sure that we cannot hold onto this interpretation any better than we did the first, the author depicts his Eve figure not as a weak and foolish woman, easily duped, but rather as a scholar of scientific bent, able to debate and use logic as well as to marshal classical sources in defense of her position. Neither is her mate the conventional virtuous-but-naïve Adam who falls because he cannot resist his wife's endearments. Rather, Chauntecleer is a conceited fool who "falls" through his personal vanity and self-indulgence.

At issue is the very popular medieval subject of the prophetic power of dreams. Chauntecleer has had a nightmare in which some kind of creature—one that he had never seen in waking life—menaces him with death. Awakened by her mate's oneiric groaning, Pertelote chastises him for being afraid of dreams; she adopts here the era's predominant medical view that dreams are caused largely by indigestion and have no prophetic value, and it is this view that leads her to prescribe her barnyard physic. Chauntecleer, citing several sources, both classical and folk, adopts the more poetic view that dreams are a powerful and trustworthy source of knowledge about the future and that, therefore, he is forewarned of a danger that awaits him.

The role reversal here created by the female figure adopting traits stereotypically associated with the male—courage, rationality, and logic—and the male figure adopting those usually associated with the female—trepidation, superstition, intuitiveness—leads the audience now to believe that the allegory is not the straight-forward one of the Garden of Eden but its inversion. At just this point, however, when we believe we have at last caught hold of the meaning of the narrative, the focus shifts again. Explaining her disdain of her husband's poltroonery, Pertelote reveals what, according to her, "women most desire":

> I cannot love a coward, by my faith!
> For, whatever women may pretend,
> What we really want, if truth be told,
> Is a real man, strong, and smart, and bold!
> And shrewd—neither miser, nor a fool. (VIII, 2911–15)

This loudly echoes the theme of the Wyf of Bath's tale, in which the young Knight is charged with discovering "what thing it is that women most desire," and the allusion is reinforced by the further echo from the Wyf's own pronouncement on the subject:

> Though my husband beat me on every bone,
> He soon won my love all over again.
> I loved him best of all of them, in fact,
> Because he was so domineering.
> If truth be told, we women are strange that way:
> Whatever cannot easily be had,
> That we want the most. (III [D], 511–18)

These obvious allusions to the "Wyf of Bath's Tale" introduce the Wyf into the "Nun's Priest's Tale" as a character and make her, momentarily at least, the subject of the allegory. The Nun's Priest does this with several pilgrims, such as his boss, the Prioress, by whom he is supposedly "hen-pecked," by giving Pertelote characteristics already associated with the Prioress in the "General Prologue."

At the same time as it inserts other pilgrims and their tales into the narrative of Chauntecleer and Pertelote, the device also inserts the Nun's Priest as a judge of character of the various pilgrims and interpreter of their tales. Not only is Pertelote now seen as a kind of Wyf, but the Wyf herself is seen as a kind of Eve through the allegorical association with Pertelote-as-Eve.

The beast that Chauntecleer has dreamed of is, of course, a fox—the very Renard of medieval tradition who always represents Satan, the enemy who first tempted man and caused his Fall. Chauntecleer falls, as well, again encouraging our simple allegorical identification with the story of the Fall. But wait! Chauntecleer refused Pertelote's advice and shunned what she urged him to eat. Instead, the vainglorious cock gave in to the blandishments of the fox concerning his beautiful voice; he closed his eyes and sang. Thus, the Fall of Man in this version is the fault not of another, but is caused by the personal vanity and sensuousness of the fallen himself, an interpretation that, while differing from folklore, is theologically correct: Adam was not an innocent victim of Eve's slyness but a willing participant in her disobedience: "Was shee thy God, that her thou didst obey?" (if we may leap ahead to Milton [*Paradise Lost*, X, 145]).

True to his promise to tell a merry tale, the Nun's Priest ends with the Christian comic view of the human condition. With his eyes closed, the crowing Chauntecleer does not see the fox spring forward and is carried off in his jaws to become his next meal. Our tragic hero becomes our comic hero, however, when having learned through his own fall how to use language deceitfully, he tricks the trickster into opening his mouth to boast of his catch. Flying to the highest branch of a nearby tree, he scolds, "He who is willfully blind when he ought to see / Deserves what fate God may decree!" (VII, 3431–32).

The multiple possibilities of meaning in this tale, the shift from one allegorical theme to another, the combination of low subject and high rhetoric, all force the audience to pay more attention to how the tale is written than to what it means. It is this that makes it self-reflexive, and it is this that associates the Nun's Priest as author most closely with Chaucer himself, who constantly calls attention to his craft, regularly breaks the spell of the story, and insists that we look at how fiction works. This is not to say that the "Nun's Priest's Tale" has no meaning or that it is meant to ridicule the idea of truth. On the contrary, the very saturation of meanings leads the audience like a thirsty man to the well, to seek a stable meaning, both of fiction and of life, in a stable authority. The Nun's Priest puts an end to his teasing authorship by pointing us, at the end of his tale, to that authority:

> For you who hold this tale a folly
> About a fox, a cock and hen,
> Seize the moral, all you good men.
> For Saint Paul says that all that is written,
> Is written for our enlightenment. (VII, 3438–42)

The importance of these lines is made clear when they are echoed by Chaucer himself as he closes *The Canterbury Tales*: "Now pray I to them who hear or read this work, that if there be anything in it of value, thank our Lord Jesus Christ from whom proceeds all understanding and all goodness. . . . For our Book says, All that is written is written for our enlightenment" (X [i] 1081–85, 1090–91).

Like *The Canterbury Tales* as a whole, the "Nun's Priest's Tale" turns us in the direction of *higher* meaning and the *higher* Author in our search for meaning, and it shows us how poetry and fiction may be the road to the truth that will not fail.

CRITICAL RECEPTION

Like many major literary figures, Chaucer has been a victim of the ideological criticism of our contemporary moment's politically correct mentality. The general thrust of this kind of criticism is the effort to "de-Christianize" Chaucer, supposedly to make him more congenial to contemporary tastes. Thus, there has emerged a Chaucer for feminists, a Chaucer for homosexuals, a Chaucer for atheists, and a crowd of other Chaucers all declaring their secular humanism. Alas for such critics, there remains the text! It is difficult to de-Christianize an author who ends one of his poems with a prayer such as this:

> Thou one, and two, and three who lives eternal
> And reign forever in three, and two, and one,
> Uncircumscribed whilst all circumscribing,
> Defend us from all harm, seen and unseen
> And make us worthy, Jesus, of thy mercy. (*Troilus and Criseyde*,
> V, 1863–67)

It is equally difficult to make a secular humanist out of an author who ascribes all good writing to God, as we have seen Chaucer do in the closing lines of *The Canterbury Tales*.

A central interest in recent Chaucer scholarship concerns the philosophical dispute so vigorous in his day between realism and nominalism. A full summary of the scholarship and a bibliography on the issue is found in "Nominalist Perspectives on Chaucer's Poetry" by William H. Watts and Richard J. Utz (1993). Whereas most critics see Chaucer as sympathetic to nominalism, Robert Myles (1994), in *Chaucerian Realism*, makes an excellent case for the author's realism. P. B. Taylor's essay "Chaucer's *Cosyn to the Dede*" (1982) takes a similar view, as do I in my book *The Canterbury Tales: A Literary Pilgrimage* (1987) and elsewhere.

The single most useful work for situating Chaucer's writing in the cultural and intellectual heritage of the Christian Middle Ages remains D. W. Robertson's *A Preface to Chaucer* (1962). Among the many excellent Chaucer bibliographies, one of the fullest and most accessible is the *Chaucer Online Bibliography*, at www.geoffreychaucer.org.

NOTE

Geoffrey Chaucer, *The Canterbury Tales*. In *The Riverside Chaucer*, ed. Larry D. Benson, 3rd ed. (Boston: Houghton Mifflin, 1987). All quotations are my translation of the original Middle English.

WORKS CITED

Chaucer, Geoffrey. 1987. *Troilus and Criseyde.* In *The Riverside Chaucer,* ed. Larry D. Benson, 3rd ed. Boston: Houghton Mifflin. pp. 471–586.

Kittredge, G. L. 1960. *Chaucer and His Poetry.* Cambridge, MA: Harvard University Press.

Milton, John. 1991. *John Milton: The Major Works,* ed. Stephen Orgel and Jonathon Goldberg. Oxford: Oxford University Press.

Myles, Robert. 1994. *Chaucerian Realism.* Cambridge: D. S. Brewer.

Robertson, D. W. 1962. *A Preface to Chaucer.* Princeton, NJ: Princeton University Press.

Stevens, Martin, and Kathleen Falvey. 1982–83. "Substance, Accident, and Transformations: A Reading of the *Pardoner's Tale.*" *Chaucer Review* 17: 142–58.

Taylor, P. B. 1982. "Chaucer's *Cosyn to the Dede.*" *Speculum* 57, no. 2: 315–27.

Watts, William H., and Richard J. Utz. 1993. "Nominalist Perspectives on Chaucer's Poetry." *Medievalia et Humanistica* 20: 147–73.

Williams, David. 1987. *The Canterbury Tales: A Literary Pilgrimage.* Twayne Masterworks Studies. Boston: G. K. Hall.

Wyclif, John. 1889. *De apostasia.* London: Wyclif Society.

BIBLIOGRAPHY

Gallacher, Patrick J. "Sense, Reference, and Wisdom in the *Merchant's Tale.*" In *Chaucer and Language,* ed. Robert Myles and David Williams, 126–42. Montreal: McGill-Queen's University Press, 2001.

Mann, Jill. *Cambridge Chaucer Companion.* Cambridge: Cambridge University Press, 1986.

— **David Williams**

G. K. Chesterton [1874–1936]

The Everlasting Man

BIOGRAPHY

Gilbert Keith Chesterton lived from 1874 until 1936. His early religious and intellectual background mirrored the increasingly common rejection of traditional Christianity by cultivated modern Britons. His upper-middle-class parents, Edward and Marie Chesterton, tended toward Unitarianism and what his brother, Cecil Chesterton, called "a vague but noble theo-philanthropy" (1908, xii). Despite some misgivings about this liberal Christianity and an attraction to more orthodox forms of Christianity, young Gilbert generally subscribed to this inherited world view. Most of his juvenilia expressed the liberalism of the French Revolution and hence condemned dogma and preached the apotheosis of humans. These views, however, were shattered by an adolescent crisis that Chesterton underwent in late 1892 and 1893. This breakdown was the pivotal event of his life and established the central themes of his subsequent thought.

At this time, Chesterton was a student at London's Slade School of Art. Here he found the shallow liberal Christianity and progressive optimism he had imbibed from his parents challenged by fashionable *fin de siècle* decadence and pessimism in a way he could not rebut convincingly. His received liberalism, with its denial of original sin, lacked the categories to comprehend and refute the reversal of traditional humane mores by aesthetes and decadents. Confronted with this cognitive dissonance, he sought a new integrating principle for his beliefs, but the alternatives he explored, like spiritualism, all drew him away from external realities and deeper within the valley of his restless mind. Chesterton soon succumbed to an idealistic form of solipsism, and his brain began to break under the pressure of thinking itself the center and author of Being. He referred to this time as "my period of madness," and contemporaneous friends also feared for his sanity (*Autobiography*, 86). Chiefly by reading authors who affirmed the basic goodness and objectivity of Being (particularly Browning, Stevenson, and Whitman), though, Chesterton began to emerge from these depths by late 1893 or early 1894. He quickly began crafting his core principles of gratitude for the elementary fact of existence and a corresponding sense of childlike wonder at every manifestation of Being. It was these metaphysical insights that drove Chesterton's intellectual and spiritual development thenceforth and that culminated in his embracing of Thomistic Roman Catholicism.

At first, however, Chesterton found the lessons of his crisis ratified religiously by a more general belief in theism and orthodox Christianity, particularly the Anglo-Catholicism that he learned from his wife, Frances, whom he met in 1896 and married in 1901. Chesterton's maddening mental self-immurement at the Slade School made Catholic sacramentalism especially attractive to him, as it stressed the synergy of spiritual truth and external, material reality. As he argued in *Orthodoxy* (1908), the incarnational idea that Being is a mixture of matter and spirit gives the orthodox Christian a balanced view of both the self and the cosmos: "The Christian admits that the universe is manifold and even miscellaneous, just as a sane man knows he is complex" (24). Hence, if the mental scales tip too far in favor of reason, mysticism restores perspective by emphasizing that everything is not rationally comprehensible. Similarly, if the spiritual grows too strong, Christianity accents the power and goodness of reason and matter. In either case, orthodox Christianity is the "philosophy of sanity" (16) because it preserves "this balance of apparent contradictions that has been the whole buoyancy of the healthy man" (28). To Chesterton, this dynamic balance is also realistic, as Christianity's complexity matches that of life: "It not only goes right about things, but it goes wrong (if one may say so) exactly where the things go wrong. Its plan suits the secret irregularities, and expects the unexpected" (82). This holistic harmony with life as lived separated orthodox Christianity from more simplistic schemes to him, for "a stick might fit a hole or a stone a hollow by accident. But a key and a lock are both complex. And if a key fits a lock you know it is the right key" (83). Yet, Chesterton also regarded this balance as precarious and felt that a firm doctrinal authority and a respect for orthodox Christian traditions were necessary to prevent deviations into heresy and insanity: "an inch is everything when you are balancing. The Church could not afford to swerve a hair's breadth on some things if she was to continue her great and daring experiment of the irregular equilibrium" (100).

Over the next fourteen years, Chesterton became increasingly concerned that Anglo-Catholicism lacked the authority needed to maintain traditional Christian dogmas against contemporary challenges to them, especially those posed by theological modernism. As the Anglican trumpets seemed more uncertain, Chesterton grew more and more impressed by Roman Catholicism's stress on a single, central determiner of dogma, epitomized by the papacy, and what he considered its consequent doctrinal constancy and unequivocal orthodoxy. In July 1922, he resolved his final theological difficulties and overcame anxiety about his wife's reaction, and he was received into the Roman Catholic Church by longtime friend Father John O'Connor (the loose inspiration for his fictional detective, Father Brown). This conversion gave Chesterton's work greater focus and depth. Now without any reservations about the world view he was advocating, he could communicate his certainty and sense of fulfillment with clear conviction, and this absence of hesitation or defensiveness broadened his perspective, as he admitted in 1926: "with fuller convictions, one comes to have larger views" (*Illustrated London News*, 129). It is thus not surprising that he wrote most of his main theological works only after 1922, including his seminal study of Thomas Aquinas (1933).

But Chesterton made noteworthy contributions to other genres throughout his entire career. Indeed, nearly every leading Catholic and Christian literary intellectual (as well as many non-Christian thinkers) from the twentieth century's first half expressed an explicit debt to his work. One of the last men of letters, he wrote prolifically and substantively in almost all literary forms, and this versatility was matched by a consistently high level of quality. If best known for the Father Brown stories, Chesterton also penned enduring novels (*The Man Who Was Thursday* [1908]), poems ("The Ballad of the White Horse" [1911]), and critical studies (*Charles Dickens* [1906]). He also helped found the political theory known as distributism, which promoted decentralized government and widespread, small-scale property ownership, thereby providing an alternative to industrial capitalism and socialism (*What's Wrong with the World* [1910]; *The Outline of Sanity* [1926]). Nevertheless, *The Everlasting Man* is generally regarded as his finest work, and it also best displays the deepening of his thought that resulted from his assent to Roman Catholicism.

MAJOR THEMES

When Chesterton died in 1936, his friend and fellow Catholic convert, Ronald Knox, preached his panegyric. In this eulogy, Knox contended that "if every other line he wrote should disappear from circulation, Catholic posterity would still owe an imperishable debt of gratitude, so long as a copy of *The Everlasting Man* enriched its libraries" (1940, 148). Eight years later, Graham Greene deemed *The Everlasting Man* "among the great books of the age," an opinion he would hold for the next four decades (1969, 106). To Evelyn Waugh, Chesterton was "primarily the author of *The Everlasting Man*" (1984, 560); he even once proposed rewriting it, being inspired by its arguments but irritated by its style (Pryce-Jones 1973, 129)! And C. S. Lewis recalled that reading *The Everlasting Man* was crucial to his conversion to Christianity, as in it "for the first time [I] saw the whole Christian outline of history set out in a form that seemed to me to make sense" (1955, 223).

Despite this catalog of applause, though, *The Everlasting Man* has received surprisingly scant sustained critical commentary, and even the best of these discussions have noted its status as a distinctly Catholic text only glancingly. Yet a more thorough examination of this work and its Catholicism is necessary, for it is a piquant theology of history, one that contravened many of its epoch's dominant intellectual paradigms and that is molded in decisive ways by Chesterton's having written it after he became a Roman Catholic. Comprehending *The Everlasting Man*, then, requires grasping the development of Chesterton's life, thought, and faith, a close reading of the book's content and context, and a survey of critical responses to it. Such a treatment of *The Everlasting Man* will thus deepen understanding of this landmark work of Catholic literature that impressed so many twentieth-century luminaries and will, perhaps, encourage future scholarship that is commensurate with its intellectual gravity and influence.

As *The Everlasting Man* is a theology of history, some understanding of this genre is necessary to comprehend Chesterton's contribution to it. A theology of history considers the purpose of history as part of the divine economy. It asserts that people are destined for eternity while being rooted in temporality, thus giving their lives a dual significance that only a theological position can clarify: "A theology of history is precisely the reliance on a theo-logic, that is, the 'whole' story is neither completely caused nor measured by men" (Hittinger 1984, 12). Since Catholic Christians especially stress the sacramental significance of the eternal becoming incarnate in time, they are particularly prone to such reflections, believing that "history has *become theology* in Christianity" (Caldecott 1998, 478). Although Catholic theologies of history date to Augustine's *City of God*, Aidan Nichols points out that the early twentieth century was a period of "Christian interest in the theology of history of an intensity unprecedented since patristic times" (1997, 33). Catholic thinkers such as Christopher Dawson, Martin D'Arcy, and Jacques Maritain all wrote searchingly on this topic during these years, and such musings also undergirded contemporaneous poetry by T. S. Eliot and David Jones, as well as J. R. R. Tolkien's epic, *The Lord of the Rings*. Chesterton's participation in this ebullition was conditioned discretely by his own spiritual journey and by other components of his cultural context.

Chesterton had been interested in history since youth and had published *A Short History of England* in 1917. The *Short History*, however, had a more telescoped vision than that of *The Everlasting Man*. Chesterton had long held that "there is no intelligible history without a religion" (*Illustrated London News*, 1910, 632), but, although the *Short History* is favorably inclined to Catholicism, its Catholic elements are more implied than stated. Even if Alzina Stone Dale is correct in suggesting that Chesterton had embraced Roman Catholicism inwardly by the time he wrote the *Short History*, it is a more tentative acceptance (1982, 209). He was not fully committed to Roman Catholicism in 1917 and chose to concentrate more on history's matter than its meaning. The *Short History* is about history, now and in England, whereas *The Everlasting Man* attempts to assert its overall significance. Only Chesterton's unambiguous adoption of a cosmology could supply the assuredness necessary to attempt such a bold project. His effort in *The Everlasting Man* to bring an explanation of all history into clear focus finds his analysis inseparable from his Roman Catholic faith, reflecting the increased confidence provided by his reception.

Like many of Chesterton's important works, *The Everlasting Man* began as a rebuttal. H. G. Wells had completed his *Outline of History* in 1919, in which he voiced the common conviction among the era's British mandarins that the purpose of past events had been to create modern humanity and society, which in turn are the embryo for even better people and civilizations in the future. Not surprisingly, then, he paid little attention to religion. Considering his age's ascendant secularism a healthier outlook due to its chronological primacy, Wells rejected the notion that past cultures could have owed their successes to something he saw as barbaric superstition. He felt that coming epochs would continue to eschew fantasies about the supernatural in favor of a humanistic moral code deriving from the best facets of Christian and Buddhist ethics. Chesterton was a persistent critic of his friend's theses. He reviewed the *Outline* for the *Times*, and he also advanced some of *The Everlasting Man*'s later arguments against it in a 1922 essay written soon after his reception, "Where All Roads Lead," which is in many respects a germinal version of the later book.[1] In 1925, he published *The Everlasting Man*, a work designed not merely as a response to Wells "but to all histories based on a belief in linear progress" (Crowther 1991, 12). As such, it is also part of the stream of romantic protest against Enlightenment rationalism that Chesterton and fellow twentieth-century orthodox Christians (like Knox, Greene, Waugh, Lewis, Dawson, Eliot, Jones, and Tolkien) swam in (Peters 2000, 146).

The Everlasting Man opens with a telling observation, as Chesterton stresses that his view of history and his religious faith are inextricably connected: "It is impossible, I hope, for any Catholic to write any book on any subject, above all this subject, without showing that he is a Catholic" (*Everlasting Man*, 141). Whereas he had claimed in the *Short History* that without religion "there would never have been any English history at all" (41), a particular faith rather than religion generally was now the key to his interpretation of history, revealing the extent of his religious development in the years separating these two books. In making religion central to his reading of history, Chesterton begins his analysis in a consciously countermodern vein, and his specific arguments also follow this path. Instead of portraying history as a linear progression to the present, he posits three irruptions of qualitative differentiation: those separating humans from animals, Christ from all other humans, and Catholic Christianity from all other religions.

In the case of human beings, he begins by rebutting Wells's claim that primitive cave drawings are a form of bestial superstition. Chesterton (anticipating recent paleoanthropologists [Fowler 1995, 21]) asserts that cave paintings demonstrate that, from the species' earliest days, people, and only people, have sought to represent nature under other forms. For him, "art is the signature of man" in that it reveals "a difference of kind and not a difference of degree" between humans and their fellow creatures: "a monkey does not begin the art of representation and a man carry it to perfection. A monkey does not do it at all; he does not begin to do it at all; he does not begin to begin to do it at all" (*Everlasting Man*, 166, 177). Chesterton thinks this distinctive trait is constant across the ages and thus helps form part of a fixed human nature that belies Wells's belief in a plastic, and progressive, human essence: prehistoric cave painters were "exactly like men and men exceedingly like ourselves" (184). Chesterton argues further that the impulses behind art and religious worship are essentially the same and that only rational beings possess them: "these natural experiences, and even natural excite-ments, never do pass the line that separates them from creative expression like art and religion in any creature except man. . . . It was unique and could make creeds as it could make cave-drawings" (181–82). To Chesterton, these artistic and sacramental urges merge further in the myths that he contends humans, and humans alone, invent. Because only humans have the powers of speech and fancy, he postulates, only they can attempt to explain their world imaginatively. Like any art form, this one also has a religious function for Chesterton, as he maintains that most myths have tried to explain the ways of the divine to humans and have often involved the salvific death of a god or heroic god figure.

Yet even the "sane heathenism" (307) of myth-makers like Virgil and ancient Roman culture—"the highest achievement of the human race" to that point— was an insufficient theophany (293). Chesterton held that the Incarnation occurred when it did because "Man could do no more" (293). With the Incarnation, a new cosmos emerged that is "larger than the old cosmos" (309). To him, Christ is the unique intersection of the human and holy trinities, being both Son of Man and Son of God. He thus fuses the material and the spiritual, the ephemeral and the eternal, within his person and thereby raises history to a higher ontological level: he makes the matter and meaning of history one. In Chesterton's view, Christ hence fulfilled all that was good in paganism, completing what was incomplete in ancient myths. Yet he also purged all falsehood from them and so inaugurated a uniquely true understanding of Being, one that is more vital because it is unencumbered by error. As he put it in a contemporaneous Father Brown story, "it divided truth from error with a blade like ice; but all that was left had never felt so much alive" (*Incredulity*, 146).[2] Christ has thus fixed forever the *telos* by which any age can be measured, for he "incarnates Truth in the historical process" (Wills 1961, 196).

Chesterton posits further that the Church Christ left behind after his Ascension continues this process. Against his day's scholars of comparative religion, Chesterton maintains in *The Everlasting Man* that Christianity distinguishes itself from all other faiths by professing to have been founded by Truth himself. He argues (in a passage that echoes Augustine and anticipates C. S. Lewis) that Christ alone of all religious founders claimed to be God; and Chesterton contends that someone whom he considers so self-evidently sane would only have made such an assertion if it were true. The Church, then, is his vicar, serving as the voice of truth in history's final stage. And just as history now advances to the eschaton without improving essentially, so an understanding of Christian doctrine develops and deepens without core dogmas being altered, for Christ's Incarnation and establishment of the Church closes the deposit of revelation and hence precludes further substantial progress in history and religion: after Christ, "nobody else has any good news; for the simple reason that nobody else has any news" (401).

Chesterton reiterates *Orthodoxy's* key metaphor to express this belief that Christianity is qualitatively different due to its exclusive possession of dispositive, unalloyed Truth: "It definitely asserted that there was a key and that it possessed that key and that no other key was like it . . . there was undoubtedly much about the key that seemed complex; indeed there was only one thing about it that was simple. It opened the door" (346–47). Chesterton's claim that orthodox Christianity is the outlook most in accord with Being's complexity had culminated in his belief in Roman Catholicism by this time, as he called Catholicism "a view of the universe satisfying all sides of life; a complete and complex truth with something to say about everything" (256). In his mind, then, the Roman pontiff holds the keys of Peter.

Because the Church "fits the lock; because it is like life," Chesterton felt that it has had the unique ability to harmonize phenomena previously considered incompatible, particularly mythology and philosophy (380–81). Whereas antiquity deemed myth and religion one thing and philosophy quite another, he declares that Catholicism rhymes these two roads to truth due to its historicity. He argues that no pagan myths claimed to be histories, but that the Gospels ground their validity in being accounts of actual events, thereby combining the mythological desire to tell tales with the philosophical search for truth: "The Catholic faith is the reconciliation because it is the realization of both mythology and philosophy. It is a story and in that sense one of a hundred stories; only it is a true story. It is a philosophy and in that sense one of a hundred philosophies; only it is a philosophy that is like life" (378). Chesterton hence specifies *Orthodoxy's* dynamic balance of spirit and reason here in the marriage of the imaginative and the rational powers under the Catholic Church's auspices, demonstrating further the refinement of his vision following his reception into the Church.

Even as Chesterton upheld what he saw as the tenuous Christian balance between philosophy and mythology, though, he discerned a modern reversion to the pre-Christian split: "there are two tides in the world today—reason running one way and imagination the other" (*Illustrated London News*, 1923, 86). Thinking that only Roman Catholicism had preserved this precarious equilibrium previously and that it alone had the requisite authority and regard for tradition to defend it unhesitatingly in his day, Chesterton considered a Catholic revival essential for a successful rebellion against its prepotent post-Christian critics (like Wells) who sought to sunder what the Church had uniquely joined. Although Chesterton had stated similar views formerly, *The Everlasting Man* uses history more explicitly than before as the foundation for contemporary evangelical hopes.

Holding that mirror of history up to nature, Chesterton deduces that Catholicism's foes had judged it dead several times in the past, "just as they do today" (383). These "deaths of the faith"—Arianism, Albigensianism, Humanist skepticism, the Enlightenment, and Darwinism—were times when Catholicism seemed to have been buried by more modern or progressive systems. But, he argues, orthodoxy returned after each heresy had departed and cannot ever be eliminated permanently because Catholicism is founded on the One who conquered death: "it had a God who knew the way out of the grave" (382). He uses these precedents deliberately to substantiate his sense that a similar Catholic renascence was occurring in his own day: "we know that also in this ending, which really did look to us like the final ending, the incredible thing has happened again; the Faith has a better following among the young men than among the old. When Ibsen spoke of the new generation knocking at the door, he certainly never expected that it would be the church-door" (387). Chesterton later extended this principle and hope to western culture, the social order he considered founded on Catholicism, referring to it in 1932 as a civilization that "does decline, and has done so any number of times . . . [but it] has a way of managing to reappear, when its enemies have in their turn decayed." His peers are hence unwise to proclaim the "final extinction" of "this everlastingly dying creed and culture," for "today it stands erect and resurrected" (*Chaucer*, 373–74).

Although Chesterton was overly sanguine about the extent of these religious and cultural revivals, that very optimism arose from the confidence engendered by his conversion to Rome. Indeed, all of *The Everlasting Man*'s main arguments were present in embryonic form in *Orthodoxy* but had remained undeveloped for nearly two decades. The notions of humans being qualitatively different from animals; Christ being qualitatively different from all humans; and his Church being a revolutionary, eternally reviving institution are all sketched briefly in the earlier book (143–47). But their elaboration awaited the deeper understanding of their significance that Chesterton acquired only with unqualified belief in Roman Catholicism. Only by embracing fully Roman Catholic teachings and traditions did Chesterton think he had sufficient vision to see the matter and meaning of history steadily and wholly.

CRITICAL RECEPTION

Critical judgments of *The Everlasting Man* have been generally favorable, if cursory. In 1925, for instance, the Catholic *Commonweal* labeled it Chesterton's "most important" book ("Chesterton's Masterpiece," 95), and reviewers from the secular *Spectator* and the Anglican *Church Times* made cognate appraisals (Conlon 1976, 417, 421). Among notable early Chesterton critics, Hugh Kenner called *The Everlasting Man* the "most valuable single record of the place of the Incarnation" in Chesterton's thought (1947, 143); Garry Wills supplied what is still the best analysis of its place in Chesterton's *oeuvre* in 1961 (1961, 180–200); and Horton Davies judged it "a devastating polemic" against evolutionary secularism (1965, 187). More recently, Adrian Hastings deemed *The Everlasting Man* the "most impressive piece of Christian literature" of the 1920s (1986, 234), while Warren Carroll called it "a Catholic classic . . . of everlasting value" (1986, 300). By the late 1990s, Patrick Allitt was dubbing it Chesterton's "most striking postconversion work" (1997, 199), and Joseph Schwartz was even considering it comparable to *City of God* (1996, 57).

A handful of authors have dissented from this critical consensus, but they resemble it in usually failing to provide in-depth analyses of *The Everlasting Man*. Most detractors have found the book's rational arguments unequal to its intuitive insights about man and God. Reviewers for both the *Times Literary Supplement* and *Punch*, for example, felt that this perceived disparity vitiated otherwise salutary observations about secular and sacred history (Conlon 1976, 413–16, 419). Lawrence Clipper echoed this criticism, deeming Chesterton out of his depth theologically in this volume and dismissing it as "a long syllogism with a faulty major premise" (1974, 110). Maurice Cowling reiterated such objections a decade later, concluding that Chesterton's ambition in *The Everlasting Man* was "beyond his capability . . . Chesterton had little talent for philosophical, theological, or theoretical statement" (1985, 320).

On the whole, though, *The Everlasting Man* has been recognized as a significant contribution to Catholic thought and literature. It is therefore all the more imperative that future scholars devote more detailed attention to this tome than it has received thus far. In composing this Catholic theology of history, Chesterton joined a venerable heritage of such commentators while dissenting forcefully from the confident agnosticism that predominated among the British literati of his day. He thus not only engaged his era's prevalent norms but also contributed to the Christian and countermodern communities of discourse that challenged these regnant convictions. *The Everlasting Man* reveals additionally the crucial shaping force that Roman Catholicism became in Chesterton's intellectual and imaginative vision following his reception into the Catholic Church. Scholars of Chesterton, religious thought, and modern Anglophone and Christian and Catholic culture will hence find much material for rich reflection within the pages of his masterwork. Perhaps, then, future ages will study *The Everlasting Man* as assiduously as past ones have admired it, for, as Waugh concluded, "It met a temporary need and survives as a permanent monument" (1984, 560).

NOTES

G. K. Chesterton, *The Everlasting Man*. In *Collected Works of G. K. Chesterton*, ed. Larry Azar, vol. 2, 136–407 (San Francisco: Ignatius Press, 1986). All references are to this edition. Used by permission of A. P. Watt, Ltd., on behalf of the Royal Literary Fund.

　　1. Compare especially "Where All Roads Lead," 51–58, with *The Everlasting Man*, 214–32.

　　2. See also Chesterton's *The Resurrection of Rome*, 357–61 and 455–56.

WORKS CITED

Allitt, Patrick. 1997. *Catholic Converts*. Ithaca, NY: Cornell University Press.

Caldecott, Stratford. 1998. "Was Chesterton a Theologian?" *Chesterton Review* 24 (November): 465–81.

Carroll, Warren. 1986. "Chesterton's Christ-Centered View of History." *Faith & Reason* 12: 299–312.

Chesterton, Cecil. 1908. *G. K. Chesterton: A Criticism*. London: Alston Rivers.

Chesterton, G. K. 1908. *Orthodoxy*. Reprint, New York: Image Books, 1959.

———. 1917. *A Short History of England*. London: Chatto & Windus.

———. 1926. *The Incredulity of Father Brown*. Reprint, London: Penguin, 1958.

———. 1987. *Illustrated London News*. November 19, 1910. In *Collected Works of G. K. Chesterton*, ed. Laurence Clipper, vol. 28, 632–35. San Francisco: Ignatius Press.

———. 1988. *The Autobiography of G. K. Chesterton*. In *Collected Works of G. K. Chesterton*, ed. Randall Paine, vol. 16. San Francisco: Ignatius Press.

———. 1990. *Illustrated London News*. April 21, 1923. In *Collected Works of G. K. Chesterton*, ed. Laurence Clipper, vol. 33, 86–90. San Francisco: Ignatius Press.

———. 1990. *The Resurrection of Rome*. In *Collected Works of G. K. Chesterton*, ed. Robert Royal, vol. 21, 281–466. San Francisco: Ignatius Press.

———. 1990 "Where All Roads Lead." In *Collected Works of G. K. Chesterton*, ed. James Thompson, Jr., vol. 3, 25–58. San Francisco: Ignatius Press.

———. 1991. *Chaucer*. In *Collected Works of G. K. Chesterton*, ed. Russell Kirk, vol. 18, 150–374. San Francisco: Ignatius Press.

———. 1991. *Illustrated London News*. July 24, 1926. In *Collected Works of G. K. Chesterton*, ed. Laurence Clipper, vol. 34, 129–33. San Francisco: Ignatius Press.

"Chesterton's Masterpiece." *Commonweal* 3 (December 2, 1925): 95.

Clipper, Lawrence. 1974. *G. K. Chesterton*. New York: Twayne.

Conlon, D. J., ed. 1976. *G. K. Chesterton: The Critical Judgments*. Antwerp, Belgium: Universitaire Faculteiten Sint-Ignatius.

Cowling, Maurice. 1985. *Religion and Public Doctrine in Modern England*, vol. 2. Cambridge: Cambridge University Press.

Crowther, Ian. 1991. *G. K. Chesterton*. London: Claridge Press.

Dale, Alzina Stone. 1982. *The Outline of Sanity: A Biography of G. K. Chesterton*. Grand Rapids, MI: Eerdmans.

Davies, Horton. 1965. *Worship and Theology in England*, vol. 5. Princeton, NJ: Princeton University Press.

Fowler, Brenda. 1995. "Where Did He Go?" *New York Times Book Review* (December 17): 21.

Greene, Graham. 1969. *Collected Essays*. New York: Penguin.

Hastings, Adrian. 1986. *A History of English Christianity, 1920–1985*. London: Collins.

Hittinger, Russell. 1984. "The Metahistorical Vision of Christopher Dawson." In *The Dynamic Character of Christian Culture*, ed. Peter Cataldo, 1–50. Lanham, MD: University Press of America.

Kenner, Hugh. 1947. *Paradox in Chesterton*. New York: Sheed and Ward.

Knox, Ronald. 1940. *Captive Flames*. London: Burns and Oates.

Lewis, C. S. 1955. *Surprised by Joy*. London: Harcourt Brace Jovanovich.

Nichols, Aidan. 1997. "Christopher Dawson's Catholic Setting." In *Eternity in Time*, ed. Stratford Caldecott and John Morrill, 25–49. Edinburgh: T. and T. Clark.

Peters, Thomas. 2000. *The Christian Imagination*. San Francisco: Ignatius Press.

Pryce-Jones, David, ed. 1973. *Evelyn Waugh and His World*. London: Wiedenfield and Nicolson.

Schwartz, Joseph. 1996. "The Theology of History in *The Everlasting Man*." *Renascence* 49 (Fall): 57–66.

Waugh, Evelyn. 1984. *The Essays, Articles and Reviews of Evelyn Waugh*, ed. Donat Gallagher. Boston: Little, Brown and Co.

Wills, Garry. 1961. *Chesterton: Man and Mask*. New York: Sheed and Ward.

— **Adam Schwartz**

Sandra Cisneros [1954–]

The House on Mango Street

BIOGRAPHY

Sandra Cisneros was born on December 20, 1954, in Chicago to parents of Mexican descent. After Alfredo Cisneros del Moral and Elvira Cordero Anguiano married, they settled in a poor southern Chicago neighborhood. Alfredo upholstered furniture and Elvira worked in a factory to support their seven children. Sandra grew up as the only girl among six brothers, an older sister having died as a child. Her brothers became three groups of two, leaving Sandra on her own. She once explained her choice to write: "I am the only daughter in a family of six sons. . . . That explains everything" ("Only Daughter," 3–4). For years she would feel excluded from her family's male community. That her brothers ignored her did not hurt Sandra as much as her father's attitude. Alfredo would tell people that he had seven sons, instead of six sons and a daughter. Sandra fought her loneliness through reading, thanks to her mother's influence; Elvira helped her daughter obtain a library card as soon as she could read.

Cisneros had few friends, because her family often traveled from Chicago to Mexico for long visits with Alfredo's family. Each time they returned, she found herself in a new apartment. Not only did Sandra not make friends, she felt disrupted by the change in cultures. In Mexico she was not accepted as Mexican, but in the United States she was not seen as an American.

Cisneros also moved in and out of various Catholic schools, marked by what she later observed as the nuns' judgmental attitude toward Chicanos. Her early days in school conditioned her to detest even the buildings. She explained to later audiences in the Foreword to *Woman Hollering Creek* that she thought the Catholic schools resembled prisons, "big, hulky, and authoritarian, the kind of architecture meant to instill terror" (xi). Her days were filled with reading and studying at home rather than interacting with classmates. The Cisneros family owned only two books, a Bible and an old copy of *Alice in Wonderland*, making Sandra's library card especially important.

Struggling to find her place, Cisneros closely observed those around her. She began as a child to collect the stories she would later include in her most popular work, *The House on Mango Street*. Cisneros lived many of the experiences related by her twelve-year-old Chicana narrator, Esperanza. Her negative experiences in Catholic schools, and the guilt inflicted by its codes, inhabit Esperanza's attitudes from the earliest scenes.

Cisneros graduated from Chicago's Loyola University, following the advice of a teacher who urged her to apply for admission to the University of Iowa's graduate writing program. She was shocked at her acceptance. Again feeling out of place at Iowa, Cisneros had an epiphany. She realized that the difference separating her from her mostly Anglo classmates, which in the past had seemed a weakness and the cause of her isolation and dissatisfaction, in actuality proved her strength. Cisneros later wrote that the child-voice of *The House on Mango Street* was born with that realization.

After obtaining a Master of Fine Arts degree, Cisneros returned to Chicago to teach in an alternative high school. Her poetry gained recognition through public readings and its appearance inside public transport vehicles in a project sponsored by the Poetry Society of America. In 1980 she published her first book, a slim volume of poetry titled *Bad Boys* with a printing of only one hundred copies.

Cisneros continued to work on *The House on Mango Street*, and in 1980 received the first of two National Endowment for the Arts awards. They contributed to her support as she lived for a time in Europe. She published *The House on Mango Street* in 1984, its short poetic chapters capturing much critical attention. A collection that brazenly mixed poetry with fiction, *My Wicked, Wicked Ways*, followed in 1987. According to Cisneros, the title represented a liberating self view. She knew her desire to construct her own future might be labeled "wicked" by some. She credits her upbringing as a Catholic in the Mexican tradition for that misconception. Any thought of "redefining" or considering herself as a sexual being inspired guilt. In one interview, she stated that, as a beginning writer, she had hoped to get rid of her haunting past. As she matured, she realized that her ghosts could become a part of her life and that she could write about that hard-earned coexistence. Her preface labels her poems "wicked," based on the "girl grief decade" of her "wicked nun years," referring to her writing as a "first felony" and her poems as her sins.

Cisneros assumed a temptress pose in the cover photograph for *My Wicked, Wicked Ways*, her flashy dress revealing cowboy boots as she sat cross-legged, holding a cigarette. The startling red colors in a glass of wine, her bright earrings, and her lined lips spurred complaints from readers; women felt betrayed by Cisneros's sex object image, and men complained that she "led them on." Cisneros countered charges of stereotyping by describing the image as powerful and independent, like her style. She wanted to counter the tradition that labeled strong women as abnormal, bad, or insane, attributing much of the blame for that flawed perception to religion.

In 1991, she published her story collection, *Woman Hollering Creek*, for which Random House advanced her a startling $100,000, the most ever paid to a Chicana writer; *Woman* won the Lannan Literary Award, while her 1994 work, *Loose Woman*, brought her a 1995 MacArthur Genius Grant. After teaching in both Texas and California, she settled in San Antonio, remarking on its perfect blend of influences from both the United States and Mexico. There she raised national attention when she painted her house purple. That traditional Chicano color was not one of the hues that code allowed in her historic neighborhood. Her arguments with the local board focused on the fact that no records had been maintained regarding the colors of San Antonio's *barrio*, an area of the city that predated her upper-class white neighborhood. The dispute faded along with the paint color, which eventually turned an acceptable lavender under the effect of the hot Texas sun.

Cisneros continued to publish articles and stories, but her next novel was delayed by the death of her father. By the fall of 2002, she was ready to begin a book tour with the anticipated *Caramelo*. Although she does not like Chicago, she returned there to debut her novel through two public readings. Laced with magic realism and the poetic notes of "Spanglish," the novel delighted critics, providing a narrator who survives through her instinct for story. Her epiphany occurs outside of a locked Catholic church, emphasizing the paradox of religion for Cisneros. While her disconnect from Catholicism's organized rites remains firm, her characters exude a personal spirituality in their use of imagination, and she never denies the strong effects of Catholicism on the Chicano culture.

Cisneros remains important as one of the first Latina writers widely published in English, as the first Latina to garner a six-figure advance, and as a writer whose nontraditional approach to fiction incorporates poetic elements and mixes English with Spanish, leaving some of that Spanish untranslated. Cisneros challenges her readers to embrace those differences and to learn from them.

PLOT SUMMARY

Cisneros obviously based young Esperanza Codero, the narrator of *The House on Mango Street*, on herself. From the book's first sentence, Cisneros's own story emerges: "We didn't always live on Mango Street." Esperanza lists the several places the family has lived, unable to recall them all, adding, "But what I remember most is moving a lot" (3). Esperanza's symbolic first name means "hope." Like Cisneros had as a child, Esperanza hoped for a real home for her large family.

When Esperanza arrives at Mango Street, the dilapidated house inspires not pride but a rush of shame. The structure symbolizes her poverty and the shame she occasionally feels for her people; she does not want to admit that she lives there. She concludes the chapter by saying, "I knew then I had to have a house. A real House. One I could point to. But this isn't it" (5). The house traditionally represents Esperanza's future as the approved domestic sphere, signaling hard physical labor for a woman. However, Cisneros subverts its tradition. She transforms that sphere to a space in which Esperanza may create her art. In chapter/vignette 23, "Bad Girl," Esperanza shares her secret desire to write with her aunt. Chapters acquaint readers with Esperanza's sister Nenny as well as with other members of her family. She introduces her family by describing each of their hair textures, emphasizing their individuality and personality. By the third chapter, readers understand the strict gender divisions that exist in Esperanza's world and the isolation that she feels with few friends and only her sister as a companion. Her neighborhood slowly comes into sharp focus through brief revelations regarding its inhabitants, such as the grocer, the raggedy men, the junk store owner and his prized music box, local children, their relatives and loose neighbors, and, of course, the nuns whom Esperanza fears.

Esperanza matures both physically and emotionally through a series of events in this *bildungsroman*. Cisneros rejects the traditional female maturation tale in which the protagonist faces challenges that relate to her learning proper behavior for acceptance into society. Instead, she claims the traditional male version, in which a boy gains personal independence through trials that earn him his freedom. Esperanza will claim her independence from the *barrio* through her writing, with creativity acting as the key that opens the door to the outer world. She wants nothing more than to leave the *barrio*, but by the book's end she understands that she will one day return because she cannot escape the environment that lives in her heart. Various buildings and enclosures represent Esperanza herself as she seeks her own structured identity.

The book's vignettes read like poetry, filled with acute imagery and edgy figurative language, framed by Esperanza's dreamy tone. Cisneros has called the stories "lazy poems" ("Do You Know Me?," 79), each of which had the potential to develop into a dense poetic format. However, their messages seem stronger as prose. A poor neighborhood holds little charm for those who must survive its challenges, including piles of disease-spreading garbage, shootings of children, the ever-present rats, and the terrible housing conditions.

Ultimately, Esperanza triumphs over her poverty, just as Cisneros did. Like Cisneros, Esperanza leaves her *barrio* in order to write truthfully of its rough beauty and challenge. Cisneros later wrote, "It's a circular thing, you leave, but you also do other work to enable other people to control their destinies" (Aranda 1990, 65).

MAJOR THEMES

From the first chapter of *The House on Mango Street*, which bears the book's title, Cisneros reveals through her autobiographical narrator the destructive effects of her Catholic school training. Ashamed of their new small house with the tiny windows that make the structure appear to "hold its breath" (4), Esperanza yet identifies with the house as a promise unfulfilled. She had so badly wanted to move out of the crowded world of apartments into a house, but her disappointment with the structure reveals her self-consciousness regarding her own value. She explains her hatred of her former crowded apartment through her nun teacher's reaction to it. Upon seeing Esperanza playing outside, the nun had stopped, pointed at the apartment building with its peeled paint and barred windows, and remarked accusingly, "You live *there*?" (5). Because of Esperanza's identity with the structure, the nun actually accuses the girl of being an unworthy. Cisneros's characterization of Esperanza's teacher as representing a religion that neither physically nor spiritually enlightens the poor Chicano community but rather increases their emotional burden through accusation informs her use of Catholicism throughout this collection. In addition, the importance of structures and Esperanza's identification with certain houses emphasize the significance of her rejection of God's house. In "Laughter," for instance, she remarks to her sister that one house looks like Mexico, a thought that brings comfort as she recognizes an aspect of herself that the teacher nun so abruptly dismisses.

Because she is yet a child, Esperanza relates to the Church and Catholicism through her school experience. When she notes in the chapter "My Name" that children at school pronounce her name as if it is made of a hard metal that hurts their mouth, she again alerts the reader to the damage done to her self-image. The passage's irony lies in the fact that her name means hope, a major theme of the New Testament. Esperanza's dream of gaining a new name by rebaptizing herself undercuts the Church's stance on baptism as a celebration and recognition of the value of all new life to a loving God. The Church has betrayed Esperanza by not fulfilling its promise of respect for her existence made on the day of her formal Baptism. She remains conscious of the Church's symbolic significance, noting in "Our Good Day" that two outcast sisters in the neighborhood wear Sunday shoes that are shined, despite the girls' disheveled appearance. However, they wear their shoes without socks, and the shoes rub painfully against their red ankles. Esperanza immediately warms to the pair, although her only friend, Cathy, tells her not to speak to them because they smell like "brooms." Here Cisneros suggests that two more young women, symbolically and painfully marked by the Church, are swept, like waste, from its protection.

In "There Was an Old Woman. She Had So Many Children, She Didn't Know What to Do," Esperanza alludes to the lack of birth control in Catholic families as she tells her tale of one very tired mother, deserted by her man and attempting to cope with her enormous brood. The children mature not respecting anything, including themselves, and the neighbors eventually weary of helping care for another's children. In her situation, the poor woman should be able to turn to the Church for emotional and physical nurture, but it is not even mentioned as a possibility for rescue. The symbolically named Refugia wedges her head between slats in a gate, probably in an attempt to escape through a gate that will not open for her. Angel attempts to fly like his namesakes, but falls from the sky, not merely landing on earth but exploding there without a whimper. Cisneros's adoption of biblical imagery to describe a child's foolish venture offers multiple interpretations. Angel's imitation of heavenly figures, encouraged by the Church, does him real physical damage, but he remains silenced by the forces, natural and spiritual, that he sought to employ. Conversely, Angel might benefit from his early lesson, learning that natural forces like gravity deserve his respect; they govern his world in a far more real manner than do the Church's spiritual forces.

At times, Cisneros departs from her negative approach to allow for the association of religious ideas with those of the imagination. In "Darius & the Clouds," while at school Darius notices the clouds in a sky Esperanza has just described as something that keeps her safe. "You can fall asleep and wake up drunk on sky" (33), she announces, adding that "here," down on earth, enough sky is lacking. To Esperanza, the clouds resemble pillows in their inviting fluffiness, suggesting a safe haven for the children and the promise of restful sleep, which can serve as an escape from the threats of their surroundings. Darius identifies God in a cloud next to one that looks like popcorn. Cisneros may suggest that God can offer comfort, but it is a God disconnected from any organized religious group. Darius's God may be claimed as his own, without the intercession required by the Catholic approach to confession and prayer. However, because Esperanza has pronounced Darius in general a fool, his wise statement may be interpreted as simple babbling.

Esperanza longs to join the "special kids" who eat in the canteen at school, although her mother refuses to make her a lunch to carry. She pleads that she will make her own lunch and argues that her absence from the home lunch table will simply make her mother love her more when she returns home after school. Her mother at last relents, and Esperanza proudly carries her rice sandwich to school, falling in line with the eat-at-school regulars, until a nun asks who had sent her. When Esperanza offers a letter from her mother, the gruff nun sends her to the aptly named Sister Superior to receive the required permission to eat at school. Esperanza views the encounter as punishment, made clear by the fact that she must stand in line with two classroom transgressors. The sister at first denies Esperanza's request because she lives close enough to the school to walk home for lunch. She demands that Esperanza climb up on a box and point out her house, but the girl is too shy. Interestingly, the box holds books, symbols of Esperanza's escape from her surroundings, but their containment in the cardboard prison marks the school as a jail where knowledge is selfishly withheld from those who need it most. As Esperanza cries, the nun points to a row of slum three-flats, asking whether the girl lives there, although Esperanza knows even raggedy men would not enter those horrid structures. Once again, a nun purposely discourages Esperanza in her attempts to develop her sense of self. Sister Superior does show some humanity when she permits Esperanza to eat in the canteen only that one day. When the girl pronounces the experience nothing special, readers understand it is not the canteen that disillusions her but rather the Catholic school's headmistress.

Esperanza experiences a real Church baptism at Precious Blood Church in the chapter titled "Chanclas," but the religious ceremony is for a cousin. During the party afterward, she experiences her own figurative rebirth, but it is into the secular world, not the religious. When her Uncle Nacho pulls her onto the dance floor wearing her new dress, slip, and socks, she feels self-conscious about her clunky oxford shoes. But she attracts the admiration of all present, including a boy "who is my cousin by first communion or something" (47), and Esperanza knows that things have changed when the boys watch her dance. That chapter precedes "Hips," in which she is led to consider her awakening by a friend named Lucy. Their discussion of the need for wide hips alludes to a sexuality that comes too early to Esperanza's world. Cisneros inserts the image of Nenny's earrings, little gold ones that her mother gave her for her First Holy Communion, a juxtaposition of the sacred and the profane, as the girls sing verses about hips and kissing women that eventually lapse back into little-girl jump rope songs. The earrings may be viewed as either comforting, marking the lingering hold of her mother on Nenny's childhood, or threatening, a symbol of maturity in the adult world that religion represents. The necessity of Catholic school, not for education and self-enlightenment but to help one avoid turning "out bad" (53), is emphasized in the following chapter, "The First Job." Turning out good was expensive business in a private school, and so Esperanza needs to work. At her job, she wears white gloves as if at her First communion, and her day will indeed offer a first of sorts. She is accosted by an oriental man who forces her to kiss him.

Religious imagery continues to contrast with its surroundings in "Elenita, Cards, Palm, Water," when Esperanza requests that a witch woman tell her fortune. The woman works in a kitchen containing multiple religious artifacts, including holy candles, a plaster cast saint figure, and a Palm Sunday cross covered with dust. The cross is mentioned as the penultimate item in the series that finally includes a voodoo hand in a picture taped on the wall. That the inhabitants of the *barrio* so easily operate guided by precepts from two violently opposed credos suggests that they accept faith wherever they find it. Cisneros also implies that all of these items represent equal superstitions, especially when the woman admonishes Esperanza to rid herself of bad spirits by sleeping beside a holy candle for one week, then spitting on the eighth day. Esperanza departs, receiving a wish for the Virgin's blessing from the witch, an unlikely representative of the Blessed Mother of God.

In a later chapter, Cisneros returns to the idea of Christmas as devoid of any religious meaning when Esperanza, now taking a keen interest in boys, feels she may soon "explode" (73) just like Christmas. Although her reference is to new life as she imagines herself new and "shiny," the comparison to tinsel, an item light and airy and void of substance, dominates. Her Christmas wish includes a boy hanging on her neck and a breeze up her skirt, hardly spiritual images. Later still, the book's sole curse word is "Christ!," and Esperanza continues to mark her move toward her first sexual experience using religious holidays as reference. When in the chapter "Sally" the title character loses her only friend due to her changing ideas, Esperanza notes that the day it happened was a Tuesday before Easter, suggesting sacrifice and isolation, two themes of the chapter.

As the book draws to a close, Esperanza helps her community mourn the death of another child, a baby reportedly taken away by Jesus. That a supposedly benevolent figure steals a life even as Esperanza learns the secret of her own identity from three female strangers who attend the wake represents Cisneros's overriding message regarding religion: it provides solace only for those who have given up and given in to life's sorrows. When one of the unknown women tells Esperanza that she understands her longing to leave the *barrio*, the girl is thunderstruck at her knowledge of that secret. Even more important is the admonition that while she may leave, she must someday return. The scene's imagery includes the scent of cinnamon clinging to the women and their smoky, dreamy appearance, suggesting participants in a ritual, although not a religious one. The three apparitions allow Esperanza to envision her future; they empower her as if a female version of the three aspects of the Godhead, the Father, the Son, and the Holy Ghost.

Cisneros's young narrator remains too immature to voice invective against the Church or to yet recognize that organization's detrimental effect on her neighborhood. Rather than empower the residents of the *barrio*, it weakens them through the administration of large doses of guilt and the lack of encouragement to better their often desperate lives. Esperanza makes her own hope by remaining open to the myriad outside influences that fill her youthful imaginative mind with a longing for a life beyond the poverty and pain that surrounds her. Catholicism's colonization of the *barrio* will not trap the girl who provides her own spiritual nurturing through creativity and vision.

CRITICAL RECEPTION

Cisneros portrayed the problems of the *barrio* in an honest manner, leading critics to remark on her "dangerous" approach. They felt that her readers might see only a young woman who felt trapped by her culture and her poverty. Cisneros explained that the story needed that realism to counteract false images of the *barrio* presented through television and the media; the *barrio* was no Sesame Street. Some reviewers reacted negatively to Cisneros's mixing of poetic technique with fiction. One *Booklist* critic wrote that her "loose and deliberately simple style," mixing poetry with prose, at times "annoys" readers with its "cuteness." This critic disagreed with others who believed that her "apparent randomness" actually represents a skilled "exploration" of the book's themes (1984, 281). Carol Muske appreciates that loose style, writing that Cisneros's "forays" in and out of poetry and prose prove "utterly spontaneous," even "volatile, a rose-in-the-teeth passion refashioned to contemporary taste" (1995, 16).

Cisneros herself has told others that when words come easily to her, they translate into fiction. When she encounters more difficulty expressing herself, poetry generally results. Whatever the disagreement over her approach, Gary Soto found it appealing. He called Cisneros "foremost a storyteller" regardless of the form she chose (1988, 21). Native American Barbara Kingsolver explained that the choice to write fiction rather than poetry is a practical one in the United States, where poets do not receive much credit: "Elsewhere, poets have the cultural status of our rock stars and the income of our romance novelists. Here, a poet is something your mother probably didn't want you to grow up to be" (1991, 3–4). *The House on Mango Street* won the Before Columbus American Book Award and has become one of the most widely read Chicana works in the United States. One of its chapters, "The Monkey Garden," is widely anthologized for high school and college readers.

NOTE

Sandra Cisneros, *The House on Mango Street* (New York: Random House, 1987). All references are to this edition.

WORKS CITED

Aranda, Pilar E. Rodriguez. 1990. "On the Solitary Fate of Being Mexican, Female, Wicked and Thirty-three: An Interview with Sandra Cisneros." *The Americas Review* 19, no. 1 (Spring): 65.

Cisneros, Sandra. 1987. "Do You Know Me? I Wrote *The House on Mango Street*." *The Americas Review* 15, no. 1 (Spring): 71.

———. 1987. *My Wicked, Wicked Ways*. Berkeley, CA: Third Woman Press.

———. 1990. "Only Daughter." *Glamour* (November): 256.

———. 1991. *Woman Hollering Creek*. New York: Random House.

Kingsolver, Barbara. 1991. "Poetic Fiction With a Tex-Mex Tilt." Review of *Woman Hollering Creek and Other Stories*, by Sandra Cisneros. *Los Angeles Times Books Review* (April 28): 3–4.

Muske, Carol. 1995. "*The House on Mango Street* (book review)." *Parnassus: Poetry in Review* 20: 409–23.

"Review of the *House on Mango Street*, by Sandra Cisneros." *Booklist* 15 (October 1984): 281.

Soto, Gary. 1988. "Voices of Sadness and Science." Review of *My Wicked, Wicked Ways*, by Sandra Cisneros. *The Bloomsbury Review* (July-August): 21.

BIBLIOGRAPHY

Ganz, Robin. "Sandra Cisneros: Border Crossings and Beyond." *Melus* 19, no. 1 (Spring 1994): 19–29.

Mirriam-Goldberg, Caryn. *Sandra Cisneros: Latina Writer and Activist*. Springfield, NJ: Enslow Press, 1998.

Olivares, Julian. "Entering *The House on Mango Street*." In *Teaching American Ethnic Literatures*, ed. John R. Maitino and David R. Peck, 209–35. Albuquerque: University of New Mexico Press, 1996.

— **Virginia Brackett**

Paul Claudel [1868–1955]

Break of Noon

BIOGRAPHY

With the possible exception of the Anglo-Catholic T. S. Eliot, who also excelled in the writing of both poetry and drama, French poet and dramatist Paul Claudel is very likely the most influential and widely regarded Catholic man of letters of the twentieth century. Like Eliot and others of Claudel's contemporaries and near contemporaries—some outstanding examples are the American poet Ezra Pound, the Anglo-Irish poet William Butler Yeats, and the Italian poet and dramatist Gabriele D'Annunzio—Claudel was caught up in and shaped by the profound secularist and materialist movements of the latter half of the nineteenth century, with their appeal to scientism and social reform. For the most part, young artists of any ilk were compelled to turn either to the so-called religion of art or to revivifying the familiar bulwarks of traditional forms and values if they reacted negatively to the smug certainties of their epoch. That many did so is witnessed in the iconoclastic modernist movement in art, literature, and music that flourished at the beginning of the twentieth century. In Claudel's case, however, these normal processes of creative individuation were accelerated by a profound conversion experience in his young manhood that quite literally changed the course of his life and thus his art as well.

Paul-Louis-Charles-Marie Claudel was born in the rural community of Villeneuve-sur-Fère in the district of Aisne, France, on August 6, 1868, the fourth child and second son of Louis-Prosper, a tax collector who had been posted to Villeneuve in 1862, and his wife, Louise, the daughter of a local physician. Although the family would leave Villeneuve for good in 1872, and although by 1882 Louise and the three surviving children (their first child, Henri, died in infancy) would take up residence in Paris to enable daughter Camille to study sculpture, Louis-Prosper's subsequent postings would keep the young Paul exposed to the less cosmopolitan lifestyles of the provincial regions of France well into his teens. Nevertheless, as the scion of a relatively middle-class family in bourgeois France, young Paul was exposed as well to the most advanced thinking of the time, and as a result his upbringing was not particularly religious, although he did take his First communion in 1882. Due to the family's frequent moves, his early education was sporadic, and the family's isolation in rural areas led him to read voraciously on his own in the modern classics—Dante, Shakespeare, Racine, Voltaire, Goethe, Keats—and among more contemporary authors such as Balzac, Hugo, and Baudelaire. Drawn to the rationalities of naturalism and the audacities of the *symboliste* movement, with their concomitant hostility to organized religion in general and the Church in particular, by the time of his fourteenth year and his entrance into the Louis-le-Grand lyceum in Paris, Paul was a self-professed and, we must assume, youthfully self-styled atheist.

The year 1886 marked a life-altering turning point in the aspiring poet's life. First, he discovered *Une Saison en infer* by Rimbaud, a poet with whose putative religious conversion he would subsequently closely identify, and he began to write himself, completing a one-act play, *L'Endormie* (*The Sleeping One*), and a short poem, "For the Mass of Men, Love's Last Sacrifice." Then, on Christmas Day of that same year, after visiting Notre Dame, he opened a Bible a Protestant friend had given his sister Camille and felt that he had been called back to the Church. He would not formally return to the Church until Christmas 1890, when he took communion, again at Notre Dame; but from that Christmas of 1886 onward he was never without a Bible. Henceforth he would see in himself, as an individual, a person at odds with the increasing secularism and materialism of his age.

During this same period, Claudel the artist achieved a modest critical renown with three plays: *Fragment d'une drame* (1888), *Tête d'or* (1889), and *La Ville* (1889). Additionally, Claudel, the budding man of the world, enrolled at École des Sciences Politiques and switched from law to political science, with plans to enter the foreign service with an emphasis in oriental languages. His first consular postings, between 1893 and 1895, were to New York and Boston. In 1895 he was posted to China, where he would remain until 1899. He continued perfecting his dramatic skills, rewriting *Tête d'or* and continually reworking the material that would eventually become *La Jeune Fille Violaine* (1892–1900). He also began composing the prose poem *Connaissance de l'Est* (*The East I Know*, 1895–1905).

The year 1901 marked another *annus mirabilis* in Claudel's development as both an artist and staunchly devout and orthodox Catholic. The year began with Claudel entering a Benedictine seminary to pursue a vocation to the priesthood and ended with his beginning a four-year liaison with a married woman. As we shall see, the details of this year are germane to the text under consideration, *Partage de Midi* or *Break of Noon*.

In 1905, the year *Break of Noon* was first composed, Claudel returned to France from a second posting in China, and on March 15, 1906, just before returning to China for a third time, he married Reine Sainte-Marie-Perrin. They would subsequently have five children.

Despite keeping up a full career as poet, dramatist, and man of letters, Claudel continued to advance his career in the French foreign service. Following upon his third posting to China, which ended in 1909, Claudel was posted to Prague (1909–1911), Frankfurt and Hamburg (1912–1914), Rome (1915–1916), Rio de Janeiro (1917–1919), and Copenhagen (1919–1921). In 1921, he returned to his beloved Orient, this time as the French ambassador to Japan, a post he held until 1927. From 1927 to 1933, he was posted to Washington, D.C., for two tours of duty as the French ambassador to the United States. He ended his diplomatic career as the French ambassador to Belgium, retiring in 1935.

Claudel was invariably prolific as a poet, dramatist, and essayist. The year 1904 saw the publication of his *Art poétique*. He completed *Cinq Grandes Odes* in 1908; and between 1913 and 1916 he completed his translation of *The Oresteia of Aeschylus*, a project that had begun with his translating *Agamemnon* from 1892 to 1894. Among his major original dramas are *The Tidings Brought to Mary* (*L'Annonce faite à Marie*, 1911), itself a rewrite of *The Young Girl Violaine*; *The Hostage* (*L'Otage*, 1911); *The Satin Slipper* (*Le Soulier de satin*, 1925); and two revisions of *Break of Noon* (1948), the last of which is the text considered here.

Claudel devoted much of the latter part of his literary life, however, to his religious writings. *A Poet Before the Cross*, a book-length meditation on the Passion and death of Christ begun in Washington, D.C., in 1933, was completed during the final year of his diplomatic career in Brussels in 1935. Asked in 1928 to write a preface to the Book of the Apocalypse, he was so inspired that, in terms of sheer volume, virtually all of his subsequent literary efforts were devoted to biblical exegesis, including studies on The Song of Songs, Emmaus, and the Apocalypse. Paul Claudel died on February 23, 1955.

PLOT SUMMARY

As the three-act play *Break of Noon* opens, it is late morning. Félicien De Ciz, a French businessman, and his wife, Ysé, are chatting with their fellow passengers Almaric and Mesa as they relax on the forward deck of a liner on the Indian Ocean bound for the Far East from France. The married couple and their two children have only recently embarked at Aden, and De Ciz, like Almaric, is heading to China to seek new business opportunities. Mesa, an ex-seminarian, is returning to China, where he had already achieved success as a ranking customs official. Ysé teases Mesa about his gold rocking chair, and when De Ciz and Ysé leave, Almaric suggests to Mesa that Ysé has a romantic interest in him. Mesa protests that she is too vulgar and brazen a flirt. Later, when Ysé and Almaric, who, by coincidence, had been lovers ten years earlier, reminisce about old times, they recall their affair with a regretful wistfulness, although Ysé insists that she loves her husband, even if she does not particularly appreciate the life he has made for her. Mesa returns from a stroll to find Ysé alone and reluctantly confesses that he knows she is attracted to him. She compels him to vow that he will not fall in love with her, but only succeeds in arousing his ardor.

Act II takes place later, in Hong Kong, where Mesa and Ysé have arranged an assignation in an obscure corner of an old Chinese cemetery. The gold chair, prominent in Act I, has become the omega-like entrance to a nearby empty tomb, and an eclipse of the sun is about to occur. Mesa had arrived early enough to get cold feet and leaves shortly before Ysé and De Ciz arrive on the scene themselves. They are in a huff over his latest business deal, for which he must leave her for a time. Despite her pleas for him to take her with him, he goes off. Incapable of not keeping their rendezvous, Mesa now returns. Ysé tells him that De Ciz will be gone for a month, but Mesa should not come to see her during that time; yet she makes him swear before a cross that he finds her to be no less desirable even though, as a married woman, she is forbidden to him. Then she goes further: he must help her become free of De Ciz, even if it means her husband's death. Mesa has no sooner balked at that prospect than De Ciz unexpectedly returns. Apparently inspired by Ysé's pleas, Mesa convinces De Ciz to take on a desk job in a customs house that would require him to be away from Ysé for several years. Unaware that Mesa is preparing to cuckold him, De Ciz accepts the offer.

Later still, in Act III, Ysé and Almaric are hiding in a ruined Confucian temple in a Chinese port city where a bloody rebellion is raging. Almaric has once again become Ysé's lover, although she has her and Mesa's love child with her, a sickly infant who will shortly die. Resigned to their fate, Almaric has set a time bomb that will take their lives as well as the lives of the rampaging mob slaughtering any Europeans remaining in the city. As the sun begins to set, Mesa shows up at the door to tell Ysé that De Ciz is dead and so they now may marry, and he announces to Almaric that he has come to take Ysé and their child away. When Almaric laughs in his face, Mesa pulls a revolver, but in the ensuing struggle Mesa is knocked unconscious.

Almaric finds a safe passage marker on Mesa's person. Thrilled that they can escape with their lives, Almaric goes off with Ysé. Alone, Mesa revives. By chance, Ysé misses the boat that would have meant her salvation, and she returns to comfort the injured Mesa. Knowing that they are soon going to die together, she apologizes to him for the pain she has caused him, but she stresses that none of it was her fault. She has done only what she had to.

MAJOR THEMES

Paul Claudel's Catholicism dominates, either as an attitude that must be explicated or a point of interest that must be dismissed, much of the criticism in English regarding the poet's work and his vision. Surely the blame (much too harsh a word, perhaps, but nevertheless an adequate one) for much of that critical attention to Claudel's faith can be attributed to the poet himself. Claudel's well-chronicled and dramatic conversion from a young, modernist pagan, worthy of the most progressive thinking of the secular age that spawned him, to a devout supplicant to the religion of his traditions and ancestry both sets him curiously among and separates him from many of his modernist contemporaries, who also struggled with issues of spiritual belief in a materialist age. (As disparate as their respective journeys were, William Butler Yeats and T. S. Eliot come immediately to mind.) Additionally, a poet and dramatist among whose last major works is a lengthy meditation entitled *A Poet Before the Cross* cannot help but make clear his spiritual allegiances and religious values in no uncertain terms.

The most profitable way to explore Claudel as a Catholic writer, however, is not to argue that it was because he was self-professedly a devout Catholic that we have an interest in the Catholicity of his work and vision but rather to discover, if we can, why Claudel's work is widely regarded as particularly Catholic, for it surely is. The peculiarly Catholic drama of what many regard as Claudel's most realistic play, *Break of Noon*, is found in the fleshing forth of the internal moral and spiritual struggles that the central character, Mesa, must endure. As the economy of the action underscores, the moral strokes are broad but subtly applied in this somewhat autobiographical work. Claudel had contemplated entering the priesthood in early 1900, entering a Benedictine seminary at Solesmes in January and then at Ligugé in September of that same year before coming to the conclusion that he had no vocation. In October, again in the French foreign service and outward bound for China, he met a young, married woman on the ship and ended up carrying on a four-year relationship with her, until October 1904, during which time she abandoned her husband and children. In a 1951 interview, Claudel would confess that the love affair in *Break of Noon* was autobiographical (Fowlie 1960, introduction to *Break of Noon*, xvi–xvii), and so it is generally assumed that Mesa is Claudel's alter ego in the drama and Ysé the married woman with whom he carried on the adulterous affair.

Mesa, the disenchanted young man and ex-seminarian, falls in love with a married woman, arranges for her husband's absence from the scene, and has a child by her, fully aware at all times that he is flirting not with her as much as with his own eternal damnation. Nevertheless, the lovers' ending up together in the closing scene seems more like the turning of a roulette wheel or the partner-changing in a French farce than the result of some cosmic, erotic destiny, and we are left to imagine that if death were not so near for both of them, the lovers might yet again part company. This is the substance of the plot, which moves forward with emotional stops and starts that could make for faulty stage-craft except for the fact that they mimic the emotional and spiritual confusions of the two lovers, primarily Mesa. Furthermore, lest the drama devolve into mere melodrama, Claudel has both De Ciz and Almaric provide credible foils to Mesa's highly refined but largely misplaced and surely misdirected spiritual sensibilities. The adventurous De Ciz is incapable of perceiving any action as right or wrong, good or evil; Almaric, an atheist, recognizes wrongdoing only enough to revel in it. Mesa confesses to a belief in God as the only significant Other and so is the most culpable because he believes in sin and then knowingly commits it.

For Claudel, consciousness of God makes ordinary life, even at the extremes of sinfulness and self-gratification, ultimately impossible; but he is a modernist and thus humanist enough to recognize and acknowledge that his characters, like all of us, are nevertheless condemned to having only those ordinary lives to lead. Such a thought may be disheartening to anyone without a religious faith as profound as Claudel's Catholicism, but it is the very essence of submission and suffering to anyone who does have such a faith. The lovers, like all of us, are condemned not by their tragedy but by their mortality. It is their innocence not to recognize as much and Claudel's religious genius that he does. Death, for Claudel, *is* the human condition, even in the throes of breathtaking physical passion. In the moral universe of *Break of Noon*, the necessity of choice is a certainty, death is a certainty, and our need to work out our spiritual redemption through our interrelationships with others is a certainty; but we reside otherwise, each of us, in a mortal darkness in which only faith in the comfort of the Resurrection can ultimately sustain the individual soul.

It is from these conflicts, more dramatized than openly expressed, that Claudel has taken the timeless formula wherein the beloved is the dramatic stand-in for the spiritual desideratum and translated it through the confusion of sexual allegiances into the very emblem of the spiritual chaos that keynotes the modern epoch. The male characters perform their otherwise tragic roles with a pathetic obliviousness to the broader implications of their actions, more like marionettes than individuals in a moral universe. Recognizing her deleterious effect on the male characters, only Ysé, the eternal female who is for the males the channel for but not the embodiment of moral evil, nevertheless tries unsuccessfully to exercise a moral power for the better. It is Ysé, for example, who makes Mesa swear that he will not love her in the first act, who begs De Ciz to take her with him in the second, and who has left Mesa for his own good in the third. Clearly, she is at the very least trying to do the right thing, but she knows that there is no way out once the trap of her and Mesa's physical desire for each other has closed upon them. Although doubtful that there is a God, Ysé believes more in the real presence and power of the spiritual than Mesa does. Despite, or because of, its bald-faced flatness, her announcement to Mesa in the first act—"Mesa, I am Ysé" (30)—resonates through the drama. What in the English has something of the palindrome about it ("Madam, I'm Adam") in its skewed syntax proves revealing: by intervening between the lovers, the self-assertive "I am" renders true union with another impossible. We are, each of us, who we are; what we are to each other is an entirely different matter; what we are to God is a mystery that we must endure.

Mesa's fatal flaw, however, is his inability to share either guilt or salvation with others as a result of his belief in, yet failed relationship with, God. By unwittingly acting as if he is the only person with a spiritual relationship with God, he cuts himself off from the spiritual growth he could have realized through Ysé. The lesson Mesa must learn, Ysé tells him, is that "others, for better or for worse, exist, and not just you alone" (109). She herself, she explains, is that embodiment of "otherness," but this too is finally only "self" if not expressed with reference to God. Thus, Claudel is able to use the sinfulness of the lovers' relationship and their consciousness of it not to moralize but to make it clear that they have left God, the ultimate Other, out of the necessary equation in which true being-in-oneness resides. Early in the play, Ysé had reminded Mesa of how two were made from one in Adam and Eve, and she tells him bluntly that she is his soul. For Mesa to grow from this relationship, however, requires a commitment that he is not prepared to make, a commitment of his soul as well as his body to Ysé's soul as well as her body. The implication again is clear: if the lovers cared for each other soul to soul as much as they do body to body, then God would enter the picture. Otherwise, they become lost in a tawdry eroticism until it is too late.

The passage of the day from midmorning to midnight, suggested in the title *Break of Noon*, highlights the essential tragedy of the human condition lived without reference to God. The original French, *Partage de Midi*, is even more telling, however. Wallace Fowlie, who translated the drama into English, informs us that *partage* is a geological term in French denoting the separation of rainwater to each side as it runs off a hill; in other words, a watershed (*Break of Noon*, xi–xiii). So, then, on the one side of the watershed in *Break of Noon*, which occurs at the end of the first act, is light and life and youthful hopefulness; after that demarcation, it is, punning aside, all downhill from there into darkness, night, despair, and death. By the play's end, only Mesa's raised hand is visible, and the audience is left in the dark, so to speak, regarding the significance of that gesture.

For Claudel, like his contemporary Joseph Conrad, we live in the flicker—immortal souls constrained by our mortality to exist in this shadow world of ours, conscious of Paradise, of a living God, but capable in the long run, it often seems, only of embracing each other at best and even then often to our own despair. In his work *Poetic Art*, Claudel writes:

> At Notre Dame, more than anywhere else, in the very midst of the filth of Paris, like Jeremiah, in his cistern engulfed under deep waters, you will have a taste of Death; how reassuring, if you raise your head, to see, instead of the sun, these enduring large streaked roses, which seem to absorb, to suspend, trophy-like—the better to exclude it—the light which might otherwise gain access. (1969, 142)

In *Break of Noon*, Claudel is most Catholic in his holding up for our examination those who, like Mesa, can see or at least imagine the light but who then deny it.

CRITICAL RECEPTION

In his important study, *Claudel: Beauty and Grace*, Angelo Caranfa makes it quite clear that, in his attempt to locate Claudel as central in modern French aesthetics, it nevertheless "is not the intent of [his] work to yield to a Catholic approach to literary criticism and aesthetics" (1989, 9). That said, Caranfa's treatment of *Break of Noon* is rife with themes, imagery, and metaphorical allusions drawn from the totems, icons, and rituals of the Roman Catholic experience. Mesa's and Ysé's death is "sacramental" and "lies in their obedience to God's law, the Incarnate Word" (87); they are "no longer exiled souls . . . because now their love is submerged into the baptismal water of Christ's Body and Blood" (88); their lives "can only be understood in terms of . . . the mystery of the Incarnation, Death, and Resurrection of Christ" (88). It is not my intention here to gainsay Caranfa's critical and interpretive conclusions but to demonstrate how Catholicism seeps into them like a staining agent that can be neither neutralized nor diluted.

Not everyone reads *Break of Noon* in such ostensibly religious—and Catholic—terms. Wallace Fowlie considers the play to be "about the meaning of love, and especially about the role of a woman in the experience of love" (*Break of Noon*, xiv). Nevertheless, he concedes that, because "Catholicism is so much a part of the genius of Claudel," we are required to see "God as the invisible Actor, the Impresario who can and does use human passion . . . for the realization of His own goal" (xix). Perhaps understandably, he does not bother to elucidate that goal.

In Richard Berchan's *The Inner Stage: An Essay on the Conflict of Vocations in the Early Works of Paul Claudel*, which focuses on the period of Claudel's conversion and its consolidation into his poetry, *Break of Noon* is seen as representing a regression from the drive toward renunciation that had informed the poet's postconversion vision thus far. Berchan writes, "If Claudel's conversion of 1886 spiritualized the love-quest of *L'Endormie* [a pastoral farce composed in 1893], opening the door to renunciation, *Partage de Midi* dramatizes a regression to the love-quest after the failure of his attempt at total renunciation" (1966, 101). As such, in this schema, the lovers' passion "condemns them to death . . . in order to achieve a spiritual union beyond death" (102)—erotic, in the best sense of that word, but hardly religious and certainly not Catholic.

We may well ask how the reading of the same text can be so much at odds in terms of an issue as essentially black and white as its moral and spiritual foundations. While it is, of course, not unusual for two critics to arrive at vastly different readings of the same text, the inescapable irony here is that Caranfa is trying to avoid reading Claudel in terms of his Catholicism alone, while Berchan is doing just that. Strange, then, that the first comes up with a very Catholic reading, and the second does not, of the same action in the same text—unless, of course, it is some genuine indication of the quicksand that Claudel's Catholicism can easily become. For example, Adrianna M. Paliyenko, in her study *Mis-Reading the Creative Impulse: The Poetic Subject in Rimbaud and Claudel, Restaged*, does not deny the weight of coincidence in the arguments supporting Claudel's identifying Rimbaud as a shaping force in his spiritual life: "The eighteen-year-old Claudel, who first read Rimbaud in June 1886, had abandoned the Catholic faith of his childhood and accepted the prevalent materialist world view. Later that same year, on Christmas Eve, Claudel had a mystical conversion experience" (1997, 2). Nevertheless, because Claudel's "mis-reading Rimbaud as a Christian poet" did not take place in the younger poet's writings until much later, from 1895 to 1910, Paliyenko attributes the "mis-reading" to Claudel's manipulating his spiritual indebtedness to Rimbaud in order to mask what was, in fact, an alteration in Claudel's view of the role and nature of the poet and of poetry: "Claudel's transformation of Rimbaud works out his own struggle with identity, notably priest versus poet" (2). For our present purposes, this averred dichotomy between the poet and the work as a moral or spiritual tool, on the one hand, and a purely aesthetic experience, on the other, accounts for the possibility that the exemplary ways in which Claudel can conceal the homiletic within the realistic and symbolic, as he does masterfully in *Break of Noon*, is as liable to confuse the reader as it did, if Paliyenko is correct, the poet himself. At the very least, it can contribute to a blending of purposes.

Harold A. Waters had already observed as much in his study, entitled simply *Paul Claudel*, wherein *Break of Noon* is both good drama (in the pathos of its flirtatious and adulterous eroticism "the play can well provide an excruciating vicarious experience for the reader-spectator" [1970, 80]) and psycho-spiritual autobiography. As Waters puts it, "Before *Partage*, Claudel was concerned with the paradox of sin's existence in a universe created by love; he saw it serving a mysterious purpose. The play and the experience behind it [Claudel's adulterous love affair of 1900–1904 following hard upon his failed endeavors as a seminarian] blended the ideas of earthly love and sin's necessity. . . [whereby] carnal love . . . excludes love toward God" (79–80). Like any artist, in other words, Claudel is quite capable of incorporating the wide varieties of personal experience, his métier, into his work, from which we readers can then derive satisfaction and direction at any number of levels, including the spiritual and the moral. For Claudel, the earthly experience is a tragedy for the soul, since it is cut off from God; the Christian solution, that salvation and redemption are found in and through Christ, not only forms the foundation of his world view but intensifies the tragedy that the earthly experience is without God. Claudel the artist, however, need not pronounce this, only demonstrate it. If this world is indeed, in the Catholic tradition, a vale of tears, then either one picks up his cross and follows Christ, or one just picks up his cross. Either way, he suffers, because life here is suffering. For a poet like Claudel, consequently, whose point of view is so staunchly and single-mindedly Catholic, the representation of the suffering, its causes in the person and in human nature, is all that is necessary to make the point.

Marie-Thérèse Killiam, in *The Art Criticism of Paul Claudel*, comes to a similar conclusion in summarizing Claudel's aesthetic: "The spiritual significance of a work of art depends on its forceful appeal to the imagination. . . . For Claudel, the quest for the self which art brings about, can only mean the quest for the soul. . . . A work of art . . . exists only in relation to its viewers, and it exerts a force of appeal on all of them" (1990, 339–40). As such, she continues, "Whether or not we accept Claudel's religious view point [*sic*], whether we accept his voyage into art as a voyage to the soul or to the unconscious, Claudel . . . shows that the quest is more important than the discovery itself, and that the meaning of art lies within all of us" (341).

The same dual purposiveness, wherein Claudel the purely secular man of letters—the aesthete, as it were—and Claudel the Catholic poet manage to cultivate the same thematic agenda, pleasing, as it were, both the groundlings and the gallery without sacrificing either his scruples or his principles, can be found in Claudel's attention to oriental settings. This attention derived originally from his time spent in the Orient as a youthful official in the French foreign service. Whether or not the oriental setting for *Break of Noon* is inspired by biography, exotica, or more profound thematic concerns based in Claudel's Catholicism, with its emphasis upon the universality of human experience, recent criticism of his use of the oriental garden reinforces the notion that Claudel may be far more a metaphysical poet and dramatist, working his ostensibly secular material within the confines of a traditional and orthodox Catholic world view, than any mere modernist innovator and experimentalist. We can see in Nina S. Hellerstein's analysis of Claudel's poetic technique, in her article "The Aesthetics of the Oriental Garden in Claudel's *Connaissance de L'Est*," an emphasis on the human place in the cosmic landscape, one that can be regarded as Catholic as much as, in keeping with Hellerstein's purposes, it finds its immediate roots in oriental traditions. According to Hellerstein, the Chinese view of the universe entails "a dynamic interaction of vital energies . . . reflected in parallel forms in their garden design, landscape painting and calligraphy" (1999, 44). Claudel was an avid student of these philosophical traditions, and Hellerstein maintains that this view finds further parallels in Claudel's own aesthetic: "The poet, like a magician, takes possession of 'des fragments de monde' [the fragments of the world] and moves them around within his mind; this mental participation in nature's structures echoes the activity of the artist . . . [who] does not passively 'copy' nature . . . but utilizes his profound understanding of its laws to 'imitate' its life-producing processes" (51–52). Here again, if we may borrow a page from Paliyenko, we encounter the priest as much as the poet in Claudel, the individual devoted to cultivating an aesthetic that is as realistic as it is moral and as moral as it is spiritual. This is a Catholic aesthetic, one that is in the world but not of it. For Hellerstein, Claudel's interest in the aesthetic of the oriental garden was more than purely technical. Rather, within the profundities of his minimalist approach is all the reductive energy of his Christian world view. Hellerstein writes, "[Claudel] contrasts the Oriental understanding of the interdependence of human and natural forces with the [western] quantitative attitude towards nature, based on the search for human domination and possession" (44).

This, in a microcosm, is the conflict among the four characters who play out their tragic roles in *Break of Noon*. It is intriguing, therefore, that the climax comes not in an oriental garden but in a Chinese cemetery, where the natural order and orderliness dominate the unruly—and deadly—games for possession and domination that Mesa, De Ciz, and Almaric play out around the attractive Ysé. Alyssa Gilbert summarizes this state of affairs quite succinctly in the article "*L'Age Mûr* of Camille Claudel and *La Jeune Fille Violaine* of Paul Claudel: Destruction and Fulfillment," in which she contrasts Claudel's early drama *La Jeune Fille Violaine* with his sister Camille's sculpture *L'Age Mûr*. In writing the play, Gilbert argues, "Claudel hoped for a two-fold accomplishment: a personal need to teach and reveal his interpretation of Christianity, and to help Camille," who gradually had become more and more caught up in a web of incipient paranoia, alcoholism, and self-destructive love affairs (1996, 28). In response to his sister's path toward disintegration, Claudel proposed the path of submission and suffering, the path upon which Mesa and Ysé ultimately find themselves as *Break of Noon* concludes. According to Gilbert,

> The two main components of Claudel's experience of Christianity were a complete submission of "self" to God and a fundamental acceptance of suffering. If both of these ways of being are adopted, then not only is eternal salvation possible, but a tentative solution for the problem of earthly existence: believers will be able to realize profound spiritual fulfillment and will be therefore willing to interact with each other peacefully. (28)

This is something the male characters in *Break of Noon* in particular are incapable of doing, torn as they are between self-gratification and ego dominance. The violence in the last scene between Almaric and Mesa merely mimics the violence going on all about them in the Chinese port city, which in turn mimics the violence of a fallen and unredeemed physical universe from which the way of the Cross—submission and suffering—redeems humankind. It is, to allude to the poet T. S. Eliot, himself alluding to Saint Paul, to be saved from fire by fire.

NOTE

Paul Claudel, *Break of Noon*, trans. and intro. Wallace Fowlie (Chicago: Henry Regnery, 1960). All references are to this edition.

WORKS CITED

Berchan, Richard. 1966. *The Inner Stage: An Essay on the Conflict of Vocations in the Early Works of Paul Claudel*. East Lansing: Michigan State University Press.

Caranfa, Angelo. 1989. *Claudel: Beauty and Grace*. Lewisburg, PA: Bucknell University Press.

Claudel, Paul. 1958. *A Poet Before the Cross*, trans. Wallace Fowlie. Chicago: Henry Regnery.

———. 1969. *Poetic Art*, trans. Renée Spodheim. 1948. Reprint, Port Washington, NY: Kennikat Press.

Gilbert, Alyssa. 1996. "*L'Age Mûr* of Camille Claudel and *La Jeune Fille Violaine* of Paul Claudel: Destruction and Fulfillment." *Claudel Studies* 23, no. 2: 23–37.

Hellerstein, Nina S. 1999. "The Aesthetics of the Oriental Garden in Claudel's *Connaissance de L'Est*." *Claudel Studies* 26, no. 1–2: 43–54.

Killiam, Marie-Thérèse. 1990. *The Art Criticism of Paul Claudel*, vol. II. American University Studies XX: Fine Arts. New York: Peter Lang.

Paliyenko, Adrianna M. 1997. *Mis-Reading the Creative Impulse: The Poetic Subject in Rimbaud and Claudel, Restaged*. Carbondale: Southern Illinois University Press.

Waters, Harold A. 1970. *Paul Claudel*. New York: Twayne.

BIBLIOGRAPHY

Murphy, Russell Elliott. 1996. "*Break of Noon* [Paul Claudel]." In *Masterplots*, ed. Frank N. Magill, revised 2nd ed., 775–78. Los Angeles: Salem Press.

— **Russell Elliott Murphy**

Elizabeth Cullinan [1933–]

House of Gold

BIOGRAPHY

The fiction of Elizabeth Cullinan flows from her life. Born in 1933 to an Irish American family in Manhattan, Cullinan grew up in an environment that paralleled in some ways the milieu of her novel, *House of Gold*. Her father, Cornelius, studied for the priesthood and then for law, worked as an insurance investigator, and had a fondness for the ponies, as does Edwin Carroll, the perennially inadequate Devlin in-law of *House of Gold*. Her mother, Irene O'Conner Cullinan, was devoted to her own mother, and Irene lived for a time with her husband and three daughters in her mother's house. Growing up in their grandmother's house, Elizabeth Cullinan and her two older sisters were reared to be obedient children who, like Winnie and Julie in the novel, gave up or "cramped" some pleasures of childhood for the well-being of the crowded household.

Cullinan attended local parochial schools and graduated in 1954 from Marymount Manhattan College. In 1955 she went to work at the *New Yorker*, first as a typist and then as secretary to William Maxwell. This was an experience equivalent to a writing internship, for at *The New Yorker* she learned her craft: precise detail, controlled structure, emphasis on relationships, cool irony. In 1960, to the consternation of her family, she moved to Dublin, Ireland, for three years (excluding a trip back to the United States for a few months after the first year). There she achieved the spatial and psychological distance needed to begin *House of Gold*, which was copyrighted in 1969 and received a Mifflin Literary Fellowship Award in 1970. In 1971, ten stories from *The New Yorker* were collected as *The Time of Adam*, and another short-story collection, *Yellow Roses*, came out in 1977. In 1982, she published a second novel, *A Change of Scene*, a first-person narrative about a twenty-six-year-old Irish American woman's three-year stay in Dublin in the early 1960s. Cullinan taught for a semester at the Writers' Workshop at the University of Iowa in 1977, one year at the University of Massachusetts, and then at Fordham University from 1979 to 1998. She continues to write.

PLOT SUMMARY

Six remaining of the nine adult Devlin children congregate in the late 1950s for a death watch at the house of their widowed, "saintly" Irish Catholic mother. The now unconscious octogenarian matriarch had raised her children with a pious religiosity that provided them with order and security but that also squelched their individuality and left them dependent and guilt-ridden.

The external plot is minimal. Dr. Hyland, a socially prominent old family friend, has cared for Mrs. Devlin gratuitously for many years. Now that she is on her deathbed, the children are unable to contact him and agonize about whether to summon a different doctor to ease her passing and ultimately to fulfill a legal requirement for a signed death certificate. The significant action is internal. In this slow-moving, highly detailed story, the author enters into the consciousness of twelve of the major characters, revealing their multiple perspectives, remembrances, meditations, and unresolved emotions about the dying woman.

To the delight of their pious mother, two of her boys became Jesuit priests; two of the girls became nuns. Father Vin, the Jesuit missionary, has died, as have Francis, the oldest, and Michael, a happy-go-lucky high school dropout who lived aimlessly for six years after his "fiancée" died from an abortion. In this hierarchal household in which religious vocation, sex, and age determine seniority, Father Phil dutifully attempts leadership while continually anticipating the pain of making mistakes. Mother Mary James and Mother Helen Marie responded in prepubescence to calls from God to seclude themselves in a convent—but not from such pharmaceutical marvels as the drug librium. Elizabeth, the devoted youngest daughter, is married to Edwin, an ex-seminarian who, kept on the periphery of Devlin family life, creates his own diversions at the racetrack. Elizabeth, Edwin, and their two girls, Julie and Winnie, until recently had lived for years on the upper floor of Mrs. Devlin's house, an "incarceration" that has fueled in particular the resentment of twenty-year-old Winnie. Tom, the favored youngest son, is a military man who arrives with his college-educated wife, Claire, and two less-indoctrinated preteen boys, Frank and Vinnie. The unmarried, irresponsible, dour, and socially inept Justin still lives at the house with his mother in a symbiotic relationship of bickering. Finally, Sister Sebastian, a selfless nursing nun from Spain, attends to Mrs. Devlin and squints at the peculiar behavior of the Devlin family.

"'Never let them [your children] see your doubts,' was what Mrs. Devlin had always said. 'Never let them know your feelings'" (108). Significantly, in this omniscient narration, Mrs. Devlin is the only main character whose unmediated consciousness is not displayed. Her words and actions are rendered through flashbacks embedded in the consciousness of other characters. True, Mrs. Devlin's interpretation of her world is reflected through a biographical sketch she penned, "The Story of a Mother," but this is a public, sanitized interpretation modeled on second-rate, moralistic Catholic fiction; it is a manipulated narrative presentation of self that is meant as much to conceal as to reveal. Accordingly, she celebrates the love of God and love of family that single out the Devlins from the general population, but she edits out, for instance, the abortion of her future daughter-in-law, and she fails to mention the wife of Francis, who lived in her house for a number of years. "The Story of a Mother" is not an expression of her thoughts but of her desires. What Mrs. Devlin really felt and thought—to what degree she is a manipulator of her children or a victim of her own Irish family upbringing—can only be conjectured.

The author's own perspective is channeled through two characters. Winnie, the reader of Russian novels, is a contemporaneous self-portrait. Although molded in the Devlin tradition of self-abnegation and deference, she strives for individuality and musters a defiant courage at the end of the novel that suggests that the Devlin family's unquestioning reverence for authority is coming to an end.

Tom's wife Claire ("clarity"—also the name of Cullinan's sister) is an outsider who can provide a critique of the Devlin household from a more mature and objective viewpoint. Claire observes that Mrs. Devlin's "house of gold" actually is depressing, a "poor plain house . . . half-crooked on the little patch of ground. And the awful reddish-brown shingling" (107). College-educated Claire (magna cum laude) recognizes that "The Story of a Mother" is a destructive fairy tale whose effect if not purpose is to control the Devlin children emotionally, psychologically, and spiritually. She is repulsed by the manipulative child-rearing philosophy of Mrs. Devlin, and vows that her own two sons will not be transformed into docile, guilt-ridden, anxious-to-please worshipers of both God and mother.

The ending of the novel is inconclusive, particularly for the children of Mrs. Devlin. There are indications that the third generation of Devlins, although scarred by the oppressive upbringing of their parents, may find the courage and resources to find a healthy balance between family, faith, and individuality.

MAJOR THEMES

The focus of *House of Gold* is *aggiornamento*. It is the Italian word Pope John XXIII used as a rationale for the Second Vatican Council: an updating, reinvigoration of the Church to embrace and sanctify the contemporary world. When asked to clarify his meaning, the pope dramatically opened a window to let in the fresh air. Although Cullinan is appropriately labeled a "Catholic" writer, *House of Gold* is a novel primarily about a family, not a Church; social relationships, not theological principles, guide her writing. But in family as in religion, a closed atmosphere can be stifling. On these smothering days in the late 1950s in July, as Mrs. Devlin is puffing out her life, opening windows is not permitted.

The title *House of Gold* refers first of all to the family residence, adorned in the color befitting Mrs. Devlin's fiftieth wedding anniversary. Particularly for those not raised within its walls, Mrs. Devlin's house of gold is stifling and oppressive; two living room windows are stuck permanently closed, and stagnation is further exacerbated by house rules governing ventilation: "the rule that said the porch windows must be shut from mid-morning to mid-afternoon, all summer" (85).

"House of gold" refers not simply to the building but also to the magic "kingdom" of Mrs. Devlin as depicted in "The Story of a Mother," her autobiographical fairy tale that conflates motherhood and a simplistic religion of duty, obedience, and certain reward. Within the walls and within the myth of the house of gold, Mrs. Devlin is venerated. Dying within her shrine bedecked with garish religious kitsch, Mrs. Devlin's sainthood is parodied when Tom's two boys, Frank and Vinnie, request their grandmother's spectacles and a lock of hair as relics. Their mother, Claire, the skeptic outsider with a distancing sense of irony, associates

Mrs. Devlin's "solid gold-leaf tea and coffee service" with the sacred altar vessels of the Catholic Mass and applies to Mrs. Devlin the Litany of Loreto, the ancient formulaic prayer in which Mary is invoked by many appellations, including "Mystical Rose," "Tower of David," "Tower of Ivory," and "House of Gold."

The Litany of Loreto is parodied in a number of ways, as ritual degenerates into formulae or hypnotic mantras; stock phrases initiate unthinking patterns, and ironically, communication with God is an evasion of human interaction. Early in the story, Father Phil's inability to establish meaningful communication with his mother causes him to fall back on the formula (27); in order not to waste time, Elizabeth "turns off" the ramblings of her sister, Mother Mary James, by retreating into repetitive ejaculatory prayer, "Jesus, Mary, and Joseph, I place my trust in Thee" (193). And at the novel's end, Justin joins in the singsong monotone of the rosary because it is better than talking, a way to fill up the hours that does not demand human engagement. The train tracks behind the Devlin house symbolize the predetermined discourse, with the train wheels producing a "monotonous rhythm: Da-da, da-dum, Da-da, da-dum," as Julie mentally chants the names: "Union Pacific. Jersey Central. Rock Island. Seabord–Through the Heart of the South. Great Northwestern. Cotton Belt–Blue Streak. Nickel Plate Road. Nickel Plate Road. Nickel Plate Road" (103), a secular Litany of Loreto that serves a similar function: the passing of the train interrupts conversation, takes away the pressure to communicate. Edwin's marginalization within the Devlin family leads him to escape into his own version of the Loreto litany based on horse racing: "*Sudden Storm. Mirage. Bold Lady*" (197). Union Pacific, pray for us. Heart of the South, pray for us. Bold Lady, pray for us. House of Gold, pray for us.

The focus on religion in the novel is not so much deeply theological as it is historical and sociological; Catholicism, the house of gold, is the preconciliar Church of the late 1950s in America. Mrs. Devlin regulates her life by the "clear cut insights of catechism" (216) and equates salvation with economic investments: vocations to religious life and devotional acts guarantee future spiritual returns. Eternal certainties, paradoxically, are predicated on mystery and authority. Never let them know your feelings or your doubts, she always said. "My order is God's order" (24), she tells Tom. Infallibility is another of her traits: Edwin, in questioning Mrs. Devlin's actions, "overstepped the mark, blamed the one none of them had ever blamed before—she'd always let them or made them blame each other" (255). Order and control, clarity and mystification, exist within a structure of intense emotional and high aspirations. Religion is the catalyst that provides the fairy tale with credibility and emotional and psychological force.

Religion is also implicated in the military virtues that Mrs. Devlin uses to structure her life: "security, discipline, loyalty and good fellowship, pomp and ceremony, and exclusiveness" (138). This exclusivity ties in with Catholicism at midcentury. The Devlins are insular, self-contained, "friendly" but not open to taking in others, as Edwin is constantly reminded; he recognizes that his mother-in-law has "managed to cut her family off from so much of what regulated the lives of other people" (256). The Devlins view Catholicism not as an engagement with the world but as an evasion of it. There is no vocation, no "calling," outside of religious life. Even in the third generation, Frankie and Vinnie, as well as Julie and Winnie, must squirm at the possibility that to be holy, to be a worthy Devlin, they too must enter religious life.

In *American Catholic Crossroads*, Walter J. Ong contrasts the insularity of "Christendom" with the open-endedness of "Catholicity." Christendom identifies itself defensively in terms of what is outside its walls. By contrast, Catholicity, Ong contends, does not wall itself in against the secular and non-Catholic world but seeks redemption through and with the world. According to Ong, the Greek-originating word "Catholic" (*katholikos*) means not "universal" (as does the Latin term "*universalis*") but "through-the-whole" (1981, 63–64). Again, the Devlin family and their religion are sealed off, just like the windows in the Devlin house. They exclude the foreigners and practice a vertical, "trampoline" religion in which one bounces to heaven without working "through" the horizontal, material and social dimensions, evading rather than interpenetrating the world. Even Father Vin's missionary activity, which seems to imply a destruction of boundaries, is in reality only a widening or an outgrowth of the aspiration to extend Christendom—to bring others within our walls, to make them like us.

What Claire preaches and Winnie begins to learn is window opening. According to Claire, the monumentality of Mrs. Devlin is her legend or fairy tale intended to provide safety and happiness, but in fact "outside of it [the legend] the two things didn't go together or stay together, anyway. Happiness meant risk, continual risk" (293). In other words, the Devlin practice of religion (conformity, duty, guilt, forced and compulsive self-denial, exclusivity) is enslaving rather than liberating, for it de-emphasizes individuality, conscience, and spiritual growth. Taking risks means making choices. It is in making choices that we achieve identity and affirm or deny God.

No character in *House of Gold* embodies this emancipatory vision of religion, but Sister Sebastian, the nurse, signals the direction that might be taken. Another outsider, she comes closest to demonstrating how religion can be a liberating rather than a stifling force. Practical and self-giving, Sister Sebastian is sensitive to the ironies of the Devlin household, but she evades the traps of judgment and guilt. Unlike the Devlins, who are purebred bloodhounds in tracking down "fault," Sister Sebastian, Justin notices, "didn't blame him for trying to get away" (327) from his mother's wake. In direct opposition to the Devlin family, in which religious vocation stems from encouragement bordering on coercion, Sister Sebastian has broken from her family, from their "rigid order, their cold discipline" (58), in order to find freedom in her religious order. "'I am not a prisoner'" (327), she tells Justin. Her self-sacrifice is freely chosen and liberating.

This is why Justin cannot be taken as a source of hope, as some have contended. Justin has greater freedom than his siblings in that he alone has cast off the fairy tale that has enslaved them, but he has no structure or purpose in which to exercise that freedom other than opposition or dissent. *House of Gold* is a critique of Catholicism but not a denunciation. The practice of religion can be authoritarian, repressive, rule-dominated, otherworldly, mechanistic, and spiritually enslaving, but religion can also inspire, enable high aspirations, provide meaning and structure, and satisfy the imagination, senses, and emotions through liturgy. Cullinan suggests not the need to forsake the Church but to transform or reconceptualize it. At the end of the novel, it remains a possibility that Sister Sebastian's gentle influence will help Justin find something meaningful by which to organize his life. More likely, he will wind up like Bob in Cullinan's short story "The Black Diamond" (1983–84), the uncle living in "absolute loneliness" on the top floor of his dead mother's house, a portrait of "monumental disgust": "too savvy and too honest to enter into the vainglorious moods of his mother's house, too timid to move beyond it, and too much at a loss there to refuse the part of decent malcontent in which he had been cast" (39).

CRITICAL RECEPTION

In the thirty-three years since its publication, *House of Gold* has prompted only a handful of extended critical commentaries, most of them appreciative. Early reviewers applauded Cullinan's tightly controlled structure, attention to meticulous detail, and ability to delineate character through slight gesture or seemingly mundane conversation; her literary forebears were considered to be Chekhov, Joyce, and Henry James. Her most commonly cited "failing" was more of a quibble: the reviewers' desire for her to expand her subject matter and themes to represent a more varied and inclusive world picture. The repressive Irish Catholic family, the domineering matriarch, the directionless uncle, the ineffective priest, the loyal but often embarrassed daughter trying to assert independence without severing family ties—these are recurring motifs that find expression in *House of Gold.*

Among the more celebratory evaluations is that of Charles Fanning: "Elizabeth Cullinan is one of the most accomplished of contemporary American writers," and *House of Gold* is "contemporary Irish-American fiction at its best" because of "its combination of precise craftsmanship and authenticity to felt experience" (1990, 334, 335). Appropriately, Fanning finds that "[h]er clear renderings of the complexity and fragility of relationships bring the fresh air of considered moral perspective of Irish-American life" (335).

On the other hand, while grouping Cullinan with Tom McHale, Jimmy Breslin, and Pete Hamill, critic Amy M. Lilly (2001), in *Dictionary of Literary Biography*, slights *House of Gold* in favor of the short stories. But Lilly provides the most complete biographical record of an author whose fiction is veiled autobiography, tracing patterns and themes found in *House of Gold* through Cullinan's short stories. Drawing upon interviews with Cullinan, Lilly supplements her analysis with insightful commentary by the author on her life and work. Similarly, in her article "Bequeathing Tokens: Elizabeth Cullinan's Irish-American Families," Eileen Kennedy (1981) extends the development of characters and themes from *House of Gold* into the stories "The Reunion," "Voices of the Dead," "An Accident," "A Foregone Conclusion," and "The Ablutions."

In "Wake Homes: Four Modern Novels of the Irish-American Family," Catherine Ward compares Cullinan's *House of Gold* to novels by Mary Doyle Curran, Maureen Howard, and Mary Gordon—all of which center on the literal or symbolic gathering of an Irish American family at a wake. Ward finds *House of Gold* to be "a masterfully crafted portrait of a dysfunctional Irish-American family" (1991, 85), less bitter than Howard's *Bridgeport Bus*, more realistic than Curran's *The Parish and the Hill*, but less analytic than Gordon's *The Other Side*. Avoiding both romanticized and caustic depictions of Irish American family life, Cullinan recognizes both the necessity and dangers of family ties.

Charles Fanning's book *The Irish Voice in America* (1990) and his article "Elizabeth Cullinan's *House of Gold*: Culmination of an Irish-American Dream"

(1980) provide useful social and literary background for the matriarch motif in Irish American literature and an analysis of how it functions in *House of Gold*. Fanning presents a detailed analysis of Mrs. Devlin's florid "The Story of a Mother" and concludes that Justin and Mrs. Devlin are "mirror images of the same paradox: he is an outsider in his own house, and she is an outsider who founded a home without ever finding one" (1980, 46).

In her perceptive analysis, "Elizabeth Cullinan: Yellow and Gold," Maureen Murphy identifies a central concern of Cullinan's novel: "It is Winnie Carroll's understanding that people have the right to be themselves, to their own identity, that is at the heart of *House of Gold*, for it urges the claims of the individual over the twin bonds of faith and family in Irish-American life" (1979, 147–48). It is important to understand, though, that individuality is in dialectical rather than oppositional relationship with family and faith. Perhaps rather than individuality, which suggests free-floating independence, what Winnie is seeking is personhood, personal identity within communities that help to define and nurture that identity.

Although only a few pages of Anita Gandolfo's *Testing the Faith: The New Catholic Fiction in America* are concerned directly with Cullinan, it is indispensable for providing literary parallels and background since midcentury on the theological, social, and devotional dimensions of Catholicism reflected in *House of Gold*. Gandolfo insightfully recognizes that "the Devlin family home is an emblem of . . . the ideology of the Golden Age of Catholicism in America. Ultimately the reader comes to understand the enormous physical and psychological cost in maintaining the 'house of gold'" (1992, 120). *House of Gold* is ranked with other forward-looking postconciliar novels that demonstrate "appreciation of the shift in theological emphasis promoted by the Second Vatican Council, an understanding of life's experiences in light of the gospel message rather than an application of static precept to life's situations" (124–25). Similarly, although providing little direct commentary on *House of Gold*, Mary R. Reichardt, in *Catholic Women Writers*, offers a very helpful social and religious context for understanding the stultifying and moribund world view of the Devlins, tainted by the "lingering effects of Jansenist Irish Catholicism" with its "guilt, self-criticism, fear of punishment, and unhealthy attitude toward sexuality" (2001, xxvii).

Most critics agree that what partly makes *House of Gold* successful is the author's attitude toward her subjects. Cullinan avoids both rant and vapid sentimentality. Although unrelenting in her exposure of suppressive familial and religious practices, it is clear that her mission is not denunciation but critique. For instance, Catherine Ward clarifies that "*House of Gold* does not imply that familial identification is always unhealthy. . . . Cullinan does not bear a grudge against the family, but she is aware of patterns of suppression, hypocrisy, and illusion" (1991, 88). And Eileen Kennedy finds a similar attitude toward religion: "if Cullinan dissects the drawbacks, the psychic scars that can be inflicted by Irish Catholicism, she is equally objective about its potential to help human beings achieve some degree of goodness, maybe of holiness" (1981, 98). Ellen Frye, in her article on *House of Gold* in *Catholic Women Writers*, agrees: "Cullinan's tone, while critical, upholds Catholicism as a stabilizing and unifying force in times of crisis" (2001, 77). In short, regarding both family and Church, Cullinan is interested not in slamming doors but in opening windows. The Devlin family myth is not the only way to be family. The Devlin's practice of religion is not the only way to practice religion.

What gives *House of Gold* its moral authority is the attempt to balance the claims of the individual and the need for structure, both in family and religion; as Anita Gandolfo recognizes, Cullinan does not "urge the reductive abolition of authority" but demonstrates "the need to bridge the distance between law and life" (1992, 124). The individualities of Father Phil, Tom, the two nuns, and Elizabeth are suppressed by the authoritarianism first inculcated by their mother and later codified by their faith and by the military. Given such imprisonment in conformity, it is understandable that Charles Fanning might conclude that Justin's "failure will be his salvation" (1990, 337); "Justin is the best equipped Devlin for the motherless world that the family is about to enter" (341). But such individuality alone is not enough. Justin rejects the Julia Devlin myth, but he has no other myth to replace it, no satisfying vision or narrative that establishes ideals, structure, rituals, and emotional peace. At the end, this is what Claire knows and Winnie begins to learn.

NOTE

Elizabeth Cullinan, *House of Gold* (Boston: Houghton Mifflin, 1970). All references are to this edition.

WORKS CITED

Cullinan, Elizabeth. 1983–84. "The Black Diamond." *Threshold* 34 (Winter): 39–43.

Fanning, Charles. 1980. "Elizabeth Cullinan's *House of Gold*: Culmination of an Irish-American Dream." *Melus* 7, no. 4: 31–48.

———. 1990. *The Irish Voice in America: Irish-American Fiction from the 1760s to 1980s*. Lexington: University Press of Kentucky.

Frye, Ellen C. 2001. "Elizabeth Cullinan." In *Catholic Women Writers: A Bio-Bibliographical SourceBook*, ed. Mary R. Reichardt, 74–80. Westport, CT: Greenwood Press.

Gandolfo, Anita. 1992. *Testing the Faith: The New Catholic Fiction in America*. Westport, CT: Greenwood Press.

Kennedy, Eileen. 1981. "Bequeathing Tokens: Elizabeth Cullinan's Irish-American Families." *Éire-Ireland: A Journal of Irish Studies* 16, no. 4: 94–102.

Lilly, Amy M. 2001. "Elizabeth Cullinan." In *Dictionary of Literary Biography*, ed. Patrick Meanor and Richard E. Lee, vol. 234, 72–78. Detroit: Gale Group.

Murphy, Maureen. 1979. "Elizabeth Cullinan: Yellow and Gold." In *Irish-American Fiction: Essays in Criticism*, ed. Daniel J. Casey and Robert E. Rhodes, 139–51. New York: AMS.

Ong, Walter J. 1981. *American Catholic Crossroads*. Westport, CT: Greenwood Press.

Reichardt, Mary R., ed. 2001. *Catholic Women Writers: A Bio-Bibliographical SourceBook*. Westport, CT: Greenwood Press.

Ward, Catherine. 1991. "Wake Homes: Four Modern Novels of the Irish-American Family." *Éire-Ireland: A Journal of Irish Studies* 26, no. 2: 78–91.

— **Thomas D. Zlatic**

Dante Alighieri [1265–1321]

The Divine Comedy

BIOGRAPHY

Dante Alighieri was born in Florence, Italy, in 1265. We have no original sources outside of Dante's own works for his childhood. Early commentators tell us that he was born into an old noble family, but his branch of that family was comfortable without being wealthy. In so far as we can discern anything of importance about his early years, we have to rely on the *Vita Nuova* (The New Life). Written about 1292, this is his earliest full-scale work. The title had echoes in the Latin tradition that would have suggested to Dante's contemporaries some type of conversion. And that is in fact what we find: a conversion that anticipates and, to a certain extent, provides some key elements to understanding *The Divine Comedy*.

The *Vita Nuova* tells the story of Dante's love for a young Florentine woman he calls Beatrice, which began when she was still a girl and continued after her early death. It consists of a number of love poems, some of which were probably composed independently and later set among passages of prose that put them in context and explain the history of which they are a part. Scholars disagree about whether this book gives reliable information about Dante's life or whether it is only a kind of vision. In any event, in the course of the story Dante comes to see Beatrice, love itself, and the conventions of medieval chivalric poetry in a new perspective. She emerges both as the inspiring lady and as a new form of holy woman related to the philosophical, theological, and even mystical flowering of medieval culture.

The erotic and the religious doubly inspire the poet as they had not inspired any writer in the West since Plato. In the very last section of the *Vita Nuova*, Dante records, "After writing this sonnet, it was given unto me to behold a wonderful vision; wherein I saw things which determined me that I would say nothing further of this most blessed one, until such time as I could discourse more worthily concerning her. And to this end I labor all I can" (Rossetti 1908, 43). Despite subsequent complications in Dante's life and the difficulties in knowing what this projected "discourse" contained at this early point, the eventual result of all those diverse studies would be *The Divine Comedy*, in which human and divine love cooperate to produce an even more astonishing vision.

A man vigorously involved in every aspect of life in his native city of Florence, which was leading the renaissance of learning in his time, Dante studied and, in various works, wrote about philosophy and theology (*Convivio*, c. 1304–1307); linguistic and aesthetic matters (*De Vulgari eloquentia*, c. 1304–1307); and sought a solution for the turmoil in the Church and the politics of the Italy and Europe of his day (*De Monarchia*, 1312–1314). This last issue was a source of deep heartache. In 1300, Dante was elected one of the Florentine priors, the highest office in the city. Owing to internal factions and papal machinations, he was exiled from his beloved Florence in 1302 and never set foot inside the city again. He passed the remaining nineteen years of his life in exile, sometimes in straitened circumstances.

Given those circumstances, his achievements were even more remarkable. Dante was not an original philosopher like Aquinas or Bonaventure, although he took some daring positions on practical and speculative matters. Most notably, he argued that the spiritual and the secular powers had equal status in their own proper spheres—a daring contention at a time when it was believed that worldly rulers received their authority from the pope. But beyond any specific position, his main contribution was to present a living vision of the medieval world with the kind of vividness that we usually associate with the high renaissance. And in various works, but especially in *The Divine Comedy* (begun around 1307 and finished just before his death), he chose to do so in the vernacular Italian so that not only the learned, but even women and children, could be nourished by the "bread of angels." Dante died in 1321 of malaria and is buried in Ravenna.

MAJOR THEMES

The Divine Comedy is the greatest Christian poem ever written and one of the two or three greatest works in all western literature. It tells the story of a character, also named Dante, who is lost in a Dark Wood and, with the help of several guides, finds his way out of his predicament by means of a journey through Hell, Purgatory, and Paradise, culminating ultimately in the Beatific Vision. In the course of his pilgrimage, the fictional Dante encounters sinners and saints, popes and kings, well-known figures from classical and contemporary history, and simple persons known only to him. The *Comedy*'s human variety and concreteness coupled with its cosmic scope produced a comprehensive vision of the medieval universe whose power has survived the demise of many of the scientific and historical views on which it was based. Simply put, *The Divine Comedy* occupies a central place in the western imagination.

But Dante's poem was meant to be more than literature, as that term is understood today. In a letter to Can Grande della Scala of Verona, one of his patrons, Dante writes that, like sacred Scripture in the Middle Ages, the poem is "polysemous," that is, interpretable in four senses: one literal and three symbolic (moral, allegorical, and anagogical). This comparison with revelation already suggests that Dante was attempting something quite ambitious. But he explains further what he means. In a purely literal sense, his subject is "the state of souls after death." Allegorically, "the subject is man according as by his merits or demerits in the exercise of his free will he is deserving of reward or punishment." This dual focus—on human life both here and in the hereafter—serves a single purpose:

"to remove those living in this life from a state of misery, and to bring them to a state of happiness" ("Epistle to Can Grande," 20–26). The happiness Dante pursues, however, consists both of a virtuous life under a good political order on earth and a supernaturally elevated life in heaven.

The *Comedy*, then, consciously strives to present far more than the spiritual development of one man. Or perhaps it would be better to say that for Dante integral spiritual development included many things that might seem secular or worldly to us. Dante's cosmos is neoplatonic and hierarchical, a great unity stretching from the Creator down to the deepest reaches of Hell—the absolute bottom of the universe. So he must negotiate—and find a place for—everything, human and divine, in the course of his journey. And the power that shows itself in every detail of this world is love: transcendent love in the impulse toward God and charity toward man; perverted and inordinate love among the damned in Hell.

The result is a unified vision of all aspects of our lives that has rarely been attempted, much less achieved, in any culture on the face of the earth. Given that goal, it is a testimony to Dante's powers of concise expression that the *Comedy* is relatively short. At around 15,000 lines, it is equal to about four or five plays by Shakespeare—no small scope but compared with other medieval works, such as the *Romance of the Rose*, a real jewel of craftsmanship. And the *Comedy* maintains interest throughout, unlike some of the more prolix medieval epics, because it consists primarily of a series of dramatic encounters with a wide variety of people.

It has sometimes been said—simplistically—that Dante settles scores in the *Comedy* by putting his enemies in Hell and his friends in Heaven. This is true in so far as his enemies embodied some serious evil. But he also found friends and other acquaintances there, not least his dear mentor Brunetto Latini, who we discover in a moving scene is damned among the sodomites. In any event, it is a more significant fact that Dante's poem displays the great and not great alike in the afterlife as all bearing eternal significance.

The Middle Ages took numbers seriously and attributed mystical significance to them. Because of the centrality of the Christian Trinity to medieval culture, the numbers one and three in particular, but also seven and nine and the multiple combinations of all these numbers, were deliberately woven into texts to indicate various things over and above the sense of the words. Dante makes use of all these devices in ways both great and small.

In terms of its large-scale structure, the *Comedy* displays obvious numerical patterns. The poem is divided into three canticles (*cantiche*): Hell (*Inferno*), Purgatory (*Purgatorio*), and Paradise (*Paradiso*). Each of these canticles in turn consists of thirty-three cantos (a section of 150 lines or so); in addition, the first canto in *Inferno* serves as a prologue to the whole poem, which brings the total number of cantos overall to an even 100. At the smaller scale, Dante uses a rhyme scheme called *terza rima*, in which sets of three rhymes are alternated and interlaced in a continuous chain reflecting the Trinitarian basis of the work and, it might be said, of reality as Dante records it. Various other small brush strokes of this kind appear throughout the poem (in *Paradiso*, for example, the name Christ comes up several times at the end of a line and rhymes only with itself so that the unique name of the Savior is seen as having no other fitting echo in Dante's whole universe). Each of these structural elements underscores that Dante has thought deeply and taken great pains to incarnate meaning in every detail.

What we might call the geography of the three canticles also shows a remarkable symmetry. As Dante descends into the depths of Hell, he sees displayed the punishments allotted to souls who succumbed to the seven deadly sins. In Purgatory, he climbs a mountain marked into seven cornices where these same sins are atoned for and purged. Finally, in Paradise, he ascends through the seven heavens, each the sphere of a planet in the medieval cosmology, on his way to the three highest heavens (the Fixed Stars, Primum Mobile, and Empyrean) and the Beatific Vision that transcends all created things.

The opening lines of the *Comedy* are among the most famous in all of world literature:

> Midway upon the journey of our life
> > I found myself within a forest dark
> > For the straightforward pathway had been lost.

Even in translation (here Longfellow's) we immediately perceive the deep resonance of the chord that Dante has struck. The middle of our life is precisely where all of us find ourselves when we discover that we need redemption. But Dante is also introducing another precise numerical meaning here. The date of this journey, we later learn, is Easter 1300. Dante was born in 1265, so he is just thirty-five when the poem opens, or midway through the "threescore and ten" (seventy) years that Psalm 90 says is the human life span. The several medieval commentators suggested that at this age we make a cosmic turn from our birth and progress into the world back toward our death and God.

Dante tries to ascend a mountain towards the sun, the traditional figure for God. But his way is blocked by three beasts: a panther, a lion, and a she-wolf, in medieval allegory symbols of incontinent appetites, violence, and fraud (drawn from Jer. 5:6). He cannot get past them and is about to give up when a figure with a hoarse voice appears. This is the classical Latin poet Virgil, who, we learn, owing to a series of women in Heaven—the Virgin Mary, Saint Lucy, and Dante's Beatrice—has been asked to help. Virgil is usually described as a symbol of human reason in the poem, and this is true up to a point. He will guide Dante through the places where human reason suffices, Hell and Purgatory. After that, Dante will need other, specifically Christian guides: Beatrice and, later, Saint Bernard of Clairvaux. Thus begins Dante's great journey.

Hell

Outside the gates of Hell, Dante and Virgil find the indifferent, those who never strove for good or evil. In Dante's view of the nature of the universe, these people have held themselves aloof from the very dynamism of love so that "mercy and justice" alike hold them in disdain. They exist in a shadowy realm that does not even have the dignity of moral evil. Those who actively chose evil are inside the gates of Hell proper, over which Dante sees what has since become a famous inscription:

> Through me the way is to the city dolent
> > Through me the way is to eternal dole
> > Through me the way among the people lost.
> Justice incited my sublime Creator

> Created me divine Omnipotence
> The highest Wisdom and the primal Love
> Before me there were no created things
> Only the eterne, and I eternal last
> All hope abandon, ye who enter here. (*Inferno*, 3.1–9)

All the lost souls that the poets subsequently meet, Virgil explains, have lost the "good of understanding." They pursued inordinate, or mistaken, or evil loves. Their state in the afterlife varies according to those choices. The virtuous pagans (canto 4), for example, live in a dignified but sad city; they had the human virtues but not supernatural joy. The famous pair of adulterous lovers, Paolo and Francesca (canto 5), are constantly whirled about like leaves in a storm. The gluttonous are immersed in a fetid swamp, and so forth. In the afterlife, the punishment, what Dante calls the *contrapasso*, fits the crime. Their transgressions are classified according to the three main divisions Dante first encountered with the three beasts: incontinence, violence, and fraud:

1. Incontinent
   lustful
   gluttonous
   avaricious
   wrathful
2. Violent
   against neighbors
   against self (suicides, etc.)
   against God
3. Fraudulent
   A. Simple (panderers, flatterers, simoniacs, diviners, peculators, hypocrites, thieves, evil counselors, sowers of discord, forgers)
   B. Malicious
      against relatives
      against country
      against hosts
      against lords and benefactors

This schematic might give the impression that Dante is merely writing a fictional version of standard moral treatises such as Aristotle's *Ethics* or Saint Thomas's *Summa Theologiae*. Dante follows his great predecessors in his large conceptualization, but one of the most remarkable features of his poem is that the people he sorts into these philosophical categories remain very highly colored and well-rounded individuals. Even people who have never read Aristotle or Aquinas find Dante's treatment lively and convincing.

Hell does not obliterate the human personality of the sinner. Indeed, some of the damned retain virtues of a kind, even if they have been eternally condemned for their sins. For example, Farinata degli Uberti, a haughty politician of Dante's time, lies in a red-hot metal coffin for his heretical materialism. But Farinata had once heroically defied his entire political faction and prevented the destruction of Dante's beloved Florence. And the poet carefully records both just retribution for the man's proud disbelief and admiration for his headstrong character: "I had already fixed my eyes on his, / And he uprose erect with breast and front / As if he held Hell in great disdain" (*Inferno*, 10.34–35, my adaptation).

Dante occasionally will do similar things even with fictional characters. Ulysses, the mythological hero of the *Odyssey*, was little more than a name to Dante, because Homer was not directly known in the West until about two centuries later. But from the bits and pieces of knowledge he had picked up, Dante knew that Ulysses had made long voyages by ship after the Trojan War. Dante imagines him restlessly unwilling to return home because of a limitless desire to experience human virtue and vices, and invents a final journey for him, to the very edge of the known world. Ulysses in this reading is an evil counselor because he convinces his men to wander endlessly. Dante himself warns at the start of *Paradiso* that we should be careful in setting out on the great sea of being so that we not lose ourselves. As Ulysses and his men draw near to the mountain of Purgatory, which rises from an island in the middle of the sea far beyond the Mediterranean and the Gates of Hercules (Gibraltar), he exhorts his men:

> Consider ye the seed from which ye sprang;
>> Ye were not made to live like unto brutes,
>> But for the pursuit of virtue and knowledge. (*Inferno*, 26.118–20)

This is true, but Ulysses has abandoned parents, wife, children, and all duties in this pursuit, and he dies with all his men in a whirlwind near the mountain.

In their own journey, Dante and Virgil finally reach the ultimate bottom of the universe, where, contrary to expectations, Satan is not roasting in fire but frozen in ice. His great batlike wings freeze him even more firmly the more he beats them in the hope of fleeing the Creator's cosmos. The poets literally climb down his body through the center of the earth and then up the other side to emerge, after the reversal this entails, at the base of the mount of Purgatory mentioned by Ulysses. And there they begin a second phase of their pilgrimage.

Purgatory

Hell was a place of stinging smoke, foul smells, and harsh sounds. Purgatory, for all the expiation and effort it calls forth, could not be more different. The minute the poets emerge on its shores they are in a realm that will increasingly restore the human relationship with the goodness, beauty, and truth of God's creation. And this shows itself in the colors and breezes, stars and vegetation:

> Sweet color of the oriental sapphire,
>> That was upgathered in the cloudless aspect
>> Of the pure air, as far as the first circle,
> Unto mine eyes did recommence delight
>> Soon as I issued forth from the dead air,
>> Which had with sadness filled mine eyes and breast.
> The beauteous planet, that to love incites,
>> Was making all the orient to laugh,
>> Veiling the Fishes that were in her escort. (*Purgatorio*, 1.13–21)

The final three lines here refer to Venus, the planet that in medieval astrology influenced love, and the sign of Aries, which in the combination alluded to were thought to be the positions these celestial signs occupied at the moment of creation. So along with the immediate appreciation of the beauty here, we are being told that the whole of this canticle is under the sign of a kind of fresh beginning for the world.

That new start also requires an embrace of humility. Dante and Virgil find as gatekeeper of Purgatory the virtuous pagan Cato, who directs them down to the water's edge, where Dante is to wash away the grime of Hell with the dew on the grass (a traditional symbol of grace) and to be girt by Virgil with a rush, the humble plant that survives the assaults of the waves by yielding to their motion. It is at first strange that Dante puts a classical figure, however virtuous, at the foot of Purgatory. This is one of Dante's innovations and perhaps is meant to reinforce the basic harmony between the classical virtues at their best and the natural virtues in the Christian system. There will be some strong suggestions of that closeness throughout the ascent.

For instance, as Dante and Virgil go through the various cornices that purge away the seven deadly sins (pride, envy, anger, sloth, avarice, gluttony, and lust), they discover the repentant sinners suffering some trial, but not as in Hell an eternal punishment. The trial usually bends the will in a direction opposite to the besetting sin. The proud, thus, are bent down under the weight of heavy rock like the corbels sometimes seen in medieval buildings. On the wall that runs around the inside of the ledge, as will be the case on the other cornices, there is a kind of frieze with three examples of the virtue of humility: the Virgin Mary saying, "Be it done unto me according to they word"; the Hebrew King David dancing before the Ark of the Covenant; and the Roman Emperor Trajan listening to the request of a humble woman. In other words, there is an example drawn from New and Old Testaments and a classical example. The pattern is repeated, with variations, on the other cornices.

But for all the correspondence between pagans and Christians on natural virtue, they are not the same. No one can climb higher on the mountain unless the sun is shining—a traditional symbol for the presence of God. Whatever people believe to be the case on earth, here it is clear that spiritual progress occurs only with the help of divine grace. Angels convey souls in swift boats to the island, and saints may suddenly help souls to leap higher. Also, other human achievements take on a different meaning here. Dante meets many artists whom he knew or had heard of—his friend the musician Casella, poets of the school to which he belonged, painters who were the immediate predecessors of Giotto. But their artistry, great as it was, is placed here in a context that takes away all reason for proud competition. Art is a wonderful human capacity, but even it, by the very logic of the poem Dante is writing, ultimately becomes a means to something that transcends not only all human achievement but the entire created universe.

It may seem odd from a modern perspective, but all this harsh training and demotion of human achievement is directed toward one goal: freedom. When the poets reach the summit of the mountain, they find there the Earthly Paradise, the original garden that God created human beings to live in. Virgil, as a pagan, can go no farther with Dante, but before he leaves, he tells the younger poet:

> Free and upright and sound is thy free-will,
> And error were it not to do its bidding;
> Thee o'er thyself I therefore crown and mitre! (*Purgatorio*, 27.140–42)

The final words signify that Dante has regained both the kingly and priestly powers that were part of the natural human endowment before the Fall. His will is so straight that he can act as it prompts him now. But natural innocence and religion will not be enough for the Christian voyage that remains. Dante needs another guide; not surprisingly, one appears immediately and it is the soul of his earthly love Beatrice. Loved and beloved are now ready for the final ascent.

Paradise

It has often been observed that the *Paradiso* is the least approachable of the *Comedy*'s canticles. Part of the difficulty stems from the sheer nature of the material. We can easily grasp the subject and form of human evil (*Inferno*) and of human striving toward uprightness (*Purgatorio*), because these are quite familiar everyday matters. But heavenly transcendence is beyond most of us. Furthermore, as Dante himself says, "the transhuman cannot be signified by words, / but let the example be enough / for whoever Grace reserves the experience" (*Paradiso*, 1.70–72). So both his subject and the manner in which to treat it present immediate obstacles.

But a poet of Dante's abundant gifts and ambitions was not to be deterred from attempting this final ascent. He will use elements that we might find surprising: notably, classical mythology and the Ptolemaic astronomy of his time— transforming them along the way—to suggest that this realm that has never been seen requires transformation on our part to appreciate. In a striking image in the same opening canto of the *Paradiso*, he prays to the "Good Apollo" (the classical god of poetry) to "Enter into my breast, and breathe there / as when you drew Marsyas / from the sheath of his members" (19–21). This is an obscure reference to a mythical singing contest that Marsyas lost; his punishment was to be flayed alive and drawn out of his own skin. In this rather violent image, Dante is praying to the real God who inspires everything to draw him out of even his normal human mode into the state that God himself desires.

In powerful images such as this, Dante build up his image of the *Paradiso* as a kind of singularity, a dense gravitational object that, at this height, attracts everything that has come before toward itself. In his "Epistle to Can Grande," Dante had stated that his purpose in writing the *Comedy* was to turn "those living in this mortal life from the state of misery and to bring them to the state of bliss" (39). For Dante, Paradise is literally that bliss, and we must therefore read this portion of the poem as an attempt to convey to us the deepest and most central reality of Dante's world. Even in this heavenly realm, Dante will need to pass through various phases—moments that will expand his capacity to take in the light of vision and literally open his mind to the widest degree imaginable— before he will actually see the full light of Heaven.

He begins a graduated ascent from the first part of this canticle through the moon, sun, and planets, as those were understood in the Ptolemaic astronomy as forming concentric circles around the earth. These, of course, also provide a good structural parallel with the circles of Hell and the cornices of Purgatory. But we learn along the way that the souls he meets really do not inhabit these planets; they appear there only as a concession to his human mode of knowing. In reality, all the souls in glory exist in the transcendent realm beyond time and space. In the first sphere, the Moon, Dante asks a woman he meets there, Piccarda, sister of his close friend Forese Donati, how she can be content with her relatively low position. He receives the answer:

> . . .'Tis essential to this blest existence
> To keep itself within the will divine,
> Whereby our very wishes are made one;
> So that, as we are station above station
> Throughout this realm, to all the realm is pleasing,
> As to the King, who makes his will our will.
> And in his will is our peace. . . . (*Paradiso*, 3.79–85)

Questions and answers like these lead on to others, and the whole process advances Dante's understanding higher into this final realm.

It gives us one idea of how far from our usual earthly conceptions this realm is when Dante first perceives its light directly—and then only as a tiny piercing point—in canto 28, only a few hundred lines from the culminating vision and end of the poem. By that point, he has encountered the great theologians Thomas Aquinas and Bonaventure in the circle of the sun; in the circle of Jupiter, some of the great rulers who brought justice to the earth. In a long episode, his great-great grandfather Cacciaguida, who died on the Second Crusade, tells him about his future exile and the moral necessity of remaining faithful in his writing to the truth. After this, Dante meets the great contemplatives and undergoes an examination on the theological virtues of Faith, Hope, and Love by the souls of the apostles Peter, James, and John. And finally he turns directly to the source of all light.

How he turns to that light is itself significant. Like lovers of every age before and since, he is moved by the light reflected in his lover's eyes and suddenly realizes that the source lies behind him. Turning around, he sees a pinpoint of light so intense that he has to turn away for the moment. And Beatrice explains to him quite simply: "From that point hangs Heaven and all of nature." The origin, sustaining principle, and goal of all things has finally become directly apprehensible to a still-mortal man. But there are still some steps to mount before the final vision.

Dante passes beyond time and space into the Empyrean, where the whole universe seems to now be turned inside out. Where previously the heavens had circled around the earth, conceived not as the most important point but the bottom of the universe, now it appears that all of creation is centered on God as the concentration of all virtues. Dante comes upon the divine Rose at this altitude as well, where all the saved souls displayed as a concession to his human weakness farther down now take their true places in heaven proper. Beatrice moves off among them and Dante's final guide comes forth: Bernard of Clairvaux. Saint Bernard was a legendary contemplative, one of the authorities Dante cited in his explanatory letter to his patron as having written, in his *On Consideration*, how it is possible to see something about the divine even in this life. The person besides Christ who mediates that vision is the Blessed Virgin Mary, and Bernard intones at the beginning of the last canto of *Paradiso* a hymn to her, asking that the final grace of vision be given to Dante but without destroying his human affections. Dante and Bernard see her granting their wish and Dante moves toward his final goal. He notes symbolic elements of the Trinity in three circles and the human form somehow joined together with them. But he cannot grasp that mystery until it grasps him in the experience that ends the sacred poem:

> As the geometrician, who endeavours
>> To square the circle, and discovers not,
>> By taking thought, the principle he wants,
> Even such was I at that new apparition;
>> I wished to see how the image to the circle
>> Conformed itself, and how it there finds place;
> But my own wings were not enough for this,
>> Had it not been that then my mind there smote
>> A flash of lightning, wherein came its wish.
> Here power failed the lofty fantasy:
>> But now was turning my desire and will,
>> Even as a wheel that is equally moved,
> The Love which moves the sun and the other stars. (*Paradiso*, 33.133–45)

CRITICAL RECEPTION

The Divine Comedy circulated in manuscript for more than two hundred years before being first printed in the sixteenth century. That history, plus disputes over the proper reading of many difficult passages, has given rise to complex textual questions. Giorgio Petrocchi's edition *La Commedia secondo l'antica vulgata* (1994) is the most up-to-date scholarly text in Italian, with his *Vita di Dante* (1983) offering the fullest, most reliable biography. Among the other biographies and brief studies, Michele Barbi's *Life of Dante* (1954), George Holmes's *Dante* (1980), and R. W. B. Lewis's *Dante* (2001) are noteworthy. Robert Hollander's *Dante, A Life in Works* (2001) repays study.

Among the many modern English translations of the *Comedy*, the Carlyle-Wickstead version has an outdated Italian text but is easy to use and provides good notes. Dorothy Sayers, John Ciardi, and Mark Musa offer readable poetic versions. Allen Mandelbaum and Anthony Esolen do the same with the Italian on facing pages. Charles Singleton's prose translation is accompanied by a good Italian text and the most copious commentary in English, with citations in the original languages and English translation of the classical and medieval sources on which Dante drew. Jean and Robert Hollander, although eccentric in the verse form, convey a sense of the energy of the original; their version also reflects current scholarly views.

For texts and translations of the other works, there are many possibilities. A good place to begin is the Princeton Dante Project (www.princeton.edu/dante/), which contains English, Italian, and Latin versions of all Dante's works and much other useful matter. A massive Italian Internet site (www.danteonline.it) also offers texts and regularly updated, searchable bibliographies. For readers of Italian, the standard reference is the *Enciclopedia Dantesca*, edited by Umberto Bosco (1970–78); in English, Paget Toynbee's *Concise Dictionary of Proper Names and Notable Matters in the Works of Dante* (1914) is helpful.

By the sixteenth century, when the *Comedy* was first set in type and printed, it was given the adjective "*Divine*," a reflection of the esteem in which it was held. Dante's memory had been preserved and fostered by Boccaccio and the

Italian humanists. But in subsequent centuries, Dante's highly colored and dramatic Christian vision was rather neglected, even in Italy. The philosopher Giambattista Vico thought of him as a kind of inspired barbarian. Elsewhere, he was positively criticized. Voltaire and Goethe found him uncongenial. Most readers could not go much past the *Inferno*. *Purgatorio*, and especially *Paradiso*, seemed much less effective to generations of Neoclassical- and Romantic-era readers. There is no easy way into this disparate material, but one useful volume is Michael Caesar's *Dante: The Critical Heritage 1314(?)–1870* (1989), which presents in English selections from various languages and periods. Modern interest in Dante has been much more positive, especially in England and America. The British poet Dante Gabriel Rossetti (1861) translated the *Vita Nuova* along with other poems in *Dante and His Circle*, which remains an attractive rendering. Beginning with Longfellow in the nineteenth century and then continued by T. S. Eliot, Ezra Pound, Allen Tate, John Crowe Ransom, and others, the medieval Dante has come into close proximity with some of the great names of modern poetry.

On the critical side, Charles Singleton in America and Paget Toynbee in England, among others, encouraged a close reading of the texts. These critics tended to emphasize the orthodox nature of Dante's work, an element that was not always evident to its first readers. In fact, early Church authorities condemned Dante for his *De Monarchia*, which posited an early version of a kind of separation of church and state. Other ecclesiastical figures looked askance at the *Comedy* for what was thought to be its excessive praise of Beatrice as Dante's *salute* (salvation) and, no doubt, for its strong criticism of the popes in Dante's day (only Sylvester II among them is not in or destined for hell in Dante's view). The Council of Trent in the sixteenth century nearly placed Dante on the *Index* of forbidden books.

Modern readers, often even those of an indisputable orthodoxy, have raised doubts about whether Dante was even a Christian. The most interesting of these works is Ernest L. Fortin's *Dissent and Philosophy in the Middle Ages* (2002); Fortin's essays in *The Birth of Philosophic Christianity* (1996) provide a shorter version of his argument. But that view is extreme and very much in the minority. Among Europeans, Erich Auerbach's *Dante Poet of the Secular World* (1961) is particularly important. Ernst Curtius's *European Literature and the Latin Middle Ages* (1967) contains a valuable chapter on Dante. On Dante's use of philosophy and theology, see Etienne Gilson's *Dante and Philosophy* (1963). Although aging, Edmund Gardner's *Dante and the Mystics* (1913) surveys a central element in Dante's thought.

The eight volumes of *Dante: The Critical Complex*, edited by Richard Lansing (2003), are uneven but contain many valuable essays: *Dante and Philosophy* (volume 3) and *Dante's Afterlife: The Influence and Reception of the Commedia* (volume 8) are of particular interest.

NOTE

Dante Alighieri, *The Divine Comedy*, trans. Henry Wadsworth Longfellow (Boston: Houghton Mifflin, 1904). Unless otherwise noted, all references are to this edition.

WORKS CITED

Auerbach, Erich. 1961. *Dante Poet of the Secular World*, trans. Ralph Mannheim. Chicago: University of Chicago Press.

Barbi, Michele. 1954. *Life of Dante*. Berkeley: University of California.

Bosco, Umberto, ed. 1970–1978. *Enciclopedia Dantesca*. 6 vols. Revised edition. Rome: Instituto dell' Enciclopedia Italiana.

Caesar, Michael, ed. 1989. *Dante: The Critical Heritage 1314(?)–1870*. London: Routledge.

Curtius, Ernst R. 1967. *European Literature and the Latin Middle Ages*, trans. William R. Trask. Princeton, NJ: Princeton University Press.

Dante Alighieri. 1904. "Epistle to Can Grande." In *A Translation of the Latin Works of Dante Alighieri*, trans. A. G. Ferrers Howell and Philip H. Wicksteed. London: J. M. Dent.

Fortin, Ernest L. 1996. *The Birth of Philosophic Christianity*, ed. J. Brian Benestad. Lanham, MD: Rowman and Littlefield.

———. 2002. *Dissent and Philosophy in the Middle Ages: Dante and his Precursors*, trans. Marc A. LePain. Lanham, MD: Lexington Books.

Gardner, Edmund. 1913. *Dante and the Mystics*. Reprint. New York: Octagon Books, 1968.

Gilson, Etienne. 1963. *Dante and Philosophy*, trans. David Moore. New York: Harper and Row.

Hollander, Robert. 2001. *Dante, A Life in Works*. New Haven, CT: Yale University Press.

Holmes, George. 1980. *Dante*. Past Masters. New York: Hill and Wang.

Lansing, Richard, ed. 2003. *Dante: The Critical Complex*. 8 vols. New York: Routledge.

Lewis, R. W. B. 2001. *Dante*. New York: Viking.

Petrocchi, Georgio. 1983. *Vita di Dante*. Bari, Italy: Laterza.

———. 1994. *La Commedia secondo l'antica vulgate*. 2nd ed. Florence: Le Lettere.

Rossetti, Dante Gabriel. 1908. *Dante and his Circle*. London: Ellis and Elvey.

Toynbee, Paget. 1914. *Concise Dictionary of Proper Names and Notable Matters in the Works of Dante*. Revised edition by Charles. S. Singleton. Oxford: Clarendon Press, 1968.

BIBLIOGRAPHY

Royal, Robert. *Dante Alighieri: Divine Comedy, Divine Spirituality*. New York: Crossroad, 1999.

— Robert Royal

Dorothy Day [1897–1980]

The Long Loneliness

BIOGRAPHY

Dorothy Day, arguably one of the most influential Catholics in United States history, may be all the more influential because, excepting God's grace, how can one account for her unpredictable conversion and radical devotion to Jesus Christ present in the poor? Her autobiography, *The Long Loneliness*, tells her story and introduces readers to the Catholic Worker movement, her remarkable and ongoing legacy that to this day is at the vanguard of radical Catholicism.

Day was born in Brooklyn, New York, in 1897. Her father, John Day, was a newspaperman who moved his family from coast to coast while writing and betting on horses. Her mother, Grace, a woman who beautifully balanced the roles of wife and mother in adverse and fortuitous times, had five children. Dorothy was the middle child. Her older brothers followed their father into newspaper journalism. So did she. Her sister Della and brother John, in their own separate ways, later followed Dorothy Day in the entanglements with people and radical causes that became her life.

During the eighty-two years of that life, much of Day's "long loneliness"—a phrase borrowed from Mary Ward, an Elizabethan English nun—came from her choice to be Catholic and her closeness to Christ in the utter radicalness of his Gospel. Although lonely, Day had an uncommon gift for engaging in and sustaining friendships. In the course of her long life, she had a motley mix of friends, including Forster Batterham, the estranged father of her only child. These relationships outline the story of her life. Day always happily received her old friends or news of them. Rayna and Raph, whom she met as a student at the University of Illinois, enjoyed the arts with her as well as a shared compulsion to work for justice. For Day, Rayna, who was later buried in Red Square, never lost her aureole. Day also stayed in touch with other friends of her bohemian youth, like the radical historian John Reed and Mike Gold and his family. From those same years, Peggy Baird and Caroline Tate finally joined her in the Catholic Church, and she never stopped praying for playwright Eugene O'Neill.

In addition to the people who touched her directly—including Eleanor Roosevelt and Diego Rivera, who made cameo appearances in her life story—Day formed true and mutual relationships, however grounded in fiction, with writers and their characters, as Robert Coles discusses in "Her Spiritual Kin," the final chapter of his book *Dorothy Day: A Radical Devotion* (1987). She seemed to engage in lifelong conversations with writers like Ignazio Silone, Romano Guardini, Charles Dickens, and Leo Tolstoy. Dostoevsky had a special place in her heart, and she also kept company with his characters: for instance, his Idiot, the brothers Karamazov, and the saintly Sonia. "By little and by little" she simultaneously lived alongside such saints as Thérèse of Lisieux, Francis of Assisi, Thomas Aquinas, and the Virgin Mary, and their words fell from her lips and pen like interjections and commas.

Yet through all the relationships Day enjoyed and sometimes suffered, her relationship with God prevailed. As a child when she stumbled on a neighbor at prayer, she had an epiphany. As a teen wandering the streets between bars and assignments for the two socialist, communist, and anarchist publications that hired her—*The Call* and *The Masses*—she ducked into churches and secretly admired the morality of the few Catholics she encountered. Throughout her twenties, whether in hot pursuit of Lionel Moise (with whom she conceived and then aborted a child), in her brief unhappy liaison of a marriage to Barkely Tober, in her settled, sexual contentment with Forster Batterham, or in contemporaneous writings and her more mature reflection, she let her readers know that she missed God. She was lonely for God and eventually willing to give all to be lonely with God.

God led her to Christ in the poor. As Day saw it, Peter Maurin, whom she met several years after her conversion to Catholicism, gave her life Gospel meaning by creating with and through her the Catholic Worker movement during the years of the Great Depression. The movement took on much of her character and convictions. Her secular commitment turned sacred. From high school on, Day had loved the poor and struggled to transform the system that made them poor. She had identified with labor and laborers and championed their cause. She had instinctively recoiled from violence, including her own, despite her sympathies with communism and socialism. In fact, she had been wary of all causes when they turned to violence as the means to accomplish justice. The Catholic Worker movement embraced and acted upon these causes, and its newspaper, the *Catholic Worker*, recorded them.

Once baptized into the Church and then indoctrinated by Peter Maurin in the practical implications of that Baptism, Dorothy Day grasped the interstices of Christ's command to love God and neighbor in a way that transformed her gift for developing and sustaining relationships into a love inclusive and indiscriminate, excepting its partiality for the poor. This active love would transform the Catholic Church in America prior to, through, and after the Second Vatican Council. As Mel Piehl describes it, in the Catholic Worker's first wave of popularity, the Church did not necessarily realize just what was happening. Piehl writes, "The Worker's success in stirring social concern among Catholics during the thirties, however, partially masked its distinctiveness. The movement was not, as first appeared, simply another Depression phenomenon, but the means whereby the unsettling perspectives of the radical Gospel first found their way into American Catholicism" (1982, 114–15). It would be tried by fire, particularly when Day opposed the United States's involvement in World War II, causing leaders in the movement to leave and nearly half its Houses of Hospitality across the country to close. Yet by this choice the movement defined itself and its Catholic stance, and Piehl concludes that "By the end of the fifties the idea that it was possible to be a good Catholic and a good liberal at the same time was no longer in question" (170).

After the publication of her autobiography, *The Long Loneliness* (1952), Day continued writing, traveled to Cuba, and was devotedly followed by fellow Catholic worker Ammon Hennacy, "the one-man revolution," and countless others. Michael Harrington brought her ideas into national prominence. She stood by the antiwar Berrigan brothers even when distressed by Phillip Berrigan's departure from the priesthood and his subsequent marriage. She supported Cesar Chavez and the United Farm Workers. She observed changes in the Church and society in the 1960s and could not tolerate well the new, secular dispositions of her followers and their propensity to loose living. Still, she had established the Catholic Worker movement and she stayed with it until her death in 1980.

Day not only lived her life fully but also wrote it down. Camus might say that she thus lived it twice. Even as a child, she had committed her life to paper in diaries and letters, and, growing up, she somehow hung onto the essence of her personal records, despite family upheaval and uprooting. From her own words we know how she both changed and remained the same. From others we know that, even after her death, she continues to change the history of the Catholic Church in the United States. She established a new model, rooted in the Gospel, for individual and corporate dissent from monolithic, mainstream, unquestioning, and conservative Catholic acquiescence. The House of Hospitality that Day founded in New York City not only weathered the changes in her Church and country but also launched over a hundred others across the United States and the world, including one in Australia. The Catholic Worker movement became like a university in the type of active, inclusive Gospel love Dostoevsky terms a "harsh and dreadful thing." It created a Catholic counterculture so admired that, despite tension with the institutional Church, Day was officially invited to participate in Vatican II and is now being considered for canonization. At this latter idea, Day would probably laugh dismissively and ask to be taken seriously. Since Catholic Worker communities are still being founded, we can be sure that some are doing just that.

PLOT SUMMARY

Dorothy Day's autobiography, *The Long Loneliness*, tells the story of a twentieth-century Grail Quest with all the incoherent coherence of a modern believer caught midstream in the living mystery of God's life in this world. As Patrick Jordan states, "Between the book's opening chapter—in which Day links writing an autobiography with going to confession—and the book's postscript—in which she ties community and conversation to receiving Communion—she leaves us with the best glimpse we need as to the *why* and *how* of her life" (2002, 16). The prologue confession and postscript communion frame Day's three main sections: "Searching," "Natural Happiness," and "Love is the Measure."

In "Searching," Day remembers family stories her mother told at the table. She recalls a maternal great-great-grandmother, Charity, and her husband, Christian, the sole survivor of nine brothers, all captains of whalers lost at sea. She dreams, romps, walks, and works her way through childhood and adolescence into the two years she studies at the University of Illinois at Urbana. She begins her professional life as a writer willing to be poor. In this section, Day captures the various locations of her life, Brooklyn and San Francisco, Chicago and Staten Island, but above all traces the topography of her inner life. The San Francisco earthquake comes alive as she describes herself left alone in her big, brass bed as it careens across her shiny bedroom floor, but it is the experience of her neighbors engaged in acts of charity after the quake that leads her to tell the event at all. Like so many of the incidents Day remembers, seismic shock comes, to borrow a phrase from Christopher Fry, "soul-size."

Finished with schooling, as a novice journalist with a heart for the masses in a time of worldwide social ferment, Day works diligently at *The Call* and *The Masses* and socializes freely with their bohemian, communist, socialist, and anarchist crowd. She fasts for the hungry in a jail outside Washington, D.C., and suffers in cells in Chicago with women of the street. She also finds herself at Benediction and praying the rosary. Taking a friend's advice, she uses the five thousand dollars she earned selling the movie rights to her novel *The Eleventh Virgin* (1924) to buy a house on Staten Island, where she settles into a new life.

In part two, "Natural Happiness," Day initially relishes her free and easy existence on Staten Island with her lover Forster Batterham and their colorful neighbors. She loves the island's gardens and campfires, and the smell of salt and seaweed on her lover as they "'lived together' in the fullest sense of the phrase" (*Long Loneliness*, 114). Awaiting the birth of their daughter, however, she finds that habits of grateful prayer have sprung in her heart like water. Day gives birth to Tamar Teresa, has her baptized, then herself receives the sacraments of Baptism, Confession, Communion, and Confirmation. Anarchist to the core, Forster will have none of it. So she chooses to leave the man she loves for God whom she loves more and in obedience to Christ's law as taught by the Roman Catholic Church.

Day lives for a while with Tamar in Los Angeles and Mexico, then returns to New York. When the advanced payment from two Catholic periodicals, *America* and *Commonweal*, takes her to Washington, D.C., to cover simultaneous mass demonstrations, she visits the National Marian Shrine on the feast of the Immaculate Conception. Realizing that, after three years as a Catholic, she has never really known one active Catholic lay person, she prays in anguish "that some way would open up for me to use what talents I possessed for my fellow workers, for the poor" (166). Immediately upon her return to New York, she meets Peter Maurin, a French peasant, active Catholic layman, and "holy hobo."

In the final section of her autobiography, "Love is the Measure," Day and Maurin found the Catholic Worker movement, building Gospel community with the poor on the Lower East Side of Manhattan. The movement rapidly spreads across America and abroad as the *Catholic Worker* newspaper circulates its story around the globe. The first issue, May 1933, prints 2,500 copies; by the end of that year, circulation reaches 100,000. The price of the paper, a penny a copy, authenticates the focus of the movement: service to and with God's beloved poor.

Peter Maurin teaches Day what he has learned as a wandering, laboring Christian, his philosophy of "cult, culture, and cultivation." Day transforms the concepts of his "Easy Essays" into their program of Christian Houses of Hospitality and farms, with regular prayer, soup lines, community, support for labor in all its strikes and struggles, and a consistent commitment to nonviolence that often translates into protest of the United States military industrial complex. Although the movement may not have been what Peter Maurin had in mind, Dorothy Day records his explanation: "Man proposes, but woman disposes" (175).

MAJOR THEMES

From Saint Augustine to Dorothy Day's contemporary and friend, Thomas Merton, the confessional autobiography is both a Catholic genre and a means of explaining faith and conversion, as in the example of John Henry Newman's *Apologia Pro Vita Sua*. From the outset, Day situates *The Long Loneliness* in that tradition. In her prefatory "Confession," she says "I can write only of myself, what I know of myself, and I pray with St. Augustine, 'Lord, that I may know myself, in order to know Thee'" (10–11). Although she writes this autobiography after two other works that approach the form—the fictional *Eleventh Virgin*, an autobiography in disguise (all copies of which she wanted to burn later in her life) and *From Union Square to Rome* (1938)—*The Long Loneliness* is clearly undertaken as a remembering of her incorporation into the Catholic Church. So she chooses to confess. Admitting that when she wrote the story of her conversion twelve years earlier in *From Union Square to Rome* she had failed to acknowledge her sins, she now wishes to tell the whole story, perhaps especially those dark passages one leaves behind in the confessional box. She invites her readers into her "ugly, gray, drab, monotonous sins" (10) so that they can appreciate how radical her turning is when she comes to believe.

Yet Day is judicious and sacramentally sensitive in what she tells and what she omits. She implicates no one but herself. Ritual naming may unconsciously govern her choices. She names some people only by their given name. On some she lingers lovingly, not only giving a synopsis of their life but also reflecting fully on that life in the context of the Mystical Body of Christ. This habit of soul she puts to the page in writing of her family and her lover and those people she meets after leaving him.

In writing of "The Generations Before," she introduces the reader to her mother, Grace. She says little about her father except that his work on a morning newspaper keeps him away from home at night. Although she mentions his parents by name, she does not name him. In recounting her mother's family lore, she says most about her own great-great grandparents, Charity and Christian. By name, they assume near-allegorical status, as if she is plumbing their stories for the roots of her own faith. Before and concluding the chapter, she quotes G. K. Chesterton, the British Catholic essayist, and the Book of Ecclesiastes. The excerpts from both sources extend and probe the meaning of her ancestors, named and unnamed. Chesterton is quoted saying, "Tradition is the democracy of the dead" (17); and Ecclesiastes, "Only this I have found that God made man right and he hath entangled himself with an infinity of questions" (17). These quotations extend Day's own life story and suggest its democratic and Scriptural framework. She is both democratic to the core and a Christian believer. In the hands of a less practiced journalist or a Catholic less grounded in the Incarnation, such philosophical interjections might lose a reader. Day can digress, but in doing so she still holds her readers' attention. Between the two quoted passages she wonders about her ancestors: is Grandfather Napoleon "now young and dashing once more and free from all pain" (17)? She is no stranger to Ecclesiastes's "infinity of questions." Consistently she balances the universal truths of faith and the sensible realities of life.

Writing of her relationship with Forster, her lover and the father of her child, presents a challenge. He is her beloved, but he also divides her life into the time before Baptism and the time after. When Day writes of herself as a woman passionately in love with him and their child, yet actively on the baptismal quest that, she senses, will divide their family, she does not separate the carnal happiness glowing in her from her growing awareness of God's insistent, loving presence. She is clear, however, that she must prefer God to man.

For all her simplicity as a narrator, Day exhibits the double consciousness intrinsic to the confessional mode of the book. Much as Geoffrey Chaucer is present in *The Canterbury Tales* as both poet and pilgrim, the Dorothy Day of the early 1950s sees herself in her earlier life through the eyes of an adult Catholic. Her devotion to the Mystical Body, spiritual sensibility, and social conscience consistently influence her voice, subject, and style. Unlike in her previous two autobiographical works, her voice this time has a resonance formed by her immersion in the lives of the poor. The literal "re-membering" of the Body of Christ in her own body and the lives of others has become her story: now she is recalling her life and enfleshing it in the light of faith. That Day already believes is indisputably true, for she authors the book more than two decades after founding the Catholic Worker movement. As Christ is God incarnate, she has long been practicing the Incarnation by grace and intent among the poor as she sees in their faces the face of Christ. She recalls the relationships that form her entire life but puts the pieces of life's puzzle together in a new way. She now sees all as members of Christ's Mystical Body.

In Christ she remembers the times before she knew him. She writes the first two sections of her book, as it were, to confess her sin in its context and without judging others and to acknowledge the very real beams of light that penetrated her life when she had no Church to call her own. From her first word on, she writes with a voice that has made its own the Word of God in the Scriptures, especially the New Testament and the writings of Christian saints and sages. As a woman in her early fifties writing about herself as a child and adolescent, she neither dispenses with nor demands of that child-self the spiritual vision or moral standards that she has now acquired by grace and fierce adherence to the Gospel. She may, however, hint at the latter. As a child, she did have a sense of right and wrong. She did not pick Miss Lynch's cucumbers nor, without permission, take her mother's change to buy a soda. Yet, as an adult, she notes censoriously that these typical moral teachings are grounded in possessions and possessiveness, that, even in the nursery, "might makes right." Sex goes even deeper, she states. She learns early that one should not have a child out of wedlock. Yet even as a little girl she seems to intuit that sex has something to do with

God, if only through observing the taboos of adults who do not talk about either religion or sex (17–18).

In the final section of *The Long Loneliness*, "Love is the Measure," we understand the hard-won integrity of her vision, the milieu of the Mystical Body in which she is writing her autobiography. From Pope Pius XII's Christmas message, she learns a distinction: "It is people who are important, not the masses" (221). The Mystical Body is the body of the poor. They are in Christ's body and he is on the Cross.

The bridge toward the Cross is grounded in her life with Forster. The crucifix is mentioned for the first time in one particularly long conversation Day recounts with Sasha and Freda, her friends on Staten Island, which is in large part a replication of a conversation the self-proclaimed agnostic Sasha had had with a Christian person on the train ride home. This story makes clear that others are aware of Day's inner life and, in fact, turn to her for help with their own questions. Freda tells her husband how their son Dickie has begun asking questions about God and church and where the world came from, and how she doesn't know what to answer. "So then he goes to Dorothy," she continues, "and she gives him a crucifix to hang over his bed and he calls it 'his friend, Jesus Christ'" (131).

In the days after Tamar is baptized, when Day is considering her own Baptism, she comes to the Cross in a more expansive and complex way. Twice she refers specifically to the Mystical Body of Christ, invoking it as both structural device and spiritual theme. Of her daughter's Baptism she writes, "Tamar had become a member of the Mystical Body of Christ. I didn't know anything of the Mystical Body or I might have felt disturbed at being separated from her" (144). In a different context, months after Tamar's Baptism, she reflects on the execution of Sacco and Vanzetti, an injustice over which Forster broods for weeks. She writes about how the country mourned their loss, especially the poor and the workers, "those who felt most keenly the sense of solidarity—that very sense of solidarity which made me gradually understand the doctrine of the Mystical Body of Christ whereby we are the members of one another" (147). For Day, there's the rub. Why is the notion of the Mystical Body not truly evident in the real Church? Her daughter is baptized, but can she follow? She is clear in her reasoning: the institutional Catholic Church is aligned with the rich, not with the masses so beloved by Christ and herself. How can she bear to lose her enduring love of the masses through receiving Baptism into that Church? She explains further, and clearly in retrospect, "I loved the Church for Christ made visible. Not for itself, because it was so often a scandal to me. Romano Guardini said the Church is the cross on which Christ was crucified; and one must live in a state of permanent dissatisfaction with the Church" (149–50).

For Dorothy Day, the Mystical Body into which she follows her daughter through Baptism is, as Guardini eloquently acknowledges, clearly itself on the Cross. Five years pass before she realizes her own personal call as a Catholic baptized into that crucified Body, the call that will cost her the rest of her life. That call will unify her developing sense of Christian spirituality with its ethical consequences in a way that takes her beyond individual conscience and sacrament into active, communal love both for the crucified Mystical Body and as that Body incarnate. In her vocation to the Catholic Worker she finds the way to embrace fully and with love the poor she had so feared losing. The social, incarnate dimension of her conscience enlarges through Day's concern for the poor long before she becomes a Catholic. She gradually familiarizes her audience with the love of the poor that God forges in her flesh from childhood. Once in the Church, she unwittingly acts as its conscience, but acts humbly, for she knows where she has been and loves those who were there with her, however little tolerance they have for her Church or understanding of her conversion.

Spiritual sensibilities pervade the whole text of *The Long Loneliness*. And no wonder. At the start, Day has established the book's focus on God, and especially the God of Francis Thompson's "The Hound of Heaven," the poetic raptures of which Eugene O'Neill once proclaimed before her in the Greenwich Village darkness (84). She knows, as did both the Victorian poet and the modern playwright, that God pursues us long before we acquiesce. Although, as she relates, her family was not church-going, the young Day did attend church on occasion. Beautiful prayers resounded in her and instinctually she was drawn to worship. As an adolescent, she wrote a letter to a friend in which she recorded that she was reading Dostoevsky but, because it was a Sunday, she should be reading the Bible. However, she states, she didn't want to read the Bible: God is love, she knows, but she prefers the "thrill that comes with the meeting of lips" (34). In retrospect, Day now wonders at such childish pretentiousness but implies how deeply these early incidents are imbedded in her spiritual sensibility.

At college, her studies and her friendships with young socialists bring her to critique religion and reject it, along with scorning the hypocrisy of comfortable Christians who fill the pews on Sunday but ignore the poor. Her early empathy with the poor and admiration for the class warfare of the communists draw on convictions nurtured through her reading of Upton Sinclair and Jack London. She has no use for a Jesus who blessed the meek: "He was two thousand years dead and new prophets had risen up in His place" (46). Yet, her very thought of him suggests that at this stage she continues to refine her conscience and spirituality. The stillness and natural beauty she experiences on Staten Island with Forster, so different from the hustle and bustle of Manhattan, further develops her contemplative self. In serenity, silence, and solitude, Day discovers an inner voice busy with discernment, dialectic, and debate. Walking to the Village, she prays the rosary given to her by a friend in New Orleans, uncertain how to do it but doing it anyway. All she knows is that it makes her happy. But, "[t]hen I thought suddenly, scornfully, 'Here you are in a stupor of content. You are biological. Like a cow. Prayer with you is like the opiate of the people'" (132).

These diverse and mature spiritual habits inculcate in Day the hospitality that becomes her personal habit and the trademark of the Catholic Worker houses. For the twenty years of the movement recorded in *The Long Loneliness*, stories tumble out of her as ideas incarnate with a life of their own, Christ's life. People show up and stay—the mad and merry, Jew and Gentile, laborer and addict. Such openness to others made her beloved by many. As she says of Tom, coordinator of the house on Chrystie Street, "People love him because he loves God and for love of God loves the poor" (235).

Day's developing spiritual sensibility manifests itself in a changing point of view. In the three sections of the book, she moves from journalistic objectivity through contemplation and conversation toward immersion in the activity of an apostle employed by the Gospel. In the first section of the book, Day sees others as if from a moving subway train, not dwelling long on anyone but caught in the whirl of the childhood and adolescence that literally take her across the continental United States and back again. Her professional life, lived at times with the poorest of the poor while writing with the iconoclastic intelligentsia of her time, moves in a blur yet inexorably toward the Catholic Worker. Yet rarely do people in this section speak in their own voices. Trotsky, Robert Minor, and the street women with whom she is jailed in Chicago, especially Mae, are singular exceptions. There are lengthy quotations from letters, books, and prayers, but people usually speak in indirect discourse. As her title to this section states, she is still searching.

In the middle section of the book, settled into her beach bungalow on Staten Island, she listens to voices. On one level, her neighbors are lovable gypsies and beach bums: Lefty, Sasha, his mother the *babushka*, his wife Freda, Malcolm Cowley and his wife Peggy, and the Mexican mother-in-law of her baby brother John. They all speak for themselves. They gripe, counsel, instruct, argue, and cajole. Day seems aware that they, unknowingly, were leading her, as much as did her catechist Sister Aloysia, into God's embrace by allowing her first to love herself as she is. These live voices sounding questions out loud about faith and other matters raise the pitch of the autobiography to a new level, one less individualistic and more communitarian. Voices ring true, and, like an eavesdropper in the gathering places of a neighborhood of friends on the beach or around a kitchen table, Day gives an intimate sense of the life shared in her beach community. What could be a more apt prelude to Baptism into the Mystical Body of Christ for both Tamar Teresa and her mother? On the other hand, however, Forster says not a word. Day observes that he became talkative only when angry, "And, his wrath, he said, was caused by my absorption in the supernatural rather than the natural, the unseen rather than the seen" (120). Despite Forster's brooding and sometimes explosive presence, natural happiness prevails and he is at its center. Day leaves us with no doubt: she loves him and their child, and she loves God with and through them. At the same time, a real relationship with God is developing within her, particularly in those times of solitude when she is "a sybaritic anchorite" (133).

From the montage watched from a moving train, through the discerning dialogue overheard on the beach that puts her on the road to the baptismal font, Day paves the way to the book's end as a whirlwind of activity incarnating the social demands of Catholicism. It is occasioned by but not dependent on Peter Maurin. Maurin serves as her mentor, Virgil to her "Divine Comedy." He teaches her a Catholic vision, rooted in his own life as a worker who has chosen to be poor. He also opens the door beyond her individual devotion to the proletariat cause to life in community with the poor. For her it is a new world. That world is the Mystical Body of Christ on the Cross, and it is real and chaotic. In the midst of the chaos, Day holds on to bright moments. Tamar grows up in this world. One night as the community conversation runs into the night, Dorothy's dear little daughter gets left in the bathtub, and the water grows cold, but the child just keeps on making soap boats and playing with her toys (237). Prayer becomes a community bond that also raises the "infinity of questions." Tamar wonders if Mary, mother of Jesus, minds if she says her prayers while standing on her head (236). Questions deserve communal answers, and so around the tables where they share meals with the poor and at the Catholic Worker farms, community members grapple with the questions of the day in the light of the Gospel. Their Gospel nourishment evolves into fidelity to active, inclusive, and nonviolent love, the practice of which transcends and often challenges the pronouncements of Church hierarchy. No matter. It is the works of mercy rather than the commandments that lure and keep people in the movement. Now the story of Day's life is no longer chronological but topical, with themes that originate in the Gospel but have meaning only in direct application to the world of the poor. The chapters in the final part of the book take on a new kind of title: labor, community, retreat. In the whirlwind of activity that is the consequence of believing, Dorothy Day herself experiences the reality of being the Mystical Body crucified.

The experience of her "long loneliness" comes in many forms, but it comes most painfully in Day's fierce adherence to Gospel pacifism, in which she is at odds with Peter Maurin and abandoned by many of her early followers. Even before the United States entered into World War II, she insisted on love of enemies and rejection of violence as a defining element of the Catholic Worker. When she persists in that stand, the movement divides. Many of her early disciples leave, and Houses of Hospitality close. Then as now, while not everyone in a Catholic Worker house may hold to the movement's radical pacifism, no one is unaware of it. Once again it is Christ, forgiving and suffering, whom they incarnate. Day asks only, "What does God want me to do? . . . Is it pride, presumption, to think I have the spiritual capacity to use spiritual weapons in the face of the most gigantic tyranny the world has ever seen? . . . Again the long loneliness to be faced" (272–73).

The book's conclusion is, in the final analysis, a movement back and forth from loneliness to communion narrated in the stream of consciousness of the Mystical Body of Christ. Here, author and subject coincide. Day alludes to Dostoevsky's Father Zossima in concluding that "the final word is love" (285). The kitchen table around which her mother Grace told stories of her ancestors Christian and Charity has come full circle to the table of living communion. Day entitled the book's last part rightly: "Love Is the Measure."

CRITICAL RECEPTION

When first published in January 1952, *The Long Loneliness* garnered favorable reviews in the *New York Times*, *Newsweek*, and the *Herald Tribune*. *Times* reporter R. L. Duffus concludes, "This book will not shock anybody. It may touch many, whatever their secular or religious faith, who lament the kindliness and sympathy that Communists found among certain left-wing groups—and betrayed" (1952, 12). At the time, Michael Harrington, a young Catholic Worker volunteer, wrote a loving review of the autobiography for the movement's own newspaper. Dwight MacDonald's subsequent two-part personal profile on Day as the radical Christian woman for *The New Yorker* no doubt attracted another audience for the book. Nearly ten thousand copies sold. (By contrast, Flannery O'Connor's brilliant southern novel *Wise Blood*, also published in 1952, barely sold 2,500 copies that year [Elie 2002, 14]).

The autobiography has since gone through two printings, 1981 and 1997, with introductions by Daniel Berrigan, S. J. and Robert Coles, respectively, neither of whom needed to stretch to celebrate the endurance and relevance of Day and her story. It is still Gospel of and for our times. Women, laborers, pacifists, and Catholics find themselves in good company with Dorothy Day. The press acclaimed the power of her story first, with the Jesuit poet Berrigan and the Harvard psychologist Coles following thereafter. Writing in 2002 on the fiftieth anniversary of its publication, Eugene McCarraher wrote, "Day's sacramental imagination can still be a sure light in our post-September 11 world. The human price exacted—in Afghani and American lives—for our 'freedom' and 'homeland security' is too easily ignored. Day's sacramental realism should lead us to ask if a freedom so purchased is not really a servitude" (2002, 13).

NOTE

Dorothy Day, *The Long Loneliness* (San Francisco: Harper and Row, 1981). All references are to this edition.

WORKS CITED

Coles, Robert. 1987. *Dorothy Day: A Radical Devotion*. Reading, PA: Addison-Wesley.

Duffus, R. L. 1952. "Behind the Slogans, She Saw the Dream in Men's Hearts." *New York Times Book Review* 111 (January 20): 12.

Elie, Paul. 2002. "Why and How Day Wrote It." *Commonweal* 79, no. 9 (May 3): 13–15.

Jordan, Patrick. 2002. "Between the Lines." *Commonweal* 79, no. 9 (May 3): 16.

McCarraher, Eugene. 2002. "*The Long Loneliness* at 50: Dorothy Day's Enduring Autobiography." *Commonweal* 79, no. 9 (May 3): 12–13.

Piehl, Mel. 1982. *Breaking Bread: The Catholic Worker and the Origins of Catholic Radicalism in America*. Philadelphia: Temple University Press.

BIBLIOGRAPHY

Cook, Jack. *Bowery Blues: A Tribute to Dorothy Day*. Philadelphia: Xlibris, 2001.

Coy, Patrick G., ed. *A Revolution of the Heart: Essays on the Catholic Worker*. Philadelphia: New Society Publishers, 1988.

Forest, Jim. *Love Is the Measure: A Biography of Dorothy Day*. Maryknoll, NY: Orbis, 1994.

Klejment, Anne, and Nancy L. Roberts. *American Catholic Pacifism: The Influence of Dorothy Day and the Catholic Worker Movement*. Westport, CT: Praeger, 1996.

Merriman, Brigid O'Shea. *Searching for Christ: The Spirituality of Dorothy Day*. Notre Dame, IN: University of Notre Dame Press, 1994.

Miller, William D. *A Harsh and Dreadful Love: Dorothy Day and the Catholic Worker Movement*. New York: Liveright, 1973.

———. *Dorothy Day: A Biography*. San Francisco: Harper and Row, 1982.

————. *All Is Grace: The Spirituality of Dorothy Day.* Garden City, NY: Doubleday, 1987.

O'Connor, June. *The Moral Vision of Dorothy Day: A Feminist Perspective.* New York: Crossroad, 1991.

Roberts, Nancy L. *Dorothy Day and the Catholic Worker.* Albany: State University of New York Press, 1984.

Thorn, William J., Phillip M. Runkel, and Susan Mountin, eds. *Dorothy Day and the Catholic Worker Movement: Centenary Essays.* Milwaukee, WI: Marquette University Press, 2001.

— **Jane F. Morrissey**

Annie Dillard [1945–]

Holy the Firm

BIOGRAPHY

Meta Ann Doak, the writer we know as Annie Dillard, was born on April 30, 1945. After what seems a relatively unremarkable youth in Pittsburgh, at age eighteen Doak left to attend Hollins College in Roanoke, Virginia. Closer scrutiny, however, reveals an unusually privileged background in a wealthy extended family and parents who proved idiosyncratic, quirky, and lively, raising Meta Ann to march to the beat of her own drummer. Yet, progressing from childhood curiosity to high school rebellions, however artful, caused alarms even for her unusual parents. With the advice of her high school, they agreed that the creative but traditional environment of a small, southern college for women offered the right balance for their exuberant, unconventional daughter (Smith 1991, 3–6). That choice of Hollins would make all the difference.

Annie Dillard appeared to burst upon the literary scene with the publication of *Pilgrim at Tinker Creek* (1974), which received the 1975 Pulitzer Prize for general nonfiction when she was only thirty. The book was represented as a personal journey to the local wilderness, an homage to Thoreau, largely brought about by a need to discover a new purpose in life after a near-fatal bout with pneumonia (Smith 1991, 8). Brought out through the help of then-husband Richard Dillard's agent, and with the assistance of *Harper's Magazine* press editor Lawrence Freundlich, the book gained its first attention through the early publication of several segments in *Harper's* and elsewhere (9). Yet, despite careful placement in the literary marketplace, *Pilgrim at Tinker Creek* still seemed to herald the sudden appearance of a native, rural genius, sometimes to the author's dismay (Parrish 1998, 158).

For the next two decades, Annie Dillard exerted a major influence on literary nonfiction, bringing new attention to the personal essay. *Holy the Firm* (1977) and *Teaching a Stone to Talk* (1982) built on her already strong reputation. *An American Childhood* (1987) concentrated more specifically on Dillard's personal past, narrating her childhood and early adolescence. In the novel *The Living* (1993), Dillard directed her substantial observational powers to the fictional history of a small community, while in *For the Time Being* (1999) she returned to the processes of philosophical and theological speculation seen in her earlier works.

Questions of nature and God fascinate Dillard. Throughout her career she has explored both the natural world and spiritual experience, along with their epiphanic intersections. Raised a Presbyterian, she demonstrates a convincing knowledge of comparative religion, reading widely in theological and mystical works (Smith 1991, 5–12). Having progressed through two marriages and the birth of a child in 1984, Annie Dillard formally joined the Roman Catholic Church in the 1990s, marrying for a third time (Smith 1991, 13; Cantwell 1992, 40).

The question remains how Meta Ann Doak metamorphosed into Annie Dillard during the years between her entry into Hollins and her completion of *Pilgrim*. Although Dillard's reputation suggests the sudden eruption of a "natural talent," her early success grew from nearly a decade of hard study (Parrish 1998, 123–26ff).[1] She has frequently acknowledged the influence of Professor Richard H. W. Dillard. Nine years younger than he, she took his poetry seminar during her sophomore year at Hollins, and they married shortly thereafter, in 1965. Richard Dillard, however, was only one among many important influences. As Nancy Parrish notes in her book on the "Hollins Group," this was a fertile creative period at the then little-known college, one that led several students to successful careers. Hollins combined the nurturing atmosphere of a small college with the vigorous coaching characteristic of larger university writing workshops. A supportive Hollins community, along with the specific early tutelage of Richard Dillard, created conditions in which the highly innovative talents of Meta Ann Doak could develop into the startling and evocative mature style of the still youthful Annie Dillard.

Attention has focused on "Annie Dillard," both as writer and subject, but Meta Ann Doak has remained a footnote, and the name shift is emblematic of Annie Dillard's "writing life" (Parrish 1998, 125–27).[2] She has created a fictional persona of herself as a "pilgrim," through which to explore issues of God, nature, life, and death. For Annie Dillard the writer, the passion is *writing*—the production and performance of a constructed textual self. For that constructed textual identity, the passion is a compelling blend of natural experience, personal reflection, and theological speculation. On occasion, Dillard's writer identity surfaces in the prose and overshadows briefly the interests of the pilgrim character. Yet Annie the writer, in creating Annie the pilgrim, has still succeeded in erasing Meta Ann, the person of fact and record.

It is easy to conflate the actual writer and the performative persona created in the writing. Certainly part of this conflation is accidental and part is the natural consequence of how readers respond to personal, creative nonfiction. Still, given her long and careful training at Hollins as well as her sophisticated early introduction to the literary market, Dillard has also consciously helped to mystify her own literary development. She has spent little time detailing the period of transition from the naive undergraduate of 1963 to the Pulitzer Prize winner of 1975. For the performance to succeed, Dillard's literary origins must remain an intriguing mystery.

Annie Dillard's work has been widely admired, and her interest in the mystical presence of God in the natural world has won her many readers. Although her influence has begun to wane, she remains a presence and, for many, a model. She is a writer of great intellectual and literary skill, educated in ways both formal and autodidactic. Furthermore, few writers can match her gift for lyrical prose, particularly in the difficult and challenging venue of the reflective, philosophical essay. Yet some of her critics have found her work affected and mannered. Readers may also experience difficulty with her apparent attempts to co-opt the suffering of others in her unrelenting search for extreme and intense material. Nonetheless, Dillard has proven herself capable of suggesting a transcendence in her prose, seeking and exploiting the opportunities for epiphany in everyday life. It remains uncertain whether her reputation will regain its earlier levels or whether it will continue to decline. Undoubtedly, she has made an important contribution to literary nonfiction. Her achievement as a prose stylist may ultimately overshadow her spiritual concerns, appropriately for one more the writer than the theologian.

PLOT SUMMARY

Holy the Firm consists of three interrelated essays focusing on images of flight, burning, suffering, and transcendence. The rugged coastlines of Washington State, along with its mountains and forests, provide an inspiring setting. Living at this breathtaking site while teaching at Western Washington University, Dillard finds a powerful landscape and a palette of compelling imagery that serve her exploration of both the transcendence and immanence of God (Smith 1991, 11). The first essay, "Newborn and Salted," revolves around the vignette of a moth dying in a candle, connecting it with other images of divine power—light, fire, and flight. This essay emphasizes the liminal nature of the site, as well as Dillard's own existence, while also introducing images of water, salt, birth, and baptism. The second essay, "God's Tooth," narrates the story of a child burned in an airplane crash, and it asks questions similar to those in the Book of Job. Images of failed flight, of falling and burning, connect with the moth of the first essay. The final essay, "Holy the Firm," builds on the images and themes from the prior two, dwelling on God's fundamental relationship to creation. Dillard returns to the questions of transcendence and immanence and relates them to the "esoteric" concept of "Holy the Firm," a substance both created and in touch with the "Absolute."

The whole poetic prose triptych draws much of its emotional energy from the centerpiece event in the second essay.[3] Young Julie Norwich (likely a pseudonym alluding to the medieval mystic and anchorite, Julian of Norwich) is riding in her father's small airplane when it suffers engine failure and crashes into the woods. Almost miraculously, she and her father escape the initial crash uninjured. Ironically, even as her father extricates Julie from the wreckage, the plane explodes and splashes her face with burning gasoline, ensuring a long period, perhaps a lifetime, of pain and disfigurement. The causes and consequences of such cruelty in fate and such indifference in the gods and/or the one God prompt much of the speculation throughout the book.

The first essay has prepared us for the crash with its narrative of the moth dying in the candle flame. Dillard so revivifies the commonplace image that we briefly forget that anyone else has ever mentioned that moths die in flames. This one dies not in a moment but throughout an evening, transformed into a new wick for the candle and flame that killed it. The passage suggests the baroque quality in Dillard's sensibilities, recalling the intensity of Bernini's *St. Teresa in Ecstasy*, for example, or Richard Crashaw's poems meditating on the wounds of Christ. The intense imagery connects with Dillard's many other powerful images of gods/God in the world.[4]

The final essay returns to some images of flight and immolation but goes further. Dillard is purchasing wine for a service at the Congregationalist church. Walking from the store, her backpack filled with what seems to be a bottled sacrament, she looks down the hillside to the beach and has a vision of Christ's Baptism. Her vision brings Dillard and the readers into an immediate and intimate closeup, and we see that in the droplets of water coating the figure of Christ are infinite, miniature worlds. The passage reveals Dillard's almost dizzying ability to move between micro and macro images, finding in the concrete moment a figure that opens to potential transcendence. Her visionary experience leads her back to issues in theology, the contrast between God as transcendent, from whom creation emanates, and God as immanent. Dillard resolves this contrast by using the difficult but unifying image of Holy the Firm, a mythical substance, conceived in esoteric theological writings. Dillard uses this image to connect and unify the potentially conflicting perspectives on God's relationship with the world.

Dillard closes *Holy the Firm* by considering how the life of Julie, the burn victim, will be lost or distorted by pain and disfigurement as well as by an even more painful rejection by the world and potential absence of romantic love. Readers are led to question not the God who allowed this to happen so much as our ignorance of divinity and its meaning in a material world. In the end, Dillard suggests that Julie may become a nun, a cloistered servant of the divinity whose purposes are so difficult to discern; this again connects Julie with the medieval mystic Julian. But at the last instant, Dillard posits a worldly redemption for Julie through either the miracles of medicine or the human emotional power to see beauty beyond disfigurement. In the book's final line, Dillard (as both writer and character) wrests the narrative from Julie, claiming that "I'll be the nun for you." This closing celebrates the intellectual mystic and the poet as the interpretive persona through whom readers come to know the transcendent *Holy the Firm*.

MAJOR THEMES

Mystical poetry resists analysis, and *Holy the Firm* is best read as prose poetry of spiritual reflection—highly meditative, intensely imagistic, and charged with symbolic possibilities. At only seventy-six pages, *Holy the Firm* may seem minor in comparison to *Pilgrim at Tinker Creek* or *An American Childhood*. Yet this slim volume contains perhaps the highest concentration of poetic and conceptual energy that can be discovered in any of Dillard's writing.

In the natural temple of the Washington coastline, in the monastic isolation of a small house, in the liminal site where sky, sea, and land meet, Dillard writes from her ongoing reading, study, and reflective exploration of fundamental questions. Paraphrased, these read like a syllabus for a course in theology: "How is God present in the world?" "What does this presence mean in the pattern of our lives, our choices, our experiences, and our relationships?" "Why do the innocent suffer horror, terror, pain, and torture as a result of the random events of the created world, the accidents that lead us to question God's purposes and our faults?" "How can we reconcile conflicting concepts of God's relationship with creation?"

Exploring such questions could lead to an unreadable work, but Dillard proves more than a match for such challenges. Having steeped herself in varied theological texts, she remains free of their abstract language. But she has scouted these sources for images and metaphors to use in constructing a literary response to theological quandaries. Dillard combines this preparation with her disciplined observations of the natural world, everything from the spider's web in her bathroom to the sweep of the horizon on the Pacific coastline. She integrates both patterns of imagery with allusions to her wide range of general reading and individual experience. The text that emerges from this complex integration is charged with both poetic and intellectual energy. Passages sing from the pages like a prose psalm, a hymn to the presence and power of God. At the end of the first essay, speaking of the immanent and more "natural" god (note the small "g"), Dillard states that "he is everything that is" and that he is "flung, and flowing, sowing, unseen, and flown" (*Holy the Firm*, 31). Her alliterative style recalls both the poetry of Gerard Manley Hopkins and the poetry and lyric prose of Dylan Thomas. The passage illustrates the literal and figurative "flight" of Dillard's writing as she strives mightily to propel her prose into a lilting form that will itself take off and take flight with the reader's imagination.

As noted, *Holy the Firm* offers a triptych of essays with the focal narrative in the central piece, the second essay entitled "God's Tooth." Julie Norwich survives a plane crash only to be burned by the random touch of flaming gasoline from an after-crash explosion. She becomes the figure of suffering humanity, struggling to explain causality and to justify divinity in a world where innocent children have their faces burned off. At pains to make Julie neither too metaphorical nor too angelic, Dillard also narrates her first meeting with the child two weeks earlier, at a local gathering. Julie had been making a minor pest of herself, in her childish and childlike fashion, especially by annoying Dillard's cat. Still, Dillard identifies with the child, admitting that "We *looked* a bit alike"; but the writer quickly acknowledges that the child's face has been "slaughtered now, and I don't remember mine" (41).

This understated passage results from careful effort. Dillard must acknowledge the concrete reality of the child, her authentic personality, to create the appropriate emotional connection for the reader. The writer must also both distance herself from the child, as image and object, and yet identify with the child's condition. Thus, in the statement quoted here, both Dillard and the child become faceless, one by accident of fate and the other by a forgetfulness (perhaps feigned). This connection is vital for the structure of the whole work, for *Holy the Firm* depends on our connecting emotionally with the loss experienced by the child but then transferring that emotion, through the persona of Dillard the pilgrim, to a generalized humanity. Only thus can we connect fully to the rather abstract problem explored by the writer—our relationship with divinity. The narrative must be a microcosm of that relationship, and so it is selected and rendered with allusions to the images of flight, burning, loss, and transcendence that run throughout the book. From this focal event, Dillard goes on to explore the fundamental questions noted above. The burned child is the emblematic image and exemplum from which Dillard will derive the meditation of the work.

For Dillard's rhetorical strategy to work, we must acknowledge our common plight with Julie, but we must not dwell on the particularities of the girl's own subjectivity. Dillard asks us to consider whether such burned children scream without lips, but we do not actually visit the child or hear her cry out. Despite the horrific directness of Dillard's description, and perhaps even because of the stark images (such as the pain drugs futilely seeping through the burned tissue and into the sheets), Dillard quickly distances us from the emotional complexity of actual human experience. The writer is hunting for an image here, and the greater purposes of poetic form and philosophical speculation must take precedence over the subjectivity of the actual victim. Indeed, not only faceless, Julie is also nameless, a figure who is given, instead, the name of the fourteenth-century English mystic writer. In addition, Julie is necessarily connected with Christ because her father is allusively named "Jesse," father of the biblical David and so in the line leading to Jesus. But the father remains even more a mere image. We witness no angst-ridden, guilty parent sitting by the bedside of the inconsolable child—this is not social realism but mystical poetry, after all. The specificity and the concreteness serve not the victims but the images deriving from the victims. The images must be believable, but we must not become too involved in the idiosyncratic and particular problems of actual lives.

The burning moth of essay one is another winged and fallen figure, as is the image of a tiny winged god, singed and smoking, brought in by the cat and rescued by Dillard. Both foreshadow Julie's story. While the latter provides a playful figure of poetic hyperbole and wit, the former transforms the old cliché into an almost mystical event (an image that connects with both crash victim Julie and the writer). The moth does not just hit the flame, burn, and fall to the ground. No, it becomes glued in the liquid wax, its body emptied of a substance turned into vapor and carbon, its shell transformed into a second wick for the candle. The incident supposedly occurred while Dillard was camping in the Blue Ridge Mountains two years earlier (an obvious allusion to her first book) and while the writer was reading a novel about the poet Rimbaud called *A Day on Fire*. From burning moth to passionate artistic engagement, Dillard segues to speak of a writer's commitment. She shifts to the writing class she teaches at Western Washington, passionately confronting her students with the question of whether or not they would give their lives to be writers, whether they would descend into the flame and allow it to hollow them out. She confesses that "They had no idea what I was saying" (18). Shortly thereafter, Dillard returns to the image of the small, hermitage-like dwelling where she lives and writes, and she conflates and balances the images and roles of nun, thinker, and artist. The room, she says, is a "skull," empty but with a good view (22). By extension, Dillard becomes the passionate intellect, the "pilgrim" mind, dwelling within that skull.

Such comments reveal Dillard's central concern—she is writer first and foremost, her interests in theology and philosophy coming in only as a close second. She will not serve two masters—she has given herself, moth to flame, as writer. By extension, Dillard represents the writer as the equivalent of the nun and the thinker, co-opting and encompassing these roles by a kind of artistic fiat. But the speculating mystic we meet in these pages is not Annie Dillard the writer but the persona of the writer in the role of nun/thinker, just one more aspect of the character Annie the pilgrim. Dillard uses these passages to reveal her view of art and the artist. In the process, readers still encounter a genuine exploration of theological problems as well as visionary responses to those problems. But always it is the poetic structure of the work and the poetic voice of the text that take precedence. In *Holy the Firm*, theological speculation serves poetry.

Having briefly revealed the writer's goals and roles in the first essay, then plunged us, in the second, into the concrete problem of how human suffering leads us to question whether and how God is present to us, Dillard proceeds in the third essay to explore and respond to the questions of transcendence and immanence. *Holy the Firm* provides the image. It is a concept, she tell us, out of esoteric theology that describes a concrete substance, deep in the core of the earth, deep in the heart of creation, and actually in contact with the Absolute. But prior to this abstract discussion, Dillard experiences a vision. She has volunteered to buy the communion wine for the small Congregationalist church where she attends but is not a member. Returning from the purchase, she describes the wine as almost radiating from her backpack. She is suffused with its light, becoming "moth," "light," and "prayer" (65). Looking down the hillside, she sees people on the shore, but this image immediately changes into a vision of Christ at his baptism. We are suddenly in intimate contact with him as he rises from the water, where the sphere of each droplet on his skin becomes its own tiny world. Imaginatively descending into one such world, Dillard witnesses the whole of creation and the wholeness of creation and eternity. Deftly and efficiently, the writer has encompassed the equivalent of the *Paradiso* of Dante's *Commedia*, the beatific vision encapsulated in a handful of lines on two pages.

Having experienced the vision, the pilgrim now can explain the conundrum. Creation emanates from a distant God, and God is also immanent, present in all creation. But both the transcendent and the immanent God remain connected in *Holy the Firm*. Supposedly a low substance, lower than salts and minerals, *Holy the Firm* is still a transcendent substance, in touch with the Absolute, with divinity, and thus it offers a solution in its solidity with both Creator and creation, both of which "socket" into *Holy the Firm* (71). This is, of course, a poetic solution, not a theological one. The problem is to satisfy the longing for spiritual wholeness as experienced by the character of Dillard the pilgrim. Dillard the writer has carefully and gracefully articulated that solution, and so the character is satisfied and the artist's problem has been solved. She speaks again of the role of artists: "There is no such thing as an artist; there is only the world" (71–72). In the subsequent rhapsodic passage, the nonexistent artist is still the essential flame that emerges from and lights the world. The artist is also a "seraph" who lights God's kingdom (72).

For Dillard, art is the true mysticism. The intensity of spirit, the power and passion of the mystic are but figures of speech, metaphors for the essential transcendence that is art itself. *Holy the Firm* is definitely a book that evolved more from Dillard's years in writers' workshops than from her perusal of theology texts. Dillard is a passionate and committed artist and a highly capable one. She has found in mystical writing a treasure trove of images, delightful and powerful, and given her passion for poetry, she cannot resist them. Solving real theological questions is rarely accomplished with such graceful prose or with such powerful closure. The problems are thorny, and the connections between abstract systems and concrete actions become awkward to negotiate. But the artist seeks symmetry, seeks form and power through the form. Dillard succeeds in her quest, but the search is not for some theological Grail. As artist, she seeks rather a gracefully rhapsodic *story* of her pilgrim character finding that Grail in *Holy the Firm*. Dillard is not a mystic determined to be a saint but a writer concerned with the captivating power that holy images and stories of saintliness can convey.

Readers would be wrong to take offense at this. Dillard has carefully foreshadowed and declared her commitments. We should have no doubt that her text is a stage on which she will perform, not a pulpit from which she will offer doctrine. Criticizing Dillard for not being a theologian would be like criticizing an actor because she is not the person she plays on stage. Dillard is a performing artist, and she chooses, in part, to construct a performative persona as a mystical pilgrim. In the process of reading, we do indeed learn something about the nature of mysticism and the theological quest, but we should not be shocked that Dillard is a performer in her prose. While often compared to writers like Thoreau, she actually shows greater similarity to artists like Spalding Gray, the writer/performer whose one-man stage shows about his own life have been made into successful films. Like Gray, Dillard uses the material of her own life to create her art, and like him, she creates a performative persona (the pilgrim), which is not to be confused either with the artist playing the part or the actual person whose life is mined for events and images. Dillard's search for serious epiphanies parallels, in one sense, Gray's search for a "perfect moment" in such films as *Swimming to Cambodia* (1987). Ultimately, Dillard is an artist, and we need to evaluate her on that basis. We may expect to be engaged, entertained, and enlightened by the sacramental union of artist with art form, which for many writers is the only theology they really know. On these grounds, Dillard does not disappoint.

As to the Catholic dimensions of Dillard's work, we are left with a problematic picture. Religious ideas in *Holy the Firm* apparently grow from a nondenominational and idiosyncratic Christianity, informed by wide, eclectic, and undirected reading in theology and philosophy. Showing some interest in "the high Churches," Dillard still demonstrates preference for the "low," which she regards as more engaged with God's presence (59). Her reading includes everything from Julian of Norwich to the Rule of Saint Benedict, but like many writers Dillard in *Holy the Firm* comes to Catholicism because it offers a cornucopia of images, metaphors, and allusions as resources for the poet's work. Conceptually, she may prefer unstructured religious situations because they provide the writer more scope for inscribing her own interpretation. Furthermore, reading Dillard does not lead many to engage in careful scrutiny of her theological concepts. She writes with such power that reading her prose is an experience of breathless abandon. The overlapping images, the flights of metaphor, the rhapsodic flow, and the rhythmic, bardic tone leave us dazzled but exhausted. This results not from the writer's "rapture" but from her conscious construction of the text that counterfeits that rapture. After such a reading experience, few are willing to plunge back in and engage in systematic analysis. Those who have been inspired will follow their inspiration, while those who have been confused or offended will think of better uses of their time.

The fundamental problem of a God both transcendent and immanent is clearly integral to much of Christianity, especially to Roman Catholicism. Dillard's solution in *Holy the Firm* seems poetically compelling but theologically awkward.

Her response to complex ideas betrays a poet's search for the strong image rather than the systematic theologian's critical examination and resolution of problems. At one point, she characteristically declares that if God is immanent then Christ is "redundant" (70). This cavalier remark is merely one example of Dillard's failure here to acknowledge the complex paradoxes inherent in the Catholic understanding of God's nature and the Trinitarian perspective on God. Christ's life and death mean more than the mere engagement of God with the created world in a physical sense. Rather, Christ offers a sacramental touch of personal divinity while sharing the common experience of humanity. Catholics believe that through Christ we know God and God experiences our created condition in a unique Person. What is more, through the sacrifice of the Cross and the Resurrection, Christ becomes Redeemer of our fallen nature and example of transcendence—from death into life everlasting. In *Holy the Firm*, Dillard seems to regard the question of God's transcendence and immanence as if it were a problem in theoretical physics rather than a question of sin, sacrament, and redemption. Dillard may have found these latter concepts less than satisfactory in her writing of *Holy the Firm*, but they are fundamental to much of Christianity, especially to Catholicism.

Thus, Dillard's theological perspective lacks much connection with a Catholic Christology. She seems equally unwilling to address and explore the third person of the Trinity, the Spirit. Reaching instead for the artistically satisfying but theologically weak concept of *Holy the Firm*, Dillard confirms once again her skill as an artist as well as her ultimate limits in explaining mainstream Christian theology. That Dillard eventually converted to Catholicism many years after these speculations may or may not have relevance here. Certainly her later and somewhat desultory work, *For the Time Being*, coming after her conversion, might have greater relevance for Catholic theology, even if it lacks the concentration of the earlier book. In *Holy the Firm*, however, we have an inspiring prose poem about Dillard's pilgrim character grappling with important theological issues. As an example of the personal theological struggle, this work can be deeply appreciated by believers of any faith, but as an example of Catholic or even Christian theology, it has obvious limits. We should appreciate it for its excellence on its own terms rather than asking it to achieve the goals of a theological treatise.

CRITICAL RECEPTION

Coming shortly after the overwhelming success of *Pilgrim at Tinker Creek*, *Holy the Firm* began and remains in the shadow of the earlier Pulitzer Prize-winning book. Receiving a warm reception, it was regarded more as a mere coda to *Pilgrim*, or perhaps as a foreshadowing of longer works to come. Critics have praised its evocative poetry, while some have complained of difficulties with its obscure theology (Smith 1991, 12). Later critics have fit the book into an overall pattern of Dillard's ongoing exploration of spirituality, but it still receives far less attention than Dillard's other works.

Several book-length studies of Dillard, along with a number of dissertations, focus on Dillard as a writer who seeks spiritual experience in the context of nature. She has been compared with Robinson Jeffers, Gerard Manley Hopkins, Kathleen Norris, Aldo Leopold, Wendell Berry, Edward Abbey, and, of course,

Thoreau. Few studies specifically examine *Holy the Firm*. Sandra Johnson (1992) does discuss the text in her book on the "epiphany" in Dillard's writing, seeing it as "neo-romantic" and connecting it with the writing of Wordsworth, Hopkins, and even T. S. Eliot. Yet Johnson concentrates more on Dillard's other writing and is interested more in the neoromantic sensibility than in the theological issues. Linda Smith's slender Twayne study, *Annie Dillard* (1991), devotes a brief, reasonably useful chapter to *Holy the Firm*, but this book also focuses mostly on the more popular works. In her book on the Hollins Group, Nancy Parrish (1998) provides an excellent case study of the writer's development and the process of writing *Pilgrim*. Parrish, however, also gives scant attention to *Holy the Firm*.

Unfortunately, a number of works about Dillard develop a worshipful tone. Even Parrish, who demonstrates a keen critical intelligence, occasionally lapses into the posture of sitting at the "guru's" feet. Mary Cantwell's 1992 profile of Dillard, for all its useful information, is perhaps the worst example of this tone. In the long run, such analyses may do more to detract from than support Dillard's reputation, making her seem more the cult icon than the accomplished writer.

Having garnered several awards, decades of positive reviews, frequent republication in anthologies, and a wide general readership, Dillard still has not become a favorite of the academic critics, except among those committed few who study the literary essay. A contemporary writer whose stylistic affinities suggest a modernist, she has provoked little interest among postmodern scholars. As a neoromantic writer focused on the interior life of the spirit, Dillard seems an inappropriate subject to scholars increasingly devoted to social and cultural approaches to literature. She is the subject of a number of scholarly articles, but they are not usually in the most influential journals. Many college students meet Dillard only through their first-year composition anthology, but few English majors engage her work in advanced courses. She remains a subject of interest but not of extensive research. *Holy the Firm* gains only a fraction of the attention given to Dillard. A spiritual reflection written at the "fringey" edge of the world, *Holy the Firm* remains a book for lonely explorers patient enough to endure its excesses and abstractions that they might share in its poetic ecstasies.

NOTES

Annie Dillard, *Holy the Firm* (New York: Harper and Row, 1977). All references are to this edition.

1. Much of chapter 4 (123–63) of Nancy Parrish's book *Lee Smith, Annie Dillard, and the Hollins Group* is devoted to an intricate description of Dillard's life and work in the Hollins community, both as a student and then as a "faculty wife" engaged in her own independent writing. The remainder of this paragraph generalizes from Parrish's detailed account.

2. Parrish explores at some length the relationship between Dillard the writer and Dillard the persona in the writing. Much of this discussion parallels my own reading of Dillard, prior to my examination of Parrish's book. We differ in that I find the blurring of distinctions between writer and persona less a sign of contemporary liminal conditions of the writer and more the result of highly controlled and self-conscious rhetorical strategy and stylistic technique.

3. Using the model of the visual triptych, I begin my discussion here with the second, central essay because it contains the focal event and image of the burned child.

I then proceed to discuss the first and third essays, as if moving first to the left and then to the right of the central triptych panel. I use this approach in both the "Plot Summary" and the "Major Themes" sections of this essay.

4. We see similar issues raised, in a more limited way, in the essay "The Deer at Providencia," from the 1982 volume *Teaching a Stone to Talk*.

WORKS CITED

Cantwell, Mary. 1992. "A Pilgrim's Progress." *New York Times Magazine* (April 26): sec. 6, 34ff.

Dillard, Annie. 1974. *Pilgrim at Tinker Creek*. New York: Harper's Magazine Press.

———. 1982. "The Deer at Providencia." In *Teaching a Stone to Talk*, 60–66. New York: Harper and Row Perennial Library.

———. 1987. *An American Childhood*. New York: Harper and Row.

———. 1999. *For the Time Being*. New York: Alfred A. Knopf.

Gray, Spalding. 1987. *Swimming to Cambodia*, directed by Jonathan Demme. Cinecom.

Johnson, Sandra Humble. 1992. *The Space Between: Literary Epiphany in the Work of Annie Dillard*. Kent, OH: Kent State University Press.

Parrish, Nancy C. 1998. *Lee Smith, Annie Dillard, and the Hollins Group*. Baton Rouge: Louisiana State University Press.

Smith, Linda. 1991. *Annie Dillard*. New York: Twayne.

— Vincent Casaregola

Isak Dinesen (Karen Blixen) [1885–1962]

Babette's Feast

BIOGRAPHY

Karen Christenze Dinesen was born in 1885 at Rungstedlund, her family's estate in Denmark. She was the second of five children born to Wilhelm Dinesen and his wife, Ingeborg Westenholz. The Dinesens were an old landowning family, and the Westenholzes made their fortune through commerce. Karen was reared amidst wealth and social privilege, an atmosphere she seemed to regard as stifling. Wilhelm Dinesen, debilitated by a disease that was probably syphilis, committed suicide when Karen was ten. This tremendous loss overshadowed what seemed to be an otherwise peaceful childhood. Dinesen was educated at home by governesses. She enjoyed telling stories and writing plays from a young age, and she published her first two stories, "The Hermits" and "The Ploughman," in 1907. Her primary ambition in this early period, however, was to paint. She studied painting at the Danish Academy of Art from 1903 to 1906 and later in Paris in 1910. Another formative experience was Dinesen's trip to Rome in 1912, which, as Robert Langbaum suggests, cast Italy in her imagination as a sensuous, exotic, and radically other landscape, an Italy that she described as "the natural setting for stories" (1964, 41).

Throughout her life, Dinesen, or "Tanne" as her family called her, chafed against the ordinariness of life. A romantic bohemian who sought heightened emotional and aesthetic experiences, she was subject to frequent mood swings and fits of melancholy. Such a disposition, although conducive to her art, did not lend itself to a tranquil personal life. As a young woman, Dinesen fell in love with her Swedish cousin, Hans von Blixen, who did not reciprocate her feelings. Blixen's twin brother, however, courted her, and eventually she agreed to marry Baron Bror von Blixen. Dinesen, now Baroness von Blixen, longed to live far away from her husband's rural Swedish estate, and the couple decided to emigrate to British East Africa and establish a coffee plantation. Against family opposition, both to the marriage and the emigration, the couple married in Nairobi in 1914.

Although the young couple was exhilarated with their new life in Africa, the marriage soon foundered. Dinesen contracted syphilis from her husband, and despite repeated treatments, the disease was incurable. She suffered painful symptoms for the rest of her life. The Blixens divorced in 1921, and Dinesen managed the farm until the Karen Coffee Company collapsed in 1931. Despite her disappointments, Dinesen embraced life in Africa. In that country, as biographer Judith Thurman describes, "was the scope, the freedom, the eroticism, the raw grandeur she had dreamed about in Denmark and of which she had felt so long deprived" (1982, 129). In 1918 she met Denys Finch-Hatton, a British aristocrat and safari guide. Their intense love affair is alluded to in *Out of Africa* (1937) and dramatized by Meryl Streep and Robert Redford in the 1985 Hollywood film based on Dinesen's memoir.

In 1931, devastated by both the sale of her farm and Finch-Hatton's death in an airplane accident, Dinesen returned to Denmark and Rungstedlund. She decided to support herself through writing, and she wrote in English under the pen name Isak (from the Old Testament, "he who laughs") Dinesen. Her first book, *Seven Gothic Tales* (1934), was, according to Langbaum, less favorably received in Denmark than in America, where it became an instant best seller. Despite the fact that Dinesen "used to complain that the Americans liked her better than her own countrymen did" (1964, 3), her first three books, including *Out of Africa* and *Winter's Tales* (1942), firmly and immediately established her literary reputation on both sides of the Atlantic. Langbaum also notes that she was, from 1957 until her death, a "leading contender" for the Nobel Prize in Literature (203). Just four years before her death, Dinesen published a second group of books in quick succession: *Last Tales* (1957), *Anecdotes of Destiny* (1958), and *Shadows on the Grass* (1961). A final story, *Ehrengard*, was published posthumously in 1963. Dinesen died in 1962.

Several aspects of Dinesen's biography are worth highlighting in relation to her authorship of *Babette's Feast*. Although Dinesen suffered from syphilis, the immediate cause of her death was malnutrition. Susan Hardy Aiken explains that Dinesen's syphilis "attacked the spinal nerves that control digestion, ultimately causing her to die of starvation." She points out the irony inherent in the fact that Dinesen "wrote that celebration of transformative consumption [*Babette's Feast*] at a time when her own body was literally devouring itself" (1990, 254–55). Yet as Judith Thurman has noted, Dinesen had a lifelong preoccupation with maintaining her delicate, birdlike figure, starving and fasting in order to achieve her physical ideal. "Fasting," Thurman argues, "became and remained for her . . . an ironic, powerful, and essentially feminine act of heroism" (1982, 66).

Dinesen's views about religion were equally complicated. She was baptized in the Danish Church but reared as a Unitarian, a faith system she later distanced herself from, explaining that "it hardly seems a religion at all" (Langbaum 1964, 39). Her attitude toward Christianity seems to have swung between repulsion and attraction. As a young woman she described herself as an atheist (Thurman 1982, 173), and long after she returned from Africa, she stated that she received her "strongest impression of religious faith from Mohammedans" (374). She considered her status, in regard to Christianity, as that of an outsider: "I think that I have really honestly sought to understand what it was . . . but any real understanding in a connected sense I have never achieved" (374). She also condemned what she described as "the poisonous tradition of dualism" inherent in Christianity, which placed the sensual and spiritual worlds in opposition to each other (374).

It may seem ironic, then, that *Babette's Feast*, which employs the themes of Eucharist, grace, and redemption in such sophisticated ways, was authored by a woman who did not consider herself a Christian. Would Dinesen have objected to attempts to classify her story within a Catholic tradition or context? Perhaps not. Aside from the fact that she drew very deliberately from Catholic ritual, imagery, and tradition in constructing her stories, Dineson demonstrated a personal fascination for Catholicism, which perhaps dates from her travels to France and Italy in her twenties. In response to her brother Thomas's suggestion that "considering her general outlook, she ought to become a Catholic," Dinesen stated that "without subscribing to any dogma she was a sort of Catholic, a Catholic priest at that" (Thurman 1982, 172). She repeated this assertion on more than one occasion; in another exchange with Thomas, she wrote, "You know that I have said that I would like to be a Catholic priest, and I still maintain this—I am not far from being one" (215). Judith Thurman suggests that Dinesen's identification with the Catholic priest arose both from her relatively isolated, independent manner of living and her role as an artist, which privileged her to "perform a great spiritual service to humanity" (215). In light of this interpretation, it seems no coincidence that Dinesen chose to represent the artist/chef Babette Hersant as a priest presiding over the Eucharist.

PLOT SUMMARY

Isak Dinesen's *Babette's Feast* made its debut in the *Ladies' Home Journal* in 1950 and was subsequently reprinted in Dinesen's final collection of stories, *Anecdotes of Destiny*, in 1958. The story was intended for an American audience, and its subject matter was suggested by Dinesen's friend Geoffrey Gorer, who told her that "Americans are obsessed with food" (Thurman 1982, 329). Fittingly, the sumptuous banquet at the heart of the story ranks among the most memorable depictions of a dinner party in literature. When Gabriel Axel's film rendition of *Babette's Feast* (*Babbette's Gastebud*, 1987) came to the United States in 1988, American viewers did, indeed, seem obsessed with food, as some high-end restaurants offered diners recreations of the Dean's birthday dinner described in the work (Rashkin 1995, 356). For all its mouthwatering description of such fancy dishes as Cailles in Sarcophage and Blinis Demidoff, however, *Babette's Feast* is no mere tribute to the delights of the palate. Dinesen's deceptively simple account of an extravagant feast in a bleak Norwegian village questions the divide between body and soul, secular and spiritual, and past and present. The story's overt comparison of feasting to the Eucharist prompts readers to reflect, in particular, upon the intersections of love and loss, grace and redemption, in the lives of ordinary men and women.

Babette's Feast is set in Berlevaag, a remote fishing village on the coast of Norway, between the years 1854 and 1883. The story commences by introducing two sisters, Martine and Philippa. Their father, the Dean, was the charismatic leader of an ascetic Protestant sect, and after his death his daughters devote themselves, as before, to a life of piety and charity among the members of his community. The sisters' quiet lives have been contained within the narrow confines of the village; each woman has had one frustrated suitor. Martine, at eighteen, had attracted a young army officer, Lorens Loewenhielm, who was passing through Berlevaag on a visit to his aunt. Struck by Martine's angelic beauty, Lorens has a vision of a better, nobler life under her influence. Through the help of his pious aunt, Lorens gains admittance to prayer meetings at the Dean's house, but he is intimidated by his surroundings and never speaks. Nor can he speak to Martine of his love: at the end of his final visit, Lorens simply bids her farewell. "[I]n this world," he says, "there are things which are impossible!" (*Babette's Feast*, 24). Although Martine never reveals her feelings for the young officer, the story makes clear that she, too, suffers a loss at his departure.

A year later, when Philippa is eighteen, a famous French opera singer, Achille Papin, arrives in Berlevaag on a sightseeing trip to the Norwegian coast. He attends the Dean's church and is immediately transfixed by Philippa's voice raised in song. Envisioning a future opera diva, he gains permission from the Dean to give Philippa singing lessons, simply describing how wonderfully she would sing to God's glory. As the lessons continue, Achille falls in love with his pupil. One day, at the end of singing a duet with Philippa, Achille kisses her. Philippa immediately asks her father to cancel the lessons. Achille sadly returns to Paris without his diva.

Fifteen years later, a third stranger arrives in Berlevaag. A woman, terrified and exhausted, appears on the sisters' doorstep. She bears a letter from Achille Papin, which explains that she, Babette Hersant, has had to flee Paris in the wake of the civil war. Babette's husband and son have been shot as revolutionaries, and Babette, who fought alongside them, has narrowly escaped with her life. Achille commends Babette to the care of the sisters, stating simply in his letter that "Babette can cook" (30). Babette insists that she will work for nothing, only food and shelter, and the sisters take her into their home. They teach Babette to make their simple, austere dishes—split cod and bread-and-ale soup—and warn her that "luxurious fare was sinful" (32). Babette's economical housekeeping saves the sisters money and time, and they now have more resources to help the poor and sick of Berlevaag.

Twelve more years pass, and Babette receives her first letter since arriving in Berlevaag. She learns that she has won ten thousand francs, thanks to a lottery ticket—her last tie to Paris—that a friend had renewed for her each year. This news saddens the sisters, who assume that their good and faithful servant will now return to Paris. They help her count and store her money, and wait for the inevitable. When Babette comes to them, begging them to allow her to cook a "real French dinner" (37) in honor of the Dean's birthday, the sisters, although reluctant, give in. Babette orders all the necessary goods from Paris, and the sisters, completely mystified as to what a real French dinner entails, begin to fear the worst, especially when a live tortoise is wheeled in. They consult with the members of their community and decide that at the Dean's birthday dinner they would try to ignore the food and "be silent on all matters of food and drink" (41).

On the evening of the Dean's birthday, twelve guests assemble for dinner, including two last-minute additions, old Mrs. Loewenhielm and her nephew Lorens. Lorens, who has since married an aristocratic woman and become a respected general, nonetheless wonders if he has made the right choices in life. He arrives at the sisters' home that evening seeking confirmation of his decision to abandon the Dean's house—and Martine—years before. Expecting a simple meal of haddock and water, the General is stunned by what appears before him: amontillado, fine champagne, turtle soup, Blinis Demidoff. He is also astonished that his fellow diners seem to take no notice of the extraordinary food. Yet the Dean's followers respond in other ways to the magic of the food and wine. The community members, strained over the years by animosity and petty quarrels, begin to reconcile their differences as they reminisce about the Dean's life and great deeds.

When the centerpiece of the meal arrives—Cailles en Sarcophage—the General suddenly remembers that he has had the dish once before, at the Café Anglais in Paris. The café's chef, a woman, was famed for transforming a meal "into a love affair of the noble and romantic category in which one no longer distinguishes between bodily and spiritual appetite or satiety" (51). At this point, the General "no longer wondered at anything" (51). At the conclusion of dinner, he rises and gives a speech on the nature of divine grace. Grace comes to us regardless of the choices we make in life, he states: "Grace, brothers, makes no conditions and singles out none of us in particular; grace takes us all to its bosom and proclaims general amnesty. See! that which we have chosen is given us, and that which we have refused is, also and at the same time, granted us. Ay, that which we have rejected is poured upon us abundantly" (52). Although the members of the Dean's community do not fully understand the General's speech, they, too, realize that they have been given "infinite grace": "They had been given one hour of the millennium" (54).

After their guests depart, the sisters return to the kitchen to find Babette "white and . . . deadly exhausted" (56). They tell her that they will remember the evening after she returns to Paris; Babette responds that she will not return, as everyone she used to cook for—the same aristocracy, ironically, she fought against as a Communard—has departed. Moreover, she spent all her lottery winnings on the feast. Babette reveals that she gave all she had not for the sisters, but for herself: "I am a great artist!" she says (58). Philippa embraces Babette and utters the same words Papin once wrote to Philippa: "In Paradise you will be the great artist that God meant you to be! . . . Ah, how you will enchant the angels!" (59).

MAJOR THEMES

Babette's Feast is, in essence, a story of redemption. As more than one critic has noted, Babette is a Christ figure—a humble, suffering servant who figuratively sacrifices herself in the preparation of the feast. Soon after Babette joins the sisters' household, "the stone which the builders had almost refused had become the headstone of the corner" (33). Years later, at the end of the Dean's birthday dinner, the exhausted Babette is described almost as a dead white corpse (56). Despite the expenditure of Babette's energy and her entire fortune, her renunciatory "sacrifice" is paradoxically framed as self-gratification: Babette begs the sisters to be allowed to perform her act of radical altruism.

Pair after pair of seemingly irreconcilable binaries shape the story: aesthetic/ascetic, body/soul, Catholic/Protestant, giving/receiving, present/past, presence/absence. These binaries, along with the bleak, wintry landscape of Berlevaag Fjord, suggest a fallen, fragmented world, one that the Dean and his followers wholeheartedly reject: "[T]he earth and all that it held to them was but a kind of illusion, and the true reality was the New Jerusalem to which they were longing" (21). Babette's feast marks a brief moment—"one hour of the millennium" (54)—when all is reconciled into a harmonious whole. While it may not be desirable to label *Babette's Feast* a "Catholic" story, as explained below, Babette's mode of redemption—the reconciliation of binaries—resonates well with certain aspects of Catholicism.

This union of opposites is most clearly exemplified by the Eucharistic imagery in the story. Although critics have compared the feast to a Protestant, Lutheran communion, less attention has been given to considering the meal within a Catholic context. And Catholic communion, I would argue, invokes and celebrates paradox in a way that many Protestant doctrines of the Eucharist do not. According to the Catholic doctrine of the Real Presence, the consecrated host looks like bread but is in actuality Christ's body; it is at once divine and human, Father and Son, corruptible and immortal. Transubstantiation is miraculous and impossible, and *Babette's Feast* also celebrates the "impossibility" of redemption. Both Loewenhielm and Papin, when they first meet Martine and Philippa, have visions of what is newly "possible." They are, of course, disappointed, but after the feast, decades later, Loewenhielm says to Martine that "tonight I have learned . . . that in this world anything is possible" (54).

Transubstantiation, as the actualization of the impossible, could seem to some as terrifyingly "magical," and the story highlights this dimension of Babette's feast as well. When the sisters agree to let Babette prepare the feast, she is implicitly compared to a witch, with her "red-haired familiar" (47). And Babette, despite her humble, quiet demeanor, is a dark, potentially violent figure who fought for her menfolk on the barricades. The sisters' "cornerstone" "had a mysterious and alarming feature to it, as if was somehow related to the Black Stone of Mecca, the Kaaba itself" (33). Since the Reformation, anti-Catholic literature has often attempted to relate Catholicism to "exotic" non-Christian religions such as Islam and Hinduism; the sisters' apprehension of the foreign, Catholic Babette gently parodies narrow sectarianism and the stereotypes it generates. The sisters' anxieties about the feast also mimic anti-Catholic depictions of the Mass. Martine dreams that the meal prepared by her papist cook will be a "witches' sabbath" (40) to poison them all; after the meal, she recalls a story about cannibalism.

Although Babette has fought with the Communards, she appears less as an agent of violence than its victim. Despite the gentle tone of the story and the beauty of the feast, it is important to remember, as critic Esther Rashkin (1995) reminds us, that each of the characters has suffered some loss. The feast does not alter the past; it does not restore Philippa and Martine to their youthful lovers, return Babette to her family and her café, or bring the Dean back among his followers. Yet while Rashkin argues that the feast serves to memorialize the dead (and hence requires a Protestant reading), the term "memorial" suggests nothing more than absence. Loewenhielm's statement, "that which we have chosen is given us, and that which we have refused is, *also and at the same time*, granted us" (52, emphasis mine), implies that, to the contrary, nothing is ever irrevocably lost. There is, at the feast, a paradoxical presence in the midst of absence. Loewenhielm, now married, will never again be Martine's lover, yet he sits once again at the Dean's table. Philippa knows that Achille Papin still thinks of her. The Dean's followers repair bonds of fellowship that had been broken through pettiness and quarrels. And Babette, despite the loss of an audience sophisticated enough to appreciate her culinary genius, continues to assert her identity and vocation: "I am a great artist!" (58), she cries, rather than, "I *was* a great artist." Seen in this light, the feast more closely resembles a Catholic Eucharist than a Protestant one. Whereas the Protestant Eucharist memorializes a sacrifice long past, Catholic doctrine teaches that Christ's sacrifice is ongoing, repeated at every consecration of the bread and wine.

Who would expect to find presence in absence, past in present, transcendence in the sensual? The characters in *Babette's Feast* receive grace where they least expect it. The Dean, surprisingly, admits the papist Achille Papin to his house, stating that God's ways are unfathomable (27). As the Dean's followers sit down to Babette's exotic meal, they comfort themselves with the thought that "grace had chosen to manifest itself there, in the very wine, as fully as anywhere" (48). While the concept of grace is central to both Protestantism and Catholicism, Catholicism's stress upon the goodness of creation (rather than upon innate depravity) encourages believers to acknowledge grace in all things and at all times. Babette's role as an artist is to awaken the senses of her audience so that they can see and understand God's grace in the world. Despite the diners' vow to "purify" themselves "of all delight or disgust of the senses," only through their senses will they apprehend God. After Babette's sumptuous meal, the diners recognize that "they had seen the universe as it really is" (54). And if, as *Babette's Feast* suggests, God can best be apprehended through the senses, rather than through Scripture or the cold light of reason, who better to perform the part of the priest than the artist, whether singer, chef, or writer?

CRITICAL RECEPTION

Surprisingly, *Babette's Feast* has received only scant attention in book-length studies of Dinesen's work. There are, however, a number of interesting essays on the work. Scholarship on *Babette's Feast* falls primarily into two categories: feminist readings and analyses of the story's Christian themes and imagery. Studies by Susan Hardy Aiken, Sara Stambaugh, Maire Mullins, and Maureen Barr all employ a feminist perspective to interpret Babette as a transgressive figure whose art has the power to redeem a limited patriarchal society. Stambaugh describes Babette as both a "Dionysian Christ" and a "proper witch" whose "miraculous feast results from feminine art, immersion in the material world, and alliance with the flesh rejected by the Dean's ascetic congregation" (1988, 81). Aiken describes the "entombed" quails that Babette serves as symbolic of "an alternative feminine form of incarnation" in which "the woman's own body is offered up, in displaced form, through her Eucharistic culinary corpus" (1990, 254). Mullins describes Babette as an "implicitly revolutionary" (1994, 225) female Christ who subverts a male exchange system with her "aneconomic" gesture (226): the giving of a gift that demands nothing in return. Barr, finally, describes Babette's "female art" as "an Achilles heel of patriarchal reality—the patriarchy's vulnerable point, where alternative versions of [woman-oriented] reality can be expressed" (1990, 27).

Scholarship on the religious dimensions of *Babette's Feast* is particularly fascinating because a survey of this literature yields, in some cases, conflicting interpretations. Robert Langbaum reads the story as a possible rebuttal to Kierkegaard's *Either/Or*. In contrast to Kierkegaard, who perceives the necessity of choice "between the sensuous-esthetic and the ethical ways of life," Dinesen's story seems to suggest that "it doesn't much matter which choice you make, that all paths can lead to salvation" (1964, 253). Other studies focus more directly on the story's Eucharistic imagery. Gossman explores two kinds of communion in the story, the "sacramental union of Christian righteousness with the happiness of artistic fulfillment" (1963, 325) as well as the union between Babette the artist and her newfound audience.

More recently, some scholars have raised the question of whether the Eucharist in *Babette's Feast* is a Lutheran-Protestant or a Catholic one. Compelling arguments have been made on either side. Mary Elizabeth Podles faults critics of the story and the movie for noticing its Eucharistic imagery without "detect[ing] its Lutheran overtones" (1992, 564). According to Podles, Babette's Eucharist is Lutheran both because it reveals a Lutheran understanding of grace—"an outpouring of unmerited, even unappreciated favor . . . raising those who correspond to it to an elevated, transfigured plane" (563)—and emphasizes salvation through consumption of the Eucharist. "For Luther," Podles states, "the import and effectiveness of the sacrament lay not in the miraculous transubstantiation of the bread and wine into the body and blood of Christ, but in the participants' eating of it" (563).

Esther Rashkin, whose psychoanalytic reading explains *Babette's Feast* as "a story about the overcoming of an inability to mourn" (1995, 357), also argues that "the feast in the text requires a puritan or 'Protestant' reading" (369). Rashkin notes how each character in the story struggles to reconcile himself or herself with some catastrophic loss. Even the feast contains references to the dead: Cailles in Sarcophage and Veuve [Widow] Clicquot champagne (363–64). Babette's feast provides a way in which the participants can acknowledge and articulate their grief over lost loves and thwarted vocations. This memorial dinner, argues Rashkin, "is a Protestant one in which the literal ingestion of bread and wine is understood as a symbolic or metaphorical communion with the flesh and blood of the dead. In this form, it is distinct from the Catholic Eucharist in which the bread and wine are believed to become the actual flesh and blood of Christ" (369).

An alternative reading, however, is offered by Ervin Beck, who suggests that Dinesen may have sympathized more with Catholicism than Lutheranism (1998, 212). The name "Babette," he speculates, may have been inspired by Saint Barbara (whose feast day, like that of the Dean, also falls in December), who is frequently depicted in Catholic iconography with the Eucharistic cup and wafer. Upon her martyrdom, Saint Barbara prayed for those who "die without benefit of the sacraments," a potential fate for "Babette's Lutheran sectarian friends in their quarreling, fallen state" (211). But Beck's most interesting arguments come directly from the text of the story. Noting that Babette first learned to cook in the home of "an old priest who was a saint," he argues that transubstantiation (the Catholic doctrine of the transformation of bread and wine into the actual body and blood of Christ) occurs in the course of the meal. Following the meal, Martine tells the story of a missionary who unknowingly eats the grandchild of a tribal chief; this story, Beck argues, "emphasizes the 'actual presence'" in Babette's feast, "another such instance of holy cannibalism" (212).

Surely, more scholarship remains to be written on the topic of Eucharistic imagery in *Babette's Feast*. But the diversity of critical views cautions readers not to be too complacent in pigeonholing Dinesen's story as either uniformly "Catholic" or "Protestant." Dinesen delighted in ecumenical dialogue; Beck points out that in 1952, around the time of the composition of *Babette's Feast*, Dinesen was inviting clergy of various religious denominations to her home for food and theological discussion. Might *Babette's Feast* be another of Dinesen's attempts at creating an ecumenical dialogue in which the best of both Catholic and Protestant traditions are fused together? To place *Babette's Feast* squarely within a single religious tradition might, in the end, overlook a vital, creative dimension of the story.

NOTE

Isak Dinesen, *Babette's Feast*. In *Anecdotes of Destiny and Ehrengard* (New York: Vintage Books, 1993). All references are to this edition.

WORKS CITED

Aiken, Susan Hardy. 1990. *Isak Dinesen and the Engendering of Narrative*. Chicago: University of Chicago Press.

Barr, Maureen. 1990. "Food for Postmodern Thought: Isak Dinesen's Female Artists as Precursors to Contemporary Feminist Fabulators." In *Feminism, Utopia, and Narrative*, ed. Libby Falk Jones and Sarah Webster Goodwin, 21–33. Knoxville: University of Tennessee Press.

Beck, Ervin. 1998. "Dinesen's *Babette's Feast*." *Explicator* 56, no. 4 (Summer): 210–13.

Gossman, Ann. 1963. "Sacramental Imagery in Two Stories by Isak Dinesen." *Wisconsin Studies in Contemporary Literature* 4: 319–26.

Langbaum, Robert. 1964. *Isak Dinesen's Art: The Gayety of Vision*. Chicago: University of Chicago Press.

Mullins, Maire. 1994. "Home, Community, and the Gift That Gives in Isak Dinesen's *Babette's Feast*." *Women's Studies* 23, no. 3 (July): 217–29.

Podles, Mary Elizabeth. 1992. "*Babette's Feast*: Feasting with Lutherans." *Antioch Review* 50 (Summer): 551–65.

Rashkin, Esther. 1995. "A Recipe for Mourning: Isak Dinesen's *Babette's Feast*." *Style* 29, no. 3 (Fall): 356–74.

Stambaugh, Sara. 1988. *The Witch and the Goddess in the Stories of Isak Dinesen: A Feminist Reading*. Ann Arbor and London: UMI Research Press.

Thurman, Judith. 1982. *Isak Dinesen: The Life of a Storyteller*. New York: St. Martin's Press.

— Maria LaMonaca

John Dryden [1631–1700]

The Hind and the Panther

BIOGRAPHY

It is remarkable that during England's so-called "Age of Reason"—when the Church of England was hedged in by Penal Laws and Test Acts, ensuring that only Anglicans could attend public school or university, vote, or hold office—the nation's two greatest poets were Catholics: Alexander Pope by birth, and John Dryden by conversion. More even than Pope, Dryden was the commanding figure in British literature of his time.

For the stage, Dryden produced comedies, tragedies, masques, farces, and opera libretti; his poetry compasses lyric, elegiac, satiric, heroic, narrative, panegyric, and epistolary modes. Through translations he made classical texts (and older English authors such as Chaucer) available to more readers than ever before. His prose includes biography, history, and, most importantly, literary criticism of a volume and sophistication so much beyond any previous writer's as to lead Dr. Johnson to call him "the father of English criticism" (1905, 410). In prose as in his couplet verse, Dryden set new standards of clarity, concision, and conversational ease: in Johnson's phrase, he found the English-language brick and left it marble (469). Yet for so prolific and popular a writer, biographical information on Dryden is scant. Few letters or anecdotes by contemporaries survive. His verse, nearly all occasional, consists of public poetry on public themes for public occasions: not for him the inward musings of a romantic poet. Yet Dryden is most fully himself in his verse, nowhere so movingly as in *The Hind and the Panther*.

Born in 1631 in the village of Aldwincle, Northamptonshire, into a family of Puritan (but still Anglican) landowners, Dryden grew up amidst the most turbulent events of English history: the Civil Wars and Interregnum, when matters of politics and religion were inevitably intertwined. Although on the Parliamentary side in the wars, his family was not rigidly Calvinist: they sent their son to Westminster School and then to Trinity College, Cambridge, where Dryden took a bachelor's degree in 1654. Both institutions fostered his deep classical and biblical learning, constant sources in his works of parallel, allusion, and a providential understanding of history.

Cambridge may also have nurtured Dryden's lifelong interest in the new natural philosophy (what we call science). One of the first members in 1662 of the newly chartered Royal Society, he wrote in 1674, "A man should be learned in several sciences, and should have a reasonable *philosophical*, and in some measure a *mathematical* head to be a complete and excellent poet" (*Works*, 1885, 15:406). From the start, Dryden was a master of arguing in verse and thoughtful about method. It was from the "modest" (versus "dogmatical") "inquisitions of the Royal Society," he said, that he drew his "skepticism"—his belief that only rarely can reason penetrate to the real essences of things or the real causes of events (*Works*, 2:307).

By tradition, Dryden's first employment was in Oliver Cromwell's secretariat; his first significant poem was *Heroique Stanzas* (1659) on Cromwell's death. Soon afterward, he hailed Charles II's restoration, predicting for Britain a new Augustan age, in *Astraea Redux* (1660) and *To His Sacred Majesty: A Panegyric on the Coronation* (1661). Much later, after his conversion to Catholicism, enemies would remind Dryden of this early shift in loyalty from Lord Protector to King, suggesting that he had always been a timeserver and turncoat. But no one thought so at the time; as Johnson said, "if he changed, he changed with the nation" (1905, 334). *Heroique Stanzas* nowhere mentioned Cromwell's religion but praised only the strong leader who returned his war-torn nation from faction to peace—the same terms in which Dryden also praises Charles.

Embarking on a literary career in Restoration England meant entering the world of patronage. We next hear of Dryden living with the courtly playwright Sir Robert Howard, whose sister Lady Elizabeth he married in 1663. In that year, too, he began writing for the stage, the sole route before copyright by which an author might make a living from his works. In two decades he produced twenty-two plays: amorous Restoration comedies, rhymed heroic tragedies, and re-workings of Shakespeare. Set among Indians, Aztecs, and Turks—in faraway locales that allowed for glancing commentary on events at home—the tragedies took full advantage of the Restoration's delight in elaborate staging and costume and in formal exchanges of opinion on such topics as empire, religious persecution, differing sexual mores, and the nature of government. Dryden's popularity in this short-lived form led to the Duke of Buckingham's famous send-up of him in *The Rehearsal* (1671) as "Bays" (that is, from the poet's traditional laurel crown), ever afterward his nickname among the enemies that so successful a career inevitably produced.

In 1668, Dryden was named poet laureate; upon further appointment as historiographer royal, Stuart patronage promised him £200 a year—when the Merry Monarch could be brought to meet his obligations. But by the middle 1670s, under contract to produce three new plays a year, Dryden tired of "the ungrateful drudgery" of writing plays: "I desire to be no longer the Sisyphus of the stage" (*Works*, 3:255, 5:195).

By the late 1670s, too, national events conspired to engender in Dryden a new seriousness, a new political and religious commitment. The changing mood appears first in dramas, then explodes in the great mock-heroic satires *Mac Flecknoe* (1676?), *Absalom and Achitophel* (1681), and *The Medal* (1682)—taken together, the funniest and most successfully savage body of satire yet to appear in English. Behind all these poems looms the Exclusion Crisis, the effort to block the publicly Catholic James, Duke of York, from succeeding his brother Charles II to the throne. In this conflict were born modern political parties: Tories (including most of the Anglican establishment) supported the divine right of anointed majesty, Whigs (often Dissenters) supported the people's right to choose their king. The Tory Dryden consistently defended "lawful established government against anarchy, innovation, and sedition," all disguises, he believed, for mere "private interest" (*Works*, 6:174).

In 1682, amidst the shower of personal abuse his satires predictably garnered, Dryden also published *Religio Laici; or, A Layman's Faith*, a Horatian verse epistle in defense of Anglicanism rooted in the same appeal to authority that undergirds his political writing. After a famous opening account of the subsidiary role of reason in faith, Dryden proceeds to defend the Anglican "middle way" against rationalist Deism on the one side and Catholicism on the other. At the heart of his case against both is the Protestant doctrine of *scriptura sola*: Deists reject revelation, which alone tells us of Christ's promises; meanwhile, Catholics elevate an untrustworthy oral tradition above the authoritative text. Zealous sectaries (always for Dryden the main enemies of peace and good order) may pervert the text, but to the Anglican,

> The *welcome News* is in the *Letter* found . . .
> It *speaks* it *Self*, and what it does contain,
> In all things *needfull* to be *known*, is *plain*. (*Religio Laici*, 366–69)

Honest interpreters can thus differ only over lesser matters and should not threaten civil peace: "For points obscure are of small use to learn: / *But Common quiet is Mankind's concern*."

Within four years—probably by late 1685, soon after the accession of James II—Dryden had rejected the main arguments of *Religio Laici* and, with his three sons, converted to Roman Catholicism. At no other turning point in his life do we so wish for some glimpse into Dryden's soul; but as usual, we have only his public pronouncements. These take the form of defenses of his newfound faith, starting in 1686 with a controversial *Defence* of some papers left by James's first wife Anne explaining her own conversion to Catholicism, followed in 1687 by *The Hind and the Panther* and in 1688 by a translation into English of the Jesuit Dominique Bouhours's *Life* of the recently canonized Francis Xavier. The result was a firestorm of abuse that continued for the rest of his life. Enemies concluded that Dryden, never sincerely devout, had (in the words of an acid personal attack by Edward Stillingfleet) "chang[ed] his Religion for Bread" (1687, 105). A century later, the Whig historian Thomas Babington Macaulay repeats the slur: "[Dryden] knew little and cared little about religion. . . . Finding that, if he continued to call himself a Protestant, his services would be overlooked, he declared himself a Papist" (1914, 2:850–52).

In fact, Dryden did not profit under the new regime, which he predicted would be short: he expected that James would soon be succeeded by his militantly Whig and Protestant daughter Mary. When William and Mary indeed came into power in 1689, Dryden lost his government posts; his sons' careers were blasted. From the start he had known that all this would happen; he wrote of Anne of York:

> The loss of Friends, of worldly Honours, and Esteem, the Defamation of ill Tongues, and the Reproach of the Cross, all these, though not without the

struglings of Flesh and Blood, were surmounted by her; as if the Saying of our Saviour were always sounding in her Ears, *What will it profit a man to gain the whole world, and lose his Soul!* (*Works*, 17:211)

As Walter Scott (no friend to Catholicism) concluded, "If we are to judge of Dryden's sincerity in his new faith, by the determined firmness with which he retained it through good report and bad report, we must allow him to have been a martyr, or at least a confessor, in the Catholic cause" (*Works*, 1:268).

The immediate effect of Dryden's choice was poverty. To support his family he returned to the stage, producing five more plays; with the help of his astute publisher Jacob Tonson, he turned as well to translation, producing (among many shorter works) versions of *Juvenal and Persius* (1693) and a monumental *Virgil* (1697). The year before his death in 1700, when growing opposition to William led some in government to seek even Tory allies such as Dryden (were the old poet willing to trim), he wrote to his cousin Mrs. Steward:

If they will consider me as a Man, who have done my best to improve the Language, & Especially the Poetry, & will be content with my acquiescence under the present Government, & forbearing satire on it, that I can promise, because I can perform it: but I can neither take the Oaths, nor forsake my Religion; because I know not what Church to go to, if I leave the Catholique. ... May God be pleased to open your Eyes, as he has opend mine: Truth is but one; & they who have once heard of it, can plead no Excuse, if they do not embrace it. (*Letters*, 1942, 123)

MAJOR THEMES

On March 25, 1686, James II ended over a century of censorship by declaring the publication of Roman Catholic books legal in England. The main agenda of his reign was to secure freedom for Catholics through repeal of the Penal Laws and Test Acts. At first, he sought alliance with the Anglican establishment, hoping to secure Catholic freedoms while leaving Dissenters subject to the old disabilities. When this effort failed, James prorogued Parliament and on April 4, 1687, issued a Declaration of Indulgence suspending the Penal Laws and Test Acts by royal prerogative, thereby granting religious freedom to all. Sectaries such as William Penn were delighted. But all knew that the suspension would last only as long as James's reign, and most Catholics feared that James's hasty policies would reap them only augmented future persecution. Even the Vatican counseled caution. That Dryden shared his coreligionists' fears comes clear in a guarded letter he wrote to his old friend George Etherege: "Oh that our Monarch wou'd encourage noble idleness by his own example, as he of blessed memory did before him for my minde misgives me, that he will not much advance his affaires by Stirring" (*Letters*, 1942, 27).

The Declaration appeared one week before *The Hind and the Panther* went to press. Many readers have suggested that James's sudden change of policy caused Dryden to revise the poem by adding new material blackening the Anglican Church. Dryden's own prose preface, however, suggests only that the Declaration might have spared him "the labor of writing many things . . . in the third part" (presumably in the Hind's long plea for religious freedom).

The poem is a beast fable in three parts, of which the third includes two further inset beast fables. Dryden defends his "mysterious writ"—his choice of this popular (if waning) genre, whose animal lore is drawn from a tradition reaching back through the Middle Ages to such ancient bestiaries as the pseudo-Aristotelian *Physiologus* and to the Bible itself—by citing the precedents of Aesop, Chaucer, and Spenser.

Part one introduces the cast and briefly raises topics to be considered in more detail later. First appears the Church of Rome, "A milk-white Hind, immortal and unchang'd," who wanders alone in a forest "once her own" (an England now Protestant). She has been savagely hunted, but although "doom'd to death" is "fated not to die," a reference not only to the temporary protection ordered by the "Lyon" (James) but also to Christ's promise never to forsake his Church (Matt. 28:20). "Not so her young," however: English Catholics have been martyred in plenty, most recently in the fraudulent Popish Plot, but (in a paraphrase of Tertullian), "Their fate was fruitful"; "the sangine seed . . . increas'd the sacred breed."

The pacific Hind is threatened by a host of factious, "innovating" predators: the reformed churches whose conflicts have for two centuries produced "Such wars, such waste, such fiery tracks of dearth" and that are now united only in their hatred of her ("No union they pretend, but in *Non-Popery*"). These include "The bloudy *Bear*, an *Independent* Beast"; "The bristl'd *Baptist Boar*"; "False *Reynard*" (Unitarians and Socinians); and, most dangerous, the Presbyterian "insatiate *Wolfe*," a "traitor and blasphemer" who "ruled awhile" (during the Civil Wars) and whose "innate antipathy to kings" still threatens to reduce the state to "the dreggs of a Democracy" governed only by private "interest."

The Wolf may pose the greatest present danger, but Dryden shrewdly sees that in the long term, because each sect takes "private reason" for its guide, it is the spiritually arid rationalism of the Fox that will at last characterize them all: "Here they began, and here they all will end." Unlike the true, sacramental faith which he has yearned for and now finally received, private reason is mere "pride," a condition Dryden diagnoses in his own past self:

> But, gratious God, how well dost thou provide
> For erring judgments an unerring Guide! . . .
> My thoughtless youth was wing'd with vain desires,
> My manhood, long misled by wandring fires,
> Follow'd false lights; and when their glimps was gone,
> My pride struck out new sparkles of her own.
> Such was I, such by nature still I am,
> Be thine the glory, and be mine the shame.
> Good life be now my task: my doubts are done. (*Hind and Panther*, 1.64–78)

Dryden traces the history of Wolfish religious persecution back to Cain, contrasts it with the good shepherding of "Pan" (Christ), and proposes in its stead James's policy of toleration (could "brutes" but be "Curb'd of their native malice to destroy"):

> Of all the tyrannies on humane kind,
> The worst is that which persecutes the mind.
> Let us but weigh at what offense we strike,
> 'Tis but because we cannot think alike. (1.239–42)

Finally enters the poem's other main character: the Anglican Panther, "noblest, next the *Hind*," "least deform'd, because reform'd the least." But for all her residual beauty and purity of conduct—"sure no Church can better morals boast"—the Panther is "without Respect" in the forest, "neither lov'd nor fear'd, / A mere mock Queen of a divided Herd": having herself rebelled, she has no "innate authority" to quell rebellion in others. Faced with common dangers, Hind and Panther agree to walk home together; their conversation that evening constitutes part two of the poem, the next day part three.

Part two displays Dryden's unmatched skill in versified debate. As in all his dialogues, there is an appearance of even-handedness, but his own side gets the longest and most persuasive speeches; the Panther's contributions grow shorter (and more short-tempered) as the Hind's grow more eloquent. Throughout, Dryden rejects the Anglican "middle way" he had so recently defended, now finding only confusion and error—"bungling biggottry"—in his own earlier beliefs. He makes the point first and most forcefully in discussing the "main question" then separating Catholics and Anglicans: that of Christ's Real Presence in the Eucharist (the true "food" for want of which the sectarian beasts are "starving"). Whereas the Church of England had previously managed to retain a studied vagueness on the issue, the new Restoration Book of Common Prayer contained a rubric specifically condemning Catholic doctrine; the Test Acts required all seeking public office to accept the host in Anglican fashion: kneeling (thus excluding Dissenters, for whom such a posture was idolatry) but also with an oath denying transubstantiation. The Hind makes clear that in all this Anglicans have "chopp'd and chang'd" their teaching ("and what may change may fall") and finds current Anglican efforts to deny such change—arguments such as that the Church of England had always found Christ's presence "real" but only in a "symbolic" sense—proof that "not onely *Jesuits* . . . can equivocate."

The Panther waspishly replies that, unlike the Hind, she never claimed infallibility, provoking a long discussion about the need for an unerring guide, since "discord cannot end without a last appeal." A loving God would not leave us unprovided: "A guide was therefore needfull, therefore made"; "Our Saviour else were wanting to supply / Our needs." The Hind is especially concerned to confute Dryden's own earlier views on the locus of religious authority as expressed in *Religio Laici*, views now given to the Panther: "Yet, *Lady*, still remember I maintain, / The Word in needful points is onely plain." In response, the Hind argues that no text is self-explanatory; all texts need interpreters. "No written laws can be so plain, so pure, / But wit may gloss, and malice may obscure"; "The sense is intricate, 'tis onely clear, / What vowels and what consonants are there." By locating authority not in God but man, Dryden's earlier views constituted an invitation to pride and factional self-interest:

> For they, who left the Scripture to the crowd,
> Each for his own peculiar judge allow'd;
> The way to please 'em was to make 'em proud.
> Thus, with full sails, they ran upon the shelf;
> Who cou'd suspect a couzenage from himself? (2.254–58)

Exasperated at her failure in argument, the Panther finally demands that the Hind "produce this vaunted [infallible] leader to our view"—to which the Hind replies (echoing Christ in Gethsemane): "*she who ye seek am I.*" In a last, long speech summarizing the debate, the Hind demonstrates that the Panther's faith lacks the four Nicene signs of the true Church (one, holy, catholic, apostolic). In a passage that sums up Dryden's lifetime of thinking about England's colonial project, the Hind pauses especially over Anglican failure in Christian witness:

> Thieves, Panders, Palliards, sins of ev'ry sort,
> Those are the manufactures we export;
> And these the Missionaires our zeal has made:
> For, with my countrey's pardon be it said,
> Religion is the least of all our trade. (2.556–67)

The Hind's words are confirmed by heavenly "fireworks," a "streaming blaze" in the sky such as Dryden claims himself to have seen on the evening of James's defeat of Monmouth (Charles's bastard son who had rebelliously sought the throne for himself). She lovingly invites the Panther to stay the night—indeed to make a permanent home with her (to reunite with Rome). The Panther, "amazed" at the Hind's voluntary poverty, accepts the lesser offer.

In part three, the previously "well-bred" Panther turns savage, definitively refusing all offers of reconciliation and making clear her deepest motivations: "envy," "malice," "ambition," "interest," "pride," and "revenge." She sarcastically congratulates the Hind on Catholicism's new (tolerated) status, her obvious jealousy earning the reply:

> Our mite decreases nothing of your store;
> I am but few, and by your fare you see
> My crying sins are not of luxury. (3.112–15)

(Catholics in fact constituted less than five percent of the population at the time.) To the Panther's comment that under a Catholic king many would of course convert "for miracles of bread," the Hind replies with what is also a defense of Dryden himself:

> Judge not by hear-say, but observe at least,
> If since their change, their loaves have been increast.
> The *Lyon* buyes no Converts, if he did,
> Beasts wou'd be sold as fast as he cou'd bid.
> Tax those of int'rest who conform for gain,
> Or stay the market of another reign. (3.223–27)

When the Panther abruptly changes tack, arguing that if few have pursued "profitable change," such small numbers must argue continuing loyalty to the Church of England, the Hind advances an alternative explanation ("shame of change, and fear of future ill") and expresses Dryden's fears of what James's immoderate policies portended: "The respite they enjoy but onely lent, / The best they have to hope, protracted punishment."

Again bested in argument, the Panther offers a short beast fable. A group of swallows plan to migrate south for the winter but are persuaded by a "Martyn," a "round-belly'd" superstitious "dunce," to stay: God may reverse the sun's course, calling back summer. (The martin is a certain Father Petres, advisor to

James II, reputed to have persuaded a group of Catholics planning emigration to remain in England.) An Indian summer (James's short reign) indeed comes, followed by sudden winter in which many swallows die and

> *Martyn* himself was caught a-live, and try'd
> For treas'nous crimes, because the laws provide
> No *Martyn* there in winter shall abide. (3.632–34)

Penetrating this malicious threat, the Hind replies with a long attack on the Penal Laws and Test Acts with which Anglicans, fearing that a tolerated Catholicism might become once again widespread, have "ground the persecuting knife, / And set it to a razor edge on life." That the Panther has done this in part by making accommodation with latitudinarians and Whigs against Catholics (thereby dangerously letting the Wolf "into her bed") is the burden of a second inset fable offered by the Hind. A wise and gentle farmer finds that his pigeons cannot bear his keeping as well a few "Domestick Poultry." Resentful of every grain given the chickens, the pigeons first libel their defenseless enemies ("An hideous Figure of their Foes they drew"), then seek to banish them, and finally, on the advice of one particularly vain, self-interested "theologue," invite their old enemies, the buzzards, to the farm, supposing that buzzards will prefer chicken meat to their own. (The "theologue" is Dryden's old enemy, the low-church Whig Gilbert Burnet, then in Dutch exile but after 1689 to ascend to a bishopric; the buzzards are all the corrupters of Anglicanism the Panther has allowed into her church by consorting with the Wolf.) At the fable's inconclusive end, the farmer (James) declares universal toleration while the buzzards are poised to eat all the birds on the farm.

Thus, *The Hind and the Panther*—appropriately, given its historical moment—ends inconclusively. The immediate future for English Catholics is bleak: the Church of England is poised on the brink of doctrinal self-liquidation; but Christ's promises to his Church remain. As night falls,

> The [Hind] withdrew, and, wishing to her Guest
> The peace of Heav'n, betook herself to rest.
> Ten thousand Angels on her slumbers waite
> With glorious Visions of her future state. (3.1295–98)

One way to interpret *The Hind and the Panther* is as a confessional poem. The middle 1680s were for Dryden a time of stock-taking in all areas of his life. In his 1685 "Ode" to the memory of Anne Killigrew, for instance, a decade before Jeremy Collier's famous attacks on the licentiousness of the Restoration stage, Dryden made a public apology for the "fat Pollutions" of his own comedies. In the same spirit of stock-taking, *The Hind and the Panther* echoes and transforms many of Dryden's earlier works (not merely *Religio Laici*). In his tragedy *Tyrannick Love* (1670), for instance, Saint Catherine upbraided the Roman emperor Maximin:

> Thus, with short Plummets Heav'ns deep will we sound,
> That vast Abyss where humane Wit is drown'd!
> In our small Skiff we must not launce too far;
> We here but Coasters, not Discov'rers are. (4.i.544–47)

Now, in *The Hind and the Panther*, as Dryden explores the riches of his new faith, that passage is transformed:

> Why chuse we then like *Bilanders* to creep
> Along the coast, and land in view to keep,
> When safely we may launch into the deep?
> In the same vessel which our Saviour bore
> Himself the Pilot, let us leave the shoar,
> And with a better guide a better world explore. (1.128–33)

The Hind contains so many rewritings of this sort as to make the poem a kind of deliberate summing-up of Dryden's career, a testament to the completion of his searching.

The Hind also contains Dryden's most moving confessional writing. In part three—in a speech by the Hind, but one wherein it is impossible not also to hear the poet's own voice—the man who for a generation had gloried in his fame as the greatest poet of his age, and who knew himself to be its most powerfully effective satirist, reflects on what his conversion to Catholicism means: loss of fame and, in an effort to cultivate Christian charity, renunciation of vindictive satire. In part two, saying "Good life be now my task," Dryden had acknowledged that while intellectual conviction is one thing, actually living the demands of his faith is quite another, especially given the "pride" that remains in any fallen creature ("Such was I, such by nature still I am"). Now, as the Hind lectures the Panther, he makes starkly clear how painful the proud poet finds the renunciations he is called upon to make:

> 'Tis said with ease, but oh, how hardly try'd
> By haughty souls to humane honour ty'd!
> O sharp convulsive pangs of agonizing pride!
> Down then thou rebell, never more to rise,
> And what thou didst, and do'st so dearly prize,
> That fame, that darling fame, make that thy sacrifice. (3.281–90)

But even this offering is, of course, not enough:

> 'Tis nothing thou hast giv'n, then add thy tears
> For a long race of unrepenting years:
> 'Tis nothing yet; yet all thou hast to give,
> Then add those *may-be* years thou hast to live.
> Yet nothing still: then poor, and naked come,
> Thy father will receive his unthrift home,
> And thy blest Saviour's bloud discharge the mighty sum. (3.291–97)

Difficult for any man, cultivation of humility and forgiveness is hardest for the satirist:

> Thus (she pursu'd) I discipline a son
> Whose uncheck'd fury to revenge wou'd run: . . .
> Instruct him better, gracious God, to know,
> As thine is vengeance, so forgiveness too.
> That suff'ring from ill tongues he bears no more

Than what his Sovereign bears, and what his Saviour bore. (3.298–305)

Thus, as Thomas Fujimura (1993) has argued, it is possible to read much of *The Hind and the Panther* as a dramatization of Dryden's own struggle: the "proud," "malicious," "vengeful" Anglican Panther embodies not only the satirist that Dryden was but what "by nature still I am"; while the forgiving Hind (whose "plain simplicity of love" leads her, when insulted, to "suppress / The boiling indignation of her breast") embodies the Christian ideal to which he knows he must strive.

CRITICAL RECEPTION

The modern response to Dryden's longest and most complex original poem is deeply divided. It has been called "the noblest of ratiocinative poems" (Hooker 1941, 73) and "the greatest poem of all times about the Catholic Church" and "one of the most deeply reflective poems in English literature" (Gardiner 1998, 3). Meanwhile, C. S. Lewis found Dryden's choice of the beast fable as a vehicle for theological controversy suggestive of a mind "bordering on aesthetic insanity" (1939, 9), while Dryden's most recent biographer deems the work, despite the magnificence of its parts, ultimately a failure, "betrayed by too many inventions, too many styles, too many conflicting purposes" (Winn 1987, 424).

Response in Dryden's own time was immediate and unanimous: "It passed rapidly through three editions. From this point of view it was a success, but in reality a *succès de scandale*; it was a poem everyone read and everyone condemned" (Young 1954, 158). The many replies were, in the fashion of the time, mainly scurrilous, mainly anonymous, and mainly attacks on Dryden's character and Catholicism.

The most enduringly famous reply was a parody by two erstwhile friends, Charles Montagu (soon to be inventor of Britain's national debt) and a young Matthew Prior. *The Hind and the Panther Transvers'd to the Story of the Country-Mouse and the City-Mouse* can be appreciated only by examining parallel passages. Dryden's opening,

> A milk white *Hind*, immortal and unchang'd,
> Fed on the lawns, and in the forest rang'd;
> Without unspotted, innocent within,
> She fear'd no danger, for she knew no sin,

becomes at the hands of Montagu and Prior:

> A milk-white *Mouse* immortal and unchang'd,
> Fed on soft Cheese, and o're the *Dairy* rang'd;
> Without, unspotted; innocent within,
> She fear'd no danger, for she knew no *Ginn*. (Prior 1971, 1:40)

The exchange on infallibility in Dryden, which begins with the Panther's "That men may err was never yet deny'd," becomes:

> *That mice may err was never yet denied.*
> That I deny, said the immortal dame,
> There is a Guide—Gad, I've forgot his Name—(Prior 1971, 1:50)

The Hind's grandiloquent *"she whom ye seek am I"* becomes "Hear, and be dumb, thou Wretch, *that Guide am I.*" The parody was so popular, Ned Ward reported, that "Nothing but *Mouse, Mouse,* was crept into every Body's Mouth" (Hooker 1941, 52).

This was the gentlest of the responses. More typical was *The Revolter, a Tragi-Comedy* (1687), in which Dryden's Anglican *Religio Laici* and Catholic *Hind* come alive and fight each other on stage: "In short, the whole poem, if it may deserve that name, is a piece of deformed, arrogant nonsense, and self-contradiction, drest up in fine language, like an ugly brazen-faced whore" (*Works*, 9:102). The anonymous author (Robert Gould) of "The Laureat" (1687) used the occasion to attack the whole of Dryden's life and career:

> Thou standst upon thy own records a knave, . . .
> The curse of ours, and scoff of future times. . . .
> Had Dick still kept the royal diadem,
> Thou hadst been poet laureat still to him. . . .
> Who ever changed more in one moon than thou? . . .
> Gold is thy god; for a substantial sum,
> Thou to the Turk wouldst run away from Rome. (*Works*, 9:105–07)

"The worst poem . . . the age has produced," Bishop Burnet declared simply (Johnson 1905, 380).

Balanced response could begin only when animosities between Protestants and Catholics dwindled into mere party rivalry of Whig and Tory. That time had not come even in Johnson's "Life" (1779), which suggests that no argument on the themes Dryden had chosen could be successful. Like Montagu and Prior, Johnson found that "A fable which exhibits two beasts talking Theology appears at once full of absurdity" (380) and, as if predicting the critical disagreements of the twentieth century, objected to Dryden's mixture of "heroic poetry" with "satire" (444). (Like most readers until Earl Miner [1967, 148–50], Johnson failed to notice how often Dryden playfully directs that satire at his own chosen genre.) Only by 1808 did Walter Scott's detailed historical knowledge, grasp of how Augustan poetry works, and distance from the original controversy make possible what remains the most adequate judgment of Dryden's accomplishment in

> the finest specimens of the English heroic stanza. The introductory verses, in particular, are lofty and dignified in the highest degree: as are those in which the splendor and majesty of the Church of Rome are set forth, in all the glowing colors of rich imagery and magnificent language. But the same praise extends to the versification of the whole poem. It never falls, never becomes rugged; rises with the dignified strain of the poetry; sinks into quaint familiarity, where sarcasm and humor are employed; and winds through all the mazes of theological argument without becoming either obscure or prosaic. (*Works*, 9:101)

But the historical moment that enabled this judgment soon passed as Dryden's topical references grew obscure and as, under the pressure of new (romantic) notions of poetry, readers lost an understanding of how Augustan verse is built.

Most modern scholarship on Dryden has been concerned to elucidate his place in the intellectual currents of his time and to demonstrate the consistency underlying his shifts of allegiance. No one now questions the sincerity of Dryden's conversion, but at the same time, as the titles of the two most important twentieth-century studies suggest (Louis Bredvold's *The Intellectual Milieu of John Dryden* [1934] and Phillip Harth's *Contexts of Dryden's Thought* [1968]), modern scholars find it easier to produce intellectual history than to grapple with Dryden's verse. The prevailing view of *The Hind and the Panther* remains admiration for the stylistic mastery of its varied parts and bemusement at the whole. Efforts to discuss the poem's unity—from Earl Miner's attempt to place it in a tradition of "discontinuous allegory" (1967, 146) to Anne Gardiner's argument (in what is otherwise the best historical reading of the poem) that it is a systematic rewriting of the Song of Songs (1998)—convince only partly. Many readers conclude with James Sutherland "We read the poem because it is a pleasure to be with Dryden; it is the mind of Dryden that we are in contact with, and the voice of Dryden that we hear throughout. This alone gives the poem any unity it may have" (1969, 191).

Until we recover an understanding of how the Augustan long poem operates, many works by Dryden (and Pope, and Thomson) will remain puzzling to us. In such an effort of historical imagination, Margaret Doody suggests, Dryden's poem will be central: "*The Hind and the Panther* may be taken as the great, the undeniable, *sui generis* poem of the Restoration era, and pondering on it may help us to understand others of that period, and of the Augustan Age in general" (1985, 80).

NOTE

John Dryden, *The Poems and Fables of John Dryden*, ed. James Kinsley (London: Oxford University Press, 1962). All references to Dryden's verse are to this edition.

WORKS CITED

Bredvold, Louis. 1934. *The Intellectual Milieu of John Dryden*. Ann Arbor: University of Michigan Press.

Doody, Margaret Anne. 1985. *The Daring Muse: Augustan Poetry Reconsidered*. Cambridge: Cambridge University Press.

Dryden, John. 1885. *The Works of John Dryden*, ed. Walter Scott and George Saintsbury. 18 vols. Edinburgh: William Patterson.

———. 1942. *The Letters of John Dryden*, ed. Charles Ward. Durham, NC: Duke University Press.

Fujimura, Thomas H. 1993. "The Personal Drama of Dryden's *The Hind and the Panther*." In *The Temper of John Dryden*, ed. Robert W. McHenry, Jr., 67–89. East Lansing, MI: Colleagues Press.

Gardiner, Anne Barbeau. 1998. *Ancient Faith and Modern Freedom in John Dryden's The Hind and the Panther*. Washington, DC: Catholic University of America Press.

Harth, Phillip. 1968. *Contexts of Dryden's Thought*. Chicago: University of Chicago Press.

Hooker, Helene Maxwell. 1941. "Charles Montagu's Reply to *The Hind and the Panther*." *ELH* 8: 51–73.

Johnson, Samuel. 1905. "Life of Dryden." In *Lives of the English Poets*, ed. G. B. Hill, vol. 1, 391–487. Oxford: Clarendon Press.

Lewis, C. S. 1939. "Shelley, Dryden, and Mr. Eliot." In *Rehabilitations and Other Essays*, 1–34. London: Oxford University Press.

Macaulay, Thomas Babington. 1914. *The History of England from the Accession of James the Second*, ed. C. H. Firth. 6 vols. London: Macmillan.

Miner, Earl. 1967. *Dryden's Poetry*. Bloomington: University of Indiana Press.

Prior, Matthew. 1971. *The Literary Works of Matthew Prior*, ed. H. B. Wright and M. Spears. 2 vols. Oxford: Clarendon Press.

Stillingfleet, Edward. 1687. *A Vindication of the Answer to Some Late Papers Concerning the Unity and Authority of the Catholick Church*. London.

Sutherland, James. 1969. *English Literature of the Late Seventeenth Century*. London: Oxford University Press.

Winn, James Anderson. 1987. *John Dryden and His World*. New Haven, CT: Yale University Press.

Young, Kenneth. 1954. *John Dryden: A Critical Biography*. London: Sylvan Press.

— Douglas Lane Patey

Andre Dubus [1936–1999]

Voices from the Moon

BIOGRAPHY

The fictional world of Andre Dubus is populated largely by the working-class men and women of the Merrimack Valley in northeastern Massachusetts, to which he had migrated from the University of Iowa with his first wife and four children in 1967. Here he put down roots as a writer and college teacher, as an ardent Red Sox fan, and as a husband and father. (Dubus was to marry twice more, first in 1975 and again in 1979, the latter union bringing him two more children.) The tenacity with which Dubus's imagination seized upon this New England locale, however, and the generous narrative voice with which he breathed consequence into the inconspicuous lives of his sales clerks and waitresses, mill workers and bartenders, ballplayers and Marine recruits, were nurtured in the American South.

Dubus's storytelling came to center on that region around Haverhill, Massachusetts, where he lived until his death in 1999 and where he taught literature and writing until 1984 at the now defunct Bradford College. But his art drew its motive force as much from that intricate, fulsome, but always potentially explosive texture of extended family relations that marked the South in which he grew up. (Both Dubus's first cousin, James Lee Burke, and his younger sister, Elizabeth Nell Dubus, are practicing novelists, as is his son Andre Dubus III.)

One can observe this commingling of the New England locale with the stubborn, intense family loyalties of the South in what is one of Dubus's most accomplished tales, "A Father's Story." At that story's conclusion, the narrator, Luke Ripley, defends before God his concealment of his daughter's unwitting hit and run murder of a young man. Ripley audaciously appeals to loyalties more primal and potent than legality or morality as he summons the supreme judge, God the Father, who witnessed the actual rather than the prospective trial and punishment of his child: "I could bear the pain of watching and knowing my sons' pain, could bear it with pride as they took the whip and nails. But You never had a daughter, and if you had, You could not have borne her passion" (*Selected Stories*, 1996, 475–76).

Dubus maintained that he wrote stories because he was human, not because he was a southerner: "all of us need to speak into the silence of mortality . . . and with stories try to finally understand . . . it" (*Broken Vessels*, 1991, 92). Those stories, nevertheless, display a southerner's, and more specifically a southern Catholic's, awe at the solemnity of marital and family relations, fatherhood and motherhood—even, indeed especially, at those awful moments when that solemnity is transgressed in adultery, one of Dubus's recurrent subjects.

Andre Dubus was born in 1936 and schooled in Lafayette, Louisiana, from the third to the twelfth grade, at the Christian Brothers' Cathedral School. This Cajun milieu of hearty family and communal ceremony united with the piety and ritualism of 1950s Catholicism to engender in him an unassailable devotion to the sacramental life of the Church, despite his tenuous official status in that Church as a three-time divorcee. Many years later, in a 1986 essay called "On Charon's Wharf," he linked the Eucharist with those mysteries of concrete, flesh-and-blood family ties in which this southern heritage had instructed him—and with the sharpened sense of mortality that attends such awareness:

> This morning . . . I placed on my tongue the taste of forgiveness and of love that affirmed, perhaps celebrated, my being alive, my being mortal. This has nothing to do with immortality, with eternity; I love the earth too much to contemplate a life apart from it, although I believe in that life. No, this has to do with mortality and the touch of flesh, and my belief in the Eucharist is simple: without touch God is a monologue, an idea, a philosophy . . . the silent touch affirms . . . the mysteries of love and mortality. (*Broken Vessels*, 78–79)

Dubus's lifelong attendance at daily Mass, and more importantly, his appropriation of sacramental ritual as a thematic and structural principle of his narratives, weathered the conflict of his burgeoning sexuality with puritanical strains in that Catholicism. In one his earliest published stories, "If They Knew Yvonne" (1969), Dubus stakes out the true character of the Eucharist, rescuing it from the theological dualism willed to his youthful protagonist by his early Catholic education. To fortify young Harry against his nascent sexuality, Brother Thomas presents the boy with a picture of Thomas Aquinas being wrenched away from the outstretched arms of a woman by two heavenly guardians. The picture's title, "Angelic Warfare," aptly characterizes the ruinous spirituality Harry adopts in response to the sorrow welling up in adolescent self-consciousness. He is further instructed to avoid intimacy with women but equally to avoid being alone, to use up his energy in any and all mindlessly physical activities, and to receive the Eucharist often as a check against concupiscence. This advice only fuels the boy's compulsion to masturbation as a palliative to his spiritual isolation. His subsequent relationship with Yvonne Millet stalls short of real intimacy, and he betrays her love in casual boasting about his sexual prowess. Harry's sister Janet astutely diagnoses the defect in the theology Harry has inherited: Harry's teachers, she insists, have made sex "introverted . . . something between you and yourself, or between you and God. Instead of between you and other people" (*Selected Stories*, 193). Harry has been taught to think of the Eucharist in legalistic and individualistic terms as an instrument for chastening desire and for securing an exclusively personal salvation. Janet conceived of the Eucharist rather as the "sacrament of love," to which she had clung for strength to tend her young sons during the five years when her husband was abandoning her for a younger woman (Lewis 2002, 37–38).

When he was eighteen, Andre Dubus moved with his parents to Lake Charles, Louisiana, near the Texas border, where he subsequently graduated from McNeese State University, majoring in English. He then accepted, in 1958, a commission in the United States Marine Corps, "a step he took to please our father," his older sister Kathryn notes (Anderson 2001, 45). A number of Dubus's essays and short stories celebrate the courage and personal tenacity elicited by the demands for physical prowess—and by implication, for sexual manliness—of emotionally distant fathers or surrogate father figures. At the same time, these stories suggest the emotional toll exacted in satisfying such expectations. "The Intruder," a very early tale republished in the late volume *Dancing After Hours* (1996), deals tragically with the sexual initiation of a psychologically fragile young boy, while the early Paul Clement stories, "An Afternoon with the Old Man" and "Contrition," evoke the painful gap between an incommunicative father and an uncertain, self-conscious son (*Adultery & Other Choices*, 1977). The harrowing story "Cadence" describes the ambiguous triumph of an older Paul Clement, who escapes the shame of failing out of Marine boot camp like his buddy Munson but on whom descends an emotionally numbing "certainty" of bodily confidence and rigidly figured identity that may mask deeper, unresolved patterns of fear and violence (*Selected Stories*, 173). Such patterns unfold in the psyches of any number of Dubus's male protagonists, unequal as they most often are to the claims of intimacy upon them and nostalgic for the more physically taxing but less emotionally complex rituals of male camaraderie. Such is the pattern notable in Hank Allison and Jack Linhart, the male protagonists of Dubus's early trilogy of novellas, "We Don't Live Here Anymore," 1975 (*Separate Flights*); "Adultery," 1977 (*Adultery and Other Choices*); and "Finding a Girl in America," 1980 (*Finding a Girl in America*).

After serving for five and a half years in the Marine Corps, rising to the rank of captain, Dubus resigned his commission in 1963, the year of his father's death. He moved to Iowa City with his first wife, Patricia Lowe, whom he had married in 1958 and by whom he had four children during his Marine years: Suzanne, Andre, Jeb, and Nicole. There he enrolled in the University of Iowa's Writer's Workshop, submitting as his thesis a novel-length manuscript called *The Lieutenant*, which he published in 1967. Shortly thereafter, however, Dubus underwent an artistic conversion to the short-story form. His oldest son Andre describes how at the age of thirty-two, while reading a large dose of Chekhov, he threw away a novel-length manuscript he had been composing and "told himself it was time he taught himself to *write*" (Anderson 2001, 11). Thereafter, Dubus accepted the position at Bradford College and moved with his family to New Hampshire and eventually to Haverhill, where he devoted himself to the arduous craft of the short story, writing on average through his mature years, his son estimates, three stories a year. Between 1975 and 1986 he composed seven collections of short stories and novellas. During this period he developed, if not a large popular following, a reputation among discerning readers as one of America's finest practitioners of short fiction, and he won National Endowment for the Arts grants in 1978 and 1985 and Guggenheim Fellowships in 1977 and 1986.

The worldly Cajun milieu of Dubus's youth and the Cajun stock from which he was descended on his father's side—his mother was of Irish descent—no doubt contributed to his robust conviviality and physicality. His short stories, novellas, and essays testify to his earthy passions for food, music, conversation, sport (especially baseball and running), the rites of male camaraderie—and especially for the pleasures of female companionship and "the achieved intimacy of . . . flesh," as Edith Allison puts it describing her ministrations to her dying lover in "Adultery" (*Selected Stories*, 411). Dubus's temperamental sensuality is deepened by a Catholic sacramentalism that instinctively aligns the motions of the spirit—and the operations of grace in assisting them—with the importunities of the body: its unplumbed reserves of endurance, its fierce loyalties and compassionate spontaneities, and its hunger—at times overweening—for fleshly exchange. The narrator of "Rose" recalls the unimaginable bodily strength displayed in a moment of unself-consciousness by a fellow Marine Corps candidate who failed out of basic training but even more the heroism displayed by a cocktail waitress (Rose) who saved her children from a fire set by a brutal, drunk husband. She is redeemed from her passive complicity in an abusive marriage when she finds the courage to challenge her husband, ultimately killing him in an analogously unconscious fit of bodily rage. Her fury is inspired by direct identification with the pain of her injured son, which liberates her to contact the mysterious depths of her own abused body.

"Well, I see the whole world as Catholic, so I can't help but see my characters through the eyes of a Catholic," Dubus told his friend and confessor Father Patrick Samway, S. J. (Anderson 2001, 123). The Catholic vision in Dubus's fiction is not so much a matter of explicit theological reflection as it is a unified vision of everyday human actions and human intercourse as the site of spiritual transformation and of the drama of grace. As Father Samway puts it, "More than any other writer I have read, Dubus unites his home and church language with his out-of-home and out-of-church language. He speaks and writes with one voice" (Anderson 2001, 125). That one voice sees the structure of reality itself as sacramental.

Andre Dubus's religious sensibility emerged all the more clearly in his later work, after the traumatic events of July 23, 1986. On that day he was struck by a car on Interstate 93 north of Boston while stopping to assist a stranded motorist. Dubus entered a protracted period of debilitating but transformative physical and emotional pain. His left leg had to be amputated above the knee, and he lost most of the functioning of his right leg. Several months later, his third wife Peggy Rambach filed for divorce, "overwhelmed," Kathryn Dubus claims, "by the strain of caring for Andre and a new baby" (Anderson 2001, 47). In a bitter court battle, Rambach won custody of their two children, Cadence and Madeleine. The twin losses left Dubus creatively paralyzed for a time, but gradually he regained his writing voice, publishing two volumes of essays and autobiographical sketches, *Broken Vessels* (1991) and *Meditations from a Movable Chair* (1998), and a final, radiant collection of stories, *Dancing After Hours* (1996). These volumes witness to Dubus's mature artistry as a prose stylist and fiction writer, to his courage and emotional honesty, and to a greater meditative depth and humility in his confrontation with his own personal failings and with our common mortality.

Andre Dubus died on February 24, 1999. In a funeral tribute, Father Patrick Samway captured something of the spiritual light that shone through all his work but especially the late stories of *Dancing After Hours* and the essays in *Broken Vessels* and *Meditations*: "Andre knew that this life is . . . far too strange, to arrive at the end of it and then be asked what you make of it and have to answer, 'Scientific humanism'. . . . Andre took it as axiomatic that one should settle for nothing less than infinite mystery and infinite delight; i.e., God" (Anderson 2001, 199).

PLOT SUMMARY

The nine sections of the novella *Voices from the Moon* focus severally on the members of the Stowe family, a working-class family in a small factory town north of Boston in the Merrimack Valley. With occasional flashbacks to the recent past, the principal action unfolds in contemporary times over the span of a single day and evening. The protagonist of the story is, arguably, the twelve-year-old Ritchie Stowe, for it is his point of view that dominates the beginning and ending of the novella, and it is he who serves as the most sensitive register of the conflicts threatening to rupture the family.

At the outset, Ritchie is pedaling to morning Mass, obsessed with the harsh exchange he had overheard the previous night between his father Greg and his older brother Larry. Already burdened by his mother's divorce from his father, with whom he lives alone, Ritchie learns that his father, forty-seven years old, plans to marry his brother, Larry's, ex-wife Brenda, like Larry in her mid-twenties. Larry's anger at the imprudent—and in Massachusetts, even illegal—union threatens to dissolve the already attenuated fabric of family life. Ritchie agonizes over preserving his sexual purity and his Catholic faith in such a sinful environment, but the humane Father Oberti cautions him not to judge his father so harshly. After leaving church, Ritchie meets up with the thirteen-year-old Melissa Donnelly, to whom he finds himself physically attracted and in whom he confides his distress.

Subsequent sections adopt the narrative point of view of the other family members while shuttling back to Ritchie as he struggles to reconcile his longing for purity with his family's promiscuities and his own dawning sexuality. Greg Stowe, the hard-working owner of two successful ice cream stores, anticipates that Larry, an aspiring dancer and actor, will quit as his assistant after the previous night's confrontation. He replays that meeting in his mind, watching Larry depart in anger, presumably for the last time. Ritchie questions his father about whether he will visit Larry, as he does Ritchie's mother, and then he seeks escape from the growing family acrimony in the sensory delights of the softball field and in the thought of Melissa.

Larry visits Brenda's apartment, reviewing in imagination the perverse pride and lust that destroyed their marriage. He had encouraged Brenda to seduce men they invited back from local bars to their apartment as a prelude to their own lovemaking. Larry breaks down in tears before Brenda, enjoining her never to reveal this grotesque act to his father. In section five, the reader inhabits Brenda's consciousness as she guiltily reviews the dark voices that compelled her own complicity in that year-long riot of destructive passion with Larry. And she assesses the solidity and stability Greg brings to her life. In the following section, Ritchie is shown once again as he feverishly empties his conflicts into the physical passion of horseback riding, struggling all the while to reconcile his love of God with his attachments to his family and with the idea of earthly satisfaction represented by Melissa.

The narrative begins to move toward more harmonious closure in section eight. Greg visits the apartment of his daughter Carol, twenty-six, who rediscovers her affection for her father amidst her ambivalence about his past selfishness and inattentions to her mother. Carol's resentment as a daughter has been muted by acquaintance with the importunities and disappointments of adult love. She encourages Greg to embrace the love of Brenda without guilt, and she dances with him as acknowledgment of her sympathy with the desires that impelled his decision. In section eight, Dubus introduces the perspective of Joan, Greg's former wife and Ritchie's mother, as she counsels her son Larry toward acceptance of his father's careless action. Her perceptiveness about the love son and father share, and about the self-hatred engendered in Larry by his penchant for dreaming about success rather than striving for it, bestows authority on her prediction that the wound between them will heal.

The narrative concludes as it began with a scene in which Ritchie confides to Melissa the events of that day, particularly his transforming vision of his father in tears. The wound that has separated spirit from flesh and heaven from earth in Ritchie's consciousness also seems closer to healing as he holds Melissa's hand on the soft summer grass beneath the stars.

MAJOR THEMES

The poem from which Dubus draws his title (Michael Van Walleghan's "A Good Excuse"), and which served as epigraph to the novella in its original publication in 1984, evokes the central conflict of the story: the struggle with those Siren "voices from the moon" that tempt the disconsolate soul—particularly that of Dubus's males—into romantic flight from the "blank field" of its own singularity and mortality.

The male protagonists in the novella desperately pursue sacred or profane voices—Gnostic voices of unworldly purity or of unachievable innocence and perfection; Gauguin-like voices tempting middle-aged weariness to an illusory paradise beyond ordinary family life; Faustian voices of time-deadening lust—until emotional exhaustion leaves them receptive to the redemptive light that shines out in the acceptance of bodily finitude. This light is mediated by the women in the novel, who instruct the men to stand still and hearken to the voice of forgiveness that inhabits the silence outside their fear and guilt and to break the daily bread of their ordinary selves in communion with other flawed, fallible mortals (Lewis 2002, 41).

The imagination of Ritchie Stowe, the twelve-year-old child of the divorced Greg and Joan, is tortured by images of his brother's ex-wife Brenda lying naked and moaning under his father. The dispersion of his family caused by the infidelities and sexual imprudence of the father—and, we learn later, of Larry and Brenda—exacerbate the strains attendant upon his own dawning sexuality and tempt him into a dichotomous spirituality like that of young Harry in "If They Knew Yvonne." While attending seven o'clock morning Mass, as he does daily, Ritchie envisions his future as a headlong, tight-lipped flight from time and the seductions of the flesh, moving "alone and with the strength of the saints through his high school years, past girls, toward the seminary" (*Selected Stories*, 290).

Ritchie's devotion to Christ in the Eucharist is sincere, passionate, and affecting. But in the shifting, promiscuous surfaces of family life amidst which his sexuality is blossoming, that devotion falls prey to a dream of angelic purity, one that threatens to elevate the Eucharist beyond the pale of earthly desire and of human weakness. Watching the "upturned and transformed" face of the celebrant Father Oberti, Ritchie longs "to consume Christ, to be consumed through Him into the priesthood, to stand some morning purified and adoring in white vestments," a thrilling and ambitious spiritual prospect but also one that threatens to exempt him from the burdens and joys of passionate human relationships (292).

The humane Father Oberti retrieves the Eucharist from these angelic "voices from the moon" when he advises Ritchie that the love of Greg for Brenda, like all love, is "always near the grace of God" and that while such love may reveal Greg's weakness and imprudence, weakness as such is not mortally sinful and should not be the cause for summary judgment. "Two of the hardest virtues for a Christian," the priest tells him, are "forgiveness and compassion," and these, he implies, are the real fruit of the Eucharist just celebrated (293).

On the deck of his house at night, the father Greg indulges fantasies of tropical escape with Brenda from the combat of daily business life and, even more, from the prospect of the passion diminishing into "the distant murmurs of tired responsibility" (307). The doubts and fears that prompt these "voices from the moon" occupy the underside of Greg's strenuous, combative personality—"self-pity, surrender to whatever urged him to sloth or indifference or anomie or despair." His decision to marry Brenda, he tells the enraged Larry in justification for allowing himself to fall in love with her, grows not out of youthful infatuation but out of the longing, all the more exigent as he enters middle age, for "completion": "It's got to do with what I've never had, and what I'll never do" (306). Just after this, Greg similarly defends his need for Brenda to Ritchie, claiming that it was "nature's way, and that a man wasn't complete without [a wife]" (309).

A reader's response to Greg is likely to be ambivalent. On the one hand, he displays emotional generosity in preserving family ties to Brenda when she had separated from Larry, and he loves Brenda and encourages her individuality rather than trying to possess her body and soul, as did Larry. On the other hand, he displays a characteristic improvidence in allowing their relationship to escalate into romance at the potential cost of family tragedy, and he insists stubbornly—and to some extent boyishly—on the unimpeachable authority of his needs. In some respects, Greg is an older, more benevolent example of those males in Dubus's stories, like Hank Allison and Jack Linhart, who allow unclarified terrors to excuse their adulterous flight from the demon of ordinariness.

Ritchie is deeply moved by the sight of his father struggling to suppress tears. He mentally compares the remorse that his father suffers at the conflict between his imperious need for Brenda's love and the love of his children that he is thereby jeopardizing to the weeping of Peter at his cowardly denial of Christ. Ritchie feels he has crossed a boundary in what he has witnessed. Like seeing his mother naked, seeing his father humbled by forces beyond his strength challenges the purity and imperviousness of Ritchie's idealizations and initiates him more deeply into "the breath and blood of being alive" (312). We find Ritchie immediately after this scene relishing with unwonted attentiveness the earth and grass on which he plays softball, relishing piquant sensory memories of Melissa's scent and mouth, and imagining his way into her desires with a greater vibrancy and intimacy.

The voice that Larry has heard is as demonic as Ritchie's was angelic, yet it is akin to it in so far as it sponsors the illusion of godlike exemption from mortality and quotidian reality. Larry is cursed, as his mother later suggests, with just enough talent to suspect his own mediocrity. Out of the obscure darkness of this self-doubt, on one of "those Faustian nights of their marriage," Larry "swayed in feigned drunkenness to a melody he had dreamed," giving birth to one of the most perverse male rituals of mortality in all of Dubus's fiction (316). In conspiring with Brenda to stage the seduction of strangers as a stimulus to their own lovemaking, Larry seeks so to aggrandize his own finite passion as to obliterate the terrible specter of his ordinariness. Lying in bed, imagining the scenario unfolding outside in the living room, he is consumed by the specious control he exercises over her and his own body—and through it, over the fears emanating from his own inner darkness. "Run slowly, slowly, horses of the night" (320), he murmurs, recalling Mephistopheles's address to time in Marlowe's *Dr. Faustus* (Lewis 2002, 41).

If Dubus is at times a little too forbearing of Greg's emotional improvidence, it is not for lack of awareness of how the energies liberated by sexual passion can turn demonic when subverted by those deeper fears engendered by consciousness of our mortality. Brenda tells Larry, in horror at what they have done, that "there is something dark in us, something evil, and it must be removed" (320). And she struggles, after their separation, to restrain that unruly part of herself that had responded so violently to Larry's invitations.

Larry's infatuation with the Faustian voice from the moon destroys his marriage, just as his jealousy and anger at his father's impending marriage to Brenda threaten now to destroy his relationship to his father. Both Ritchie and Larry, as well as Greg, are rescued from destructive fantasies of innocence, lust, or self-pity by women who comprehend the fear that has driven them into retreat from the "blank field" of ordinariness (Lewis 2002, 42).

Ritchie's mother Joan is able to relieve her elder son of the unreasonable burden of eminence that he has laid on himself and that prevents him in turn from forgiving his father. She knows how much Larry depends upon the approval of others, especially his father, to confirm his gifts and talents. She knows too, with the greater balance and clarity born of her new independent life of satisfying work, the objective good that endures, beyond her dead marriage, in Greg and in Larry and her other children. She loved and lived with Greg for twenty-seven years, she tells Larry, because he never wanted to be "the son of a bitch" he all too often was and because "it was exciting watching him struggle" with his own failings (351). From the vantage point of her long acquaintance with the importunities of her husband's and her children's temperaments, Joan distills a voice of the earth to quell the unreasoning anger of her son. She draws a redemptive wisdom from the silence she now savors in her solitary life, a silence that terrorized Larry into those Mephistophelean dreams of lust: "So when I'm alone at night— and I love it, Larry—I look out my window, and it comes to me: we don't have to live great lives, we just have to understand and survive the ones we've got" (355).

The thirteen-year-old Melissa Donelly preaches a comparable sermon to Ritchie through her affectionate witness to the turmoil he has endured. Ritchie has been struggling, as Joan did, to extract from the silence and solitude of his disintegrating family life a source of joy and transcendence. In the sports of riding and cross-country skiing—and especially in the Eucharist—he had been able "to make his spiritual solitude physical" and thereby a medium of communion with the natural world he inhabits (338). Through Christ's assistance, he believes, it might also be a source of communion with his errant family. But love of Christ precluded love of Melissa, Ritchie had persisted in thinking. Eventually, however, Ritchie's Siren dream of purity proves incompatible with his love for his incorrigibly imperfect father, with his own irrepressible sexuality, and with Melissa's kindness and affection, all the more efficacious for its alluring incarnation of the love he treasures in the Eucharist. His concluding meeting with Melissa has ritual overtones of penitential reconciliation as he discovers her physical person as a medium of tenderness and generosity of spirit rather than a stumbling block to spiritual progress: "He saw in the stars the eyes of God too, and was grateful for them, as he was for the night and the girl he loved" (358).

In section seven of the novella, an analogous healing takes place in Greg, through the ministrations of his daughter Carol. Abashed at the emotional wreckage he has left in his wake by his announced union with Brenda, Greg seeks out Carol in a mute appeal for understanding and forgiveness, all the while anticipating her disapproval of the love he is reluctant to relinquish. Carol harbors nostalgia for her father as she once saw him as a girl. For a moment, she is tempted to conceal her own lover's shirts in her closet and to take a drug so as to blot out the past and escape into a simulacrum of that innocent, childlike love—still another Siren voice of the moon. Instead, she summons up the courage to enter the present moment. She shares a drink with her father and then, with the assistance of a second drink, eases into the tangle of his, and her own, emotional vulnerabilities. Carol draws upon the strength bestowed by her own sexual experience both to acknowledge her deep affection for her father and to rise above resentments at the bearish self-centeredness with which he had pursued his own will in the past, trampling over that of her mother. The love Carol has shared with others enables her to understand, even in the face of the pain it causes Ritchie and Larry, the urgency of her father's need after two years of lonely separation from her mother. She can see her father as he exists in Brenda's eyes and can acknowledge the gift that Brenda's love represents to "an aging and grateful bear" whose weaknesses and past failures in love threaten the far greater pain and self-destructiveness of despair (341): "When you had loved several times, there was a great urge to give up and say it did not exist and had never existed, that it had always been a trick of nature to keep itself going" (343).

Aware of the potency of this temptation through her own failed romances, Carol transposes the discussion of the day's tumultuous events from the ineffectual level of Greg's halting and inevitably self-exculpating words to the ecstatic plane of ritual. She invites him to dance, as she once danced with him innocently as a child before her mother, and as she now dances with him as a woman fully conscious of the appeal he has to Brenda. Her confirmation of the trustworthiness of his impulses, her warrant that he may credit himself with falling in love, occur in the context of an ordinary family ritual that at the same time partakes of ceremonious, grace-filled action. Their dancing immediately triggers associations in Greg with a religious source of mercy and forgiveness. "Do you go to Mass at all?" he asks the incredulous Carol, out of the blue (345). Unlike Carol, Greg still feels the reality of the sacred in Eucharistic ritual but cannot conceive any "fit" between his own errant nature and that liturgical act. But as the Frank Sinatra recording concludes and their dancing ceases, Greg appears to have assimilated the religious force of Carol's admonition to allow himself to "be happy" (345), and at a level much deeper than that of verbal self-analysis (Lewis 2002, 42–43).

This climactic scene invokes an image of harmony and reciprocity that pervades Dubus's late stories. The act of dancing is a symbol of the joy and transcendence accessible to those entering into time more deeply through ritual action: through those sacraments of everyday existence in community that are seen as informed by the paradigmatic action of the Eucharist. "*Like dancing,*" Rusty thinks at the conclusion of "Blessings," after she has negotiated the harrowing memories of the prior year's boating disaster in the Caribbean and as she approaches the bed of the sleeping husband who had braved that violence on her behalf (*Dancing After Hours*, 70). Emily Moore, the protagonist of "Dancing After Hours," envisions the possibility of a blessed equipoise of body and spirit under the same image: "if the heart with intrepid fervor could love and love again, using the sexual organs in its dance, she wanted to be able to exalt its resilience" (212). The atmosphere in which Lu Ann Arcineaux moves at the end of "All the Time in the World," embracing in chaste anticipation the gift of Ted Briggs, resonates to an enchanted music like that on Prospero's isle: "She did not believe in fate, but she believed in gifts that came; they moved with angels and spirits in the air" (96). Music and dancing, the arts most intimately wedding the body to time, suffuse the narrative space of a number of these late stories, in which male and female jointly mediate, jointly celebrate their liberation from the destructive rituals prompted by the specter of mortality. These narratives more explicitly assimilate the bread and wine of ordinary human passions to the structure of the Eucharistic anamnesis—the ritual remembering of Christ's salvific passion—that had always shaped the deep structure of Andre Dubus's imagination (Lewis 2002, 43–44).

CRITICAL RECEPTION

Over the course of the thirty-two years from 1967 to 1999, while publishing eleven volumes of fiction and two volumes of essays, Andre Dubus acquired a discriminating audience that recognized him as one of the modern American masters of the short story and novella. Critics consistently acknowledge the economy of his prose, the distinctive pitch of his narrative voice, and the accuracy with which he renders his characters' feelings. They universally praise his ability to portray in sharp, realistic detail the way people look within the convincingly rendered world north of Boston that became his prime fictional province.

As much as for his talent in capturing the physical and moral texture of a given time and place, Dubus draws praise for the power and directness of feeling with which he conceives his characters, most of them unequal to the hard circumstances of their lives. In particular, critics marvel at his daring and understanding in imagining his way into the subjectivity of his women—characters like Rose and Molly in the stories so titled, of Edith Allison in "Adultery," and of Joan Stowe, the mother in *Voices from the Moon*. When it was republished in *Selected*

Stories in 1989, *Voices from the Moon* was admired for its virtuosity in presenting the story so intimately through the consciousness of the several family members.

Dubus, it has been suggested, treads close to the sentimental in the very intensity of his compassion for his characters, exempting them, some maintain, from the full measure of the consequences warranted by their situations and choices. Occasionally, critics complain that Dubus's engulfing compassion threatens to undercut the moral stakes of the extreme situations he sets up in his stories. Most critics, nevertheless, judge that this compassion is a great source of strength and understanding, and that in erring on the side of sympathy Dubus's work is a welcome alternative to the relentless irony of mainstream modern fiction.

Increasingly, commentators have come to link this quality of compassion to Andre Dubus's Catholic religious sensibility. For all the pain and turmoil his fiction characteristically traces, Dubus does not despair. The consciousness of human weakness and sin that permeates his stories is matched by an understanding of grace at work in the healing of the wounds his characters habitually inflict on themselves and on those closest to them. This awareness grows particularly emphatic in the late fiction and essays, written subsequent to his tragic accident. A recent collection of scholarly studies in a special issue of *Religion and the Arts* (2002) analyzes the nature of his religious vision, in particular its Catholic sacramental character.

NOTE

Andre Dubus, *Voices from the Moon*, in *Selected Stories*, 288–358 (New York: Vintage, 1996). All references are to this edition (with the exception of the epigraph cited from the original edition of *Voices from the Moon* (Boston: David R. Godine, 1984). Permission is granted by *Religion and the Arts* to quote from my previously published article in that journal (listed below).

WORKS CITED

Anderson, Donald, ed. 2001. *Andre Dubus: Tributes*. New Orleans: Xavier Review Press.

Dubus, Andre. 1975. *Separate Flights*. Boston: David R. Godine.

———. 1977. *Adultery & Other Choices*. Boston: David R. Godine.

———. 1980. *Finding a Girl in America*. Boston: David R. Godine.

———. 1991. *Broken Vessels*. Boston: David R. Godine.

———. 1996. *Dancing After Hours*. New York: Random House.

———. 1998. *Meditations from a Movable Chair*. New York: Random House.

Lewis, Robert P. 2002. "'No More Male or Female': Bodiliness and Eucharist in Andre Dubus's Stories." *Religion and the Arts* 6, no. 1–2: 36–51.

O'Donnell, Brennan, Paul J. Contino, and Jane Kelly Rodeheffer, eds. 2002. *The Work of Andre Dubus*. Special Issue. *Religion and the Arts* 6, no. 1–2.

BIBLIOGRAPHY

Kennedy, Thomas. *Andre Dubus: A Study of the Short Fiction*. Boston: Twayne, 1988.

— Robert P. Lewis

William Dunbar [c. 1460–c. 1518]

Poems

BIOGRAPHY

William Dunbar is among Scotland's greatest "Makars." (The Scottish term *makar* refers to one who "makes" or creates poetry.) Dunbar wrote about eighty-five poems, most or all of them while living at the court of James IV, who reigned from 1488 to 1513. Critics are in general agreement that the poet is the William Dunbar named in the records (*Acta*) of St. Andrew's University who "determined" in 1477 (completed the equivalent of a modern baccalaureate degree) and "graduated" (received a master's degree) from the same university in 1479. Since a young man could not enter the university before his fourteenth year and usually "graduated" at age twenty, William Dunbar probably was born about 1460 (Baxter 1952, 9–11).

Nothing more is known about the poet's life until his name turns up in *The Treasurer's Accounts*, the records of expenditures for maintenance of the royal household. Records of *The Treasurer's Accounts* written between 1500 and 1513 make occasional mention of the poet, usually listed as "Maister William Dunbar," and these indicate that "Dunbar was a 'servitour' of James IV, receiving miscellaneous fees, and a 'pension,' or annual salary" (Bawcutt 1992, 6). Of special interest is the *Accounts* entry of March 1503 stating that Dunbar received a monetary award for saying his first Mass (Baxter 1952, 79–80), offering proof that the poet was an ordained priest.

Yet it was the court of James IV, not the Scottish church, which provided the primary backdrop for Dunbar's poetry. "Dunbar's view of the world was from the vantage point of the court," states Edmund Reiss (1979, 46), and "Dunbar lived his entire professional life intimately bound to one king and his immediate circle" (Norman 2001, 191). Moreover, Dunbar's poems contain "vivid images of himself, his friends and his enemies at the court of James IV" (Bawcutt 1998, 1:1). Dunbar's role at the court is not entirely clear, but most likely poetry was "subordinate to . . . other duties," such as "sometimes serving as a chaplain, clerk, letter writer, envoy, or notary" (Bawcutt 1992, 80).

In addition to being named in the St. Andrew's *Acta* and *The Treasurer's Accounts*, Dunbar is mentioned in two legal documents indicating that "he occasionally acted in the law courts as a *procurator*, or advocate" (Bawcutt 1998,

1:3). A "Mastir Willlyaim Dumbar" is named as a procurator selected to represent Sir John Wemyss in a family lawsuit in 1502, indicating that Dunbar was "a 'lovitt,' or trusted associate and legal representative of this Fifeshire laird" (Bawcutt 1992, 6). Dunbar's name also appears as that of a witness for a transfer of Edinburgh property in a document dated March 13, 1509; this citation provides evidence of the poet's being "an Edinburgh citizen, perhaps himself a property-owner . . . and, most significantly, a chaplain" (6–7). No other facts about Dunbar's life have been found. Earlier scholars sometimes used passages in particular poems to argue that Dunbar was of noble birth, had been a Franciscan friar, or had served as a member of the Scots Guard in France. But such claims remain undocumented (6).

What is clearly discernible in many of Dunbar's poems is that the poet considered himself impoverished and that he greatly desired a benefice. The possibility of a benefice is mentioned in the *Treasurer's Accounts* entry of 1500 when Dunbar's first "pension" is granted (Bawcutt 1998, 1:2). Dunbar wrote several poetic petitions requesting money from the king, often using humor in his requests, and sometimes he complained about not having a benefice. In one petitionary poem (number 68), his first-person speaker complains that when he was a boy being bounced on his nurse's knee, he was called a "bishop," but now, having reached a mature age, he finds that "A sempill [simple] vicar I cannot be" (lines 62–64). In the meantime, others have been more fortunate, including, "Iok that was wont to keip the stirkis" (Jock accustomed to looking after the young bullocks), who now has a long list of church appointments, and also "vplanis Michell" (country-boy Mitchell), who has been assigned two or three ecclesiastical positions (lines 66–72). Then the speaker fervently asks, "How sould I leif, and I not landit / Nor yit with benefice am blandit?" (How am I to survive since I have no inherited property and have not been provided with a benefice?) (lines 76–77).

In spite of his pleas, there is no record that Dunbar ever received a benefice. The reasons "have been attributed to Dunbar's lack of wealthy and noble kinsmen" at a time when "Nepotism was . . . widespread in the Scottish church" (Bawcutt 1998, 1:3). Such abuses were discussed at the Fifth Lateran Council (1512–1517), and the attending bishops sought reform, urging in particular "the enforcement of its decrees regulating the mode of life and morals of clerics and putting restraints on the number of incompatible benefices one cleric could hold" (Minnich 2001, 5). But such efforts came too late for Dunbar, who had the misfortune of serving under a king notorious for placing his nearest kin in high ecclesiastical positions. In one instance, James negotiated to have the Archbishop of Glasgow created a cardinal so that he could arrange for his own brother, the Duke of Ross, to be elected to the "primatial see" at the age of twenty-one (C. Mackenzie 1936, 40). After that attempt was foiled by Ross's unexpected death, James created a greater scandal by trying to ensure that his illegitimate son, Alexander Stewart, would become archbishop of Saint Andrews. Alexander was born in about 1497 to Marion Boyd, one of James's many mistresses (Baxter 1952, 98), and was only sixteen when the Duke of Ross died; James arranged for the "see" to be kept open until after the young prince had completed his education in Padua and Siena. When Alexander returned to Scotland in 1509, he held the title "Archbishop-elect" and "two years later was made Chancellor, appointed legate . . . by Pope Julius II, and given the Abbey of Dunfermline and the priory of Coldingham *in commendam*," upon which "James IV now transferred his support of the see of Glasgow to Saint Andrews" (C. Mackenzie 1936, 40). It was during the same years that Dunbar was writing petitionary poems in the hope of obtaining a modest benefice. Although history is silent about whether Dunbar attained his dream, it does reveal that James's aspirations for Alexander were thwarted: the young archbishop died at the age of twenty-six, fighting alongside his father at the Battle of Flodden (40).

James IV was also killed at Flodden, the disastrous battle of September 9, 1513 resulting from James's invasion of England. Some critics have suggested that Dunbar died alongside his king. However, there is no proof that the poet was at Flodden or even alive at the time. The last entry containing Dunbar's name in *The Treasurer's Accounts* is dated May 14, 1513, although records from August 1513 until June 1515 have not survived (Bawcutt 1998, 1:3). All that can be said with certainty about Dunbar's date of death is that he was dead by 1530, the year Sir David Lindsay completed *The Testament and Complaynt of our Souerane Lordis Papyngo*: that work makes mention of Dunbar as deceased (Baxter 1952, 214–25).

MAJOR THEMES

Unlike most medieval poets, Dunbar did not create a major opus; instead, his reputation rests on a collection of approximately eighty-five poems that are greatly diverse in subject matter, genre, verse form, tone, and level of diction. Even though Dunbar was a priest, there are only seven poems in the extant canon that are overtly religious in nature. It is likely that additional religious poems were lost or destroyed during the Reformation (Bawcutt 1992, 164). Of course, there are many other poems in the Dunbar canon that befit the poet's "priestly profile," especially the short moral poems. Yet some clearly do not, even though one critic argues that "at the heart" of all of Dunbar's poems, "no matter whether they are in the form of humorous banterings, grotesqueries, celebrations, or allegories," there "lies a moral sense that ultimately views everything human in terms of eternal values and ultimate truths" (Reiss 1979, 69). But this seems an extreme view. It is nearly impossible to imagine a moral or religious purpose for many of Dunbar's satiric and petitionary poems or for those two or three exhibiting the sentiments and language of medieval courtly love literature. Yet some of Dunbar's secular poems do seem to contain disguised priestly exhortations. In these, Dunbar apparently perceived his role as a Scottish Nathan to a Renaissance King David: like the prophet Nathan, Dunbar employed poetic allegory to open his king's eyes to his transgressions.

It is in this role of king's prophet that Dunbar uses secular poetry to caution James IV about inappropriate sexual behavior. In the short satiric beast fable beginning, "This hindir nycht in Dumfermling" (number 76), Dunbar derides the silly, amorous escapades of a wily red fox and a young and tender lamb. As Bawcutt notes, the "poem is traditionally interpreted as referring to some amorous exploit of James IV, who was a notorious philanderer" (1998, 2:469). Even within the stately heraldic dream vision poem known as "The Thrissil and the Rois" (number 52), which Dunbar wrote to honor the royal wedding of James IV (the Scottish Thistle) to Margaret Tudor (the Tudor Rose of red and white),

James is gently reminded to honor his wedding vows—to keep the sacrament of Marriage. Within the poem's allegorical vision, Dame Nature advises the Thistle to behave like a king: to "be discreit," to avoid nettles and weeds, and to hold no other flower in as high regard as the young rose (Evans 1987, 103).

There is a more general priestly exhortation hidden in Dunbar's dark poetic comedy of the dance of the "Sevin Deidly Synnis" (number 47). Since the action of the poem takes place on Shrove Tuesday, the night before Ash Wednesday and the last time for carnival activities before Lent, it prepares its hearers for Lenten prayers and fasting even as it amuses them. The setting is hell, where the seven cardinal sins are shown dancing with their human victims for the entertainment of devils. Using a kind of "grotesque realism, that special literary manifestation of carnival," Dunbar shows how the sins are integrated into human behaviors (Evans 1991, 358). Dunbar's purpose, in the midst of the demonic carnival, is "to show the monstrosity of evil, to bring its disgusting and horrifying nature to the surface, and at the same time to show its intrinsic meanness and destructiveness" (Ross 1981, 172). So in spite of its robust humor, the poem provides a warning to sinners and prepares them psychologically for Lent. As C. S. Lewis explained, "Dunbar and his contemporaries seriously believed that such entertainment awaited in the next world those who had practiced (without repentance) the seven deadly sins in this" (1954, 95).

This poem, in fact, is just one of many of Dunbar's poems—moral, religious, and satiric—to focus in some way, directly or indirectly, on the human need for the sacrament of Penance. While Dunbar devotes two religious poems to the sacrament itself, in many others he reminds humans of the brevity of life and their need to confess and do penance if they hope to receive eternal life. It is possible that Dunbar wrote some of these poems at the request of James IV. Historians indicate that James was "oppressed continually by a sense of his sins," especially for "the part he had played in the faction which had brought about his father's lamentable death at Sauchieburn" (Baxter 1952, 98). Although it is not clear that James IV was in any way responsible for the actual murder of his father, James III, it is believed that he had, while in the hands of his father's enemies, made an "audacious assertion of his own kingship" and had demonstrated "his determination to unseat his father" (Nicholson 1974, 530). For penance, James IV wore an iron belt around his waist (531) and usually made "a Lenten retreat to the Stirling friary of Observant Franciscans, which he founded in 1494 and supported with generous gifts" (Bawcutt 1998, 2:489). Perhaps also it was as an act of atonement that James oversaw the construction of many churches during his reign, including the beautiful Chapel Royal at Stirling Castle in 1501 (Macdonald 1989, 94). Surely, this king would have valued poetry that emphasized the human need for confession.

Such exhortations constitute the essence of Dunbar's many brief but finely honed moral poems, which frequently conclude with a call to confession. Dunbar's moral poems are written in short, simple verses with refrains, sometimes in Latin, borrowed from Scripture and the liturgy. Their voice resembles that of Qoholeth, the wise "preacher" of Ecclesiastes. In fact, in the short poem beginning, "O wreche, be war" (number 42), Dunbar appropriates the most familiar refrain from that Wisdom book: *Vanitas vanitatum et omnia vanitas* (Vanity of vanities, all is vanity) (Eccles. 1:2).

Dunbar's most common motif in his moral poems is mutability in the world. Repeatedly, the preacher's voice emphasizes the need to recognize the brevity of life and to prepare for death by confessing sins and doing penance. Such is the pattern in the poem beginning with the Latin line, "Memento, homo, quod cinis es" (Remember, man, that you are ashes) (number 32), an idea reinforced by the poem's Latin refrain, "Quod tu in cinerem reuerteris" (since you will revert into ashes). In the course of the poem, the speaker emphasizes the inevitability of death, citing examples of dead heroes of the past and naming such pairs as Hector and Hercules and David and Absalom. The speaker warns that even before the current year is over, the reader could become an ugly "tramort" (corpse); he also explains that no castle or tower can keep out "The dragone Death, that all devouris" (line 28) and reminds readers that the only "possession" to accompany them in death is "guid deid" (good work). The poem concludes with the following advice: "Go speid the [thee], man, and the confes, / With humill hart [humble heart] and sobir teiris [tears]" (lines 37–38). By doing so, the reader will be prepared to meet "Thy ransonner with woundis fyve" (that is, Christ, whose five wounds have paid the ransom for [redeemed] the sinner) (line 45).

Dunbar's greatest artistic achievement in his moral poems is the "Lament for the Makaris" (number 21). Here Dunbar explains the brevity of life in a poetic "dance of death." To each of the poem's *terza rima* stanzas is added the Latin refrain, "Timor mortis conturbat me" (The fear of death greatly disturbs me). As the poem begins, the speaker complains that he is currently troubled "with gret seiknes" and observes that "this fals warld" is "bot transitory" (line 5). A poetic dance of death follows, revealing members of the various estates who participate in the dance. While the first to dance are princes and prelates, the poem quickly narrows its focus to poets, particularly those poets with whom Dunbar identifies. The list begins with "The noble Chaucer, of makaris flour" (line 50), and the list grows increasingly personal as Dunbar mentions dead poets of his own generation. In the penultimate stanza, the speaker makes a logical deduction: "On forse [necessity] I man [must] his nyxt pray [next prey] be" (line 95). The poem does not end here but rather with the familiar priestly exhortation: since it is impossible to escape death, we should prepare for it spiritually so that we may live eternally.

The theme of confession, as previously noted, is also of considerable importance in Dunbar's religious poems. According to Priscilla Bawcutt, Dunbar's religious poems "differ from the moral ones not only in their Christocentric subject matter but in their emotionalism and, most strikingly, in their rich symbolic imagery . . . symbolism not peculiar to Dunbar, but . . . a shared Christian language" (1992, 166). The shortest of the religious poems is a single eight-line stanza beginning with the word "Saluiour" (Savior) (number 60), an indication that the poem is a short prayer. It is also a confessional prayer and reflects concerns that the poet perhaps had while living within the splendor of Scotland's Renaissance court. The "I" in the poem confesses that he has sinned by allowing his intelligence to be swayed by sensuality but adds that some "spark" of light and spirituality has inspired him, awakening his "wit" (intelligence), and so "reason" directs him to confess. The speaker then prays for "grace" and for "space" (a quantity of time) to make amends. He also asks for "Substance with honour," an enigmatic phrase perhaps describing what Dunbar desired his poems to be, especially since the speaker asks that he will not cause harm to anyone.

Two of Dunbar's religious poems provide instructions for people making confession: "The Maner of Passyng to Confessioun" (number 41) and "The Tabill of Confessioun" (number 83). Dunbar perhaps wrote the poems in response to the decree of the Fourth Lateran Council (1215) that "had made it mandatory for all parishioners to confess mortal sins once a year privately to their parish priests" (Bawcutt 1998, 2:485). It has been suggested that in both poems, Dunbar's purpose is "to aid readers in the examination of their conscience before making confession to a priest," and so "the I [in the poems] represents the voice of a typical sinner, and should not be identified with that of the poet" (485). Yet, even if Dunbar is using the "I" as the voice of a kind of Everyman figure, it is unlikely that Dunbar, a priest, would consider himself exempt from making confession.

"The Maner of Passyng to Confessioun" (number 41) consists of ten seven-line stanzas and is a Lenten poem: "O synfull man, thir ar the fourty dayis / that euery man sulde wilfull pennence dre" (should willingly endure penance). The poem's content is appropriate to the season, for it contains useful advice for anyone making confession. The speaker explains that the Lord Jesus had established the precedent for fasting when he fasted in the wilderness for forty days. Then the speaker stresses the importance of confessing all of one's sins. Reflecting the viewpoint of a priest, he warns that if a confession is incomplete, the priest will be unable to advise the penitent appropriately; the effect, he states metaphorically, will be that of one blind man being led forth by another. He continues with another analogy: just as a physician cannot heal a bodily wound until it is examined and cleansed, so a priest, the physician of the penitent's soul, cannot impose an appropriate penance until all the sin is exposed. In the final stanza, the speaker introduces another topic of importance—making confession while one is still young: "Quhill thou art abill [able] baith in mynde and toung." The speaker explains that it is of less merit to make a confession when one has not been exposed to temptation, "Quhen thou art ald and ma na wrangis wyrke" (may commit no sins).

Dunbar's other confession poem, "The Tabill of Confessioun" (number 83), is a much longer poem consisting of twenty-one eight-line stanzas. It also is a poetic prayer. The poem is so doctrinally correct, referring to all seven sacraments of the medieval Catholic Church, that during the Reformation it was modified in some manuscripts and early prints "in order to conform to Protestant dogma" (Bawcutt 1998, 2:485). For example, the scribe working on the Maitland manuscript during the Reformation had actually copied two lines of the stanza on the seven sacraments until he apparently realized the danger and "simply scored the lines out," while Bannatyne, creator of another Reformation manuscript containing Dunbar's poems, "more subtly revised Dunbar's verses so that only two sacraments should appear" (Macdonald 1989, 92).

In the opening lines, the first-person speaker is at prayer as he cries, "To the, O marcifull saluior myn, Iesus." The refrain line, "I cry the marcy [mercy] and laser [time] to repent," is also an element of the prayer, asking not only for Christ's mercy but also for time to do penance. In much of the rest of the poem, the speaker alludes to almost every conceivable sin, beginning with the cardinal sins:

> Off the sevin deadly synnis dois me schrif [do I confess]:
> Off prid, inwy [envy], of ire and covatice,
> Off lichory, glutton, with sleuth. (lines 18–20)

In addition, the speaker refers to some popular devotional practices, including the five wounds of Christ. It is noteworthy that during Dunbar's time, the cultic "devotion to the five wounds of Jesus (in his hands, feet, and side) was at its height" and "associated . . . with veneration and repetition of the name Jesus" (Bawcutt 1998, 2:486). Those who used the five wounds as a devotional aid considered them a symbol of Christ's compassion for sinners (486). Particularly moving is the final verse of the poem: the speaker compares himself to a ship sailing through violent storms and prays that Christ will bring his ship to the blessed port.

Dunbar's remaining religious poems have as their themes the Virgin Mary and the life of Christ, and at least three of these are among his greatest poems. Dunbar's remarkable poem honoring the Holy Mother, "Ane Ballat of Our Lady" (number 16), is also a prayer. Following in the tradition of the great Latin hymns associated with Saint Bernard of Clairvaux, Dunbar's hymn is more directly indebted to John Lydgate's English Marian poems. Like Lydgate, Dunbar adopted the "aureate" style for his hymn. The term *aureate*, introduced into English by Lydgate, means "gold-adorned," and this gilded style was used to honor its subject (Ebin 1988, 25). Dunbar's poem is adorned with Latinate phrases and sings with internal rhyme: "Hodiern, modern, sempitern, / Angelicall regyne" (lines 5–6). Dunbar uses only two end rhymes in all seven of his twelve-line stanzas. Moreover, the structure of the poem adds to its substance, for taken together, the seven stanzas constitute a poetic rosary. The only break in the rhyme scheme of each stanza, occurring always in the ninth line, is the opening of the rosary prayer, *Aue Maria, gracia plena* (Hail Mary, full of grace). Dunbar amplifies that prayer line in the fourth stanza, which is the central stanza of the seven, by providing verbal variation on the words "Hail Mary":

> Hale, qwene serene, hale, most amene,
> Haile, hevinlie hie emprys [high empress of heaven],
> Haile, schene, vnseyne with carnale eyne [shining one, unseen by
>   carnal eyes],
> Haile, ros of paradys [rose of paradise]. (lines 37–40)

In addition to this great hymn to the Virgin, Dunbar wrote three poems that honor Christ. His beautiful lyric on Christ's nativity (number 58) opens with the Latin Advent versicle, *Rorate, celi, desuper*! Dunbar translates the Latin, from Isaiah 45:8, in the poem's second line, "Hevins distill your balmy schouris." Bawcutt notes that "Dew or rain falling from heaven was a common medieval symbol for the Incarnation" (1998, 2:412). In the third line, Dunbar introduces Christ as "the brycht day ster" (star), an image he borrowed from Revelation 22:16, in which Christ is called "the bright and morning star" (2:412). Moreover, the Latin refrain, which concludes all seven of the poem's eight-line stanzas, similarly echoes the Advent liturgy borrowed from Isaiah's messianic prophecy: "Et nobis Puer natus est" (And unto us a Son is born).

The poem, so musical in sound and rhythm, calls for general rejoicing over the most glorious moment in the history of creation. The third stanza calls upon all the orders of angels, the stars, planets, firmament, and celestial spheres, along with the four elements. Then sinners (that is, mankind) are told to be glad and also to do penance (line 17) because Christ's blood will save them and release them from their bondage to the devil. The fourth stanza invites "all clergy" to bow down before the new baby. The birds of the air are instructed to sing because the "dully nycht" (dark night) has passed away and "Aurora," personifying a new dawn, has come to pierce the clouds of darkness. Then with a pun on the word *son*, the poet proclaims: "The son is rissin with glaidsum lycht" (line 39). The sixth stanza calls upon the flowers of the earth to spring up in honor of the blessed fruit "sprung" from "the rose Mary" (line 40). And in the seventh and final stanza, the poet bids all of heaven to sing along with all the regions of the air, all fish in the deep, all birds in the sky. He concludes by inviting all creation to sing *Gloria in excelsis*. It is noteworthy that both of these hymns of praise contain seven stanzas, for seven is the number of perfection in Christian symbolism.

Far different in tone is Dunbar's somber poem on Christ's Passion (number 1). It is much closer in theme to Dunbar's confession poems. "Ane Ballat of the Passioun" is a dream vision that makes real the sufferings of Christ. In the opening stanza, the narrator-dreamer establishes the time as Good Friday and states that he is kneeling at an altar within a cloister chapel. As he contemplates the crucifix before him, he experiences a sense of being present at the Passion; in the ensuing dream, he becomes an eyewitness. He describes in great detail each of the tortures inflicted upon the body of Jesus and thereby provokes an emotional response in the reader. The poem's refrain, "O mankind for the luif [love] of the [you]," emphasizes the causal relationship between Christ's suffering and the redemption of mankind. In the second portion of the poem, the dreamer experiences an allegorical passion that corresponds to Christ's real one. By means of personification allegory, Dunbar describes the steps humans must take as they seek salvation: Contrition, Compassion, Pain, Pity, Conscience, Confession, Repentance, and Penance all visit the dreamer. The dreamer's psychological "passion" parallels Christ's real Passion in several ways: Compassion strikes at him (line 98) just as the Jews had beat Jesus (line 29); Contrition blinds his eyes with tears (lines 99–100) just as Jesus is blinded by blood streaming down his face from wounds inflicted by the crown of thorns (line 47). Remembrance confronts the dreamer, showing him the instruments of torture that had afflicted Christ's body: "corse [cross] and nails scharp, scurge and lance, / And bludy crowne" (lines 107–08). Critic Antony Hasler observes that "the subject observing the Passion becomes a series of metamorphoses of allegorical space; the engaged witness is transformed into the stage for a psychomachia, to emerge finally as the house fit for Christ to enter" (1989, 197). Indeed, the poem's final two stanzas tie together Christ's actual Passion and the dreamer's allegorical experience. The dream concludes when the dreamer is awakened by what feels to him like an earthquake: "The erde did trymmill quhair I lay" (line 138); in this way, the literary dream vision is brought to an end with an awakening device, but the dreamer's sensation is also a continuation of the immediate aftermath of the real Crucifixion as described in Saint Matthew's Gospel (Matt. 27:51).

The last of Dunbar's trio of Christ-centered poems celebrates the Resurrection (number 10). As Priscilla Bawcutt has observed, "Done is a battle on a dragon blak" is "undoubtedly the most popular of Dunbar's religious poems, appealing alike to believers and non-believers" (1992, 178). In this poem, Dunbar employed the alliterative ballad form, and he reveals Christ to be the triumphant hero overcoming evil: "Our campioun Chryst confoundit hes his force" (lines 1–2). Christ is hailed as the victorious champion over death and evil; his foe, personified as a black dragon, is derived from apocalyptic symbolism. The Latin refrain line, "Surrexit dominus de sepulchor" (the Lord has risen from the tomb), completes all five of the eight-line stanzas; it is liturgical, having been used in the Easter Mass and also "in the liturgy during the weeks following Easter" (Bawcutt 1998, 2:310). Dunbar's intent is to explain that the Resurrection is a victory for the human race because "The yetis [gates] of hell ar brokin with a crak" (line 3). Evil is personified not only as the black dragon, but Lucifer is equated with the cruel serpent (line 10) and the old "kene" tiger (line 11). Similarly, Christ is referred to as the sacrificial lamb (line 18) who becomes a lion risen up again (line 19). Bawcutt notes that Dunbar's poem is one of a "small cluster of Scottish poems on this theme" but "stands out from the rest, rather as did *Rorate celi*, for its finer craftsmanship" (1992, 183).

CRITICAL RECEPTION

Just as it has been difficult to find facts about Dunbar's life, so also has it been difficult to establish Dunbar's poetic canon. Priscilla Bawcutt, Dunbar's most recent editor, indicates that "no autograph of Dunbar's poems exists" and "only a few texts date from Dunbar's own lifetime or shortly after" (1998, 1:4). She also notes that although "Dunbar's poetic genius was recognized by his immediate contemporaries" he was all but forgotten after the Reformation and throughout most of the seventeenth century (1:3–4). He was not rediscovered until some of his poems were published in Allan Ramsay's *Ever Green* of 1724 (1:4). After that, Dunbar's reputation gradually increased. At the end of the nineteenth century, the Scottish Text Society produced its three-volume edition of Dunbar's poetry, and Dunbar soon gained recognition as one of Scotland's greatest poets. He received considerable scholarly attention during the twentieth century, including the praise of Scotland's great modern poet, Hugh MacDiarmid. During the twentieth century three "complete" editions of his poems were published (by W. Mackenzie [1966], J. Kinsley [1979], and P. Bawcutt [1998]). Bawcutt's is the most recent and should remain the definitive edition for many years. To be as accurate as possible, Bawcutt took all the texts of Dunbar's poems printed in her edition directly from manuscripts and early prints instead of from earlier editions (1:11). She also made an effort to correct errors made by some of Dunbar's earliest editors after she discovered that Ramsay had tampered with Dunbar's texts and that verses in some of the religious poems were "adjusted by post-Reformation copyists to conform with Protestant dogma" (1:11–12). Also during the twentieth century, four critical books about Dunbar were published (by Scott [1966], Reiss [1979], Ross [1981], and Bawcutt [1992]).

As for criticism of Dunbar's religious poems, the confession poems and the poem on Christ's Passion have fared the worst. There has been almost no published criticism of the confession poems, although Bawcutt believes that the "Tabill" (number 83) "is more than a dry tabulation of sins, and is suffused with emotion, particularly in the refrain and in the final prayers" (1998, 2:485). Criticism of the "Passioun" poem for the most part has been harsh. John Pinkerton, Dunbar's eighteenth-century editor, described it "as stupid as need be" (2:367–68), and many recent critics have not been much kinder. James Kinsley finds that it displays "a passionless rhetoric" (1979, 108), and Tom Scott describes the physical details of the Crucifixion as "a sado-masochistic exercise which cannot be imaginatively responded to without sacrifice of sensitivity" (1966, 286). Yet Aeneas Mackay, editor of the Scottish Text Society edition, called it the "most impressive" of the religious poems (1893, cxl), and Agnes Mure Mackenzie called it a "fine thing . . . nowise conventional," comparing its stark details to a Flemish painting (1933, 66–67).

Dunbar's poems on the Nativity and Resurrection, on the other hand, have received positive evaluations. C. S. Lewis observed that the Nativity hymn "might almost claim to be in one sense the most lyrical of all English poems . . . the hardest . . . simply to *read*, the hardest not to sing" (1954, 95). Bawcutt admires the "forceful rhythms" of the Resurrection poem and also its imagery, which she describes as "theologically orthodox yet deployed in such a way as to have the force of myth—bold, arresting, and mysterious" (1992, 178). C. S. Lewis gave this poem highest praise, finding in it "speech of unanswerable and thundering greatness" and adding that the poem "vibrates with exultant energy," having "the ring of a steel gauntlet flung down" (1954, 96).

Modern readers have also been impressed by the *aureate* diction of "Ane Ballat of Our Lady." Lois Ebin praises Dunbar for taking "the strategy of Lydgate's Marian lyrics to the absolute limits, placing an even greater emphasis . . . on the poet's role in transforming his matter into poetry" (1988, 87). Moreover, modern Scottish poet Tom Scott, so frequently critical of Dunbar's subject matter and technique, describes this poem as "a carillon of joyful bells" and states emphatically that "The Scots language has never produced anything so extravagantly exuberant" (1966, 304).

NOTE

William Dunbar, *The Poems of William Dunbar*, ed. Priscilla Bawcutt (Glasgow: Association for Scottish Literary Studies, 1998, 2 vols.). All references are to this edition. Used by permission of the Association for Scottish Literary Studies.

WORKS CITED

Bawcutt, Priscilla. 1992. *Dunbar the Makar*. Oxford: Clarendon Press.
Baxter, J. W. 1952. *William Dunbar: A Biographical Study*. Edinburgh: Oliver and Boyd.
Ebin, Lois A. 1988. *Illuminator, Makar, Vates: Visions of Poetry in the Fifteenth Century*. Lincoln: University of Nebraska.
Evans, Deanna Delmar. 1987. "Ambivalent Artifice in Dunbar's *The Thrissil and the Rois*." *Studies in Scottish Literature* 22: 95–105.

———. 1991. "Bakhtin's Literary Carnivalesque and Dunbar's 'Fasternis Evin in Hell.'" *Studies in Scottish Literature* 26: 354–65.

Hasler, Antony J. 1989. "William Dunbar: The Elusive Subject." In *Bryght Lanternis: Essays on the Language and Literature of Medieval and Renaissance Scotland*, ed. J. Derrick McClure and Michael R. G. Spiller, 194–205. Aberdeen, Scotland: Aberdeen University Press.

Kinsley, James, ed. 1979. *The Collected Works of William Dunbar*. Oxford: Clarendon Press.

Lewis, C. S. 1954. *English Literature in the Sixteenth Century Excluding Drama*. Oxford: Clarendon Press.

Macdonald, Alasdair A. 1989. "Religious Poetry in Middle Scots." In *The History of Scottish Literature: Origins to 1660*, ed. R. D. S. Jack, vol. 1, 91–104. Aberdeen, Scotland: Aberdeen University Press.

Mackay, Aeneas J. G. 1893. Introduction. In *The Poems of William Dunbar*, ed. John Small and Walter Gregor, xi–clii. 3 vols. Scottish Text Society. Edinburgh and London: William Blackwood and Sons.

Mackenzie, Agnes Mure. 1933. *An Historical Survey of Scottish Literature to 1714*. London: A. Maclehose & Co.

Mackenzie, Compton. 1936. *Catholicism and Scotland*. 1971. Reprint, Port Washington, NY: Kennikat Press.

Mackenzie, W. Mackay, ed. 1966. *The Poems of William Dunbar*. 1932. Revised edition, London: Faber and Faber.

Minnich, Nelson H. 2001. "The Last Two Councils of the Catholic Reformation: The Influence of Lateran V on Trent." In *Early Modern Catholicism: Essays in Honor of John W. O'Malley, S. J.*, ed. Kathleen M. Comerford and Hilmar M. Pabel, 3–25. Toronto: University of Toronto Press.

Nicholson, Ranald. 1974. *Scotland: The Later Middle Ages*. Edinburgh: Oliver & Boyd.

Norman, Joanne S. 2001. "William Dunbar's Rhetoric of Power." In *The European Sun*, ed. Graham Caie, Roderick J. Lyall, Sally Mapstone, and Kenneth Simpson, 191–200. East Linton, Scotland: Tuckwell.

Reiss, Edmund. 1979. *William Dunbar*. Boston: G. K. Hall.

Ross, Ian Simpson. 1981. *William Dunbar*. Leiden, The Netherlands: Brill.

Scott, Tom. 1966. *Dunbar: A Critical Exposition of the Poems*. Edinburgh: Oliver & Boyd.

— Deanna Delmar Evans

T. S. Eliot [1888–1965]

Four Quartets

BIOGRAPHY

T. S. (Thomas Stearns) Eliot was born in St. Louis in 1888 and spent his childhood summers at the Eliot home in Gloucester, Massachusetts. He died in England in 1965, having embraced British history, tradition, and culture without ever losing his deeply American roots. A Harvard graduate (1910), he read philosophy and literature in France and worked in publishing in London. In 1915, he married Vivienne Haigh-Wood and began a deeply strained and anguished relationship. A decade after her death in 1947, Eliot secretly married Valerie Fletcher and seemed to attain a degree of serenity and comfort in their marriage. Emily Hale, a third crucial woman in Eliot's life and a mystical presence especially in *Burnt Norton*, the first of the *Four Quartets*, remained pivotal in Eliot's life and imagination.

In the years of World War I and the early 1920s, Eliot's literary and moral imagination reflected a certain pessimism and even despair. In his family's Unitarianism, Eliot found no resonant antidote. In the ironically titled poem "The Love Song of J. Alfred Prufrock" (1917)—Prufrock neither invites nor expresses authentic love—Eliot delineates modernity's anxiety and confusion. *The Waste Land* (1922), a poem at once observant, learned, and ambitious, explores humanity's fragmentation, loss of faith, and spiritual desolation in the wake of World War I. And in 1925, another poem, "The Hollow Men," intensified this world of neutrality, torpor, and drift.

Yet the searching, religious echoes in these poems clearly reflect the depth of Eliot's preoccupation with what the theologian Paul Tillich calls "ultimate concern," an intense, experiential conviction that God's seeming absence paradoxically speaks to his presence. Eliot's reading of and admiration for such religious mystics as Saint John of the Cross and Pascal and such deeply Christian and Catholic thinkers as Saint Augustine and Dante are evident by their resonances even in his early poems. In Rome in 1926, Eliot had knelt emotionally before Michelangelo's *Pietà*. Later, he would discern a pattern of grace in his disenchantment, struggles, and eventual conversion to the Anglo-Catholic Church and to the faith, hope, and love it embodied and professed. In 1930 on Ash Wednesday, Eliot confessed this faith, and in 1934 his *Choruses from "The Rock"* confirmed the degree to which hollowness had given way to substance, despair to faith, and loss to the discovery—or the recovery, Eliot would insist—of the joy of grace and salvation.

SUMMARY

Four Quartets constitutes the deepest and most sustained of Eliot's meditations on his own—and humanity's potential—journey from despair to a suffering and knowledge that become genuinely redemptive. Like the tradition of meditation in which each of the quartets is steeped, each poem begins with a composition of a particular place and ends with a prayerful utterance. Each place is at once crucial to Eliot's inner life and resonant with significance for all of us as readers of and potential sharers in Eliot's vision. Each of the four poems first appeared separately: *Burnt Norton* in 1936, as war clouds gathered in Europe; *East Coker* at Easter, 1940, as England suffered through the Blitz's rain of death and destruction by Hitler's bombs and rockets; and *The Dry Salvages* in 1941. Originally, Eliot had planned for only three quartets. But in 1942, a fourth, *Little Gidding*, appeared, at once a further exploration, extension, and prophetic vision of the deeply moral and religious concerns of the preceding three poems. Despite their individuality, the quartets are united by artistic patterns that Eliot elsewhere calls a condition of "stillness and reconciliation" (Gordon 1999, 391). Like the mystery of conversion itself, discrete experiences and holistic form, single images and broader coherence, moments and eternity, humanity and divinity enhance each other and ultimately—and mystically and paradoxically—reconcile.

In the 1930s, Eliot visited and in certain instances revisited the English places whose names form the titles of the quartets. The Dry Salvages, a shelf of rocks off Cape Ann, Massachusetts, is the only American place-name used. It had maintained an indelible place in Eliot's childhood, memory, and imagination. Each place and poem remains indispensable to *Four Quartets*' deeper pilgrimage and ultimate and communal destination.

Burnt Norton

In this first quartet, centered in a strikingly beautiful rose garden in Burnt Norton in Gloucestershire, Eliot draws on his experience of an idyllic time he shared there with Emily Hale, whom he clearly loved. The quartet's five parts, or movements, invoke the mystery of time, a garden simultaneously echoing the Fall as well as Eden's prelapsarian innocence, and childhood's wonder crystallized in joy and the sound of laughter. A strain of melancholy runs through *Burnt Norton*, as if time's cycles are as futile and devoid of purpose as they were for Saint Augustine before his conversion. Yet the biblical and archetypal garden, childhood, and laughter's presence simultaneously invoke more joyful memories and hold out a promise for a vision of time redemptive and salvific.

East Coker

The major paradox of *East Coker* is that Eliot's concern with his specific, historical ancestral home—the village of East Coker in Somerset is the place from which Andrew Eliott began his journey to the New World—served to inspire Eliot's, and England's, faith and perseverance during the most desolate hours of the Blitz. Published at Easter 1940, the poem was reprinted in May and June and sold nearly 12,000 copies within a year (Gordon 1999, 353). Dame Helen Gardner commented on its powerfully moving impact, and Mary Lee Settle, an American novelist in wartime London, recalled that Eliot had wrought from a feeling of hopelessness "a promise like steel." Indeed, his "miraculous effrontery of spirit," she reflected, made Eliot "our lay priest" (quoted in Gordon 1999, 391).

The spirit and hope of *East Coker* resonate in its conviction that such seeming ends as affliction and death in fact can provide new and redemptive beginnings; that memory and visions of home provide our deepest identity and continuity; and that our humility constitutes not only virtue but wisdom. Here, Eliot invokes the mystics'—and Saint Paul's—valuing of patience and waiting as a way to apprehend the theological virtues of faith, hope, and love. Despite melancholy and sadness, laughter once again resonates from the garden. Despite the elusiveness of words, the presence of the Word endures. Despite the strong sense of loss, permanent values remain. Despite evil and suffering, Eliot invokes in a central and striking way the paradox of Good Friday in all its mystery of darkness and hope, despair and salvation. And in this light, despite the soul's frequent sense of isolation and lostness, Eliot hopes for—and sees—a greater unity and a "deeper communion."

The Dry Salvages

Here, Eliot locates life's ebb and flow, dangers and wonder, in the river and the sea and in the dynamism of the soul's voyage. His childhood memories of the Mississippi River's near-divine power and the rocks off Cape Ann inform the symbolism—and concrete literalness—of the fishermen who risk shipwreck and death each time they embark from Gloucester. With its deeply biblical echoes of fishing and mystery, this quartet crystallizes a vision of life as a dangerous voyaging whose end is salvation. Invoking Saint Bernard's prayer to the Virgin at the end of Dante's *Paradiso*, the speaker here entreats her blessing on all seafarers—on all humanity. From childhood, Eliot knew the Salvages represented danger—the largest rock constantly visible, the "Dry" at times hidden by the tides—yet he knew as well, even if subconsciously, the presence of promise and grace. The sea's immensity and wildness also serve to point to a Guide, a Protector.

Atop a hill in Gloucester, visible from the sea, stands a Roman Catholic Church called Our Lady of Good Voyage. Atop the church is a statue of the Virgin cradling a sailing ship, embodying a beacon-like faith, hope, and love, and signifying the mariner's hope for a secure harbor, a safe deliverance and return. A photograph of this statue graces the pages of Sebastian Junger's *The Perfect Storm* (1998), a harrowing account of the voyage and destruction of the fishing boat the *Andrea Gail*, harbored in Gloucester and lost in a ferocious storm in 1991. Cradling the ship in one hand and blessing all voyagers with her other upturned hand, the Virgin makes concrete the deepest longings and prayers of this quartet. In this setting of seafaring and the hope of reunion, life and death, and in the divine light of the Virgin and Christ, Eliot accentuates the deepest source of all hope. It is at once a "hint half guessed" and a "gift half understood"—the mystery of the Incarnation (*Four Quartets*, 199).

Little Gidding

Like Dante and the *Paradiso*, Eliot sees *Little Gidding* as a written act of faith, a witness and testament to a transcendent grace and deliverance. Here, Eliot anchors his vision in a seventeenth-century religious community in Huntingdonshire. In publishing *Little Gidding* in October 1942, Eliot voyaged beyond his originally planned structure of three quartets. Unlike the other three, the name for this quartet signals no autobiographical and personal connection to Eliot. Although, as in the first two quartets, the place is again located in England, it is as if Eliot seeks to move beyond the personal in a most striking way in order to address and invoke a broader and deeper unity and blessedness.

Eliot did visit Little Gidding, and the quartet resonates with Eliot's cherishing of and gratitude for this small Anglican community founded by two brothers and their sister, Nicholas, John, and Susanna Ferrar. Indeed, Nicholas was a good friend of the poet George Herbert, and as he lay dying Herbert asked Nicholas to arrange for the publication of a volume of Herbert's poems, later called *The Temple*. Herbert's poem "Redemption" has strong affinities with *Four Quartets*, as does the poem "Love," which also profoundly influenced the interior life and conversion of the modern mystic Simone Weil.

Eliot clearly was moved by the devotion of the Ferrars and their community of some sixty souls. This devotion continued beyond Nicholas's death in 1637 and the near-destruction of the church at Little Gidding in 1646, when it was ravaged by its iconoclastic enemies. Despite this persecution, John and Susanna Ferrar continued their community's devotional life until their deaths in 1657. In this community's devotion, suffering, and perseverance, Eliot sees and symbolizes the communion of saints, the gathering of believers that marks the keeping of faith, and the keeping and sharing of the faith, the ultimate truth and revelation from whose essence life itself is generated and by which it is sustained.

It is not surprising and in fact wholly fitting that Eliot wrote and rewrote more drafts of *Little Gidding* than of any other quartet. For here he brings to bear the paradoxical symbols and dialectic of temporality and ultimacy, flux and permanence, fire and rose, endings and beginnings. Here, the sacramental presence of the Incarnation reconciles moment and eternity, and a once-destructive fire resembling the fires of the Blitz becomes the refining and redemptive fire of the transforming Holy Spirit. And here, the once isolated and despairing soul becomes part of a deeper and more vital communality generated by a divine "Love" and called into being by a divine voice that seeks the soul's response and ultimately its salvation. In this light, we again experience the garden, river, and sea—all informing and illuminating the souls whose community begins and ends in God. Eliot's closing prophecy and assurance—that "all" shall be "well"— is itself an end and a beginning, a form of hope rooted in Christ's promise, as in his assurances that "I will not leave you orphans" or "I will be with you always, even unto the end of the world." Eliot's "all shall be well" is taken from the writing of the fourteenth-century English mystic Julian of Norwich, who also lived in troubled times and who heard these words of comfort and peace spoken to her by Christ. Striking here is that for all his intellectual and doctrinal commitment to the Catholic faith and tradition, it is to the mystics and to Pascal's emphasis on the heart's having reasons that reason cannot fathom that Eliot turns at these vital moments. To be sure, Eliot neither minimizes nor dismisses the power of affliction, whether his own or humanity's shared wounds. Yet for him, this affliction is transformed and redeemed by Christ's own crucifixion and resurrection. Eternal life, not temporal death, constitutes the last word in humanity's ancient and current narrative.

MAJOR THEMES

For many contemporary writers and their audiences, Eliot argued, the Christian faith had become an anachronism. The secular mind and imagination, he insists in his essay "Religion and Literature," are "simply unaware of, simply cannot understand the meaning of, the primacy of the supernatural over the natural life" ([1932] 1975, 28). Eliot's conversion to Anglo-Catholicism constituted his recovery of an ancient faith deeper, more resonant, and more transcendent than his family's rationalistic Unitarianism. At once intellectual and emotional, this historic faith meant for Eliot an embracing of doctrinal truth, of tradition, and of a sacramentalism whose rituals celebrate a Eucharistic vision of life, death, and eternal life. The Church embodied for him the mysticism of Saint John of the Cross, Pascal, and Simone Weil—for whose *The Need for Roots* he wrote an admiring introduction—and an intellectual and affective continuity rooted in Scripture and tradition. In Eliot's vision of this tradition and continuity, he accents, as do Dante and Augustine before him, life as a pilgrimage from sin to redemptive grace and a God who is not absent but a God of mystery, supernatural revelation, and presence.

Eliot's affinity for the work of Simone Weil stems from his affinity for Pascal and Saint John of the Cross. For Weil, the heart of all prayer, and even all study, is attentiveness—an opening of one's mind, heart, and spirit to the presence of grace. We do not search for God in an active, restless way, she insists, but rather God descends to us when we are serene and at peace, expectantly awaiting him. Throughout each of the quartets, we discover Eliot's valuing of this same meditation, prayer, attentiveness, and expectation. These habits constitute the counter to the fragmentation, atomism, and restlessness of modernity. Our hearts are restless, Augustine insists in his *Confessions*, until they rest in God. So too for Eliot. The habits of the heart must embrace meditation and contemplation in order to cultivate, and to welcome, that "peace at the center" of which Quakers and the Church speak so consistently. The soul's stillness and watchfulness are at the heart of Eliot's vision of grace and salvation.

Just as the Catholic Church's tradition values meditation—it is not, as sometimes popularly thought, the province of Buddhism or other eastern philosophies or religions—it also recognizes that any serious meditation must acknowledge and encounter the "dark night of the soul." Simone Weil's wrenching experiences of loss and affliction, like Pascal's, testify to the strange and paradoxical ways in which good and evil, suffering and joy, are interwoven. The human mind, says Pascal, is at once the "glory and shame" of the universe. As Weil reflects on the person and mystery of Christ, she returns again and again to Christ's affliction on the cross, on the depth and extent of his suffering and abandonment.

Throughout *Four Quartets*, Eliot's acute awareness of sin as well as grace, evil as well as good, death as well as redemption, is strikingly clear. Indeed, his awareness of the presence of grace accentuates rather than dismisses the actuality of sin, just as the joy of the Resurrection transcends but does not minimize the agony of the Crucifixion. The river can be a destroyer as well as a deliverer. The seas through which fishermen voyage can be terrifying and chaotic as well as serene. Ordinary life can be benevolent at its prosaic heart or it can hold within itself hollowness or even horror. As with the great mystics and all true believers, Eliot fully realizes that the virtues of humility and of faith, hope, and love are daily challenged by faithlessness, egotism, and the will to power and destruction.

For Eliot, the very tradition of the Church itself serves to provide a counter to the isolated Cartesian ego so dominant in the imagery of the modern world. Eliot knows that the very word "modern" is an ancient word and that each of us is part of a broader tradition and traditions that have helped to shape us. Indeed, in his essay "Tradition and the Individual Talent" ([1919] 1975), Eliot argues that all writers affect by their writing the place and importance of their predecessors and those who will follow them. Although Marx and Lenin found tradition an oppressive and stultifying force, a dead hand suppressing the needs and desires of the living, Eliot sees tradition as a liberating and enhancing presence. Viewed rightly, tradition can free us from the egocentric and the parochial. G. K. Chesterton believes that "orthodoxy" is not oppressive but, in fact, a "romance," a wondrous affirmation of values permanent and perennial (the title of his best-known book is, simply, *Orthodoxy*). And at orthodoxy's heart, he writes, is the value of tradition: "Tradition means giving votes to the most obscure of all classes, our ancestors. It is the democracy of the dead. Tradition refuses to submit to the small and arrogant oligarchy of those who merely happen to be walking about" ([1924] 1959, 48). Dissenting from those who equate "progress" with the "modern," then, Eliot, like Chesterton, affirms those values the Church finds permanent and perennial. And dissenting from those who champion the autonomous ego as the supreme reality and arbiter of all judgments, Chesterton and Eliot emphasize the vital place of tradition—and especially the Christian and Catholic tradition—in defining who we are and who we ought to be. However fallen we are, Eliot insists, we need always to be reminded that we are made in God's image and that this recognition is at once astonishing, sobering, and salvific.

To accentuate the importance of continuity and tradition rather than isolation and atomism is also to make clear that for Eliot the Church values and crystallizes the essence of memory and community. As noted, in each of the quartets the presence of memory is both striking and pervasive. Eliot's memories of his times at Burnt Norton and East Coker, his childhood memories of the rocks off Cape Ann—even his memory of sailing around them at one point—retain a deep and affective resonance. For Eliot, memory may be potentially and actually redemptive. He may well have assented to Dostoevsky's valuing and even cherishing of memory as a deeply spiritual and redeeming presence. As Dostoevsky's hero Alyosha says to a group of children at the end of *The Brothers Karamazov*, "You must know that there is nothing higher, or stronger, or sounder, or more useful afterwards in life, than some good memory, especially a memory from childhood, from the parental home. You hear a lot said about your education, yet some such beautiful, sacred memory, preserved from childhood, is perhaps the best education. If a man stores up many such memories to take into life, then he is saved for his whole life. And even if only one good memory remains with us in our hearts, that alone may serve some day for our salvation" (1991, 774).

Continuity, tradition, and memory all presuppose and point to the importance of community—tradition, after all, might well be seen as a communal rather than an entirely individual memory—and for Eliot throughout *Four Quartets* the value of community occupies a central and dynamic place. Indeed, the operative pronoun in the work, and especially in *Little Gidding*, is "we" rather than "I." Community serves to subvert atomism and egotism and to affirm, through love and service, our obligation to others and to the common good. Certainly in his own life, Eliot's longing for love and his struggles to sustain it are evident and powerful. In *Four Quartets*, the speaker's desire to address and embrace others and to overcome his solely private concerns constitute a recurring theme. And surely his decision to forge ahead with *Little Gidding* as the fourth of his quartets, with its anchor the seventeenth-century religious community that so engaged Eliot's moral imagination and vision of a life lived with and for others, witnesses the holistic nature of Eliot's commitment to a "deeper communion." Kristian Smidt, among other commentators, rightly notes that the Catholic sacrament of Penance appears most frequently in Eliot's work and that the Eucharist comes next: "And one of the chief things that Eliot sought in the Church and its doctrine of immortal bliss was clearly a sense of communion" (1961, 208). In an increasingly secular age, then, Eliot apprehends through the Church and its traditions the value of meditation and attentiveness, the affirmation that grace overcomes the most grievous evil and sin, and the power of charity and communion. If the communality of our shared pilgrimage is indeed key for Eliot, key also is his conviction that a Christological and Eucharistic reality centers and illuminates the very nature of pilgrimage. Voyaging remains arduous, yet the presence of the Virgin provides a sacred and sacramental assurance that faith and grace will prevail and that suffering, finally, is not futile but redemptive. The divine attentiveness to and identification with humanity's travail through the mysterious yet concrete events of the Incarnation, Crucifixion, and Resurrection make certain that affliction is not an end but a beginning. The ultimate harmony to which the end of *Little Gidding* points, the unity of fire and rose, is apocalyptic, and its tone of promise and assurance reflects the Book of Revelation: the redeemed, once lost and now found, "shall hunger no more, neither thirst any more; neither shall the sun light on them, nor any heat. For the Lamb which is in the midst of the throne shall feed them, and shall lead them unto living fountains of waters: and God shall wipe away all tears from their eyes" (Rev. 7:16–17; Authorized Version).

CRITICAL RECEPTION

Since it proved impossible to separate the form and style of Eliot's poetry from the deep religious commitments—indeed, the act of conversion itself—that shaped them and provided their reason for being, the poetic and critical responses to Eliot in general and to *Four Quartets* in particular inevitably reflect his critics' most profound presuppositions about and attitudes toward religious institutions and traditions and the essence of faith itself. Such poets as Karl Shapiro and William Carlos Williams criticized Eliot, Williams particularly because he believed Eliot's embracing of British culture and history had meant his rejection of his American background and identity. Hemingway too was highly critical of Eliot, yet when he converted to Catholicism because of his second wife he began to address deeply religious questions closely linked to Eliot's struggles and vision. Indeed, Santiago— or Saint James—the old fisherman in Hemingway's *The Old Man and the Sea*, as well as the novella's mystical resonances of fishing and the sea are often illuminated by *The Dry Salvages*. Santiago's suffering, hope, and prayers to the Virgin call to mind this segment of the *Four Quartets*, and even as Hemingway criticizes Eliot it is clear that he, like most modern novelists and poets, feels his influence.

In acknowledging Eliot's influence, certain writers insisted they were most influenced by his early poems rather than by "Ash Wednesday," *Four Quartets*, or *Choruses from "The Rock"*—that is, they experienced deeply and shared Eliot's delineation of despair and lostness but not his religious conversion and commitments. At its best, this attitude simply represents a disagreement with Eliot's faith and the objects and ends of this faith. At its worst, it represents a form of bad faith that holds that disbelief and despair are true to modern experience but any religious response to them must be false or escapist—precisely the perverse view that C. S. Lewis satirizes so mordantly in *The Screwtape Letters*. For those whose religious ideas and experiences figure importantly in their writing, then, including W. H. Auden, Flannery O'Connor, Dag Hammarskjold, and many others, Eliot remained and remains tremendously significant for his ideas and convictions as well as for his style. Eliot's championing of Dante, for example, contributed to a significant surge of critical interest in Dante even though a current of interest had always proved consistent. But for those indifferent to traditional religious experience, institutions, or values, or even hostile to them and sympathetic only to the secular and often the reductive, Eliot seemed alien. Paradoxically, many of these critics could fervently embrace such ideologically dogmatic systems as Marxism and prize its restrictive lens as a way of interpreting literature even as they criticized Eliot's Catholicism. Yet, given Eliot's acute sense of the ironies and paradoxes of the human condition, he was not surprised by such contradictions. Eliot's biographer Lyndall Gordon astutely locates the critical and social situation: "Eliot took up a stance unlikely to charm the audience of his day, of pilgrim, prophet, and preacher. The models . . . by which he measured himself—Augustine . . . Ezekiel, Elijah, Dante—were heroes of other, more religious ages. The 'lost' generation followed him willingly to the brink of despair, but wondered at his inclinations when he went beyond it. His exhortations sounded odd in their ears, dogmatic, irrelevant, as he went in search of higher love" (1999, 232).

Yet even as certain critics noted the difficulty of Eliot's vision for readers "in a secular age," they acknowledged the power and importance of *Four Quartets*:

Eliot is primarily occupied with the Christian conception of how man lives both "in and out of time," of how he is immersed in the flux and yet can penetrate to the eternal by apprehending timeless existence within time and above it. No less central to his mind is the doctrine of Incarnation, of God become man through the Savior, since Eliot holds that the nineteenth century substitution of

Deification, of man becoming God through his own potentialities, led ineluctably through hero worship to dictatorship. (Spiller 1963, 1357)

In this light, while "it was easy to say that Eliot's religious poems were not widely representative of the age," it is also undeniable that "in a period of breakdown, moving into the shadow of war, they constituted some of the most sustained, if most somber, devotional poetry since the seventeenth century" (1357).

Indeed, for the poet, critic, and dramatist Robert Lowell, Eliot's struggles with faith and doubt, angels and demons, provide a spiritual experience of strong concreteness. Lowell finds Eliot's conceptions of Christ and the Virgin "icy," yet he stresses that his religious vision speaks to our experience in a way ideology cannot: "death and rebirth are at the heart of his poems, in a rather universalist and symbolic guise that perhaps ignores any creed. Eliot has hit on one of the very few things that are still alive in religion: I don't see how man will ever quite be able to get rid of purification, contemplation, and rebirth. Our orthodox sciences—sociology, social reform, psychiatry—and our orthodox prophets— Freud and Marx—still leave this loophole; alas, they must" ([1987] 1990, 193–94). Here, Lowell minimizes Eliot's creedal dimensions, yet he emphasizes the centrality of his religious concerns as well as their perennial universality. Elsewhere, Lowell calls the experience in *Four Quartets* "dramatic and brutally genuine. It is one of the very few great poems in which craftsmanship and religious depth are equal" (1990, 130). As for his friendship with Eliot, Lowell speaks movingly of Eliot's humility and charity, virtues that not all of Eliot's critics have stressed or even acknowledged: "I have never met anyone more brilliant, or anyone who tried so hard to use his brilliance modestly and honestly. One could go on for a long time recalling his gentle, unobtrusive acts of kindness" ([1987] 1990, 194).

For Louis Untermeyer, writing shortly after the publication of *Four Quartets*, the poem's difficulty, power, and beauty are interwoven: "The accent of 'Four Quartets' is grave, sometimes sadly nostalgic, but it is by no means lugubrious. The music as well as the meaning is solemn, and it will not be to everybody's taste. Eliot's counterpoint of private expression and impersonal mysticism is not easy to follow. But few will question the beauty of the communication; few will doubt the perfection of the poet's art" ([1943] 1990, 95–96). In placing *Four Quartets* in the setting of the English poetic tradition, Reginald Snell returns to the vital importance for Eliot of the Incarnation. The quartets, he writes, "provide . . . the theme of a meditation, in which the intellectual and emotional elements are admirably balanced and mutually forfeited, upon the mystery of the Incarnation" ([1944] 1990, 100).

"Fulfilled" rather than "forfeited," Eliot might have argued, but there is no denying how crucial the Incarnation remains in Eliot's mind, heart, and imagination. Indeed, Paul Goodman wonders whether Eliot's perennial desire for simplicity—yet a simplicity emerging through awareness and suffering—might be bound up with his most ultimate vision of the divine. Paradoxically, "perhaps the divine commitments are simple things after all, and all that is easiest is best. I wonder if he did not experience this when he composed the beautiful cadences of these 'Quartets'" ([1943] 1990, 94). In this light, one of the most profound images and sounds of *Four Quartets* may be the children's laughter and, underlying and participating in it, the incarnate mystery of the Christ Child.

Writing nearly four decades apart, Roy Harvey Pearce in 1961 and Alfred Kazin in 1997, and writing often with differing presuppositions, both critics see Eliot as a key figure in American (and British) literary history. Furthermore, both see Eliot's religious vision and *Four Quartets* as key to our understanding of him. For Pearce, Eliot consistently seeks "the relation of the word to the Word," the discovery and recovery of spiritual meaning (1961, 432). In this light, Pearce argues, Eliot joins "the great religious poets of the Anglo-European tradition, against whose work, in a sense, so many American poets in their ineluctable egocentrism had set themselves. What marks him as somewhat different from the poets in the Anglo-European tradition is the very insistence and self-consciousness of his drive toward the religious poem" (314). Given the drive of Eliot's soul, says Pearce, and the deep nature and essence of Eliot's concerns, "in retrospect, then, Eliot's early poetry seems not only to lead to but to require the Quartets" (314). And in writing the *Four Quartets*, Pearce insists, Eliot intensified the implications of several imaginative and religious patterns of thought and tried to push them to their "farthest limits (who could conceive of going farther than 'The Rock' or the Four Quartets?)" (433).

In *God and the American Writer*, Alfred Kazin explores the ways in which American writers apprehend, explore, and dramatize divinity. In the dialectic between God and the soul, the nature and essence of time are persistent concerns. For Eliot and Whitman, Kazin argues, time remains a "promise" and "something to be fulfilled," and in this conviction they are "characteristically American" (1997, 115). Yet the past remains critical as well. For, says Kazin, "It was exactly his own past in St. Louis along the Mississippi and summers off the Atlantic that entranced Eliot in the personal memories that pervade Four Quartets. To bring back the past was to transcend it into the larger circle of God's will that crowned belief in the Incarnation (another interweaving of past and future, based on the union of spirit and flesh)" (114). As we come to the end of *Little Gidding* and hence of *Four Quartets*, Kazin argues, the music of the poetic lines becomes especially beautiful. And this beauty in turn emerges from Eliot's experience of forgiveness. Says Kazin, "Four Quartets is for me the great elegy that Eliot wrote in order to forgive himself at last. So much is forgiven. . . . What has so long been divided in himself is now united—as in the Incarnation of God in man" (213). Again we are reminded that in Eliot's work his frequent references to Penance are followed by references to Communion, to the Eucharist. If Eliot was able to forgive himself it was made possible, he knew, only because God had forgiven him. And since Eliot insists that to be truly real the personal must extend to the impersonal, the partial to the mystical, the moment to the eternal, it is clear that the divine forgiveness extends to the failings and sins of all humanity. In the end—and therefore in the beginning, Eliot would say—*Four Quartets* affirms that through the mystery of the Incarnation all is reconciled and that love, finally, overcomes pain and affliction and even death itself.

NOTE

T. S. Eliot, *Four Quartets*. In *Collected Poems 1909–1962*, 173–209 (New York: Harcourt Brace, 1991). All references are to this edition.

WORKS CITED

Chesterton, G. K. [1924] 1959. *Orthodoxy.* Garden City, NY: Doubleday.

Dostoevsky, Fyodor. 1991. *The Brothers Karamazov,* trans. Richard Pevear and Larissa Volokhonsky. New York: Random House.

Eliot, T. S. [1932] 1975. "Religion and Literature." In *Religion and Modern Literature: Essays in Theory and Criticism,* ed. Edward E. Ericson and G. B. Tennyson, 21–30. Grand Rapids, MI: Eerdmans.

———. [1919] 1975. "Tradition and the Individual Talent." In *Selected Prose of T. S. Eliot,* 37–44. New York: Harvest/Harcourt Brace and Company.

Goodman, Paul. [1943] 1990. "T. S. Eliot: The Poet of Purgatory." In *T. S. Eliot: Critical Assessments,* ed. Graham Clarke, vol. 3, 92–94. London: Christopher Helm.

Gordon, Lyndall. 1999. *T. S. Eliot, An Imperfect Life.* New York and London: Norton.

Junger, Sebastian. 1998. *The Perfect Storm.* New York: Harper.

Kazin, Alfred. 1997. *God and the American Writer.* New York: Knopf.

Lowell, Robert. [1987] 1990. "Two Controversial Questions." In *T. S. Eliot: Critical Assessments,* ed. Graham Clarke, vol. 1, 192–94. London: Christopher Helm.

———. 1990. "Four Quartets." In *T. S. Eliot: Critical Assessments,* ed. Graham Clarke, vol. 3, 128–30. London: Christopher Helm.

Pearce, Roy Harvey. 1961. *The Continuity of American Poetry.* Princeton, NJ: Princeton University Press.

Smidt, Kristian. 1961. *Poetry and Belief in the Work of T. S. Eliot.* New York: Humanities Press.

Snell, Reginald. [1944] 1990. "T. S. Eliot and the English Poetic Tradition." In *T. S. Eliot: Critical Assessments,* ed. Graham Clarke, vol. 3, 97–100. London: Christopher Helm.

Spiller, Robert, et al., eds. 1963. *Literary History of the United States.* 3rd ed. New York: Macmillan.

Untermeyer, Louis. [1943] 1990. "Eight Poets." In *T. S. Eliot: Critical Assessments,* ed. Graham Clarke, vol. 3, 95–96. London: Christopher Helm.

— **Thomas Werge**

Shusaku Endo [1923–1996]

Silence

BIOGRAPHY

Shusaku Endo was one of the leading Japanese writers of the twentieth century. He was extraordinarily prolific: between 1955, when he began writing, and his death in 1996 he published almost two hundred books, including over fifty novels and seventeen short-story collections, in addition to scores of books of essays, criticism, travel accounts, plays, and screenplays. He received virtually every literary award available in Japan, and in 1995, just a year before his death, he was awarded the Bunka Kunsho, the Order of Culture, which is Japan's highest honor for its artists. He was a recipient of the Dag Hammarsjkold Prize and of honorary doctoral degrees from three Catholic universities in the United States: Santa Clara, Georgetown, and John Carroll. His novels have been translated into dozens of languages, and his most acclaimed novel, *Silence*, was chosen by Harper Collins publishers as one of the one hundred most influential religious books of the twentieth century.

Endo was nominated on several occasions for the Nobel Prize for Literature, and it was assumed throughout Europe that he would be the next Japanese author to receive the award. The Japanese press, in fact, clustered outside his Tokyo home in 1994 as the Swedish Academy prepared to make its announcement. When word arrived that the prize had gone to a younger Japanese author, Kenzaburo Oe, Endo was asked to comment on the selection. His response is telling: "Oe writes brilliantly about the search for salvation in a world devoid of God." Although this remark likely struck most Japanese readers as high praise, it can only be regarded as a bittersweet appraisal coming from an author who wrote so brilliantly about the search for salvation in a world that *has* God but commonly turns a deaf ear to his voice.

Endo was one of only a handful of novelists in Japan determined to search for salvation in a world *with* God. He was, simply put, the foremost Christian writer in Japan during the twentieth century. But being the "foremost Christian writer" in a country where just barely over one percent of the population belongs to any Christian denomination does not have quite the same meaning as it does in the western world. Endo was a voice crying in the spiritual wilderness of his own land. But his was a voice that was heard not only within the small Christian community but by a great many in Japan. It is quite likely that no one has been more instrumental than Endo in creating a positive image of Christianity in Japan. Thanks to him, thousands of Japanese no longer regard Christianity as a peculiar, exotic faith; because of his writings, it is now possible to talk of a Japanese brand of Christianity that has attracted the interest of many of his countrymen. Endo was also directly responsible for the baptisms of dozens of his compatriots in the literary and intellectual worlds of Japan. He was, in every positive sense of the term, the real "godfather" of the Japanese Church.

Endo was born on March 27, 1923, in Tokyo, but his earliest memories were not of Japan. When he was quite young his father was transferred to Dalian, a city in occupied Chinese Manchuria. As a result, his childhood memories were all of a foreign city that was a peculiar mixture of Russian, Chinese, and Japanese elements. Already in his childhood, Endo encountered the uneasy intermingling of different cultures, and as a young boy he had to ask himself what it meant to be Japanese.

At a young age, Endo had personal experience of the pain of betrayal and discord. His parents' marriage collapsed, and he had to endure night after night of his mother weeping in the darkened parlor or practicing her violin with such angry fervor that her fingertips often bled. When he was ten, his mother took her two boys and returned to Japan, moving in with her sister's family in Kobe in the wake of her divorce. Endo's aunt was a devout Catholic, and at her encouragement his mother began to seek comfort by attending Mass, and before long she was baptized. She pursued her new faith with the same intensity that had drawn blood from her calloused fingers on the violin strings. She forthwith sent her sons to catechism class, and Endo was baptized at the age of eleven by a French priest. Years later, he would describe his acceptance of Christianity as an act akin to having his mother dress him up in an ill-fitting suit of western-style clothes. His chief task as a writer, he has claimed, has been to retailor those foreign clothes to fit his Japanese body. It is of some significance that Endo as a Japanese has always insisted that it is the clothes, and not his body, that have to be changed. He has never defined Christianity as a bulky western suit that he needed to grow into; rather, the process he describes is one in which the suit itself is trimmed and fitted to the contours of his body. It is also important to note that Endo's baptism came in 1935, at a time when the tides in Japan were swiftly turning against the importation of foreign goods and foreign beliefs and beginning the process of pushing the alien elements out in preparation for a ritual cleansing of the land through warfare.

During the war, the conflict was personalized for Endo, and on many occasions his classmates or teachers would demand to know what choice he would make when he finally was called upon to choose between the divine emperor of his native land or the God of the foreigners. He naturally developed an antipathy toward a Japan that would force a weak individual such as himself to make this kind of moral decision under the threat of coercion. The torturing of individuals to force them to choose one way of belief over another would become the primary motif in *Silence*.

A serious case of pleurisy kept Endo from the draft, and after the war he began his study of French Catholic literature at Keio University. In 1950, through the good offices of a French priest, he was in the first group of Japanese chosen for overseas study after World War II. He lived in France for almost three years, studying Catholic writers at the University of Lyon. But his essays and stories about this period make it clear that he was never comfortable being treated by French churchgoers as the great hope for the conversion of heathen Japan. His studies merely served to persuade him, as foreign sojourns have often persuaded Japanese intellectuals, that a thick, unscalable wall separates western Christian culture from the polytheistic culture of Japan.

As if to affirm that he would never succeed in his attempts to be both Japanese and Christian, Endo succumbed to a serious lung ailment in Lyon and had to return to Japan. Shortly thereafter, he began to write. His first novella, *White Men*, earned him a prestigious newcomer prize, and in 1959 he published his first major novel, *The Sea and Poison*, a scathing indictment of the lack of moral conscience that allowed Japanese doctors during the war to vivisect a downed American pilot. That year he also began producing a prolific series of "entertainment" novels, the first being *Wonderful Fool*, featuring a bumbling Frenchman in Japan whose love and self-sacrifice are reminiscent of Christ.

In 1960, Endo took another trip to Europe—to gather materials for a study of the Marquis de Sade, ironically enough—and there suffered a major relapse of his pleurisy, resulting in two and a half years of hospitalization and three operations that left him with only one lung. The emotional pain of the war years, enduring the taunts of his fellow Japanese and the betrayal by his Church, was now magnified by his protracted experience with physical pain. In the novels published after his long hospitalization, Endo displayed considerably more sympathy for those who are weak in both body and spirit, and it was from this point forward that he began to etch in the features of his forgiving, accepting Christ. It is, as many critics have pointed out, an image very much influenced by his feelings of deep gratitude and reverence toward his own mother. But it goes deeper than that: Endo is clearly seeking to create an image of Christ to which his countrymen can relate, and that softer, compassionate figure that emerges in his novels, speaking through the silence, has had a profound impact on many Japanese people today.

At the same time, Endo began to focus on the struggle between the frail but believing individual and the many social institutions that seem designed solely for the purpose of crushing the meek and gentle of the world. Those two themes— the brutality of man-made institutions and the forgiveness that comes from a maternal Christ—merge most powerfully in *Silence*, written in 1966. *Silence* became an immediate and enduring best seller and firmly established Endo's literary importance. The novel received the prestigious Tanizaki Prize and encouraged its author to continue writing novels exploring faith, human weakness, and the ways in which the original encounter with the Catholic padres has proven emblematic of the interaction between Japan and the West over succeeding centuries.

In 1980, Endo attained further literary accolades for a historical novel, *The Samurai*, the second of his major serious works to be based on historical events from the "Christian Century." This novel follows the temporal and spiritual journey undertaken in 1613 by a group of Japanese envoys who traveled with a Catholic priest to Mexico, Spain, and Rome, encountering both the kings of the earth and, finally, the King of Heaven. The novel earned Endo the important

Noma Prize, and shortly after its publication he was elected to the Japan Academy of Arts. From 1985 to 1989 he served as the president of the Japan P. E. N. Club, and in 1988 he was named a "Person of Cultural Merit" by the Japanese government. His last major novel, and one of his best, *Deep River*, was published in 1993. Endo's health deteriorated steadily after the novel appeared. From a hospital bed in the wake of a stroke he was notified in October 1995 that he had received the Order of Culture, the highest honor Japan pays to its artists. He died less than a year later, on September 29, 1996.

PLOT SUMMARY

Silence follows the facts of history closely. It opens at a critical turning point in the interaction between Catholic missionaries and a Japanese government growing increasingly wary of foreign influences in their otherwise tightly ordered society. Japan's "Christian Century" began with the arrival of the dynamic Jesuit priest, Francis Xavier, on the shores of Japan in 1549. Xavier was enthusiastic about the prospects for spreading Catholic beliefs throughout Japan. Although reliable figures are hard to come by, it seems very likely that somewhere between 400,000 and 500,000 Japanese were baptized as Catholics by the year 1600. Given all the differences of culture, language, religious background, and so many other factors, such a high level of success is truly remarkable.

In 1592, however, when Spanish Franciscans were allowed into Japan, they spent nearly as much time publicly condemning the Portuguese Jesuits as they did teaching the Gospel of love. Dutch traders who landed at Nagasaki poured more oil on the fire by suggesting to the Japanese warlords that the typical Catholic pattern was to send first the missionaries, then the conquering armies. Because the Jesuits had continued their customary practice of converting samurai leaders so that their vassals would follow suit, it appeared to the rulers of the country that it was indeed risky to have powerful warlords shifting their loyalties to a foreign God and his emissaries.

Consequently, in the early seventeenth century they adopted a series of policies aimed at eradicating Christianity among the Japanese people. The first official persecution came on February 4, 1597, when twenty-six Christians at Nagasaki—seven Europeans and nineteen Japanese converts—were lashed to crosses and then pierced through the side with long spears. Other forms of torture and execution were devised and used on both native converts and foreign missionaries, including crucifixion, torment in boiling hot springs, and the infamous torture of "the pit," which figures prominently in *Silence*. Christians were tied and suspended upside down over a pit filled with all manner of foul material, and a cut was made behind their ears to prevent hemorrhaging. This proved to be one of the most effective means by which foreign priests were "encouraged" to apostatize.

Entire populations in villages where Christians were thought to lurk were paraded out by the authorities and forced to trample and spit upon an image of Christ or the Virgin known as the *fumie*, meaning literally an "image to trample upon." This was an image sometimes made of brass and mounted in a wooden plaque. Others were simple drawings on paper. Those who refused to trample were tortured or killed. The ritual of trampling on the *fumie* was repeated at least once a year in every suspect village throughout the remainder of the feudal period.

Official Catholic records claim around 3,100 martyrs, but there were no doubt many more. That figure does not include the nearly 30,000 men, women, and children slaughtered in the Shimabara Rebellion of 1637, an uprising of mostly Christian peasants in Kyushu. Thousands of others, whether because of torture or because they were vassals who dutifully followed their masters into and then back out of the Church, would be counted among the ranks of apostates. There were even several prominent European priests in Japan who succumbed to the violence and renounced their Church, a fact that plays a significant part in Endo's novel. Although a few on the tiny islands off Nagasaki continued for over two centuries to practice a metamorphosized, underground form of their religion, Christianity was essentially snuffed out in Japan by the late 1630s and did not reemerge until around 1870.

The central character in *Silence* is a Portuguese priest named Rodrigues who comes to Japan in the early seventeenth century at the height of the persecution of Christians, hoping to find out what has become of the stalwart priest Ferreira who trained him but now is rumored to have broken under torture. Rodrigues and his companion Garrpe go underground to minister to the beleaguered Japanese flock. They are guided through the verdant hills of the Nagasaki region by a sniveling, cowardly Christian convert named Kichijiro, who himself seems to them a Judas figure because his fear of torture impels him to trample repeatedly on the *fumie*.

Over time, one after another of the Japanese Christians shepherded by Rodrigues is captured and tortured. Garrpe, too, drowns in the ocean in an attempt to rescue a Christian woman. Rodrigues keeps expecting God to thunder out of the heavens, to send flocks of angels to embrace the martyred dead, to intercede on behalf of the suffering innocents. Throughout it all, God seems to maintain a stoic silence.

Rodrigues is presented as something of a Christ figure himself—coming to save the downtrodden in Japan. At a point at which he is beginning to question God's existence, he is finally betrayed to the authorities by Kichijiro and is taken to meet his mentor Ferreira, who has indeed abandoned the Church as an institution. Ferreira tells Rodrigues that the Japanese have no conception of God for they "do not have the ability to conceive of an existence that transcends the human." In the country's churches, he continues, "the Japanese were not praying to the Christian God. They twisted God to their own way of thinking in a way we can never imagine" (*Silence*, 240–41; revisions to translation mine). In another encounter between Rodrigues and his apostate mentor, a broken Ferreira tells Rodrigues, "This county is a more terrible swamp than I ever imagined. No matter what kind of seedling you plant in this swamp, the roots begin to rot; the leaves grow yellow and wither. And we planted the seedling of Christianity in this swamp" (237; revisions mine).

Endo imposes his own form of narratorial silence onto Rodrigues. Although the early chapters, in which Rodrigues feels the greatest personal fulfillment (and pride) by enduring persecution to tend his flock, are told in the first person, after his capture the narrative turns to the third person, then finally to utterly impersonal historical accounts in which Rodrigues as an individual voice is essentially lost. In losing himself, however, Rodrigues lives the core Christian paradox by coming to a recognition—a recognition that comes to him in the form of God breaking through the silence at his moment of greatest agony—that in sacrificing himself for others he emerges victor.

The high point of the novel comes when Rodrigues is brought before the *fumie* and encouraged by Ferreira to trample on it. The blameless Japanese Christians being tortured in the pit will be spared if Rodrigues will simply place his foot on the image. "For love Christ would have apostatized. . . . You are now going to perform the most painful act of love that has ever been performed," Ferreira taunts him (269). But as he prepares to trample, Rodrigues hears a voice:

> The priest raised his foot. In it he felt a dull, heavy pain. This was no mere formality. He was about to trample on what he had considered the most beautiful thing in his life, on what he had believed the most pure, on what was most filled with the ideals and the dreams of man. How intense the pain in his foot! And then the Christ in the bronze spoke to the priest: "Go ahead and trample. It's all right to trample. I more than anyone know the pain in your foot. Trample. It was to be trampled on by men that I was born into this world. It was to share men's pain that I carried my cross."

> When the priest placed his foot on the fumie, dawn broke. And far in the distance the cock crew. (271; revisions mine)

Cryptic historical records form the conclusion to the novel. Although buried in the archives of the persecutions, Rodrigues—jailed, given a Japanese name and wife, and forced to identify captured Christian icons—emerges victorious, continuing his surreptitious mission from his cell, reasserting his beliefs and succumbing over and over again to tortures and tramplings. Although victim to human weakness, he realizes that he has a role to fill: "Even now I am the last priest in this land. But Our Lord was not silent. Even if he had been silent, my life until this day would have spoken of him" (298).

MAJOR THEMES

The dramatic situation in *Silence* forces the reader to take sides in interpreting Endo's message. We either have to agree with Ferreira that the Japanese spiritual soil is not conducive to the sprouting of Christian faith, or we have to accept Rodrigues's insistent assertion that the Japanese have not given the seed of Christianity a chance to grow. This whole dialectic culminates in the great dramatic scene in *Silence*, which is, of course, Rodrigues's struggle as he is seduced by Ferreira into stepping on the *fumie*. Most frequently quoted from the novel are the adroitly phrased debates that rage back and forth between a desperate Rodrigues and his former mentor-turned-chief tormentor, the apostate priest Ferreira. The two of them, trained so effectively in the persuasive logic approach to proselytization, have a field day with one another, twisting reason and positing new arguments to win the day over the opponent. Both are in fine form, and although Rodrigues has been physically drained by days of being hung upside down in a pit filled with excrement, the battle of words seems to revive his sense of himself as a man called to convert the unbeliever. The verbal clash between these two lingers in the brain.

But what lingers in the heart are the groans. While Ferreira and Rodrigues are sharing tea and sophistries, Rodrigues keeps hearing sounds that he believes belong to people snoring off in the distance. Finally, Ferreira tells him it is not snoring but the groans of innocent Japanese Christians being tortured in the pit, a torture that will cease only if Rodrigues will step upon the image of Christ. Far more important in *Silence* than the question of whether the broken Ferreira or the soon-to-be-broken Rodrigues will emerge victor in the verbal crusades is the issue of those groans breaking the "silence," as if they were the voice of God attempting to break through the hard, egotistic shells of these two foreigners. Catechismic conflicts are being waged between the rational western prelates—meanwhile, the common people are suffering. No theological debate that ignores, even threatens to drown out, the cries of the Japanese peasants moaning from the pit has any efficacy in the view of the human condition presented in Endo's fiction.

Therein lies the great and wonderful irony of the novel—that in giving up himself by placing his foot upon the face of Christ, Rodrigues is setting aside all the religious debates that lead only to conflict and is performing an act of compassion that will literally succor the weak and help to bind up the wounds of the suffering. By "losing his life" as a Catholic priest, Rodrigues has found the meaning of his mission to Japan, which is simply to make the lives of the humble and the powerless more bearable. And the ultimate enemy to such a simple act of charity is none other than the institutions of the mundane world—the brutal Japanese government, the dogmatic Church organization—that would grind individual sufferers under their feet in order to achieve their separate aims.

Endo suggests in the crucial *fumie* scene that there is divine permission and forgiveness granted to Rodrigues for what he is about to do. Repeatedly in his fiction, Endo asserts that God is determinedly trying to get through to his children, trying to use the sufferings of others and the wounds we leave in the lives of those we wrong to communicate his will to us. In *The Girl I Left Behind*, a novel Endo wrote just a few years before *Silence*, for instance, a young man who has manipulated a woman for his own satisfaction wonders after the fact: "why do I feel so lonely? If [that girl] had taught me anything at all, it was that every single person with whom we cross paths during our journey through life leaves an indelible mark on us. So does loneliness stem from such marks? Furthermore, if . . . God . . . truly exists, does He speak to us through these marks? But still I have to ask, what is the source of my loneliness?" (1994, 192).

In *Silence*, the young Portuguese priest Rodrigues comes to Japan full of his mission, full of self-assurance—full, ultimately, of himself. The voice of his own ego is screeching so loudly in his ears that he cannot discern the whisperings of the still, small voice trying to inform him of the hazards of his own self-absorption. He has not yet been sufficiently humbled by his trials to be inwardly quiet, thereby allowing the voice of God to speak to him through the silence. And when his faith is tested in Japan as he watches innocent Japanese Christians being tortured and killed, all he can do is look up at the heavens and demand to know why God remains silent. Unfortunately, all his hollering deafens him to the cries of others, which are, ultimately, the echoes of God's own voice.

The passion of Rodrigues consists of a progressive smoothing down of the sharp corners of his selfish ego and his overly confident Eurocentrism, and by the end of the story, when he too has to decide whether to trample on the sacred image, the man who stands with his foot poised to grind into the face of "the most beautiful thing in his life . . . what he has believed most pure . . . what is filled with the ideals and the dreams of man" (*Silence*, 259) has himself been "silenced"; it is no longer the voice of his own desires and aspirations and ambitions that he hears with such impassioned exclusivity, and his torture by the Japanese authorities, culminating in his realization that others are suffering because of his stubborn willfulness, has finally been of sufficient intensity to convince him that he has been wrong in caring first about himself. And so, it is not God who is "silent" in this novel. Rather, it is Rodrigues who is reduced to "silence" and taught, thanks to his tribulations, that the way to emulate Christ is not to shout his words to others but to quietly perform his acts of compassion for others, forgetting self and its incessant, high-decibel demands.

Another figure of critical importance in the story is the weak, drunken Japanese apostate, Kichijiro. Like the novel itself, this character is complex and much misunderstood. It is easy to dismiss him as the typical Judas figure, repeatedly betraying his family, his faith, and Rodrigues because of his fear of physical torture. But Endo finds great significance in the fact that Kichijiro, despite his spineless, self-serving acts of betrayal, will never abandon Rodrigues, just as Christ will never leave him alone in his suffering. Kichijiro tramples time and again on the *fumie*, but he always returns to be with Rodrigues in order to share in, and thereby lessen, his torment. This pathetic, sniveling figure is surely a type of every frail mortal who keeps yearning after some ideal of spiritual purity that is always just out of reach or that the travails of life keep pushing beyond our grasp. Perhaps the key to understanding the significance of this character to Endo is the author's unabashed comment, "Kichijiro is me."[1]

Kichijiro is, perhaps, each one of us. He lives in agony, caught between a vision of distant celestiality and the all-too-human imperfections that continually remind him he has fallen short. Yes, Kichijiro keeps falling down; the Japanese word Endo uses throughout the novel for "apostatize" literally means to "fall over" (*korobu*). But Kichijiro repeatedly struggles back to his feet and places himself in harm's way so that he can remain beside Rodrigues. As Endo has commented, "Over and over again, he fell and then stood up again, fell and rose again. That's what faith is, I think: what we believe in even as we keep on repeating our many mistakes."[2] Kichijiro is no hero, but he is certainly human. In this struggle to remain a companion to another who is in pain, Endo glimpses the ultimate redemption of a weak human being like Kichijiro. And like himself. And like us.

The careful reader of the novel, listening to hear what message Endo is trying to convey through *Silence*, will find sufficient evidence that his lifelong project was not to demonstrate the inability or unwillingness of God to communicate with his children; rather, his focus was on the repeated and varied attempts God makes to transmit his will by breaking down the soundproof walls that humans erect through their own selfish and willful attitudes and behaviors. The message that finally emerges in and through *Silence* is simple: stop hurting one another. Bind one another's wounds. Do what Christ would have done. God speaks in *Silence*, and he seems to have quite an eloquent, moving, and persuasive command of Japanese.

The "voice in the silence" is an apt description of one of the most profound thematic strains running through all of Endo's writing. Perhaps his most significant contribution to Japanese literature can be found in his insistence that there is something more to the human experience than the relations between one human being and another. Japanese literary and religious traditions are remarkably silent themselves about communication between humans and god, even though Japanese mythology suggests that mortals are direct descendants of divinity. Nature, as the repository of a higher essence, has repeatedly, almost incessantly, been praised in Japanese verse. Japanese poets regularly turn their gaze toward natural phenomena such as rainstorms and fragile cherry blossoms to mirror the subtle swings of their private emotions. But even the most careful reader would have difficulty locating tales in any form that try to humanize the gods or suggest verbal exchange between humans and a higher being.

Endo is virtually alone among contemporary Japanese writers in suggesting that human actions are not self-contained, that there is a higher level of judgment, transcending even the tightly structured social order in Japan, and that every act of evil or of faithlessness is viewed by God. One can look long and hard and still fail to locate another Japanese author who so assiduously intimates that human actions of every stripe are observed from an outside perspective—that there is, in fact, an eye (and perhaps even a voice) of omniscience that stands apart from the narrow, self-centered, autobiographical voice of both traditional and modern Japanese narrative. In both the structures of his works—which frequently alternate between points of view—and this exalted perspective, Endo hints at the existence of a personage who observes every human act with a unique blend of sorrow and compassion. The sorrow precedes the compassion and is often muted in Endo's early writings, but the compassion is most certainly there.

CRITICAL RECEPTION

Japanese literary critics were uniformly enthusiastic about *Silence*. The gripping drama of the story, the grimy humanness of the characters, the carefully wrought historical setting—all these elements combined to elicit positive responses to the novel. Equally uniform, however, was a misunderstanding of the underlying theme of the book—that God does exist and that he does speak to his children in the midst of their mortal agonies. In fact, most common among critics was the tendency to regard the title of the book as a direct explication of its theme: that if there is a God, he has left us alone to make our own choices and to suffer in isolation.

One might assume that the novel would find a sympathetic audience among the tiny minority of Catholic readers in Japan. Initially, however, just the opposite was the case. Some conservative Catholic readers, including clergymen, found the book offensive, and in some congregations reading of the novel was discouraged. Perhaps the most sensitive issue for these believers is what they perceived as a disrespectful treatment of the many thousands of early Christians who died as martyrs. If the novel was misinterpreted by otherwise enthusiastic critics and denounced by many Christians in Japan as false in its theological premise (one critic even suggested there was more of "Protestant" Pure Land Buddhism in the novel than of Catholicism), what sort of reading audience made the book an immediate best-seller?

The rather surprising answer is that the novel became something of a cult classic among left-wing college students in Japan during the mid-1960s. It was read as a metaphorical account of the persecution and torture of Japanese Marxists beginning in the 1930s and continuing throughout the war years. Many leftist intellectuals were called in and interrogated by the secret police, beaten, and otherwise abused (the death of Marxist author Takiji Kobayashi at the hands of the police in 1933 was the first warning shot against political dissension), and large numbers of leftists were compelled under threat of physical reprisals to recant publicly their antigovernment sentiments. The postwar generation of politically charged youth read *Silence* as an account of these earlier martyrs to their cause.

By the late 1970s or so, however, a more liberal wing had emerged within the Catholic Church in Japan, and a number of prominent priests—especially Endo's good friend and spiritual advisor, Yoji Inoue—spoke out on behalf of the novel and its author's more open views toward the possibility of creating a uniquely Japanese form of Christianity. The book also caught on in English translation, particularly after Graham Greene praised its power, and it is regularly taught in college courses on world literature, on Asian history, and on theology. Endo's writings have developed a small but loyal readership throughout the United States and Europe, where his voice calling for a "re-tailoring" of Christianity resonates powerfully.

NOTES

Shusaku Endo, *Silence*, trans. William Johnston (London: Peter Owen, 1976). All references are to this edition.

1. Comment made by Endo at a symposium held at John Carroll University the day before he was awarded an honorary degree. See *Journal of the Association of Teachers of Japanese* 27, no. 1 (April 1993): 88.

2. In 1992, Endo cooperated in the production of a film titled *Haha naru mono: Ningen no dohansha* (Mothers: Companions to Mankind), the primary aim of which was to dispel misconceptions about the meaning of *Silence*. This quotation is from an interview with Endo that is part of that video (produced by President Inc., Tokyo, 1992).

WORK CITED

Endo, Shusaku. 1994. *The Girl I Left Behind*, trans. Mark Williams. London: Peter Owen.

BIBLIOGRAPHY

Boscara, Adriana. "The Meaning of Christianity in the Works of Endo Shusaku." In *Tradition and Modern Japan*, ed. P. G. O'Neill, 81–90. Tenterden, England: Paul Norbury Publications, 1981.

Endo, Junko. "Reflections on Shusaku Endo and *Silence*." *Christianity and Literature* 48, no. 2 (Winter 1999): 145–48.

Gessel, Van C. "Endo Shusaku." In *Dictionary of Literary Biography*, vol. 182: *Japanese Fiction Writers Since World War II*, ed. Van C. Gessel, 197–213. Detroit: Bruccoli, Clark and Layman, 1997.

———. "Endo Shusaku: His Position(s) in Postwar Japanese Literature." *Journal of the Association of Teachers of Japanese* 27, no. 1 (April 1993): 67–74.

———. "Hearing God in Silence: The Fiction of Endo Shusaku." *Christianity and Literature* 48, no. 2 (Winter 1999): 149–64.

———. *The Sting of Life: Four Contemporary Japanese Novelists*. New York: Columbia University Press, 1989.

———. "Voices in the Wilderness: Japanese Christian Authors." *Monumenta Nipponica* 37, no. 4 (Winter 1982): 437–57.

Mathy, Francis. "Shusaku Endo: Japanese Catholic Novelist." *Thought* 42, no. 167 (Winter 1967): 585–614.

———. "Shusaku Endo: The Second Period." *Japan Christian Quarterly* 40, no. 4 (Fall 1974): 214–26.

Rimer, J. Thomas. "That Most Excellent Gift of Charity: Endo Shusaku in Contemporary World Literature." *Journal of the Association of Teachers of Japanese* 27, no. 1 (April 1993): 59–66.

Sano Hitoshi. "The Transformation of Father Rodrigues in Shusaku Endo's *Silence*." *Christianity and Literature* 48, no. 2 (Winter 1999): 165–76.

Updike, John. "From *Fumie* to Sony." *New Yorker* (January 14, 1980): 96–102.

Williams, Mark. *Endo Shusaku: A Literature of Reconciliation*. London and New York: Routledge, 1999.

———. "From Out of the Depths: The Japanese Literary Response to Christianity." In *Japan and Christianity: Impacts and Responses*, ed. J. Breen and M. Williams, 156–74. Basingstoke, England: Macmillan, 1993.

Wills, Elizabeth. "Christ as Eternal Companion: A Study in the Christology of Shusaku Endo." *Scottish Journal of Theology* 45 (1992): 85–100.

Wills, Garry. "Embers of Guilt." *New York Review of Books* (February 19, 1981): 21–22.

— Van C. Gessel

Desiderius Erasmus [c. 1469–1536]

The Praise of Folly

BIOGRAPHY

Desiderius Erasmus was probably born in 1469 and was certainly born in Rotterdam, whence came the Latin surname "Roterodamus" under which he published his voluminous work. Like many geniuses of his time, he was illegitimate, the youngest of two sons born to a priest called Gerard and a woman from Gouda in southern Holland. He went to school first in Gouda, then at Deventer, and, after the death of his father, at 's-Hertogenbosch. His early education consisted of the standard subjects taught in primary schools of the late fifteenth century: Latin, rhetoric, and some dialectic. He was taught by the humanist Alexander Hegius for a brief time at Deventer, a school influenced by the *devotio moderna*, the fourteenth-century pietistic movement emphasizing Christ as a model for daily living.

In 1487, Erasmus was sent to an Augustinian monastery at Steyn, outside Gouda, an environment he found austere and uncongenial and upon which his many subsequent complaints about the shortcomings of the institutional Church were partly founded. Letters from this period of Erasmus's life reveal a taste for and wide reading in both classical authors and the Fathers of the Church; however hostile he found the monastery to refinement and learning, it was certainly during his own brush with monasticism that he began to acquire the training to accomplish his life's work: the reconciliation of *bonae litterae* with *sacrae litterae* and the application of philological scholarship to the text and exegesis of Scripture. Indeed, Erasmus's first extant work, *De contemptu mundi*, completed sometime in the late 1480s, is a traditional eulogy of life in the cloister. Not until the 1490s, when he wrote *Antibarbari*, a dialogue on the question of whether it is possible to study and appreciate the writers of antiquity and at the same time remain a faithful Christian, did he explicitly attempt to reconcile classical civilization with Christian piety in a way unrelated to monastic life. By then, he himself had departed from the monastery.

The initial departure took place in 1493, when Erasmus was appointed secretary to the bishop of Cambrai, whose planned trip to Rome required the services of a Latinist. Although the journey to Rome never materialized, Erasmus seems to have remained for a time in the bishop's circle in the southern Netherlands, but he left this appointment for Paris in 1495. It had been his intention to take a doctorate in theology; instead, he discovered a decided aversion to the kind of scholastic theology then taught at the Sorbonne and was welcomed into the circle of Robert Gaguin, the diplomat and historian who imported Italian humanism to the court of Louis XI. Erasmus remained in Paris until 1499, when he accepted a post in London as tutor to William Blount, Lord Mountjoy (himself later tutor to the future Henry VIII). Through Mountjoy, Erasmus was introduced to the most influential English humanists of the day: John Colet, William Grocyn, Thomas Linacre, and Thomas More. His friendship with More, in particular, proved to be important and lasting, and the English humanists in general seemed to provide Erasmus with the intellectual and cultural stimulation, as well as the personal recognition, for which he had longed in Europe.

Between 1500 and 1509, Erasmus traveled almost continuously: from London to Paris, from Paris to the Netherlands and back, and finally to Italy—itinerant habits that characterized the rest of his career. He was by this time a professional scholar, although this meant scraping together a living as a tutor and lecturer and enduring a state of near impoverishment. He worked just as much as he traveled, producing editions with scholarly commentaries of Cicero, Plutarch, Lucian, and others. The *Handbook of the Christian Soldier*, a manual commissioned by the wife of the master of arms at the court of Burgundy and designed as a summary of faithful conduct in the secular world, was written in 1501 and was one of his most widely read and enduring works. He had set out in 1500 to learn Greek, not only so that he could provide a Latin translation of the New Testament based on the original Greek but also so that he could begin an edition of the works of Jerome, his favorite of the Church Fathers. Both the first printed Greek edition of the New Testament, with Latin translation and extensive annotations, and his nine-volume edition of Jerome first appeared in 1516. His *Adages*, a collection of Greek and Latin proverbs accompanied by frequently brilliant essays on letters, culture, and Christian faith, was first published in 1500 and greatly expanded in 1509; he would add to and revise it for the rest of his life. It was perhaps on this work that Erasmus's reputation most depended; it won him a wide readership even outside scholarly circles. It is largely owing to the popularity of such works as the *Adages*, the *Colloquies*, and *The Praise of Folly* that Erasmus was able at the end of his life to leave an estate of five thousand florins, invested with the Duke of Württemburg and the city of Geneva, to be distributed to the poor, the disabled, the aged, girls in need of dowries, and impecunious students (McConica 1991, 81).

Even before the publication of the enormously expanded *Adages* in 1509, Erasmus's reputation was growing, and he was awarded a doctorate soon after arriving in Turin during his Italian travels of 1506 to 1509, a mark of his increasingly famous accomplishments. This sojourn in Italy was followed by an extended stay in England (1509–1514). In 1509 he composed *The Praise of Folly*, which was published in Paris in 1511. In a letter to Thomas More usually published along with later editions of *The Praise of Folly*, Erasmus explains that he got the idea for the book while crossing the Alps on his way to England: as he was thinking about his English friends, indeed, of Thomas More himself (whose name sounds like the Greek word for folly, *moria*), he struck on the notion of praising folly and dedicating the work to his friend because of More's "pleasure in jokes of this sort" (*Praise of Folly*, 2). Another letter to Martin Dorp, a grammarian with theological pretensions, further describes how he wrote the whole book while staying at More's house in London. Following the first edition in 1511, the work was reprinted thirty-seven times during Erasmus's lifetime, including greatly expanded and somewhat revised editions in 1512, 1514, 1515, 1516, 1521, 1522, and 1532. By 1549 it had been translated into Czech, French, German, Italian, and English.

The *Praise of Folly* was not only instantly successful; it was also instantly controversial. Its frank portrayal of greed and abuse among the clergy, from mendicant friars right up through the pope himself, earned Erasmus not just fame but also suspicion. Dorp, in 1515, was the first to accuse the book of impiety; he also rejected Erasmus's edition of the Greek New Testament as an enterprise that cast doubt on the authority of the Vulgate translation. Like the *Colloquies* (dialogues first published in 1518 as exercises for budding Latinists learning to cultivate an elegant style), in which such practices of the unreformed Church as the sale of indulgences and the blind worship of saints are frequently satirized, *The Praise of Folly* is not spoken in Erasmus's own voice, but this literary subtlety made no difference to readers inclined to see heresy in loyal criticism.

Controversy, indeed, would dog Erasmus's heels for the rest of his life, as his ideas about using Greek manuscripts to correct the Vulgate translation of the New Testament and his protests against clerical ignorance, greed, and disregard for authentic Christianity (as he and other humanists conceived of it) put him increasingly at odds with the institutional Church. Having physically and emotionally left the cloister in 1493, he resisted in 1514 a command from his prior at Steyn to return to his order there. In 1517, he was granted papal permission to pursue his goals outside the monastery, although he remained an Augustinian canon in good standing. While he had many admirers and defenders of his Greek New Testament, his work on Jerome, and his advocacy of studying Scripture in the original languages, he had many enemies as well. Theologians in Paris and Spain attacked passages from the translation of the New Testament, together with its annotations, and seized (often out of context) on the subtle but unmistakable criticisms of the ecclesiastical establishment in *The Praise of Folly* and *Colloquies* in order to seek and, by 1531, obtain official condemnations of much of Erasmus's work.

Despite these condemnations, Erasmus consistently maintained his independence from Luther and other reformers whose dissatisfaction with medieval Catholicism led to a decisive break with the existing ecclesiastical structures. In a well-known exchange with Luther, *The Free Will* of 1525 (answered by *The Bondage of the Will* the following year), Erasmus explicitly set himself against what he regarded as the perverse theology and ill-advised radicalism of the German reformers. While it was possible for him to respond with cautious admiration to Luther's ideas before the 1520s, the increasingly divisive atmosphere of the period between 1520 and 1530 led Erasmus to distance himself from the movement to break with Rome. In *On Repairing the Unity of the Church* (part commentary on Psalm 83, part discussion of how to reform the Church from within), Erasmus clarified his view of schism: "He who separates himself from the community of the church and goes over to heresy or schism is worse than the man who lives an impure life without doing violence to the dogmas" (*Collected Works of Erasmus*, vol. 63, 513).

Erasmus's attempts to steer a middle way between a Church in need of reform and a Protestant movement too divisive for his taste were not altogether successful. Throughout the 1520s and into the 1530s he warded off attacks from both Catholics and Protestants while growing increasingly isolated, a voice of moderation in an era of extremes. His reply when the Swiss reformer Ulrich Zwingli invited him in 1522 to become a citizen of the city of Zurich poignantly describes his place in the theological disputes of his time: "I wish to be a citizen of the world, to be a fellow-citizen to all men—a pilgrim better still" (*Collected Works of Erasmus*, vol. 9, 185). By 1535, his friend More had been executed in England and the reform movement had stirred political unrest and violence across Europe. In the early 1530s, Erasmus moved, in the words of one biographer, "from one exile to another" (Augustijn 1991, 159), searching for a hospitable community in which to work and publish. He traveled from Basel to Freiburg, then back to Basel in 1535, settling finally at the home of his friend and printer, Hieronymous Froben. There, he died during the night of July 11–12, 1536.

MAJOR THEMES

The Praise of Folly is compact but richly textured and stylistically complex. It is a paradoxical encomium, a declamation in which Folly, personified as a woman, extols her influence over the human race. Although the work itself contains no formal divisions, the speech Folly delivers is usually regarded as following a loosely structured three-part argument that most, if not all, men and women are fools—that folly, in fact, undergirds the whole human condition. In the first part (pages 1–76), Folly shows that, without her, men and women would suffer such despair that life would scarcely be possible; in the second part (76–115), she offers numerous examples of how she enables secular and ecclesiastical leaders in particular to ignore their own sins so as to misdirect the affairs of everyone else; and finally, in the last part of the speech (115–37), she declares that she even enables the practice of Christian faith and is responsible for the attainment of the beatific vision. The work ends with Folly's claim that she cannot provide the epilogue that is customary when concluding a public declamation because she has forgotten everything she has said.

While the structure of the work is deceptively simple, its method is notoriously complex. The paradoxical encomium was a classical genre, but we know of only two precedents for the idea of making the speaker the subject of the speech: Aristophanes's *Plutus*, in which Poverty praises herself, and Lucian's *Phalaris*, spoken by the tyrant of Acagras in praise of his own tyranny. To this formal paradox, Erasmus has added a brilliant irony that has no model in classical or medieval literature—Folly's topic makes her oration at once an obvious piece of self-flattery (the joke is on Folly) and a biting critique of society at large (the joke is on us).

The classical form of the paradoxical encomium is enriched by Erasmus's use of such medieval festive forms as the *sottie* and *sermon joyeux*. These were skits performed in France from the late fifteenth through the seventeenth centuries under the leadership of a "Prince of Fools" or a "Mother Folly," and they typically included a parade or roll-call of fools along with a mock sermon or a farce delivered before a serious performance of a morality play or saint's life. Another likely influence on the ironic reversals and cynical/comical revelations of Folly's argument is the Feast of Fools, which enjoyed robust popularity from the twelfth through the sixteenth centuries, despite ecclesiastical disapproval. During these celebrations, the lower clergy at many cathedrals chose a "bishop" or "pope" to conduct a parody of the usual liturgical proceedings and sometimes to deliver a mock sermon.

With its examination of how Church and secular leaders (both noble and academic) exhibit folly as they govern the world, the middle part of Folly's oration also depends on the medieval satire of the estates, in which representatives of all classes of society are caricatured and their corruption exposed (Miller 1974, 503–7). Folly's acerbic survey of her numerous devotees in the bodies politic and ecclesiastical omits few professions from the roster of fools. Grammarians, rhetoricians, lawyers, theologians, monks, cardinals, popes, courtiers, and kings: all are numbered among the parade of followers Folly marshals "to make it perfectly clear that no mortal can live happily unless he is initiated into my mysteries and has gained my favor" (*The Praise of Folly*, 115).

The Praise of Folly thus draws together a number of themes important to Erasmus's thought. Erasmus's vision for a Christlike society depended on both an accurate understanding of the Scriptures and a thorough cleansing of those offices and institutions that had, in his view, fallen away from Christian ideals. In its satiric mode, *The Praise of Folly* attempts that purgative function. At the same time, as Clarence H. Miller, the work's most important modern translator and editor, asserts in his introduction to the Yale edition of the work, "no other brief, integral work of Erasmus condenses the humanists' program for educational, religious, and theological reform better than the *Folly*" (xi). Without denying the deep, at times even bitter, criticism of the Church that pervades *The Praise of Folly*, we may observe in it the even deeper concern of its author to promote what he believed was a more authentic Christianity than was sometimes exhibited by the established Church of his time.

Certainly the emphasis in the second part of the work is on purgation. As Folly lists the many ways in which the ruling classes conduct the business of government, the universities, and the Church, the satire becomes so biting that she must finally remind herself that she is supposed to be praising her own influence, not damning the faults of others: "But it is no part of my present plan to rummage through the lives of popes and priests, lest I should seem to be composing a satire rather than delivering an encomium" (115). Nowhere is the corrective and purgative thrust of Folly's speech more apparent than in her criticisms of professional theologians, criticisms that amount to a mirror image of Erasmus's own preference for philology and rhetoric over what he regarded as arid and frequently absurd scholasticism. Here is Folly's demonstration, for instance, of her influence over the scholastic theologians:

[They] explicate sacred mysteries just as arbitrarily as they please, explaining by what method the world was established and arranged, by what channels original sin is transmitted to Adam's posterity, by what means, by proportion, in how short a period of time Christ was fully formed in the virgin's womb, how accidents subsist in the eucharist without any domicile. But such questions are run-of-the-mill. There are others which they think worthy of great and "illuminated" theologians, as they say. If they ever encounter these, then they really perk up.... Whether the following proposition is possible: God the Father hates the Son. Whether God could have taken on the nature of a woman, of the devil, of an ass, of a cucumber, of a piece of flint? And then how the cucumber would have preached, performed miracles, and been nailed to the cross? (88–89)

Such stinging ridicule is only part of Erasmus's method, however, and thus only partly accounts for what his work has to say about Christian faith and piety. Folly both mocks the schoolmen (and everyone else) for their foolishness and insists in the first part of her speech that foolishness is essential to life, a contradiction that does not bother her at all but may bother the reader. Folly's argument for her place at the center of life's sustaining illusions turns in part on the medieval trope that all the world's a stage, that the actor playing the king may also play the beggar. In yet another of her maddening ironies, Folly points out that anyone who attempts to expose the illusion risks being dismissed as a fool:

If at this point some wiseman, dropped down direct from heaven, should suddenly jump up and begin shouting that this figure whom everyone reverences as if he were the lord god is not even a man because he is controlled by his passions like an animal . . . I ask you, what would he accomplish except to make everyone take him for a raving lunatic? Just as nothing is more foolish than misplaced wisdom, so, too, nothing is more imprudent than perverse prudence. . . . True prudence, on the other hand, recognizes human limitations and does not strive to leap beyond them; it is willing to run with the herd, to overlook faults tolerantly or to share them in a friendly spirit. But, they say, that is exactly what we mean by folly. I will hardly deny it—as long as they will reciprocate by admitting that this is exactly what it means to perform the play of life. (44)

Folly's cynical (and accurate) reminder that prophets are without honor in their own countries hints at a still deeper paradox in the work. The Platonic idea that appearances mask reality is linked to what Augustijn has called "the central theme" in Erasmus's thought, an idea Erasmus himself called "the philosophy of Christ" (1991, 75). Erasmus used the term for the first time in the most famous of his *Adages*, "The Sileni of Alcibiades." In that adage, Erasmus explains that the wooden boxes carved in the ancient world to resemble the grotesque goat god Silenus contained, when opened, precious and beautiful objects; even so, says Erasmus, Christ himself concealed in a humble, human exterior the riches of divinity. So Folly presents the idea of the *theatrum mundi* as a way of explaining that

All human affairs, like the Sileni of Alcibiades, have two aspects quite different from each other. Hence, what appears "at first blush" (as they say) to be death, will, if you examine it more closely, turn out to be life; conversely, life will turn out to be death; beauty will become ugliness; riches will turn to poverty; notoriety will become fame; learning will be ignorance; strength, weakness; noble birth will be ignoble; joy will become sadness; success, failure; friendship, enmity; what is helpful will seem harmful; in brief, you will find everything suddenly reversed if you open the Silenus. (42–43)

In this passage, the paradox of the Silenus is used to reinforce Folly's case that society is held together by illusions that, if stripped away, would render life unlivable. But the figure also suggests a further paradox that Folly takes up in the last part, again ignoring its apparent incompatibility with the rest of what she has said: unlike the other kinds of folly she has described, the folly of Christians does not facilitate social life but rather mitigates against it. Whereas before she has insisted on the conformity of all her followers, she now asserts that Christian fools "conflict in their whole lifestyle with the entire company of other mortals" (133). That this company must include even representatives of the institutional Church, whose outward shows of wealth may not correspond to inward riches, is made evident from the middle part of Folly's speech. The satire of the middle part thus serves to bridge the gap between two conflicting views: that folly enables the self-delusions and deceptions that make social life possible, and that it delivers the Christian believer from the degraded conditions of human society through those moments of self-transcendence that foreshadow the beatific vision (Miller 1974, 506–8).

The paradox that worldly greatness does not always (or often) correspond to heavenly exaltation—the paradox of the Cross itself—was at the heart of Erasmus's thought and certainly informs his criticisms of the ecclesiastical establishment of late medieval Catholicism in *The Praise of Folly*. Delivered in the voice of Folly, in words so complicated by irony, satire, and contradiction that they themselves might be regarded as a kind of Silenus box, the point is easy to miss. But it is unmistakably present in every word Folly speaks, as long as the reader is willing to take those words with the dash of wit and the grain of salt she offers as seasoning.

CRITICAL RECEPTION

Commentary on and reaction to *The Praise of Folly* span nearly five centuries, and the work remains one of the most important in the western tradition. Nevertheless, as Cornelis Augustijn has said, "Almost everyone knows the *Praise of Folly* (*Moriae encomium*) by its title. Few know the book itself" (1991, 57). The status and meaning of Erasmus's masterpiece—indeed, of the author himself—have often acted as a kind of lightning rod for readers who attempt to pin down Folly's elusive double meanings and multilayered pronouncements in the service of controversies within the institutional Church and beyond. Critical reception falls roughly into three eras: one tracing the period of the European religious wars, in which *The Praise of Folly* was frequently condemned by the Church and defended only by moderate reformers, mostly in Basel; one following the Enlightenment, in which Erasmus's work, including *The Praise of Folly*, was admired for its commitment to social reform without authoritarian dogma or recourse to violence; and finally one that began in the early twentieth century and has produced renewed appreciation of the work's literary greatness and importance to the history of Christian thought. All three periods are helpfully and comprehensively chronicled in Bruce Mansfield's three-volume *Interpretations of Erasmus*, published by the University of Toronto Press between 1979 and 2003.

In the century following Erasmus's death, the fortunes of *The Praise of Folly* were bound up with the controversies in which western Christendom were then entangled. Having condemned the book as heretical in 1527 and 1533, the Sorbonne did so again in 1542 and 1543; these condemnations in turn led to *The Praise of Folly*'s appearance on the *Index of Forbidden Books* published at Trent in 1564. Popes Paul IV, Sixtus V, and Clement VIII all reiterated this negative judgment on the orthodoxy of the work and its author. Such official condemnations naturally colored the reception of *The Praise of Folly* by both Catholic and Protestant readers for at least two centuries. A nine-volume edition of Erasmus's collected works was published by Froben at Basel in 1538–1540 and included an appreciative preface written by Erasmus's friend Beatus Rhenanus, but no further such collections appeared until the Leiden edition published by Jean Le Clerc in 1703–1706. The enlarged critical perspective of the twentieth century on Erasmus's life and works, including his controversial masterpiece, owes a great deal to the publication by P. S. and H. M. Allen of Erasmus's voluminous correspondence, including his many defenses of *The Praise of Folly* (1997). Erasmus scholarship has been greatly advanced in the last fifty years by the Latin editions published at Amsterdam (1969–) and the ongoing efforts of the University of Toronto to translate all of Erasmus's works into English (1974–).

The Praise of Folly is certainly now regarded as a seminal work of Christian humanism, but even in criticism of the last one hundred years attitudes toward the work tend to be a measure of attitudes toward the Protestant Reformation itself. From one point of view, *The Praise of Folly* offers a welcome critique of medieval ritualism and scholasticism, a forerunner of the Reformation and even the Enlightenment. On the other hand, the work may be regarded as presenting too indirect a criticism of medieval Catholicism and therefore as betraying the reformers' project. Johann Huizinga's important and influential biography of Erasmus, first published in Dutch and translated into English in 1924 under the title *Erasmus of Rotterdam*, hints at both views in his assessment of the work. For Huizinga, Erasmus's objections to unreformed Catholicism were achieved only by balancing precariously between the satiric and the sacred, especially at the end of the work: "It was an unrivalled feat of art neither to lose the light comical touch, nor to lapse into undisguised profanation. It was only feasible by veritable dancing on the tightrope of sophistry. In the *Moria*, Erasmus is all the time hovering on the brink of profound truths" (1957, 75–76). Although this statement resumes the general portrayal of Erasmus's wavering allegiance to one church or another, Huizinga's discussion also identifies an important crux in twentieth-century interpretations: how to understand Folly's remarks on Christian ecstasy at the end of her declamation. Huizinga regards Folly's oration as beginning with and returning to the theme of "salutary folly, which is true wisdom" (74), and in that sense offering a *jeu d'esprit* with serious intent. While he thinks *The Praise of Folly* Erasmus's best and most important work, Huizinga also considers it essentially a jest.

In his brief but lucid *Erasmus*, James McConica is more willing to endorse the work's place in the author's formidable contribution to Christian scholarship and piety. Although McConica regards the work as "imperfect," not a product of Erasmus's "mature thought," he sees it as taking its reader "more deeply than any other of [Erasmus's] creations to the inner recesses of his mental world" and "ending unexpectedly with a statement of his religious ideals" (1991, 89). In fact, the careful attention now paid to the thematic unity of *The Praise of Folly* and the meaning of the work's last section has been a significant part of the twentieth-century reevaluation of Erasmus's importance as a Christian scholar and theologian (Mansfield 2003, 225). This reassessment has been enabled by erudite and sensitive discussions of the interplay of Christian and classical ideals that is so integral to *The Praise of Folly*'s method. Studying the Renaissance fool in *Praisers of Folly; Erasmus, Rabelais, Shakespeare*, Walter Kaiser has analyzed Folly's use of what he calls "transvaluation," a method that "finds its authorities in Socrates, who claimed that ignorance was wisdom, and in Christ, who claimed that death was life" (1963, 60). As Kaiser explains, transvaluation works by reversals, paradox, and the concealment/disclosure of eternal truth in humble form: "When Stultitia praises drunkenness, we are certainly not to think that Erasmus is advocating Bacchanalian orgies. What we are to see is that he is redefining the nature of sobriety and happiness and truth itself" (54–55).

Like McConica, other scholars have argued that it is possible to find places where Erasmus conceals nothing about his religious views, however unlikely a mouthpiece he has found for them. In *Ecstasy and the Praise of Folly*, M. A. Screech's learned reading of the last few pages of Folly's oration, the author argues that Erasmus intended to moderate the satiric thrusts of the rest of the work with a straightforward endorsement of ecstatic, mystical experience at the end. For Screech, Folly speaking of the conversion of Saint Paul or the Transfiguration is Folly speaking in a different register from the biting satire of the first two parts of her oration: these experiences "play a central role in the Christian religion . . . at the climax of the *Moria*, and in Erasmus' theology generally" (1980, 219).

Screech's judgment is shared by Sister Geraldine Thompson, whose *Under Pretext of Praise; Satiric Mode in Erasmus' Fiction* examines Erasmus's use of irony in *The Praise of Folly* and some of the dialogues. In Folly's characterization of the beatific vision as a form of Christian madness, according to Thompson, "there is no irony at all" (1973, 70). Marjorie O'Rourke Boyle has pressed this view even further, arguing in *Christening Pagan Mysteries: Erasmus in Pursuit of Wisdom* (1981) that the ecstatic vision at the end of the work echoes and Christianizes Folly's early association of herself with the vernal greening of the world— Folly as pagan mystery goddess foreshadows the visionary experience of the Christian believer and allows Erasmus to reconcile classical wisdom with Christian faith.

While such interpretations have certainly served to restore Erasmus's reputation as a serious theologian, they may understand too literally the last part of a work that is unified more by its consistent sense of paradox than by its final rhapsody on Christian madness. Clarence H. Miller (who has both edited the Latin text of the work and translated it into English) has pointed out that Folly departs from the paradoxical encomium not once but twice: the first time in the second part, when her discursive mode becomes so satiric that she has to remind herself that she is supposed to be delivering another kind of speech, and the second time when she speaks of the beatific vision (1988, 283–84). In fact, Folly employs three styles throughout her oration, styles that Miller has identified as "casual, formal, and plain," and while these correspond roughly to the three parts of the work, none overwhelms the others; none is precisely coincident with Erasmus's own voice (285).

Not to hear Erasmus's own voice in Folly's claim to preside over Christian happiness is not the same as denying the theological seriousness underlying the work; it is simply to observe the difference between the kind of systematic theology to which Erasmus himself took exception and the kind of rhetorical hermeneutics he practiced. Emphasizing, like Miller, the theological implications of rhetorical concerns, Walter Gordon, in *Humanist Play and Belief: The Seriocomic Art of Desiderius Erasmus* (1990), has examined the way in which *The Praise of Folly* combines controlled, rhetorical wordplay with contemplation of the absolute, arguing that playfulness and piety in the first and third parts are linked and balanced in dialectical form. Gordon finds a dramatic conflict informing Folly's declamation throughout, especially in the central image of the *theatrum mundi*: when Folly imagines a divine intruder interrupting "the play of life" to reveal the illusions that sustain her followers, she anticipates the visionary madness of the last part.

Part of the genius of Folly's oration is thus to link the playful with the sacred, a method that has frequently had the effect of confounding its most ponderous critics but that has not, in the end, obliterated its place among the masterpieces of western Christendom. *The Praise of Folly* remains one of the wisest works of the sixteenth century.

NOTE

Desiderius Erasmus, *The Praise of Folly*, 2nd ed., trans. and intro. Clarence H. Miller (New Haven, CT, and London: Yale University Press, 2003). All references are to this edition. Used by permission of Yale University Press.

WORKS CITED

Allen, P. S., and H. M. Allen, et al., eds. 1997. *Opus epistolarum Des. Erasmi Roterodami*. 11 vols. Oxford: University of Oxford Press.

Augustijn, Cornelis. 1991. *Erasmus: His Life, Works, and Influence*, trans. J. C. Grayson. Toronto: University of Toronto Press.

Boyle, Marjorie O'Rourke. 1981. *Christening Pagan Mysteries: Erasmus in Pursuit of Wisdom*. Toronto: University of Toronto Press.

Erasmus, Desiderius. 1974. *Collected Works of Erasmus*. Multiple editors. Toronto: University of Toronto Press.

———. 1979. *Moriae encomium*, ed. Clarence H. Miller. Vol. 11 of *Opera omnia Desiderii Erasmi Roterodami*. Amsterdam: North-Holland Publishing Company.

Gordon, Walter M. 1990. *Humanist Play and Belief: The Seriocomic Art of Desiderius Erasmus*. Toronto: University of Toronto Press.

Huizinga, Johann. 1924. *Erasmus of Rotterdam*. New York: Charles Scribner's Sons.

————. 1957. *Erasmus and the Age of Reformation*. New York: Harper.

Kaiser, Walter. 1963. *Praisers of Folly; Erasmus, Rabelais, Shakespeare*. Cambridge, MA: Harvard University Press.

Mansfield, Bruce. 1979. *Phoenix of His Age; Interpretations of Erasmus c. 1550–1750*. Toronto: University of Toronto Press.

————. 1992. *Man on His Own: Interpretations of Erasmus c. 1750–1920*. Toronto: University of Toronto Press.

————. 2003. *Erasmus in the Twentieth Century*. Toronto: University of Toronto Press.

McConica, James. 1991. *Erasmus*. Oxford: Oxford University Press.

Miller, Clarence H. 1974. "Some Medieval Elements and Structural Unity in Erasmus' *The Praise of Folly*." *Renaissance Quarterly* 27: 499–511.

————. 1988. "Styles and Mixed Genres in Erasmus' *Praise of Folly*." In *Acta Conventus Neo-Latini Guelpherbytani; Proceedings of the Sixth International Congress of Neo-Latin Studies*, ed. Stella P. Revard, et al., 276–87. Binghamton, NY: Medieval and Renaissance Texts and Studies.

Screech, M. A. 1980. *Ecstasy and the Praise of Folly*. London: Duckworth.

Thompson, Geraldine. 1973. *Under Pretext of Praise; Satiric Mode in Erasmus' Fiction*. Toronto: University of Toronto Press.

— **Katherine G. Rodgers**

William Everson (Brother Antoninus) [1912–1994]

The Veritable Years: Poems 1949–1966

BIOGRAPHY

William Everson lived a rich and varied life as a farmer, poet, hand-press printer, Dominican monk, and professor. A leading member of the San Francisco Renaissance, he was hailed by friend and mentor Kenneth Rexroth as "the finest Catholic poet writing today" (1957, 8). Everson was born on September 10, 1912, to an agnostic father and a Christian Science mother. Although his mother, Francelia Marie Herber, had been raised a Catholic in Adrian, Minnesota, she gave up her childhood faith upon her marriage to Louis Waldemar Everson, a Norwegian immigrant who had been previously divorced. They moved west, eventually settling in Sacramento, where William, the second of their three children, was born. Although the children attended Christian Science Sunday school, as a young adult William turned to his father's agnosticism.

The first religious conversion of his life came in the fall of 1934 through the unlikely means of Robinson Jeffers's poetry while Everson was a student at Fresno State College. Thirty years later, Everson would write to his friend Lawrence Clark Powell on the occasion of Jeffers's death, "He was my spiritual father. It was he who broke my own father's agnosticism, and proved to me that there is a God. It was he who taught me how to worship . . . who woke up my soul . . . who made me a religious man, gave me the dignity of faith in life and in God. Without him I would probably never have found my voice as a poet" (Bartlett 1988, 191).

Thus, early on, Everson discovered at the same instant his religious sensibility and his vocation as poet. In 1935, he dropped out of college to return to the San Joaquin Valley, where he had grown up, with the intentions of marrying his high school sweetheart, Edwa Poulson, purchasing land to plant a vineyard, and writing poetry in earnest. The poems he wrote and published during the next few years as *These Are the Ravens* (1935), *San Joaquin* (1939), and *The Masculine Dead* (1942), focused on his native California landscape and anticipate, in their celebration of the sacral nature of the earth and its rhythms and rituals, the religious poetry that he would begin writing later in life after his conversion to Catholicism.

After the outbreak of World War II, Everson was sent as a conscientious objector to work in the forestry service at Camp Angel in Waldport, Oregon, in 1943. There he became the director of the Fine Arts Project and, along with several other artists, he founded the Untide Press. Here he would print his next four books, including the comprehensive *The Residual Years: Poems 1940–1941* (1944). It was also here that Everson's lifelong interest in hand-press production began, manifesting itself after his conversion in the foundation of his Seraphim Press at the Dominican St. Albert's House of Studies in Oakland, where he would begin his monastic life.

Upon his release in 1946, Everson's marriage had ended and he had sold his farm. He moved to the San Francisco Bay area where he thrived in the burgeoning literary atmosphere. Kenneth Rexroth enthusiastically embraced his poetry and became his mentor during these years, helping him to edit an enlarged edition of *The Residual Years*, which was published by New Directions in 1948 and led to national recognition of Everson's poems. Here he also met Mary Fabilli, poet and graphic artist, who would be the means of his conversion to Catholicism. Everson and Fabilli, a lapsed Catholic, married in June 1948 even as she was beginning to return to the faith of her childhood. He attended Mass with her occasionally, at first to please her, but soon he began to feel drawn to "the personal element in Catholicism." Just as Robinson Jeffers had broken his agnosticism, Mary "broke both my Jeffersian pantheism and my Lawrentian erotic mysticism. . . . [H]er whole touch was to personalize, to humanize; she had that laughing sensibility of the personal dimension in the human physical and natural context" (Bartlett 1988, 112). On Christmas Eve of 1948, Everson experienced a mystical vision while attending Midnight Mass with Mary at St. Mary's Cathedral: "That was the night I entered into the family and fellowship of Christ—made my assent, such as it was—one more poor wretch who had nothing to bring but his iniquities" (113). Almost immediately upon his conversion, Everson began writing a new strain of poetry that explored the spiritual and psychological terrain of religious experience, thus beginning the body of work that would ultimately be collected as *The Veritable Years: Poems 1949–1966*.

Everson's joy at conversion, however, was mixed with sorrow. He and Mary realized that they could not remain together since their marriage would not be recognized by the Church. After much agonizing, they separated in June 1949, and on July 23, Everson was baptized. The following year, Everson moved to Maurin House of the Oakland Catholic Worker and spent fourteen months ministering to the city's poor, work he found uncongenial and dispiriting. He sought spiritual direction from Father Leo Osborn, a Dominican at St. Albert's College, and began to feel he had a vocation for life in a religious order. In 1951, he was accepted as a *donatus*, a lay monk without vows, and began a new life as Brother Antoninus. This new identity would define his work, both as poet and printer, for the next eighteen years.

Everson's monastic life was marked by a series of spiritual crises as he wrestled with his vocation, and these internal struggles became the subject matter of his poems. For the first few years at St. Albert's, Everson was obsessed with his ambitious but ill-fated project to print the newly approved Latin translation of the *Psalter* in its entirety. In the spring of 1954, after two and a half years of intense labor, the project was only one-quarter finished. Beset by seemingly insurmountable technical problems, Everson abandoned work on the *Psalter* and experienced his first crisis of faith. After an abortive attempt at studying for the priesthood, he began reading the work of Carl Jung, partly in an attempt to understand his own troubled psyche. The writings of Jung left a profound impression on Everson and would introduce a new element into his poetry.

Even as he was living the sequestered life of a monk, Everson's reputation as a poet was growing. In 1957, Kenneth Rexroth announced the arrival of the "Beat Generation" in the second issue of *Evergreen Review*, in which he proclaimed Everson "the most profoundly moving and durable poet of the San Francisco Renaissance" (8). Everson, under the persona Brother Antoninus, began to give public poetry readings and was becoming a celebrity. In 1959, *The Crooked Lines of God*: *Poems 1949–1954*, his first full-length collection of Catholic poems, was published and nominated for a Pulitzer Prize. The same year, *Time* magazine dubbed Antoninus "the Beat Friar," and his religious poetry began to receive national attention. In 1962, another collection followed, *The Hazards of Holiness: Poems 1957–1960*, containing poems that dramatized the spiritual crisis and recovery he had experienced during those years.

In 1960, Everson's life and work began to take a new turn when he met Rose Moreno Tannlund, an attractive Mexican divorcee who came to Everson for spiritual counsel. From the intense spiritual, emotional, and physical relationship that ensued emerged Everson's celebrated erotic sequence and his last full-length collection of Catholic poems, *The Rose of Solitude* (1967). His relationship with Rose forced him to question his calling to live a celibate life, and he found himself in turmoil again. In 1963, in the hope of renewing his vocation, he entered the novitiate in Kentfield to prepare to take the vows of a First Order brother, which would make him a permanent member of the Dominicans; however, for the third and final time, his relationship with a woman altered the course of his life. In the fall of 1965, eighteen-year-old Susanna Rickson came to Everson for spiritual direction and the poet immediately fell in love with her. After a tortured relationship, during which time Susanna attempted to leave Everson and returned pregnant with another man's child, he decided once and for all to leave behind the monastery and to marry. On December 7, 1969, during a poetry reading at the University of California at Davis before an audience of 300 people, Brother Antoninus removed his Dominican habit and announced his return to secular life. The following week the couple wed and Everson went to live with Susanna and her infant son, Jude.

Thus began the third movement of William Everson's life and work. The poems he wrote during these years were eventually collected and published posthumously as *The Integral Years: Poems 1966–1994*. These poems, like all of Everson's earlier work, are autobiographical in nature. They deal with the aftermath of his abandonment of monastic life, celebrate married love, and explore the emerging theme of the poet's vocation as shaman. In addition, although Everson necessarily left the Church and its sacraments behind after he married, his love and his hunger for God are as palpable in his postmonastic poems as they are in his ostensibly Catholic poems.

In 1971, Everson became poet-in-residence at Kresge College of the University of California at Santa Cruz. He and Susanna moved to a rustic spot a few miles north of the campus where he kept a primitive cabin he named "Kingfisher Flat."

Here the poet could work in peace and seclusion immersed in the life and rhythms of the landscape he loved. In addition to lecturing and teaching classes on fine press printing, Everson worked busily during these years collecting and editing the poems of his early and middle years, wrote many editorial and critical works centering particularly on Robinson Jeffers, and produced a number of hand-press projects. In spite of the crippling symptoms of Parkinson's disease that began to afflict him in 1977, Everson remained active, writing, printing, and performing public readings close to the end of his life. He died at Kingfisher Flat on June 2, 1994, and was buried on his birthday at the Dominican cemetery in Benicia, California.

MAJOR THEMES

The work of William Everson's long career as a poet is varied and ambitious. To borrow Ralph Waldo Emerson's phrase from "The Poet," Everson "dared to write his autobiography in colossal cipher" (1971, 21). In his Preface to *The Veritable Years*, first published in 1978, Everson described his life as "a mythic journey through time," a rite of passage following the archetypal model of "separation-initiation-return" (xxxv–vi). These three phases of his life are represented by the three volumes he arranged and published under the collective title *The Crooked Lines of God: A Life Trilogy*. Volume I, *The Residual Years (1934–1948)*, contains the secular poems written before his conversion. Volume II, *The Veritable Years (1949–1966)*, features the Catholic poems, many of which were written while Everson was a *donatus* of the Dominican Order. Finally, Volume III, published posthumously as *The Integral Years (1966–1994)*, contains some poems Everson wrote in his last years as a Dominican as well as poems he wrote during the years after 1969 when he married and resumed secular life.

The Veritable Years lies at the crux of Everson's spiritual autobiography and represents, according to most critics and readers, his finest work. These poems are passionate expressions of the consolations and desolations Everson experienced after his conversion to Catholicism. The reader of these poems becomes witness to a powerful *psychomachia*. Everson describes the drama they convey: "A man wrestling first with God, then with his own shadow, sometimes confusing them, generates a strange and fitful light, a lurid apocalyptic glare" (xxxvii). Everson's description is telling in a number of ways. First, it implicitly acknowledges the influence of Carl Jung on his development during this period of spiritual and psychological turmoil, an influence that Albert Gelpi suggests accounts for "the distinctiveness of Everson's achievement . . . the Dionysian character of his Christianity" (1998, xxi). Second, it explicitly acknowledges the apocalyptic nature of the poems. Everson is engaged in various ways throughout *The Veritable Years* in a life-and-death struggle for his own salvation. In the tradition of many great religious poets who have come before him (John of the Cross, John Donne, Gerard Manley Hopkins, and T. S. Eliot, to name but a few), Everson is using language to explore the dark shadow-world of his own sinful soul and trying to discover therein some small sign of God's presence. What makes Everson's struggle even more deeply personal than those recorded by his forbearers is his frank, relentless grappling with his powerful sexual urges.

This leads, ultimately, to his attempt to reconcile the demands of the flesh with those of the spirit in explicitly sexual terms.

Finally, the poems of *The Veritable Years* are remarkable in that they contain key themes evident in his earlier poems, but they are modified as he tries to reconcile them with his Christian beliefs. A defining element of the secular poems of *The Residual Years* is Everson's profound sense of place. Ross Labrie characterizes Everson's passion for the California landscape still evident in the religious poems of *The Veritable Years* as the poet's attempt to create a synthesis between Catholicism and the "pantheistic romanticism" of his youth (1997, 92). Thus, Everson's depiction of nature is a unique mingling of romantic myth and Catholic incarnational theology.

These major themes—Catholic theology, American romanticism, Jungian psychology, and erotic mysticism—are all present in *The Veritable Years* but are manifested in varying degrees as the reader moves through the volume. As with the three volumes marking the three phases of his life, Everson organized the six books that make up *The Veritable Years* chronologically and indicated parenthetically the years of composition rather than the year of each volume's publication: *The Crooked Lines of God (1949), The Savagery of Love (1950–1954), River Root / A Syzygy (1959), The Hazards of Holiness (1957–1960), Eros and Thanatos (1962),* and *The Rose of Solitude (1960–1966).* Each book offers a distinctive voice and vision as Everson moves from the surety and delight in his newfound faith (evident in the celebratory "Triptych for the Living," written just after his conversion experience), through the unexpected reawakening of his sexuality after joining the Dominicans (evident in *River Root / A Syzygy,* a graphically descriptive paean to the holiness of conjugal sexual relations), through the resultant dark night of the soul (dramatized in *The Hazards of Holiness*), and finally through the acceptance of his own need for sexual love (evident in the erotic mysticism of *The Rose of Solitude*). Altogether, the collection contains seventy-three poems (the longest of them, *River Root / A Syzygy,* is nearly twenty pages in length) that are framed by a prologue, "At the Edge," and an epilogue, "Who Is She That Looketh Forth as the Morning." These two poems serve to unify the volume and to emphasize further Everson's spiritual and aesthetic development.

The prologue is a free-verse meditation on the urgency of salvation, one that will come only through the frank acknowledgment of death and the relentless pursuit of God. Originally a prologue to one of Everson's longer poems on his conversion, "The Falling of the Grain," Everson moved it, enabling it to serve as the keynote to *The Veritable Years* to introduce into the collection the persistent Christian theme of dying into life. It also stands in dialectical relationship to the epilogue. The latter is a formal lyric narrating the emergence of a mythic female figure from the sea, her impregnation by the Holy Spirit, and the beginning of "the blaze of birth" that will result in the coming of the God who "tramples death." Thus, the volume begins with death and ends with the promise of new life; it begins in lamentation and crisis and concludes with God answering the poet's pleas; and it begins with the spontaneity of free verse and concludes with the contained passion and peace conveyed by stately pentameter quatrains. The epilogue also bears the mark of Everson's increasing interest in combining traditional Christian symbols with Jungian archetypes as he tries to forge a more universal language to carry eschatological vision. Thus, the two poems provide a welcome symmetry to the volume and also reflect the great aesthetic and stylistic range of the poems they frame.

The earliest poems of the collection are the most orthodox in their treatment of religious material. "Triptych for the Living," the first poem, is a three-part meditation on the Incarnation. The poet imagines the announcement of Jesus' coming to the shepherds in Part I, "The Uncouth," his violent birth in Part II, "The Coming," and the journey of the Magi in Part III, "The Wise." The subject of the poem came directly out of Everson's conversion experience on Christmas Eve, when he found himself drawn into rapt contemplation of the figures in the crèche.

Although Everson claims no special spiritual kinship with Saint Ignatius of Loyola, "Triptych," along with many other poems in the volume, is reminiscent of the practice of Ignatian meditation. In his *Spiritual Exercises*, Ignatius calls upon the exercitant to imagine important moments in the life of Christ, to achieve composition of place that he might see, smell, hear, touch and taste as many aspects of the scene as the imagination permits, and to enter into the action. Everson accomplishes all of this admirably in the trilogy of poems, identifying first with the miserable poverty of the shepherds, then with the agony of birth for Jesus and for his parents, and finally with the exhaustion and exhilaration of the wise men as they find the God they sought, "fl[inging] themselves down in the dung and dirt of that place, / And kissed the ground" (114). Again, even as Everson writes about biblical figures, the autobiographical element is evident: clearly he is writing of his own poverty, his own pain, and his own joy at finding Christ at last. Several other early, postconversion poems, such as "The Flight in the Desert," "The Making of the Cross," and "The Massacre of the Holy Innocents," treat biblical subjects similarly and with comparable success.

Another traditional genre evident in the volume is the devotional poem. Once again, Everson's approach to this genre is characteristically his own. One of his most compelling poems, "A Canticle to the Waterbirds," is a hymn to the sacredness of creation as manifested in the ordinary birds that populate the Oakland estuary. The circumstances of composition are, once again, noteworthy. The poet had been living for fourteen months in West Oakland at the Catholic Worker Maurin House. By the summer of 1950, he found daily exposure to the squalor and debasement of humanity dispiriting, and in the hope of a cure, he had begun an intense program of nearly continuous prayer. During this period he experienced the vision of the waterbirds, joyful and faithful creatures of God "among the deserted factories and warehouses, and out along the silent piers," and the poem came to him (Bartlett 1988, 123). As with Hopkins a century before him, the poet's "heart in hiding / Stirred for a bird" (1995, 117). However, the voice of the poem resembles the oracular utterance of Everson's American predecessor, Walt Whitman, more than the interior praise of Hopkins. It is a catalog of creatures in which the poet takes delight in the sheer act of naming. The particularity of his address to each bird isolates it, momentarily, and asks the reader to acknowledge it as sign and sacramental symbol of our common "creaturehood" (Labrie 1997, 101). Jesus spoke of God's care for the sparrow; Everson echoes Christ's providential message as he sees it embodied in the birds of his native place.

"The Mate-Flight of the Eagles" similarly introduces creatures native to California into a biblical story. Ross Labrie notes that "although the poem is ostensibly set in Palestine, the eagle imagery suggests an American landscape, thus integrating Everson's primary subject, the Crucifixion, with his own environment" (1997, 102). The reader also finds in this poem manifestations of another of Everson's preoccupations, his increasing interest in erotic mysticism. The poem participates in a long tradition, most evident in the writings of John of the Cross, in its use of erotic imagery to describe divine love; however, Everson grafts upon this tradition Jungian theory. The mating eagles in the sky join to form "one cross," thus beginning a stream of imagery depicting the cross as an archetype of the masculine and feminine conjoined, both phallic symbol and wound, thus depicting Christ as androgynous God, both bridegroom and bride. In the course of the poem, sexual consummation becomes "the archetype of religious consciousness" (102).

Everson had been interested long before his conversion, in part because of his early exposure to the poetry of Whitman and Jeffers and in part because of his strong sexual instinct, in "a kind of religious sexuality, a sense of the universal life-force compelling all things in the sexual rhythm" (Gelpi 1998, xxi). This tendency was further encouraged by his intermittent reading of depth psychology, beginning in 1946 when he read Wilhelm Reich. His interest in the anima/animus, the idea "that each man carries a spontaneous product of the unconscious which is the feminine within him, while each woman's unconscious has . . . a masculine imprint" (Bartlett 1988, 183), is evident in poems as early as 1952. (This is well before his acquaintance with Jungian scholar Father Victor White in 1955 at St. Albert's College and before his sustained reading of Jung beginning the following year.) In two other poems of this early period, "The Encounter" and "Annul Me in My Manhood," the speaker of the poem "becomes the woman before God, his/her whole being called into activity by His totally mastering love" (Gelpi 1998, xxv). This early acknowledgment of the woman within will lead, gradually, to the anima's becoming his "primary archetypal focus in the struggle toward transcendence" (Gelpi 1998, xxiv).

Everson's full immersion in Jungian thought came about, in part, as a result of the depression he experienced in 1954 and 1955 as he began to reconsider his vocation. His project to print the *Psalter* on his hand press had failed, he had given up the idea of the priesthood after much consideration, and he had stopped writing poetry (Bartlett 1988, 153). During this period, he was asked to serve as spiritual counselor to a couple whose marriage was failing and was thus required to go out into the world and have personal contact with women. This aroused in the celibate Everson his dormant sexuality, further causing him to reevaluate his decision to live in an entirely masculine world void of the feminine principle. Father White suggested to him a course of reading that eventually led him to *God and the Unconscious*. As he began to question the traditions of orthodox Catholicism, Everson began to adopt a new mythology and to envision the doctrines of the Church in what he believed to be a more universal way.

The immediate result of all of this intellectual and spiritual turmoil was his breakthrough poem, *River Root / A Syzygy*, "one of the most sustained erotic poems in the English language, and certainly the most religious" (Harryman 1998, 329). In fact, so intense and frank is the depiction of the sexual act between the two married protagonists that Everson did not attempt to publish the poem while he was still a Dominican. The poem is a third-person narrative that begins with Everson's characteristic expansive vision of nature. It is set at the confluence of two great rivers, the Missouri and Mississippi, each of which represents the creative masculine principle in this American Eden. The speaker describes at length a night of lovemaking, the husband and wife clearly identified as Adam and Eve figures, the eternal masculine and feminine principles. Most startling, perhaps, and yet most Catholic, is the repeated insistence of God's presence in every act of love:

> For the phallus is holy
> And holy is the womb: the holy phallus
> In the sacred womb. And they melt.
> And flowing they merge, the incarnational join
> Oned with the Christ. The oneness of each
> Ones them with God. (131)

Finally, the poem culminates in the engendering of a child, through whom the two become both one and three, a paradox conveyed through imagery of the Holy Trinity. According to Albert Gelpi, "Amongst the Antoninus poems collected in *The Veritable Years*, *River-Root* can be seen as a watershed: the turning away from the often austere asceticism of the years just after conversion back down again to primal nature, now transfigured in the mystery of the Incarnation . . . at once a recovery and synthesis and turning point. It opened the way back to poetry—and to the world" (1998, xxvi).

River Root anticipates the erotic mysticism that culminates in the final series of poems in *The Veritable Years*, the poems published collectively as *The Rose of Solitude*. Once again, it is helpful for the reader to recall the circumstances of Everson's life at this time. In October 1959, Everson began counseling Rose Moreno Tannlund. Within months, their intense spiritual relationship had developed into an erotic obsession for Everson. The plot of the poem is autobiographical, tracing a monk's love affair with a Mexican woman. After breaking his vow of chastity with her, she leads him to repentance and confession, and they part: he to return to his cell, she to begin another relationship. As in *River Root*, the poet depicts sexual love with great intensity, only this time he describes it as a personal experience using first-person narration. Once again, the female body is a conduit of the sacred; the poet celebrates "The Sign of God evoked from the splendid flesh / Of the Rose revealed" (244). The protagonist's desire for the rose that mysteriously resides both outside himself and within his own heart is inextricably tied to his suffering from the very beginning of the poem: "I have nailed myself to the Mexican cross, / The flint knife of her beauty" (245). The poet is gradually transformed, in the course of the sequence's five sections "into the Christ-figure, the poet crucified" (Bartlett 1989, 42). The two central symbols of the poem, the cross and the rose, represent feminine aspects of the poet's self with which he ultimately becomes reconciled, just as the anima/animus must be reconciled if the individual is to achieve psychic wholeness (38):

> Rose!
> Reality unfolded!
>
> On the four wings of the Cross,
> In the ecstasy of crucifixion,

In the blood of being,
In the single burn of beauty

BE!

So that
In you,
The consummate
Vision of Other:

In you
I AM! (310)

Here in this passage near the end of *The Veritable Years* we see all four of Everson's major themes converge: Catholic theology (evident in the centrality of the Incarnation to salvation), romanticism (evident in the notion of the natural object, the rose, as an embodiment of God), Jungian psychology (evident in the unification of the masculine and feminine principles within the singular figure of the androgynous Man-God), and erotic mysticism (evident in the realization of divine love by means of erotic love). Furthermore, the volume concludes as it began, autobiographically. Within two years of the publication of *The Rose of Solitude*, Brother Antoninus left the Dominican order to marry Susanna Rickson and return to the secular world. The reader has been brought along the journey, from the poet's postconversion leap into religious life to his psychological and spiritual preparation for a return to secular life. With the first poems of *The Veritable Years*, Brother Antoninus is born; through the last poems, we witness him dying into a new life.

CRITICAL RECEPTION

The Catholic poems that would eventually be collected in *The Veritable Years* were greeted, as each volume was published, with both enthusiasm and reserve. Kenneth Rexroth, who had inaugurated the entry of Everson's secular poems into national notice in 1948, helped to bring the poet's religious poems to the attention of readers and reviewers in 1957 with his celebrated "San Francisco Letter." He praised the originality of the poems, their "gnarled, even tortured honesty" and "rugged, unliterary diction" (8).

The Crooked Lines of God, published two years later, was greeted with favorable reviews in a number of high-profile publications, including the *New York Times Book Review*, and was nominated for a Pulitzer Prize. However, a number of reviewers found fault with Everson's poems. Rosemary Deen, writing for *Commonweal*, appreciated the "blunt honesty" that Rexroth so admired but found the poet's "eccentricities of diction," his "reliance on the shock of conjoining sexual and religious figures," and the lack of careful craftsmanship troubling (1960, 656–57). John Engels, in his review in *Poetry*, acknowledged the power of personality that lies behind these poems but described it as an element that is so strong "the reviewer must be wary" for "one is constantly tempted to forget about the poems and talk about the man." As was evident in the enormous popularity of the poetry readings he gave throughout the country during these years, a popularity acknowledged and further fueled by *Time* magazine's feature on "the Beat Friar" in May 1959, the public attraction to Everson/Antoninus had as much to do with the charismatic persona of the poet/monk as with the poetry itself. Finally, though, when one looks at the poems, Engels argued, the reader finds that Everson lacks the "judicious detachment," "austere craftsmanship," and "formal discipline" necessary to realize the experience he is trying to embody, and that Brother Antoninus's voice is monotonous and too derivative of his masters Whitman, Hopkins, and the Old Testament poets (1962, 254).

The Hazards of Holiness (1962) and *The Rose of Solitude* (1967) were greeted with a similar mixture of admiration and condemnation. Janet Fiscalini found the poet's "fluent violence" and "consciously muscular language" in the former volume adequate to carry the power of some of the experiences the poems describe, yet these were weakened, in her estimation, by "passages of straining rhetoric or simply despairing baldness" (1962, 101). William Dickey, in an angry review, described the latter volume as "a pretentious and dishonest book ... 125 pages of overheated verse, and a lengthy prose preface which may represent the fullest statement of a narcissist theology yet made in our time." Once again, Everson's language is at issue, which Dickey claimed is "like its substance, overblown" leading in some cases to "distortions which can best be called grotesque" (1968, 693). Finally, Robert Creeley, in a more measured review in *Poetry*, acknowledged his dislike of the excessive drama and conscious rhetoric of the poems but also introduced the idea that one's response to these tortured poems depends upon "the reader's own relation to the literal facts dealt with, the faith in God which is the issue" (1963, 43). Creeley's corrective helps to account for the great divergence of opinion among contemporary reviewers on the value of Everson's Catholic verse. Certainly one's attitude toward religious faith and the capacity of poetry to carry and convey that faith will enter into the reader's experience of the poems, and the reviewers who are most forgiving of Everson's flaws as a craftsman are those who admire the project he is undertaking.

In 1978, when all of these poems were collected and published again as *The Veritable Years*, along with a number of poems that had not been previously available to the public, critics attempted to assess the value of the Catholic poems anew. While there was still disagreement, a general shift toward a greater appreciation of the poems was evident. James Finn Cotter in the *Hudson Review* condemned the poems that had been so popular upon their initial publication, posing the rhetorical question, "Did Everson's reputation depend on the verbally sensational, the mock-biblical, and the autobiographical shock rather than on content and style?" (1979, 117). He concluded with the damning statement that the poems exploit the Christian tradition rather than explore it. Such a judgment stands in stark opposition to Albert Gelpi's claim for Everson's poems made in the introduction to *The Veritable Years*: "if T. S. Eliot is the most important religious poet in English in the first half of the twentieth century, Everson/Antoninus is the most important religious poet of the second half of the century" (1998, xix).

Here, in these two divergent positions, we can see the crux of the dispute among critics of the Catholic poems from 1957 to present. Those readers who attempt to evaluate the poetry independent of the life and of the man inevitably find it lacking, whereas those who consider the life and the work to be of a piece herald its greatness. Rexroth defended Everson's autobiographical genius from the beginning, evident even in his pre-Catholic poems. Gelpi, in his studies of Everson's Catholic poetry, accentuates Everson's identity as a "romantic individualist, trusting reason less than the undertow of passion and instinct to write out a life-long poem, as Whitman did a century ago, of the struggles with himself to realize himself," a vocation that corresponds to the Jungian theory of the emergence of the self Everson adopted during his monastic years (1998, xix). Ross Labrie includes Everson in his book-length study, *The Catholic Imagination in American Literature*, tracing the parallel development of the poet's life and work as he moves from pantheist to Christian, and focusing on the Catholic poems as "spiritual documents" that are "convincing as poetry and are often heightened by fine workmanship" (1997, 110).

Recent scholarship on the poems of *The Veritable Years* is dominated by a few dedicated scholars. Lee Bartlett, Everson's biographer and, perhaps, the chief champion of his work among present-day scholars, and Albert Gelpi, Alan Campo, and Ross Labrie, have provided much helpful factual information about Everson's life and work in their revealing interviews and thoughtful studies on Everson's romanticism, erotic mysticism, and Jungian influences. In addition, Gelpi has recently edited a new selection of poems spanning Everson's career, *The Dark God of Eros: A William Everson Reader* (2003), as part of the California Legacy Project. After several decades of neglect by anthologies, from which Everson's poems have been omitted, perhaps Gelpi's new edition, like *The Veritable Years*, will serve to introduce a new generation of readers to the work of this remarkable American Catholic poet.

NOTE

William Everson (Brother Antoninus), *The Veritable Years: Poems 1949–1966*, with a foreword by Allan Campo, introduction by Albert Gelpi, and afterword by William Harryman (Santa Rosa, CA: Black Sparrow Press, 1998). Used by permission of Black Sparrow Books/David R. Godine, Publisher, Boston. All references are to this edition.

WORKS CITED

Bartlett, Lee. 1988. *William Everson: The Life of Brother Antoninus*. New York: New Directions.

———. 1989. "God's Crooked Lines: William Everson and C. G. Jung." In *The Sun Is But A Morning Star*, ed. Lee Bartlett, 23–45. Albuquerque: University of New Mexico Press.

Bartlett, Lee, and Allan Campo, eds. 1979. *William Everson: A Descriptive Bibliography*. Metuchen, NJ: Scarecrow Press.

Cotter, James Finn. 1979. "Familiar Poetry." *Hudson Review* 32, no. 1 (Spring): 109–22.

Creeley, Robert. 1963. "Think What's Got Away." *Poetry* 52, no. 1 (April): 42–48.

Deen, Rosemary. 1960. "Poetry of Conversion and the Religious Life." *Commonweal* 71, no. 24 (March 11): 656–57.

Dickey, William. 1968. "Intention and Accident." *Hudson Review* 20, no. 4 (Winter): 687–98.

Emerson, Ralph Waldo. 1971. "The Poet." In *The Collected Works of Ralph Waldo Emerson*, ed. Alfred R. Ferguson and Jean Ferguson Carr, vol. 3, 3–24. Cambridge, MA: Belknap Press.

Engels, John. 1962. "Two Religious Poets." *Poetry* 99, no. 4 (January): 253–58.

Fiscalini, Janet. 1962. "Antoninus' Night." *Commonweal* 77, no. 4 (October 19): 100–01.

Gelpi, Albert. 1998. "Introduction: Everson/Antoninus: Contending with the Shadow." In *The Veritable Years: Poems 1949–1966*, by William Everson, xix–xxxiii. Santa Rosa, CA: Black Sparrow Press.

———. ed. 2003. *The Dark God of Eros: A William Everson Reader*. Berkeley, CA: Heydey Press.

Harryman, William. 1998. "Afterword: The Flesh of Divinity—'River Root' and *The Veritable Years*." In *The Veritable Years: Poems 1949–1966*, by William Everson, 329–40. Santa Rosa, CA: Black Sparrow Press.

Hopkins, Gerard Manley. 1995. "The Windhover." In *Gerard Manley Hopkins: A Selection of His Finest Poems*, ed. Catherine Phillips, 117. Oxford: Oxford University Press.

Labrie, Ross. 1997. *The Catholic Imagination in American Literature*. Columbia: University of Missouri Press.

Rexroth, Kenneth. 1957. "San Francisco Letter." *Evergreen Review* 1, no. 2: 4–9.

— Angela O'Donnell

Rumer Godden [1907–1998]

In This House of Brede

BIOGRAPHY

British author Rumer Godden's long life and prolific writing career were an ongoing adventure of crossing boundaries—geographically, culturally, religiously, and artistically. The many journeys of her ninety-one years took her not only to live much of her life abroad from her native England but eventually to convert to Roman Catholicism. She wrote seventy books. With her 1969 novel *In This House of Brede*, Godden would undertake as a literary subject one of the faith's arguably most secret, mysterious, and misunderstood forms of practice: the contemplative monastic vocation of women called to consecrated religious life.

She was born Margaret Rumer Godden on December 10, 1907, in Eastbourne, Sussex. Her parents, Arthur Leigh Godden and Katherine Norah Hingley Godden, took the infant Margaret and her elder sister Jon to India, where Arthur Godden was employed as a clerk in navigation, and the family lived near rivers in the Assam and Bengal regions. After a one-year stay with relatives in England, the Godden sisters returned to India in 1914 to avoid the bombings of London during World War I. The childhood world Rumer Godden knew in India was one of happy adventure, a comfortable sense of belonging that taught respect for other cultures, extended family ties, and informal learning (Wybourne 2002, 88–89). An aunt tutored the Godden children, which later included two more sisters, Nancy and Rose.

Jon and Rumer returned to England in 1920 to go to boarding school. They chafed at its confines and endured a particularly negative experience at an Anglican convent school that left Rumer with disdain for the High Anglican Church (Rosenthal 1996, 7–8). After transfers to several schools, the Godden girls enrolled at the day school, Moira House. There, young Rumer encountered a teacher, Mona Swann, who affirmed and nurtured her talent for writing, leaving her with what would be a lifelong inspiration (Godden 1987, 45–48).

Artistic in an expansive way, Rumer energetically pursued dance and music as well as writing. She studied dance in London in 1927, then moved to Calcutta and opened a dance school in 1928, where her contact with wealthy Indians made her aware of the need for Indian independence (Wybourne 2002, 89). It was a busy time for Rumer, with a successful, innovative venture that was an unusual endeavor for a young woman. Her social life in Calcutta was also a whirlwind to the point of turbulence—she became pregnant by a carefree stockbroker, Laurence Sinclair Foster, and having refused an abortion, married him in 1934. The marriage was shaky from the start, and financial pressures took their toll. Born prematurely, their son died within four days, producing lifelong grief for Rumer; yet 1935 brought the birth of a daughter, Jane, as well as the publication of a first novel, *Chinese Puzzle*. Her second novel, *The Lady and the Unicorn*, was issued in 1936, but marital strain continued because of finances, the demands of the growing family, and Laurence's lack of support for Rumer's writing and unconventional ideas (90). In 1938, Rumer returned to England to give birth to a second daughter, and a year later, she published a best-selling novel about a band of British Anglican nuns who found a convent in India, *Black Narcissus*.

After the outbreak of World War II, Laurence persuaded a reluctant Rumer to return with the children to Calcutta. There she confronted the dual crises of his hitherto unrevealed financial difficulties. Laurence had concealed totally his failed gambles on the stock market, departing suddenly to join the army and leaving Rumer to be confronted by hordes of creditors—he secretly liquidated their assets and sold their property (Godden 1987, 162–63). Her substantial earnings from the international best seller *Black Narcissus* went principally to pay her husband's debts. Subsequently, Rumer and the children settled in Kashmir, where she sought to establish a life that balanced single motherhood, writing, small business ventures, and her own particular form of cross-cultural domestic simplicity. Beset by the frustrations of a crumbling marriage and the grieving aftermath of a miscarriage, she sought comfort in work and her new home. She started a small herb farm, yet even then stability was not hers to be had in the foreign land that she had called home: a servant attempted to poison her family, allegedly for political reasons (229–33).

As the war ended, Godden left the farm and her failed marriage to begin a new phase of her life. The mid- to late 1940s brought her back to England and also brought her more literary and professional success. She published another best-seller, *The River*, in 1946, and *Black Narcissus* was made into a major film. She also began writing children's books and autobiographies.

After marrying James Haynes-Dixon in 1949, Godden began a series of moves both physical and spiritual (Wybourne 2002, 92–95). All the while writing prolifically, she relocated to several homes in pursuit of a comfortable sense of place and family connections. In 1957, for reasons she did not clearly explain for the record, Godden converted to Roman Catholicism. In 1961, she sought the prayers of the oldest Benedictine community for women in England, Stanbrook Abbey in Worcester. A friendship between writer and monastery formed that would take Godden further with her depictions of convent life than she had gone before, this time into the cloister as well as into the heart of a troubled, restless pilgrim who aspires to an unlikely vocation and a spiritual home. Impressed by the nuns she came to know as real persons and accomplished women, Godden spent several years living near the Abbey as a Benedictine oblate (one who follows the Benedictine Rule as much as possible in lay life), working on the novel that would be entitled *In This House of Brede*. The book would later be adapted to the screen in a 1975 television film starring Diana Rigg.

After her husband's death in 1973, Godden endured profound grief (Wybourne 2002, 94). She would return again to the complicated vocations of nuns with the 1979 novel *Five for Sorrow; Ten for Joy*. She spent her last years in Scotland, near her daughter, and continued to write. She died there in 1998, having left explicit instructions for quality champagne to flow after her Requiem Mass (95). The Stanbrook Abbey nuns, on whose example she had drawn inspiration for her fiction, had remained her friends. Of Godden's unconventional spiritual journey, one Benedictine offered this view: "[I]t is not difficult to guess how attractive the honesty and tolerance of the Rule of St. Benedict was to one whose personal history had its share of mistakes and failures. Rumer was never conventionally 'pious,' but it was as a Benedictine oblate that she finally entered the room of the spirit and quietly closed the door behind her" (95).

PLOT SUMMARY

In This House of Brede's title derives from the traditional answer that an aspiring novice is taught to give when arriving at the monastery door: "to try my vocation in this House of Brede." Its overall narrative structure is complicated by the layering of memory and inner reflection and by its many subplots and characters. *In This House of Brede* is essentially the story of a woman's unlikely midlife renunciation of worldly success, her entrance into a Benedictine contemplative order in rural England, and her ongoing struggle with personal loss, religious formation, and spiritual growth. Because the protagonist has indeed entered a monastic community, the novel brims with detailed depictions of the personal stories and struggles of the other nuns and novices who are drawn together in this shared lifestyle of the monastery and Benedictine tradition. These interpersonal dynamics and individual dilemmas invigorate the plot with tension, color, depth, and variations in character.

The novice with the unlikely vocation, Philippa Talbot, leaves behind in the London of 1957 a life of achievement, power, sophistication, and mystery. Having been a "woman of the world" in a positive sense, she is well traveled, educated, fashionable, accomplished, and admired. A war widow, she appears to subdue the pain of personal loss by pouring her energies into her career, yet vague, disturbing flashbacks invade her consciousness. As a successful professional who makes her mark as an executive in the mid-twentieth century (before such options were readily available to women), she is an exceptional and singular figure of authority. Yet at forty-two, she tires of this success and seeks a radically different life beyond the limelight. Having converted to Catholicism, she has made retreats at Brede Monastery and decides to enter the order. With the resolve that has characterized her administrative career, the formidable Mrs. Talbot calls her staff into her office one by one to tell them of her shocking plans. She gives away personal objects that have established her sense of status and identity and finds a suitable caretaker for both her cat and her flat. She says farewell to friends and dines with a former lover, steadily and frankly preparing for life without the comforts of fine food, alcohol, and good tea (and presumably, male companionship). After a train ride to Brede, she stops by a local pub to fortify herself with final rounds of whiskey and cigarettes before, supposedly, leaving behind the world at the monastery door.

Philippa enters alongside another unlikely candidate, Elspeth Scallon, a young woman of great physical beauty and exceptional musical talent who, as Sister Cecily, must persevere in her ardently desired vocation despite the protests of her overbearing mother. Sister Cecily must also resist the persistent attention of the wealthy young farmer who still wants to marry her; even after she is clothed as a nun, she must firmly protest his advances through the grille of the visitor's parlor. The third postulant in their class is Sister Hilary, a sturdy, cheerful young woman whose family's high social standing seems to prepare her well for life in a monastery that is not without its own traditional perpetuation of secular class structure, despite the sacred vow of poverty. Sister Hilary, though, is quite adaptable to a life based on structure, duty, and defined roles, and her character provides a foil for the other two more complicated postulants.

Once inside the convent door, the new postulants are greeted by a community in upheaval over the impending death of the long-ruling Abbess Hester. After this death, Abbess Catherine is elected and moves the community forward with pragmatism, insight, and humane, evenhanded resolve. A financial crisis arises relating to the late Abbess's extravagance in commissioning a stone altarpiece by a renowned sculptor. Other clandestine wrongs unfold, including the mismanagement of funds by an unstable nun with a troubled relative in need of money. At the time of great crisis, the necessary funds appear by way of an elaborate providential development that may seem contrived to a reader unaccustomed to miracles: a simple wooden cross that had traditionally been worn by the Abbess, ever since it had been given to them by an aristocrat imprisoned during the French Revolution, is broken and reveals a valuable ruby hidden within.

Ninety-six nuns in various positions and phases of life constitute the community of Brede Monastery at the time of Philippa's entry. Their interactions, personal struggles, and conflicts move the story forward through the years of formation for Sisters Philippa and Cecily. The choir nuns have their learned, specialized roles as councilors and are set apart from the claustral sisters, who handle the domestic work; this division of labor creates a class system. Individual nuns pursue special projects suited to their interests and abilities in such fields as scholarship, creative writing, music, weaving, and gardening. Squabbles and even bitter conflicts and rivalries ensue, and despite the regular program to tame pride, egos flare up in the predictable course of daily prayer and work. Moments of humor, frank utterances, and glimpses of personalities beyond the enforced piety and uniformity of habits are regularly revealed.

At the center of these events is the question of whether the aspiring nuns in formation will persevere in their vocations. Periods of crisis and doubts arise that force the sisters to realize that they have not entered a monastery to avoid personal pain but, in fact, to confront it more keenly and prayerfully. After the choir's director finds herself overly fond of the beautiful and musically gifted young Sister Cecily, the elder nun leaves Brede for another monastery. As she grows to become first Sister Cecily and then prepares for profession as Dame Cecily, the formerly earnest yet naive young woman must turn away from the pressure to leave the monastery and marry a man who still loves her. Her uncertainty extends all the way to the time of her Solemn Profession, as she feels intensely the desire to have a home and children of her own yet realizes how much greater and truer is her vocation as a nun.

Larger developments within the community arise and are resolved alongside the novel's main focus: first, the transformation of the powerful Mrs. Talbot into the humble and struggling sister in formation whose patterns of thought and action are difficult to change and whose inner torment troubles her greatly; then the reconfiguration of Dame Philippa, a professed member of the community who eventually is able to overcome the obstacles and suspicion of the community so that she can finally integrate the strong leadership, analytical ability, and cosmopolitan experience of her former life with her profession as a Benedictine nun. Dame Philippa learns that, although she must strive to live the precepts of humility and obedience and other "conversions of manners," she cannot leave her essential nature behind: she regularly solves problems of various types, including preventing the suicidal death of a sister in crisis and attempting to handle the business affairs of the order. Yet Sister Philippa experiences her own inner crisis, the torment of memories unresolved after her young child's accidental death. When the daughter of the nanny whose negligence had, in part, caused the death of Philippa's son enters Brede Monastery (ironically inspired by the publicized example of the famous former Mrs. Talbot), Sister Philippa must confront her past fully and faithfully, which in community brings her to the critical process of forgiveness and healing.

The novel concludes with a move that brings Dame Philippa back to her origins in a renewed and religious way that appears at odds with her initial expectations of removal from the world and of vowed stability to Brede Monastery. Fourteen years after entering Brede, Dame Philippa consents to leave for Japan, where she had spent her childhood and learned Japanese, so that she might guide a fledgling Benedictine community of newly professed Japanese nuns in the establishment of a monastery there. She is again in charge, a position that she had sought to withdraw from in religious life, yet she is obedient to a call greater than her own will and more original than her own vision and plans. This redirection draws together fully who she has been in the world and who she is in religion. As the novel ends, the sea that Philippa never expected to view again after entering Brede Monastery becomes her passage to a surprising yet fitting new religious mission.

MAJOR THEMES

With its setting in a Benedictine monastery, *In This House of Brede* is an explicitly Catholic novel. Its religious nature, however, transcends the obvious and pervasive references to Catholic tradition in order to encompass a larger view of the workings of providence, the unexpected growth of religious vocation, the complexities of spirituality, and the human struggle to resolve pain, anger, and pride in order to grow in mercy and faith. In this way, *In This House of Brede* is foremost a novel of mystery—not in the conventional sense of the genre (in spite of the mystery alluded to in Philippa's traumatic flashbacks) but in the religious mystery of providence at work in the direction of lives into vocations and in the daily orderings of events and circumstances by a sense of divine power. Most obviously, the novel reveals in detail and demystifies many behind-the-grille realities of a cloister and its veiled inhabitants, complete with the human foibles and desires of the individual sisters. More profoundly, however, the novel explores the mystery of religious vocation and of unpredictable turns of providence that shape and remake life itself.

Philippa is herself a mystery: a woman of exceptional, aloof power, yet one with a troubled past and a difficult process to attempt in religious life. As an unlikely candidate for the convent, Philippa must struggle as she undergoes a radical alteration of lifestyle and established identity. She must not only renounce her material success but also resolve to surrender or redirect many of the very qualities that have allowed her to succeed in the past: independence, confidence, analytical problem-solving, originality, and experience. This process alone would interest readers who wonder about the inner workings of the monastery and who might be content to read on to see if Philippa and her companion postulants will persevere to Solemn Profession of perpetual vows. Yet such a superficial view of this transformation would be unsatisfying for readers, as it would diminish the psychological development of the characters and superficially reduce nuns to pious figures cloaked in habits of dress and prescribed or stereotyped patterns of behavior. Instead, perhaps the most unpredictable and satisfying religious and literary dimension of *In This House of Brede* is that it is not the story of the protagonist's total negation of self in order to become a nun. Rather, the surprising reversals to and reconnections with Philippa's past that become a part of her new identity as a nun suggest a larger and more realistic view of the spiritual journey toward maturity and integrity in religious life, both for Philippa and for the monastic life represented.

Clearly, Brede Monastery, for all of its enclosure and structure, is not a refuge from life's petty distractions, frustrations, and serious problems. Indeed, it is a place that connects the problems of the world with the grace of God through prayer, the witness of profession, and occasional counsel offered from beyond the grille. Godden's inventive yet realistic presentation of this truth debunks the popular stereotypes of convent life as an easy escape and of the misperceived motivations of those who enter. Philippa Talbot may leave behind the world for the monastery; Sister Philippa, however, must use her vocation to bring help to the world and, at times, help *from* the world *to* the monastery. The community faces crises and challenges throughout the story, and it is often Philippa who engineers the necessary solutions. In living out fully her commitment to God and to the community, she must draw on and use her talents and knowledge from her previous life as the powerful, capable Mrs. Talbot. Indeed, it is significant that unlike most postulants, Philippa does not change her name upon entry into the monastery, for her religious formation and spiritual growth ultimately call her to reclaim her past and to integrate all aspects of her identity in order to live out fully both her life and her religious vocation.

Despite her desire to remove herself from the "pinnacle" of leadership, Philippa cannot escape the part of her nature that allows her to analyze problems and lead others to solutions. In this sense, her vocation as a nun is not simply renouncing pride and embracing obedience but is a delicate process of finding ways to integrate her former life experiences with her vocation so as to meet the challenges before the community. When the troubled Dame Veronica swallows a potentially fatal dosage of medication, it is Philippa who discovers the crisis and subsequently intervenes to save her life. Philippa's demeanor of urgency and her tone of efficient authority in summoning the Abbess are directly described in the narrative as the lingering presence of "the old decisive Mrs. Talbot" (150). When Sister Philippa proposes an unpopular plan to allow portions of the monastery grounds to be sold, she refers directly to her professional experience and convinces the Abbess but then faces harsh opposition from senior sisters who deem her ideas too worldly for the monastery's good. As her frequent critic Sister Agnes complains, "That was Mrs. Talbot speaking, not the Sister Philippa we are hoping and trying to adapt to our ways" (174). Later, Dame Philippa transcends this conflict and uses her former professional contacts to negotiate an academic book contract for Sister Agnes's scholarly work on the Holy Cross imagery (328).

At another point, Philippa counsels Penelope Stevens, the uncertain young married woman who worked in her office as a typist and who later is pressured by her husband to undergo an abortion. Philippa stands up to the husband on his wife's behalf in a conversation that is interrupted by the news that Penny has experienced complications and is gravely ill, a crisis that compels the entire community to pray for her. Later, it is again Dame Philippa who welcomes back the couple, who finally have a baby. It is the former executive and professed nun who both provides career counseling for the unemployed husband ("It seemed odd from behind the grille to show someone how to write an appraisal of a marketing situation" [300]) and prays to the Sacred Heart for the couple's protection. Frequently, Mrs. Talbot's talents become the tools of Dame Philippa's ministry. As McTurk, her former boss and supporter through the transition, reminds her, Philippa must remain essentially herself at her best in this new life of formation: "To deny your gifts would be cheating. We can overcome our second natures, my dear, but not our first, and you were born to responsibility, to lead" (178). While Philippa protests that she seeks the self-effacing, obedient status of a nun, she gradually learns to integrate her talents and religious vocation. Despite tensions, suspicion, and misunderstandings, the community finds room and support for both Sister Philippa and her premonastic experience.

Yet Philippa's spiritual progress also demands confrontation with her past pain and the resolution of personal crisis through monastic bonds and mercy. The major challenges of unresolved grief and the necessity of forgiveness emerge as significant themes within the larger context of her story. Her secret struggle throughout much of the story is her grief and anger that cannot fully be suppressed by her determined resolve, causing the inner pain to surface in troubling flashbacks. Her son's life and accidental death have remained a secret that she has kept even from her religious superiors. The entrance into Brede Monastery of the daughter of the negligent nurse poses a crisis for Philippa, who finds herself unable to welcome the young novice, Sister Polycarp. This crisis is one of the novel's most dramatic reminders that the monastery does not offer an escape from reality. As Philippa's secret memory finally unfolds, her superiors and we the readers learn that the event took place at a time when Philippa worked abroad in the United States. During a stay in California while she was recovering from an illness, her young son was playing with a gold nugget that led him to fall into an abandoned mine, beyond rescue, despite the fact that he was supposed to have been supervised by a nurse. This image comes to epitomize loss in the world, the fragility and transience of earthly life, and the vulnerability of human connections and interdependence that must include mercy.

Having been confronted by her superiors, Dame Philippa still balks at welcoming the negligent nurse's daughter as a sister in religion. Finally, Philippa's illness—a severe bout of chicken pox and influenza—brings about a physical and emotional healing through her enduring the illness alongside Sister Polycarp, who openly expresses her sorrow and regret over the boy's death and finally moves Philippa to accept her and to forgive the nurse and her family. Philippa emerges from the infirmary both humbled and healed. Changed in both the physical and emotional sense, she is finally able to accept both Sister Polycarp and her own past. The illness brings physical renewal that suggests ritualistic acts of purification and rebirth (Philippa has her first full bath in six years, then dons a new habit). Moreover, the emotional detoxification that comes with forgiveness is essential to her integration of her secular past and her religious vocation (280).

The novel's historical elements, directly encompassing the Second Vatican Council and the papacy and death of John XXIII, present the Catholic Church in transition. This period of change touches Brede Monastery not simply through its rare glimpses of television news and official ties to Rome but in the internal state and projected adaptation of the monastery. New issues emerge within Brede's walls regarding traditions set forth by the Benedictine Rule and the spirit of change and revitalization that is circulating throughout the Church. By the novel's end, the nuns of Brede are not yet exiting the religious life, but they do begin to debate seriously and vigorously the manner in which they should remain there. Their habit is slightly updated, but many of the nuns balk at the suggestion that women religious exchange traditional dress for cardigan sweaters and give up the veil for hairdressing that one nun likens to an appearance that is "dowdy and blowsy, like Edwardian nurses" (346). Other complaints arise over the transition from Latin to the vernacular in worship and over the nature of monastic work and the structure of social class within the monastery. The long-standing hierarchical distinctions between choir and claustral nuns are questioned; tradition and learning are upheld but are weighed against a more egalitarian and unified spirit of community. The complexities of these issues are given personal and emotional weight in the dialogue among the novel's diverse characters. In this sense, the novel is of significant historical interest in understanding the immediate challenges and questions posed by Vatican II.

Moreover, multicultural views of both the world and Catholicism emerge in the novel's final movement of Philippa from Brede to Japan. Godden's depictions of Japanese culture and its people are arguably strained with stereotypes and patronizing in comic and awkward attempts at dialogue and characterization. However flawed in this presentation, the novel's inclusion of another culture, the mention of its Catholic history (including the early martyrdom of Japanese Christians), and the suggestion that the Catholic mission might have a positive role in enriching the spiritual qualities of life in Japan's postwar period of economic growth are interesting variations on the traditionally Eurocentric depictions of Christian monastic life. The absence of a genuine awareness of cultural diversity and a lack of sensitivity to other peoples, as well as the failure to pursue interreligious dialogue here, all allude to the historical difficulty and misguided attempts at Catholic missionary connections—a problem for both the novelist and the Church.

In the end, the nuns of Brede Monastery endure, struggle, and grow in their vocations. Whatever larger questions surround them are left alluded to but largely unexplored, including issues regarding the future of the Rule, its reinterpretation, the expanded scope of the order's mission, and the role of women in the Catholic Church. Brede Monastery continues to change those who enter; by the novel's conclusion, the order's conservative elements voice concern that their younger sisters will change Brede's traditions. As the awkward, unabashedly working class yet forthright and faithful Sister Polycarp argues seriously (when, in one of her more comic escapades, she is reprimanded for pulling up her skirts in front of a neighboring farmer while she chases a monastery calf back into its pen), "'Nuns have legs and arms and heads and hearts, and it's time the world knew it'" (262). The Catholic Church and secular society were only beginning to acknowledge the reality of this statement in 1969, the year of the publication of *In This House of Brede*. It could be argued that the reality of Sister Polycarp's statement is still being processed, or even ignored, by both the Catholic Church and mainstream culture. The novel creates a vivid fictional space in which readers not only can peer through the visitors' grille but also engage and observe some of the struggles of women religious as they negotiate the austere beauty and strength of tradition, the uncertain and immediate changes of Vatican II, and the timeless inner struggles of faith, vocation, community, and very human experiences.

CRITICAL RECEPTION

Godden was, in her lifetime, largely regarded as a writer of high-quality popular fiction, and *In This House of Brede* was and is considered one of her major works. Time has not elevated her books to the status of major literary classics, but a work such as *In This House of Brede* does continue to interest and engage a wide readership. Reviews from major periodicals at the time of the novel's publication reflect that period's cultural ambivalence regarding organized religion, its traditions, and the often limited roles it had allotted to women. Subsequent critical attention in both literary and religious circles, while limited, reveals more appreciation for the narrative complexity and spiritual significance of the novel as well as for the importance of Rumer Godden as an original voice in literature.

The critical reception of the novel at the time of its release was lukewarm in both secular and Catholic publications. The novel's most serious flaw, in the opinion of several critics, is its failure to develop the depth, passion, and high art required for the kind of religious story that Godden seems to be attempting. "To state it baldly, this is not a religious novel, though intended to be," contends Millicent Bell in *The New York Times Book Review* (1969, 5). Bell argues that the novel's lack of "spiritual struggle" (5) and its failure to explore "sin and redemption" make it less religiously significant than more artful works with secular settings (34).

Likewise, some critics find the novel's religious nature to be greatly diminished by perceptions of Godden's workmanlike handling of several key elements: the timely miracles that too mechanically resolve the plot complications of monastic crises; the characterization and psychological development of the nuns; and the overall representation of the monastery as a spiritual place. Bell finds the resolution of the monastery's financial crisis through the discovery of the ruby within the cross to be a cheap literary trick that diminishes the event's religiosity. This convenient development she dismisses as "a denouement which will not seem fortuitous only to the most naive piety" (34). In this view, the intellectual and artistic challenge of presenting and accepting the workings of providence becomes one of emotional and spiritual complexity, and Bell finds such complexity lacking in Godden. Bell acknowledges the mysterious maneuverings of God, but she does not witness in Godden's novel the "full participation of the suffering, striving, human spirit" that she believes essential for convincing literature about religious growth and transformation (34).

In his review in *America*, Jerome M. Vereb regards the novel more favorably but voices similar complaints regarding the forced workings of plot and the lack of emotional depth. Godden's representations of divine providence, he contends, are "sometimes facile" in ways that make them unconvincing and emotionally flat. He also views the novel's characterization as often strained and underdeveloped (1969, 274).

The novel's representation of the cloister also fails to satisfy some critics. A *New Yorker* critic likens Godden's Brede Monastery to a "fastidious, womanly boarding school" and claims that the novel's setting lacks the development and the essential character of a convent in its social and spiritual integrity (1969, 178). Vereb upholds the fundamental authenticity of Godden's representation of Benedictine monastic life but finds the overall spirit of Brede limited and remote (1969, 274).

Significantly, critical views from the perspective of Catholic women religious offer more positive views of Godden's Brede Monastery. Sister Mary Catherine Vukmanic, O. S. U., writes, "Rumer Godden has caught in her novel the rich echoes of this life," referring to the fullness of life that can be experienced in monastic tradition (1970, 334). Vukmanic identifies as a possible weakness the novel's "too labored effort at verisimilitude" so that it becomes perhaps less an accurate depiction of the monastic life than "its apologetic" (334). Sister Catherine Wybourne, O. S. B., notes that Godden researched monastic life thoroughly and drew extensively on her firsthand knowledge of the 1960s era of Stanbrook Abbey, and *In This House of Brede* received the blessing of Stanbrook's Abbess in 1968 (2002, 94).

Over the long term, literary criticism of a more scholarly nature has also offered a richer view of the overall spiritual and psychological depth and artfulness of *In This House of Brede*. Referring specifically to this novel as an extraordinary literary achievement of inventive style, Hassell A. Simpson discusses Godden's complex narrative voice that often blends temporal perspective in a way that he terms "the technique of near-omniscience" (1973, 121) through which past, present, and future merge in the representations of consciousness. Simpson praises the novel's "convincing immediacy and the sense of great richness in detail, of total immersion in the fictive experience" that make the temporal complexity all the more remarkable (122). He likens its effect to that of Virginia Woolf's *Mrs. Dalloway* and notes that, while Godden has been influenced by Woolf, James Joyce, and Marcel Proust, she is an original and successful stylist in her own right. Overall, Simpson lauds the effectiveness of Godden's narrative style, calling *In This House of Brede* "a compelling and original novel" (122). Moreover, Simpson praises the novel's success in avoiding some significant flaws to which literary works that attempt religious themes are vulnerable: "preachiness" and "false piety" (114).

Thematic representations of motherhood, child mortality, and religious recon-figuration of both mother and child emerge in Lynne M. Rosenthal's discussion of the novel. Noting that the name "Brede" can mean "childbearing," Rosenthal cogently argues that, however removed from the monastic life children and moth-erhood might appear, the loss of a child is central to Philippa's story (1996, 85–86). The central image of the golden nugget, pursued by the child, is interpreted by Rosenthal as the love of mother and child (86). This bond, Rosenthal suggests, is one that Philippa will learn to confront as loss so that "she will ultimately transform into love of the Mother Church, where she will find her true home and restored childhood" (86). Such a reading certainly argues for the deeply realized psychological and spiritual development of the novel's protagonist, the inclusion of suffering and grace in its plot development, and the spiritual richness of the monastic experience—all of which arguably counter the earlier complaints of other critics.

NOTE

Rumer Godden, *In This House of Brede* (London: Macmillan, 1969; New York: Viking, 1969). All references are to this edition.

WORKS CITED

Bell, Millicent. 1969. Review of *In This House of Brede*, by Rumer Godden. *New York Times Book Review* (September 27): 4–5, 34–35.

"Books Briefly Noted." *New Yorker* 45 (November 1, 1969): 178.

Godden, Rumer. 1939. *Black Narcissus*. London: Peter Davies; Boston: Little, Brown.

———. 1979. *Five for Sorrow; Ten for Joy*. London: Macmillan; New York: Viking.

———. 1987. *A Time to Dance, No Time to Weep*. London: Macmillan; New York: William Morrow.

Rosenthal, Lynne M. 1996. *Rumer Godden Revisited*. New York: Twayne.

Simpson, Hassell A. 1973. *Rumer Godden*. New York: Twayne.

Vereb, Jerome M. 1969. Review of *In This House of Brede* by Rumer Godden. *America* 121 (October 4): 274.

Vukmanic, Sister Mary Catherine, O. S. U. 1970. Review of *In This House of Brede*, by Rumer Godden. *Review for Religious* 29: 334.

Wybourne, Catherine, O. S. B. 2002. "Rumer Godden: Oblate Novelist." In *Benedict in the World: Portraits of Monastic Oblates*, ed. Linda Kultzer, O. S. B., and Roberta Bondi, 87–95. Collegeville, MN: Liturgical Press.

— Victoria Carlson-Casaregola

Caroline Gordon [1895–1981]

The Malefactors

BIOGRAPHY

Caroline Ferguson Gordon was born on October 6, 1895, at Merry Mont in Todd County, Kentucky, the home of her maternal grandmother, Caroline Ferguson Meriwether, after whom she was named. She was the second of three children and the only daughter of Nancy Minor Meriwether and James Morris Gordon. The Meriwether family and its "connections" typified the patrician southern planter society fallen on hard times in the decades following the Civil War. Short on cash but long on pride, short on men but long on indomitable women bent on survival and the perpetuation of memories they considered sacred, her family welcomed "Little Miss Carrie" into a world of material deprivation exacerbated by the recent memory of prosperity and influence, but also into a world abundant in stories, food for a fertile imagination. Throughout her writing career, Gordon's fiction would be enriched by recollections of "the old neighborhood," despite the fact that she left the South while still in her twenties, returning only sporadically.

Gordon received a degree of education unusual for a young woman of her time and circumstances. Her parents ran a classics school for young men during her childhood, and she attended classes there, revealing a gift for reading Latin and Greek at an early age. She attended Bethany College near Wheeling, West Virginia, receiving a bachelor's degree in classical studies in June 1916. After the Armistice and an unsuccessful attempt at teaching high school, Gordon again broke with convention, moved away from home to live with a relative, and began a career as a newspaper journalist. A prolific reviewer of books, especially books by southern writers, Gordon reviewed an early issue of *The Fugitive*, a literary journal published by a group of Vanderbilt University students in the early 1920s. Shortly thereafter, she met and fell in love with one of the Fugitive poets, Allen Tate. When Tate left Nashville to seek his fortune as a writer in New York in 1924, Gordon did the same. They were married in 1925, and their only child, Nancy, was born in September of that year.

Gordon and Tate lived the life of starving artists in New York among a number of young authors who would attain fame as the leading writers of the day. From

1928 to 1929 they lived in Paris on Tate's Guggenheim Fellowship. During that time, Gordon became the secretary for a well-known English writer, Ford Madox Ford, grandson of the Pre-Raphaelite painter, Ford Madox Brown. While his estimation of his own literary reputation may have exceeded that of his contemporaries, Ford was, for Gordon, a link to those writers on whose work she modeled her own early fiction, for he had personally known the great writers of the previous generation, such as Henry James, James Joyce, and George Bernard Shaw. Ford was instrumental in helping Gordon publish her first fiction; she remained deeply indebted to him throughout her writing life.

Gordon and her family returned to the United States in the winter of 1929. If they had been unable to make a comfortable living in New York in the 1920s, they were even less comfortable in the early days of the Great Depression. In 1930 they returned to the South and, with financial help from her brother-in-law, they purchased a rundown house on the banks of the Cumberland River near Clarksville, Tennessee. Although they retained ownership of the house for several years, they did not actually stay in it for long, returning to Paris in 1932, this time on Gordon's Guggenheim Fellowship. While they were in residence at Benfolly, however, their home became the center of an energetic community of writers or, put another way, an endless stream of houseguests. Gordon experienced a constant state of anxiety during this time. She had published her first stories and her first novel, to critical if not popular acclaim, and she struggled to find the time to write while responding to the obligations she felt as host, spouse, and parent. The stress took a deep psychological toll on Gordon and her marriage. She and Tate divorced in 1946 after years of vehement and explosive emotional discord. They remarried less than a year later, demonstrating a deeply rooted, perhaps irrational, passion for one another that drew them together even as it made their mutual life impossible.

Although the struggle continued for decades, Gordon ultimately produced nine novels and three volumes of short stories. She did not attain the degree of recognition or popularity achieved by several writers close to her who, indeed, benefited substantially from her editing and advice, including Katherine Anne Porter, Flannery O'Connor, and Walker Percy. In 1947, at the age of fifty-two, Gordon took a stance that would put her further at odds with popular opinion. Already facing the endemic discrimination against women in intellectual and academic circles, she placed herself squarely in the path of that other largely unexamined yet socially acceptable prejudice among intellectuals: Gordon became a Roman Catholic. Tate followed her three years later. They were among a host of poets and writers who did the same, most notably Gordon's friend from their early days in New York, Dorothy Day, Thomas Merton, Katherine Anne Porter, Robert Lowell, and others. Her already small readership continued to dwindle, but her commitment to the craft of fiction did not. In fact, she considered her conversion and subsequent consideration of spiritual themes in her writing a logical extension of the imaginative journey she had been on since the beginning of her writing career. She expressed it aphoristically by saying, "My stories are all one story," and for her the one story was the "primal plot" of human redemption.

In 1954, Gordon and Tate were living in Rome on a Fulbright grant. Their marriage was unraveling, accelerated by their excessive drinking. Gordon was working on the manuscript of her eighth and penultimate novel, *The Malefactors*.

She began seeing a Jungian psychoanalyst, under whose direction she recalled and explicated her dreams and examined deeply ingrained patterns of self-destructive behavior. This total immersion in Jungian thought, especially the concepts of the collective unconscious and archetypes, profoundly affected Gordon's fiction. In *The Malefactors*, the three major tendencies of her literary imagination converged: her own history, her act of faith in Christianity, and her understanding of the "underground stream" of consciousness that unified all three. The novel, published in 1956, represented for her the culmination of a lifetime of work. She felt that she had dropped her most valuable possession down a well when the novel was essentially ignored.

Although Gordon would always consider Princeton home, since she owned property there and her daughter and son-in-law, Nancy and Percy Wood, and grandchildren lived there, she spent most of the 1960s and 1970s in various visiting writing professorships across the country. Her wandering ended at the University of Dallas, where she taught creative writing until her health failed. In 1978 she joined the Woods in San Cristóbal de las Casas, Chiapas, Mexico, where they had retired to run a guesthouse. Gordon died on April 11, 1981, and was buried in Mexico.

PLOT SUMMARY

The Malefactors begins with a country fête in honor of a prize-winning, pure-bred, Red Poll bull. The animal is owned by Vera Claiborne, a wealthy, middle-aged woman married to Thomas Claiborne, a well-known poet whose creative powers appear to have evaporated in the luxurious idleness of their Bucks County estate. The fête reunites the Claibornes with other local inhabitants of the neighborhood and with a number of people from their pasts who come as houseguests. This group includes several old friends from their newlywed days in Lost Generation Paris and some distant relatives. Nostalgia drives the conversations as old acquaintances are renewed, but memories also shed a harsh light on the unhappiness the couple feels beneath the veneer of genteel contentment they project to their guests.

Among the house party guests is Jungian psychoanalyst George Crenfew, a distant cousin of Tom's; they grew up together in rural Tennessee. In their youthful days in Paris, George had been married to Catherine Pollard, who is also in attendance. After Catherine left George in Paris, she underwent a religious conversion to Roman Catholicism. She is well known for her faith-based outreach to the destitute of the Bowery of New York. In the opening pages of the novel, Tom meets the train of yet another guest, Cynthia Vail, a younger, distant cousin of Vera's who has recently separated from her husband, a college professor at a small school in the Midwest.

In the days following the fête, Tom and Cynthia initiate an affair. Soon thereafter, he leaves Vera and moves into a Manhattan flat with Cynthia. For a time his long writer's block disappears: he calls in favors from friends and is able to reestablish himself as a magazine editor. Eventually, Vera confronts the couple, after which she takes up temporary residence at a communal farm in upstate New York run by Catherine Pollard's charitable organization. Soon thereafter, Tom terminates the affair with Cynthia and, as his life seems to spin out of control, he consults George, more in his capacity as a therapist than as a family member. At the novel's conclusion, Tom follows Vera to the farm, where she rebuffs his attempt to reconcile. Furious, he leaves and, while driving, undergoes an intense psychological episode. As a result, he returns to the farm to wait for the morning and another opportunity to speak with Vera.

For all the simplicity of the literal action, the real plot of the novel is the movement of Tom's consciousness. Already in a state of spiritual malaise, Tom undergoes a complete psychological breakdown that is well under way when the novel begins. The narration of Tom's consciousness is frequently interrupted by seemingly random memories and, as his condition deteriorates, by hallucinations. Because Gordon situates the narrating voice within Tom's consciousness, it is sometimes difficult for the reader to distinguish between Tom's present experiences and his imagined or remembered experiences. Gordon crafts this extremely complex narrative with deliberation and skill, portraying consciousness as a realm in which the phenomena of sensory input, memory, and imagination coexist free of temporal boundaries.

At the climax of the novel, Tom sees with new eyes, which precipitates a reversal of the disposition of his consciousness. As the novel concludes—to paraphrase—he firmly resolves to amend his life.

MAJOR THEMES

Examining *The Malefactors* in the context of Gordon's work as a whole reveals it to be less anomalous than it first appeared. The novel continues themes present in Gordon's fiction from the very beginning, most notably the heroic tradition. The heroes of her novels evolve from men of action drawn from tragic paradigms to men of letters whose heroic combat is internal. Concomitantly, her paradigm for heroic action evolves from one of classical tragedy to one of Christian comedy, specifically, to that of Dante's *Commedia*. Within that context, *The Malefactors* employs a uniquely western mode of the imagination, variously called sacramental or figural. It has as its paradigm the Incarnation and the memorial act that makes present the reality of Christ in the Eucharist.

In this mode, figures of the fiction, quite autonomous in themselves, manifest another intangible reality and meaning. This meaning is conveyed in a network of resemblances that are recollected when a figure assumes a stance or performs an action that calls to mind similar actions. In Jungian terminology, such an action is called archetypal because it ultimately refers to basic human actions or patterns of behavior that seem to be common and unchanging. The activity of memory is inseparable from this embodiment of meaning, since it is by the perception of the resemblances that an illumination of the archetypal reality occurs. This process dissolves the temporal boundaries between past and present and between present and future. Understood in this way, memory allows for an intimacy in all levels of reality or a permeability of being by an unchanging, timeless meaning. Writing before the explosion of postmodern scholarship in the poetics of autobiography or the deconstruction of consciousness in fiction, Gordon plundered the texts she knew for technical models to accomplish this difficult task. She turned to the works of Augustine, Dante, and Catherine of Siena for thematic paradigms and for technical precedents.

From Augustine's *Confessions*, Gordon derived her understanding of memory as creative consciousness, as a realm in which both the past and the future are made present. For Augustine, the plot of grace at work in the human soul is revealed in memory: a way of seeing not only the past as coincident with the present but also the future—*telos*—implicit in the past and therefore the present as well. This understanding allows for the permeation of intangible reality—grace—into every level of human experience. Augustine's *Confessions* is a work of poetic imagination, with memory providing its imaginative form. The narration progresses in the classical dramatic fashion articulated by Aristotle, containing complication, resolution, peripety, and recognition. From the perspective of memory, Augustine can see and recount the working out of a divine plan in his own life as well as in the lives of those who touched him. The central act of his coming to belief in the Gospel lends a form, a plot line, to recollections that might otherwise seem unrelated or haphazard.

But Augustine has done more than write his memoirs or an autobiography. He has also recorded the action of grace in his life. From the vantage of enlightened memory he sees grace shaping his life from the beginning, at times when he could not possibly experience its influence directly. Romano Guardini calls this the "retaining of corporeal things in an incorporeal manner" that invoke the idea of sleep and the "wakability" of memories (1966, 11). Equating memory with "creative consciousness" (11), Guardini refers to memories as more permanent and more accessible to the mind than the outer realm of merely existing objects. Persons and objects in the outer realm become more or less significant as they are perceived to be more or less instrumental in shaping the interior drama of the self actively confronting the self (27). This explains Augustine's selective memory and reinforces the suggestion that his narrative was shaped along classical lines for unity of plot. It also elucidates the paradigm for Gordon's fictional technique.

Dante's *Commedia* also exemplifies this concept in the metaphor of the interior journey—the movement of the soul by the power of grace. The dissolution of the barriers of time results in what has been called a figural mode of imagination that gives an imperfect glimpse of "God's point of view." In such a view the figure and its fulfillment—its fullness of meaning—may be seen as one. As a result, all realms of existence may be consecrated to symbolic purpose, for in the imagination all existence can be a bearer of meaning, a metaphor for divine love. And, as love is known in the totality of human experience, the acquisition of meaning in this figural method occurs on a radically personal plane, a level at which intangible reality is known so intimately that it has tangible effects.

Gordon crafted such figures of meaning out of a diversity of human experience. Her characters symbolize an insubstantial reality without losing their human qualities. That symbolic meanings could be embodied in a living person as well as an imagined one is accidental but consistent with her understanding of the figural imagination. Consequently, Gordon felt free, as Dante was free, to blend knowledge and lore of various types that convey the meaning she intended. Obscure saints' legends, Jungian psychological archetypes, her personal friends—all these may and do become figures of meaning in the poetic process and coexist in the realm of imagination. Gordon also saw in the *Commedia* the same selectivity of memory that Augustine employed in pruning the final shape of the narrative.

Contemporary readers of the novel who mistook the depiction of characters who resembled existing persons of Gordon's acquaintance for *roman à clef* failed to see the archetypal reality figured in characters who outwardly resemble Dorothy Day, Hart Crane, Allen Tate, and others.

In 1947, Gordon converted to Roman Catholicism. During the 1940s, her reading interest had focused on medieval studies; she was reading Dante and medieval poetics and commentary. It was no surprise, then, that her newfound faith led her to examine medieval Christian writings in addition to secular ones. Her study of the writings of medieval Christian female mystical writers profoundly altered the form of her subsequent imaginative writings. This change is first seen in *The Malefactors*, in which her obviously close study of the life and work of the late medieval Christian mystic, Saint Catherine of Siena, is clear.

In her characteristically straightforward prose, Gordon explores the anything-but-straightforward interior life of the novel's protagonist, Tom Claiborne. Clear and active memory is never far beneath the surface of Tom's consciousness, and because he is psychologically maladjusted and frequently intoxicated, it often intrudes into his consciousness. The intimacy of experience is played out in the realm of Tom's unconscious experience, however. Tom recurrently dreams of being plunged, helpless, into a river and of leaving the river to enter a series of caves where several figures out of his past appear: his father, his father-in-law, his first "literary" friend, and others. The dream recalls the archetypal *katabasis*, the descent into the underworld, presented as typically heroic. It is also the Jungian stream of consciousness. These two senses of the primordial water symbol converge with the river of death, which may be avoided by traveling on the bridge of eternal life—itself a metaphor for Christ—found in the writings of Saint Catherine of Siena. This specifically Christian level of meaning functions in two ways. First, it places the heroic action in a moral context, placing the soul at stake with a heroic confrontation with death. Second, and more significantly, it forms the bridge between the mythic and Christian modes of imagination by showing that, as the archetypal actions are repeated, levels of meaning incrementally and cumulatively accrue to them and are all contained in the present action.

Saint Catherine of Siena is introduced early in the novel by the character that bears her name, Catherine Pollard. The presence of Saint Catherine in *The Malefactors* is twofold: first, her remarkable life is echoed in Catherine Pollard's; second, and most significant, the controlling metaphor of her major work, the *Dialogue*, forms the structure of Tom Claiborne's interior journey. Claiborne is a writer with southern roots, living off his wife Vera's inheritance in prosperous but paralyzing luxury in Bucks County. He initiates a marriage-shattering affair with her cousin in a vain attempt to break through a complete writer's block. Catherine Pollard is an acquaintance from Tom and Vera's early days as newlyweds in Paris. She had been married briefly to Tom's cousin but has since become a Roman Catholic and an outspoken social activist. On a literal level, the character of Catherine Pollard resembles Dorothy Day, but her outspoken nonconformity coupled with passionate religious fervor is reminiscent of her namesake saint as well. Both these persons are figured in Catherine Pollard; they become presences in the imaginative field of the novel. Ultimately, Gordon presents Catherine Pollard in an even more cumulative posture, when, at the climax of the novel, she appears in

Tom's dream as an archetype of the primordial feminine, providing the anchor to which the drifting soul clings and embodying the femininity of earth itself.

In the *Dialogue*, the river of death runs beneath the bridge of salvation, which Saint Catherine allegorically describes as the body of Christ. The figurative connection between body and stone is the first of the essential imaginative connections that Gordon makes. Saint Catherine's phenomenological rendering of the experience of a drowning soul is subtle and sophisticated:

> But those who do not keep to this way travel below through the river—a way not of stones but of water. And since there is no restraining the water, no one can cross through it without drowning.

> Such are the pleasures and conditions of the world. Those whose love and desire are not grounded on the rock but are set without order on created persons and things apart from me [Christ] (and these, like water, are continually running on) run on just as they do. Though it seems to them that it is the created things they love that are running on by while they themselves remain firm, they are in fact continually running on to their end in death. (1980, 67)

Gordon echoes Saint Catherine's depiction of the phenomenon of being buoyed along by a current, making figures on the bank appear to be moving to the person in the water, when Tom's recurrent dream of being submersed in a river is recounted for the first time:

> A man and a river. A river broader than the Amazon. . . . Sometimes the man stood on the bank, with another person—was it a woman?—beside him. But oftenest he moved with the current, riding sometimes in a boat, or plunged deep in the waves. . . . The current flowed smoothly. The man seemed at one with its movement until a certain moment when another current flowing into the stream enveloped his moving limbs with waves so soft, so arresting, that he stayed his course and, looking off over the broad, rippling expanse, saw on the bank (in the dream it was always the left bank) the cavern yawning. The dream always ended with that moment. He . . . had known it only as a place that would welcome him, that yawned for him if he ever left the main stream and swam toward it. (*Malefactors*, 134)

In these dream sequences, Tom encounters several "figures" from his past moving by him. The most important of these is Horne Watts, a homosexual, alcoholic poet who committed suicide by drowning. The allusion to Hart Crane is self-evident, but the allusions to Saint Catherine's bridge and river metaphor are more relevant. Madness, drunkenness, and flight are the consistent images associated with Horne Watts. His great work, which consumed his consciousness, was the poem "Pontifex." He thought of himself as the bridge builder, constructing the way to transcendence from his own imagination. He could not sustain the image; his creative powers failed him and, in despair, he abandoned life by committing suicide. It is not until Horne's life is a memory in Tom's consciousness that its full meaning is revealed. In Tom's dream, Horne rips off his head and plunges into an abyss, trying to lure Tom into the same action. Finally, he does lead Tom out of the river and onto the solid ground. Horne saves

Tom from his own fate by showing him that the right road is found not with one's own powers but by surrendering to a transcendent power that manifests itself as feminine.

In the climactic dream sequence, after tearing off his head—a symbol of hubristic Gnosticism and Faustian imaginative power—Horne moves, bringing Tom with him, out of the water to a cave on the opposite bank:

> There was somebody in the cave beside him, somebody who was leaning over to lay a hand on his shoulder, to whisper in his ear. "Yes," he said, and got up and walked with his guide over the chill, dry dust to the bank of the stream, and slipped into the current and, his guide still beside him, swam until they came in sight of the other cave on the far bank. . . . It was larger than the cave they had quitted. . . . The large column in the middle of the cave was not a stalagmite in the form of a kneeling woman. It was a woman, who, still kneeling, turned her head to look at him. "What is it?" he said. "What is it Horne? What does she want with me?" Horne only pressed his shoulder, smiling, and pointing to the woman. (310)

The stalagmitic shape of the woman-stone suggests the stone steps of Saint Catherine's bridge. When waking from the dream, Tom will recognize the woman-stone as Catherine Pollard. When he goes to her, Catherine puts Tom on the road to the truth—that is, to Vera, his wife.

For Gordon, subject matter and method merge at this point. Tom comes to a point of crisis and illumination by seeing that his life resembles all life and that all life is ordered by a pervasive, shaping force. The author adds Tom Claiborne and the other characters of the novel to the network of resemblances so that readers of the novel draw the same conclusion. But Gordon has done more than that by extending the bridge of resemblances a step further. Bearing resemblances not only to archetypal paradigms but also to real, living persons, Tom Claiborne, Catherine Pollard, and Horne Watts incarnate a radical personalization of meaning; they present the understanding of human life itself as metaphor, as bearer of substantial, intangible meaning. To perceive the resemblances to the past, to other imaginative creations, and to a specific human life, and to acknowledge the con-naturality of that life with one's own, is to apprehend Gordon's ambitious fictional project. In the end, Gordon aimed for the same effect as the medieval writers, both sacred and secular, whose works she studied: to render invisible the barrier between immanent and transcendent realms of being and to portray their interaction. It prepares for, although it may not precipitate, an Augustinian "*Tolle, lege*" experience.

In the epigram of *The Malefactors*, Gordon quotes Jacques Maritain: "It is for Adam to interpret the voices that Eve hears." Recent readers of Gordon's work tend to read this as emblematic of her subjection to a patriarchal social system that stifled her talent, as if to say that Eve lacks the higher thinking skills possessed by Adam. Closer reading of the work bespeaks the opposite meaning. Eve directly accesses supernatural reality; she is a mystic. Consequently, she possesses the prescience, insight, and wisdom that Adam lacks and must acquire and parse. The contemporary term would be to "deconstruct." The broad tropes of Gordon's later fiction indicate that Adam fails to do this at his peril. While it would be fair to say that *The Malefactors* sounds a hortatory note, in Gordon's later fiction the tone evolves from cautionary to celebratory. The hero moves bravely into perilous circumstances from which the lady saves him.

Caroline Gordon's published fiction subsequent to *The Malefactors* continues to elaborate this theme. The association of the mystical image of the bridge with the Joycean stream-of-consciousness portrait of the interior life of a modern artist typifies the ingenuity and risk-taking of a writer at the height of her imaginative powers. Until the end of her life in 1981, Gordon would continue to draw lessons in narrative technique from medieval Christian female mystics, especially Julian of Norwich, whose *Showings* Gordon assiduously studied, developing an identifiably feminine narrating consciousness. In doing so she moves beyond what she herself acknowledged as the masculine, effaced narrative technique learned from Flaubert, James, and Joyce that she employed in her early fiction.

In Gordon's fiction and in her writing life, mysticism is the bridge to a significantly more profound awareness of the role of the feminine in the communication of transcendent reality. In the climactic vision of the woman-stone in *The Malefactors*, Gordon first reveals the theme that dominates her final writings: she identifies the salvific stone, the alternative to "death by water" that Saint Catherine depicts as Christ, with a woman, thereby symbolically identifying the Mystical Body of Christ as female, as does Julian in the most profound and mysterious of her showings. Incipient in this idea is the theme that Gordon expanded in her next and final novel, *The Glory of Hera* (1972): the hero in perilous circumstances is saved through the efficacy of women, rather than vice versa. *The Glory of Hera* is a dramatic presentation of the archetypal pattern Gordon perceives at the heart of western culture—the Heracles myth. This final novel, several excerpts of which were published before her death, is a further specification of the human metaphor. In this fiction, Gordon offers the totality of her own life as the known term of the metaphor in which meaning is grounded and may be apprehended.

CRITICAL RECEPTION

The Malefactors was the second novel Gordon published after her conversion to Catholicism. Although *The Strange Children* (1951) and some of her short fiction made use of some knowledge of the lore of the Church, never before had her works held orthodoxy so close to the heart of the matter. For many, even among her Catholic reviewers, this commitment was seen as detrimental to her otherwise nearly faultless craftsmanship. In a review of *The Malefactors*, Leonard Downs wrote, "Behind all this, almost from the very beginning, stands the Church and the faith . . . and one always knows it is the Church that will win in the end" (1956, 47). It is true that the Church plays an extremely important role in the enveloping action of the novel, but simply to posit that it "will win in the end" is a gross oversimplification.

Other writers were equally vague in their perceptions of the novel. The *Kirkus* review of January 16, 1956, called it "bewildering" (16); and the *New Yorker* of March 17, 1956, speculated that Gordon had written a satire (180). Another Catholic reviewer, Laverne Gay, writing for *Books on Trial*, could not accurately recount the main events of the plot (1956, 286).

Willard Thorp's review of *The Malefactors* in the *New Republic* was an exception to the widespread misreading. Along with a helpful key in understanding the oblique action of the novel, he offered this honest praise: "By those who care about the craft of fiction, *The Malefactors* will be judged the finest of Miss Gordon's novels, if not her most ingratiating. Because of its nearly flawless construction it will probably be taught as a model of craftsmanship before it goes into a second printing" (1956, 21). It has never reached a second printing.

Another exceptional contemporary review of the book appeared in *Commonweal*. There, Father John Simons provided as clear and precise an explication of *The Malefactors* as could be wished. He articulates a theme that is crucial to an accurate reading of the novel: "From the point of view of art . . . what matters is less what happens than the strategy by which it is accomplished— the power of poetry by which the originating vision is sustained and subdued, and through which the reader is compelled to a clear eyed acquiescence" (1956, 54).

Vivienne Koch presented another serious contemporary view. She complimented "the handling of intellectual themes through the method of symbolic naturalism" (1956, 646), pointing to this as clearly distinct from "the drab, humorless and methodical exposés of husbands, lovers, and party politics or academia, which some American lady writers have mistaken for fiction" (646). She acutely delineates the dynamically charged interplay between the psychic and spiritual forces unleashed under the polished smooth surface of the book. The review concludes with praise for the very thing the majority of reviewers condemned—the portrayal of spiritual conversion—by saying, "To make experience that is remote to most of us viable, concrete and valid, by feeling and by art, is a good and rare thing to do" (651).

Ashley Brown's "The Novel as Christian Comedy" remains the most important critical work on *The Malefactors* to date. A lengthy comparison of *The Malefactors* and Dante's *Commedia*, it is the cornerstone on which all criticism of the novel must build. Brown notes that *The Malefactors* was originally subtitled "a Comedy" (1964, 162), making Gordon's indebtedness to Dante beyond question. He points out that *The Malefactors* can be seen in juxtaposition to the *Purgatorio*, which explores the psyche in terms of its earthly existence:

> During the course of the novel the protagonist undergoes a spiritual experience like that of Dante in the *Purgatorio*: his state of mind allows him to reach far into the past to reconstruct the events which have brought him to his present condition, and at the end he has a vision which anticipates the *Paradiso Terrestre* [the Earthly Paradise]. To put it another way, there is a condensation of past, present, and even future into one continuum. And this is made possible only by novelistic means. (163)

While Brown's point-for-point association of characters in *The Malefactors* with figures from the *Purgatorio* is oversimplified and not completely accurate, he is nonetheless correct in saying, "It is evident that Miss Gordon has attempted something almost unprecedented in modern fiction: she has made the dead characters as important as the living" (168).

That Gordon dealt frankly in *The Malefactors* with material considered highly controversial for any writer, much less a Catholic writer in the 1950s, went inexplicably without comment among the contemporary reviewers. The novel portrays an openly gay man very sympathetically and depicts occult activities that border on the Satanic. While Dorothy Day objected strenuously to these depictions, especially to the inference that the character based on her was involved in them (leading Gordon to make some revisions to the manuscript before it went to press), there was no mention among any of the Catholic commentators of either of these aspects of the novel. Gordon's satiric and hilarious portrayals of Freudian psychotherapy and of what is now known as biotechnology were likewise scarcely acknowledged.

The general critical neglect of Gordon's work was interrupted briefly in 1971 and 1972 pursuant to the publication of her last novel, *The Glory of Hera*. The most significant contribution was Brainard Cheney's "Caroline Gordon's *The Malefactors*" (1971). A kind of apologia for the book, it reviewed the extant criticism of the novel thoroughly and gave a fine explication. With that, the last word on *The Malefactors* appeared in print until "*The Malefactors*: Caroline Gordon's Redemptive Vision," by John Desmond in late 1982.

During the late 1980s and 1990s, Gordon attracted the attention of feminist scholars, becoming the subject of three "literary biographies" of the type that have come to be associated with revisionist cultural studies. Each of these books focuses on the vicissitudes of Gordon's personal and professional life and undervalues her artistic achievements. Her conversion to Catholicism is dismissed as the *coup de grace* to what might have been a successful career. Her fiction, especially her later work, receives cursory, simplistic, and often inaccurate readings. *The Underground Stream: The Life and Art of Caroline Gordon*, by Nancylee Novell Jonza (1995), is the best of these. I published a detailed study of the influence of mystical writing on Gordon's later fiction, entitled "Hera Consciousness: Narrating Strategies in Caroline Gordon's Later Fiction" (Henderson, 1998). In 2002, Anne M. Boyle published *Strange and Lurid Bloom: A Study of the Fiction of Caroline Gordon*, only the second book-length study of Gordon's fiction.

NOTE

Caroline Gordon, *The Malefactors* (New York: Harcourt, Brace, 1956). All references are to this edition.

WORKS CITED

Anonymous review of *The Malefactors* by Caroline Gordon. 1956. *Kirkus* 24 (2) (15 January): 16.

Anonymous review of *The Malefactors* by Caroline Gordon. 1956. *New Yorker* 32 (4) (17 March): 180.

Boyle, Anne M. 2002. *Strange and Lurid Bloom: A Study of the Fiction of Caroline Gordon*. Madison, NJ: Fairleigh Dickenson University Press.

Brown, Ashley. 1964. "The Novel as Christian Comedy." In *Reality and Myth: Essays in American Literature in Memory of Richmond Croom Beatty*, ed. William E. Welker and Robert L. Walker, 161–78. Nashville: Vanderbilt University Press.

Catherine of Siena. 1980. *The Dialogue*, trans. Suzanne Noffke, O. P. New York: Paulist Press.

Cheney, Brainard. 1971. "Caroline Gordon's *The Malefactors*." *Sewanee Review* 74 (Summer): 360–73. Reprinted, 1971, in *Rediscoveries*, ed. David Madden, 232–44. New York: Crown.

Desmond. John. 1982. "*The Malefactors*: Caroline Gordon's Redemptive Vision." *Renascence* 35: 17–38.

Downs, Leonard. 1956. Review of *The Malefactors*, by Caroline Gordon. *Jubilee* 4, no. 1 (May): 47–48.

Gay, Laverne. 1956. Review of *The Malefactors*, by Caroline Gordon. *Books on Trial* 14, no. 6 (March): 286.

Guardini, Romano. 1966. *The Conversion of Augustine*, trans. Elinor Briefs. Chicago: Henry Regnery.

Henderson, Kathleen Burk. 1998. "Hera Consciousness: Narrating Strategies in Caroline Gordon's Later Fiction." *Logos: A Journal of Catholic Thought and Culture* 1, no. 4 (Fall): 104–44.

Jonza, Nancylee Novell. 1995. *The Underground Stream: The Life and Art of Caroline Gordon*. Athens: University of Georgia Press.

Koch, Vivienne. 1956. "Companions in the Blood." *Sewanee Review* 64 (Autumn): 645–51.

Simons, John W. 1956. "A Cunning and Curious Dramatization." *Commonweal* 64, no. 2 (April 16): 54–56.

Thorp, Willard. 1956. "The Redemption of the Wicked." *New Republic* 134, no. 8 (April 30): 21.

— **Kathleen Burk**

Mary Gordon [1949–]

Final Payments

BIOGRAPHY

Mary Catherine Gordon, born in Far Rockaway, on New York's Long Island, in 1949, is the daughter of a Jewish immigrant, David Gordon, and a woman of Italian-Irish descent, Anna Gagliano. She grew up in Valley Stream, a working-class, Irish Catholic neighborhood. Her father, who had converted from Judaism to orthodox Catholicism before she was born, instilled in Mary a devotion to both Catholicism and intellectualism, introducing his daughter to Latin, Greek, and world literature. Despite the effects of polio, Anna worked outside the home while David stayed home with Mary, during which time he founded and wrote for a number of right-wing Catholic magazines before he died in 1957, when Mary was seven. In her memoir of her father, *The Shadow Man* (1966), Gordon details the painful search for her father's true history amidst the lies he told her and the discovery that he did not graduate from Harvard and Oxford as he claimed; in fact, he did not even finish high school.

After her father's death, Anna and Mary moved in with Anna's elderly Irish mother and her sister, both also afflicted with polio. Gordon describes this time as one of loss and pain: she was sent to a parochial Catholic school where the nuns discouraged her from developing the intellect her father had nurtured. The sheltered women she lived with concurred with the nuns: Gordon has noted in several essays and interviews that whenever she did something disturbing, her Irish grandmother, aunt, or mother would say, "That's the Jew in you."

Gordon won a scholarship and escaped to the largely Jewish and secular Barnard College in New York City, only a train ride away from her home on Long Island but a world apart intellectually and politically. As a college student in the late 1960s, she was exposed to the protests against the Vietnam War and the belief in sexual freedom associated with the era, and during this time she promptly lost her political naïveté, her virginity, and her Catholic faith. After college, she attended graduate school in Syracuse, New York, and began to draft her dissertation on Virginia Woolf while also publishing poems and short stories. While teaching composition at Duchess Community College, Gordon wrote her first published novel, *Final Payments*, named one of the outstanding books of 1978 by the *New York Times Book Review* and nominated for the National Book Critics Circle Award. She was twenty-nine years old.

Gordon is the author of five novels, two books of essays, a collection of short stories, a collection of three novellas, and a memoir about her father in addition to numerous uncollected essays and reviews. In the past, she has received the Lila Acheson Wallace Readers Digest Award and a Guggenheim Fellowship. For the 2003–2004 academic year, she was named a Fellow at the Radcliffe Institute of Advanced Study at Harvard University, where she is at work on a project titled "Transatlantic: A Collection of Novellas." Gordon is married to Arthur Cash and has two children, David and Anna, named after her parents. Since 1988, she has been teaching writing and literature at Barnard, where she is Millicent C. McIntosh Professor of English.

Today, Gordon reluctantly accepts the label of "Catholic novelist," acknowledging the influence of Catholicism in her life and in her writings: "I think I learned the importance of story. I think I learned the pleasure-bearing aspect of language. I think I had experiences of real formal beauty in Catholic liturgy. I think I knew about secrets and lies, although I didn't know that I knew it. And I think I didn't expect that human life was about happiness" (quoted in Lee 1997, 218).

PLOT SUMMARY

Final Payments opens with a typical Irish American trope: the funeral of the protagonist Isabel's father, Joe Moore. Moore was a professor of theology at a local Catholic college who often spent long evenings arguing theology with the parish priests. After his wife died, he raised the then two-year-old Isabel to be an intellectual equal and to respect the authority of the pre-Vatican II Catholic Church. At age nineteen, Isabel is caught in bed with one of her father's prized students: Moore has a stroke and Isabel spends the next eleven years caring for him. Her self-sacrifice is seen as natural by the orthodox Catholic parish to which she belongs, as well as by her father and herself: they both wait in vain for the clear symbol of her sin, a baby. After her father's death, Isabel is twenty-nine and free to leave the security of her orthodox Catholic father's house to enter the world of the early 1970s. The story follows Isabel over the few months after Joe Moore's death as she attempts to create a new identity and to move beyond her guilt at forcing Margaret, the housekeeper Moore hired after his wife's death, to leave so she can be alone with her father. Isabel's escape from a closed, orthodox world to a modern, secular one is disorienting to her, and she proceeds to have sex with two married and, like her father, authoritative men. Her involvement with Hugh, whose wife Cynthia is a match for Margaret in her odiousness, leads her to escape once again, this time back to Margaret, presumably to care for her as penance for her adultery and to assuage her guilt. The novel ends during Holy Week and Easter, with Isabel's realization that she has distorted the meaning of Catholic charity and self-sacrifice, and with her giving Margaret a check for all the money her father had left behind. She then makes another escape, this time to her childhood friends Liz and Eleanor, with whom she will hide while she loses the guilt-induced weight she gained during her penance with Margaret. Although the novel's ending implies that she may return to Hugh, who has since left his wife, Isabel's future is ultimately left open-ended.

MAJOR THEMES

Mary Gordon was reared in the orthodox Irish Catholic Church that changed drastically with Vatican II. She is an identifiable Catholic writer in both her moral sensibility and her subject matter. In her fiction and essays, Gordon explores the relationship between being a woman, a Catholic, and a writer and the tensions that result from these very different positions. Particularly in her first two novels, *Final Payments* and *The Company of Women* (1980), Gordon creates heroines who try to redefine the Church's definitions of faith, hope, and love—the three cardinal virtues—in the modern world. Gordon portrays a Church whose morality is based not on Jesus' compassionate ethic of care but on an often abstract ethic of judgment; yet, she then reveals the immaturity of an extreme ethic of care. Ultimately, it is only by integrating both ethics (transformed into orthodox Catholicism and secular feminism in Gordon's fiction) that her heroines have a chance to take responsibility for their own lives.

In *Final Payments*, the protagonist is formed by a patriarchal religion—and is dominated by the letter rather than the spirit of the Catholic concept of goodness. Isabel feels a distorted sense of guilt over her good looks and her luck, and this guilt, exacerbated by a seemingly guilt-inducing Catholicism, forces her constantly to seek absolution and penance for her "good fate." After leaving the expected role of "good girl," caring for her ailing father, Isabel needs to redefine what it means to be good in a secular world. For example, she forces herself to endure the odor of a homeless woman in Grand Central Station, a woman who obviously has not been graced with good fortune. She also reluctantly takes an unexpected and unappealing job offer because she fears showing ingratitude to chance; and she feels sorry for the vengeful Cynthia, wife of her lover Hugh, for having had less luck than she. All this leads up to her greatest sacrifice, what she thinks of as a pure act that repeats her celibate retreat of caring for her father, this time with the unlovable, selfish Margaret. Gordon displays here a distrust of free will despite a desire to believe in it: the dilemma for her characters is how to access their often subconscious wills. They seem to fall back on what is defined as their Irish Catholic fatalism or the security of their childhood Church whenever they can no longer take responsibility for themselves. This is the paradox in Gordon's fiction: her characters do not have to be determined by their cultural and religious heritages, but, inevitably, they are.

This fatalism is emphasized when Gordon dualistically distinguishes between an Irish Catholic world and an American Protestant one, setting the dramatic tension for Isabel's quest for assimilation into what she—and her fellow Irish American characters—perceives as a homogenous, monolithic American mainstream. The distinction between Irish Catholic and American Protestant cultures is based as much on economic class as on differences in world view. Gordon uses associative descriptions, as F. Scott Fitzgerald does, to emphasize the essential Irishness of her characters despite the fact that they are second- or third-generation Irish, as if such physical traits represent a kind of biological determinism. Isabel's friend Eleanor, for example, has "thin, Irish lips invented for mourning," while

Liz's "mouth was another kind of Irish trick, brimming with mockeries" (15). Isabel, Liz, and Eleanor all have their arguments with the Church, and not one of them receives the sacraments. But because Liz, at least, was married in the Church, her mockery and jeering are considered acceptable, "an Irish tradition, a lightning rod that channeled the energy of doubt to a safe grounding" (88). Gordon deliberately encloses the juxtaposition of mockery, melancholy, and mirth in many of her women characters within the Irish Catholic circle in order to make a greater distinction between Catholic and Protestant characters as well as to illustrate the vast cultural differences that Isabel must navigate in the non-Catholic world.

Two non-Catholics that Isabel encounters are Hugh, her married lover, and her coworker Lavinia, whose name bespeaks her old American past. Besides having, according to Isabel, "wonderful bones," Lavinia says "'damned' like a Protestant, like an American" (120, 134). Here Isabel is responding as much to a class difference as to a religious one, for Lavinia comes from a wealthy background. Because she identifies with immigrant Irish Catholics rather than native-born Americans, Isabel lacks Lavinia's sense of place as well as her self-confidence. At other times in the novel, Isabel feels almost a foreigner compared to Protestant Americans. She fears that during a get-acquainted lunch with Lavinia she will need to justify the years she gave up to care for her father to a woman who could not, she believes, understand. And later, she ponders her first celebration of Thanksgiving: "It was a Protestant holiday, an American holiday, my father had said, and we were Catholics, with a tradition that was rich and ancient and had nothing to do with cold, thin-blooded Puritans sitting down somewhere in New England" (160). Isabel's attempt at leaving her Catholic world is inevitably foiled: her clearly noted lack of high cheek bones fating her to live outside the perceived privileged circle of "real" Americans.

Continuing the distinction between the Protestant American/secular and Irish Catholic/deterministic world views, Gordon makes clear the need for mystery in our lives despite the modern desire to eliminate it. Often, her female protagonists take a destructive path in their desperation to fulfill this need: they attempt to live a contemporary spiritual life according to the orthodox Catholic Church but end up practicing a doctrine that is not only ineffective in the secular world but no longer even exists in the modern Church. Isabel's memory of her spiritually dogmatic father is deflated by Hugh's psychoanalysis, and rather than release her father's hold on her, as perhaps was Hugh's intention, it creates a larger distance between her and her lover: for instance, she had always thought that her father's dislike of nature was mysteriously related to Catholicism, but Hugh points out that it was more likely a negative reaction to a harsh rural childhood. Upon this, Isabel thinks to herself, "Where I had seen a compelling mix of tradition and original thought, Hugh had seen the slow damage of family relations. It made it so much simpler—and less interesting—this being able to understand things" (160). While Isabel's quest in the outside, secular world is an attempt to escape the restrictions of the Church, she finds the constructions of a pragmatic society equally confining.

Yet the limited roles for women accepted by the Church are in their definitiveness quite comforting. When Isabel's father has a stroke, presumably as a result of her affair with his student, she automatically assumes the role of one who is atoning for perceived sins and spends the next eleven years caring for him, rarely leaving home. The Church has given her an identity as well as a means of expiation for her "sin." Later in the novel, the Vatican II Church is depicted: there are now new rites, a familiar language, and none of the mystery that Gordon visualizes as the darkness of the traditional Church in contrast to the lightness of the modern Church, where everything is knowable. "I remembered the adjustment my eyes used to have to make, from the darkness of the confessional to the comparative light of the church. But now there was no adjustment necessary: both lights were the same," Isabel muses (226). She fears that there is no longer a place where people, words, and things have meaning, that there is no universal order or authority beneath or above the surface of life.

Isabel is searching for the authority she gave up and lost in the orthodox Catholic Church. Unfortunately, the result of searching for the motive in every action, the meaning in every word, can be paralyzing or lead to self-deception, as it does for Isabel's friend Eleanor. Isabel's other friend, Liz, says that life is a matter of tricking oneself to make it bearable. Liz's husband John, on the other hand, is successful because he can act; he is not paralyzed by the inability to choose, nor is he self-deceptive. Liz says of her husband, "he has no solidity," and like the "lightness" of the modern confessional, he also has no mystery, meaning, depth, or significance. He is, therefore, the opposite of Isabel's father, who had authority and "signified all over the place" (69–70). In the secular world, everything is random and physical, with no clear symbols or signs, no authority or center.

Another dualism that the novel presents are the two predefined roles of women accepted in the orthodox Catholic Church, that of Martha and Mary, roles that Isabel attempts to reconcile. In her article "'The Impulse of a Few Words,'" Margaret Hallissy notes that Gordon has conflated two Marys in the New Testament, Mary of Magdalene, the prostitute, and the Mary who listens to Jesus while Martha serves him; thus, Gordon's Mary is at once a sensual, spiritual, and intellectual woman, and her Martha character is the domestic woman (2001, 272). Isabel's father, Professor Moore, raises Isabel to fulfill Mary's role while relegating Margaret to the Martha role of housekeeper. Yet, after she is caught in bed with her father's student, Isabel fatalistically compares herself to Mary Magdalene, and both she and her father expect her to be pregnant, as punishment for her sin and confirmation of the identity he has thrust upon her willing shoulders: "I thought my fate as inevitable as hers [Mary's], as forcefully imposed, as impossible to question. I could no more refuse my father than Mary could have refused the angel coming upon her" (195). Isabel never does succeed in her domestic role, a failure ignored by her father but recognized and disdained by her married lover, Hugh, who chastises her for letting a coffee cup get moldy. And because she has been raised to seek male approval at all costs, Isabel describes Hugh's rudeness as the actions of "an angry God" (172).

This need for a male authority in Isabel's life is also depicted as an effect of her Catholic upbringing. Because the Church is able to keep its members by providing a sense of community and refuge so powerful that its loss could be debilitating, it can breed childish dependence, as Isabel notes: "Both Father Mulcahy and my father were children, and their love made the exhausting demands of a child's. Perhaps it was because they were so used to loving God, Who found nothing exhausting" (60). This childishness is seen in Isabel, too: she seeks in men the security and authority she craves. The loss of the authority of the Church is disorienting; thus, she is attracted to men who mimic that authority, yet at the same time she is convinced of the eventual loss of that authority.

Final Payments reflects Gordon's disappointment in the "modernizing" of the Church that came after Vatican II: instead of providing an escape or a road map to the modern world, the Church has joined it, precisely what Isabel has feared. This fear stems from the loss of the omnipotent Church: the Church had once been involved in every milestone of life, providing a sense of community and refuge so powerful that its absence is debilitating. Isabel's quest, therefore, is to find a new shelter. Since the Church was also intertwined with memories of her father, she seeks to recover it in men and sex, only to fear losing them, too. Because the loss of her father and her faith seems to have begun with her having sex with her father's student, she sees sex and now love with Hugh as the precursor to loss, so she runs back to Margaret for "the safety of her inability to inspire love" (243). Although Isabel sees the Catholic Church's values as getting her into this mess, her attachment to those values does not allow her to dismiss them entirely.

When Isabel has sex with the two married men, John and Hugh, she fights the resultant self-induced guilt. She thus confirms the Irish Catholic tendency to equate sex and sin as well as its fear of being seen as selfish and of losing pleasure once it is gained. Isabel is forced to both seek the extremes of sexual freedom and retreat into the extremes of self-denial. After her affair with Hugh is discovered by his wife, who recognizes and manipulates Isabel's sense of guilt and sin, Isabel retreats from the secular, Protestant world into a traditional, orthodox Catholic one for a bizarre reenactment of her role as caretaker for her father. She moves in with Margaret, her father's old housekeeper, who embodies the worst of Catholicism: its self-absorption, dogmatic beliefs, and sentimentalism (such as its images of the bleeding Jesus). Yet Margaret was also a part of Isabel's past, when the world was smaller, less free, but more certain. By living with Margaret, Isabel can atone for her several perceived guilty acts—firing Margaret, sleeping with her father's student, and leaving her father's house.

The bulletin board at her Catholic high school taught Isabel that "Love is measured by sacrifice" and that charity is doing God's work of loving even those who are unlovable; yet she recognizes the impossibility of such an impersonal love: "who wants to be loved in God?. . . . We want to be loved for our singularity" (175). Yet the adult Isabel deliberately forgets this awareness when she seeks to replicate the love and charity she gave to her father for eleven years. She is not seeking to be charitable to Margaret, whom she does not love, but she needs absolution for stealing Hugh from his wife and her father from Margaret. Isabel takes hostility of the body and the Church's call for charity too far; thus, her supposed act of charity in caring for Margaret is effectively more selfish than any physical pleasure—and more destructive. She is denying the flesh, finding shelter in celibacy, as she did when she cared for her father, and retreating to a pure, theoretical type of charity, without any real love for the individual, with its safety from loss and real human connection. Such denial is accomplished in part by Isabel's regression to passive, childish actions during this time, such as overeating and oversleeping. By the end of her stay with Margaret she has not only allowed herself to be given a haircut that is twenty years out of date, but she also gains enough weight to effectively enforce her celibacy.

At the end of the novel, Isabel adjusts to the modern and more secular notions of charity and self-sacrifice: instead of giving away her "self," she gives of herself, signing over to Margaret the money she inherited from selling her father's house. With this act, she adopts the Protestant definition of monetary charity over the Catholic, Marian definition of total self-sacrifice. Two events save Isabel, allowing her to adopt this new definition of self and charity without discarding the Church altogether: her attendance at the Good Friday Mass dedicated to the memory of the death of Christ, where Isabel reencounters the Church through the Gospels, and her meeting with Father Mulcahy. Father Mulcahy is depicted as part spiritual and part secular (over the "smell" of him as a priest is the "secular smell of his Old Spice" [55]), and although he deals with these contradictions with alcohol, he is the only representative of the Church who is kind and gives Isabel the reinterpretation of the Scriptures that offers her true guidance: that self-respect and not self-hatred is a spiritual and secular good. He tells Isabel that God also cares for the physical, warning the depressed, overweight young woman who had cut off her hair as part of her penance, "God gave you beauty. If you waste it, that's a sin against the fifth commandment." "Thou shall not kill? What does that have to do with it?" Isabel questions in response. "It means slow deaths, too," Father Mulcahy replies (242). Isabel's epiphany during Holy Week allows her to move from the absolute meaning of Jesus' words ("The poor you have always with you") to a relational or situational meaning. As John Neary notes, she recognizes that religious truths need story and metaphor to be completely understood: "Isabel's strikingly insightful, though also strikingly personal, interpretation of Jesus' cryptic words is based on her seeing the words relationally, both in relation to the other characters within a Biblical story [Mary and Martha, Judas] and in relation to her own current, particular situation" (1990, 107).

Isabel finally leaves Margaret's house with the help of her friends, Liz and Eleanor. She still remains a part of an Irish Catholic culture, separate from the Protestant Americans who, although she learns from them, she does not truly understand. At the end of the novel, although she resists the parts of her religious and cultural heritage that are restrictive, she is not leaving them entirely because she is "saved" by her two Irish Catholic girlhood friends, recreating and revising the Trinity, as many critics have noted.

Rather than seeing *Final Payments* as an attack on traditional Catholic values and an expression of anger at the loss of those values with Vatican II, we can see it as an acceptance of one of the goals of Vatican II: to allow the Gospel and its lessons to speak directly to people rather than merely disseminating a list of rules. Vatican II gave Catholics more moral responsibility, seemingly taking away a stable authority on the one hand but allowing more personal choice on the other. What Isabel learns from Father Mulcahy is that she is looking in the wrong place: that she has to create her own order and values, and that she can look directly at Christ's words, unfiltered by the Church.

CRITICAL RECEPTION

Since its initial publication, *Final Payments* has sold more than 60,000 hardcover copies and well over a million in paperback. Literary critics either love or hate Mary Gordon's work: she is either praised for being relentlessly honest in

her portrayal of the cold Irish Catholic family, or she is accused of being superficial and angry in her depiction of anything Catholic. But most initial reviews were
positive, focusing particularly on Gordon's poetic writing, humor, and depiction
of Irish Catholicism. Some critics, surprised by a twentieth century novel with
the nineteenth century themes of morality, goodness, and self-sacrifice, compare
Gordon to Jane Austen, Doris Lessing, or Flannery O'Connor. However, not all
critics agree. Charles Fanning argues that novels like *Final Payments* and Gordon's
later work, *The Other Side* (1989), are filled with hostile generalizations about
the working-class Irish and, in the former book, about all Irish people. For
example, religious working-class Irish are seen as fearful of intellectualism, and
as for the Irish in general, "Unhappiness was bred into the bone" (*Other Side*,
160). For Fanning, these stereotypes are not only false but "mean-spirited" (1990,
330). However, dismissing the accusation of stereotyping, John Leonard admits
that Mary Gordon's portrayal of Irish Catholics made him face the coldness of
Irishness that "I ought to know and wish I didn't" (1978, C31).

Several critics are particularly disturbed by what they perceive to be a negative
portrayal of Catholicism in the novel: they berate Gordon's characters as self-
absorbed, caring too much for personal happiness. John Mahon believes that the
heroines cannot find shelter in God so they seek it in loveless sex and in friendships
with women (1989). James Wolcott notes that Gordon's "Catholic imagery is used
decoratively, for ticky-tack symbolism" (1981, 21); Brenda Becker complains that
Gordon's heroines are the "wilted flower of Catholic girlhood just aching for
defloration at the hands of modernity" (1981, 29). Finally, Carol Iannone argues
that all Gordon is doing is replacing Catholic orthodoxy with feminist orthodoxy
(1985). But Marcia Seabury asserts that this is not true: Gordon's fiction always
ends on an ambiguous note, feminism is not presented as the new orthodoxy,
and there is "no easy, self-centered resolution" in her works (1990, 37).

NOTE

Mary Gordon, *Final Payments* (New York: Random House, 1978). All references
are to this edition.

WORKS CITED

Becker, Brenda L. 1981. "Virgin Martyrs." *The American Spectator* 14 (August):
    28–32.
Fanning, Charles. 1990. *The Irish Voice in America: Irish-American Fiction from the
    1760s to the 1980s.* Lexington: University Press of Kentucky.
Gordon, Mary. 1980. *The Company of Women.* New York: Random House.
———. 1989. *The Other Side.* New York: Penguin.
Hallissy, Margaret. 2001. "'The Impulse of a Few Words': Authority, Divided Self, and
    Language in Mary Gordon's *Final Payments* and *The Company of Women.*"
    Christianity and Literature 50, no. 2 (Winter): 269–91.
Iannone, Carol. 1985. "Fiction: The Secret of Mary Gordon's Success." *Commentary*
    79, no. 6 (June): 62–66.
Lee, Don. 1997. "About Mary Gordon." *Ploughshares* 23, nos. 2–3 (September 22):
    218–25.

Leonard, John. 1978. "The Saint as Kill-Joy" (Review of *Final Payments* by Mary Gordon). *New York Times* (April 4): C31.

Mahon, John. 1989. "Mary Gordon: The Struggle with Love." In *American Women Writing Fiction*, ed. Mickey Pearlman, 47–68. Lexington: University Press of Kentucky.

Neary, John M. 1990. "Mary Gordon's Final Payments: A Romance in the One True Language." *Essays in Literature* 17 (Spring): 94–110.

Seabury, Marcia Bundy. 1990. "Of Belief and Unbelief: The Novels of Mary Gordon." *Christianity and Literature* 40, no. 1 (Autumn): 37–55.

Wolcott, James. 1981. "More Catholic Than the Pope." *Esquire* (March 3): 21, 23.

BIBLIOGRAPHY

Bennet, Alma. *Mary Gordon*. New York: Twayne, 1996.

— Stacey Lee Donohue

Graham Greene [1904–1991]

The Power and the Glory

BIOGRAPHY

Graham Greene was born in Hertfordshire, England, in 1904 and educated at Berkhamsted School, where his father was headmaster, and later at Balliol College, Oxford. After university he worked as a journalist, initially in Nottingham and then in London, where he joined the staff of *The Times* as a subeditor in 1926. The same year saw an important event in Greene's life, his conversion to Catholicism, and the following year his marriage to Vivien Dayrell-Browning. Both experiences were later to involve complex and rather strained relationships. In 1935 he walked across the interior of Liberia, describing his itinerary in a classic among travel books, *Journey Without Maps*, which appeared in 1936. Once back in England, he became first the film critic of *The Spectator* and later, in 1940, its literary editor. He was commissioned by two publishing firms (Longman's in London and Viking in New York) to investigate the ongoing severe persecution of religion in certain areas of Mexico, an experience that was to have a profound influence on his writing. On the basis of this experience, he published both another major travel book, *The Lawless Roads* in 1939 (called *Another Country* in the United States, this book offers an interesting companion piece to *The Power and the Glory*) and his finest novel, *The Power and the Glory*, in 1940. During World War II, Greene worked for the British Foreign Office, largely in Sierra Leone. In the postwar years he continued to travel the world and work as a journalist, reporting from such trouble spots as Indochina and Kenya. In 1966 Greene was made a Companion of Honor in Britain, and in 1969 he was made a Chevalier de la Legion d'Honneur in France. He spent many of his later years in Antibes, on the French Riviera, and died in 1991.

PLOT SUMMARY

In the most anti-Catholic region of the postrevolutionary Mexico of the late 1930s, the Church is illegal and priests are shot. In a rundown port, an English dentist, Tench, meets an evasive and rather sly stranger who is there to meet "a friend of a friend," a man called Lopez. Tench tells him that a man of that name had been shot a few weeks ago. They go to Tench's house and drink illegal brandy. A child arrives and asks the stranger to visit a dying woman some miles away, and he sets off reluctantly to do so. A hard-faced, impeccably dressed lieutenant of police learns from his chief that another priest, who has spent six years in an American seminary and can pass for a gringo, is supposed to be in the area, as is also an American criminal on the run. Of the two, the lieutenant would prefer to catch and kill the priest, who in his view is more harmful. To do so, he proposes to search the whole state, executing a hostage in every uncooperative village. Five or so priests have already been summarily shot. One, Padre José, has conformed to the new state requirements, abandoned his priest-hood, and married. There is a first glimpse of a practicing Catholic family, which will be important later on.

Upstate, a riverside banana plantation run by Captain Fellows, an English World War I veteran, is visited by the lieutenant, who insists that it is the planter's duty to report the priest if he seeks shelter. Once the police have left, Fellows's very composed thirteen-year-old daughter tells him that the man is hidden in the barn. He is fed and given a beer and allowed to stay until dark. He then leaves and eventually gets shelter and coffee (there is no food) in a peasant hut where no priest has been seen for five years, and he secretly hears confessions. Later, he reaches his home village, where his seven-year-old illegitimate daughter lives, a girl ancient before her time. The village has recently been visited by the Red Shirts, and he can feel the villagers' reluctance to let him stay. The Mass he says before dawn is interrupted by a message that the police are on their way. The village is surrounded before he can escape, and his former woman hides him in her bed, giving him an onion to bite on to hide the smell of wine. The police take a hostage, and the priest creeps away when they have gone. On the track he takes he meets the wheedling, feverish mestizo who guesses that he is a priest and will later betray him.

In the city he manages to buy illegal wine, which he needs for Mass, and brandy. All the wine is drunk in a session with the chief of police and the governor's cousin. He is later caught with the dregs of the brandy and jailed—unrecognized— by the lieutenant. The time spent in the festering, filthy, stinking cell gives a clear picture of the priest's mind. As he is made to empty the foul slop pails from the cell, he meets the mestizo, a "guest of the Governor," enjoying free food and beer there because he has seen the wanted priest and is intending to betray him "outside," as the reward will be greater.

Eventually, the priest manages to leave the town and returns, starving, to the now-deserted Fellows's house, where he fights a dog for a raw bone. Feverish and exhausted, he struggles on into the next state, where religion is permitted, collapsing outside a church. As he recovers, he spends some time with the Lehrs, an American Protestant brother and sister, hears confessions, baptizes, and says Mass before leaving for Las Casas. The half-caste, who has found out where he is and is to guide him there, tells him that the American gangster is dying and has asked for a priest. The priest feels that he must go, although he knows that it is almost certainly a trap, and he manages to give the dying and indifferent man conditional absolution, unaware that the lieutenant of police is watching him. He is taken away, and during his time in prison the two men talk seriously, with neither giving way, but at least with mutual respect. The renegade Padre José is asked to see his former colleague but, ridiculed by his wife, he fearfully refuses. When the priest, the last in the state he has fled, is taken out to be shot, he thinks in his last moments about how he has lived and failed to be what he should have been: a saint. In a house in the town, a young boy who hates soppiness and loves tales of blood and guts opens the door to let in another shabby man with an odd, frightened smile—the next hunted priest.

MAJOR THEMES

Greene probably stands out as the English writer closest to the stereotypical modern Catholic novelist. At the time when he was at his most productive, English Catholicism was isolated, united, proselytizing, orthodox in attitudes and practice, and needing to explain itself because it was not understood by the non-Catholic population. As a distinctly untypical member of a minority group, Greene was to some extent doubly an outsider. Over the last hundred years or so it has not been unusual to have Catholic writers in England, but there have been none quite like Greene. A further complication is that his writing has often been deeply shaped by antipathies: the banality and boredom of the world without God, facile optimism, conventional piety, pharisaism, and the pathetic inadequacy of human attempts to explain our nature and our life. There is often an acute sense of absence and emptiness in his fiction, which is, however, interspersed with a hazy, dim, and clouded perception of what our true life might be. *The Power and the Glory* is a powerful depiction of that permanent tension.

Thematically, the novel is simple on one level, complex on another. From the narrative point of view it is, as the plot summary above suggests, an account of the events in the closing stages of the life of a fugitive, a man hunted down by the police, betrayed, captured, and finally shot in a prison yard. The story is told economically, simply, and effectively, the somber and compelling mood encapsulated in the evocative, cinematic writing Greene so often favors, from the setting in the port where the story opens to the scene of the execution the English dentist Tench witnesses from his surgery window.

But parallel to the economical and cinematic narrative there is an accompanying reflection, largely in the priest's mind, sometimes in his talk with others (such as the lieutenant of police), but occasionally also in their thoughts. This, the interweaving of narrative and reflection on fundamental questions, is what gives the novel its complexity and rich texture. As well as being caught up in and carried along by a compelling narrative, the reader is involved in the inner struggles, thoughts, feelings, and self-understanding of a man whose life has been overturned by powerful inner and outer events, in his searing pity for the poor of Mexico, the harshness and doomed nature of his own situation, and the contemplation of the death that awaits him.

In a later reflection on his writing called *In Search of a Character*, Greene declared that he would not claim to be a Catholic writer but "a writer who in four or five books took characters with Catholic ideas for his material" (1961, 56). In *The Power and the Glory*, this is precisely what he did. In the midst of his own failures and weaknesses and the existential mess of the world around him, the priest still clings to the basic tenets of his faith. His situation is not an illustration of a problem in moral theology but a compelling picture of a human being trying, with the distinctly battered faith he still has, to make some sense of human nature and his own experience and to relate in some meaningful way to these facts. There are no comforting illusions left. He has lost all the certainties of his former respectable middle-class lifestyle and status, and what the secular state has to offer is useless and deeply damaging. Both the bourgeois piety that once surrounded him and the political slogans penciled on the girlie calendar in the police station are meaningless. The shattering experiences of his own life (persecution, his sins, the vitiating sense of his own inadequacy, and the loss of all comforting illusions) make him wonder what men and women are, what their value is, and how they can, do, or should relate to each other and to God.

One of the major themes of the novel is a conscious and recurring exploration of the idea that the true awareness of another as a person inevitably brings with it a sense of the complexity of being and a feeling of sympathy and shared humanity. The simple schematic representation produced by convention and social, political, religious, and psychological clichés disappears. Received ideas crumble and are replaced by a sense of another complex, different, and yet not alien reality, and the suffering and pain of a different subjectivity become apparent and can be shared. While he is in prison, the priest both feels pity for the other inmates and can understand why the pious middle-class woman who speaks to him is appalled by her incarceration with the unlovely dregs of Mexican society; he understands that her upbringing and the shock of her experience prevent her from seeing them as her fellow human beings. "When you visualized a man or woman carefully," he thinks, "you could always begin to feel pity . . . that was a quality God's image carried with it. . . . Hate was just a failure of the imagination" (*The Power and the Glory*, 131). Here, as in Greene's other major novels, understanding and pity follow once the other is seen as a person.

Without that necessary view, a human being is often merely an awkward, embarrassing, squalid, and possibly dangerous object. The "failure of the imagination" creates an inability to see the reality and detail in another human being, another image of God. In some of his novels, such as *A Burnt-Out Case*, Greene has described an absence of faith and its concomitant detachment, noninvolvement, and solitude. Here, it is their opposites, even if they are imperfectly, confusedly, and clumsily sensed, that dominate, and the chief among them is the importance of every individual human being. The priest, for example, is willing to sacrifice his own salvation for that of his illegitimate daughter, the tiny speck of life for whom he prays, doomed to a life of physical and moral squalor, violence, and perhaps despair, and who is seen in a totally different way from that in which the politicians, the police, and the anticlericals, who are all concerned with more important things, could ever see her. God, and his image, the view of man faith can give, are mysteriously and indissolubly linked. The priest sees and tries to express, half in the terminology of his own theological training and half in specific images, what binds totally disparate people together. The unity, which is there because all human beings are alike in the sense that they are in some way like God, can be seen but not fully explained by reason. Given his premises, however, it is not in itself irrational. Greene gives us an insight into his thinking: "But at the centre of his own faith there always stood the convincing mystery—that we are made in God's image. God was the parent, but he was also the policeman, the criminal, the priest, the maniac and the judge" (101). We are alike and can see others as persons because we are all "made in God's image." Man is like God and is *capax Dei* because there is a reflection of God in him. What Greene is saying in the thoughts he gives the priest is that, however remote the likeness may be, it is there and ultimately it is what makes all human beings human.

In Greene, the individual is part of the overall human situation—his experience is that of humankind in general, and more often than not both are unsatisfactory, spoiled by sin. The priest's crowded prison cell is a microcosm of the whole world. "This place," he thinks, "was like the world: overcrowded with lust and crime and unhappy love: it stank to heaven, but he realized that after all it was possible to find peace there, when you knew that the time was short" (125). And it is not only the priest who feels that. Fellows, the expatriate Englishman who wants nothing more than "a life of ease, safety, tolerance and complacency" (136), is anguished by the thought of the dangers—"the horrors of seventy years ahead"—that await his young daughter, Coral, and knows that her present innocence, her "false air of impregnability" (31), and her happiness are doomed. It is a world we have to accept, where even the priest no longer feels much as he consumes the body and blood of God in a state of sin, for "life breeds its excuses." There is innocence in it—Coral Fellows, the boisterous and bloodthirsty young son of the practicing Catholic family, even the lieutenant of police all share that quality to varying degrees—but sin is ubiquitous, pervasive, ancient, inevitable, dreary in its sameness. The priest has something to say about it. In the hut with the mestizo who will betray him, unable to avoid the latter's shambling and repellent confession, the "awful jumble of the gross, the trivial and the grotesque" (97), he reflects on the unchanging nature of sin, of whatever particular kind it may be, and the need for any love capable of including human sinfulness to be enormous and all-embracing. He also sees the danger of sin, which dehumanizes the human personality and cuts if off from God, the source of its true humanity. Without the supernatural, the natural disintegrates, and we become the unreflecting slaves of random sensation and undirected impulse. The result, the priest knows, is that "one day they [his failures] would choke up, he supposed, altogether the source of grace" (60). Not only the more visible sins do this, he reflects. Perhaps even the frequent habitual venial sins are a more effective barrier to grace than the gravest mortal ones.

The perception of his own weakness and sinfulness marks a change in both the priest's own way of seeing himself and of knowing and relating to others. Foolishness cannot damn, but neither can it enlighten. The gifts of lucidity are won at the price of anguish and loss. What he learns by seeing himself as he saw others and others as he saw himself is our mutual responsibility for each other. It comes from a perception that God leaves us to get on with our task alone. He remains a hidden God, abandoning his lost and bewildered priest to the here and now, the world of innocence and guilt, sin and conscious responsibility.

In *The Power and the Glory*, holiness and faith are more important than piety. The latter, which Greene seems to use in the sense of a conventional religiosity, can thrive to the detriment of charity and understanding. Paradoxically, his characters' faith is often sharpened and focused by an encounter with another person's refusal or inability to believe. Here, when the hunted priest is finally captured and interrogated, he is both appalled by his own inability to communicate his faith and made more aware of what it means to him and what its consequences are. When the lieutenant tries to persuade Padre José to hear his colleague's last confession and brings the condemned man a bottle of forbidden brandy, we are once again reminded of what we have learned about the apparently nihilistic and ruthless man: that his religious experience has been a powerfully negative one, and that his unbelief is as deep, strong, and intuitive as the priest's faith. The interplay of faith, doubt, and despair help the priest see that a movement toward a truer and fuller humanity is possible, however limited it may be. As he reflects on his own life in the moments when he is being led out to be shot, he thinks about what he could have done:

> He felt only an immense disappointment because he had gone to God empty-handed, with nothing done at all. It seemed to him, at that moment, that it would have been quite easy to have been a saint. It would only need a little self-restraint and a little courage. He felt like someone who has missed happiness by seconds at an appointed place. He knew now that at the end there was only one thing that counted—to be a saint. (210)

That particular sentiment is the most Catholic of Greene's utterances and indicates a profound reflection on the self, its nature and destiny, and its relationship with other selves and God. A man, with all his weaknesses, has gone to his martyrdom with humility, dignity, and faith. Sanctity, like truth, will out. The novel, like the Gospels, shows human beings in both their weakness and their profundity as they move toward the sanctity needed to perfect their humanity.

CRITICAL RECEPTION

The critical literature on Greene in general and *The Power and the Glory* in particular is abundant and varied. This specific work is generally regarded both as one of Greene's most overtly Catholic books and universally as probably his best novel. John Updike's (1991) fine introduction to it in the Penguin Twentieth-Century Classics series shows why. Many other critics, including some novelists, share his view, and most of the criticism of Greene has been enthusiastic and respectful, even where, like Updike's essay, it has not been totally sold on the religious angle. Some critics have admired the power and skill of Greene's writing, accepting his Catholicism as an integral element of that power even when they reject it as a system of belief or morality.

Francis L. Kunkel (1973), for example, says that although the novels are explicitly Catholic, they are in no sense narrow, cozy, complacent, or moralistic but confirm Greene's own statement that he had no a priori edifying intention in writing his novel but was simply driven by the destiny of his character. And John Atkins (1957), who admires Greene but has some harsh things to say about him, is willing to forgive him his sins for the sake of his sheer readability, pointing out that his personal slant stimulates the reader and makes him discount the prejudices and idiosyncrasy.

But not all criticism of this aspect of Greene's work has been favorable. A Catholic reading some of the more antagonistic articles and books is likely to suspect that their authors probably took a guilty pleasure in reading Greene's

Catholic novels, feeling perhaps that although they enjoyed them at the imaginative level of spontaneous response they were being to some extent manipulated by an inbuilt ideology that they neither fully understood nor trusted but in which, for the moment, they had to suspend their disbelief. Later, at the stage of more conscious and systematic analysis, they perhaps exorcised their guilt by joyfully exposing that ideology for the unsatisfactory and unconvincing thing they wanted it to be. If that is true, it says a great deal about Greene's power as a writer. What makes serious imaginative literature more deeply convincing than a polemical or ideological tract is that it offers a picture of lived experience rather than a statement of an argument. It is precisely such experience that forms the basis of the novel.

Although Greene himself said of *The Power and the Glory* that it was his only novel written to a thesis, he never said what the thesis was. Is the book to be seen exclusively or primarily as an apologia for the Catholic Church or Catholic dogma? As an uplifting picture of a thoroughly decent clergyman? As an anticommunist tract? As a suggestion of the humane social reforms needed in the Latin America of the 1930s? As a political satire? To read it in any such exclusively reductionist way would be simplistic and distorting. What it is, of course, is a narration of and reflection on the lived experience of a weak, fallible, and perhaps rather unimpressive man who, in harsh and brutal circumstances, achieves a love for his fellow human beings that goes beyond liking, interest, philanthropy, or general well-wishing. What it shows is what for centuries the Church called charity, that supernatural virtue by which we love our neighbor as ourselves for God's sake. In his own way, and in his own circumstances, that is what the priest experiences, all the more keenly, it would seem, because his own failings are so clear to him. That, if there is one, must be the "thesis" of *The Power and the Glory*.

A critical reading of the novel requires not only an intelligent but also an informed response, particularly if the reader wants to reflect on its religious dimension. To see clearly the tensions and struggles involved, the reader needs a deep appreciation of such concepts as grace, sin, redemption, forgiveness, faith, hope, charity, and despair. We all achieve that understanding to varying degrees, and some of the criticism of Greene from this point of view has, as I have already suggested, been misleading and determined to point out that the religious element is usually somehow, in John Updike's phrase, "faintly stuck on" (1991, v). Occasionally, even the most articulately formulated commentaries on Greene's novels have been clever rather than intelligent or enlightened. Greene has been accused of sleight-of-hand and of deliberately using paradoxical aphorisms. In his initially witty but ultimately rather distorting account of some of Greene's fiction, Donat O'Donnell (the pen name of Conor Cruise O'Brien) alleges that a "quietistic three-card-trick" and false syllogisms are implicit in the novels (1954, 246–47). Readers might come across David Pryce-Jones's (1963) simplistic ideological attack on certain of the novels, including *The Power and the Glory*, or Elizabeth Sewell's (1954) perhaps more acceptable contention that Greene simply romanticizes Catholicism as a literary device, a point also echoed in John Atkins's book (1957). Unsympathetic critics have seen the religious element in Greene's novels as contrived, unconvincing, paradoxical, and out of step with an intelligent humanistic skepticism. They may choose to see it in that light, but they should also ask in what sense, in the words David Pryce-Jones uses, "success equals failure, failure equals success" (1963, 112), and why the life and death of the priest in *The Power and the Glory* transcends such facile categories.

In their misunderstanding of the importance of paradox and theology in Greene's writing, such critics miss the point others have seen. Success in a perhaps trivial area is sometimes paid for by failure in more profound ways, and failure in destructive or egotistical areas may lead to greater wisdom and charity. It is permissible to question, criticize, or reject Greene's views but not to misrepresent them, and thoughtful Catholic readers with an intelligent and informed approach to their faith and a sense of the appeal of powerful fiction will make up their own minds on this particular point.

NOTE

Graham Greene, *The Power and the Glory*, intro. John Updike (London: Penguin, 1990). All references are to this edition.

WORKS CITED

Atkins, John. 1957. *Graham Greene*. Rev. ed. London: Calder and Boyars.
Greene, Graham. 1955. *The Lawless Roads*. London: Heinemann.
———. 1961. *In Search of a Character*. London: Bodley Head.
Kunkel, Francis L., ed. 1973. *The Labyrinthine Ways of Graham Greene*. Rev. ed. Mamaroneck, NY: Appel.
O'Donnell, Donat [Conor Cruise O'Brien]. 1954. *Maria Cross: Imaginative Patterns in a Group of Catholic Writers*. London: Chatto and Windus.
Pryce-Jones, David. 1963. *Graham Greene*. Edinburgh and London: Oliver and Boyd.
Sewell, Elizabeth. 1954. "Graham Greene." *Dublin Review* 108: 12–21.
Updike, John. 1991. Introduction to *The Power and the Glory*, by Graham Greene, v–xii. Penguin Twentieth-Century Classics. London: Penguin.

BIBLIOGRAPHY

Evans, Robert O., ed. *Graham Greene: Some Critical Considerations*. Lexington: University of Kentucky Press, 1967.
Lodge, David. *Graham Greene*. New York: Columbia University Press, 1962.
O'Prey, Paul. *A Reader's Guide to Graham Greene*. London: Thames and Hudson, 1988.
Sherry, Norman. *The Life of Graham Greene*. Vol. 1: London: Jonathan Cape, 1989; New York: Viking Penguin, 1989. Vol. 2: London: Jonathan Cape, 1994.
Stratford, Philip. *Faith and Fiction: Creative Process in Greene and Mauriac*. Notre Dame, IN: University of Notre Dame Press, 1964.
Whitehouse, J. C. *Vertical Man: The Human Person in the Novels of Graham Greene, Sigrid Undset and Georges Bernanos*. New York: Garland, 1990. Rev. ed. London: The Saint Austin Press, 1999.

— J. C. Whitehouse

Ron Hansen [1947–]

Mariette in Ecstasy

BIOGRAPHY

Ronald Thomas Hansen was born on December 8, 1947, in Omaha, Nebraska. One of five children, Hansen has three older sisters and a twin brother, Rob. His father worked as an electrical engineer at the Omaha Public Power District. Hansen's wife, Bo Caldwell, is also a writer. In interviews, Hansen often repeats that his Nebraska roots, his role as a twin, and his Catholicism are the three defining characteristics of his identity.

In a recent collection of essays, *A Stay Against Confusion: Essays on Faith and Fiction* (2001), Hansen points to a variety of experiences and influences that shaped him as a person, as a Catholic, and as a writer. These wide-ranging influences include the nineteenth-century Jesuit poet Gerard Manley Hopkins and the contemporary novelist John Gardner. Hansen also emphasizes the importance of cinema and the *Spiritual Exercises* of Saint Ignatius Loyola. When Hansen recounts his childhood, he describes the role of the Church with playful nostalgia. In kindergarten, he embellishes a classmate's story about a chapel with special effects during show and tell. In the same year, he also appears on stage as the narrator Saint Luke in his class's Christmas pageant. The Mass in particular, he notes, held a powerful influence for him:

> Looking back on my childhood now, I find that church-going and religion were in good part the origin of my vocation as a writer, for along with Catholicism's feast for the senses, its ethical concerns, its insistence on seeing God in all things, and the high status it gave to scripture, drama, and art, there was a connotation in Catholicism's liturgies that storytelling mattered. (2001, xii)

The product of Catholic school education, Hansen attended Holy Angels grade school in Omaha, Nebraska, the Jesuit-run Creighton Prep, and Creighton University, where he earned a bachelor's degree in English in 1970. At Creighton, he was the editor of the literary magazine and a cartoonist for the school newspaper. He received his master of fine arts degree from the University of Iowa in 1974, did further graduate work at Stanford, and received a master's degree in spirituality from the University of Santa Clara in 1995. He is currently working on a master of divinity degree at the Jesuit School of Theology at Berkeley.

Upon graduation from Creighton, Hansen entered the army, served as a second lieutenant, and worked as a senior officer in the casualty branch. As a casualty assistance officer, he was responsible for accompanying and escorting the dead bodies of United States soldiers back to their families. Hansen's army experiences served as the model for Owen Meany's army position in John Irving's *A Prayer for Owen Meany*. In fact, Irving, with Hansen's permission, borrowed material from Hansen's unpublished novel, "The Escort," and incorporated it into his own novel.

After leaving the army, Hansen attended the Iowa Writer's Workshop in 1972, working with the writers John Irving and John Cheever, among others. Later, while attending the Vermont-based Bread Loaf Writers Conference in 1979, he met John Gardner, a writer who profoundly influenced him. He began publishing short stories in the 1970s, supporting himself in a variety of jobs, including as a house painter and college textbook salesman. In 1979 he published his first novel, *Desperadoes*. Since then, he has written five novels, a collection of short stories, a collection of essays, a children's book, several screenplays, and a variety of essays, book reviews, and short stories. He has also edited two anthologies of contemporary American short stories. *Mariette in Ecstasy* was published in 1991. Hansen's fiction defies simple classification, for he has written westerns, a spiritual mystery, historical fiction, and romance. His writing has received numerous awards, including the Award in Literature from the American Academy and Institute of Arts and Letters in 1989. He has also been a finalist for the National Book Award (1996) and for the PEN/Faulkner Award (1984).

Hansen has taught fiction and screenwriting at Stanford University, the University of Michigan, the University of Iowa, Cornell University, the State University of New York at Binghamton, and the University of California at Santa Cruz. He is currently the Gerard Manley Hopkins Professor in Arts and Humanities at the University of Santa Clara.

Hansen, whose twin brother Rob was a member of the Jesuits from 1966 to 1975, affirms the central role that Catholicism has played in his education, in his writing, and in his personal life. He points to Gerard Manley Hopkins and Thomas Merton as spiritual influences. He is a daily communicant who is active in the religious community at the University of Santa Clara. He once stated in a *Mars Hill Review* interview with Scott Sawyer, "I can honestly say that every time I've been happiest in my life, it's been when I've had a close relationship with God and a real affinity with Jesus" (1996, 127).

PLOT SUMMARY

The central action of *Mariette in Ecstasy* takes place in upstate New York at the turn of the century, from August 1906 to February 1907. This short novel begins with the entrance of the seventeen-year-old postulant, Mariette Baptiste, into the Sisters of the Crucifixion. In choosing a religious vocation, Mariette follows the footsteps of her much older sister, Mother Céline, the current prioress at the convent. The decision displeases Mariette's father, Doctor Henri Baptiste, a widower who is not happy that his only other child is also joining the convent.

Mariette disturbs convent life immediately with her physical beauty, her charm, and her spiritual fervor. She is too much of everything: too devout, too flirtatious, too full of pride. Within weeks, she attracts both admiration and resentment from other members of the community. She is not only brighter than the other novices, she also openly seeks religious experience as a treasure to be ardently sought after and won. Ironically, it is her fervor that most disturbs the other nuns: they understand Mariette's pride and prettiness, but they cannot come to terms with her untempered religious passion.

Soon after Mariette's sister, Mother Céline, grows ill and dies of cancer on Christmas Eve, Mariette experiences the stigmata, the wounds of Christ. Mariette's recurrent stigmata and its accompanying ecstatic moments disturb and divide the convent. Her fellow nuns do not know whether they are in the presence of the miraculous or of fraud. And Hansen's novel, to its credit, does not provide easy answers for the reader. Readers looking for evidence of duplicity or premeditation on Mariette's part can find ample evidence, from the bloody crucifix above her bed to the convent's mealtime readings of Julian of Norwich's *Revelations of Divine Love*, in which Julian describes the stigmata as a gift. At the same time, a vial of Mariette's dried blood inexplicably turns back to liquid, and her wounds come and go without a satisfying rational explanation.

The convent's attention becomes fixated on the secular consequences of the stigmata as much as the stigmata itself. A power struggle develops between Mariette and the Mother Superior, Sister Saint-Raphaël. News of the miracle leaks into the local community. The local priest, Père Marriott, conducts an investigation by interviewing members of the community. Even Mariette's father is brought in as a doctor to examine his daughter's wounds. Evidence accumulates on both sides, appears inconclusive, and eventually Sister Saint-Raphaël is forced to dismiss Mariette from the convent. Whether or not she is miraculous cannot be determined; that her presence is utterly disruptive to what had once been a quiet, unassuming cloister certainly can be.

As the book concludes, the reader sees brief snapshots of Mariette as she grows older, remaining unmarried, tutoring local school children, and tending to her aging father. In time, her father dies and she is left alone, a solitary figure understood by no one around her. The novel ends in 1937, with Mariette writing to Mother Philomène, the newly chosen prioress at the convent. The letter demonstrates her devout, unwavering, and almost unworldly love for Christ, who, unlike all others, has never abandoned her.

MAJOR THEMES

The title of *Mariette in Ecstasy* points to the central event of the book: the profound spiritual rapture of a young nun as she experiences direct communion with Christ and is given the stigmata, his wounds on the cross. The novel resists facile explanations, and the pivotal question that the book asks is not simply whether Mariette's stigmata is genuine but how a person's faith is tested by an authentic religious experience. Indeed, the immediacy of Mariette's miracle overwhelms the humble cloister, which is ill-equipped and unwilling to deal with the transcendent in its midst. Faith is tested, human frailty is exposed, and religious passion and spiritual timidity collide within the convent's walls. Many of the Sisters of the Crucifixion regard Mariette's stigmata as an intrusion into their quiet lives rather than as an event that inspires devotion or brings them closer to God. In one of the novel's signature lines, Mother Saint-Raphaël explains to Mariette, "God gives us just enough to seek Him, and never enough to fully find him" (*Mariette in Ecstasy*, 174). Mother Saint-Raphaël offers the voice of hard-won experience. She conveys her genuine desire to shepherd and protect her convent as she rationalizes her decision to expel Mariette. Yet the reader recognizes that, perhaps, her remark conveys jaded wisdom, the half-hearted comment from one hesitant to fully embrace the miraculous in her midst.

Hansen's novel succeeds on many levels: as a religious mystery, as a spiritual coming-of-age story, and as a glimpse into the lives of cloistered nuns. The author offers a complex, lyrical narrative that links the quiet movements of the natural world to the daily routines that define life in the nunnery. It is this quotidian life of the Sisters of the Crucifixion that first demands the reader's attention. The opening pages provide a directory of the convent's members and their daily schedule, which begins at two o'clock in the morning with Matins and concludes at eight in the evening when "The Great Silence" begins. The convent, although dedicated to the life of the spirit, is part of a vibrant, colorful world teeming with life. The rhythms of the natural world speak to the rhythms in the life of the Sisters of the Crucifixion. Consider the opening of the novel:

> Upstate New York.
> August 1906.
> Half-moon and a wrack of gray clouds.
> Church windows and thirty nuns singing the Night Office in Gregorian chant.
> Matins. Lauds. And then silence.
> Wind, and a nighthawk teetering on it and yawing away into woods.
> Wallowing beetles in green pond water.
> Toads. (3)

Somehow it is all of a piece: the yawing of the nighthawks, the chanting of the nuns. The association with nature anchors the convent in this world; at the same time, one senses the remoteness and timelessness that characterize cloistered life. And the reader is soon to understand that although these nuns may be admirably devout, they are flesh-and-blood creatures, too, susceptible to colds, agues, and imagined illnesses, concerned with petty jealousies and the intrigues of friendships.

Mariette's entrance into the convent highlights the nuns' connection to the physical world. Physically beautiful, Mariette is sensual and open. Spiritual exercises take on a tactile quality for her, and even before the stigmata Mariette knows that her body is a site of worship. In the hours before she enters the convent, Mariette stands before her mirror, undresses, and assesses the sacrifice she is making for Christ: "she is held inside an upright floor mirror, pretty and naked and seventeen. She skeins her chocolate-brown hair. She pouts her mouth. She esteems her full breasts as she has seen men esteem them. She haunts her milk-white skin with her hands. '*Even this I give you*'" (8–9).

Mariette is seeking the intimacy of a lover as she pursues a relationship with Christ. And as the above passage illustrates, sensuality and religious yearning become inextricably linked in this novel. Furthermore, that Mariette exploits her beauty and charm, currying favor with the other nuns and the local priest, does not go unnoticed. She is indeed a flirt, as one sister calls her; another admits her "particular attachment" to Mariette. Mariette revels in the attention. Vain and clever, she seems willing to use these things to her advantage. In one of the more compelling and troubling scenes in the novel, Mariette and her fellow sisters perform a romantic scene from the Song of Songs. They enact a sensual exchange between bride and bridegroom, titillating their audience of fellow novices. Mariette concludes the performance by imploring her audience, "'if you should ever find my Beloved, what shall you tell him . . . ? That I am sick with love'" (84–85). Spiritual intimacy has become sexualized; daily life in the convent has become grand drama. There is an illicit quality to the performance that attracts the young sisters, who may wonder if is it wrong to be sick with love when Christ is the object of one's affections.

That Mariette's devotion borders on the fanatical is undeniable. That she possesses an element of spiritual pride is true as well. But it would be a mistake to label her religious passion insincere. She regards her religious vocation as a gift. By her own admission, Mariette has had a special relationship with Christ since her confirmation. She confesses to Père Marriott that from a young age she has been "praying to understand his passion. Everything about it. To have a horrible illness so I could feel the horrors and terrors of death just as Christ did" (40). Mariette's impressive spiritual devotion attracts as much attention as her physical charms. Other nuns note her goodness, her "Christian perfection." Only her sister, Mother Céline, afraid of playing favorites, remains aloof. Her new father, Père Marriott, instructs her to write him confessional letters detailing her thoughts and reflections. Mariette compels the attention of the convent. Everyone watches Mariette, whether because they believe she is a shining beacon of pure religious light or because they are impatiently waiting to see her flaws exposed.

If the idea of balance—spiritual, physical, and emotional—occupies an important thematic place in the novel, one can see how it plays out in the sophisticated narrative Hansen constructs as well. Specifically, the narrative achieves a balanced focus between the internal and external lives of the nuns. Readers are admitted into Mariette's deepest reveries, her most heartfelt raptures; they are also offered carefully rendered descriptions of the mundane—an older nun toothlessly chewing her coffee-soaked bread, a Guernsey cow trudging across a field. Hansen often achieves this balanced effect by taking a cinematic approach to his narrative, especially at the beginning of each of the novel's three parts and then intermittently throughout. It is as if a camera's eye begins by focusing first on the exterior of the convent and the natural world that surrounds it and then moves inward, pausing to note what a certain nun is doing at a particular moment. This panoramic perspective allows Hansen to capture the individual soul as both part of and separate from the larger world.

The mundane and the mystical seem curiou ly balanced throughout as well. In part, Hansen constructs a narrative out of the day-to-day details of cloister life. He includes lists of the convent's members, detailing their names, ages, and positions. He reproduces Mariette's announcement of entrance into the community and the death announcement of Mother Céline. He reprints the letters that members of the community write. Even the passage of time differs in the convent, as it is marked by the liturgical calendar, not a secular one. At the same time, several distinct narrative features contribute to the sense of spiritual mystery that permeates the convent. The poetic presentation of words and the use of white space on the page reflect the silences and gaps that characterize cloistered living. So, too, the use of short sentences, sentence fragments, and brief paragraphs manages to convey the solitariness of cloistered life. Perhaps these are minor details, but together, they help create a sense of otherness and timelessness. And because of them, the narrative almost literally entrances, and it is as quiet as a softly spoken prayer.

The forward motion of the novel is balanced by Père Marriott's "Extracts of an Inquiry into Certain Wonderful Events at the Priory of Our Lady of Sorrows Having to Do with Mariette Baptiste." These extracts, which are inserted throughout the novel, are Père Marriott's interviews with Mariette and the other nuns in the convent as he attempts to ascertain the validity of Mariette's stigmata. The effect of the interpolated inquiry does more than foreshadow Mariette's impending stigmata; it puts the reader in the privileged position as one who observes and evaluates the miraculous simultaneously. The inquiry also contributes to a heightened sense of narrative suspense and tension, and the interruptions to the plot reflect the disruptive effect that Mariette's presence has on the convent. Mariette is felt in both her absence and in her presence, in her body and in her spirit. Finally, the believer's tone that occasionally characterizes Père Marriott's inquiry will be balanced by Dr. Baptiste's clinical and cynical examination of the wounds.

When Mariette enters the convent wearing her mother's wedding dress, renouncing her earthly father for a heavenly one, Hansen calls attention to the entangled family relationships that underlie the story. Mariette's older sister Annie is also her Mother Superior, the Reverend Mother Céline. Her father has made his displeasure in her joining the convent known; however, the local priest, Père Marriott, who seems to share Mariette's name, assumes the role of paternal mentor. She has taken on Christ as her bridegroom and a convent full of strangers as her sisters. Mariette's spiritual drama is a complicated family affair. Thus, although Mariette's stigmata is not unexpected, because of the interpolated inquiry, it is noteworthy that it begins almost immediately after her sister's death.

In his essays "Stigmata" and "Writing as Sacrament" (both reprinted in *A Stay Against Confusion*), Hansen discusses the historical background of the stigmata and his interest in it as a religious phenomenon. Several interesting facts emerge: women are seven times more likely than men to experience the stigmata; it occurs far more prevalently in Europe (Italy, in particular); and the Catholic Church has rarely authenticated claims of it. More importantly, in these essays, Hansen identifies the source material for Mariette's character: Saint Thérèse of Lisieux's *Story of a Soul*; the collection of letters, *Lettres Portugaises*; Gemma Galgini's *Letters and Ecstasies*; and the stories of other religious women who experienced the stigmata. Such source material provides a fruitful foundation for Hansen, who writes, "Cribbing and stealing from hundreds of sources, I finally allowed my factual sources to be distorted and transmuted by figurative language, forgetfulness, or by the personalities of the fictional characters" (2001, 9).

Mariette's ecstasies provide the spiritual and narrative core of this book. Almost immediately after her sister's funeral, early on Christmas morning, Mariette is in the oratory intensely and intently praying when the stigmata begins. In a trancelike, ecstatic state she walks over to Père Marriott's house and then "holds out her blood-painted hands like a present and she smiles crazily as she says, 'Oh, look at what Jesus has done to me!'" (*Mariette in Ecstasy*, 112). Christ's wounds from the cross appear on Mariette's body, and she bleeds from her hands, feet, and side. The sisters are at a loss to explain the wounds, which disappear almost as suddenly as they come.

The convent is thrown into an uproar, and each nun seeks her own confirmation of Mariette's God-given saintliness or of her essential duplicity. The ecstasies themselves are inexplicable, and they raise many more questions than they answer. Naturally, the sisters want to know if the stigmata is genuine or fake, why God would choose a young girl for such a blessing, and if Mariette has received the stigmata because she was particularly holy or, instead, if the stigmata has conferred God's special grace on her. Mother Saint-Raphaël, who often serves as the voice of reason, articulates the bewilderment many of the nuns feel. Even if the stigmata is real, Mother Saint-Raphaël argues, its purpose and presence is unclear—even to the aptly named Sisters of the Crucifixion. The nuns' emotions run the gamut from unadulterated reverence to hateful jealousy. Many of the sisters take a perverse pride in self-abnegation, and thus, to some, there is something spiritually indulgent about Mariette's passion—whether real or not—that runs counter to the austere life of the convent.

This is a spiritual drama about more than one person. The entire community and their faith—collectively and individually—are involved. Père Marriott and Mother Saint-Raphaël are unable to take a neutral attitude for very long. Furthermore, the issue of belief is complicated by the personalities involved. Although she will come to believe, Mother Saint-Raphaël is skeptical from the beginning, and she cannot tolerate the disruption to her community. Mariette has already shown herself to be at times manipulative, disingenuous, and calculating, but she is also committed to Christ. One father—the priest—believes her, while the other—the doctor and scientist—does not. As the novel progresses, evidence to support each claim grows. An anonymous letter from "A Worried Priest" accuses Mariette of deceit; an unnamed nun in the confessional states that she is in league with Mariette and that they have engineered "a cruel deception" (153). To Hansen's credit, the narration does not judge but simply presents the occurrences as if they did happen. Despite the accusations of deceit—or because of it—Mariette seeks out the ecstatic moments, for they are unmediated communion with the divine. She explains to Père Marriott, "In prayer I float out of myself. I seek God with a great yearning. . . . And when I have gotten to a fullness of joy and peace and tranquility, then I know I have been possessed by Jesus and have completely lost myself in him. Oh, what a blissful abandonment it is!" (128). Such raptures are powerfully seductive. Mariette swoons as she loses herself in the profound, overwhelming presence of Christ.

In the end, it is simply not clear whether this is a premeditated spiritual drama penned by Mariette's own duplicitous hand, a genuine mystical experience that is covered up and quelled by the small-mindedness and petty jealousies of the sisters, or the unconscious self-deception of a mixed-up, immature young girl who cannot distinguish feelings of growing sexuality from religious fervor and thus wills the stigmata onto herself. We can allow Ron Hansen the final word on this issue, though. He writes, "Mariette Baptiste was, for me, the real thing, a stigmatic" (2001, 177–78).

The novel ends with a letter Mariette sends to the new prioress, Mother Philomène, a friend and novice when Mariette was in the convent. It has been thirty years since Mariette left the Sisters of the Crucifixion. The letter, a bittersweet testimony to Mariette's impressive, difficult, and undying love for Christ, also communicates her still keen sense of loss for having been expelled from the convent. She writes to Philomène in the book's powerful final words: "And Christ still sends me roses. We try to be formed and held and kept by him, but instead he offers us freedom. And now when I try to know his will, his kindness floods me, his great love overwhelms me, and I hear him whisper, Surprise me" (179).

To the end, Mariette remains somehow both open and inaccessible; to the end, she remains a mystery.

CRITICAL RECEPTION

When it was published, *Mariette in Ecstasy* was seen as a departure for Hansen, whose two earlier novels, *Desperadoes* (1979) and *The Assassination of Jesse James by the Coward Robert Ford* (1983), can be classified as historical westerns. Nevertheless, Hansen maintains that a Christian perspective underlies most of his fiction, even though critics may not be quick to detect this. No one could mistake the centrality of faith in *Mariette in Ecstasy*. Hansen himself confesses that he worried that the book would not find a wide audience and that it would be dismissed by critics because of its overtly Catholic nature.

Hansen's fears were not realized: *Mariette in Ecstasy* became a best seller, and critics were often fulsome in their praise. The novel was selected by the *Nation* as one of the best books of 1992. Furthermore, not only did critics praise *Mariette*, they often insightfully identified those elements that make the novel such compelling fiction: Hansen's masterful plotting and characterization, his lyrical use of language, and the surprising manner in which a profound spiritual drama unfolds amidst a less than receptive community of nuns. For example, Patricia Hampl wrote in the *New York Times*, "Mr. Hansen succeeds—miraculously, it is tempting to say—in sustaining his portrait of Mariette's spirituality as well as her charm amid this drama" (1991, 12). Peter S. Prescott of *Newsweek* commented, "the unexpected appearance of visible proof of the truth of Christianity is an unendurable burden to professing Christians," and "these are mediocre people confronted by the miraculous" (1991, 66).

So, too, reviewers highlight Hansen's use of language to evoke the simultaneous sense of the mysterious and mundane that defines monastic life. Elizabeth McDonough writes in *America* that "Hansen's sparse prose is compelling and actually borders on the poetic" (1992, 66). Patricia Hampl comments, "Ron Hansen has written a novel whose language is so exquisite that the book runs the danger of being praised only for its diamond-like prose, which is often as pleasing at the most crystalline poetry" (1991, 11). Ultimately, the merits of this novel escape easy classification: it succeeds as much on the strength of its lyric simplicity as its does on its complex and unique evocation of transcendent experience.

NOTE

Ron Hansen, *Mariette in Ecstasy* (New York: HarperPerennial, 1992). All references are to this edition.

WORKS CITED

Hampl, Patricia. 1991. "Her Imitation of Christ." *New York Times Book Review* (October 20): 11–12.

Hansen, Ron. 2001. *A Stay Against Confusion: Essays on Faith and Fiction.* New York: HarperCollins.

McDonough, Elizabeth. 1992. "Recent Fiction." *America* 166, no. 3 (February 1): 66–67.

Prescott, Peter S. 1991. "An Innocent's Blessing." *Newsweek* 118, no. 17 (October 21): 66.

Sawyer, Scott. 1996. "Puzzling Out the Graced Occasions: An Interview with Ron Hansen." *Mars Hill Review* 1, no. 6 (Fall): 124–39.

BIBLIOGRAPHY

Abood, Maureen. "Everybody's Got A Hungry Heart." *U. S. Catholic* 66, no. 11 (November 2001): 18–22.

Nelson, Shirley. "Stewards of the Imagination: Ron Hansen, Larry Woiwode and Sue Miller." *Christian Century* 112, no. 3 (January 25, 1995): 82–85.

O'Leary, John. "Hansen, Ron." In *Contemporary Novelists,* ed. Windisch Brown, 6th ed., 440–41. Detroit: St. James Press, 1996.

Vorda, Allan. "A Hard Kind of Play: An Interview with Ron Hansen." In *Face to Face: Interviews with Contemporary Novelists,* ed. Allan Vorda, 107–25. Houston: Rice University Press, 1993.

— **Mark Cronin**

Jon Hassler [1933–]

North of Hope

BIOGRAPHY

Jon Hassler gives life to his native state in his fiction. This "son" of Minnesota was born in Minneapolis on March 30, 1933, to Ellen (née Callinan) and Leo Blaise Hassler; before he was a year old, the family moved to the small Minnesota town of Staples. His father was a grocer and his mother a teacher and librarian. Jon was their only child. In his memoir, *Good People*, Hassler describes himself as having "had the good fortune to be reared in a cocoon of goodness" (2001, 8).

Hassler writes fondly of his parents in *Good People* and attributes some of his success as a novelist to "gifts" he inherited from them: a "sense of language, a sense of story, and a sense of humor" from his "Irish" mother, and "industry, perseverance, and patience" from his "German" father (12). His parents reared him as a Catholic. He attended parochial school in Staples and claims to have been "a champion believer," accepting "every fact, myth, and holy opinion taught me during those four years of parochial school" (1995, 79). The Hasslers moved to Plainview, Minnesota, when the novelist was ten, and there he served as an altar boy. Although Hassler has fond memories of Plainview, he also discovered in that town a "strong current of religious animosity running under the surface of daily life" (2001, 65), a subject he addresses in his semiautobiographical novel, *Grand Opening* (1987).

After high school graduation, Hassler enrolled at St. John's University, a men's college in Collegeville, Minnesota. St. John's houses on its campus, along with the college, a seminary, a monastery, and the world-renowned Hill Monastic Library. Although coeducational programs between St. John's and the nearby women's College of St. Benedict are commonplace today, such programs did not exist during the novelist's student days. Undoubtedly, it was during his college years that Hassler became well acquainted with the environment of a masculine religious community, and he draws upon that knowledge in some of his fiction, including *North of Hope* (1990). An English major, Hassler received his bachelor's degree from St. John's in 1955.

After college graduation, Hassler became a public school teacher. He taught English in three Minnesota towns but confesses that his first job in Melrose left him discouraged and he quit after the first year (Plut 1997, 34). The next year, Hassler accepted a position at the high school in Fosston, a small town in northwestern Minnesota founded by Scandinavian immigrants. Hassler recalls that there were few Catholics there. He says, "It was like moving from Rome to Oslo. . . . The superintendent said to me, 'You're the first Catholic we've ever hired at this school, but English teachers are really hard to get'" (35). Hassler spent three years at Fosston and then completed his career as a high school English teacher in Park Rapids, a town set in the midst of Minnesota's lakes and pine forests. Hassler's move to Park Rapids was to have a great impact on his writing career, as he himself acknowledges: "The rest is history, as they say, because I made Park Rapids the setting for *Staggerford*" (35). Hassler spent six years teaching at Park Rapids High School and later owned a "small, clapboard cabin" some eight miles west of Park Rapids, where he would spend the first twenty-five summers of his writing career (2001, 76).

During his years as a high school teacher, Hassler also became a family man. In August 1956, he married Marie Schmitt, and within a few years was the father of three children—Michael, Elizabeth, and David. The marriage ended in divorce twenty-five years later, and Hassler has since remarried.

Although fatherhood and public school teaching undoubtedly brought extra stress into his life, Hassler still found time to enroll in a graduate program at the University of North Dakota, earning a master's degree in English in 1960. With his new credentials, Hassler explored college teaching opportunities and obtained a position as an English instructor at Bemidji State College (now Bemidji State University); he taught in Bemidji between 1965 and 1968. Some of his experiences in Bemidji (which became his fictional "Rookery") are transformed into fiction in the comic novel, *Rookery Blues* (1995), and its sequel, *The Dean's List* (1997).

During those years, Hassler also wrote some poetry, which was privately published in 1968 in a slender volume entitled *Red Oak and Other Poems*. Since then, Hassler has observed that poetry is not his forte, but he does believe that his experiments with writing poetry helped him in his fiction writing: "It turned out I wasn't a very good poet, but I think it was good for me. I think it sharpened my sense of language" (Powers 1990, 7–8). Hassler also took an interest in drawing and painting, especially landscapes, and sometimes would sell his artwork at local art fairs. Undoubtedly, his skill in recreating landscapes has had an impact on the prose landscapes found in his novels.

In the fall of 1968, Hassler left Bemidji and took a position at Brainerd Community College (now Central Lakes College), and he taught in Brainerd until 1980 (Plut 1997, 34). The move to Brainerd proved fortunate because there Hassler began to write fiction.

Hassler, who says he can trace his desire to be a writer back to the age of five, did not actually begin writing fiction until he was thirty-seven, and he vividly recalls the moment he began: "I, upon waking one morning in September 1970 . . . [heard] a voice in my head saying, half your life is over, Hassler, you'd better get started. Obediently, therefore, after teaching my eight A.M. class that day . . . I went to the campus library with a pen and notebook and began to write" (*My Staggerford Journal*, 1999, 3). During the next five years, Hassler published six stories in literary quarterlies (although he claims to have received eighty-five rejections as well). His "first big break," he says, came when a New York agent, Harriet Wasserman, saw one of those stories and volunteered her services "if he should ever write a book" (Plut 1997, 35).

Hassler was granted a sabbatical leave for the 1975–76 academic year with the object of writing a novel, and he was further encouraged when he received a grant from the Minnesota State Arts Board for his sabbatical project. The events of that year, recorded in a journal, were later edited and published in the memoir, *My Staggerford Journal*. In the spring of 1976, Hassler finished *Staggerford*, a novel focused on the heroic behavior of high school English teacher Miles Pruitt. The novel also introduces Hassler's best-loved character, Agatha McGee, an elementary parochial school teacher and opinionated Catholic who is highly critical of the post-Vatican II Church. Wasserman found a publisher, Atheneum Press, and *Staggerford* received the Novel of the Year award from Friends of American Writers in 1978.

In 1980, Hassler was invited to teach at his alma mater, St. John's University, where he became a tenured professor of English and writer in residence. He retired from St. John's in 1988, being named Regent's Professor Emeritus. Thus came closure to a teaching career that had spanned forty-two years in Minnesota. Hassler the writer, however, has not retired and continues to publish.

To date, Hassler has published eleven novels and continues to be recognized for his literary achievements. Since 1986, Ballantine has reissued all of Hassler's novels in paperback (Plut 1997, 35). Hassler received a prestigious Guggenheim Foundation fellowship in 1980 to complete *The Love Hunter* (1981), and *Grand Opening* was chosen Best Fiction of 1987 by the Society of Midland Authors. He was named the "Distinguished Minnesotan" by Bemidji State University in 2000 and has received several honorary Doctor of Letters degrees—from Assumption College (Massachusetts) in 1993, the University of North Dakota in 1994, and the University of Notre Dame in 1996.

The dramatic quality of Hassler's fiction has been recognized by filmmakers and theatrical producers. A screen version of Hassler's comic novel, *A Green Journey* (1985), in which Agatha McGee falls in love with an Irish priest, was produced in 1990 as an NBC Movie of the Week under the title, *The Love She Sought*, with Angela Lansbury and Denholm Elliot in the leading roles. Hassler's fiction has also been the subject of live stage productions performed by the Lyric Theater in Minneapolis. In 2000, the Jon Hassler Theater and Rural America Writers' Center was established in Plainview, where more of Hassler's fiction is being performed.

While Hassler's reputation as a novelist continues to flourish, his physical health has been on the decline. In 1993, Hassler was diagnosed with Parkinson's disease. More recently, the Parkinson's diagnosis has been rescinded; however, Hassler has learned that he suffers from a rarer but no less debilitating disease, multiple system atrophy. Not one to wallow in self-pity, the novelist has accepted his health difficulties and continues to write.

PLOT SUMMARY

North of Hope is Hassler's sixth novel. Its primary setting is the winter landscape of northern Minnesota. The cold of winter provides an appropriate backdrop to the psychological "winter of discontent" suffered by the central protagonist, Father Frank Healy. The novel spans some thirty years of Frank Healy's life. In the "present" of the novel, Frank Healy is forty-four years old and experiencing a midlife crisis during which he reexamines his life choices, including his choice to become a priest. In the process, he frequently remembers events from his past that have had an impact on his life.

Frank Healy's emotional crisis began when Aquinas Academy, located on the same campus where he had attended seminary, closed for economic reasons. Frank had been assigned to Aquinas after ordination because the bishop perceived him to be a "born teacher," and Frank had taught there for twenty years, also serving as a coach and eventually as headmaster. When Aquinas closed, the bishop had insisted that Frank see a therapist; the therapist told Frank he suffered from "short-term depression." But Frank describes his condition as "my big leak," explaining to the therapist, "I've sprung a very big leak, and my spirit is draining away" (*North of Hope*, 109). Frank, at his own request, is assigned to serve as a parish priest at St. Ann's church in Linden Falls, the small town where he had grown up under the tutelage of Father Adrian Lawrence. Father Adrian, now a monsignor, is still a priest in Linden Falls, although age has diminished his mental capacities. Father Adrian has gained the disparaging nickname Loving Kindness, since he always preaches on that topic. Frank now shares the parish manse with Adrian and a housekeeper.

Along with the Linden Falls assignment, Frank also volunteered to serve at the small mission church of Our Lady at Basswood, a nearby Indian reservation. In accepting the Basswood assignment, Frank saw himself as following in the footsteps of his childhood hero, Father Frank Zell, a nineteenth-century missionary to the Ojibway Indians, a saintly priest known for his excessive fasting who had frozen to death on the reservation lake as he sought to bring Mass to the Native Americans. Frank finds the Basswood church in a state of great disrepair and its few remaining members having to deal with a variety of modern problems, including poverty, drugs, and alcoholism, along with some resentment toward the "white man's religion." The Basswood portion of the novel constitutes an important secondary plot that quickly becomes entangled with the main plot.

One night, Frank, finding the furnace broken at Our Lady, tries to sleep on a cot in the nearly frozen sanctuary. Noticing a light in the nearby house of the reservation physician whom he has not yet met, Frank goes there and is welcomed by a somewhat inebriated Dr. Tom Pearsall. As the physician attempts to mix Frank a drink, the priest notices the physician's wife on the stairs; he instantly recognizes her as Libby Girard, a girl from his high school days who was the only girl he had ever loved. She also recognizes Frank and calls him "my best friend." The remainder of the novel will prove the accuracy of that description.

The major plot complications of the novel stem from the longtime love and friendship of Frank Healy and Libby Girard. The first part of the novel serves as a prelude to the Frank-Libby romance. It was "love at first sight" when Frank first laid eyes on her at the movie theater the summer before his senior year in high school. Both Frank and Libby were lonely young people greatly in need of love and a sense of belonging. Frank's mother had died of leukemia just before his eleventh birthday, and his father had drawn into himself. Libby came from an unstable home, having moved many times in her young life. But when she turns to Frank for physical affection, he becomes disconcerted and, although clearly attracted to her, causes her to feel rejected. Libby then finds a more willing source of affection, a local football hero named Vernon Jesson. As Frank starts his senior year, he learns that Libby has quit school to marry Vernon because she was pregnant. When Frank sees Libby with her baby, a girl named Verna, he believes he is "over her" and goes off to the seminary, which he believes himself destined for because he had learned from Eunice Pfeiffer, Father Adrian's former housekeeper, that his mother's last words were, "I want Frank to be a priest" (18).

While Frank is at Aquinas seminary, Libby comes to see him one afternoon with Verna, now a toddler, and tells him that she has left Vernon. She urges Frank to run away with her, but Frank, embarrassed by her visit, refuses. When she leaves, he prays that he will never see her again. His prayer is answered for twenty-three years. But then on that cold night in Basswood, Frank finds Libby living on the reservation.

As Frank soon learns, Libby's marriage to Dr. Pearsall is in trouble. Tom Pearsall is working at the reservation clinic only to avoid serving jail time for involvement in a Chicago narcotics scandal; moreover, as Libby will eventually learn, he is involved in drug trafficking with the Basswood criminal element, especially a former justice of the peace turned bartender known as Judge Bigelow. Tom and Judge are among Hassler's most evil characters, neither possessing any redeeming qualities. On that fateful night, Frank also learns that Verna, still Libby's only child, is a greatly troubled young woman, involved with many men and suffering from drug and alcohol addiction.

Frank soon finds himself enmeshed in all of Libby's problems. After he had rejected her at the seminary, Libby had found work as a nurse's aide and had married Harris Highsmith, a self-made businessman nearly three times her age. While Highsmith had sent Libby to nursing school, he had left her nothing when he died except the discovery that he had been molesting Verna since the child was seven. Frank also learns that Verna has been intimately involved with Tom Pearsall, her current stepfather. When one of Verna's lovers is found dead, she is suspected of murder but soon is admitted to the Hope Unit at the local hospital, a special unit for mental patients and those suffering from addictions. During Verna's hospital stay, Libby grows increasingly dependent on Frank. It also becomes increasingly evident that Frank still loves Libby.

In his own mind, Frank attempts to rationalize their relationship: "Libby is Tom's wife and my bond with her has nothing to do with sex because it's a pure mingling of souls" (194). But Frank's vow of chastity is severely tested sometime later, on a night when Libby attempts to seduce him by standing naked before him. When Frank resists her, Libby is stung by the rejection. Overcome by shame and believing the world would have been better off had she never been born, she decides to commit suicide. Frank saves her life only after he experiences what seems a miraculous moment of prescience.

Father Adrian provides some comic relief to the Frank-Libby relationship. While Frank is troubled by his love for Libby, Father Adrian worries about his fantasized romance with popular singer Jo Stafford, with whom he has imaginary conversations. While Verna is in the hospital, Father Adrian nearly dies of a heart attack. Frank rushes to his bedside and there realizes how much he loves the older man. When Father Adrian recovers, he suggests that Verna come live at the manse after being released from the hospital, the manse serving as a kind of safe haven. At the manse, Verna is able to recover fully enough to enroll at a community college.

It is while Frank is dealing with his feelings for Libby that an elderly and much troubled Eunice Pfeiffer confesses to Father Adrian that she had slightly altered Frank's mother's dying words. What she had actually said was, "Eunice, I hope Frank will want to be a priest." Father Adrian insists that Eunice tell Frank. When Frank learns the truth, he is surprised by his lack of emotion, which he interprets as a "sign." The final chapter of the novel shows a return to normalcy at the manse. Frank's "big leak" apparently is closed; his vocational crisis is resolved. It seems certain that he will remain in the priesthood while continuing to maintain a chaste but loving friendship with Libby.

Although there is no sequel to this novel, Hassler later made Father Frank Healy a minor character in *The Staggerford Flood* (2002). In that novel, Frank has become the parish priest in Staggerford and helps Agatha McGee with her guilt about having told a lie in order to save a village. In the same novel, Hassler alludes to Libby and Verna, showing that both are functioning as useful citizens: Verna is a popular travel agent and Libby a caring nurse.

MAJOR THEMES

North of Hope is unquestionably Hassler's most complicated novel, and most of its themes are serious even though sometimes softened by humor. Just as all of Hassler's novels have something of Minnesota in them, so also do they reflect Hassler's Catholic beliefs. Hassler tends to find humor in Catholic characters who are rigid in their beliefs, especially about maintaining certain customs. Agatha McGee of the Staggerford novels, for example, is the target of Hassler's mild humor when she expresses her aversion to Vatican II reforms and longs for the Latin Mass. There is less of that kind of Catholic humor in *North of Hope*, although there is a trace of it, such as when Frank is disconcerted by the young bishop who plays the trumpet in a jazz band. Father Adrian, of course, provides comic relief in this intense novel, but often his childlike, innocent behavior underscores the novel's more serious themes. Hassler has accurately described *North of Hope* as "more intense" than any other book he has written, noting that it is "colder" and "longer" (Brown 1997, 194).

A major theme in *North of Hope*, reinforced by the setting of a winter landscape, is depression and its debilitating effects on the human spirit. It is evident in Father Healy's "big leak," in Verna's promiscuity and addiction, and in Libby's feelings of worthlessness culminating in her attempted suicide. The setting of the cold landscape aids Hassler in his purpose, serving almost symbolically as a way of depicting the characters as beyond the reaches of hope, as the title of the novel implies. Much of the conflict in the novel is psychological, stemming from Frank's troubled emotional state. Libby also suffers from depression and associates her condition with having to live at Basswood; she sees herself as "banished" to a "wilderness of lost hope" (163). The central theme of hope-lessness is clearly delineated in the scene following Frank's saving of Libby from her most hopeless and destructive act, attempted suicide. Frank has taken her to the Hope Unit of the hospital, and once settled in her room, Libby talks about her feelings:

> "Frank, have you ever been hopeless?"
> "Sort of."
> "Have you ever felt like killing yourself?"
> "No."
> "Neither had I, until this winter. It's like hope doesn't reach this far north."
> "But it does, Libby. Hope goes wherever you want it to go."
> "For you it does, but not for me. Not this winter. That's why I need you." (498)

This passage not only reveals Libby's depression and her dependence on Frank, but it also suggests that Frank, by helping Libby, has found healing for himself. His capacity to love has saved them both. He was able to reach Libby before she could destroy herself through what seems a miraculous premonition of Libby's intention, which would have been impossible without love. So by saving Libby, Frank himself finds renewal that closes the "leak" in his spirit. In short, the episode reveals the power of Christian love to overcome the obstacles of despair.

Not only does Hassler reveal various manifestations of depression in the characters of this novel, but he also explores antidotes to depression, most notably the powerful effect of hope on the human psyche, especially when comb-ined with the related Christian virtues of faith and love (the three virtues exp-licated by Saint Paul in I Corinthians 13). This powerful combination—faith, hope, and love—is shown to offset the destructive effects of depression and despair.

Hassler reinforces this dominant theme humorously in episodes displaying the childlike faith and innocence of Father Adrian Lawrence. While the nickname Loving Kindness has been given to the older priest as a term of derision, and understandably so, this man is also shown to embody faith, hope, and love in his life; indeed, the "fruit" of those virtues may be described by the term "loving kindness." In an earlier novel, *Grand Opening*, Hassler had revealed the simplicity of Christ in the town idiot. Similarly, in *North of Hope*, he portrays Father Adrian Lawrence as a "fool for Christ." Possessing the faith of a child, Father Adrian prays daily for seven hundred five departed souls. There is gentle humor in Adrian's sug-gestion that "the Church impose a sunset law on prayers for the dead" (349), but there is also a subtle seriousness in Adrian's explanation of why he prays for one of them, the executed murderer Gary Gilmore: "Let's hope our Lord is healing him with loving-kindness" (503). Frank, whose complex internal psychological battle seems beyond the ken of Father Adrian, is able to recognize the virtues of the elderly priest. Sitting in Adrian's hospital room, after the older priest's nearly fatal heart attack, Frank prays that God will not take Adrian from him. He realizes that the elderly man has been a source of strength for him since he was eleven years old. At that moment, he is able to comprehend fully Adrian's virtues and weaknesses: "Never a vigorous man. Not a brilliant man. Not a man whose pass-ing will be noticed far and wide. But steady. Trusting. Self-satisfied without being self-absorbed. Devout. Good-natured. Undemanding. Even-tempered. Loving. Holy" (284).

While Father Adrian is shown to be less than a great priest, he does possess the one quality that Frank discovers is essential in a "good" priest—loving kindness. The power of loving kindness is made evident when Verna receives healing of her wounded spirit at the manse. There, for the first time in her life, Verna experiences the warmth of a loving family. Earlier in the novel, Libby had stated that if Verna "were ever to be reclaimed, rehabilitated, redeemed, it would take more than her mother's solicitude. It would take a miracle" (159). It is such a miracle that loving kindness brings about at the manse.

While Father Adrian Lawrence represents the embodiment of loving kindness, some of the other characters seem like modern renditions of vices from a medieval morality play; the "fruit" of their labor is destruction of themselves and of others. The most notable of the villains are Dr. Tom Pearsall and Judge Bigelow. Both had contributed to Verna's promiscuity, and together they engage in drug trafficking on the reservation. Both are morally indifferent to the pain and destruction caused by their selfish acts. Ironically, each is linked with a profession intended to benefit mankind. Tom is a physician, and Bigelow is a former justice of the peace. But as Libby once told Frank, Tom was never interested in "the practice of medicine" because "[h]e's got a very low level of compassion" (193), and Elaine LaBonte, a Basswood resident, perceptively describes Judge as "bad in the heart" (177). Hassler also placed a grotesque character in the novel to emphasize further the debilitating effect of alienation and loneliness on the human spirit, a dwarf called Toad Majerus whom Bigelow had bullied and made into his "toadie." Majerus reveals the great need every human being has when he tells Libby, "you never know how good it feels to belong someplace unless you spend most of your life belonging no place" (178). But it is also evident that Toad in his isolation has attached himself to a false prophet when he recites his parody of the Twenty-third Psalm: "The Judge is my shepherd, I shall not want" (181). Eventually, Judge's evil proves too much even for Toadie; the dwarf quite literally turns the table and destroys him. Tom Pearsall also receives his just deserts for taking part in Judge's drug trafficking deal. He has an automobile accident and freezes to death in a hole made in the frozen Basswood lake, a scene reminiscent of the lowest circle in Dante's *Inferno*.

Another Catholic theme in the novel, closely intertwined with those already discussed, is an exploration of the question of a priest's role in the modern world. A large portion of Frank's vocational dilemma is a search for the answer to this question. Frank had confessed to his bishop after Aquinas Academy closed that, during his twenty years of teaching, he had not accomplished what he considered the "real" work of a priest: "Things like bringing hope to the hopeless. Consolation to the sad. Love to the unloved" (170). But in contributing to the healing of Verna and in saving Libby from the ultimate act of self-destruction, Frank finally does succeed in such accomplishments.

Of course, a major facet of this theme has to do with vow-taking, especially the Catholic priest's vow of celibacy. The issue is paramount in the Frank-Libby relationship and also receives comic treatment when Father Adrian confesses to Frank that he has had "lewd thoughts" about Jo Stafford and fears for his soul. But Hassler's treatment of this theme is not so much to argue about whether the vow should be rescinded in the modern Church but to explore the limits of compassionate human love.

CRITICAL RECEPTION

All of Hassler's novels, not just *North of Hope*, are influenced by the author's Catholic upbringing. Hassler has said that the Bible is not an influence on his writing but that the Mass and the rituals of the Church are (1997, 196). Anne M. Cormier asserts that although "not overtly religious, many of Hassler's finely crafted novels portray Roman Catholic culture with an evenhandedness rarely found in more cynical modern writing" (1998, 18). Charlotte Hays shows appreciation for the "incisive portraits of American Catholicism in . . . [Hassler's] novels" (2001, 25), calling Frank Healy "a priest of our own time" whose "struggle isn't with the bottle or the cantankerous bishop but with his vow of celibacy and his very vocation" (26). Yet contemporary critics in general have been slow to discover the importance of Hassler's fiction.

The first serious critical article on Hassler's novels was published by Anthony Low, who points out that Hassler "often writes about grim, dark subjects and tormented souls" and "is never sentimental." But he adds that Hassler's novels "are often funny, and they end in joy" (1994, 59). Low suggests that it is the pervasive Catholicism in Hassler's novels that has prevented their becoming "fashionable" with critics and academics, those "who pride themselves on establishing canons and drawing up student reading lists" (61). He argues that Hassler should be recognized as more than a "regional writer," even questioning the validity of that term: "[S]crupulous fidelity in representing a region, a landscape, a people, and a culture is not incompatible with universality. A certain kind of realism, of fidelity to truth, material and moral, is precisely what makes great art universal" (60). Low concludes that Hassler is "one of the few of his kind extant: a Christian realist, in both the literary and the older philosophical meanings of the term" (61).

Critic W. Dale Brown would agree. He finds that "Hassler's stories reveal moral dilemmas and the stuff of real life," that Hassler "treats aging and romance and marital fidelity in small-town settings that might be most anywhere. And . . . [he] considers the role of religion as well" (1997, 184).

C. W. Truesdale offers special insight regarding how Hassler's treatment of Catholicism unfolds in his novels:

> What Hassler chooses to depict—aside from the interiors of churches and parish residences—is not the ritual of the mass itself but the human dimensions of his clergy, their inner conflicts, the vows they make and are supposed to live by, and their failures and compromises. Hassler takes a cool, virtually objective stance towards these characters—so much so that, were he not a true insider, he could almost be a non-Catholic or unbeliever writing these stories. What has fascinated him from the beginning of his career as a writer is the difficulty priests and lay people alike have in living according to long-held beliefs, principles, and vows. (1994, 56)

Yet, what is perhaps most memorable about Hassler's novels is that each, to varying degrees, reflects an optimistic spirit. In this respect, Hassler's novels differ from many important novels of the twentieth century, which frequently show

their protagonists without faith and suffering from alienation. Such novels typically offer a despairing view of the modern world. But Hassler, as one librarian
explained, is "A writer that makes you glad to be alive" (quoted in Low 1994, 59).

Hassler's novels have been favorably recognized in an increasingly broad critical
world. Contemporary Catholic novelist Andrew Greeley has said that *North of
Hope* "is unquestionably the best book about the Catholic priesthood since
Graham Greene's *The Power and the Glory* and Jon Hassler is certainly one of
the best Catholic novelists since Graham Greene" (quoted in Truesdale 1994,
49). But critic C. W. Truesdale believes it "very reductive and limiting to see
Hassler as primarily a Catholic writer." He argues:

> Hassler has a real genius for comedy that goes far beyond his rootedness in
> Catholic tradition—a rootedness that is certainly important in his work but is
> finally irrelevant to his excellence as an artist. Most of his characters are indeed
> Catholic, at least the main ones, but it is their breadth, depth, and humanity
> which ultimately engage the reader whether or not he or she is Catholic. (65)

Perhaps the last critical word on this subject should come from Hassler himself.
In a published interview with editor W. Dale Brown in *Of Fiction and Faith*,
Hassler classified his work as "Catholic, Christian, Regional" (1997, 188). When
Brown reminded Hassler that Catherine Bailey had called his work a body of
"life-affirming fiction" and added that he believed that a part of Hassler's popularity "must be attributed to something fairly rare these days: the assumption that
faith, religious faith, is one of the realities at work in human life" (188), Hassler
did not disagree. Hassler acknowledged that "There's something in my books that
comforts people or consoles people" (190). Brown then asked, "Fall, redemption,
judgment. Does . . . [your fiction] fit there?" Hassler replied, "Yes, I'd be pleased
to have my fiction categorized there" (191), and added that even though he
had not set out to write of such topics, "forgiveness [and the] possibility of
grace" play a major part in his storytelling (192).

NOTE

Jon Hassler, *North of Hope* (New York: Ballantine, 1990). All references are to
this edition.

WORKS CITED

Brown, W. Dale, ed. 1997. *Of Fiction and Faith: Twelve American Writers Talk
     about Their Vision and Work*. Grand Rapids, MI: Eerdmans.
Cormier, Anne M. 1998. "The Wit, Wisdom and Wonder of Writer Jon Hassler."
     St. Anthony Messenger (November): 17–21.
Hassler, Jon. 1995. "Remembering Houses." In *Imagining Home: Writing from the
     Midwest*, ed. Mark Vinz and Thom Tammaro, 77–86. Minneapolis: University
     of Minnesota Press.
———. 1997. "Happy Man." In *Of Fiction and Faith: Twelve American Writers
     Talk about Their Vision and Work*, ed. W. Dale Brown, 183–97. Grand
     Rapids, MI: Eerdmans.

————. 1999. *My Staggerford Journal*. New York: Ballantine.
————. 2001. *Good People*. Chicago: Loyola University Press.
————. 2002. *The Staggerford Flood*. New York: Viking.
Hays, Charlotte. 2001. "Hope on Ice: The Felicitous Fiction of Jon Hassler." *Crisis* 19, no. 5 (May): 24–27.
Low, Anthony. 1994. "Jon Hassler: Catholic Realist." *Renascence: Essays on Values in Literature* 47, no. 1: 59–70.
Plut, Joe. 1997. "Of Colleges, Characters, Lake Country Journal 1, no. 1: 34–38.
Powers, Michael. 1990. *An Interview with Jon Hassler*. With a Bibliography by Larry Dingman. Minneapolis: Dinkytown Antiquarian Bookstore.
Truesdale, C. W. 1994. "On the Novels of Jon Hassler." *South Dakota Review* 32, no. 1 (Spring): 47–87.

— Deanna Delmar Evans

Hildegard of Bingen [1098–1179]

Scivias

BIOGRAPHY

Hildegard of Bingen was born in 1098 in what today is known as Germany's Rhineland, at Bermersheim near Alzey. She was of noble birth, although not of the highest rank of nobility. It is said that as the tenth child in the family her parents gave her as a "tithe" to the Church; others say she showed religious promise very early on in life. At the age of eight, Hildegard entered a life of religious seclusion, either as an oblate or an anchoress, and was placed under the guidance and tutelage of an older relative who was a committed anchoress, Jutta of Sponheim. From childhood on, Hildegard was said to have exhibited a visionary gift; however, she told very few people about it, and Jutta was probably one of them. Another whom she confided in was her friend and confessor Volmar, a monk at the Abbey of Disibodenberg, where the anchorhold was located.

As Jutta became widely known for her wisdom, other girls joined Hildegard, and the anchorhold was transformed into a small community of Benedictine women, in which Hildegard was professed as a nun at the age of fifteen along with the group. The women's monastery was attached to the Abbey of Disibodenberg, a Benedictine monastery for men, in the tradition of the many double monasteries that existed at this time. The women's monastery, however, was much smaller than that of the men.

Upon Jutta's death in 1136, Hildegard was elected leader of the community and called *magistra*, meaning "teacher," which is the role Jutta had carried out before her. Hildegard was thirty-eight years old at the time and had spent thirty years immersed in religious life, praying the Scriptures and psalms, singing the Divine Office, and steeped in the Benedictine world of "work and prayer." The imagery of her later writings also gives evidence that she had at least limited access to her surroundings outside the monastery.

At the age of forty-two, in 1141, Hildegard received an overwhelming vision from God, whom she calls the "Living Light" in her writings. God commanded her to write and speak what she had seen and heard in the visions. She initially resisted this call from God. But resistance made her ill, and so she began to work on her first mystical-visionary treatise, the *Scivias*, after a considerable personal struggle. In 1146 she wrote to the greatest spiritual authority of the twelfth century, Bernard of Clairvaux, asking his opinion regarding the truth of her visions. Both Bernard and the institutional Church authorities confirmed their validity and importance in 1147.

Hildegard continued to write books on a wide variety of subjects, including two other visionary works besides the *Scivias*. Her play, the *Ordo Virtutum*, was the first medieval morality play written and performed between the ninth and fourteenth centuries. In addition, she penned practical works about the natural world, the treatment of illnesses, and the importance of diet for health. She also wrote several lives of the founding saints of the monasteries to which she belonged and commentaries on the Benedictine Rule. From her forty-second year on, Hildegard felt both a call from God and a commission from the Church to prophesy when the Living Light wished to communicate with the people of God.

Hildegard lived in a particularly tumultuous time, with both the political and religious realms in constant upheaval. She composed commanding letters to those in power and was highly influential with political and religious leaders because they shared her conviction that she spoke the literal words of God. Her influence was not limited by location, although travel was difficult in the twelfth century: she wrote more than four hundred letters to people of all ranks, situations, and genders as far away as England and Jerusalem.

Hildegard founded her own monastery, the Rupertsberg, in 1150 after receiving a command from God. During this tense period in her life, she was in the middle of writing *Scivias*, a book that required ten years to complete. Her move with her nuns to Rupertsberg was highly unpopular with the monks of Disibodenberg, who profited by her presence both spiritually and materially. Moreover, she did not know if Volmar would be allowed to come as confessor to the nuns, and her favorite sister and friend, Richardis, was made abbess elsewhere not long after the move and died shortly thereafter. However, Hildegard continued to be joined by many women in the monastery she founded. Later in her life, her community was extended to a new convent not far away at Eibingen. The current Abbey of St. Hildegard is located on this site near in the modern city of Eibingen, or Bingen.

In her lifetime, Hildegard may have initially gained a kind of celebrity for her composition of what would ultimately be a cycle of about seventy-seven songs, called the *Symphonia*. A letter exists from Odo of Soissons, written in 1148 in Paris, about this musical work. It was composed for the Liturgy of the Hours, the liturgical chant sung constantly in the course of a Benedictine day that gives the day its structure. According to Hildegard, her music came to her directly from the Living Light, just as her other visions did. Hildegard regarded music as a bridge between this world and the divine realm; she believed that she and her sisters were glimpsing a bit of heaven when songs of praise were sung in the daily Divine Office. In fact, the heavenly choir of angels is an important symbol in her work and has profound meaning for her understanding of the unity of heaven and earth.

Later in her life, Hildegard was invited by Church authorities to preach publicly, an unusual commission for a woman and especially for a cloistered nun. She thus undertook four extensive preaching tours, speaking in town squares as well as in monasteries. In her preaching, she spoke with the voice of authority that came from her visions but also from a prophetic calling or voice that is uniquely her own. She was considered a magnificent, if terrifying, preacher who brought many back to the faith and away from the heresies of the times.

Hildegard died in 1179 at the advanced age of eighty-one despite having suffered from chronic illness throughout her life. In her lifetime she was known as the "Sybil of the Rhine" in acknowledgment of her prophetic and visionary gifts. Although canonization proceedings were begun, they were left incomplete due to reforms in the canonization process at the time; it seems as though her cause was lost in the process. Nevertheless, although not formally canonized by the Church, she is officially venerated as a saint in Germany today, and even outside Germany she is often referred to as Saint Hildegard of Bingen.

SUMMARY

Scivias (1152) is impressive as a work of overall stylistic symmetry despite having been composed over ten years and in difficult circumstances. The short title is an abbreviation of the longer phrase *Scito vias Domini*, or "Know the Ways of the Lord." Divided into three parts of unequal length but equal importance, the book is structured carefully for Hildegard's theological purposes. It is her first treatise of what ultimately became a "set" of three treatises of visionary-theological character. The latter two books in this trio are the *Liber vitae meritorum*, or the "Book of Life's Merits" (1163), and *De operatione Dei*, or "The Works of God" (1174).

Part one of *Scivias* concerns the creation of the world in its goodness by God and humankind's Fall, which brings sin into the world. It is lyrical in its description of paradise and inventive in its language, imagery, and the immediacy given to the theology of the Fall and the realities of sin. Hildegard envisions not only the Fall of humanity but the Fall of the angels as well; this is an early indication that her work will always include every dimension of the created order. Despite the Fall, she considers creation to be a wonderful gift, an abundance of God's *viriditas*, or "lush greenness." She uses such wordplay throughout the work to link the startlingly alive greenness of the earth to other ideas such as strength, virtue, virginity, and Christ's birth from a virgin—all words that are similar in the Latin original.

Part two concerns the pivotal event of the Christian faith, the Incarnation of Christ, through which salvation comes. Where Eve failed, the Virgin triumphs: in Mary, Jesus becomes man for the sake of humanity. This focus on the Incarnation is especially meaningful for Hildegard because of her desire to combat Catharism, a Gnostic heresy of the time that condemned the body and all physical things. It is clear that Gnosticism is distasteful to her both theologically and personally; she is very down to earth in the way she sees life despite the gift of her visions, which can seem ethereal at times. For Hildegard, the Incarnation of Christ is the manifest love of God in and for the world; the Savior redeems God's creation in his Resurrection.

Part three considers the tribulations of the Church as it suffers from sin in the world and from persecution; it also contrasts these trials by depicting the support of those who remain faithful, helping to build the Kingdom of God. Many of Hildegard's illustrations literally look like buildings and ramparts in this section. Here is where virtue and vice are strongly contrasted, an opposition she will return to in a later work. But the outcome is never in doubt: at the end of time, there will be the inevitable triumphal coming of the Kingdom of God. Hildegard's images are unique for her era because of their lack of conformity to any contemporary artistic motifs: for example, she often uses female figures as metaphors, and she portrays her visions surrounded by circles that remind the modern reader of eastern mandalas.

MAJOR THEMES

Hildegard's *Scivias* was read first by her confessor, then her abbot, and finally her archbishop. As luck would have it, Pope Eugenius was visiting the Archbishop of Trier at a crucial time in 1148. The pope not only confirmed that Hildegard's visions were indeed from God, he also insisted that she must keep writing these visions down as they came to her. This approval demonstrated to the wider community that Hildegard's visions were indeed extraordinary yet also orthodox in content and, as such, to be respected as a gift from God. The pope's sanction gave both Hildegard and the Church a very clear idea of her role as a visionary writer.

The entirety of the *Scivias* is lavish in its imagery in both words and in colorful illustrations, or miniatures, which were part of the original manuscript. While we can see the work and imagination of Hildegard's inspired writing here, it is very clear from the start that she regarded *Scivias* primarily as an exact transcription of God's words. Therefore, the subjective or personal element of Hildegard herself rarely appears except in the description of the revelation she receives and in her use of quotations from biblical or Church authorities. We hear more of her own character and voice elsewhere. This is an important element of the *Scivias* as a literary work: the book is a clear portrayal not only of the drama of salvation but also of the gifts Hildegard has received and how she puts them to use. She is emphatically clear about when God is speaking and when she, as visionary, is interpreting or narrating God's words and that these instances are different in kind. In fact, Hildegard insisted to her biographers that she never went into trances or ecstasies but saw a "double-vision" in which the things of everyday life and the things of heaven were experienced simultaneously.

Scivias cannot be considered without raising the issue of whether or not Hildegard's visions were the result of migraine headaches, as some scholars have contended. Ironically, this supposition is often seen as a theological "deal-breaker." If, on the one hand, Hildegard did suffer from migraine, then the visions can be explained scientifically and without recourse to religious experience; if, on the other hand, she did not, then the visions must have come from God. The most authoritative voice speaking for the migraine theory comes from the medical rather than the theological community. In his book on migraine, *Migraine: The Evolution of a Common Disorder*, the prominent neurologist Oliver Sacks concludes that it is likely that Hildegard had migraine. Yet he also concludes that it essentially does not matter. Why? Because Sacks states that it is not what our malady or diagnosis is in itself that matters nearly as much as what we choose to do with it (1970, 57–58). This medical view is in full harmony with the theological view that the Spirit of God expresses itself as it wills, in whatever incarnate being and under whatever conditions are present. If Hildegard had migraine, she did not so much "suffer" from it as receive great joy from its symptoms. If she did not have it, then the likenesses are coincidental. Neither hypothesis confirms or denies the divine origin of her visions or the authenticity of her call to prophesy. Indeed, if migraine did not cause her to suffer but rather gave meaning and shape to her life, then perhaps the pain associated with the symptoms was spiritually lifted from her through the working of God's grace. This is certainly a legitimate and rational approach from the Catholic perspective, which maintains the link between revelation and reason, properly understood (as explained by Saint Thomas Aquinas). It also explains in more depth what it truly means to be "incarnated" in the theological sense of the word, leaving behind any soul-body dualism that we might bring to these issues.

Scivias is both an impressive work and one that it is difficult for contemporary readers to penetrate with ease. Its wording is difficult and is made more so by Hildegard's interesting use of grammatical constructions. It is full of allusions, especially to biblical sources, which are at times commented on explicitly and are at other times references that the author's original readers or hearers were expected to know. Its syntax is occasionally tangled, its tone at times ponderous, and the explanations, more elliptical than direct, often leave readers more confused afterward than at the start. While overall it is an inspirational work of great individuality—no less than a lofty retelling of the salvific structure of the cosmos and a work of poetic insight—it cannot be called an easy introduction to Hildegard. There are two translations in English that, if used in conjunction, give the best sense of the original Latin. The first is that of Mother Columba Hart, whose volume of the *Scivias* appears in the Paulist Press Classics of Western Spirituality series. The second is that of Bruce Hozeski (1986), whose translation is at times ruined by the contextual interpretation of his editors, Bear and Company, and not by the translator. Large portions are very faithful and readable translations.

In addition to all these considerations, the historical time in which *Scivias* was written is essential to an understanding of both its style and its content. Hildegard believed that God had chosen her, a woman, to speak forth strongly to "a womanish time" when Christians were not heeding or hearing the words of God (*Letters* 1994, 26, 49). In her age, there was also a firm belief in apocalyptic prophecies, and Hildegard's was the most powerful of these. Apocalyptic prophesy is a curious but particular genre that focuses its attention on the imminence of divine judgment and the coming of the Kingdom of God, which will abolish all error, sin, and darkness, although not without a period of struggle on the part of humanity. A precise time for the ending of the world is not given but rather an expectation that its destiny is fully in God's hands. *Scivias* is a proclamation to an age drifting away from the knowledge and truth of God, to the peril of individuals and collectively to the Church herself. It stands as a reminder and as a call to repentance so that people might hear in a new way the Gospel that had always been true but was, in Hildegard's opinion, not currently being followed.

Part of the originality of Hildegard's work lies in her unique claim to prophetic insight, and part of it lies in the use of allegorical figures with which she emphasizes her points in both the miniatures and the text. These figures are all the more striking because of their femininity: *Ecclesia* (Church), *Synogoga* (Synagogue), *Caritas* (Charity), and *Sapientia* (Wisdom) are all female figures to Hildegard. If it were not for the visual images accompanying the text, we might be tempted to explain the abundance of feminine imagery on the strength of the argument that these nouns actually are all feminine in Latin. Some figures, like the Church, were traditionally perceived as feminine: the Church is the bride of Christ, the *sposa Christi*. Some, like Wisdom, are from the Old Testament. Other figures are individual to Hildegard's visionary works. Whatever their origin, these female figures become powerful forces in the narrative and its accompanying illustrations because they are vital to the visions Hildegard received. They are one reason for her widespread appeal today.

Besides this liberal use of feminine imagery, there is very little in Hildegard's *Scivias* that may be considered dubious in its theological content; she may be innovative, but she is so only in her expression of traditional doctrines. Rather, her unique expression enriches her work, and she appealed to people in her own time as in ours through her creative use of metaphor and in her confidence in proclaiming the message of the Living Light. Hildegard's work is thoroughly Catholic in both spirit and detail. She derives her structure from the traditional understanding of the work of God in creation, Incarnation, salvation, and in the coming of God's kingdom. Moreover, she speaks as a prophet in the manner of the Old Testament prophets, calling back those who have strayed from the central mysteries of the faith and warning them to return to a loving God who, as the Living Light, causes all things to exist.

Yet another important theme in *Scivias* is later developed more fully in Hildegard's third theological-visionary treatise, *De operatione Dei*. Her major image here is that of the cosmos, the world with its four directions and its center, totally encompassed by the figure of a man with arms outstretched. God is encompassing the created world, and the microcosm (the small part we inhabit) is placed in the context of the macrocosm (the full sum of God's being and his creation). Hildegard repeatedly uses imagery from the material world around her to emphasize the goodness of the world: rocks, minerals, precious stones, blooming plants, and the stars in the sky convey the wonder of God's marvelous work in creation and, ultimately, re-creation. She is not hesitant to be equally as graphic when depicting what we can do to the goodness of the world: we sin, and thus cause a foul stench to arise or we fall into a loathsome pit (an image from vision four of *De operatione Dei*). She also emphasizes that even those in the Church hierarchy may sin. The worse the degree of sin, the more "leprous" and "corpse-like" they become (*Scivias*, 238).

Central to an understanding of the structure of *Scivias* is Hildegard's theme of the link between the macrocosm and the microcosm in the Incarnation. Her vision of the Church, kneeling to receive the body and blood of Christ from the side of the crucified Christ in heaven (Vision 6, 235–38), is stunning in its complexity. It touches on the sacrifice of Christ, the sacrifice of the Church, the Church as the bride of Christ, the Real Presence of the Eucharist made so by the words of the liturgy and the actions of the priest, and many other doctrinal truths. For Hildegard, the Incarnation is the pivotal point of all of history: it brings balance back into existence, it links the microcosm and the macrocosm, and it allows God to pervade this still fallen world.

A final theme in *Scivias* is that of eschatology, or the last things. Hildegard, as we have seen, is clear about the drama of salvation: salvation history has been initiated by God and will end when God so wills it. Her apocalyptic visions of the end of time, like those of the Old Testament prophets, remind her readers that God, while loving and merciful, is also a just judge. In the end, virtues will be adorned as with jewels and the smell of sweet fragrance, while vices will be ugly, deformed, strangled, and reek of dreadful odors. The Last Judgment is justice done by God. Hildegard writes her visions to remind humanity that there is yet time to see the beautiful rather than embrace the foul things in life, the latter of which may bring temporary pleasures but ultimately will strangle and defeat us.

Scivias becomes far richer when read in the context of Hildegard's other two theological-visionary works, for in this way we can see the incremental progression, modification, and restatement of her main themes. Looking at all three works also raises a number of interesting textual and literary issues. The primacy of image over text moves from the centrality of the illustrations in understanding the *Scivias*, to the more imaginative use of the visual in the *Liber vitae meritorum*, and finally to a meshing of text and image in *De operatione Dei*. Although asserted in differing tones throughout the three works, the source of Hildegard's authority to write and preach remains the same: the direct words of God that impel her to the task.

CRITICAL RECEPTION

In her time, Hildegard was famous as the Sybil of the Rhine, the prophetess of God, a visionary authority whose words were to be taken seriously. An example of the potency of her prophetic power can be seen in her relationship to Frederick Barbarossa, the Holy Roman Emperor and one of the most feared men of the day. Hildegard was able not only to gain from him a perpetual grant for the land for the Rupertsberg convent, protecting her from retaliation should she lose favor, but she also chastised him in her letters as though he were an intemperate little boy when he meddled in Church affairs, calling him both "infant" and "madman."

With this kind of notoriety, one wonders, then, why Hildegard virtually disappeared from popular view after the thirteenth century and did not resurface again until the nineteenth century. At that time, her writing was rediscovered piece by piece and her manuscripts started to be examined by scholars. Some of this foundational scholarship was performed by the nuns of the Abbey of St. Hildegard, especially by Sister Adelgundis Führkötter, an Eibingen nun who became interested in the order's foundress. Führkötter wrote out of curiosity at first, and then with scholarly fervor for her subject. She published seminal works on Hildegard's approach to the cosmos (1987), on Hildegard's variety of works (1972), and on the miniatures that were used to illustrate *Scivias* (1977). All have been recently reissued.

By the late twentieth century, Hildegard had attracted a whole new following of readers who were especially appreciative of her holistic attitude toward the entire cosmos in its essential relationship to God. However, this new adulation has not always been faithful to Hildegard's actual voice and message. While she affirms creation as God's work, she is not merely the simplistic "nature lover" we see, for example, in such works as Matthew Fox's *Illuminations of Hildegard of Bingen* (2003). Fox, who along with his followers views Hildegard as an advocate of creation spirituality, often misquotes her and thus misleads readers regarding her actual words. Unfortunately, this book, while full of errors, is also the only readily accessible source of Hildegard's color illustrations from *Scivias*. Another book to be avoided is Renate Craine's *Hildegard: Prophet of the Cosmic Christ* (1997), because it takes as its thesis the idea of the "Cosmic Christ" in creation spirituality rather than deriving its central themes from Hildegard's work itself.

Today, Hildegard has received a wide reception among both scholars and general readers alike. Much of the scholarly work done initially on her works was highly technical and thus not accessible to the average reader; much of it continues to be this kind of analysis and criticism. Such work may be especially valuable for readers who have a particular interest and training in music. For more general readers, a number of recent studies present Hildegard to modern readers in a highly accessible way. Barbara Newman's *Sister of Wisdom* (1987), for example, is a readable yet highly erudite account of Hildegard's use of and relationship to feminine imagery. It considers this imagery in the light of Hildegard's times, avoiding the error of others who would cast her as a type of twentieth-century "feminist" heroine. Newman has made many valuable contributions to Hildegard studies, both in academic circles and in books that are appreciated by the general public. She has also written the critical edition of Hildegard's *Symphonia* (1998), which should be considered the standard text on the lyrics of Hildegard's songs in Latin and English translations, one poetic and the other literal. Other recommended critical texts include Sabina Flanagan's *Hildegard of Bingen: A Visionary Life* (1989), Fiona Maddocks's *Hildegard of Bingen: Woman of Her Age* (2001), and my own *Hildegard of Bingen: An Integrated Vision* (2001).

There are quite a few translations of Hildegard's opus into various languages, and the translations in English vary in quality. Aside from the two versions of the *Scivias* mentioned above, there are several recommended collections of Hildegard's works, each of which gives the reader a sense of Hildegard's message and show-cases her considerable talents. These are Sabina Flanagan's *Secrets of God: Writings of Hildegard of Bingen* (1996), Fiona Bowie and Oliver Davies's *Hildegard of Bingen: Mystical Writings* (1990), and Penguin's *Selected Writings: Hildegard of Bingen* (2001).

For readers of the *Scivias*, Hildegard's collected letters and her biography also help put many things into context. Translated by Joseph Baird and Radd Ehrmann, volume one of *The Letters of Hildegard of Bingen* was published in 1994 and volume two in 1998; a third volume is forthcoming. A recommended biography is *The Life of Hildegard of Bingen*, edited by Hugh Feiss (1996), which is a compilation and translation of several of Hildegard's contemporary biographies.

Hildegard would no doubt be shocked at the "appropriation" of her ideas and their misrepresentation when taken out of context by some popular writers. Her life has, unfortunately, been fictionalized in unacceptable ways. Joan Ohanneson's *Scarlet Music: Hildegard of Bingen* (1997), for example, is a fictional account that has had huge success but reads into Hildegard's interior life feelings and emotions that are more based on the conjectures and concerns of a twentieth-century writer of light fiction than appropriate to the historical Hildegard. For example, this novel describes how Hildegard was harshly "ripped away" from her loving parents, and it speculates about her sexual feelings for a certain cleric who, in reality, did not even enter her life until a later point. It is disappointing to note that this book's commercial success has afforded the author, as with Matthew Fox, the dubious distinction of being an "expert" on Hildegard. On the other hand, the fictional *The Journal of Hildegard of Bingen*, by Barbara Lachman (1995), can make for interesting reading as long as it is accompanied by more accurate historical accounts.

Finally, Hildegard has been portrayed in two recent films. One, produced by the Washington National Cathedral in 1989 and entitled *Hildegard of Bingen*, is a very good four-part documentary. The second, Vision Video's 1995 *Woman of Vision*, is a lavishly produced, meticulously costumed epic that juxtaposes fine scenes of liturgical chant appropriate to the period with completely inaccurate portrayals of the sequence and importance of events in Hildegard's life. All is subordinated to the film's obvious agenda: to portray Hildegard as a leader in a wholly feminine approach to God, a veritable crusader for women's rights.

Hildegard was always self-consciously aware of her extraordinary gift, but she never used it without the discernment and approval of Church authorities; she advocated stability in religious vocation, despite her unusual life, to those inspired by her example. Her theology is entirely centered on Jesus' Incarnation and in the consequent overlapping of heaven and earth in our experience of God. Part of the delight of Hildegard's writing is in its embracing of the created world in all its beauty, in her visions of the Church as a female figure, and in her almost dizzying use of imagery to portray the history of the universe from a Christian perspective. However, if not placed in proper context, we miss much of the impact she had on her peers as well as that which she can, and does, have on us today. It is essential that we do not overlook the full treasure of the riches she has to offer us.

NOTE

Hildegard of Bingen, *Scivias*, trans. Mother Columba Hart (New York: Paulist Press, 1990). All references are to this edition.

WORKS CITED

Bowie, Fiona, and Oliver Davies, eds. 1990. *Hildegard of Bingen: Mystical Writings*. New York: Crossroad.

Craine, Renate. 1997. *Hildegard: Prophet of the Cosmic Christ*. New York: Crossroad.

Feiss, Hugh, trans. 1996. Gottfried of Disibodenberg, et al. *The Life of Hildegard of Bingen*. Peregrina Translation Series. Toronto: Peregrina.

Flanagan, Sabina. 1989. *Hildegard of Bingen: A Visionary Life*. London and New York: Routledge.

———. 1996. *Secrets of God: Writings of Hildegard of Bingen*. Boston: Shambala.

Fox, Matthew. 2003. *Illuminations of Hildegard of Bingen*. 2nd ed. Rochester, VT: Inner Traditions International.

Führkötter, Adelgundis, ed. 1972. *Hildegard von Bingen*. Salzburg: Otto Müller Verlag.

———. 1977. *The Miniatures from the Book Scivias, Know the Ways*. Turnhout, Belgium: Brepols.

————. 1987. *Kosmos und Mensch aus der Sicht Hildegards von Bingen*. Mainz, Germany: Verlag der Gesellschaft für Mittelrheinische Kirchengeschichte.

Hildegard of Bingen. 1986. *Scivias*, trans. Bruce Hozeski. Santa Fe, NM: Bear and Co.

————. 1987. *Hildegard of Bingen's Book of Divine Works, with Letters and Songs*, trans. Bruce Hozeski; ed. Matthew Fox. Santa Fe, NM: Bear and Co.

————. 1994. *The Book of Life's Merits*, trans. Kent Kraft. New York: Garland Press.

————. 1994/1998. *The Letters of Hildegard of Bingen*, trans. Joseph Baird and Radd Ehrmann. 2 vols. New York: Oxford University Press.

————. 1995. *Liber Divinorum Operum*, ed. Albert Derolez and Peter Dronke. Turnhout, Belgium: Brepols.

————. 2001. *Selected Writings of Hildegard of Bingen*, trans. Mark Atherton. New York: Penguin U.S.A.

King-Lenzmeier, Anne. 2001. *Hildegard of Bingen: An Integrated Vision*. Collegeville, MN: Liturgical Press.

Lachman, Barbara. 1995. *The Journal of Hildegard of Bingen: A Novel*. Reprint edition. New York: Harmony/Bell Tower.

Maddocks, Fiona. 2001. *Hildegard of Bingen: Woman of Her Age*. New York: Doubleday.

Newman, Barbara. 1987. *Sister of Wisdom: St. Hildegard's Theology of the Feminine*. Berkeley, CA: Scholar's Press.

————. 1998. *Symphonia: Critical Edition*. Revised edition. Ithaca, NY: Cornell University Press.

Ohanneson, Joan. 1997. *Scarlet Music: Hildegard of Bingen: A Novel*. New York: Crossroad/Herder and Herder.

Sacks, Oliver. 1970. *Migraine: The Evolution of a Common Disorder*. Berkeley, CA: UCLA Press.

— **Anne H. King**

Gerard Manley Hopkins [1844–1889]

Poems

BIOGRAPHY

Unknown as a poet when he died at forty-four, the Jesuit priest Gerard Manley Hopkins is now acclaimed as a major English writer and, with Browning and Tennyson, among the finest poets of Victorian England. He also stands among the greatest poets of nature and of religion in the English language. His experiments in rhythm, sound, and wordplay influenced such major twentieth-century poets as W. H. Auden, Dylan Thomas, and Seamus Heaney, and his poems, difficult as they are, have been translated into many languages. Hopkins is now world famous, renowned for both his content and his technique.

Born on July 28, 1844, in Stratford, Essex, near London, Gerard Hopkins was the oldest child of Manley and Kate Hopkins. (His middle name was not used until *Poems of Gerard Manley Hopkins* was published in 1918; he signed his name "Gerard Hopkins" or "Gerard M. Hopkins," often followed by "S. J.") His father ran a successful maritime insurance firm and wrote insurance manuals, a history of Hawaii, a play, literary essays, songs, and books of poems. His mother, born Kate Smith, enjoyed history and music, knew some Italian and German, and wrote entertainments for her children. Devoutly Anglican and moderately High Church, the family was comfortable and given to books, art, and music. In 1852 they moved to Hampstead, then a village north of London, where young Gerard developed a love of words and sketched both nature and architecture. From 1854 to 1862 he attended the nearby Highgate School, and in 1863 he won a scholarship to Balliol College, Oxford.

Hopkins's Oxford years—1863 to 1867—were among his happiest, as he studied classical literature and classical "Greats" (history and philosophy). He kept a journal rich in images, words, and sketches and made lifelong friends, especially Robert Bridges, later a physician and poet laureate. Deeply religious, Hopkins gradually moved from the High Church theology of E. B. Pusey through the stringent piety of H. P. Liddon to the Roman Catholic Church, into which he was received on October 21, 1866, by John Henry (later Cardinal) Newman. His Oxford poetry was competent but not distinguished, his best works being "Heaven-Haven" and "The Habit of Perfection." In June 1867, he left Oxford with a "First" (a first-class degree) in Greats.

His next year was unsettled as he pondered his vocation. From September 1867 to April 1868, he taught at Newman's Oratory School in Birmingham, but he felt overworked and lacked time to read. He left there on April 15, and after a Jesuit retreat made three decisions: to burn his poetry as a sacrifice to God, to become a religious and a priest, and to be a Jesuit rather than a Benedictine. On May 11, he burned his poems—his journal recorded the "slaughter of the innocents" (*Journals*, 1959, 165)—but few were actually lost since Robert Bridges and others had copies.

After touring Switzerland with an Oxford friend, Hopkins entered the Jesuit Order at Manresa House, Roehampton, London, on September 7, 1868. As a novice he made the thirty-day retreat following the *Spiritual Exercises* of Saint Ignatius Loyola and learned Jesuit spirituality and Jesuit life. Taking vows of poverty, chastity, and obedience on September 8, 1870, he went to study philosophy at St. Mary's Hall, Stonyhurst College, in rural Lancashire. In class, he learned Suarezian Thomism, and in his reading he discovered the philosophy of John Duns Scotus, which stressed a being's unique individuality (*haecceitas* or "thisness") and confirmed Hopkins's love of distinctiveness. From 1873 to 1874, he taught rhetoric to young Jesuits at Roehampton; then, on August 28, 1874, he went to St. Beuno's College in North Wales to study theology. Amid Wales's lovely hills and valleys, his talent first exploded into brilliant and major poetry.

The spark was a shipwreck reported in the London papers: the *Deutschland* had foundered in the Thames estuary on the night of December 7, 1875, drowning some sixty crewmen and passengers, including five German Franciscan nuns exiled under Bismarck's *Kulturkampf*. Moved by their deaths and prompted by his rector, Hopkins began his first great poem, "The Wreck of the Deutschland," one of literature's finest odes. It was his first mature experiment with "sprung rhythm" (which counts only a line's stresses and permits any number of unstressed syllables). The next year was Hopkins's *annus mirabilis* as a poet. Between February 23 and September 8, 1877, he wrote eleven celebratory sonnets about God and nature, including his famed "God's Grandeur," "The Starlight Night," "As kingfishers catch fire," "Spring," "The Windhover," "Pied Beauty," and "Hurrahing in Harvest." These Welsh years, 1874 to 1877, were his happiest as a Jesuit and as a poet.

To his sadness, Hopkins had to leave St. Beuno's a year early. Always eccentric, in his third-year examination he chose to defend Scotism instead of the Suarezian Thomism he was taught, and his grades, although passing, were not adequate for a fourth year of theology. Ordained a priest on September 23, 1877, he taught schoolboys at Mount St. Mary's College in Derbyshire, then, six months later, university-level students at Stonyhurst College. From 1878 to 1881, pressing manpower needs and the English Jesuits' makeshift planning sent him to parishes in London, Oxford, Bedford Leigh (near Manchester), Liverpool, and Glasgow. He often felt tired and overworked, although his tasks were not always demanding. He continued to write memorable poems, more restrained than his Welsh sonnets and often rueful: "The May Magnificat," "Duns Scotus's Oxford," "Binsey Poplars," "Henry Purcell," "Felix Randal," "Spring and Fall," and "Inversnaid." He also wrote brilliant sermons, sometimes too clever for his congregations. In October 1881 he returned to Roehampton for his Tertianship, a final year of Jesuit spiritual training. Although producing no extant poems, this year was peaceful and happy, and Hopkins wrote essays on the *Spiritual Exercises* and on what he called the "Great Sacrifice" involved in God's creation and Christ's Incarnation.

After his final vows on August 15, 1882, his life was more stable: he spent his remaining years at Stonyhurst College (1882–1884) and University College, Dublin (1884–1889). At Stonyhurst he taught the classics to university-level students but, despite relatively light tasks, still felt tired and jaded. Some poems are melancholy—"Ribblesdale" has selfish humans and a frowning earth—while others are hopeful, even sunny, such as "The Leaden Echo and the Golden Echo" and "The Blessed Virgin compared to the Air we Breathe." In 1883 he met the Catholic poet Coventry Patmore, and his letters to him, to Bridges, and to the Anglican canon R. W. Dixon contain literary criticism of high quality.

In February 1884, at the request of the Irish Jesuits, Hopkins went to Dublin for his most permanent, and final, post as Professor of Greek at University College (teaching) and Fellow of the Royal University of Ireland (grading examinations from all over Ireland). The teaching post seemed ideal: a stable professorship at a degree-granting institution in the area of his Oxford studies. But University College, and Ireland itself, brought anguish. Founded in 1851 by Newman as the Catholic University of Ireland, University College was near collapse and had been entrusted to the Irish Jesuits in 1882. They gave it new life, bringing Hopkins and European Jesuits to the faculty. But Hopkins was an English patriot, and the Irish were campaigning for "Home Rule," an ambiguous slogan used to unite nationalist groups of disparate goals. Besides political irritation, Hopkins endured other woes: ill-prepared students, the smoke and difficult climate of Dublin, a sense of being an outsider, trouble with his eyes, exhaustion from grading hundreds of examinations, loss of contact with God in prayer, months of deep depression, and ultimately the waning of poetic inspiration. Despite good friends and happy times, his Dublin years were troubled.

In 1884, a holiday in the West of Ireland renewed his love of nature and music, and he planned to translate Saint Patrick's "Confession." In 1885, despite a holiday in England with his family, bad headaches afflicted him. His worst period lasted from early 1885 into 1886, with his melancholy reflected in his searing "Terrible Sonnets" or "Sonnets of Desolation," including "To seem the stranger," "I wake and feel," "No worst, there is none," and "[Carrion Comfort]." More reflective is "To what serves Mortal Beauty," and relief appears in "Patience, hard thing" and "My own heart let me more have pity on." Terrifying in content yet perfect in poetic form, these sonnets express both psychological anguish and the absence of God.

Hopkins had many joys: visits with friends in Dublin and County Kildare, holidays in England with his family and friends such as Bridges and Patmore, and summer trips to Wales and Scotland with an Irish Jesuit. In 1886 he wrote the darkly musical "Spelt from Sibyl's Leaves" and the bittersweet "On the Portrait of Two Beautiful Young People." He also began a series of unfinished projects: an essay on Dixon's poetry, notes for a scientific journal, musical compositions, a verse play in alexandrines, a book on "Homer's Art," and essays on Greek rhythm, Aeschylus, Sophocles, Patmore, Irish dialect, and "Statistics and Free Will." But he did finish three expanded sonnets, "Harry Ploughman" (1887), "Tom's Garland" (1887), and "That Nature is a Heraclitean Fire and of the comfort of the Resurrection" (1888). In the last, after contemplating human death, Hopkins drew solace from resurrection in Christ.

In January 1889, he was again melancholy, worrying during his retreat about his weakness and his few accomplishments, even though he recognized that Christ shaped his life. His final four poems, all traditional sonnets, manifested a new compression of style: "In honour of St. Alphonsus Rodriguez," "Thou are indeed just, Lord," "The shepherd's brow," and "To R. B."—this last a perfect sonnet to Robert Bridges about his loss of poetic inspiration. He died seven weeks later, on June 8, 1889, a victim of typhoid. He would have turned forty-five years old on July 28th of that year.

All his life, Hopkins regularly sent his poems to Robert Bridges, who postponed publication until he thought the literary world was ready for Hopkins's original-ity. *Poems of Gerard Manley Hopkins* was finally published in 1918, edited by Robert Bridges.

MAJOR THEMES

Hopkins's poems fall naturally into four periods: Early Poems (1860–1875), Welsh Poems (1875–1877), Middle Poems (1878–1883), and Dublin Poems (1884–1889). In the Early Poems he is an apprentice; therefore, a survey of his major themes best focuses on his mature poems, beginning with "The Wreck of the Deutschland" (1875–1876). This survey, too simply divided into sacred and secular, should begin with his synthesis of the sacred and the secular into his grand theme, the presence of God shining through all creation. Except for this incarnational theme and the themes of selfhood and psychological anguish, Hopkins's poetic themes are not notably original. His distinctive quality comes rather from the freshness and strength of his language, from the music of his words and rhythms, and from his unusual perspectives as he sees his themes from quirky angles and presents them with often quirky metaphors.

"Incarnationalism" is so named to parallel the Incarnation (or enfleshment) of Christ: because the divine Christ took on human flesh, he united divinity with physicality, thus giving a divine dimension to every physical thing—violets, stones, trout, oil, humans. Hopkins expresses this incarnational union in various ways. "The world is charged with the grandeur of God," asserts "God's Grandeur," as Hopkins presents God's presence as an electric charge with countless sparks. In "As kingfishers catch fire," Christ is a stage actor who "plays" to "the Father through the features of men's faces." "Pied Beauty" cries out, "Glory be to God for dappled things," celebrates God's presence in even the strangest things, and ends with a simple "Praise him." Yet God also brings pain: Hopkins is honest enough to admit that God causes suffering as he acts in the world, for the nun in "The Wreck of the Deutschland" suffers from "God's cold." Hopkins's incarnational-ism is consistent and intellectually honest.

Two of Hopkins's famous word coinages, "inscape" and "instress," reflect his incarnational theology. "Inscape," which denotes both a being's unique inner individuality and external shape, is theologically grounded in God's act of creating and preserving each individual being. "Instress," which denotes a being's active drive to sustain its inscape and express it to a perceptive observer, is theologically grounded in God's self-expression and self-proclamation in and through creation. This incarnational vision, pervasive in the Welsh poems, is at the center of Hopkins's spirituality and of his art.

Hopkins's themes may now be divided into sacred and secular. His sacred themes involve God, the Virgin Mary, the saints, sin, redemption, and the sacraments. In portraying God, Hopkins is highly Trinitarian. He begins "The Wreck" by invoking God the Father as master and creator: "Thou mastering me / God! giver of breath and bread; / World's strand, sway of the sea; / Lord of living and dead; / Thou hast bound bones and veins in me, fastened me flesh." He then turns to the Son, Christ, who brings Hopkins both terror ("the frown of his face / Before me") and warm love ("the heart of the Host") and who brings the shipwrecked nun both suffering ("the unshapeable shock night," "God's cold") and eternal life ("shé has thée for the pain"). Near the end of the poem, Hopkins again turns Trinitarian as he calls on "the Christ of the Father compassionate." The Holy Spirit appears most memorably in "God's Grandeur," in which nature remains fresh and morning dawns "because the Holy Ghost over the bent / World broods with warm breast and with ah! bright wings." The Trinity as three appears in "The Wreck" as "God, three-numberèd form" and "three of the thunder-throne" and in "(Margaret Clitheroe)" as "The Utterer, Utterèd, Uttering." Yet overall, it is Christ whom Hopkins most often names, praises, and invokes with inventiveness and variety: "O Christ, O God," "hero of Calvary," "Orion of light," "martyr-master," "Christ, King, Head," "Jesu heart's light, / Jesu, maid's son," "Double-naturèd name," "Miracle-in-Mary-of-flame," "prince, hero of us, high-priest," "our thóughts' chivalry's thróng's Lórd," "O maid's child," "our Saviour," "first, fást, last friend," "O Hero savest," "Lord of the Eucharist," "God's infinity / Dwindled to infancy," "O thou terrible," "Christ our King," "God-made-flesh," "Jesus Christ sacrificed / On the cross," "truth," "immortal diamond."

Hopkins also celebrates Mary and the saints. In "The Wreck" Jesus is "maid's son," "the heaven-flung, heart-fleshed, maiden-furled / Miracle-in-Mary-of-flame." Two lovely, rhythmic poems praise Mary, "The May Magnificat" and "The Blessed Virgin compared to the Air we Breathe." As for the saints, he dedicates poems to the early martyrs Dorothea and Thecla, to the English Margaret Clitheroe, the Welsh Winefred and Beuno, and the Spanish Jesuits Francis Xavier and Alphonsus Rodriguez.

Hopkins's sense of sin is strong, recurring, even nagging. His early Oxford poems are guilt-ridden, and even his Welsh poems worry about sin. "The Wreck" recalls his fear of hell, and the rapturous "Spring," so positive in its octave, prays in its sestet that God capture young men and women for himself before they "sour with sinning." "The Sea and the Skylark" contrasts the beauty of sea and bird to the "shallow and frail" Welsh town of Rhyl where humans break "down / To man's last dust, drain fast towards man's first slime." Some poems end with sinfulness, others foresee redemption in Christ. "In the Valley of the Elwy" visualizes a kindly judge who balances sin and goodness and gently prays, "God, lover of souls, swaying considerate scales, / Complete thy creature dear O where it fails." "The Wreck" knows God's "mercy" and calls both Father and Son "compassionate." Another shipwreck poem, "The Loss of the Eurydice," addresses Christ as "O Hero [who] savest," confident that "prayer shall fetch pity eternal." Redemption is most striking and brilliant in "That Nature is a Heraclitean Fire": "at a trumpet crash, / I am all at once what Christ is, since he was what I am, and / This Jack, joke, poor potsherd, patch, matchwood, immortal diamond, / Is immortal diamond." In other poems Hopkins reflects on the sacraments as aids to redemption, sometimes in passing, sometimes quite centrally: Baptism (in "The Loss of the Eurydice": "these daredeaths, ay this crew, in / Unchrist, all rolled in ruin"); Penance (in "The Wreck": "the / Comfortless unconfessed of them"); the Eucharist ("The Bugler's First Communion," or in "Felix Randal": "I had our swéet repríeve and ránsom / Téndered to him"); Marriage ("At the Wedding March"); and the Sacrament of the Sick (in "Felix Randal": the blacksmith "mended / Being anointed and all").

Hopkins's crafted prose, especially his sermons and spiritual writings, express many of these themes in theological terms and vibrant language. In a Liverpool sermon of 1880, he asked, "What is a Paraclete?" and answered,

> A Paraclete is one who comforts, who cheers, who encourages, who persuades, who exhorts, who stirs up, who urges forward, who calls on; what the spur and word of command is to a horse, what clapping of hands is to a speaker, what a trumpet is to the soldier, that a Paraclete is to the soul: *one who calls us on*, that is what it means, a Paraclete is one who calls us on to good. (*Sermons*, 1959, 70)

In 1882, at the end of his Tertianship, he reflected on the Trinity and creation: "God's utterance of himself in himself is God the Word, outside himself is this world. This world then is word, expression, news of God. Therefore its end, its purpose, its purport, its meaning, is God and its life or work to name and praise him" (129). Most original theologically is an 1881 comment about Christ and the Trinity in which he asserts that sacrifice is of the very essence of the Trinity:

> To give God glory and that by sacrifice. . . . is a consequence and shadow of the procession of the Trinity, from which mystery sacrifice takes its rise. . . . It is as if the blissful agony or stress of selving in God had forced out drops of sweat or blood, which drops were the world. . . . The sacrifice would be the Eucharist, and that the sacrifice might be truly victim like, like motionless, helpless, or lifeless, it must be in matter. (197)

Hopkins was a preacher of eloquence and a theologian of creativity.

Hopkins's secular themes include nature, ecology, adults and children, selfhood and self, mental suffering, and (since he is so experimental) poetry itself—its words, sounds, rhythms, and forms. His nature poems, sometimes with sacred or moral dimensions, celebrate stars, birds, spring, weeds, trees, the sea, a cow, trout, chestnuts, fields, clouds, hills, a stallion, streams, fern, even mud. His poem "Spring" is rhapsodic: "Nothing is so beautiful as Spring— / When weeds, in wheels, shoot long and lovely and lush." Given their sheer number and variety, he shows a special fondness for birds, as in "The Windhover": "I caught this morning morning's minion, king- / dom of daylight's dauphin, dapple-dáwn-drawn Falcon, in his riding / Of the rólling level únderneáth him steady áir." It is typical that many natural wonders—weeds, a cow, moles on fish skin, mud—are not at all beautiful: his famous "Pied Beauty" makes a point of celebrating "all things counter, original, spáre, strange; / Whatever is fickle, frecklèd (who knows how?)."

Two nature poems are highly ecological. In "Binsey Poplars," Hopkins grieves that "my aspens dear" are "áll félled, félled, are áll félled." "O if we but knew

what we do," he continues, "when we delve or hew– / Hack and rack the growing
green!" The land is permanently bereft: "After-comers cannot guess the beauty
been" of this "rural scene, a rural scene, / Sweet especial rural scene." Two
years later, from Scotland's Loch Lomond, he again pleads for conservation in
"Inversnaid." Describing a stream as a "dárksome búrn" with "a wíndpuff-
bónnet of fáwn-fróth / . . . over the broth / Of a póol so pítchblack," he reflects,
"What would the world be, once bereft / Of wet and wildness? Let them be left, /
O let them be left, wildness and wet; / Long live the weeds and the wilderness yet."

Many poems—often his most tender works—concern adults and children.
Some are moralistic or religious, some praise favorite figures of the past (Duns
Scotus, Henry Purcell), but most recall his friends, parishioners, and students. "In
the Valley of the Elwy" recalls "a house where all were good / To me" and where
a "comforting smell breathed at very entering." "Felix Randal" memorializes a
Liverpool blacksmith, "big-boned and hardy-handsome," whom Hopkins tended
in his final illness. "Harry Ploughman" vividly describes a farmer's physical grace,
and "Tom's Garland" worries about "the Unemployed." "The Handsome Heart"
praises a generous boy in a church sacristy, and "Brothers" shows a student watching his younger brother in a school play and hoping he won't make a mistake.
One of Hopkins's tenderest and most accessible poems, "Spring and Fall," is
dedicated "to a Young Child," Margaret, who grieves for the loss of autumn's
golden leaves without realizing that she really grieves for her own mortality: "It
is Margaret you mourn for."

Hopkins, follower of Duns Scotus, wrote enthusiastically of self and selfhood.
Fascinated by the self, he turns to images of camphor, alum, and ale to describe
its uniqueness, and in "As kingfishers catch fire" cries out, "Each mortal thing
does one thing and the same: / Deals out that being indoors each one dwells; /
Selves–goes its self; *myself* it speaks and spells." In "To what serves Mortal
Beauty," "men's selves" are the "world's loveliest," and "self flashes off frame
and face." He charts the decay of self in his Terrible Sonnets. In "No worst,"
his fear of madness makes him cry out, "O the mind, mind has mountains; cliffs
of fall / Frightful, sheer, no-man-fathomed." In "I wake and feel," his self-loathing
has him taste like "gall" and "heartburn," and his lost contact with God makes his
prayers "like dead letters sent / To dearest him that lives alas! away." A gentler
self returns in "My own heart": "Soul, self. . . , poor Jackself," "let joy size"
(grow) until that moment when God's smile again "lights a lovely mile."

For an experimental poet like Hopkins, a final theme—rarely expressed as
the content of a poem but surely that—is poetry itself, its words, images,
sounds, rhythms, and forms. He chooses the uncommon word for stunning effect:
"the moth-soft Milky Way." He makes the common word shock: "I am gall, I
am heartburn." He omits needed words—"O hero savest"—and creates new
words and combinations: "fallowbootfellow," "churlsgrace," "onewhere,"
"wíndpuff-bónnet of fáwn-fróth," "dapple-dáwn-drawn Falcon." Images and
metaphors are unexpected, even earthy: "dappled-with-damson west," "hope
had grown grey hairs," "down-dugged ground-hugged grey [clouds]," "the ooze
of oil / Crushed," "brinded cow," "a stallion stalwart, very-violet-sweet," "heartburn," "thóughts agáinst thoughts ín groans grínd," "manwolf," "Time's
eunuch," "voids with shame." His rhymes are original, even strange: he rhymes
"Saviour" with "gave you a" and "boon he on" with "Communion" and even

breaks words for a rhyme: "king- / dom" rhymes with "wing," and "sing" with "ling- / ering." His "sprung rhythm" permits unusual freedoms, as when he echoes the sound of axes against the "Binsey Poplars" in a strong, harsh five-stress line of only six syllables: "Áll félled, félled, are áll félled." And he so played with form that, disregarding length yet keeping the basic rhyme pattern, he wrote sonnets of ten lines plus four syllables ("Pied Beauty"), nineteen lines ("Harry Ploughman"), twenty lines ("Tom's Garland"), and twenty-four lines ("Heraclitean Fire"). Such experimentation makes the words, music, and structure of his poetry as distinctive a selving as his more explicit comments on self and selfhood, and his experiments become themselves a theme. In "To R. B." (Robert Bridges), his last poem and one of his few about poetry, he uses a metaphor from music to describe his mind as "a mother of immortal song" and his poetry as "the roll, the rise, the carol, the creation." Surely this presents language, sound, and technique as theme—a major theme and a major glory of Hopkins.

CRITICAL RECEPTION

From the first edition of *Poems*, small errors marred the texts, and the first reliable text is the revised fourth edition of 1967, coedited by Norman H. MacKenzie. Only he and Catherine Phillips have worked carefully from the manuscripts, and only their editions are trustworthy; MacKenzie's Clarendon Press edition is definitive. MacKenzie also edited facsimiles of the poetic manuscripts, invaluable for studying Hopkins's imagination and the stages of a poem's development. MacKenzie (1981) and Paul Mariani (1970) wrote the best commentaries, Robert Bernard Martin (1991) and Norman White (1992) the best biographies. Of these, Martin is the smoother writer, White the more thorough researcher, but both lack a religious understanding of Hopkins. Mariani, a poet himself and biographer of poets, is writing a new biography that should restore the balance. Bernard Bergonzi (1977) produced the best short biography.

Critics initially portrayed Hopkins as a modern poet. A 1919 reviewer in *New Witness* called him "more modern than the most freakish modern would dare to be. . . . the last word in technical development" (Maynard 1919, 259). The second edition of *Poems* in 1930 brought him greater notice, and the New Critics and later the Kenyon Critics acclaimed Hopkins in the 1930s and 1940s: for them, his complex experiments made him the quintessential modern poet in need of explication. By way of balance, Wendell S. Johnson (1968) and Alison G. Sulloway (1972) later read him as a Victorian immersed in his age's anxious preoccupations with self, society, and meaning. Later yet, Jude V. Nixon (1994) and Tom Zaniello (1988) linked him with his Victorian contemporaries, and Walter J. Ong, S. J. (1986), studied his fascination with self in view of nineteenth-century philosophy, Victorian self-consciousness, and Catholic and Jesuit values.

Other critics of the 1940s, to make him more accessible, placed Hopkins in broader contexts. W. H. Gardner (1948) set his eccentricities within the English poetic tradition, and W. A. M. Peters, S. J. (1948), studied his mind, his view of reality, and his poetry. Geoffrey H. Hartman (1954) and J. Hillis Miller (1963) wrote broad essays that linked him with other writers and brought him much attention. Alan Heuser (1958) saw his creative vision as primitive and mystical, rooted in the Pre-Raphaelite sensibility and Greek philosophy. Elizabeth

W. Schneider (1968), finding critics still not in substantial agreement, shunned any artificial unity and studied major poems on which critical agreement had not yet been reached.

A number of critics, early and late, presented Hopkins as a Jesuit and Catholic poet. Opposing the dichotomizing of priest and poet, John Pick (1942) argued the unity of poet, priest, and Jesuit in his deeply religious poetry. Alfred Thomas, S. J. (1969), gave the historical details of life in Hopkins's Jesuit communities from 1868 to 1882. David Anthony Downes (1990) argued that Jesuit spirituality and Ignatian meditation patterns greatly influenced his art. Robert Boyle, S. J. (1961), affirmed that his mature metaphors, symbols, and rhythms expressed the divine life flowing into the just person. James Finn Cotter (1972) explored his use of, and place in, the Christian tradition. Jeffrey B. Loomis (1988) affirmed his inner power as spiritual and sacramental, especially with the Eucharist. Others linked spirituality and style. Marylou Motto (1984) thought his patterns of language or "voice" expressed a religious affirmation. Maria R. Lichtmann (1989) studied themes of parallelism and contemplation to find an interplay of form and spirit. Virginia Ridley Ellis (1991) sought the source of his poems' power, and by studying his manuscript revisions she argued the force and importance of his religious belief.

Recent critics have studied other aspects of Hopkins—philosophy, poetics, intellectual and religious contexts, language—and his poems have been analyzed in terms of various literary theories. Hopkins scholars teach and write in many countries: Korea, Japan, Australia, Canada, the United States, Ireland, Scotland, Wales, England, the Netherlands, France, Spain, Italy, Poland, Russia, and Israel. An unusual overview, edited by Joaquin Kuhn and myself (2002), presents fifty-five essays from thirteen countries done in the reader-response mode. Other essay collections, most of high quality, are more traditionally academic. A journal is also dedicated to the poet, *The Hopkins Quarterly*, which was founded in 1974 and publishes essays, reviews, and bibliographies mainly on Hopkins but also on his circle, Bridges, Dixon, and Patmore.

NOTE

Gerard Manley Hopkins, *Gerard Manley Hopkins: The Major Works*, ed. Catherine Phillips. Oxford World Classics Series (Oxford: Oxford University Press, 2002). This edition of the poems is recommended.

WORKS CITED

Bergonzi, Bernard. 1977. *Gerard Manley Hopkins*. Masters of World Literature Series. London: Macmillan.

Boyle, Robert, S. J. 1961. *Metaphor in Hopkins*. Chapel Hill: University of North Carolina Press.

Cotter, James Finn. 1972. *Inscape: The Christology and Poetry of Gerard Manley Hopkins*. Pittsburgh, PA: University of Pittsburgh Press.

Downes, David Anthony. 1990. *The Ignatian Personality of Gerard Manley Hopkins*. Lanham, MD: University Press of America.

Ellis, Virginia Ridley. 1991. *Gerard Manley Hopkins and the Language of Mystery*. Columbia: University of Missouri Press.

Gardner, W. H. 1948. *Gerard Manley Hopkins (1844–1889): A Study of Poetic Idiosyncrasy in Relation to Poetic Tradition.* 2 vols. London: Oxford University Press.

Hartman, Geoffrey H. 1954. *The Unmediated Vision: An Interpretation of Wordsworth, Hopkins, Rilke, and Valery,* New Haven, CT: Yale University Press.

Heuser, Alan. 1958. *The Shaping Vision of Gerard Manley Hopkins.* London: Oxford University Press.

Hopkins, Gerard Manley. 1955. *The Correspondence of Gerard Manley Hopkins and Richard Watson Dixon,* ed. Claude Colleer Abbott. London: Oxford University Press

———. 1955. *The Letters of Gerard Manley Hopkins to Robert Bridges,* ed. Claude Colleer Abbott. London: Oxford University Press.

———. 1956. *Further Letters of Gerard Manley Hopkins,* ed. Claude Colleer Abbott. London: Oxford University Press.

———. 1959. *The Journals and Papers of Gerard Manley Hopkins,* ed. Humphry House. London: Oxford University Press.

———. 1959. *The Sermons and Devotional Writings of Gerard Manley Hopkins,* ed. Christopher Devlin, S. J. London: Oxford University Press.

———. 1990. *The Poetical Works of Gerard Manley Hopkins,* ed. Norman H. MacKenzie. Oxford: Clarendon Press.

Johnson, Wendell Stacy. 1968. *Gerard Manley Hopkins: The Poet as Victorian.* Ithaca, NY: Cornell University Press.

Kenyon Critics. 1945. *Gerard Manley Hopkins.* Norfolk, CT: New Directions.

Kuhn, Joaquin, and Joseph J. Feeney, S. J., eds. 2002. *Hopkins Variations: Standing round a Waterfall.* Philadelphia and New York: Saint Joseph's University Press and Fordham University Press.

Lichtmann, Maria R. 1989. *The Contemplative Poetry of Gerard Manley Hopkins.* Princeton, NJ: Princeton University Press.

Loomis, Jeffrey B. 1988. *Dayspring in Darkness: Sacrament in Hopkins.* Lewisburg, PA: Bucknell University Press.

MacKenzie, Norman H. 1981. *A Reader's Guide to Gerard Manley Hopkins.* Ithaca, NY: Cornell University Press.

Mariani, Paul. 1970. *A Commentary on the Complete Poems of Gerard Manley Hopkins.* Ithaca, NY: Cornell University Press.

Martin, Robert Bernard. 1991. *Gerard Manley Hopkins: A Very Private Life.* New York: Putnam's.

Maynard, Theodore. 1919. "The Artist as Hero." *New Witness* 13: 259–60.

Miller, J. Hillis. 1963. *The Disappearance of God: Five Nineteenth-Century Writers.* Cambridge, MA: The Belknap Press of Harvard University Press.

Motto, Marylou. 1984. *"Mined with a Motion": The Poetry of Gerard Manley Hopkins.* New Brunswick, NJ: Rutgers University Press.

Nixon, Jude V. 1994. *Gerard Manley Hopkins and His Contemporaries: Liddon, Newman, Darwin, and Pater.* New York: Garland.

Ong, Walter J., S. J. 1986. *Hopkins, the Self, and God.* Toronto: University of Toronto Press.

Peters, W. A. M., S. J. 1948. *Gerard Manley Hopkins: A Critical Essay Towards the Understanding of his Poetry.* London: Oxford University Press.

Pick, John. 1942. *Gerard Manley Hopkins: Priest and Poet.* London: Oxford University Press.

Schneider, Elizabeth W. 1968. *The Dragon in the Gate: Studies in the Poetry of G. M. Hopkins*. Berkeley and Los Angeles: University of California Press.

Sulloway, Alison G. 1972. *Gerard Manley Hopkins and the Victorian Temper*. New York: Columbia University Press.

Thomas, Alfred, S. J. 1969. *Hopkins the Jesuit: The Years of Training*. London: Oxford University Press.

White, Norman. 1992. *Hopkins: A Literary Biography*. Oxford: Clarendon Press.

Zaniello, Tom. 1988. *Hopkins in the Age of Darwin*. Iowa City: University of Iowa Press.

— Joseph J. Feeney

John of the Cross [1542–1591]

The Dark Night of the Soul

BIOGRAPHY

Saint John of the Cross—poet, mystic, spiritual director—sought to live and write the dream of a divine life of passion. He is generally considered both a remarkable sixteenth-century Spanish poet and an unflinchingly driven, selfless Catholic monk. Together with Saint Teresa of Avila, he founded the Discalced ("Barefoot") Carmelites, a reform movement dedicated to following the original rule of Saint Albert, a thirteenth-century Patriarch of Jerusalem.

Thomas Merton called John "one of the greatest as well as the safest mystical theologians God has given to His Church" ([1950] 1981, 55). Edith Stein (1960) found great comfort for her soul in his writings. As a Doctor of the Catholic Church, John has received recognition for making a significant contribution to the Church: his writings and teachings are useful for all generations. As a poet, he is often considered one of the best, if not the best, Spanish poet. His influence on some of the finest modern and contemporary poets can be seen in works by T. S. Eliot, Robert Lowell, Seamus Heaney, and others. His sensually romantic poems of divine love appeal to a broad audience, both secular and religious, while his life story of dedication and suffering for his convictions continues to win over each new era of readers inspired by his personal drama of religious politics, poetic excellence, intense suffering, and unquestionable spiritual consecration.

John was born on June 24, 1542, as Juan de Yepes y Alvarez in Fontiveros, Spain. His father, Gonzalo de Yepes, raised in a wealthy silk merchant family, sacrificed his inheritance to marry Catalina Alvarez, a silk weaver's daughter. Gonzalo died when John was still a child. The family, which included two older brothers (Francisco and Luis, who died of malnutrition), had to scrape by to survive, moving to different towns, often living among the poor in Muslim barrios. John attended a practical training school for orphans and disadvantaged children, the Colegio de los Niños de la Doctrina in Medina, to acquire skills for various trades to support the family. Various biographers note his inaptitude for the manual trades, which resulted in his not being placed with skilled laborers. Instead, John was assigned as a sacristan in the Augustinian convent of the Magdalena, helping the nuns and begging for alms.

When he was seventeen, John began working at the Plague Hospital de la Concepcíon, a smallpox facility in Medina del Campo. He worked for seven years at the hospital and enjoyed the compassionate ministry. While there, he received patronage from the hospital's administrator, Don Antonio Álvarez de Toledo, to attend a Jesuit college with the understanding that he would not neglect his responsibilities at work. Following four years of studying classical languages, the humanities, and religion, John decided in 1563 to join the Carmelite Order and took the name Juan de Santo Matía. John then attended the University of Salamanca, one of the most highly regarded academic institutions in Europe. Ordained as a priest in 1567, he considered joining the Carthusians instead of entering the secular priesthood.

In 1567, his meeting with Teresa of Avila proved to be a watershed moment that redirected the entire course of his life, engaging him in the Carmelite reform. Teresa had been ardently working with nuns and wanted a male associate who could bring the reform to the men. Although twenty-seven years older than John, Teresa perceived a kindred spirit. She invited him to apprentice in the practicalities of the reformed life at Valladolid before beginning a Carmelite reformed monastery in a dilapidated farmhouse in Duruelo. Taking his vows as John of the Cross in 1568, he joined with two Carmelites from Medina, José de Cristo and the Prior, Antonio de Jesús. After renovating the farmhouse and establishing a small community of monks, he started a college of the Reform at Alcalá de Henares and briefly served as its rector.

When Teresa was commissioned to the Convent of the Incarnation, she invited John to join her as spiritual director and confessor to the nuns. He served there from 1572 to 1577. Teresa may have been closer with her confessor Jerónimo Gracián, yet she and John were good friends and coworkers despite occasional disagreements between them. Teresa's admiration and respect for the younger friar is evident in a letter dated December 1578. She writes of John,

> He is, indeed, the Father of my soul, and one of those who have done me the greatest good by their Words . . . you may, I assure you, have the same confidence in him as you have in me, and you will be pleased with him. He is very high in the interior life, and what is more, joins the widest experience to the most profound knowledge. (quoted in Bruno 1936, 211)

The intensity of John's fervor coupled with his strong messages of the *via negativa*, or "negative" way to God, and total commitment to sanctification, simplicity, and poverty often create an impression of a harsh and austere man. More complex portraits also describe his love for nature, going on picnics and prayer walks with other friars, making time to carve and draw, as well as designing the interior layout of several monasteries.

As so often happens with many reform movements, opposition soon arose and attempts to impede the reform increased. A General Chapter of the Carmelite Order met in Piacenza in 1575 and mobilized to end the Discalced Order. John was imprisoned twice for refusing to reject the Teresian reform. First, when he was thirty-three, Calced brothers kidnapped and imprisoned him at Medina del Campo until the papal nuncio intervened. And then again, in December 1577, he was kidnapped, blindfolded, and transported to the Calced Carmelite Priory in Toledo, where, under the direction of Father Tostado, he was confined in a tiny cell with no windows and only a peekhole in the ceiling for light. Verbal castigations and regular beatings by the monks (at first daily) caused wounds that did not heal for years. For six months he received simple meals of bread, water, and sardines. When a more benevolent jailer was assigned, John received a change of clothes, some writing materials, and permission to walk outside. During his imprisonment, John began writing the "Cántico Espiritual" (Spiritual Canticle). After nine months, he escaped by climbing the monastery wall and hiding at the nearby convent of Carmelite nuns in Toledo. John continued to work in various monasteries and to write. In 1578, he was appointed prior of El Calvario near Beas de Segovia. In 1579, he established a college of the reform at Baeza. He was confirmed as prior of Los Mártires three times, appointed as a first, second, and third definitor, a Vicar Provincial, and *consillario* at different locations. He started Discalced houses in numerous cities and towns, including Manchuela, Madrid, Seville, Córdoba, and Caravaca.

During a period of eight years, from approximately 1577 to 1586, he wrote most of his works, including *Llama de amor viva* [*Living Flame of Love*], *Subida del Monte Carmelo* [*The Ascent of Mount Carmel*], *Noche Oscura* [*Dark Night of the Soul*], and "Cántico Espiritual." We also have twelve poems and thirty-two letters (John destroyed much of his correspondence with Teresa, and during an investigation of his character, many nuns and monks disposed of any letters they had received from John). Writing, as Teresa was, during the years of the Inquisition, he sought to provide teachings on prayer for the nuns and monks when so many of the available books in the vernacular had been banned.

After Teresa's death, John found himself caught in a struggle to determine the vision and future of the Discalced. With Gracián, John supported the moderate position. In 1591, trumped up allegations began surfacing in efforts by Nicolás Doria and his assistant Diego Evangelista to defame John's character (suggesting sexual impropriety) and see him deposed as a principal leader of the reform. Per order of the Chapter of 1591, he lost his offices and was almost expelled from the Carmelites. Sent into solitude at La Peñuela in the Sierra Morena, John became ill with sores and wounds on his legs and shoulders as well as an infection that spread to his back. He was given the decision to move to either Baeza or Ubeda, a foundation directed by one of his opponents, Father Francis Crisóstomo. Although he was known at Baeza, he chose Ubeda, where he was neither known nor taken care of. Crisóstomo often expressed irritation at the inconvenience of John's presence, and the poet saint's final months were marked by the prior's inhospitable treatment. Even at the end of his life, he received an answer to his oft-quoted prayer that he shared with his brother Francisco when they were together for the last time in Segovia: "Lord, what I wish you to give me are sufferings to be borne for your sake, and that I may be despised and regarded as worthless" (quoted in Bruno 1936, 320). When John realized he would die soon, he approached Crisóstomo, who served him so poorly, and asked forgiveness for being a burden. Biographical accounts relate that the prior was amply overwhelmed with remorse, repented, and asked forgiveness.

John died on December 14, 1591, at the age of forty-nine. He was beatified on January 25, 1675, canonized on December 26, 1726, declared a Doctor of the Church by Pius XI on August 24, 1926, and made the patron poet of Spain in 1952.

SUMMARY

The phrase "dark night of the soul" has, in general usage, come to signify going through a difficult time, a period of depression, or a season of despair and hopelessness. And while the concept as John conceived it in *Noche oscura* or *The Dark Night of the Soul* refers to those difficult, lonely, and hard-pressing trials of life, his emphasis always involves one's relationship with God and focuses on love and union with the Beloved. The difficulties one endures are those that purge self-absorption and self-centeredness to liberate the spirit within for God-centeredness. The hard times and the sufferings are but conduits of future blessings.

The *Dark Night* is both a poem and a commentary that together constitute the saint's articulation of mystical life in Christ. Written as a companion piece to *The Ascent of Mount Carmel*, *Dark Night* uses the same poem but with its own commentary. *Ascent* focuses on active pursuit of the spiritual life, and *Dark Night* highlights passivity, our human incapacity to progress without the divine movement and unction of God to effectuate change and transformation.

John wrote the poem first and then, years later, at the request of Madre Ana de Jesús and the nuns at Beas, he added more than one hundred pages of prose commentary on his eight stanza poem. It is sometimes asserted that *Dark Night* was written while John was in jail. Most scholarship, however, indicates that John wrote the poem around 1579, not long after escaping from the Toledo convent. He did write several poems during his incarceration: parts of "Cántico Espiritual" as well as "Super Flumina Babilonis" (By the Waters of Babylon) and "Romance Sobre el Evangelio" (Romance on the Gospels).

John divides *Dark Night* into two books that follow the two types of dark nights. The two books reflect the order in which the soul must pass, first through the Night of Sense and, once through, into the Night of the Spirit. John describes the two nights as

> two kinds of darkness or purgation in spiritual persons according to the two parts of the soul, the sensory and the spiritual. . . . Hence the one night or purgation will be sensory, by which the senses are purged and accommodated to the spirit; and the other night or purgation will be spiritual, by which the spirit is purged and denuded as well as accommodated and prepared for union with God through love. (*Collected Works*, 311)

In book one, he elaborates the many weaknesses and unsanctified frames of mind to which beginners on the path are susceptible. Book one also covers the sufferings one must endure in the Night of Sense and the anticipation of God's indescribably wonderful blessings of delight. In book two, John reviews the imperfections of proficients (those who have already advanced on the spiritual path) and the afflictions and warfare of the Night of the Spirit. He also expounds his concept of the secret ladder.

Major themes and images of the *Dark Night* include love, union with the Beloved, light and darkness, freedom, self-denial, pain and suffering, aridity (a sense of deprivation of spiritual support), passivity, attachments and detachments, *Todo y Nada* (all and nothing), journey, and delight. Like many Christian mystical writings, *Dark Night* draws heavily from themes in the Song of Songs, especially the bridal imagery and symbolism. Also present are numerous references to biblical and theological writers, teachers, poets, and individuals, such as Saint Augustine, Saint Bernard, Saint Dionysius, Job, Jeremiah, Isaiah, Ezekiel, Jonah, King David, and Mary Magdalene.

While the first night, the Night of Sense "is common and happens to many" (311), John contends that few enter the Night of the Spirit because it requires great self-diminishment and self-denial; such personal abnegation is too difficult for most. And the greatest difficulty could arise from a lack of awareness about the higher purpose of suffering. Toward the end of the work, John explains that he has sought to expose the night so that many more could know what they are experiencing, better grasp what is involved in spiritual maturity, and be less surprised and, perhaps, better able to make it through. "The reason I undertook this task," he writes, "was to explain this night to many souls who in passing through it do not understand it" (382).

John never finished the commentary for the entire poem and ends his discourse with stanza three. Some critics argue, as does E. Allison Peers, that John could easily have finished his explanations because he lived for many years after completing the manuscripts we now have (1990, 193).

MAJOR THEMES

An important dimension of John's faith, as expressed in *Dark Night*, is not institutional conformity but a Christocentric and sovereign God-centered vision. John extols the individuality of each believer and his or her ability to progress in spiritual understanding and relationship with God. The goal he sets for the soul in process is complete renewal, "renewed with divine qualities and delights" (*Collected Works*, 335) and the enjoying of "the sweet and delightful life of love with God" (297).

To be transformed into the image of Christ and arrive at union with him, the soul must be cleansed of all sins and failings. Before John discusses the cleansing process of the two nights, he outlines the many foibles and frailties of beginners in the way of the Cross. A beginner may exhibit and wrestle with several, or even all, of these spiritual imperfections. Here John employs a persuasive and clever rhetorical angle. By starting with an extended treatment of the spiritual imperfections, he leaves little room for anyone to claim exemption from the necessity of passing through the fires of the dark night. And he directly states that he wants everyone to "see the need there is that God put them in the state of proficients" (311).

Beginners in the "dark night" are not necessarily new converts but believers who are still young in their inner transformation; they are souls who have not progressed through the nights to the state of proficients (those who are already contemplatives) or to the state of the perfect (those who have entered "divine union of the soul with God" [298]). The beginners John describes in the *Dark Night* are quite a collection of agitated, arrogant, and aspiring spiritual persons. They often love the pursuit of spiritual sweetness and consolation—until it becomes difficult, ungratifying, or seemingly ineffectual. The propensity for vexation, disappointment, depression, bitterness, weariness, and discontent sidetracks their initial zeal and devotion. There are some patient, peaceful, and humble beginners, but they are a minority in John's view and must still go through the dark night process for the shaping of their souls.

John constructs a spiritual psychology to assess the ways people think about themselves and react to their own progress and that of others. His is not a cynical or comical portrayal in the vein, for example, of an Annie Dillard, Kathleen Norris, or Flannery O'Connor. Rather, he is straightforward and direct. The confessional curtains are drawn back to give us entrée into the hearts and minds of sixteenth-century nuns and monks as John perceived them.

The discussion of sin and imperfection revolves around the seven capital sins, but with a twist. John does not focus on worldly temptations and falterings but on understanding how these seven sins manifest themselves in spiritual temptations and lusts. There are the proud, the luxurious (also translated "lustful"), the greedy, the angry, the gluttonous, the envious, and the slothful. All of their sins are "imperfections that have to be purged by means of the dark night" (303).

Whether it is pride or greed, luxury or sloth, John illustrates the three enemies of the soul (the world, the flesh, and the devil) fast at work, hindering progress, and needing purgation. And then, having established this need, he moves on to describe the suffering of purgation and how illumination begins. He attempts to clarify the confusion and strangeness a person may encounter when the night, also known as "the illuminative way or way of infused contemplation" (327), begins. While prayer and other spiritual exercises once seemed sweet and even easy, souls in this stage lose the immediate connection to such delights and "suffer considerable affliction in this night, owing not so much to the aridities they undergo as to their fear of having gone astray. Since they do not find any support or satisfaction in good things, they believe there will be no more spiritual blessings for them and that God has abandoned them" (316). Repeatedly, John urges the reader to refrain from worry and action, to appreciate the weaning process as part of God's plan to impart holy strength, greater love for God, peace beyond comprehension, and infused contemplation.

What seems to the soul so severe and adverse, and so contrary to spiritual pleasure, works in it so many blessings. Souls may feel abandoned and perishing, a Jonah in the ocean beast's belly, but in John's economy the night of so much pain is truly a night of healing to prepare the soul to become "united / The Lover with His beloved, Transforming the beloved in her lover" (296). Hence, if John never diminishes the awfulness and pain of suffering, he does transform it into a positive part of life inasmuch as its purposes and benefits make all difficulties shrink in comparison:

> [E]ven though this happy night darkens the spirit, it does so only to impart light concerning all things; and even though it humbles a person and reveals his miseries, it does so only to exalt him; and even though it impoverishes and empties him of all possessions and natural affection, it does so only that he may reach out divinely to the enjoyment of all earthly and heavenly things, with a general freedom of spirit in them all. (346)

Here, and throughout *Dark Night*, John often engages these inverse relationships through a rhetoric of paradox reminiscent of biblical discourse found in the Gospels and epistles.

John is a master at both specifying generalities and generalizing the specifics of spiritual experience. The *Dark Night* moves back and forth between categorizations of spiritual dynamics, progressions, virtues, failings, and acknowledgments of the difficulty of expressing fully the complete experience of the soul's journey to union with the Beloved. It is "a matter so difficult to treat and expound," John writes, "for hardly anything has been said of it, in sermons or in writing, and even the experience of it is rare" (311, 312). This ineffable dilemma, or "knot," as he names it in "De la Communicacion de los tres personas" (On the Communion of the Three Persons), does not stop him from making the attempt, and one way he does so is through an embedded classification system. John's classifications include two nights (sense and spirit); three enemies (world, flesh, devil); three states (beginner, proficient, perfect); seven capital sins; two kinds of friendship (sensual, spiritual); four benefits the soul obtains; four passions of the soul (joy, grief, hope, fear); two kinds of imperfection (habitual, actual); three kinds of good ordained for the soul; five reasons why the soul walks securely in darkness; ten steps of the mystic ladder of divine love; three faculties (understanding, memory, will); three chief colors (white, green, purple); three theological virtues (faith, hope, charity); two manners; two parts; two houses of the soul (sensual, spiritual); and three properties of the spiritual night.

By such listings, John provides a means for ordering spiritual realities. Lists function to control information and construct understanding. The irony is that John attests to the unknowability of all spiritual information in full and the uncontrollable dimension of religious experience. His lists are scattered throughout the text. They do not play an overarching organizational role; instead, they are interwoven into the discussion, as are the Scriptures, personal anecdotes, and, most notably, the poem itself, which can seem lost, obscured by John's lengthy narrative. While John writes a commentary on his poem, it is not poetic analysis. Rather, as Antonio de Nicolás explains,

> The prose commentary is not, properly speaking, a commentary on the poetry, but rather adds to it a different sense, a different direction, that the poetry on its own does not have. The prose commentary is a description of the spiritual practice, while the poetry is art, but art achieved through the same method of spiritual practice. It is therefore obvious that no commentary may be substituted for the poetry. Though the poetry may be read after the commentary. (1989, 57)

The two dark nights last far longer than any night in ordinary time. It is possible to suggest that the nights are experienced both in time and space. John indicates that the nights have a duration, albeit of unknown length. In book one he writes, "Yet we cannot say certainly how long the soul will be kept in this fast and penance of the senses" (328). Typically, the Night of Sense lasts a long time before those who make it through enter the Night of the Spirit. And the ending of the Night of Sense does not immediately open the door to the Night of the Spirit.

The nights have a location, a destination, and a geography in the soul of a person. John provides an archeological tour of the interior life where the heart of God and the heart of a person meet. Both the soul and the nights are often described in spatial terms; the soul is the house of a person's being ("My house being now all stilled" [295]), and the nights are a "land without a way" (323), landscaped with gardens, prisons, and ladders that the soul must journey through. One could be anywhere in the world and recognize the reference points. There is nothing particularly Spanish or Moorish in John's place descriptions of the night;

familiar biblical and religious imagery abound instead. For John, the dark night is the straight and narrow road of Matthew 7:14. In his prologue, he describes the happy follower who finds it: "The soul must ordinarily walk this path to reach that sublime and joyous union with God. Recognizing the narrowness of the path and the fact that so very few tread it—as the Savior Himself says [Matt. 7:14]—the soul's song in this first stanza is one of happiness in having marched along it to this perfection of love" (296). The dark night is something one "enters" (306). It is a place of darkness and light. It can also be a place of warfare and a "dungeon" (341). It is a "road" (369) and it has a secret ladder (368). It requires climbing the ladder and descending. It is a "dry and desert land" (323). It both takes place in a house and it is a house (387). It is "dark water" that "serves God himself as a tabernacle and dwelling place" (367). It is a hiding place (367). It is a place of visitation (385).

John's metaphors of place can also be seen in directional analogies of going deeper or soaring higher. Mary Giles notes that the image of ascent is the cornerstone of writings by Spanish mystical theologians (2001, 58). For John to ascend means also to descend, and he contends that the spiritual journey is a constant series of ups and downs (Dark Night, 372). The secret ladder provides a clear example of this:

> We can also call this secret wisdom a "ladder" because as the same steps of a ladder are used for both ascent and descent, so also the same communications this secret contemplation produces in the soul extol it in God and humiliate it within itself. Communications which are truly from God have this trait: they simultaneously exalt and humble the soul. For on this road, to descend is to ascend and to ascend is to descend, since he who humbles himself is exalted and he who exalts himself is humbled. (371)

The dark night is a significant sacred space ordained for divine activity that permits, for those who make it through, the ultimate meeting place with God. While the dark night happens in the soul, invisible to all but God, John writes of the soul in terms that allow accessibility to the workings of divine activity and its consequent acts of knowing. The soul, for John, is the ultimate knowing place, what Wendy Wright describes as the "intimate inside where deep meaning could be accessed" (1999, 47). Wright proposes, as geographers, landscape architects, philosophers, and others also have, that "any space can be transformed into a meaningful 'place' through the capturing and storing of experiences" (45). She also points out that the incarnational paradigm is of central importance for the Church and that "Christianity has long defined the body as meaningful, indeed sacred space" (45). So, too, for John, the body is a pivotal crossroad for his mystical vision that combines a twofold path of the sense and spirit with the now well-known threefold progression of purgation, illumination, and union. The body is both a sacred and a profane place that, once cleansed through purgation and emptied of self and its unholy contents, can be illumined and filled with true love.

CRITICAL RECEPTION

An extensive amount of research exists on John's works, life, influence, theology, and spiritual practice. For a comprehensive bibliography of Spanish, French, and English scholarship, see A. Robert Lauer-Flores's compilation, "Bibliografiá sobre San Juan de la Cruz." Introductions to collected and selected works editions by Kieran Kavanaugh (1991), Antonio de Nicolás (1989), E. Allison Peers (1934–1935; 1959; reprint 1990), and Benedict Zimmerman (1928) provide useful manuscript and biographical information. Father Bruno's biography, *St. John of the Cross* (1936), still provides an engaging account of John's life, relationships, and religious context. Other important biographies are the *Vida de San Juan de la Cruz* by Crisógono de Jesús Sacramentado (1958) and *St. John of the Cross: His Life and Poetry* by Gerald Brenan (1973).

There are numerous studies that compare the teachings and mystical paths of John and Teresa of Avila. These include *The Crucible of Love* by E. W. Trueman Dicken (1963), *Fire Within* by Thomas Dubay (1989), and *John of the Cross and Teresa of Avila: Mystical Knowing and Selfhood* by Edward Howells (2002). Howells outlines the epistemologies of John and Teresa's works. He seeks to understand their "mystical anthropology" and answer the question, "If the soul can feel and know God mystically in the interior part, in a distinct set of operations from those of ordinary experience and knowledge, while the ordinary operations are retained in the exterior part, can it be said to remain a single soul?" (2). He concludes that it is the "dynamism of the Trinity" that "solves the problem of the division in the soul and becomes the central feature of Teresa and John's anthropology" (4). His work is very helpful for clarifying important differences and similarities in John's and Teresa's views of mystical knowing and union. Anthologies and articles on mysticism also contain discussions, notably Bernard McGinn's multivolume *A History of Christian Mysticism* (1992) as well as *The Silent Cry: Mysticism and Resistance* by Dorothee Soelle (2001) and *The Poet and the Mystic* by Colin Thompson (1977).

In "Spanish Mystical Practice and Writing in the Middle Ages and Early Renaissance," Jane Ackerman situates John, along with Teresa and other Christian mystical writers, in a country also inhabited by Islamic and Jewish mystics. She stresses the "diversity of mystical activity" (1997, 4) and acknowledges the current impossibility of determining direct influence or crossover among the different religious traditions. Ackerman also describes John's writing as a composite of "many Christian vocabularies, including the language of scholastic theology, a biblically-inspired language of love (amply developed in earlier Christian spiritual writing, and notably in the writings of Bernard of Clairvaux), as well as the ancient Christian traditional language of the via negativa" (28).

Other analyses of John's writing style and poetic voice are provided by de Nicolás, who demonstrates how John uses methods of meditation in his poetry to assist readers to remember his teachings. By organizing "memory points" for building images and using "easy rhythms of rhymed verse" (1989, 57), de Nicolás proposes that John "builds his poetic experience using the same method he uses to build his spiritual life" (63).

Discussions of the *Dark Night* often appear in essays about the contemplative life and religious writing. In *God and the Imagination*, Paul Mariani analyzes the Italian form of the *Dark Night* in his essay, "The Intensest Rendezvous: On the Poems of John of the Cross." Mariani informs us that *Dark Night* is "made up of eight identical stanzas, rhyming ababb, each stanza consisting of lines of seven, eleven, seven, seven, and eleven syllables. It's an Italian form—the lira—transposed to Spanish by two Castilian poets active during the first half of the sixteenth century and anthologized by one Sebastian de Córdoba in 1575" (2002, 219).

In *The Darkness of God: Negativity in Christian Mysticism*, Denys Turner devotes a chapter to a psychological reading of the *Dark Night*. He compares John's description of the passive night with characteristic symptoms of depression. Turner concludes that we cannot define the dark night of the soul as simply "depression" because, while the similarities certainly exist, the outcome of the process for each is radically different. Depression despairs at its loss of self. In contrast, Turner points out, "when the passive nights pass, all is transformed" (1995, 243).

Donna Buhl Le Grand seeks to understand why John's poetry, so highly esteemed and discussed in the twentieth and twenty-first centuries, received little to no recognition in the eighteenth and nineteenth century canon of Spanish literature. She contends that his use of a variety of poetic styles did not match the preferred Italian forms and that his corpus did not fit the constructions of Spanish national identity as a "homogenous culture that subscribed to one unifying religion" (1993, 448). Conversely, she argues that his acceptance at the turn of the twentieth century reflects the same concerns of national identity and unity but with a different era's agendas and anxieties: "Mysticism, and particularly John of the Cross, came to represent and prove national and Catholic identity and religious homogeneity at a time when the Church was struggling to maintain control of culture and ideology" (450). Le Grand also argues that the reason the *Dark Night* has received more notice than John's other poems may be because it is written in the preferred Italian form.

Online World Wide Web sites now provide access to most of John's writings as well as bibliographies, biographies, and religious and literary criticism. The Teresian Carmel of Austria, The Institute of Carmelite Studies publications (ICS), New Advent, the Catholic Information Network, and the Christian Classics Ethereal library house some of the largest collections and links.

NOTE

WORKS CITED

Ackerman, Jane. 1997. "Spanish Mystical Practice and Writing in the Middle Ages and Early Renaissance." *Studia Mystica* 18: 1–35.

Brenan, Gerald. 1973. *St. John of the Cross: His Life and Poetry*. Cambridge: Cambridge University Press.

Bruno, Father. 1936. *St. John of the Cross*. London: Sheed and Ward.

Crisógono de Jesús Sacramentado. 1958. *Vida de San Juan de la Cruz*. 12th ed. Madrid: Biblioteca de Autores Cristianos. 1991. Translated by Kathleen Pond as *The Life of St. John of the Cross*. London: Longmans.

de Nicolás, Antonio T. 1989. *St. John of the Cross: Alchemist of the Soul*. York Beach, ME: Samuel Weiser.

Dicken, E. W. Trueman. 1963. *The Crucible of Love: A Study of the Mysticism of St. Teresa of Jesus and St. John of the Cross*. London: Darton, Longman and Todd.

Dubay, Thomas. 1989. *Fire Within: St. Teresa of Avila, St. John of the Cross, and the Gospel—On Prayer*. San Francisco: Ignatius Press.

Giles, Mary E. 2001. "A Spirituality of Pilgrimage: The Camino de Santiago and Spanish Mysticism." *Studia Mystica* 22: 54–82.

Howells, Edward. 2002. *John of the Cross and Teresa of Avila: Mystical Knowing and Selfhood*. New York: Crossroad.

John of the Cross. 1934–35. *The Complete Works of John of the Cross*, trans. E. Allison Peers. 3 vols. London: Burns and Oates.

———. 1959. *Dark Night of the Soul*, trans. E. Allison Peers. 1990. Reprint. New York: Image Doubleday.

Lauer-Flores, A. Robert. "Bibliografia sobre San Juan de la Cruz." Available online at http://faculty-staff.ou.edu/L/A-Robert.R.Lauer-1/BIBSANJUAN.html.

Le Grand, Donna Buhl. 1993. "Mystic Poetry in Literary Historiography: The Case of San Juan de la Cruz." In *Romance Languages Annual*, ed. Jeanette Beer, Charles Ganelin, and Ben Lawton, vol. 5, 445–50. West Lafayette, IN: Purdue Research Foundation.

Mariani, Paul. 2002. *God and the Imagination: On Poets, Poetry, and the Ineffable*. Athens: University of Georgia Press.

McGinn, Bernard. 1992. *The Foundations of Mysticism, Origins to the Fifth Century*. New York: Crossroad.

Merton, Thomas. [1950] 1981. *What is Contemplation?* Springfield, IL: Templegate.

Peers, E. Allison, ed. and trans. 1990. *Dark Night of the Soul: A Masterpiece in the Literature of Mysticism by St. John of the Cross*. New York: Doubleday/Image.

Soelle, Dorothee. 2001. *The Silent Cry: Mysticism and Resistance*, trans. Barbara and Martin Rumscheidt. Minneapolis, MN: Fortress Press.

Stein, Edith. 1960. *The Science of the Cross: A Study of St. John of the Cross*, trans. Hilda Graef. Chicago: Henry Regnery.

Thompson, Colin P. 1977. *The Poet and the Mystic: A Study of the Cántico Espiritual of San Juan de la Cruz*. Oxford: Oxford University Press.

Turner, Denys. 1995. *The Darkness of God: Negativity in Christian Mysticism*. Cambridge: Cambridge University Press.

Wright, Wendy. 1999. "Hearts Human and Divine: Women's Sacred Place." *Studia Mystica* 20: 43–55.

Zimmerman, Benedict. 1928. Introduction to *The Ascent of Mount Carmel*, by St. John of the Cross, trans. David Lewis, 1–21. London: Thomas Baker.

— **Elizabeth Bachrach Tan**

James Joyce [1882–1941]

A Portrait of the Artist as a Young Man

BIOGRAPHY

James Joyce, the Irish novelist, is perhaps one of the most significant of modern writers. He revolutionized the form and structure of the English novel, and his novels had an enormous impact on other twentieth-century writers. Rather than presenting action and thought, he used "stream of consciousness" (or "interior monologue"), a narrative technique also adopted by such writers as Virginia Woolf and William Faulkner. Joyce attempted to record the random thoughts and feelings flowing through the mind of one or more characters. His sentences, especially those in the later works, were frequently structured in a disorderly and disjointed manner. His fictional treatment of sex and religion triggered charges of blasphemy in some critical and religious circles. Joyce was a modernist in his departure not only from traditional literary forms and subject matter but also from established societal values.

Joyce was born in a south Dublin suburb on February 2, 1882, the eldest of ten children, to John Stanislaus Joyce (1849–1931), an improvident tax collector, and Mary Jane Murray (1859–1903). In 1887, the family moved to Bray, a town fifteen miles south of Dublin. From 1888 to 1891, Joyce was educated at Clongowes Wood College, a strict Jesuit school at Sallins, County Kildare. In 1891, the year when Charles Stewart Parnell died, Joyce composed his first printed poem, "Et Tu, Healy," to commemorate the Irish hero's death. In 1892, the family moved to Blackrock and then to Dublin. After briefly studying at the Christian Brothers' school on North Richmond Street, Joyce attended Belvedere College, another Jesuit school, from 1893 to 1898. Although Joyce attended Catholic schools in preparation for a priestly life, he left Belvedere with serious doubts about the Roman Catholic faith.

In 1899, Joyce entered University College in Dublin, a Jesuit institution founded by Cardinal John Henry Newman. There he studied modern languages, including English, French, and Italian. In April 1900, Joyce's "Ibsen's New Drama," a review of Henrik Ibsen's *When We Dead Awaken*, was published in the London *Fortnightly*. The next year, Joyce privately published the article "The Day of the

Rabblement," in which he attacked the Irish Literary Theatre for not having produced any dramatist of European stature. While a student at University College, Joyce finally broke away from Roman Catholicism and its teachings and the provincial patriotism that he observed in Ireland. During this time, he also read extensively and resolved to become a writer. Among his fellow students at University College was Oliver Joseph St. John Gogarty, a poet and surgeon who appears in *Ulysses*.

After graduation from university in 1902, Joyce went to Paris to study medicine but spent most of his time reading and writing. He soon returned to Ireland and wrote book reviews for a Dublin newspaper. In 1903, he went to Paris again but was recalled home for his mother's death. In 1904, he briefly taught at a Dalkey school, published several poems and sketches, and won a prize in a music contest. In the same year, he fell in love with Nora Barnacle, a Galway girl who was working as a waitress at Finn's Hotel in Dublin. Since he was opposed to marriage as an institution, Joyce decided to make his way in Europe; the couple's official marriage was not to take place until July 4, 1931. He and Nora left Dublin in 1904, traveling through London and Zurich to Pola, Italy, where Joyce began teaching English at the Berlitz school. The next year, he was transferred to the Berlitz school in Trieste, Italy; his son Giorgio and his daughter Lucia Anna were born there in 1905 and 1907, respectively. In 1905, his brother Stanislaus joined him in Trieste. Joyce made trips to Ireland in 1909 and 1912. In 1913, he began corresponding with Ezra Pound, who was one of the enthusiastic reviewers of Joyce's fiction.

In 1914, Joyce's first important work, *Dubliners*, was published in London. A collection of short stories set in Dublin, the book reflects the author's concern with life among the Irish lower middle class. Among the well-known stories from *Dubliners* are "Araby," in which a boy's tender passion for a woman ends in disillusionment, and "The Dead," a story about Gabriel Conroy's epiphany at the end of a party. *A Portrait of the Artist as a Young Man* was published in New York in 1916; it came out in London the next year. First serialized in *The Egoist* (from February 2, 1914, to September 1, 1915), the novel is largely an autobiographical work based on the author's early life. In the work, Joyce appears as the central character, Stephen Dedalus.

In 1915, Joyce took his family to Zurich, Switzerland, which was neutral in World War I; the family stayed there until 1919. He gave private English lessons while working on the early chapters of *Ulysses*, his best-known novel. In 1918, *The Little Review* in New York began serializing *Ulysses*. In 1919, Joyce returned to Trieste but soon moved to Paris. *Ulysses* was published in Paris in 1922 and later in New York in 1934. The French translation of the novel came out in 1929. In *Ulysses*, which recreates the events of a single day in Dublin in 1904, Joyce draws ironic parallels between Homer's epic hero, Odysseus, and the modern antihero, Leopold Bloom.

Joyce, who had eye troubles since the late 1900s, had become nearly blind by 1933. His last novel, *Finnegan's Wake*, was published in 1939 in England and the United States after parts of it had been serialized as *Work in Progress*. The story focuses on the Dublin tavern-keeper Humphrey Chimpden Earwicker's stream of consciousness; Joyce uses puns in many different languages, which makes the novel highly inaccessible for the general reader.

Joyce's other works include three volumes of poetry: *Chamber Music* (1907), *Gas from a Burner* (1912), and *Poems Penyeach* (1927). His *Collected Poems* appeared in 1936. His single play, *Exiles* (1918), is written in the manner of the Norwegian dramatist Henrik Ibsen. Part of the first draft of *A Portrait of the Artist as a Young Man* was released as *Stephen Hero* in 1944 (enlarged in 1955). Joyce went to Switzerland in 1940 to escape the German occupation of France. He died of a perforated ulcer in Zurich on January 13, 1941.

PLOT SUMMARY

In *A Portrait of the Artist as a Young Man*, the protagonist Stephen Dedalus is a student at Clongowes Wood College, a strict Roman Catholic school in Ireland. Although he plays football with his schoolfellows, he is not interested in the game; his mind frequently wanders. Sensitive and introverted, he is teased by other boys—for having a strange name; for kissing (and then for not kissing) his mother before bed. Stephen is relieved to go home for the Christmas vacation. At the dinner table, his father and Mr. Casey have a bitter argument with his aunt, Dante Riordan, over Irish politics and religion. They squabble over the Irish nationalist politician Charles Stewart Parnell (1846–1891) and over the Catholic priests' involvement in Irish politics. According to Dante, the adulterous Parnell was a traitor to Ireland and a public sinner, and the priests were right to abandon him. Stephen's father and Mr. Casey defend Parnell, arguing that the corrupt Irish priests should be eliminated. When the two men use foul language mocking the priests, Dante warns them that Stephen will "remember all this when he grows up—the language he heard against God and religion and priests in his home" (*Portrait*, 33).

Back at Clongowes, Stephen has accidentally broken his glasses. Father Dolan, the prefect of studies, insists that Stephen is lying about the glasses, calls him a loafer, and paddles the terrified boy in class. Instigated by his classmates, Stephen reports the cruel and unfair incident to the rector. The rector agrees that Father Dolan made a mistake and assures the boy that he will take care of the matter. Stephen comes back to the playground, tells his schoolfellows of the conversation with the rector, and is received by them as a hero.

Due to his father's financial difficulties, Stephen is not sent back to Clongowes. The family moves to Dublin, and Stephen attends Belvedere College, a prestigious day school in the city. The English professor announces in class that Stephen's essay includes a phrase that is heretical, and the boy renounces it. After school, Stephen is beaten up by some of his classmates for being a heretic and for claiming Byron to be the greatest poet. With the prize money he earned for his compositions, Stephen buys groceries and presents for his family. He also takes the family out, redecorates his room, lends money, and buys books. When all the money is spent, however, his household returns to the usual state of sordidness, and he goes back to his old life as a student. A feeling of helplessness drives him to seek sexual adventures in the city—and he surrenders his body and mind to a young prostitute.

Father Arnall's hellfire sermons, delivered during a retreat, have a decisive impact on Stephen's spiritual journey. The sermons focus on death, judgment, hell, and heaven—mostly on hell. Stephen, who still lives in sexual sin, is seized with feelings of remorse, guilt, and shame. He is so repulsed by his lustfulness that he vomits in his room. Then he offers a tearful prayer of repentance to God and resolves to live a life dedicated to him. Stephen confesses his sins, especially his sexual impurity, to an old priest. After receiving absolution from the priest, Stephen's spirit is exalted.

Stephen tries his utmost to live a life of piety and self-restraint, although he occasionally wonders if his heart has really changed. The director of the college, impressed with Stephen's religious devotion, appeals to him to join the Jesuits. The priesthood, according to the director, is the most noble—and powerful—vocation. Stephen momentarily entertains the idea of joining the order, but the prospect of a life fettered by priestly responsibilities repels him. He loves sensual beauty too much to renounce this world, and he is willing to fall into its lures. Stephen crosses the bridge over the river Tolka, turning a cold eye toward the shrine of the Virgin Mary. In a moment of ecstasy, he hears a voice calling his name from beyond the world and finds his true vocation—not a religious but a literary one. On the seashore, Stephen encounters a young girl, "the angel of mortal youth and beauty," who inspires him to cry out in "profane joy" (171, 172). He has been born again, not through religion but through art.

The setting of the final chapter of the novel is University College, where Stephen is a student. He is known among students as an arrogant loner who has refused to sign the petition for world peace. Stephen, who has now found his salvation in art, equates the artist with God. Both condescend to their creatures. As the novel closes, Stephen is ready to leave Ireland in search of freedom from his home, church, and country.

MAJOR THEMES

A Portrait of the Artist as a Young Man is an artist novel (*Künstlerroman*) tracing the childhood, adolescence, and young manhood of Stephen Dedalus, who leaves his native environment behind for a literary career in Europe. His spiritual journey is not toward the Celestial City of God but toward the Tower of Ivory, the world of artistic perfection. Growing up in nineteenth-century Ireland, Stephen witnesses the squalor, cruelty, and hypocrisy of his surroundings. The novel chronicles why and how Stephen renounces a priestly career and pursues an artist's life.

Stephen's decision to become an artist has much to do with his inquisitive, sensitive, and independent mind. As a young pupil at Clongowes, he feels that his schoolfellows look "very strange" (13). A brilliant boy, he even speculates on such cosmic issues as what lies beyond the universe. At the same time, Stephen genuinely tries to be a good boy, keeping all the rules at school. He prays and goes to bed on time to avoid going to hell after death; he also feels that it is a terrible sin to steal a monstrance.

At Belvedere, several classmates assault Stephen for not agreeing with their low opinion of Byron. When the tormentors leave him with scornful laughter, Stephen "[stumbles] after them half blinded with tears, clenching his fists madly and sobbing" (82). Despite their cowardice and cruelty, he bears no anger toward them; he feels that some power is stripping him of that anger. Indeed, the object of his pursuit—"intangible phantoms"—is completely different from those of the other children of his age. His battle is "against the squalor of his life and against the riot of his mind" (83). Although his father and teachers urge him to become a gentleman and a good Catholic, what they say is "hollowsounding" in his ears (91).

Closely related to the theme of the artistic vocation is the protagonist's loss of the Christian faith, especially the Irish Catholic faith. Growing up in a religious environment, Stephen initially takes his faith for granted. However, a series of events leads him to renounce Christianity. Stephen quickly learns that Irish Catholicism is a bitterly controversial, politically charged institution and that there are fundamental differences even among family members and friends in their understanding of politics and religion. When Dante, his aunt, contends that the pastors of the Church deserve respect, Mr. Casey calls them "princes of the church" but Stephen's father calls them "sons of bitches" and "lowlived dogs" (33, 34). When Dante accuses Parnell of betraying the trust of his people, Mr. Casey counters that it was indeed the privileged bishops and priests of Ireland who sold the aspirations of their country. Mr. Casey's face glows with anger, and Stephen "feels the glow rise to his own cheek as the spoken words [thrill] him" (38).

Stephen's schooling in Catholic institutions also contributes to his loss of faith. He witnesses and suffers from the cruelty and meanness of the teachers. In Father Arnall's Latin class, a student fails to give the right answer, so the teacher makes him kneel in the middle of the class, calling him "one of the idlest boys" he has ever met. Then, Father Dolan suddenly appears, asking, "Any boys want flogging here, Father Arnall? Any lazy idle loafers that want flogging in this class?" As Father Dolan strikes Stephen's hands with the "pandybat" for idling, the boy is frightened, ashamed, and enraged (47–48).

By the time Stephen leaves Ireland, he has become an agnostic. When Cranly, one of his friends at University College, asks him whether he believes in the Eucharist, Stephen's reply is negative. Cranly then asks him if he disbelieves in the Eucharist. Stephen's answer is, "I neither believe in it nor disbelieve in it." Cranly wonders whether Stephen has ever felt love toward anyone or anything; and Stephen gloomily replies, "I tried to love God. It seems now I failed. It is very difficult. I tried to unite my will with the will of God instant by instant. In that I did not always fail. I could perhaps do that still" (239–40).

The problem of an unquestioning piety is a major concern in *A Portrait of the Artist as a Young Man*. Dante is a devout Catholic, but her unconditional reverence for Irish Catholicism arouses contempt from Stephen's father, Mr. Casey, and Stephen himself. She passes a quick judgment on Parnell's character, seasons her argument with Bible verses, and antagonizes Protestants. In the second chapter, we also see a pious person in Stephen's uncle, Charles. A good-natured man, he regularly brings the boy to the chapel, where he prays. Stephen kneels at his side, respecting but not sharing his piety; he often wonders what his old uncle prays for so seriously.

Alienation, a universal theme in modern literature, is also conspicuous in *A Portrait of the Artist as a Young Man*. Stephen is estranged from his family, from his schoolfellows, from society, and from his country. The opening pages of the novel clearly reveal his isolation and self-absorption. While he plays football with the other boys, he "[keeps] on the fringe of his line, out of sight of his prefect, out of the reach of the rude feet, feigning to run now and then" (8). In the playroom, he sits "in a corner . . . pretending to watch a game of dominos" (13–14). When he returns from his successful audience with the rector, his school-mates celebrate his triumph; as their cheers die down, however, Stephen feels "alone" (59).

Stephen's isolation continues in the succeeding chapters and is increasingly accompanied by intellectual pride. He does not want to play, he is bothered by the noise of children at play, and their "silly voices" make him acutely feel that he is "different" from others. He is happy only when he is "alone or in the company of phantasmal comrades" (84). He lives in the world of philosophical speculation and fantasy.

Based on Stephen's apparent hostility to Irish Catholicism and on Joyce's departure from the Church, one may reasonably assume that *A Portrait of the Artist as a Young Man* is an anti-Catholic novel. However, the novel will still appeal to open-minded Catholic readers who take the challenges of modernism/postmodernism seriously. In this age of pluralism and diversity, can the Church still proclaim Christ as the only way to salvation? Does the Church have the moral authority to dictate human conduct? Has humanity grown beyond the Christian faith? Should the Church be involved in politics? Is the Catholic hierarchy still an acceptable moral voice? Unlike sentimental or pietistic Christian writers, Joyce tackles these questions head-on.

A Portrait of the Artist as a Young Man has also contributed to writing that rebels against a "repressive" Irish Catholic or Catholic school upbringing. For example, in her *Memories of a Catholic Girlhood* (1957), Mary McCarthy reveals the cruel and hypocritical aspect of the Catholic education that she received as an orphan. In *Pagan Babies and Other Catholic Memories* (1982), Gina Cascone recalls questionable religious practices that she observed in her nine years of attending a Catholic school. More recently, Frank McCourt, author of the best-selling *Angela's Ashes: A Memoir* (1996), indicts the Irish Catholic Church for its supposedly relentless power over its followers. Controversial in Joyce's time, such works dismissive of or hostile toward a pre-Vatican II Catholic childhood constitute a familiar, even popular, genre today.

CRITICAL RECEPTION

James Joyce has been compared to William Shakespeare in his mastery of English. Virtually no other writer surpasses him in his experimental use of language and in his unconventional narrative techniques. In 1998, the editorial board of the Modern Library voted *Ulysses*, *A Portrait of the Artist as a Young Man*, and *Finnegan's Wake* as the best, third best, and seventy-seventh best English-language novels, respectively. Armin Arnold considers Joseph Conrad, D. H. Lawrence, and James Joyce as the three outstanding English novelists of the first half of the twentieth century (1969, 2).

A Portrait of the Artist an a Young Man is Joyce's first full-length book written in the stream of consciousness technique. Numerous critics have praised the novel for its innovative style. Herbert Fuller, for example, finds in *A Portrait of the Artist as a Young Man* eloquent statements on the "priesthood" of art. The religion that Stephen embraces, however, is not "a religion of art" but "a religion of Man." Self-fulfillment requires worshiping one's own creativity; worshiping God is thus to deny oneself (1958, 123–24). In J. I. M. Stewart's view, the book is as monumental as Henry Fielding's *Joseph Andrews*, George Eliot's *Middlemarch*, and Samuel Butler's *The Way of All Flesh*. Joyce's novel is unsurpassed, however, in its originality. Stephen Dedalus is presented to readers with "a hitherto unexampled intimacy and immediacy"; he is aware of people around him only when they affect "his own interior chemistry." Joyce chooses diction, syntax, and rhythm in a way that stresses "the contours of the underlying emotion" (1960, 18–19). Helmut Bonheim comments along the same lines: "Joyce's style is indeed admirably suited to his central theorem: that the more positive and creative aspects of a civilization are developed by those who, by fighting against society as it is, fight for it, by those who envision the future as substantially different from the present" (1964, 15).

Harry Levin, Herbert Sherman Gorman, and William York Tindall defend Joyce as a Catholic moralist. Noting that Father Arnall's powerful discourse on hell is the "ethical core" of the novel, Levin claims, "Joyce is orthodox enough to go on believing in hell" (1941, 57). According to Gorman, Joyce could not help being a Catholic novelist: "Roman Catholicism is in [Joyce's] bones, in the beat of his blood, in the folds of his brain and he cannot rest until it is either removed or clarified. It is his misfortune that it may never be removed. It will pervert his nature but it is there, twisted out of all resemblance to itself even in the frankest passages." Gorman concludes, "The vivid, highly-functioning mind of the Stephen Dedalus of *Portrait of the Artist as a Young Man* is the mind of a Mediaeval Catholic" (1924, 75). Tindall claims that regardless of Stephen's (or Joyce's) opinion of the Church, Joyce is clearly accepting of traditional morality: "Disapproving of the Church's morality, he approves of the morality that the Church approves of and professes. No wonder that Thomas Merton, the Trappist, was helped on his way to holiness by Joyce. No wonder that Catholics, despite their original dismay, are turning more and more to Joyce" (1959, 72). (Thomas Merton, it should be noted, was edified by reading Father Arnall's sermon: it was a spur in his decision to convert to Catholicism.)

Much has been written about the protagonist, Stephen Dedalus, as a Catholic. According to Herbert Howarth, Stephen is a Christ figure who leaves a messianic message in the last pages of the novel: "By writing his own story he says three things to the Irish: let me show you how backward you look to me; let me show how I have fortified and sharpened myself, imitate me; see how I have sacrificed myself for you" (1958, 254–55). Richard Ellmann points out that Stephen's departure from Irish Catholicism is an act of rebellion against a "father church" which is "harsh, repressive, [and] masculine," but Joyce found a mother figure in the Virgin Mary, whose love was suited to wretched sinners (1959, 304). According to Joseph Campbell, Stephen's departure from the Church is a heroic act. Stephen is willing to act alone and bear the consequences, burning in hell for eternity. This, in Campbell's view, is courage—"the courage of facing complete shipwreck, shipwreck on the rocks, disaster, schizophrenic disintegration, hell, anything" (1993, 48).

Some critics condemn Stephen Dedalus as a character. Wyndham Lewis, for example, expresses an utter contempt for Stephen; he cannot find more "lifeless" and "irritating" characters than "the deplorable hero of the *Portrait of the Artist* and of *Ulysses*." Characterizing Stephen as a "grotesque figure," Lewis argues that Stephen lacks heroism and that the author's "effort to show him in a favorable, heightened light throughout, destroys the naturalism, and at the same time certainly fails to achieve the heroic" (1927, 99–100). Another critic, Caroline Gordon, considers Stephen a prideful sinner like Lucifer who falls from grace. Noting that *A Portrait of the Artist as a Young Man* has been misread for a whole generation, she argues that the novel is "not primarily . . . a picture of the artist rebelling against constituted authority, but rather the picture of a soul that is being damned for time and eternity caught in the act of foreseeing and foreknowing its damnation" (1957, 213).

On the other hand, Wayne C. Booth neither praises nor condemns Stephen. According to Booth, it is impossible for Joyce's novel to be both a portrait of the soul freed from bondage *and* a portrait of the soul chaining itself up. Based on his analysis of textual evidence, Booth concludes that Joyce was ambiguous in his position on Stephen's flight: the author was "always a bit uncertain about his attitude toward Stephen" and that readers "simply cannot avoid the conclusion that to some extent the book itself is at fault, regardless of its great virtues" (1961, 328–35).

The source of Father Arnall's sermons at Belvedere College has received some critical attention. According to James R. Thrane, the primary—perhaps the only—printed source of the hellfire sermon was the English version of an Italian tract titled in translation *Hell Opened to Christians, To Caution Them from Entering into It*, written by Giovanni Pietro Pinamonti, a seventeenth-century Jesuit (1960, 173). Don Gifford identifies two equally important sources for the sermons: Pinamonti's tract, which provided the specific patterns and language of the sermons; and Saint Ignatius of Loyola's 1548 book *The Spiritual Exercises*, which provided the sermons' narrative structure. Piamonti's meditations consist of two parts. Part I, "On the Sensory Pain Suffered by the Damned," consists of three sections: "The Prison of Hell," "The Fire," and "The Company of the Damned." Part II, "On the Pain That Stems from the Eternal Loss of the Beatific Vision," comprises four sections: "The Pain of Loss," "Remorse of Conscience," "The Pain of Execution," and "Eternity." In turn, *The Spiritual Exercises* suggests four weeks of meditation on (1) Sin and Its Consequences (Hell); (2) Christ's Life on Earth; (3) Christ's Passion, and (4) His Risen Life. Gifford notes that Father Arnall's sermons concentrate heavily on *The Spiritual Exercises'* first week, with some attention also given to the second week (177–78).

During the past three decades, much has been written about *A Portrait of the Artist as a Young Man* from new interpretive angles: psychoanalytic, feminist, reader response, deconstruction, poststructuralist, and new historicism, among others. According to Joseph A. Buttigieg, *A Portrait of the Artist as a Young Man* as a modernist classic needs to be reread in a postmodern context. A revisionist reading of the novel means "liberating [the work] from the boundaries within which traditional literary interpretation, and more specifically New Criticism, have confined it" (1987, 18). Chester G. Anderson finds a number of Freudian symbols and motifs in the novel. Stephen exhibits such symptoms as castration fears, phobias, fetishes, paranoia, homosexual wishes, and masochism (1976, 135). M. Keith Booker applies Mikhail Bakhtin's theory of polyphony, or "dialogics," to Joyce's fiction, tracing the intertextual dialogue between Joyce and such literary predecessors as Homer, Rabelais, Dante, Goethe, Shakespeare, and Dostoevsky.

Dostoevsky, for example, viewed the Orthodox Church in Russia as an evil institution that relies on violence and intimidation for its survival; Joyce felt the same way about Irish Catholicism. Like Dostoevsky, Joyce considered Catholicism as an imperialistic force in his home country (1995, 186). According to Kevin J. H. Dettmar (1996), Joyce's *Dubliners* is postmodern, while *A Portrait of the Artist as a Young Man,* a later work, is modernist. This "lapse" in Joyce's early career indicates his two contradictory spirits, "the high modernist purpose and the low postmodern play"; *Portrait* is "the work, which holds up least well in an age of postmodern readers" because of its dependence upon the modernist paradigm (108).

One may wonder if all of these reader-based, self-reflective, or self-reflexive analyses are equally valid. There is no denying, however, that postmodern approaches have enriched and broadened readers' understanding of *A Portrait of the Artist as a Young Man* as a multilayered novel. The fact that Joyce's novel keeps challenging—and confusing—readers proves that it is truly a classic work. One may never arrive at the exact meaning of the novel, but then a well-wrought work of fiction, like life itself, is sometimes inexplicable and inexhaustible. Indeed, the study of Joyce's works has become a field that promises possibilities for almost limitless cultivation.

NOTE

James Joyce, *A Portrait of the Artist as a Young Man: Text, Criticism, and Notes,* ed. Chester G. Anderson (New York: Viking, 1968). All references are to this edition.

WORKS CITED

Anderson, Chester G. 1976. "Baby Tuckoo: Joyce's 'Features of Infancy.'" In *Approaches to Joyce's Portrait: Ten Essays,* ed. Thomas F. Staley and Bernard Benstock, 135–69. Pittsburgh, PA: University of Pittsburgh Press.

Arnold, Armin. 1969. *James Joyce.* New York: Frederick Ungar.

Bonheim, Helmut. 1964. *Joyce's Benefictions.* Berkeley: University of California Press.

Booker, M. Keith. 1995. *Joyce, Bakhtin, and the Literary Tradition: Toward a Comparative Cultural Politics.* Ann Arbor: University of Michigan Press.

Booth, Wayne C. 1961. *The Rhetoric of Fiction.* Chicago: University of Chicago Press.

Buttigieg, Joseph A. 1987. *A Portrait of the Artist in Different Perspective.* Athens: Ohio University Press.

Campbell, Joseph. 1993. *Mythic Worlds, Modern Worlds: On the Art of James Joyce,* ed. Edmund L. Epstein. New York: HarperCollins.

Cascone, Gina. 1982. *Pagan Babies and Other Catholic Memories.* New York: St. Martin's.

Dettmar, Kevin J. H. 1996. *The Illicit Joyce of Postmodernism: Reading Against the Grain.* Madison: University of Wisconsin Press.

Ellmann, Richard. 1959. *James Joyce.* New York: Oxford University Press.

Fuller, Edmund. 1958. *Man in Modern Fiction: Some Minority Opinions on Contemporary American Writing.* New York: Random House.

Gordon, Caroline. 1957. *How to Read a Novel.* New York: Viking.

Gorman, Herbert S. 1924. *James Joyce: His First Forty Years.* New York: Viking.

Howarth, Herbert. 1958. *The Irish Writers, 1880–1940*. New York: Hill and Wang.

Levin, Harry. 1941. *James Joyce: A Critical Introduction*. Norfolk, CT: New Directions.

Lewis, Wyndham. 1927. *Time and Western Man*. London: Chatto and Windus.

McCarthy, Mary. 1957. *Memories of a Catholic Girlhood*. New York: Harcourt.

McCourt, Frank. 1996. *Angela's Ashes: A Memoir*. New York: Scribner's.

Stewart, J. I. M. 1960. *James Joyce*. London: Longmans, Green.

Thrane, James R. 1960. "Joyce's Sermon on Hell: Its Source and Its Backgrounds." *Modern Philology* 57: 172–98.

Tindall, William York. 1959. *A Reader's Guide to James Joyce*. New York: Noonday Press.

— John J. Han

Sor Juana Inés de la Cruz [1648–1695]

Response to Sor Filotea

BIOGRAPHY

Poet, dramatist, and essayist, Sor Juana Inés de la Cruz was born Juana Ramírez de Asbaje on her grandfather's hacienda in the village of San Miguel Napantla, located near the volcano Popocatépetl, outside Mexico City. Because most of the documents relating to Sor Juana's life were lost during the Mexican revolution of the 1860s, much of what we know about her is based on autobiographical statements that she incorporated into her most famous prose work, *Response to the Most Illustrious Poetess Sor Filotea de la Cruz* (1691), and a short biography written by the Jesuit Diego Calleja that was published in 1700 in Spain in the final volume of her collected works.

Until recently, it was believed that Juana was born in 1651, but newly recovered documents suggest that she was probably born in November or December 1648, the illegitimate daughter (then known as a "child of the Church") of Isabel Ramírez and Pedro Manuel de Asbaje. About her father, little is known except that he was a Basque, possibly of noble descent, and that he had fathered two previous daughters by Juana's mother. While much has been made of Juana's illegitimacy, as Octavio Paz explains in his monumental critical biography of Sor Juana, in seventeenth-century Mexico "sexual orthodoxy was much less rigorous than religious orthodoxy" and there was "nothing particularly censurable" in children being born out of wedlock ([1982] 1988, 68). Known as a capable, strong woman who ably managed the family hacienda after her husband's death, Juana's mother subsequently bore three more illegitimate children by another man yet was throughout her life considered a respectable member of *criollo* (creole) society.

From an early age, Juana was strongly attracted to reading and learning. As she tells us in her *Response*, she was "so inflamed with the desire to know how to read" that at the age of three she tricked her older sister's instructor into thinking that she had her mother's permission for instruction. She also tells us in her *Response* that she read the "many and varied books" in her grandfather's library and later asked her mother for permission to dress as a man so that she could attend the university in Mexico City, where only men were admitted.

Sometime between the ages of eight and ten, Juana went to live in Mexico City in the family of Juan de Mata, who was married to her mother's sister. It was through the Matas that in 1664 Juana was introduced to the court of the newly arrived viceroy and vicereine of New Spain, Don Antonio Sebastian de Toledo and Doña Leonor Carreto. Impressed by her learning and wit, they gave her the position of lady-in-waiting, and for the next several years Juana enjoyed all of the privileges that such a position entailed, including the opportunity to continue her education beyond that of most women in seventeenth-century Mexico.

In 1668, with the tenure of the viceroy and vicereine drawing to a close and her own situation at court uncertain, Juana decided to enter the religious life. At first she joined the Convent of San José de las Carmelitas Descalzas (Discalced Carmelites), but the harshness of the order's rule was apparently too much for her and she returned to the court after just three months. Through the intercession of her spiritual advisor, the Jesuit Antonio Nuñez de Miranda, Juana received a substantial dowry that allowed her entrance to the Convent of Santa Paula of the Order of San Jerónimo of the Hieronymite Sisters of the Immaculate Conception, where well-to-do seventeenth-century *criolla* women who desired the religious life could pursue their vocations in a luxury similar to that they had experienced at home. Indeed, as Paz and others have documented, the nuns at San Jerónimo received frequent guests in the convent locutory, wore expensive jewelry, ate well, managed estates, accepted expensive gifts, lived in spacious quarters, and even employed servants and owned slaves. Accompanying Juana to the convent, for example, were a mulatto slave and her child whom Juana had been given by her mother and whom she later sold (Paz [1982] 1988, 128). It was in the Convent of Santa Paula that Juana Ramírez took the name by which she was thereafter known—Sor Juana Inés de la Cruz.

During the quarter century that Sor Juana spent as a religious at San Jerónimo, she earned an unparalleled literary celebrity that gained her the titles of "Tenth Muse," "Minerva of America," and "Phoenix of Mexico." Known for her witty plays about courtly life, secular love poetry, sacred songs, and baroque allegories, Sor Juana attracted the patronage of a series of viceroys and vicereines who brought her writings to Spain, where they were eventually published in three volumes (1689, 1692, and 1700) and received even greater critical applause than they had in the courts of Mexico where they originally circulated.

Eventually, Sor Juana's celebrity outside the convent drew upon her the full wrath of a male ecclesiastical system that frowned upon women, particularly nuns, who aspired toward authorship in the field of secular letters. Separated from her friends at the viceregal court and her admirers in Spain, and perhaps threatened by a possible Inquisitorial investigation, Sor Juana renewed her vows to the religious life and devoted her remaining days to works of self-mortification and charity. Among other things, she suspended her learning, sold a collection of valuable musical and scientific instruments as well as her prodigious library (reputed to be one of the largest private libraries in the New World), and donated the money to help alleviate the sufferings of Mexico's poor. Sor Juana died on April 17, 1695, of the plague after attending to the needs of other nuns who had previously fallen ill.

SUMMARY

The controversy that eventuated in the publication of Sor Juana's *Response to Sor Filotea* and that caused its author so much trouble in her last years began as a conversation in the locutory of the Convent of San Jerónimo, which, as Paz has noted, was "frequently visited by homilists, theologians, and other distinguished personages, both clerical and secular" and more closely resembled a literary "salon" than a cloister ([1982] 1988, 121–22). In this particular case, Sor Juana had apparently offered commentary on a sermon delivered some four decades earlier in Peru by the renowned Portuguese Jesuit missionary Antonio de Vieyra (1608–1697) about the greatest of Christ's so-called *finezas* or "gifts" to humanity. In his sermon, Vieyra disputed the views of three Church fathers—Saints Augustine, Thomas Aquinas, and John Chrysostom—on the subject. During her conversation on Vieyra's sermon, Sor Juana is said to have defended the views of the earlier theologians and, after refuting the argument of the Jesuit, offered her own opinion on the subject. According to Sor Juana, Christ's greatest *fineza* was the favors that God withholds, rather than grants, to humanity.

Hearing Sor Juana's discourse and opinions either in person or through others who were present in the locutory for the original conversation, Manuel Fernández de Santa Cruz y Sahagún (1637–1699), then bishop of Puebla, requested that Sor Juana send him a written account of her ideas about Vieyra's sermon and Christ's *finezas*. In response to the bishop's request, Sor Juana provided her opinions in an ostensibly informal letter with the understanding that she recorded her ideas at the explicit command of the bishop and that her letter was meant only for the bishop and not for the public. Under the pseudonym of a fictitious nun named "Sor Filotea de la Cruz," the bishop in turn published Sor Juana's letter in a pamphlet titled the *Athenagoric Letter of Sister Juana Inés de la Cruz* (1690)— "Athenagoric" means "worthy of the Greek goddess Athena." Along with the letter, Santa Cruz also published a mild indictment of Sor Juana for devoting herself too much to literary pursuits unbefitting her station as a nun and requesting instead that she redirect her energies toward prayer, works of charity, and theological studies.

Although friendly in tone and disguised by a pseudonym, Santa Cruz's criticism of the acclaimed nun drew the attention of Mexico's ecclesiastical elite, many of whom had long resented Sor Juana's prominence, including the powerful archbishop of Mexico City and noted misogynist, Francisco de Aguiar y Seijas. It was to defend herself against the criticism of the likes of Santa Cruz and Aguiar y Seijas that Sor Juana the following year wrote her famous *Response to Sor Filotea*, in which she provides an autobiographical account of herself and a justification of her life's work both as a nun and as a writer.

MAJOR THEMES

Of central interest to most twenty-first-century readers of Sor Juana is her writing about women and their intellectual standing in society. Considered by some to be the "first feminist of the New World" (Merrim 1991, 7), Sor Juana was one of the first writers, female or male, to challenge openly the many misogynist assumptions that dominated the patriarchal structures of her day. Indeed, whether through allusions and literary encoding or through direct references to prominent women, including mythological figures and female intellectuals and leaders, Sor Juana shows a constant concern about feminist issues. Some of her most important poems were dedicated or addressed to the vicereines of New Spain, and a satirical poem known by its opening words, "Misguided Men," in which Sor Juana criticizes those men "who will chastise a woman when no blame is due" while "oblivious" to the fact that these same men "prompt" what they "criticize" (*Poems, Protest, and a Dream*, 149), has had such a popular impact that, according to Ilan Stavans, "it is even today memorized in part by schoolchildren in Mexico and throughout Latin America" (xxxii). In virtually all of Sor Juana's works, then, appear concerns about the rights of women, and critics are certainly correct in pointing to the importance of these concerns when assessing Sor Juana's place in literary history.

It is in her *Response*, however, that Sor Juana most directly articulates her views of women and their standing in society and the relationship between these views and Catholicism. Addressing "Sor Filotea's" accusations that Sor Juana has endangered her soul by devoting herself to a level of learning only befitting to men, Sor Juana argues that women are in all respects as capable and deserving of education as men. In her argument, Sor Juana quotes Scripture on the subject, specifically Saint Paul's injunction that elder women should seek knowledge and serve as instructors to their younger sisters and the writings of Church Fathers such as Saint Jerome, who took a special interest in seeing that women received an education. In addition, she also points to the many learned women who have had a positive impact on society throughout history, including Hypatia, Zenobia, and the Sibyls (from classical history); Esther, Anna, Deborah, and Abigail (from the Bible); Queen Isabella, Christiana Alexandra, and the Condesa of Villaumbrosa (from contemporary culture); and Saints Teresa of Avila, Gertrude, and Birgitta (from Christian history).

In making her argument, Sor Juana draws particular attention to Saint Paul's statement, "Let women keep silence in the churches," interpreting Paul's intention behind this statement as applying to men as well as women. According to Sor Juana, Paul's phrase "*keep silence* is intended not just for women, but for *all* incompetents" (51), for, she explains, "a fool may reach perfection (if ignorance may tolerate perfection) by having studied his title of philosophy and theology and by having some learning of tongues, by which he may be a fool in many sciences and languages" (49). Included among these men are, she states, "the evil Pelagius, "the intractable Arius," and "the evil Luther," all of whom, she further asserts, would have done well to follow Paul's instructions to "keep silence in the churches" (49).

Further to reinforce her interpretation of Paul, Sor Juana points to Paul's praise for such learned women as Fabiola, Marcella, Pecatula, and Leta, who involved themselves in the instruction of other women. Applying these Pauline principles to her own day, Sor Juana notes "how much injury might have been avoided in our land if our aged women had been learned, as was Leta, and had they known how to instruct as directed by Saint Paul" (53). Without the benefit of "learned elder women," Sor Juana continues, fathers are forced to use men to teach their daughters such basic skills as "reading, writing, counting, the playing of musical instruments, and other accomplishments, from which," she asserts, "no little harm results, as is experienced every day in doleful examples of perilous association"

(53). "Such notorious peril," maintains Sor Juana, "could be prevented if there were learned elder women, as Saint Paul wished to see, and if the teaching were handed down from one to another, as is the custom with domestic crafts and all other traditional skills" (54–55). Anticipating the "higher" biblical criticism of the nineteenth century, Sor Juana concludes her remarks by providing a historical context for her interpretations of Paul. "Historical fact," she explains while citing Eusebius as her source, "is that in the early church, women were charged with teaching the doctrine to one another in the temples and the sound of this teaching caused confusion as the Apostles were preaching and this is the reason they were ordered to be silent" (55).

While the tendency among scholars has been to situate Sor Juana's feminist concerns as fundamentally, even innately, opposed to the religious beliefs and institutions of Catholicism, such a view tends to be reductionistic. Instead of crediting Sor Juana with the imaginative power to explore and negotiate sometimes conflicting forces within her life and culture, it reduces her considerable genius to a psychological conflict between the necessity of conforming to the mandates of a Catholic belief system erroneously assumed to be opposed to reason and women's rights and her own experiences as a learned, intelligent women whose intellectual vitality included an equally passionate spiritual life. As Asunción Lavin explains, "Sor Juana was a devout and sincere believer, who, like most other people of her times, was deeply concerned with the salvation of her soul." According to Lavin, Sor Juana regarded her vocation as a nun "as a secure road to perfection and salvation" (Merrim 1991, 66).

With the same intensity that she argues for the importance of women's contribution to the world of learning, Sor Juana also articulates the sincerity and depth of both her Catholic faith and her vocation as a nun. For Sor Juana, being a Catholic and a nun is as important as being a feminist and a woman of letters. Indeed, just as feminist concerns permeate the writings of Sor Juana, so too do her faith and commitment to Catholicism. In the words of Elena Feder, Sor Juana was a "sincere believer" (1992, 478), and as George H. Tavard explains in his study of Sor Juana's theology, throughout her works Sor Juana "holds onto the anchor of faith" (1991, 213). Despite substantial criticism from a variety of sources, explains Tavard, there is not so much as a "hint that her theology might be at fault" (167). According to Tavard, even Sor Juana's secular "myths are tested and controlled by the revelation given once and for all in Jesus Christ and known in the Scriptures through the Church" (213).

Likewise, Jean Franco notes that Sor Juana was "a nun living within a system of patronage that she neither resisted nor opposed." "The center of Sor Juana's world," continues Franco, was "held together by the mythical power of the divine church and its kingdom on earth represented in the New World by the clergy and the viceregal court whose power Sor Juana did much to legitimize." Far from being "a lone sniper" who resisted traditional authority, Sor Juana was "at times, the very voice" of that authority, and, continues Franco, "it is important to stress that most of Sor Juana's poems were written within the conventions of court or Church and under their patronage" (1989, 49–50). Even Nina M. Scott, who describes Sor Juana as a "supremely intellectual woman who dared to verbalize a radically feminist stance in a time and context most unpropitious to her" (1985, 511), states that "Sor Juana never doubted her orthodoxy" (513).

In addition to her *Athenagoric Letter* and *Response*, most, if not all, of Sor Juana's works deal with Catholicism and issues of faith, and many of her writings were written specifically for the Catholic Church, including numerous poems, lyrics, and hymns (*villancicos*) to Mary and other saints. Many of these works were commissioned by the Church and sung or recited at ecclesiastical functions. Sor Juana also composed several of what Pamela Kirk terms "sacramental dramas" (known in Mexico as *autos sacramentales* and *loas*) about the mysteries of the Eucharist and related theological and liturgical subjects (1998, 36). Moreover, as Jean Franco explains, it is almost impossible to disentangle the secular from the religious in Sor Juana's writing. According to Franco, in the works of Sor Juana "courtly relations were apt to be transcoded into the religious" and "the religious was transcoded into the courtly" (1989, 26). Such is certainly the case, for example, with Sor Juana's *Allegorical Neptune*. Written in 1680 to explain the significance of an arch she was commissioned to construct in honor of the installation of Tomas de la Cerda, Marquis de la Laguna, as the viceroy of New Spain, this was printed with the blessings of the Church and is as much a work about the importance of Catholic leadership as it is about the classical mythologies that inspired the arch.

Such is also the case with Sor Juana's *Response*. With the same intensity and eloquence with which she defends her views on the rights of women, she also defends the authorities and dogmas of Roman Catholicism. Describing herself as first and foremost "an humble nun, the lowliest creature of the world," Sor Juana never questions the authority of the Church (*Poems, Protest, and a Dream*, 5). About Bishop Santa Cruz's ("Sor Filotea's") "most holy admonition" that she devote herself less to literary activities and more to her duties as a nun, Sor Juana states that she took his advice "to heart" as a "sensible warning" worthy of serious consideration (9). In addition, she states that she wrote "nothing except when compelled," that she "wish[ed] no quarrel with the Holy Office," and that she "tremble[d]" lest she "express some proposition that will cause offense or twist the true meaning of some scripture" (11). And about the relationship between her vocation as a Catholic nun and her writing, Sor Juan says, "I esteem more highly my reputation as a Catholic and obedient daughter of the Mother Church than all the approbation due a learned woman" (62–63).

While such statements, as many scholars have assumed, may indeed be in part rhetorical posturing designed to gain sympathy for the "ignorant" but well-intentioned efforts of a "humble nun" (11), throughout the *Response* Sor Juana also asserts that the greatest gift that God has given her was the "mercy of loving truth above all else" (11), and just as we do not question the sincerity of Sor Juana's feminist convictions, so too we have no good reason to doubt that she sincerely sought orthodox communion with the Church. All of Sor Juana's published works, it should be remembered, were printed with the *imprimatur* of the Church, and the last volume of her works to be published during her lifetime (1692) contains the affidavits of what Octavio Paz describes as "a team of theologians and literati," all of whom affirmed that the works of Sor Juana were in keeping with Church theology ([1982] 1988, 433).

From a Catholic perspective, however, it is important to note that Sor Juana herself justified her views on women through Catholic theology and Scriptural exegesis, and, as some Sor Juana scholars have failed to realize, rather than assuming that "two rival beliefs were at war within her: Christianity and feminism, her religious faith and her love of philosophy" and that in the end "feminism and philosophy triumphed" (422), Sor Juana saw nothing incompatible between faith and feminism. Throughout her *Response*, Sor Juana affirms her commitment to Catholicism and her vocation while simultaneously using Catholic thinking to justify her feminism.

For Sor Juana, the link between these two systems was reason, and in her *Response* Sor Juana uses her own life to illustrate how reason itself dictates that faith supports feminism and feminism enhances faith. For as long as she can remember, Sor Juana states that she was "inflamed with the desire to know" (*Poems, Protest, and a Dream*, 13) and that in her "the desire for learning was stronger than the desire for eating" (15). After entering the convent, she says "that inclination exploded in me like gunpowder" (17). Even when an abbess ordered her to cease her studies, she could "look at nothing without giving it further examination" (41). Aristotle, she writes, "would have written more" had he "prepared victuals," for even in the kitchen there were profound, even mystical, lessons to be learned about biology, geometry, and chemistry that enhanced rather than detracted from faith.

Just as, she explains, "all things issue from God, Who is at once the center and the circumference from which and in which all lines begin and end" (23), so too does reason lead to God. Indeed, Sor Juana thanks God for "will[ing]" that her passion for learning "be turned towards letters and not to some other vice" (27). For this reason, too, Sor Juana argues, the Church Fathers promoted the education of women and valued the contributions of learned, pious women to the faith. If the women of her day were dissuaded from learning, as, for example, Sor Juana had been by her Mother Superior, such authorities were themselves to be censured by the Church for failing to use their reason to see the will of God in the contributions that wise, learned women had to offer society and the Church. Although she does not explicitly say so, included in this number would be the bishop of Puebla himself, who while publishing her *Athenagoric Letter* as a criticism of her and simultaneously granting it his *imprimatur*, acted less out of reason than insecurity about the reasonings of a "humble nun." Reasonable men, she implies, should welcome the input of reasonable women, and if they did, both the Church and the world would be better off.

Much debate exists regarding why in her last few years Sor Juana, as far as we know, stopped writing and seems to have turned her attention primarily to prayer, self-mortification, and works of charity. Did she, as Nina Scott, among others, has suggested, "lose confidence in herself" and "bow to the will of her superiors" (1985, 518)? Did she, as Dorothy Schons, among others, has suggested, having accomplished what she wished to accomplish as a writer, turn her attention to matters of "heart" and "conscience" (1991, 55), hoping to die "in the odor of sanctity, revered and loved by all" (57)?[1] Or did she perhaps, as Octavio Paz ([1982] 1988) speculates, remain defiant to the end, only pretending to forsake the life of the mind in order to preserve herself from possible imprisonment and torture by the Inquisition and its officers?[2]

Most likely, the truth will never be known for certain, but in several testimonials that she wrote, some signed in her blood, which managed to survive the indiscriminate destruction of Church records during the Mexican revolution of the mid-nineteenth century, evidence indicates that Sor Juana's commitment to Catholicism was as strong as her commitment to education and literature. If, as scholars have generally concurred, Sor Juana's *Response* is the culmination of her thinking, "a courageous document that serves both as mirror to her overall odyssey and as a farewell letter" (*Poems, Protest, and a Dream*, xi), then a revisiting of the rhetoric and message of the *Response* in the light of its Catholic themes may very well offer a key to understanding her contribution to the historical development of both feminist and Catholic literary traditions in the Americas. Rather than a text that is assumed to posit an inherent, essentially irresolvable conflict between feminism and Catholicism, the *Response* can perhaps best be seen as Sor Juana's culminating attempt to explain to both her peers and to posterity that reason dictates a compatibility, not an incompatibility, between these two spheres of thought and action that characterized her entire career as intellectual and nun. Sor Juana—brilliant, devout, and progressive—understood this concept, and as George Tavard explains, contemporary Catholicism, especially in the United States, "could well use" the help of this important but still relatively unknown author as "a critical counterpoint to its self-image" as a religion insensitive to feminist concerns (1991, 1).

CRITICAL RECEPTION

Scholarship on Sor Juana is vast, complex, and controversial. Recognized in her own day as one of the most important writers of both New and Old Spain, she later fell into nearly two and a half centuries of obscurity and neglect, only to be reclaimed in the middle of the twentieth century as one of the great literary voices of the "Golden Age" of Spanish literature. Even at the height of her literary celebrity during the seventeenth century, Sor Juana was controversial. Praised in the halls of the viceregal court of Mexico and among the aristocracy and intellectual leaders of Spain as one of the most eloquent and erudite of Spanish writers, she was simultaneously criticized and condemned by many within the Mexican ecclesiastical hierarchy for devoting herself too intensely to the production of secular literature unbecoming her status as a woman and a nun.

Because the bulk of Sor Juana's manuscripts and correspondence (which is reputed to have been voluminous) has been lost, a complete, definitive text of all her works is currently an impossibility. The standard edition of Sor Juana's writing is today considered to be the four-volume *Obras Completas de Sor Juana Inés de la Cruz*, published between 1951 and 1957 in Mexico. Excellent English editions include *A Sor Juana Anthology* (1988), edited and translated by Alan Trueblood, and *Sor Juana Inés de la Cruz: Respuesta and Selection of Poems* (1994), a "critical edition" edited and translated by Electra Arenal and Amanda Powell. For the general as well as the scholarly reader, a paperback anthology published in 1997, *Poems, Protest, and a Dream*, translated by Margaret Sayers Peden and with an introductory essay by Ilan Stavans, offers an excellent and readily accessible introduction to Sor Juana's major works.

While considerable biographical work has been done on Sor Juana, Octavio Paz's massive *Sor Juana or, The Traps of Faith*, first published in Mexico in 1982 and translated into English in 1988, dominates all biographical and critical studies that follow. Although Paz's interpretation of Sor Juana's life and works has itself been controversial, he offers an extraordinarily readable account of the woman that places her within the context of seventeenth-century viceregal New Spain and provides compelling interpretations of most of her writings. Any reader of Sor Juana scholarship should undoubtedly begin with Paz's book. An earlier book, Gerald C. Flynn's *Sor Juana Inés de la Cruz* (1971), provides a general introduction to Sor Juana and her works.

More recent scholarship on Sor Juana has tended to explore the tension between the feminist, secular dimensions of her writings with their religious themes and her vocation as a writer/nun, with most scholars tending to interpret her within one context or the other. Two books by Stephanie Merrim—one a critical study titled *Early Modern Women's Writing and Sor Juana Inés de la Cruz* (1999) and the other a collection of essays titled *Feminist Perspectives on Sor Juana Inés de la Cruz* (1991)—establish a feminist construction for reading Sor Juana. Other important feminist studies include Jean Franco's *Plotting Women: Gender and Representation in Mexico* (1989) and Nina M. Scott's "Sor Juana Inés de la Cruz: 'Let your Women Keep Silence in the Churches'" (1985).

A book that focuses primarily on the Catholic dimensions of Sor Juana's life and works is George H. Tavard's *Juana Inés de la Cruz and the Theology of Beauty: The First Mexican Theology* (1991). As John F. Crossen has indicated in an essay on Sor Juana's Catholicism published in Mary R. Reichardt's *Catholic Women Writers: A Bio-Bibliographical Sourcebook* (2001), Tavard's book is considered to be the standard study of Sor Juana from a Catholic perspective. In *Sor Juana Inés de la Cruz: Religion, Art, and Feminism* (1998), Pamela Kirk also provides a sensitive and authoritative study of the relationship between religion and feminism in Sor Juana's works.

Other critical studies help situate Sor Juana within the context of seventeenth century literature or focus on the technical contributions of her writing. Excellent examples of these studies include Alfred Arteaga's "Chiasmus of the Woman Writer: Sor Juana Inés de la Cruz" (1993); Elena Feder's "Sor Juana Inés de la Cruz; or, the Snares of (Con)(tra)di(c)tion" (1992); Julie Greer Johnson's "Humor in Spain's American Colonies: The Case of Sor Juana Inés de la Cruz" (2000); Bradley J. Nelson's "Dialogism and the Sonnet: Silence, Reading and the Ethics of Knowledge in Sor Juana Inés de la Cruz" (1999); Nina M. Scott's "Sor Juana and Her World" (1994); and Grady C. Wray's "Seventeenth Century Wise Women of Spain and the Americas: Madre Ágreda and Sor Juana" (2001).

NOTES

Sor Juana Inés de la Cruz, *Poems, Protest, and a Dream*, trans. Margaret Sayers Peden and intro. Ilan Stavans (New York: Penguin, 1997). All references to Sor Juana's writings are from this anthology.

1. See also Lavin's opinion about the possibility that Sor Juana may have willingly submitted to "a self-holocaust of humility and penitence." According to Lavin, despite Sor Juana's unremitting commitment to the life of her mind and her some-times outspoken feminist views, she was always "a dutiful nun who complied with the daily routine, performed the conventional assignments to which she was appointed, obeyed her superiors, and befriended her sisters in religion" (Merrim 1991, 79).

2. Viewing the testimonials that Sor Juana signed, supposedly with her blood, as nothing more than "examples of devout formulas" (469) that are "lamentable both

as literature and as religious language," Paz argues that Sor Juana could not, "no matter how severe her opinion of her own life and behavior, have believed" what she signed (465).

WORKS CITED

Arteaga, Alfred. 1993. "Chiasmus of the Woman Writer: Sor Juana Inés de la Cruz." In *Literature and Quest*, ed. Christine Arkinstall, 89–103. Atlanta: Rodopi.

Crossen, John F. 2001. "Sor Juana Inés de la Cruz." In *Catholic Women Writers: A Bio-Bibliographical Sourcebook*, ed. Mary R. Reichardt, 181–86. Westport, CT: Greenwood Press.

Feder, Elena. 1992. "Sor Juana Inés de la Cruz; or, the Snares of (Con)(tra)di(c)tion." In *Amerindian Images and the Legacy of Columbus*, ed. Rene Jara and Nicholas Spadaccini, 473–529. Minneapolis: University of Minnesota Press.

Flynn, Gerald C. 1971. *Sor Juana Inés de la Cruz*. New York: Twayne.

Franco, Jean. 1989. *Plotting Women: Gender and Representation in Mexico*. New York: Columbia University Press.

Johnson, Julie Greer. 2000. "Humor in Spain's American Colonies: The Case of Sor Juana Inés de la Cruz." *Studies in American Humor* 3: 35–47.

Sor Juana Inés de la Cruz. 1951–1957. *Obras Completas de Sor Juana Inés de la Cruz*. Vols. 1–3, ed. Alfonso Mendez Plancarte; Vol. 4, ed. Alberto G. Salceda. Mexico City: Fondo de Cultura Economica.

———. 1988. *A Sor Juana Anthology*, ed. and trans. Alan Trueblood. Cambridge, MA: Harvard University Press.

———. 1994. *Sor Juana Inés de la Cruz: Respuesta and Selection of Poems*, ed. and trans. Electra Arenal and Amanda Powell. New York: Feminist Press.

Kirk, Pamela. 1998. *Sor Juana Inés de la Cruz: Religion, Art, and Feminism*. New York: Continuum.

Merrim, Stephanie, ed. 1991. *Feminist Perspectives on Sor Juana Inés de la Cruz*. Detroit: Wayne State University Press.

———. 1999. *Early Modern Women's Writing and Sor Juana Inés de la Cruz*. Nashville, TN: Vanderbilt University Press.

Nelson, Bradley J. 1999. "Dialogism and the Sonnet: Silence, Reading and the Ethics of Knowledge in Sor Juana Inés de la Cruz." *Romance Languages Annual* 10: 744–50.

Paz, Octavio. [1982] 1988. *Sor Juana or, The Traps of Faith*, trans. Margaret Sayers Peden. Cambridge, MA: Harvard University Press.

Schons, Dorothy. 1991. "Some Obscure Points in the Life of Sor Juana Inés de la Cruz." In *Feminist Perspectives on Sor Juana Inés de la Cruz*, ed. Stephanie Merrim, 38–60. Detroit: Wayne State University Press.

Scott, Nina M. 1985. "Sor Juana Inés de la Cruz: 'Let Your Women Keep Silence in the Churches.'" *Women's Studies International Forum* 8: 511–19.

———. 1994. "Sor Juana and Her World." *Latin American Research Review* 29: 143–54.

Tavard, George H. 1991. *Juana Inés de la Cruz and the Theology of Beauty: The First Mexican Theology*. Notre Dame, IN: University of Notre Dame Press.

Wray, Grady C. 2001. "Seventeenth Century Wise Women of Spain and the Americas: Madre Ágreda and Sor Juana." *Studia Mystica* 22: 123–49.

— **James A. Levernier**

Julian of Norwich [c. 1342–c. 1416]

Revelations of Divine Love

BIOGRAPHY

During the fourteenth century, while England was engaged in the Hundred Years' War with the Continent, a thirty-year-old English woman saw sixteen "showings," or visions. Soon after this event, the young woman recorded the contents of these revelations in a text entitled *A Book of Showings*, or *Revelations of Divine Love*. Fifteen to twenty years later, she composed a longer, more detailed account of the same sixteen visions and locutions.

Very little biographical information is known about this young woman, not even her name. The bubonic plague raging throughout England and all of Europe left little time for record keeping, and numerous collections of information needed to be destroyed and buried to contain its spread. At some point in her life, the woman became an anchoress and led a life of seclusion in a little room built onto the Church of St. Julian at Norwich. She took the name Julian after the patron saint of this church and lived according to the Rule of Life for anchors and anchoresses. The anchoress pledged to live her entire life within the confines of this room, eating a diet of cheese and bread. The room had a dirt floor, and she was provided with a shovel for sanitation purposes and a cat to keep the church mice in check. The Rule of Life delegated set hours for prayer and visitation and governed the reception of the sacraments as well as dress and diet. Simple cottage industries provided a small income. Since Julian was able to read and write, she may have copied manuscripts in addition to composing her own manuscript on her revelations.

Anchorholds had three openings with a curtain over each of them. Through one window, Julian could look into the church proper and see the altar for the celebration of the Eucharist and the tabernacle housing the consecrated bread, containing the body of Jesus. Her life as an anchoress reflected this Jesus, who was also housed as a captive for love in the little room of the tabernacle on the altar. The second window opened into a room where a maid servant could prepare her meals and slip food through the window. The servant would also secure necessities such as medicine, clothing, and the goods for her manual labor.

The third window allowed people to approach the Lady Julian for spiritual counsel. During times of deeper penance and solitude, such as Lent and Advent, the window was covered with a black cloth with a white cross on it. This signaled to the visitors that the anchoress would not be available for conversation, not even spiritual conversation. From the *Book of Margery Kempe*, we learn that a hermit at Lynn advised the English mystic Margery Kempe to seek spiritual direction from the anchoress Julian at Norwich, who was known for her well-balanced personality and spiritual wisdom. Margery Kempe records a series of conversations that she had with the anchoress on how to live as a devoted wife and mother. She had been prone to travel to places of pilgrimage, leaving her family members behind to care for themselves. Julian instructed her to grow in trust and the love of God within her family situation.

It is not known whether Lady Julian embraced the anchoritic lifestyle before or after she wrote the later edition of the *Revelations*, but civil records of the Norfolk County records office indicate that a woman by the name of Julian remained in the anchorhold at Norwich until her death sometime between 1416 and 1419. Various wills in the county records leave a legacy to the anchoress at Norwich, but some believe two more women by the same name were housed in the little room after the death of the author of the *Revelations*. City and county records also indicate that the anchoress at the Church of St. Julian was the first anchoress in town and that the number of anchoresses in Norwich rose to twenty-six in Julian's lifetime. This fact bespeaks high praise for this woman whom many chose to imitate.

Evidently, Julian received training in rhetoric and literature after her mystical experience, because the style of the second edition of her text indicates a marked growth in her literary skills between 1373 and 1393; her knowledge of Scripture and other spiritual literature also advanced during this period. Perhaps some confessor or preacher who perceived her spiritual and intellectual capabilities tutored her. Or she may have received education from the Benedictine nuns at Carrow, since the anchorhold at the Church of St. Julian was under their care. Although the specific details of Julian's life remain unknown, there is no doubt that some kind of training in Scripture, as well prolonged hours of contemplative prayer, influenced her writings, especially the longer edition of the *Revelations*. Her text also shows how the local color of the town, including the fishing industry, textile mills, dye making, and the hospitals and castles, filled with dying victims of the plague, flavored her descriptions.

Julian was the first person to write a theological treatise in the English language. Her message was not only for scholars versed in Latin and Norman French but for the plain folk as well. Living at the same time as the Middle English poet Geoffrey Chaucer, Julian created her own God-talk, framing words in a new way. Her creative expressions are not only original to her, but some of her word pictures have never been used again in the history of the English language.

Julian of Norwich was an optimist grounded in reality. Her visions of divine love presented a new context for the mystery of sin and the sufferings and pains resulting from it. This anchoress, whose life remained so hidden, leaves behind just one message, that of God's love. She is silent now, and only the Word that flowed from her pen remains. And this Word is Love.

SUMMARY

Revelations of Divine Love is a record of sixteen visions witnessed by Lady Julian in May 1373. The anchoress Julian of Norwich is suddenly taken ill and believes that she is dying. A priest arrives to administer the last rites, and he tells the anchoress to look at the crucifix. The crucifix seems to begin pouring blood copiously over Julian and her bed as the visions begin. Julian simultaneously sees Jesus crowned with thorns and the Virgin Mary at the moment she agrees to become the mother of the Redeemer. While Julian watches these two visions, God places something the size of a hazelnut in her hand. She realizes this small object is the whole of creation, but it seems tiny compared to the immensity of God.

Suddenly, God's presence sheds light on a scene of the bottom of the sea, and Julian sees how a sinner resembles a person drowning. Nevertheless, a person can feel protected even at the bottom of the sea as long as one realizes God is present in every situation.

Then, Julian sees the convergence of all time and all space into one point, indicating how God is present in all of reality, working in and through it. God performs every act that ever was, is, or will be, and each of these actions proceeds according to God's will and intentions. Although puzzled by the absence of sin in this vision of all things, Julian discovers how sin is the absence of something that ought to exist.

After this, streams from the scourged body of Jesus flow over the entire creation, washing away sin. God uses blood for cleansing instead of water in order to elevate human nature and manifest the depths of divine love.

Still gazing at the crucifix, Julian hears a locution saying that the fiend is overcome by the death of Jesus. The devil loses so much ground from his victims' acts of repentance that he would actually be farther ahead if creatures never sinned. Julian laughs when she sees that the power of the devil is locked in God's hands.

The sixth vision shows an exemplum of a lord entertaining some guests. God tells Julian a king can thank a servant privately, or he can give more honor with a public recognition, or better yet, a king can call his servant "friend." Likewise, God freely chooses how he will honor each person.

Soon, Julian experiences quick emotional shifts between consolation and desolation. The changes are so rapid that she realizes these experiences are not based on anything she herself has done. God allows creatures to vacillate so they learn to rely on him instead of themselves.

Julian feels physical and spiritual pains in her own body as she watches a scene of Mary and some of the disciples of Jesus grieving at the foot of the cross. Jesus explains how the depth of her love for him is determining the depth of the pain she is feeling, and that the Virgin Mary suffers more pain than anyone at the sight of Jesus' suffering because of her great love for him. Jesus absorbs all the pain in the world as if it were his own.

Despite his pain, Jesus radiates joy because of the love with which he suffers for the world: if he could suffer more for us he would. Still experiencing the pain of Jesus in her own body, Julian begins to radiate joy as she looks at the radiant face of Jesus. Suddenly, "three heavens" appear, revealing the delight that the Trinity takes in seeing creatures respond to divine love.

Jesus looks down at Julian from his cross and leads her through the wound in his side into his heart. There, she discovers a shelter large enough for all men and women of all time. Jesus points to his mother, who has stayed beneath the cross all this time, reflecting the joy that is in the heart of her son, Jesus. Through a series of "I am" statements, Jesus shows how his humanity exists within the mystery of the Trinity and how each person of the Trinity longs for the intimate union with every single person that has ever existed. The creature also longs for this deep union, but seeing the glorified state of God makes a person painfully aware of guilt and sin. God allows this sense of guilt because it breaks the vicious pride that truly prevents union with God. In fact, awareness of one's personal weakness draws forth the compassion of God. The devil blames creatures for their failures in order to discourage them from seeking union with God. By contrast, God longs to shower his creatures with mercy and peace. In fact, God promises two "Great Deeds" that will overcome sin. One Deed will remain secret until the end of time, but the other Deed will unfold gradually in the course of time as creatures begin to understand how God's will has been operating in everything that has ever happened. God has already cured the sin of Adam, which is the greatest sin that has ever occurred, so God can certainly cure the lesser sin of Adam's children.

The fourteenth and longest revelation begins with a *ratiocinatio* on trust in God. Through a series of questions and answers, God teaches Julian that he is the source of her desire for union with him and the source of her prayer. In the longer text of the *Revelations*, Julian develops an allegory about a lord and his servant, describing the relationship between God and the sinner. A description of the threefold motherhood of God expands the themes of creation and redemption presented by the servant allegory. The image of a beautiful child stepping out of a sticking mud pit and gliding up to heaven culminates this story of redemption. The child represents a soul being lifted from the pain of sin in death to end the cycle of sin.

The evening after Julian experienced the showings, the fiend enters her bedroom. She had been feverish the whole day, and now the devil tells her that she has been suffering from delusions all day. Suddenly, Jesus also appears, reassuring her with a final vision that validates all she had seen and experienced the previous day. Jesus shows Julian her soul resembling a large city, with the God-Man sitting on a throne in the center of the city. Julian sees the Trinity taking delight in all it has accomplished in this holy city, which is actually the soul of all creatures. Jesus tells Julian the trials of life will never overcome her because God reigns in the kingdom of her soul.

For fifteen years, Julian wondered if she was supposed to act on these messages. Were these mysteries revealed to her for some particular reason? She asks God for some indication so she can know what is expected of her. So, fifteen years after the initial revelations, God tells her the revelations occurred simply to show his love for her. That is, God wanted her to know not only that he loved her, but he wanted Julian to realize how important it was to him to have her *know* that he loved her. To know we are loved has redeeming value.

MAJOR THEMES

The study of the structure of mystical writings is a key step in understanding the meaning of a text based on mystical experience. A mystic experiences God in a medium beyond language and ordinary logic and then uses a literary construct and plot to hold this experience in order to convey it to others. Theologians and exegetes examine literary structure and plot to reach behind these literary devices to come into closer contact with the original mystical experience, coded within the plot and drama of various literary and theological genres.

In her *Revelations of Divine Love*, Julian of Norwich presented a simple report of the sixteen visions and locutions she experienced. After many years of prayer and reflection, she then produced a text four times the length of her original report. This later, more mature text developed a more explicit use of the theological method known as the four "senses" of Scripture. Saint Paul had already used this method in his epistles. The monasteries of the Middle Ages relied on this method of study, while the universities developed a scholastic form of questions and answers called the *disputatio* and a circular form of questioning known as the *ratiocinatio*. While Julian incorporated both monastic and scholastic techniques in her teaching, the four senses of Scripture provided the overarching structure of her book. Like a giant erector set, each line of Julian's text builds the foundation for the next layer of spiritual teaching.

The four senses of Scripture were as natural as breathing in Julian's time. Rather than imposing an artificial structure on her mystical revelations, they provide a subconscious filter for her mystical teaching. The first, the historical or literal sense of Scripture, considered historical events as carriers of God's messages and God's self-revelation. Rather than seeing historical events as past occurrences, all the words and events that took place in public and private revelation were like husks of corn that contained kernels of truth. Then, the three remaining senses of Scripture, the spiritual senses, peeled away this outer husk in order to access the deeper, hidden truths of revelation. The three spiritual senses were considered an integral part of the entire revelation, as essential as the original historical event.

Julian's initial description of her sixteen revelations supplied the historical sense for her *Revelations of Divine Love*. She then developed the second sense of Scripture, the allegorical sense, by describing the scenes in great detail and explaining the significance of each detail. This unveiling of details was regarded as the development of theological doctrine. The details contained more of the teaching, and Julian unwrapped them in order to reveal more of the doctrine. The allegorical level focused primarily on a conversion of the intellect, the transformation of one's way of thinking about God.

The moral or tropological sense of Scripture built upon the allegorical sense. This moral level focused on union with God. That is to say, the good actions of believers flowed from their relationship with God and their degree of intimacy with him. Sacraments were perceived as the primary means of developing a profound union with God. The only way fallen creatures could do good and avoid evil was to unite their poor actions to the actions of Christ, and Christ is identified with Holy Mother Church. Julian's development of the image of our "mother Jesus" on the cross is an example of this moral level of exegesis. The moral level centered on the transformation of one's actions based on a transformation of one's whole being.

The final sense of Scripture, the mystical or anagogical, anticipated the beatific vision. This mystical level is usually portrayed as the heavenly Jerusalem with the

Lamb of God lighting up the heavenly city. Julian's final vision portrays this heavenly city as a vision of her own soul. The anagogical stage centered on the transformation of one's desires. Longing and thirsting for God were the primary means of attaining this spiritual transformation.

While the major framework of the *Revelations* consisted of an exegesis of the Scripture text based on loving God with all one's heart and soul and loving one's neighbor as oneself, within this overarching construct Julian used a number of patterns of the four senses in miniature. Like Chinese boxes that contain a series of smaller boxes within larger boxes, Julian's images contain layers of meaning. Peel back one layer and one finds a whole new layer of meaning beneath it waiting to be unfolded. At times, Julian of Norwich developed these images using the scholastic *conflatio*, a series of concentric repetitions, each supplying one more piece of the truth as it repeats lines like the round of a song that adds one more word with each new repetition. At other times, Julian employed the scholastic techniques of *disputatio* and *ratiocinatio*. As Julian wove together the monastic and scholastic pedagogical techniques, she fashioned a new kind of theology, integrating spiritual transformation with the academic disciplines. An examination of some of the major themes and techniques in her text provides examples of this integration.

Julian's treatment of sin illustrates her use of imagery as a means of developing Catholic doctrine. To understand the horror of sin in its fullness, one first needs to see the beauty of its opposite, the goodness of God permeating creation and the intimate level of union with God experienced before the fall from grace. In revelations one and three, God shows Julian all time and space—past, present, and future—converging into one "point," into a unity, and he indicates that he is present in each moment of time. God also reveals that he is the one who has performed all actions that were ever performed, are now performed, or will be performed. By presenting the whole creation as an object as small as a hazelnut in the presence of God in revelation one and as an even smaller point in revelation three, a simple contrast in size becomes a theological statement. This is a key example of Julian's genius. The size points toward the immensity of God and also his closeness and his loving concern for something so small. This image shows that God is everywhere, in and through every facet of his creation. This universal presence of God is the peculiarly Catholic understanding of sacramentality. Sacramental life is intensified in the liturgy, the official worship of the Church, but it is also occurring in the living and breathing of everyday life. Creation is penetrated with both the immanence and the transcendence of God. God is so close, he is in the very air his creatures breathe. At the same time, God is beyond this world's grasp, in the distant heavens. The simultaneous intimacy and grandeur of God are reflected in nature, which points beyond itself to the supernatural.

Once Julian senses this grandeur and intimacy of God, she recalls her sinfulness and deeply regrets her failures. It seems that sin is the only thing that can hinder union with God, and she wishes God had never allowed sin to enter into creation. It is only after sensing intimacy with God and the joy this brings to the creature that one can feel the tragedy of sin, which is the loss of this intimacy with God. The pain of losing this closeness to God is so intense that creatures cannot bear the loss without the help of God.

The allegory of the lord and the servant in revelation fifteen illustrates the drama of sin within the structure of a longer, extended exemplum. Exempla were homiletic images and parables designed to organize Scriptural teachings. This parable, an extended allegory, merges sacramental theology and Scriptural principles as it describes the relationship between God and the sinner. The servant, who is eager to please the lord by gathering for him the choicest fruit of the garden, falls and gets injured. The lord is so grateful to the servant for enduring so much extra pain and suffering in order to get the harvest ready that he decides to reward the servant more than he would have if everything had gone according to the original plan. The servant represents the man Adam who fell into sin, and he also represents the New Adam, Jesus Christ, who "fell" into the womb of the Virgin at the moment of the Incarnation. The fruit in the garden represents men and women who are not yet fit to be presented to the lord of the garden. The lord, who sits on barren soil as he awaits the return of the servant, is the Creator, banished from his true home in the souls of his creatures. The servant who worries about displeasing the lord as he lies on the ground unable to move would have received immediate relief had he been aware of how lovingly the lord was looking on him, delighted by his efforts. The blindness caused by the fall makes the creature feel he is separated from God, even though God knows of his good intentions.

The themes of creation, incarnation, and redemption developed in the lord-and-servant allegory become more elaborated in Julian's images of the mother-hood of God. Julian learns that there is a threefold motherhood within the Trinity, reflecting the operations of nature, mercy, and grace, and there is the motherhood of Jesus, inviting the soul into deeper union with God. Julian urges her audience to imitate a child who relies on its mother more than itself, thereby developing the Scriptural theme of loving God with all one's heart and soul, even in the face of one's own weakness and sin. At the same time, this image of motherhood extends her teaching to the moral level of union with God, portrayed by the sacramental feeding on the body and blood of Mother Jesus. Julian encourages her listeners to cherish the weakness in themselves that attracts God's motherly love. When we feel lost and unable to find the way to God, then we can simply call for help and Mother Jesus will lift us like children onto his lap. If a child is too weak to respond to its mother, it can grab onto her and cry with all its might. This is how a helpless creature loves God with all its heart and soul and might when it feels too weak to do anything for itself. The image of motherhood reflects the theological balance between Word and Sacrament that is so characteristic of Catholic theology.

Building on the allegory of the lord and the servant, Julian states that the Doomsday, or Day of Judgment, will focus on victory over sin. Instead of condemning creatures for all the sins of their lives, God will enlighten everyone so that they will marvel at how each one has conquered sin. Each sin that has been overcome will be like a jewel, in some sense shaping one's glorified state. Yet, even though the sinner can profit from sin that is conquered, it is better to avoid sin at any cost. Considering the pain and suffering that sin caused Jesus and recognizing the damage that sin causes to the self and others, creatures can never justify willful sinfulness. But evil committed by creatures is never as powerful as goodness, which has its origin in God.

In a revelation unique to Julian, God foretells a Great Deed that will rectify sin on the last day. Only God knows what the nature of this Deed will be, but when it comes to pass, creatures will at last learn how "all is well" with creation, despite the scourge of evil. However, God chooses not to reveal the details of this Deed in time. God will also perform another Deed that is separate from the Great Deed. Little by little, this action of God will be revealed as it begins to occur. Believers will learn that God sees hearts differently than humans do, because he does not blame sinners the way that creatures blame one another.

Julian's vision of Mary remaining at the foot of the cross incorporates her role in the redemptive act. She shares the pain of the Passion and death of her son as she also shares his intercessory role. At the foot of the cross, Mary participates in the Eucharistic sacrifice of the New Covenant. She sees the blood of her son flowing over creation, cleansing it of sin and transforming the earth. The blood of her son not only covers sin but transforms the sinner and the sin. Mary participates in the rebirth of creation. When Mary gave birth to her son Jesus, she also gave birth to all members of the Mystical Body of her son who live within him. At the foot of the cross, the new Body of Christ, the Church, springs forth from the wound in the side of Christ. The waters of baptism and the blood of the New Covenant pour over the sin of the world, forgiving sin once and for all. This sacramental outpouring of blood and water is the root of the Catholic Church's radical forgiveness, a forgiveness that is total.

The forgiveness of sin, however, is not a denial of sin. The extreme measures taken by God to redeem sinners underscore the seriousness of sin, but the love of God is more powerful than the harm caused by sin. To take the Passion and death of Jesus seriously is to believe that God is not only powerful and loving in the creation of the world but that he is even more powerful and more loving in the restoration and transformation of creation. Mary, at the foot of the cross, believes in God's love for her more than any other creature ever has. As a result, God can do for Mary what he also wants to do for other creatures, but only Mary has allowed God to do all he desires to do in her being. God's will has been accomplished through Jesus and it has been accomplished in Mary, and this will can also completely transform heaven and earth, as soon as creatures stop thwarting it.

Julian of Norwich's final revelation shows her soul as a city, with God seated on a throne in the middle of the city. In the allegory of the lord and the servant, the lord, seated on barren soil, symbolizes God awaiting the readiness of creatures to admit him to his true home in their souls. This final revelation of divine love, which is similar to the Book of Revelation's portrayal of the New Jerusalem, is also the final, mystical level of Scripture, completing the text's literary and theological structure. God himself is the light in the city; he is the teacher of the soul, enlightening it from within. This light is the love radiating from the presence of the Lamb, who is Christ. This light is the Father, Son, and Holy Spirit. This concluding stage of Scriptural exegesis is also the divine liturgy of heaven that descends into every soul that is saved. The liturgy of the New Jerusalem is the liturgy of Holy Mother Church. The hosannas of heaven and earth unite at the feast of the New Covenant that forgives sin and transforms heaven and earth. Not only earth but also heaven is changed by this marriage of heaven and earth.

Julian of Norwich integrates this monastic, contemplative mode of theologizing with a scholastic *ratiocinatio* in her book's epilogue. Like a snowball growing in size and momentum as it repeats its circular movement, her conclusion finds its precision and power in a series of circular questions, with each set of questions and answers fine-tuning another aspect of the mystery of divine love. Julian introduces this *ratio* by telling us that, for more than fifteen years, she has wondered if God revealed these mysteries to her for some particular reason, and she asks God to enlighten her. Then God gives Lady Julian one last affirmation concerning her showings. The revelations occurred because God wanted to show his love for her. The message itself is Love and the person revealing it to her is Love. If she continues to ponder the revelations, she will learn nothing other than Love. Love is the meaning of the revelations. The concluding round of questions and answers draws the reader into the eternal round dance of the Trinity, where Father loves Son, and Son loves Father, and the resulting love between them is the Spirit who prolongs the gaze of Love. The overflowing love of the Trinity has spilled forth into creation, which is the fruit of divine love. These lines mirroring the eternal round dance of love within the Trinity illustrate how divine love draws creation back to its origins in God. They tell the story of how God finds a lasting home within his creation, in the inner city of each soul that will be saved. It is the story of the union of the human with the divine. It is the story of a Love without beginning and a Love without end.

CRITICAL RECEPTION

Edmund Colledge, O. S. A., and James Walsh, S. J., present a technical study of Julian's theological genius and literary expertise in a 200-page "Introduction" to the Middle English edition of *A Book of Showings to the Anchoress Julian of Norwich* (1978). Colledge and Walsh also provide a theological critique of Julian's *Showings* with their modern English translation of the short and long texts. They supply a historical picture of fourteenth-century politics, literature, and culture and portray Julian as a woman of letters at a time when this was a rarity. Relying heavily on their own expertise in medieval manuscripts, Colledge and Walsh illustrate Julian's originality in both content and presentation of doctrine. They stress her attentiveness to sacred Scriptures, especially the Wisdom literature, Gospel of John, and epistles of Saint Paul.

Another study of the Middle English texts with pictures of the major manuscripts in various copyists' penmanship is *Julian of Norwich, Showings of Love: Extant Texts and Translations*, edited by Sister Anna Maria Reynolds, C. P., and Julia Bolton Holloway (2001). The fresh translations provide a variety of insights.

Carthusian monks, who preserved Julian of Norwich's manuscripts through the centuries, have fostered research and publication on Julian through the University of Salzburg in Austria. This university press has published a series of scholarly, yet readable, volumes that remain available in college and university libraries. Brant Pelphrey's *Love Was His Meaning: The Theology and Mysticism of Julian of Norwich* (1982) concentrates on the personal nature of the relationship between God and his creatures as a means of understanding sin and redemption. He presents a condensation of this original study in a more recent edition published by Glazier, *Christ Our Mother: Julian of Norwich* (1989).

Another key study in the series of the University of Salzburg's Elizabethan and Renaissance Texts is my volume, *An Understanding of Love according to the Anchoress Julian of Norwich* (1983). I illustrate here how Julian's classical theology of love integrates her personal prayer experiences with the Scriptures and tradition, presenting the eternal mystery of God and man's love for each other in simple, nontechnical terms. My study underscores the difference that the presence of God can bring to any situation in life and shows how God's presence forms the basis for Julian's teaching on the meaning of suffering.

Christopher Abbot's *Julian of Norwich: Autobiography and Theology* (1999) presents a precise critique of Julian's theology and the genre of autobiography in building a bridge between theology and spirituality. His study lends itself to the tradition's teaching on the individual's union with God and the Church's more recent teachings on a collective spirituality, in which one's holiness consists of leading others to holiness. Julian was aware of the importance of a collective spirituality that fosters a concern for the holiness of all believers.

Ritamary Bradley (1992) and Sheila Upjohn (1989) discuss major, practical themes in Julian that are very helpful to those already familiar with Julian's text. Paul Molinari, S. J. (1958), provides good historical background and commentary on the whole of the *Revelations*. Molinari is particularly strong on relating Julian's intuitions as a mystic to the formulated doctrines of the Church.

Gloria Durka (1989), Brendan Doyle (1983), Austin Cooper (1988), Robert Llewelyn (1982), and Elizabeth Ruth Obbard (1995) present selected texts of the *Revelations* as a means of exposing the wider public to a taste of Julian's spirituality in her own words. Durka, Cooper, and Llewelyn present commentaries with their selections, and Obbard illustrates her text and captures Julian's spirituality in choice two- or three-word titles for each citation. My forward in Doyle's short anthology situates Julian's place among the German, French, and Italian mystics of her time.

Reading a variety of the modern translations may be a fruitful means of capturing the spirit of Julian of Norwich's mystical teaching. Clifton Wolters (1982), Father John-Julian, O. J. N. (2003), and M. L. del Mastro (1977), like the Reynolds and Holloway (2001) and Colledge and Walsh (1978) texts cited above, each bring Julian of Norwich into the twenty-first century with their adaptations and translations of the *Revelations*.

Through her *Revelations of Divine Love*, Julian of Norwich was a pioneer in situating the genre of mystical revelations within the discipline of theology and the Church's magisterial development of doctrine. She developed a colorful theological language that remains unique to her, and she has foretold a Great Deed that will make all things well. She presents to the world a God willing to suffer for those he loves, a God whose smile transforms pain into joy.

NOTE

Julian of Norwich, *Showings*, trans. Edmund Colledge, O. S. A., and James Walsh, S. J. Classics of Western Spirituality Series (New York: Paulist Press, 1978). All references are to this edition.

WORKS CITED

Abbot, Christopher. 1999. *Julian of Norwich: Autobiography and Theology.* Cambridge: D. S. Brewer.

Bradley, Ritamary. 1992. *Julian's Way: A Practical Commentary on Julian of Norwich.* London: HarperCollins.

Colledge, Edmund, O. S. A., and James Walsh, S. J., eds. 1978. *A Book of Showings to the Anchoress Julian of Norwich*. 2 vols. Toronto: Pontifical Institute of Mediaeval Studies.

Cooper, Austin. 1988. *Julian of Norwich Reflections on Selected Texts*. Mystic, CT: Twenty-Third Publications.

Del Mastro, M. L. 1977. *Juliana of Norwich: Revelations of Divine Love*. Garden City, NY: Doubleday/Image.

Doyle, Brendan. 1983. *Meditations with Julian of Norwich*, foreword by Patricia Vinje. Sante Fe, NM: Bear and Co.

Durka, Gloria. 1989. *Praying with Julian of Norwich*. Winona, MN: St. Mary's Press.

John-Julian, Father, O. J. N. 2003. *A Lesson of Love: The Revelations of Julian of Norwich*. New York: Writers Club Press.

Llewelyn, Robert. 1982. *All Shall Be Well*. New York: Paulist Press.

Molinari, Paul, S. J. 1958. *Julian of Norwich: The Teaching of a 14th Century Mystic*. New York: Longmans, Green.

Obbard, Elizabeth Ruth. 1995. *Introducing Julian, Woman of Norwich*. London: New City.

Pelphrey, Brant. 1982. *Love Was His Meaning: The Theology and Mysticism of Julian of Norwich*. Salzburg: Institut für Anglistik und Amerikanistik, Universität Salzburg.

———. 1989. *Christ Our Mother: Julian of Norwich*. Vol. 7. Way of the Christian Mystics Series. Wilmington, DE: Michael Glazier.

Reynolds, Anna Maria, C. P., and Julia Bolton Holloway, eds. 2001. *Julian of Norwich, Showings of Love: Extant Texts and Translations*. Florence: Sismel.

Upjohn, Sheila. 1989. *In Search of Julian of Norwich*. London: Longman and Todd.

Vinje, Patricia Mary. 1983. *An Understanding of Love according to the Anchoress Julian of Norwich*. Vol. 92, no. 8. Elizabethan and Renaissance Studies Series. Salzburg: Institut für Anglistik und Amerikanistik, Universität Salzburg.

Wolters, Clifton. 1982. *Julian of Norwich: Revelations of Divine Love*. New York: Penguin.

— Patricia Mary Vinje

Christopher J. Koch [1932–]

The Year of Living Dangerously

BIOGRAPHY

Christopher John (C. J.) Koch is an Australian novelist who began by publishing verse and has also produced film scripts from a number of his novels. His books have won notable awards and been translated into many foreign languages, especially European and Asian. Born in Hobart, Tasmania, on July 16, 1932, Koch is of Irish, English, and German ancestry. He was educated at various schools, including the Irish Christian Brothers college, St. Virgil's, in Hobart, and the Hobart State high school. He later attended the University of Tasmania, where he received a baccalaureate degree in arts in 1954.

Following graduation and extensive travel in Asia and Europe, Koch completed his first novel while living in London. Entitled *The Boys in the Island* (1958; revised 1974), it was a work of seminal importance for it showed the first signs of the author's deep interest in spiritual realities. It contains many of the elements that have marked his subsequent novels—the contest between reality and illusion; the fatal power of false religion; the concern with dualities, especially in culture and belief; and the special quality and appeal of a remote island (Tasmania) detached from a larger mainland (Australia) and distant from its ancestral culture (Europe).

On his return to Australia, Koch joined the Australian Broadcasting Corporation (ABC) as a radio producer, but he left in 1960 for a year in California when he was awarded a Stanford Writing Fellowship. He and his wife Irene subsequently moved to Italy, where their son Gareth was born, and Koch finished his second novel, *Across the Sea Wall* (1965; revised 1982). This work was something of a precursor to *The Year of Living Dangerously* in that it evokes the experience of Indo-European cultures and religions through the eyes of a young Australian, Catholic in background, who stops off in Asia on the traditional journey to Europe.

Koch resumed his work with the ABC in 1962, finally serving as federal head of radio for schools. In 1968 he spent two months in Indonesia as an advisor to UNESCO, an assignment that, combined with the experiences of his brother Philip as a reporter in Jakarta during the 1960s, helped to crystallize his interest in Indonesia as the setting for another novel. But his career in broadcasting was too all-absorbing to allow the necessary time and imaginative space for composing novels, and he resigned from the ABC in 1972 to pursue writing full time. Moving to Launceston in his home state of Tasmania, he produced his third novel, *The Year of Living Dangerously*, in 1978. Its publication marked Koch's literary reemergence after a silence of thirteen years, and the work was greeted by enthusiastic reviews and prestigious awards. It was later adapted into a movie of the same title (1982) starring Mel Gibson and scripted by Koch, David Williamson, and Peter Weir. The screenplay was nominated for an Academy Award.

In 1980, Koch moved back to Sydney, where he wrote his fourth novel, *The Doubleman* (1985), for which he earned one of Australia's most esteemed literary prizes, the Miles Franklin Award. Like all his novels, *The Doubleman* emerged slowly. Even as a full-time writer, Koch is known for his painstaking craftsmanship. He devotes many years to each book, carrying out careful research, preparing sketchbooks as well as notebooks, and engaging in constant revision. "I want to give," he has said, "the same attention to prose as I would to verse" (Jones 1985, 9). His professional diligence is also evidenced in his revisiting earlier novels and producing revised editions at a much later date. In *The Doubleman*, Koch deals overtly with spiritual themes, especially the collision in contemporary culture between Christian faith and realism and a resurgent paganism abounding in illusion. He also demonstrates his poetic ability to evoke a sense of place, prompting the comment by Graham Greene that Koch's description of his Hobart boyhood made Tasmania "part of my memory" (Collins 1985, 16).

In 1987, Koch published a book of essays, *Crossing the Gap*, which affords vital insights into his background and development as a writer and which was shortlisted in Great Britain for the Hawthornden Prize. The following years, during which Koch lived in the Blue Mountains west of Sydney and again in Tasmania, were devoted to a major writing project that began as a single work but that gradually transmuted into two novels. The first volume, *Highways to a War* (1995), won Koch a second Miles Franklin Award for his story of a Tasmanian photojournalist in modern Indochina. It attracted comparison with *The Year of Living Dangerously* in its study of brave idealism and betrayal, culminating in the tragic Christian symbolism of the hero's crucifixion at the hands of the communist Khmer Rouge. Its companion novel, *Out of Ireland* (1999), traces the adventures of a nineteenth-century ancestor of the photojournalist, an Irish political prisoner consigned to convict Tasmania.

While completing these two works, Koch remarried and moved again to Sydney. His latest book, *The Many-Coloured Land* (2002), is a personal memoir that sheds further light on his fiction by blending a study of his Irish roots with a critical appreciation of present-day Ireland.

PLOT SUMMARY

The Year of Living Dangerously is set in Indonesia during the final turbulent months of President Sukarno's rule. Taking its title from the name Sukarno himself gave the fateful year of 1965, the novel is narrated in the first person by a reporter named Cook. It centers on a group of journalists in the capital of Jakarta, in particular the Australian radio and television correspondent Guy Hamilton and the Chinese-Australian cinecameraman Billy Kwan. Technically a dwarf, Kwan fulfills, in Koch's plan, the function of the medieval court jester (commonly a dwarf), namely, "to tell people truths they didn't want to hear" (Kerr and Edmonds 1985, 4). He is an enigmatic figure who keeps secret files on various subjects and people, including his friends. A convert to Catholicism, he is also attracted to Islam. He feels a mystical attachment to the Indonesian poor and cherishes the vision of Sukarno as their savior. He invests a similar hope in Hamilton, sacrificing his own love for an English girl, Jill Bryant, an attaché to the British Embassy, by cultivating her relationship with Hamilton. Kwan also arranges a scoop for Hamilton, an exclusive interview with the Indonesian Communist leader D. N. Aidit, as a way of boosting his reputation in Jakarta, not for the purpose of self-aggrandizement but to enlarge Hamilton's power and desire to do good.

Eventually, Kwan becomes disillusioned, first with Sukarno and then with Hamilton. He loses faith in the Indonesian president's affinity with the poor and, in a dramatic scene, falls to his death from a hotel window on which he has hung the beseeching banner, "Sukarno, Feed your People." Yet his faith in Hamilton's goodness is posthumously vindicated: the journalist falls in love with Jill Bryant and, finding her pregnant, pleads with her not to have an abortion. As a violent Communist coup takes place in Jakarta, overthrowing Sukarno, and is followed by a successful countercoup, Hamilton is seriously injured, but he risks permanent blindness in one eye to accompany Jill to England.

The novel interweaves various themes—Christian tradition and Hindu mythology, Indonesian politics and Communist ideology, European ancestry and Australian identity—in ways that are mutually illuminating. It finds a symbolic basis in the *wayang kulit*, the ancient Javanese shadow play in which puppets depict the timeless interplay of good and evil. Important scenes take place in the Wayang Bar of the Hotel Indonesia, and the dramatic patterns of the *wayang* itself provide a narrative structure and moral frame of reference for the human characters and conflicts in the novel.

MAJOR THEMES

The Year of Living Dangerously has acquired for Christopher Koch and Indonesia something of the aura and of the obligatory reading for foreign correspondents that *The Quiet American* has for Graham Greene and Vietnam. This is not simply because of its treatment of a critical episode in modern Indonesian history but for its revealing study of realities about human life, particularly in the context of spiritual longings and moral demands and the interplay of eastern and western cultures. In the words of Les Murray, Koch's novel captures "the tropical darkness of Conrad or Graham Greene, the spiritual night in which Western souls are brought to strange extremes." Murray notes that nearly all of the novel's most significant moments occur at night, "away from the sun, by street light, airport lights, hotel candlelight or the dim oil lamps of the Jakarta slums" (1978, 21). In such a setting, the concluding comment of one of Koch's characters is of salutary importance: that westerners no longer have many answers, for they believe in nothing but their pleasures (*The Year of Living Dangerously*, 289–90).

From the outset, Koch has enjoyed renown for the resonant power of his imagination, tutored by his early experience as a landscape painter and a poet.

He also writes for the ear as well as the eye: he is captivated by the "wonderful rhythms and resonances" of the King James Bible (Baker 1989, 211) and has long been sensitive to "the great sound of poetic prose in English" (Pinwell 1983, 2). In *The Year of Living Dangerously* there are memorable passages that evoke the sights, sounds, and smells of Indonesian life:

> Flares, flares everywhere, in the flatland darkness, where gabled villas with orange-tiled roofs hid behind crumbling walls, and a dark, drain-like canal moved with evil slowness. On an area of muddy ground beside the highway, the lights from the *pasar* [bazaar] burned uncertainly: kerosene and gas pressure-lamps set on the counters of many little stalls under tattered awnings. Above them, the final awning of the heat extended motionless. (20)

Koch is also alive to the extended power of religious language. He makes frequent use of words with unmistakably Christian overtones—as when he describes Billy Kwan's "heavy sound camera on its brace" as "the cinecamera-man's cross" (5) and his voice as assuming, at different times, "a tone of litany" (21) and "a tone of liturgy" (97). Even the author's preparation of *The Year of Living Dangerously* gave rise to a religious statement reflective of a personal sense of divine providence, as when he told an interviewer, just after the publication of the novel, that "those long years of waiting and writing 'might be God's plan for me'" (Frizell 1978, 12).

Koch's original intention was to set the novel not in Indonesia but in Australia (under the title of *The Dwarf of Melbourne*). Only after this project failed did he relocate to Asia his story of a dwarf of mixed nationality and spiritual tension. The change proved abundantly fruitful. For one thing, it supplied a charismatic leader (Sukarno) with whom Billy Kwan could identify. Koch saw the potential in enlisting an actual historical figure and situation. Just as Stendhal and Tolstoy had chosen the Napoleonic Wars, so Koch found he could use the Indonesian crisis as a valuable backdrop for the moral and political dramas being played out. He was struck by the phenomenon of violent hero worship—of how certain individuals are moved to destroy heads of state or famous figures, such as the Kennedy brothers and John Lennon, and who do so at times not out of feelings of hostility but rather admiration and even reverence. Koch wanted to explore the "[w]orship of leader-figures, and what becomes of those who worship them" and "the fact that the worshippers are lately given to assassinating their idols" (Koch 1987, 20).

In Kwan's eyes, Sukarno was an inspiring embodiment of his people's hopes and needs. When he spoke to the crowds, "it's a mystical communion. . . . He's got this passion for his people—and it's a *poetic* passion" (*The Year of Living Dangerously*, 97). The Indonesian leader was known by many names, which were recited in the manner of a litany— "like an old lady's at prayer" (12)—by mocking western journalists in the Wayang Bar. But one name in particular—of Sukarno as "the Main Bearer of the People's Suffering"—was endorsed by Kwan: "[I]t's not just words," he says feelingly (13). To a fellow journalist Kwan explains the transcendent significance of the Indonesian president: "[W]hen a great poet writes about his country, he actually gives it a soul it didn't have before, doesn't he . . .? Well, Sukarno's done the same thing in his speeches. He's *created* this country"

(13). Sukarno was thought to have wandered incognito through the poor sections of Jakarta at night as a way of keeping close to his people. "They're the bread of life to me," Sukarno says (134), adopting a spiritually resonant phrase and adding a vital Christian element to his Hindu and Muslim legacy (Henricksen 2003, 169).

Kwan himself imitated his hero. He is obsessively concerned about the poor of Jakarta. "As a Christian," he remarks, "I have to be concerned about [the poor]—they're my brothers" (*The Year of Living Dangerously*, 95). In the face of such poverty, he asks Hamilton, "What then must we do?" It is the question posed by the people to John the Baptist (Luke 3:10), but Hamilton fails to recognize its source or import. Kwan makes clear that the virtuous response is always personal and direct—"if a man had two coats, he should give one to a man who had none" (21). His understanding of Christian social justice is to eschew large abstractions or grand theories in favor of personal involvement, to "deal with whatever misery is in front of you—and the little bit of good that you do adds its light to the sum of light" (22). In one of the most poignant parts of the novel, he shows care for an abandoned Indonesian woman, Ibu, and her sick child, giving her money for medicine but declining her overtures for prostitution as repayment (125).

Indonesia also afforded Koch a religiously charged cultural setting within which such mysteries as the universal longing for God and proneness to betrayal could be vividly depicted and the meaning and significance of Catholicism in an Asian environment could be sharply explored. The novel contains numerous references to these metaphysical dimensions. In a powerful prelude to his death, Kwan seeks to explain to Hamilton the quasi-divine calling that he claimed for him:

> There are only two sorts of men, Hamilton—men of light and men of darkness. You were incomplete—I knew that. You were mainly concerned with yourself. But you *were* a man of light, and that's why I chose you. . . . All that matters now is to know what light is, and what darkness is. And you knew. If we lose the capability of sensing that, we lose everything. We worship shadows, we worship foulness. (235–36)

Kwan recognizes such "foulness" in the twentieth century as bound up especially with sexual indulgence and destruction. He sees "the abuse of the body and neglect of the spirit as our current folly" (128), believing that the abuse of the body spells the death of love. Most of the western journalists frequenting the Wayang Bar show sexual aberrations of one kind or the other, whether it is a fondness for underage boys, an addiction to visiting prostitutes, or a voyeuristic viewing of bare-breasted Javanese women along the old canals of Jakarta at night. At one point, Kwan suggests to Hamilton the spiritual ramifications of sexual obsessiveness:

> Desire, lust, then anger: that's the sequence for the sensual man, and for our whole society. . . . [I]t's not for nothing that evil's so much tied up with losing our sexual integrity. It's through our bodies that we most easily enter Hell. How else? When we abuse each other's bodies, then we become demons. Poor sick monkeys! But the spirit doesn't die, of course; it just becomes a monster. (236)

Koch recognizes the Christian belief in the unity of body and soul epitomized in the Incarnation of Christ, which gave to the body an imperishable dignity, and he is acutely aware of the ways in which frustrations of the spirit unleash monstrous surrogates. Koch discerns, in modern western society, an increasing "reaching back to paganism: to worship of the earth, and to the myths and beliefs and values of the pre-Christian world. . . . with an accompanying absorption in witchcraft, magic and the occult" (1987, 121). While he has explored most fully in another novel, *The Doubleman*, the vulnerability of western people to bogus beliefs and spiritualities, he hints frequently in *The Year of Living Dangerously* at the deadly effects of spiritual confusion and fragmentation. In a diary entry, Billy Kwan ponders fearfully the apparent flirtation that Sukarno is having with Communism: "Why, Sukarno, if you are a true son of God, can you no longer see the danger you are courting? Unless we love God and reverence life, we are bound for extinction" (132).

Koch has termed *The Year of Living Dangerously* "basically a Catholic novel" (Pinwell 1983, 2). While he is at pains to avoid any impression that art should be an instrument of propaganda, he strongly affirms the importance of the novelist having serious moral concerns (Kerr and Edmonds 1985, 4). Koch voices these concerns especially through Billy Kwan, and he has readily acknowledged the religious motives of his main character: "Kwan is a Catholic, a bad Catholic, confused, unsure about his belief, but he is a radical Catholic. He's trying to be a one-man Catholic reform movement in the slums of Jakarta. Of course, he's misguided and so on, but Kwan's belief that you can alter the situation in front of you is a very essential Christian belief" (Pinwell 1983, 2). Kwan is a convert. "The Jesuits," he confides to Hamilton, "didn't have *me* as a child" (*The Year of Living Dangerously*, 95). A crucifix hangs on his bungalow wall, and Saint Augustine's *Confessions* and the works of Teilhard de Chardin form his current reading. As an unusual person, a borderline dwarf four feet six inches tall, he has a sharp sense of the divine hospitality of the Catholic Church. He calls it "the only Western institution that doesn't get uncomfortable with anybody" (95). Yet he is concerned at its apparent decline and feels tempted to leave Rome for Islam: "I don't think the Faith is much good unless it's passionate. Lately I have a feeling the Church has spent its passion. If it has, it's no place for me. There's something rather fine about Islam, don't you think? The passion's still there. I'm attracted to it" (95).

Koch's personal religious odyssey has given a special edge to this awareness of religious passion. When he abandoned Christianity in his teenage years, he became "spiritually adrift" and prey to alternative faiths. In the following years, while he worked on *Across the Sea Wall*, there was, he recalls, "an enormous force in Hinduism for me—particularly having spent some time in India at a young age—and it rushed into the vacuum, as it's done for so many people" (Baker 1989, 196). His recovery of Catholic belief in his late twenties reflected not only his awareness of spiritual hunger, both in himself and among many nonbelieving writers, but also the unique power of Christ to satisfy it. "[F]inally," he recalled, "I found that the shadow of God is always there." Reading the New Testament was "incredibly powerful." He knew that "Christ just won't go away, and I think that's what it comes down to" (195). Nor will Christ go away for his character Billy Kwan. Kwan underwent a series of religious shifts—"he's been," in the words of a fellow journalist, "a Buddhist, a Methodist, and then he entered the Church of Rome" (*The Year of Living Dangerously*, 68). Yet, in his attitudes and instincts he remains, finally, a Christian, reflecting Koch's belief that, without proselytizing, *The Year of Living Dangerously* ultimately propounds "the Christian ethic and Christian message" (Henricksen 2003, 171–72). As Koch has observed, "There are other channels for religiosity, and Eastern religions have their channels, but Christ remains the one channel we can't easily ignore. At least, it's too late for me to try to do so" (Baker 1989, 195).

Kwan is a divided figure not only in religious allegiance but in other ways as well. He himself admits that "he wore two faces" (*The Year of Living Dangerously*, 98): he is of mixed race, an Australian born half-Chinese; he is a mystically inclined prophet who compiles confidential dossiers and manipulates events and relationships; and, as a dwarf, he is "a man imprisoned in a child's body" (128). Such dualities of character and culture are an important feature of Koch's fiction, evident as well in later novels such as *The Doubleman*, *Highways to a War*, and *Out of Ireland*. They have allowed the author to examine and try to mend the fractures of the human heart reflected in the Christian doctrine of original sin. Besides Kwan, dualities certainly characterize each of the main characters in *The Year of Living Dangerously*. Guy Hamilton is a divided nature—English-born and raised in Singapore and Australia but haunted by a romanticized British past. He is also divided in character, a competent journalist who is chiefly interested in furthering his career in a foreign post but who possesses a passion for news that is almost metaphysical, a "yearning . . . for that vast, ultimate event which would change everything" (274), a "lust for that final event, intense as an ascetic's lust for visions" (276). Yet Hamilton shows a profound lack of spiritual openness in other ways. At one point, in conversation with Kwan, he "was no longer listening; he was welcoming back the full flow of indifference that was his natural state" (152). He shows a selfish unconcern in personal relationships, a condition that Kwan diagnoses as an inability to love and strives to cure by orchestrating a romance between Hamilton and Jill Bryant. Kwan also persuades Jill to proceed with the baby she and Hamilton have conceived when she is planning to fly to Singapore for an abortion (192). Hamilton typifies, in the words of Bernard Wall, "modern Western man at his most developed stage: restless, involved in interminable activity, and fundamentally unhappy" (1969, 133). Yet when Hamilton suffers an eye injury during the attempted coup, he "struggles through an unaccustomed prayer" of petition (*The Year of Living Dangerously*, 280). Such an act signifies his rejection of the self-sufficiency that Kwan had sought to challenge. Hamilton flies with Jill to Europe—for marriage and the child preserved from abortion—although he knows that his confused identity will finally only be settled by his return to "the other hemisphere" of Asia and Australia (295).

Similarly, the historical figure Sukarno, who plays such a symbolic role in the novel, is "a man of dualities" (130). He is the product of a Muslim father and a Hindu mother, and he is a Javanese aristocrat who prizes the peasants of Indonesia and is revered by them in return. At the end, however, he is a rather pathetic figure, described by the narrator as "old and tired and full of sins" (265) in his state of enforced exile following the coup. Yet unlike dictators like Hitler and Stalin, whom time has reduced to an almost subhuman quality, Sukarno has a charm and vitality that induce a kinder historical judgment, making his sins "venial rather than mortal" (263).

Billy Kwan comes to a tragic but noble death that captures the essential meaning of his life and represents an unmistakable affirmation of goodness. Echoing the exhortation of Christ in his final instruction to Saint Peter, "feed my lambs, feed my sheep" (John 21:16–17), Kwan raises a banner on the Hotel Indonesia imploring Sukarno to "feed [his] people" (249). He then falls sacrificially to his death.

Apart from Kwan, the other presence of Catholicism in *The Year of Living Dangerously* is supplied by the novel's narrator, Cook. Koch integrates him skillfully into the plot by assigning him the function of a confidant, especially in the Wayang Bar where the western journalists congregate after hours. Cook describes himself as a "father confessor," which he supposes even a lapsed Catholic can readily fulfill "after years of observing the role in that coffin-shaped booth where all solutions to anguish seem possible—at least for a time" (57). The Wayang, with "its changeless red candles flickering at intervals around the black mirror-surface of the bar," becomes Cook's confession box (57).

Its Indonesian background also invests the novel with layers of myth and legend, especially through the classical themes and characters of the *wayang kulit*, the ancient Javanese play in which puppets perform in front of illuminated screens. During the season of the dry monsoon, these shadow plays light up throughout the Indonesian countryside. But the puppets are not simply for play: "their shadows are souls" (121), especially in revealing the ultimate conflict that takes place between the *wayang* of the left (evil) and the *wayang* of the right (goodness). Koch has said that, in the course of writing the book, he was not tempted to embrace Hinduism or adopt a position of syncretism, even though he readily concedes that his Christian faith has waxed and waned over the years (Baker 1989, 194–95), but he found eastern mythology a rich source of metaphor and symbolism. "European writers," he noted, "have long been able to give symbolic underpinning to their work from Graeco-Roman myth. . . . I found I was able to draw on Indo-European myth in the same way" (quoted in Tiffin 1982, 330). Inspired by James Joyce's use of Homer's *Odyssey* as a substructure for *Ulysses*, Koch adopted a classical Indonesian *wayang* play, *The Reincarnation of Rama*, as the framework for *The Year of Living Dangerously*. Its patterns came to serve as a unifying and dramatizing device in the novel and provided the structure of a modern morality play.

The three parts of the *wayang* correspond to the three chapters of the novel and are reflected in the vital stages of the book: first, the audience scenes, set in Jakarta's Wayang Bar, similar to the opening court scenes of the play, in which the characters exhibit youthful folly as they try to find their way; second, the hero's painful search for enlightenment, analogous to that part of the *wayang* in which the puppet master arranges other people's lives—indeed, lives through other people, as Billy Kwan seeks to do—and uses turmoil as an instrument of spiritual progress; and third, the climax, which brings wisdom and spiritual maturity, as reflected in the shadow play's great battle between good and evil and the resolution of dilemmas (Koch 1987, 24–25).

The principal characters in *The Year of Living Dangerously* correspond to *wayang* characters. Kwan himself is the Dwarf Semar, who is comical but also wise and is based on the old Javanese god Ismaya. In the wake of Kwan's death, three of the *wayang* puppets he keeps in his bungalow are discovered broken on the floor, "as though they had been flung down in a rage" (*The Year of Living Dangerously*, 254). They are significant as a metaphor of disillusionment and represent the three people who have most disappointed Kwan—King Kresna (Sukarno), Arjuna (Hamilton) and Princess Srikandi (Jill Bryant). At the same time, Kwan's Christianity is illustrated by the Bible found open on a table in his bungalow, with a revealing passage, marked in black pencil, from the Book of Revelation (13:10) that makes clear the grim fate of those who take life and liberty and proclaims the importance of patience and of faith in the saints.

Indonesia also provided Koch with a setting in which the intermingling of religion and place could be delineated. Koch's upbringing in the cool remoteness of Tasmania has always enlivened him to the influence of geography and culture on national identity and spiritual outlook. In *The Year of Living Dangerously*, he recognizes, through the mouth of Billy Kwan, the peculiar impact of distance and isolation on Indonesia—and on Australia: "Spiritually, this place [Indonesia] is still a colony—not of Holland; of Hindustan. It's the old Hindu kingdoms that are most real here. And it's like all colonies—like Australia; because Java's one remove from the cultural source, there's a slackening—something missing. Even the air goes slack. A country of second-hand" (96). More provocatively, Koch suggests that climate can affect virtue. The oppressive heat of Asia can cause a certain aloofness, the uncontrollable perspiration in any human contact forming a barrier to sympathy and affection: "It's easier to be cruel in the tropics: perhaps this is why there's less charity there" (194).

Finally, Indonesia provided a political environment that heightened the drama of Koch's story but also allowed him to penetrate the realm of politics and identify the deeper causes of political unrest at that time, in particular the force of Marxism in representing an assertion of material goals at the cost of spiritual values and traditions. Billy Kwan is anxious about the looming Communist coup, sensing the savagery of an Islamic backlash. "That's what the Communists in this country underestimate," he tells Hamilton, "the fury of the Muslims at being told there's no God" (96). He confides to his diary his estimate of what is at stake: "[Comrade Aidit] and his cadres would stamp out the ancient dreams which are the spiritual life-blood of the country. The myths would be perverted into propaganda, the life of the spirit stilled in the name of the full belly, and love of God made an offence. Islam would be extinguished, and so would joy" (132).

Koch has noted, in his book of essays, that it is part of the Christian novelist's role "to salvage joy wherever it's to be found, among the rubbish and waste and pathetic incongruities of life; and to show as well the results of its displacement; to identify those counterfeits that come to us in its place, whispering their lies of fulfilment, power and love" (1987, 142). Indeed, conveying intimations of joy would seem to be a key purpose in his fiction. Yet the experience of joy is not to be confused with earthly enjoyment. It is not a natural mood but a supernatural condition, more synonymous with holiness than with happiness. While joy was the "small publicity of the pagan," averred G. K. Chesterton, it "is the gigantic secret of the Christian" (1961, 159). Koch's efforts to salvage joy in *The Year of Living Dangerously* are akin to the achievement of Georges Bernanos in *The Diary of a Country Priest*, a novel that Koch has rated among the last great novels by an orthodox Catholic in the twentieth century. Koch's description of Bernanos's priest-protagonist could be applied, *mutatis mutandis*, to Billy Kwan:

> His passionate love of God spreads and glows through the account until squalor gives way to formidable light. . . . Like St. Francis, he's a fool for God, and his wretched death is a triumph. . . . He makes the comfortable bourgeoisie of his parish uneasy, since his faith is uncompromising and revolutionary, just as Christ's was; just as the Incarnation itself was: a revolutionary fact shaking reality forever, bringing joy to those who wish to accept it. (1987, 140)

In *The Year of Living Dangerously*, Christopher Koch offers a contemporary picture of the salvaging of joy after indulgence in counterfeits. The novel has gained the appreciation of a discerning readership for over a quarter of a century, reflecting Georges Bernanos's vision of a "Catholic novel" as showing "the life of faith . . . at grips with the passions" and allowing the reader to "feel the tragic mystery of salvation" (Speaight 1973, 71–72).

CRITICAL RECEPTION

The publication of *The Year of Living Dangerously* gave rise to wide critical acclaim, both in Australia and internationally. Both Koch's fellow authors and professional critics were generally lavish in their praise. The major Australian poet Les Murray observed that the book "glows with the lucidity of very mature art" (1978, 21). Anthony Burgess found the novel distinctive "in its author's capacity to make an exactly caught phase of history symbolic of a larger reality," and he pronounced Billy Kwan to be "one of the most memorable characters of recent fiction" (1978, 1359). Larry McMurtry called the novel a "richly and fully realized work of fiction, well conceived and beautifully executed" (1979, 42). *The Year of Living Dangerously* won two notable literary prizes in Australia, the National Book Council Award and The Age Book of the Year, and it is frequently listed for study on school syllabi.

A movie version of the novel appeared in 1982, and a stage adaptation was performed at the Festival of Perth in 1999, stimulating a wider exposure and appreciation of the novel and helping to ensure its consistent appearance in print. There have been various scholarly articles on Koch's output, and a number of illuminating interviews, especially that by Candida Baker (1989). The first full-length study of Koch's writings, *Island and Otherland: Christopher Koch and His Books*, by Noel Henricksen, was published in 2003. Henricksen presents a well-researched and judicious assessment of Koch's novels and an extensive bibliography. A lengthy chapter on *The Year of Living Dangerously* sheds light on the background and themes of the novel and includes a selection of Koch's color sketches of Asian life that highlight the visual power of his imagination so evident in the novel.

NOTE

Christopher J. Koch, *The Year of Living Dangerously* (Vintage/Random House Australia, 1978). All references are to this edition. Used by permission of Random House Australia and Christopher Koch.

WORKS CITED

Baker, Candida. 1989. *Yacker 3: Australian Writers Talk About Their Work.* Sydney: Picador.

Burgess, Anthony. 1978. Review of *The Year of Living Dangerously*, by Christopher J. Koch. *Times Literary Supplement* (November 24): 1359.

Chesterton, G. K. 1961. *Orthodoxy.* London: Fontana.

Collins, Martin. 1985. "A Lifetime of Living Dangerously." *Weekend Australian Magazine* (June 29–30): 16.

Frizell, Helen. 1978. "The Re-emergence of a Major Novelist." *Sydney Morning Herald* (December 2): 12.

Henricksen, Noel. 2003. *Island and Otherland: Christopher Koch and His Books.* Melbourne: Educare.

Jones, Margaret. 1985. "From Politics . . . to Pixies and Cults." *Sydney Morning Herald* (April 26): 9.

Kerr, David, and Phillip Edmonds. 1985. "Christopher Koch Speaking." *Weekend Australian Magazine* (April 6–7): 4.

Koch, Christopher J. 1987. *Crossing the Gap: A Novelist's Essays.* London: Chatto and Windus.

McMurtry, Larry. 1979. Review of *The Year of Living Dangerously*, by Christopher J. Koch. *Washington Star* (February 7): 42.

Murray, Les. 1978. Review of *The Year of Living Dangerously*, by Christopher J. Koch. *Sydney Morning Herald* (October 21): 21.

Pinwell, William. 1983. "Author's Conflicts in the Year of Living Dejectedly." *Weekend Australian Magazine* (January 8–9): 1–2.

Speaight, Robert. 1973. *Georges Bernanos: A Study of the Man and the Writer.* London: Collins and Harvill.

Tiffin, Helen. 1982. "Asia, Europe and Australian Identity: The Novels of Christopher Koch." *Australian Literary Studies* 10 (May): 326–35.

Wall, Bernard. 1969. *Headlong into Change: An Autobiography and a Memoir of Ideas Since the Thirties.* London: Harvill Press.

— Karl Schmude